Tenth Edition

Behavior Modification

What It Is and How to Do It

Garry Martin

St. Paul's College, Winnipeg, Manitoba

Joseph Pear

University of Manitoba

Routledge
Taylor & Francis Group

LONDON AND NEW YORK

First published 2015, 2011, 2007 by Pearson Education, Inc.

Published 2016 by Routledge
2 Park Square, Milton Park, Abingdon, Oxon OX 14 4RN
711 Third Avenue, New York, NY 10017, USA

Routledge is an imprint of the Taylor & Francis Group, an informa business

ISBN: 9780205992102 (pbk)

Cover Designer: Brenda Carmichael, PreMedia Global, Inc.

Library of Congress Cataloging-in-Publication Data
Martin, Garry
    Behavior modification : what it is and how to do it/Garry Martin, St. Paul's College, Winnipeg, Manitoba, Joseph Pear, University of Manitoba.—Tenth edition.
        pages cm
    ISBN 978-0-205-99210-2 (alk. paper)—ISBN 0-205-99210-2 (alk. paper)
1. Behavior modification.   I. Pear, Joseph,   II. Title.
    BF637.B4M37 2015
    155.2'5—dc23
                                                        2014012903

DEDICATION

To
Jack Michael, Lee Meyerson, Lynn Caldwell, Dick Powers, and Reed Lawson,
who taught us so much and made learning so enjoyable

and

Toby, Todd, Kelly, Scott, Tana, and Jonathan, who live in a better
world because of such dedicated teachers

CONTENTS

PREFACE

About the Title of This Book

The title of this book is intended to reflect the tremendous depth and breadth of the entire field of behavior modification in a manner that is friendly and unintimidating. As emphasized throughout the book, behavior modification encompasses both applied behavior analysis and cognitive/behavior therapy. More than that, however, it also embraces the positive ways in which all of us influence the behavior of others. At the same time this book is not simplistic or "light weight." On the contrary, especially in the "Notes for Further Learning," it provides in-depth coverage of the latest research and theories on the complex and controversial issues in the field, and it endeavors to do so in a manner that is readily comprehensible to readers at a wide range of levels and with various interests—from students in their early college or university years to those in postgraduate studies, from the general reader to the serious scholar, and from novices to professionals in the area.

About the Tenth Edition of This Book

This tenth edition of *Behavior Modification: What It Is and How to Do It*, like its predecessors, assumes no specific prior knowledge about psychology or behavior modification on the part of the reader. Those who want to know how to apply behavior modification to their everyday concerns—from solving some of their own personal behavior problems to helping children learn life's necessary skills—will find the text useful. Mainly, however, this book is addressed to two audiences: (a) college and university students taking courses in behavior modification, applied behavior analysis, behavior therapy, the psychology of learning, and related areas and (b) students and practitioners of various helping professions (such as clinical psychology, counseling, education, medicine, nursing, occupational therapy, physiotherapy, psychiatric nursing, psychiatry, social work, speech therapy, and sport psychology) who are concerned directly with enhancing various forms of behavioral development.

From our separate experiences over the past 48 years in teaching members of both groups, we are convinced that both groups learn the principles of behavior and how to apply them most effectively when the applications are explained with reference to the underlying behavior principles on which they are based. For this reason, as our title implies, this book deals equally with both the principles and the tactics (i.e., the rules and guidelines for specific applications) of behavior modification.

Our goals and the manner in which we have attempted to achieve them can be summarized as follows:

1. *To teach the elementary principles and procedures of behavior modification.* Thus, we begin with the basic principles and procedures, illustrate them with numerous examples and applications, and increase the complexity of the material gradually. Questions for Learning distributed throughout each chapter promote the reader's mastery of the material and ability to generalize to situations not described in the text. These questions can also be used for examination purposes in formal courses.

2. *To teach practical how-to skills, such as observing and recording; recognizing instances of reinforcement, extinction, and punishment and their likely long-term effects; interpreting behavioral episodes in terms of behavioral principles and procedures; and designing, implementing, and evaluating behavioral programs.* To accomplish this, we provide Application Exercises that involve other people and teach the reader about analyzing, interpreting, and developing programs for the behavior of others; and Self-Modification Exercises, which encourage the reader to analyze, interpret, and develop programs for his or her own behavior.

3. *To provide advanced discussion and references to acquaint readers with some of the empirical and theoretical underpinnings of the field.* This material is presented in the "Notes for Further Learning" section at the end of each chapter. These sections can be omitted without harm to the continuity of the text. Separate Questions for Learning on the Notes are provided for those instructors who wish to use them and as aids for students who wish to broaden their understanding of behavior modification. Instructors can also use information given in the Notes sections as springboards for lecture material.

4. *To present the material in such a way that it will serve as an easy-to-use handbook for practitioners concerned with overcoming behavioral deficits and excesses in a wide variety of populations and settings.*

The book is divided into six parts:

Part I (Chapters 1 and 2) introduces the behavioral orientation of the book and describes major areas of application of behavior modification techniques for improving a wide variety of behaviors of individuals in diverse settings.

Part II (Chapters 3–16) covers the basic principles and procedures of behavior modification. Each of the chapters begins with a case history drawn from the fields of child development, developmental disabilities, childhood autism, early education, coaching, or normal everyday adult adjustment. Numerous examples of how each principle operates in everyday life and how it can operate to the disadvantage of those who are ignorant of it are also given.

Part III (Chapters 17–19) provides more sophisticated perspectives on the principles discussed in Part II. Chapters 17 and 18 discuss ways in which to combine and apply the principles. Chapter 19 provides a behavioral view of motivation and includes insights on applying various motivational operations. Each of these three chapters also begins with a case history.

Part IV (Chapters 20–22) presents detailed procedures for assessing, recording, and graphing behavior and for evaluating the effects of behavioral treatments using single-subject research designs. Many instructors prefer to present much of this material quite early in their courses—sometimes at the beginning. Therefore, we have written these chapters so that they can be read independently of the rest of the book; they do not depend on any of the other material. We recommend that students be required to read these chapters prior to carrying out any major projects for their courses.

Part V (Chapters 23–26) deals with how the basic principles, procedures, and assessment and recording techniques are incorporated into effective programming strategies. In keeping with the rigorously scientific nature of behavior modification, we have placed heavy emphasis on the importance of empirically validating program effectiveness.

Part VI (Chapters 27 and 28) focuses on the profession of behavior therapy. This part of the book is not intended to teach students how to do behavior therapy, but rather to build the student's awareness of the field of behavior therapy and how it utilizes the principles of behavior modification. Chapter 27 discusses aspects of cognitive behavior therapy, acceptance and commitment therapy, and dialectical behavior therapy. Chapter 28 reviews behavioral and cognitive behavioral treatments of major psychological disorders.

Part VII (Chapters 29 and 30) expands the reader's perspective of behavior modification. Chapter 29 presents an overview of the history of behavior modification. Chapter 30 discusses the ethical issues in the field. Some instructors might think that these two chapters belong near the beginning of the book. However, we believe that the reader is more prepared to fully appreciate this material after obtaining a clear and thorough knowledge of behavior modification. Moreover, in this edition we have presented some basic historical highlights in Chapter 1 (see below), but go into history in more detail in Chapter 29. Although we placed the chapter on ethical issues at the end of the book, it is not because we believe that this topic is less important than the others. On the contrary, we stress ethical issues throughout the book, and, thus, the last chapter provides a reiteration and elaboration of this vital subject. We hope that after reading the concluding chapter, the reader will be fully aware that the only justification for behavior modification is its usefulness in serving humanity in general and its recipients in particular.

Changes in the Tenth Edition

First, in Part II ("Basic Behavioral Principles and Procedures"), as suggested by several reviewers, we placed Respondent (Classical, Pavlovian) Conditioning in Chapter 3 (versus Chapter 14 in the 9th edition) in order to help the reader contrast it with Operant Conditioning principles and procedures now described in Chapters 4 through 14. Respondent and operant conditioning comparisons and interactions are still discussed in Chapter 15.

Second, we made a couple of changes in the sequence of operant conditioning chapters to be consistent with suggestions from reviewers and to make it easier for the reader to understand how some of the operant principles and procedures relate to each other.

Third, at the end of each of the operant conditioning chapters in the 9th edition we identified different types of pitfalls—distinct ways in which lack of knowledge of a principle or procedure can be problematic. In the tenth edition, as suggested by a reviewer, we give these pitfalls specific names to make it easier for the reader to remember them.

Fourth, as stated in Chapter 1, with the increasing prominence of Applied Behavior Analysis (ABA) we refer to ABA and behavior analysts increasingly throughout the book.

Fifth, as suggested by several reviewers and many of our students, we added more everyday examples to better illustrate the application of behavior principles in the everyday life of university students.

Sixth, throughout the book, we added many new up-to-date references to reflect recent developments in the field, and added some new notes to the "Notes for Further Learning" sections at the end of each chapter, and deleted old notes when warranted.

Finally, all chapters were revised to cover recent developments in this expanding field and to enhance the readability of the text. Some of the specific chapter revisions we made were as follows: In Chapter 1, we added "Some Historical Highlights of Behavior Modification," and expanded the comparison of behavior modification to applied behavior analysis and cognitive behavior therapy. In Chapter 2, as suggested by four of the reviewers, we adjusted the length of some of the sections so that they are more easily handled. In Chapter 3 on respondent (classical, Pavlovian) conditioning (formerly Chapter 14 in the 9th edition), we added a new application of overcoming fear in a figure skater, and introduced operant learning (as a precursor to principles and procedures of operant conditioning in Chapters 4 through 14). As suggested by several reviewers, Chapter 4 on positive reinforcement was shortened and simplified in several ways. In Chapter 5, as suggested by a reviewer, we explained that we are far more commonly influenced by conditioned than unconditioned reinforcers. Chapter 6 on operant extinction was updated with current references. The "Shaping" chapter (Chapter 10 in the 9th edition) is now Chapter 7. We moved this chapter back to this spot, which is where it used to be in earlier editions, because shaping naturally follows reinforcement and extinction. Chapter 8 on schedules of reinforcement received considerable revision to make it easier for readers to understand the differences between the various schedules. As suggested by reviewers, Chapter 9 on stimulus discrimination and stimulus generalization was shortened and updated with recent references. Chapters 10 (Fading), 11 (Chaining), and 12 (Differential Reinforcement Procedures to Decrease Behavior) were edited and updated with recent references. In Chapter 13, Punishment, we redefined a "punisher" so that the new definition includes a response-cost punisher, and we updated the section "Should Punishment Be Used?" Chapter 14 (Escape and Avoidance Conditioning) and Chapter 15 (Pavlovian and Operant Conditioning Together) were revised to make the concepts easier for students to understand. To Chapter 16, Generality of Behavior Change, we added a new lead case that is more relevant to college students, and we made the writing less technical as suggested by a reviewer. Chapters 17 through 22 were very positively evaluated by reviewers, and they received some minor editing and new references. Chapter 23 on functional assessment was rewritten and updated in many respects. For Chapter 24, Planning, Applying, and Evaluating a Behavioral Program, the reviewers were very positive about the writing style but thought that it needed some examples. We therefore started off with a brief description of a case of overcoming a dog phobia in a 5-year-old child, and we referred to that case several times throughout that chapter to illustrate the various guidelines for programming. In the 9th edition, Chapter 25 on token economies included a section titled "Initial Steps in Setting Up a Token Economy," followed by a section titled "Specific Implementation Procedures." Because of the overlap of these two sections, we combined them into one section titled "Setting Up and Managing a Token Economy." As suggested by reviewers, we altered the writing style to make it less formal, and shortened the chapter. In Chapter 26 on self-control, we updated some of the examples to make them more relevant to college students. In Chapter 27 we added discussion of dialectical behavior therapy. In Chapters 27 and 28, we updated the discussion of behavioral treatment of common clinical problems with outpatients. In Chapters 29 and 30, we added a number of stylistic changes to make the chapters more readable.

Acknowledgments

Writing the ten editions of this book was made possible by the help of many individuals. We gratefully acknowledge the cooperation and support of Dr. Glen Lowther (former Superintendent) and the staff at the Manitoba Developmental Centre and Dr. Carl Stephens (former CEO) and the staff at the St. Amant. Much of the material in this volume was generated while the authors were involved in these institutions; without the support of these staff members, this book would not likely have been written.

Grateful acknowledgment is due to our many students for their constructive feedback on the current and earlier editions. We also thank Jack Michael, Rob Hawkins, Bill Leonhart, and Iver Iversen and his students for their many excellent suggestions for improvements on earlier editions. For this edition, special thanks are due to Ashley Boris for her cheerful and efficient word processing and to Frances Falzarano for her excellent substantive and stylistic comments.

thanks are due to Ashley Boris for her cheerful and efficient word processing and to Frances Falzarano for her excellent substantive and stylistic comments.

We are grateful to the following reviewers, whose helpful criticism improved this tenth edition:

Wendy Wilson of University South Florida
Amy Conner Love of Clarion University of Pennsylvania
Sherry Broadwell of Georgia State University
Ann Rost of Missouri State University

We also express our appreciation to the very capable editorial and production team at Prentice Hall/Pearson Education.

Finally, we thank the Knowledge Translation Branch of the Canadian Institutes of Health Research which facilitated the preparation of this edition with a grant (KAL 114098) to Joseph Pear.

To the Student

This book is designed to help you learn to talk about and apply behavior modification effectively. You need no prior knowledge about behavior modification to read and understand this text from beginning to end. We are confident that students at all levels—from beginners to advanced—will find the text informative and useful.

Behavior modification is a broad and complex field with many ramifications. Realizing that some students will require or want a deeper knowledge of behavior modification than others, we have separated the more elementary material from the material that demands more thought and study. The former material is presented in the main body of the text. The latter material is presented at the end of each chapter in the section called "Notes for Further Learning" (NfFL). The numbers in the margin of the main text refer you to the corresponding numbered passages in the NfFL sections. How you use these sections is up to you and your instructor. You can ignore them altogether and still obtain a good working knowledge of the principles and tactics of behavior modification because the main text does not depend on the material in the NfFL sections. We believe, however, that many students will find these sections very informative and that many instructors will find the material useful in stimulating class discussion and imparting additional background information.

Another major way in which we have attempted to help you learn the material is by providing guidelines on the use of all the behavior modification methods discussed in the text. These guidelines should prove useful as summaries of the material as well as in helping you to actually apply the methods described in the text. To assist in your learning we have also provided a glossary of important behavior modification terms at the back of this book.

Most chapters present numerous Questions for Learning and Application Exercises (including "Self-Modification" Exercises). The Questions for Learning are intended to help you check your knowledge of the material when preparing for quizzes and exams. The Application Exercises are intended to help you develop the practical skills you will need to complete behavior modification projects effectively.

To help make your study productive and enjoyable, we progress from the simpler and more intrinsically interesting material to the more difficult and complex material. This is also true of the writing style. But a word of caution: *Do not be misled by the seeming simplicity of the earlier chapters.* Students who conclude that they are skilled behavior modifiers after they have learned a few simple behavior modification principles unfortunately end up proving the old maxim that "a little knowledge is a dangerous thing." If we personally had to pick the most important chapter in this book in terms of the knowledge and skills that define a competent behavior modifier, it would probably be Chapter 24. We therefore strongly suggest that you reserve judgment about your abilities as a behavior modifier until you have mastered Chapter 24 and all the preliminary material on which it is based.

We would also point out that—as emphasized in Chapter 30—organizations that regulate behavior modification have appeared and gained in stature and influence in the past few years. If you are considering applying behavior modification on any level, we strongly recommend that you check with the

Behavior Analyst Certification Board (www.bacb.com) to determine how you may obtain the necessary qualifications.

With those words of caution, we wish you much success and enjoyment as you pursue your studies in this exciting and rapidly expanding field.

G.L.M.

J.J.P.

TO INDIVIDUALS USING THIS BOOK TO STUDY FOR THE BEHAVIOR ANALYSIS CERTIFICATION BOARD® EXAMINATIONS

For individuals using this book to study for the Board Certified Behavior Analyst® (BCBA®) or the Board Certified Assistant Behavior Analyst® (BCaBA®) exam, the following are the chapters in this book where the content for the task list may be found:

Topics from the Fourth Edition Task List*	Relevant Chapters
Section I: Basic Behavior-Analytic Skills	
A. Measurement	1, 20, 21
B. Experimental Design	1, 22,23
C. Behavior-Change Considerations	24
D. Fundamental Elements of Behavior Change	3–19
E. Specific Behavior-Change Procedures	3–5, 10, 11, 13, 14, 17–19
F. Behavior-Change Systems	2, 7, 8, 10, 25, 26
Section 2: Client-Centered Responsibilities	
G. Identification of the Problem	1, 23, 24, 27, 28
H. Measurement	20–24
I. Assessment	20–24, 27, 28
J. Intervention	24–28, 30
K. Implementation, Management, and Supervision	24, 25
Section III: Explain and Behave in Accordance with the Philosophical Assumptions of Behavior Analysis	
Define and Provide Examples of Basic Concepts	1, 3-19, 29
Distinguish Between the Verbal Operants	19

*Adapted from the Fourth Edition of the Behavior Analysis Certification Board® Task List. The Task List can be downloaded from: http://www.bacb.com/Downloadfiles/TaskList/BACB_Fourth_Edition_Task_List.pdf

CHAPTER 1

Introduction

LEARNING OBJECTIVES

After studying this chapter, you will be able to:

- Define *behavior, behavior modification,* and *behavioral assessment.*
- Describe how behavior modifiers view traditional psychological concepts such as intelligence and creativity.

- Summarize historical highlights of behavior modification.
- Discuss the relationship between behavior modification, applied behavior analysis, and behavior therapy.
- State some common misconceptions about behavior modification.

Many of society's best achievements—from democratic government to helping the less fortunate, and from great works of art to important scientific discoveries—as well as some of its most pressing health and social challenges—from unhealthy lifestyles to environmental pollution and from racism to terrorism—are firmly rooted in behavior. But what is behavior? Before attempting an answer, consider the following scenarios:

1. *Withdrawn behavior.* A class of nursery school youngsters is in the playground. While most of the children are playing, one little boy who has been diagnosed with autism sits quietly by himself, making no effort to join in the fun.
2. *Ineffective studying.* With two term papers due next week and a midterm exam at the same time, Sam is wondering how he is ever going to make it through his first year at university. Yet he continues to spend several hours each day on Facebook and YouTube.
3. *Performance nervousness.* Karen, a 14-year-old gymnast, is waiting for her turn to perform on the balance beam at a championship. Showing signs of extreme nervousness, she thinks to herself, "What if I don't perform well? What if I fall on my backflip? I can't believe how my heart is pounding."
4. *Campground littering.* Tom and Sally have just arrived at the place where they intend to set up camp and are looking in disgust and amazement at the litter left by previous campers. "Don't they care about the environment?" asks Sally. "If people keep this up," Tom says, "there won't be any nature left for anyone to enjoy."
5. *Migraine headaches.* While preparing dinner for her family, Betty was vaguely aware of a familiar feeling creeping up on her. Then, all at once, she felt nauseous. She looked around fearfully, knowing from past experience what to expect. "Tom, Joe," she called to her sons watching TV in the living room, "you'll have to finish fixing dinner yourselves—I'm having another migraine."
6. *Staff management.* Jack and Brenda were having coffee one morning at the Dairy Queen restaurant they owned. "We're going to have to do something about the evening staff," said Brenda. "When I came in this morning, the ice cream machine wasn't properly cleaned and the cups and lids weren't restocked." "That's only the tip of the iceberg," said Jack. "You should see the grill!"
7. *Irrational thinking.* Mary, after getting a poor mark on her first exam in her first year at college, thought, "I'll *never* be a good student. I *must* do well in *all* of my courses. My professor must think I'm an idiot."

Close inspection shows that each of the above vignettes involves some sort of human behavior. They illustrate a few of the many problems with which specialists in behavior modification are trained to deal. Each of these types of behavioral problems and many others are discussed in the following pages. Behavior modification, as you will see, is applicable to the entire range of human behavior.

What Is Behavior?

Before we can talk about behavior modification, we must first ask, what do we mean by behavior? Some commonly used synonyms include "activity," "action," "performance," "responding," "response," and "reaction." Essentially, **behavior** is anything that a person says or does. Technically, behavior is any muscular, glandular, or electrical activity of an organism. (**Note to reader: Throughout the text, key terms appear in bold type. We encourage you to master them as you encounter them.**) Is the color of someone's eyes behavior? Is blinking behavior? Are the clothes someone is wearing behavior? Is dressing behavior? If you said no to the first and third questions and yes to the second and fourth, we are in agreement. One of the goals of this book is to encourage you to begin thinking and talking specifically about behavior.

How about getting an "A" in a behavior modification course, or losing 10 pounds; are those behaviors? No. Those are *products of behavior*. The behavior that produces an "A" is studying effectively. The behaviors that lead to weight loss are resisting overeating and exercising more.

Walking, talking out loud, throwing a baseball, yelling at someone—all are *overt* (visible) behaviors that could be observed and recorded by an individual other than the one performing the behavior. As will be discussed in later chapters, the term *behavior* can also refer to *covert* (private, internal) activities that cannot be readily observed by others. However, in the field of behavior modification, private or covert behaviors do *not* typically refer to behaviors done in private, such as undressing in one's bedroom with the door locked and the blinds closed. Nor do they usually refer to secretive actions, such as cheating on an exam. Rather, in behavior modification they more commonly refer to activities that occur "within one's skin" and that therefore require special instruments or procedures for others to observe. For example, just before stepping onto the ice at an important competition, a figure skater might think, "I hope I don't fall," and he or she is likely to feel nervous (increased heart rate, etc.). Thinking and feeling are private behaviors, and are discussed further in Chapters 15, 27, and 28. Covert as well as overt behaviors can be influenced by the techniques of behavior modification.

Sometimes we think in words, called *private self-talk*, as illustrated by the figure skater in the previous paragraph. At other times we think by imagining. If you were asked to close your eyes and imagine a clear, blue sky, with a few white fluffy clouds, you would be able to do so. Imagining and private self-talk, in addition to being called *covert behaviors*, are sometimes referred to as *cognitive behaviors*.

Characteristics of behavior that can be measured are called *dimensions of behavior*. The *duration* of a behavior is the length of time that it lasts (e.g., Mary studied for 1 hour). The *frequency* of a behavior is the number of instances that occur in a given period of time (e.g., Frank planted 5 tomato plants in his garden in 30 minutes). The *intensity* or *force* of a behavior refers to the physical effort or energy involved in emitting the behavior (e.g., Mary has a strong grip when shaking hands). Strategies for measuring dimensions of behavior are discussed in Chapter 21.

Questions for Learning

(**Note to reader: You will encounter sets of questions in each chapter. Because these questions are designed to enhance your learning, we encourage you to: [a] pause in your reading; [b] prepare answers to those questions; and [c] learn those answers. Doing so will help you to master the content of this book.**)
1. What is behavior, generally and technically? Give three synonyms for behavior.
2. Distinguish between behavior and products of behavior. Give an example of a behavior and a product of that behavior that are not in this chapter.
3. Distinguish between overt and covert behaviors. Give two examples of each that are not in this chapter.
4. What are cognitive behaviors? Give two examples.
5. Describe two dimensions of behavior. Give an example of each.

Summary Labels for Behavior

While we have all learned to talk about behavior in various ways, we often do so in general terms. Terms such as *honest, carefree, hardworking, unreliable, independent, selfish, incompetent, kind, graceful, unsociable,* and *nervous* are summary labels for human actions, but they do not refer to specific behaviors. If, for example, you were to describe a man as nervous, others might know generally what you mean. But they would not know if you were referring to that person's tendency to chew his fingernails frequently, his constant fidgeting when sitting in a chair, the tendency for his left eye to twitch when talking to someone of the opposite sex, or some other behavior. In later chapters we discuss ways to measure specific dimensions of behavior.

For behavior modification specialists, many terms that are commonly used by psychologists, such as *intelligence, attitudes,* and *creativity,* are also summary labels for behavior. What do we mean when we say that a person is *intelligent*? To many people, intelligence is something that you are born with, a sort of "inherited brain power" or innate capacity for learning. But we never observe or directly measure any such thing. On an intelligence test, for example, we simply measure people's behavior—their answers to questions—as they take the test. The word *intelligent* is best used in its adjective form (e.g., "he is an *intelligent* speaker," "his speech is *intelligent*") or its adverb form (e.g., "she writes *intelligently*") to describe how people behave under certain conditions, such as taking a test, not as a noun for some "thing." Perhaps a person described as intelligent readily solves problems that others find difficult, performs well on most course examinations, reads many books, talks knowledgeably about many topics, or gets a high score on an intelligence test. Depending on who uses the word, *intelligence* can mean any or all of these—but whatever it means, it refers to ways of behaving. Therefore, in this book we avoid using the word *intelligence* as a noun. (For further discussion of a behavioral approach to intelligence, see Williams, Myerson, & Hale, 2008.)

What about an *attitude*? Suppose that Johnny's teacher, Ms. Smith, reports that he has a bad attitude toward school. What does Ms. Smith mean by this? Perhaps she means that Johnny frequently skips school, refuses to do his classwork when he does attend, and swears at the teacher. Whatever she means when she talks about Johnny's "bad attitude," it is clearly his behavior with which she is really concerned.

Creativity also refers to the kinds of behavior that a person is likely to engage under certain circumstances. The creative individual frequently emits behaviors that are novel or unusual and that, at the same time, have desirable effects. (For a behavioral approach to creativity, see Marr, 2003.)

Summary labels commonly used to refer to psychological problems include *autism spectrum disorder, attention-deficit/hyperactive disorder, anxiety, depression, low self-esteem, road rage, interpersonal difficulties,* and *sexual dysfunction.* There are positive reasons that summary terms or labels for behavior patterns are so frequently used in psychology and in everyday life. First, they may be useful for quickly providing general information about how an individual might perform. We would expect that a 10-year-old child who has been labeled as having a severe developmental disability, for example, would not be able to read even at the first-grade level. Second, the labels may imply that a particular treatment program will be helpful. Someone with road rage might be encouraged to take an anger-management program. Someone who is unassertive might benefit from an assertiveness training course. However, the use of summary labels also has disadvantages. One is that they may lead to *pseudo-explanations* of behavior (*pseudo* means false). For example, a child who inverts words while reading, such as "saw" for "was," might be labeled as *dyslexic.* If we ask why the child inverts words, and we are given the answer, "Because he is dyslexic," then the summary label for the behavior has been used as a pseudo-explanation for the behavior. Another name for pseudo-explanation is *circular reasoning.*

A second disadvantage of labeling is that labels can negatively affect the way an individual might be treated, such as by focusing on an individual's problem behaviors rather than strengths. Suppose, for example, that a teenager consistently fails to make his bed, but reliably mows the lawn and places the garbage cans on the street on pickup days. If the parents describe their son as "lazy," that label may cause them to focus more on the problem behavior than to praise the positive behaviors. In some societies, racial minorities have been given the negative label "lazy" even when they were the ones doing most of the hard physical work in those societies.

In this book, we strongly stress the importance of defining all types of problems in terms of **behavioral deficits** (too little behavior of a particular type) or **behavioral excesses** (too much behavior of a particular type). We do so for several reasons. First, we want to help you to avoid the problems of using general summary labels discussed earlier. Second, regardless of the labels attached to an individual, it is *behavior* that causes concern—and behavior that must be treated to alleviate the problem. Certain behaviors that parents see and hear, or fail to see and hear, cause them to seek professional help for their children. Certain behaviors teachers see and hear prompt them to seek professional help for their students. Certain behaviors that can be seen or heard cause governments to set up institutions, clinics, community treatment centers, and special programs. And certain behaviors that you emit might cause you to embark on a self-improvement program. Third, specific procedures are now available that can be used to improve behavior in schools, in workplaces, and in home settings—in fact, just about anywhere that there is a need to establish more desirable behaviors. These techniques are referred to collectively as *behavior modification.*

Questions for Learning

6. From a behavioral point of view, what do terms like *intelligence* or *creativity* refer to? Give an example of each.
7. What are two positive reasons that summary terms for behavior patterns are used frequently in psychology and in everyday life?
8. What are two disadvantages of using summary labels to refer to individuals or their actions? Give an example of each.
9. What is a behavioral deficit? Give two examples that are not in this chapter.
10. What is a behavioral excess? Give two examples that are not in this chapter.
11. What are three reasons why the authors describe behavior problems in terms of specific behavioral deficits or excesses?

What Is Behavior Modification?

Behavior modification involves the systematic application of learning principles and techniques to assess and improve individuals' covert and overt behaviors in order to enhance their daily functioning. Behavior modification has seven main characteristics. First, the most important characteristic is *its strong emphasis on defining problems in terms of behavior that can be measured in some way, and using changes in the behavioral measure of the problem as the best indicator of the extent to which the problem is being helped.*

Second, *its treatment procedures and techniques are ways of altering an individual's current environment* to help that individual function more fully. The physical variables that make up a person's environment are called *stimuli* (plural of *stimulus*). More specifically, **stimuli** are the people, objects, and events currently present in one's immediate surroundings that impinge on one's sense receptors and that can affect behavior. For example, the teacher, other students, and the furniture in a classroom are all potential stimuli in a student's environment in a classroom setting. An individual's own behavior can also be a part of the environment influencing that individual's subsequent behavior. When hitting a forehand shot in tennis, for example, both the sight of the ball coming near and the behavior of completing your backswing provide stimuli for you to complete the forehand shot and hit the ball over the net. Things that a therapist might say to a client are also a part of that client's environment. But behavior modification is much more than *talk therapy* or *verbal psychotherapy* (such as psychoanalysis or client-centered therapy). Although both behavior modifiers and "talk" therapists talk to their clients, their approaches to therapy differ in several important ways. One difference is that a behavior modifier is frequently actively involved in restructuring a client's daily environment to strengthen appropriate behavior, rather than spending a great deal of time discussing the client's past experiences. While knowledge of a client's past experiences might provide some useful information for designing a treatment program, knowledge of the current environmental variables that control a client's behavior is necessary for designing an effective behavioral treatment. Another difference between behavior modifiers and "talk" therapists is that a behavior modifier frequently gives homework assignments to clients in which the clients change their own everyday environments for therapeutic purposes. Such homework assignments are discussed in Chapters 26, 27, and 28.

A third characteristic of behavior modification is that *its methods and rationales can be described precisely.* This makes it possible for behavior modifiers to read descriptions of procedures used by their colleagues, replicate them, and get essentially the same results. It also makes it easier to teach behavior modification procedures than has been the case with many other forms of psychological treatment.

As a consequence of the third characteristic, a fourth characteristic of behavior modification is that *the techniques of behavior modification are often applied by individuals in everyday life.* Although, as you will read in this book, appropriately trained professionals and paraprofessionals use behavior modification in helping others, the precise description of behavior modification techniques makes it possible for individuals such as parents, teachers, coaches, and others to apply behavior modification to help individuals in everyday situations.

A fifth characteristic of behavior modification is that, to a large extent, *the techniques stem from basic and applied research in the science of learning in general, and the principles of operant and Pavlovian conditioning in particular* (e.g., see Pear, 2001). Therefore, in Part II we cover these principles in considerable detail and show how they are applicable to various types of behavior problems.

Two final characteristics are that *behavior modification emphasizes scientific demonstration that a particular intervention or treatment was responsible for a particular behavior change, and it places high value on accountability for everyone involved in behavior modification programs:* client, staff, administrators, consultants, and so on.* Thus far we have discussed behavior modification in an abstract way. That is, we have talked about the general approach that behavior modifiers take toward behavior. But how do behavior modifiers determine which behaviors to modify? The answer to this question is that they make use of procedures collectively called "behavioral assessment."

What Is Behavioral Assessment?

In the preceding section, we said that the most important characteristic of behavior modification is its use of measures of behavior to judge whether or not an individual's behavior had been improved by a behavior modification program. Behaviors to be improved in a behavior modification program are frequently called **target behaviors**. For example, if a university student sets a goal of studying 2 hours out of class for each hour spent in class, studying is the target behavior.

Behavioral assessment involves the collection and analysis of information and data in order to (a) identify and describe target behaviors; (b) identify possible causes of the behavior; (c) guide the selection of an appropriate behavioral treatment; and (d) evaluate treatment outcome. One type of behavioral assessment that has become especially important is termed *functional analysis*. Essentially, this approach (discussed in Chapter 23) involves isolating through experimentation the causes of problem behavior and removing or reversing them. As the interest in behavior modification has expanded during the past five decades, so has the demand for guidelines for conducting behavioral assessments. For more information on behavioral assessment, refer to Chapters 20, 21, and 23, or the books by Cipani and Schock (2011), Fisher, Piazza, and Roane (2011), and Ramsay, Reynolds, and Kamphaus (2002).

NOTE 1
[Margin notes refer to "Notes for Further Learning" at the end of the chapters.]

Questions for Learning

12. Define behavior modification.
13. What are stimuli? Describe two examples that are not in this chapter.
14. State seven defining characteristics of behavior modification.
15. What is meant by the term *target behavior*? Give an example of a target behavior of yours that you would like to improve. Is your target behavior a behavioral deficit to increase or a behavioral excess to decrease?
16. Define behavioral assessment.

Some Historical Highlights of Behavior Modification

In addition to the term *behavior modification*, other terms that have been used to describe the application of learning principles to help individuals improve their behavior include *behavior therapy*, *applied behavior analysis*, and *cognitive behavior therapy*. Although these terms overlap in many ways, there are also some rather subtle distinctions between them. In this section, we will briefly describe some of the early history of these terms and the distinctions that have come to characterize them. (A more detailed history is presented in Chapter 29.)

Pavlovian Conditioning and Early "Behavior Therapy"

If you have taken an introductory psychology course, you may recall that in the early 1900s a Russian physiologist, Ivan P. Pavlov, demonstrated with a dog that pairing a stimulus such as a bell with food (which caused salivation) taught the dog to salivate to the bell alone. Pavlov's research initiated the study of a type of learning now known as classical, Pavlovian, or respondent conditioning (described in Chapter 3). In a landmark experiment in 1920, Watson and Rayner demonstrated Pavlovian conditioning of a fear response in an 11-month-old infant. Although attempts to replicate the Watson and Rayner experiment were unsuccessful, a subsequent landmark experiment by Mary Cover Jones (1924) clearly demonstrated the "de-conditioning" of a fear in an infant. Over the next 30 years, a number of experiments demonstrated that our fears and other emotions can be influenced by Pavlovian conditioning. Then, in the 1950s in South Africa, a psychiatrist named Joseph Wolpe, drawing heavily on Pavlovian conditioning and the work of Mary Cover Jones, developed a behavioral treatment for specific phobias, which are intense irrational fears such as a fear of heights or closed spaces. In 1960, Wolpe's approach was first referred to as *behavior therapy* by the British psychologist Hans

---

*We thank Rob Hawkins for these last two points.

Eysenck. In the early 1960s, Wolpe moved to the United States and his behavior therapy approach for treating anxiety disorders gained in popularity. Applications of behavior therapy to treat a variety of psychological disorders are described in Chapter 28.

Operant Conditioning and Early "Behavior Modification"

Pavlovian conditioning involves reflexes—automatic responses to prior stimuli. In 1938, B. F. Skinner distinguished between Pavlovian conditioning and operant conditioning—a type of learning in which behavior is modified by its consequences (rewards and punishers). In 1953, in his book *Science and Human Behavior*, Skinner offered his interpretation of how basic learning principles could influence the behavior of people in all kinds of situations. In the 1950s and 1960s, practitioners, influenced by Skinner, published a number of papers that demonstrated applications of operant conditioning principles to help people in a variety of ways. These applications were given the name *behavior modification*. Examples of these applications include helping an individual to overcome stuttering, eliminating excessive vomiting of a child with intellectual disabilities, and teaching a child with autism to wear his prescription glasses. In 1965, Ullmann and Krasner published an influential collection of such readings in a book titled *Case Studies in Behavior Modification*, the first book with "behavior modification" in its title.

Applied Behavior Analysis

NOTE 2 The year 1968 saw the publication of the first issue of the *Journal of Applied Behavior Analysis* (*JABA*). *JABA* is the sister publication of the *Journal of the Experimental Analysis of Behavior* (*JEAB*), which deals with basic behavior analysis. In an important editorial article in the first issue of *JABA*, Baer, Wolf, and Risley identified the *dimensions of applied behavior analysis* as including: (a) a focus on measurable behavior that is socially significant (e.g., littering, parenting skills); (b) a strong emphasis on operant conditioning to develop treatment strategies; (c) an attempt to clearly demonstrate that the applied treatment was responsible for the improvement in the behavior that was measured; and (d) a demonstration of generalizable and long-lasting improvements in behavior. Over the years, the term *applied behavior analysis* has become increasingly popular (Bailey & Burch, 2006). In fact, some authors maintain that *behavior modification* and *applied behavior analysis* are now "two terms used to identify virtually identical fields" (e.g., Miltenberger, 2012). We, however, present a different point of view in this book.

Cognitive Behavior Therapy

Do you ever find yourself thinking, "Why do I always screw things up," or "Why does the worst always happen to me?" The well-known cognitive therapist Albert Ellis considered such statements to be irrational—after all, you don't always screw things up and you do some things well. Ellis believed that such irrational thoughts could cause a variety of troublesome emotions. His approach to therapy was to help people identify such irrational beliefs and to replace them with more rational self-statements (Ellis, 1962). Independently of Ellis, Aaron Beck assumed that dysfunctional thinking could cause depression and other problems, and he developed a therapeutic procedure that was similar to that of Ellis. Beck (1970) referred to strategies for recognizing maladaptive thinking and replacing it with adaptive thinking as *cognitive therapy*, and he contrasted cognitive therapy with behavior therapy (Beck, 1970). In the 1970s and 1980s, the term *cognitive behavior modification* was commonly used to refer to this approach (e.g., Meichenbaum, 1977, 1986). However, during the last two decades, the term *cognitive behavior therapy* has become the more common term for this approach. Cognitive behavior therapy is discussed in more detail in Chapters 27 and 28.

Current Use of "Behavior Modification" and Related Terms

The term **behavior analysis** refers to the scientific study of the laws that govern the behavior of human beings and other animals. Behavior analysis is the science on which behavior modification is based. As mentioned above, the terms *applied behavior analysis* and *behavior modification* are often used interchangeably, and many individuals who specialize in these areas call themselves *applied behavior analysts*. The terms *behavior therapy* and *cognitive behavior therapy* also are often used interchangeably. However, many individuals who practice behavior therapy or cognitive behavior therapy would not consider themselves to be applied behavior analysts, nor would they likely be considered as such by many certified behavior analysts. An additional consideration is that *behavior modifier*, *behavior manager*, and *performance manager* are terms often used to refer to an individual who, without formal training in behavior modification, deliberately tries to improve someone's behavior. The "behavior modifier" in such instances might be a teacher, parent, spouse, peer, roommate, supervisor, colleague, or a person modifying his/her own behavior. With this brief review of terms in mind, in this book we use the term *applied behavior analyst* when referring to someone who has had considerable formal training in applied behavior analysis, the term *behavior therapist* when referring to someone who has had considerable formal training in the application of behavior therapy or cognitive behavior therapy for treating psychological disorders, and the term *behavior modification* as the systematic application of learning principles and techniques to assess and improve individuals' covert and overt behaviors in order to enhance their daily functioning. Thus, in our view, the term *behavior modification* is broader than and encompasses the other terms referred to above (for further discussion along these lines, see Pear & Martin, 2012, and Pear & Simister, in press).

Questions for Learning

17. Briefly describe Joseph Wolpe's contribution to the early history of behavior therapy.
18. Briefly describe B. F. Skinner's early influence on behavior modification?
19. State the four dimensions of applied behavior analysis.
20. What was Aaron Beck referring to with respect to the term *cognitive therapy*?
21. How is the term *applied behavior analyst* used in this book?
22. How is the term *behavior therapist* used in this book?

Some Misconceptions about Behavior Modification

You probably encountered the term *behavior modification* before reading this book. Unfortunately, because numerous myths or misconceptions exist pertaining to this term, some of what you might have heard is likely false. Consider the following statements.

Myth 1: Use of rewards by behavior modifiers to change behavior is bribery.
Myth 2: Behavior modification involves the use of drugs and electroconvulsive therapy.
Myth 3: Behavior modification only changes symptoms; it doesn't get at the underlying problems.
Myth 4: Behavior modification can be applied to deal with simple problems, such as toilet-training children or overcoming fear of heights, but it is not applicable for dealing with complex problems such as low self-esteem or depression.
Myth 5: Behavior modifiers are cold and unfeeling and don't develop empathy with their clients.
Myth 6: Behavior modifiers deal only with observable behavior; they don't deal with thoughts and feelings of clients.
Myth 7: Behavior modifiers deny the importance of genetics or heredity in determining behavior.
Myth 8: Behavior modification is outdated.

In various sections throughout this book you will encounter evidences that help to dispel these myths or misconceptions.

The Approach of This Book

The main purpose of this book is to describe behavior modification techniques in an enjoyable, readable, and practical manner. Because it has been written for people in helping professions as well as for students, we intend to help readers learn not merely about behavior modification but also how to use it to change behavior. As stated previously, behavior that someone would like to improve can be classified as either behavioral deficits or behavioral excesses, and can be overt or covert. Below are examples of each type.

Examples of behavioral deficits

1. A child does not pronounce words clearly and does not interact with other children.
2. A teenager does not complete homework assignments, help around the house, work in the yard, or discuss problems and difficulties with her parents.
3. An adult does not pay attention to traffic regulations while driving, thank others for courtesies and favors, or meet his/her partner at agreed-upon times.
4. A basketball player, encouraged by the coach to visualize the ball going into the net just before a foul shot, is unable to do so.

Examples of behavioral excesses

1. A child frequently gets out of bed and throws tantrums at bedtime, throws food on the floor at mealtime, and plays with the TV remote.
2. A teenager frequently interrupts conversations between his parents and other adults, spends hours on Facebook, text messaging and talking on his/her cellphone, and uses abusive language.
3. An adult watches TV continuously, frequently eats candy or other junk food between meals, smokes one cigarette after another, and bites his/her fingernails.
4. A golfer often thinks negatively (e.g., "If I miss this one, I'll lose!") and experiences considerable anxiety (i.e., heart pounding, palms sweating) just before important shots.

To identify a behavior as excessive or deficient, we must consider the context in which it occurs. For example, a child drawing on paper is showing appropriate behavior, but most parents would consider it a behavioral excess if the child repeatedly draws on the living room wall. A normal teenager might interact appropriately with members of the same sex, but be extremely embarrassed and have difficulty talking to members of the opposite sex—a behavioral deficit. Some behavioral excesses—for example, self-injurious behavior—are inappropriate no matter what the context (although with some imagination, one could think of extreme situations in which even self-injurious behavior would be appropriate). In most cases, however, the point at which a particular behavior is considered deficient or excessive is determined primarily by the practices of one's culture and the ethical views of concerned individuals.

To summarize, the behavior modification approach focuses primarily on behavior and involves current environmental (as opposed to medical, pharmacological, or surgical) manipulations to change behavior. Individuals who are labeled as having a developmental disability, autism, schizophrenia, depression, or an anxiety disorder, for example, show behavioral deficits or excesses. Similarly, individuals who are labeled lazy, unmotivated, selfish, incompetent, or uncoordinated also show behavioral deficits or excesses. Behavior modification consists of a set of procedures that can be used to change behavior so that these individuals will be considered less of whatever label has been given them. Some traditional psychologists who are not trained in behavior modification have shown an excessive interest in labeling and classifying individuals. Regardless of the label given, however, the behavior of the individuals who are labeled is still there and is still being influenced by their environments. The mother in Figure 1.1, for example, is still concerned about what to do with her child and how to handle the problem. That is where behavior modification comes in.

Some Ethical Issues

As behavior modification has evolved, a number of ethical or moral concerns have become increasingly prominent. These are concerns that one should always bear in mind when applying behavior modification. Various groups and/or organizations, such as the Association for Behavioral and Cognitive Therapies, the American Psychological Association, and the Association for Behavior Analysis International, have addressed the ethical issues involved in the application of behavior modification (see also Bailey & Burch, 2011). In this section, we highlight ethical guidelines that you should keep in mind when reading subsequent chapters. In the final chapter of this book we present a more detailed discussion of the relationship between cultural practices, ethics, and behavior modification.

Qualifications of the Applied Behavior Analyst/Behavior Therapist

Applied behavior analysts/behavior therapists should receive appropriate academic training, including supervised practical training, to ensure competence in behavioral assessment, designing and implementing treatment programs, and evaluating their results.

Definition of the Problem and Selection of Goals

Target behaviors selected for modification must be those that are the most important for the individual and society. Ideally the client will be an active participant in the identification of target behaviors. Where this is not possible, competent impartial third parties should be identified to act on behalf of the client.

FIGURE 1.1
The experts "helping" mother with her child?

Selection of Treatment

Applied behavior analysts/behavior therapists should use the most effective, empirically validated intervention methods with the least discomfort and fewest negative side effects.

Record Keeping and Ongoing Evaluation

Applied behavior analysts/behavior therapists should perform a thorough behavioral assessment before applying the intervention. The intervention should include ongoing monitoring of target behaviors as well as possible side effects, and an appropriate follow-up evaluation after the treatment is concluded. It is the monitoring of data by concerned parties and clients that is the cornerstone for ensuring ethical and effective treatment programs by applied behavior analysts/behavior therapists.

Questions for Learning

23. List four myths or misconceptions about behavior modification.
24. List four subtopics that address ethical issues in behavior modification programs.
25. State two guidelines to ensure that target behaviors for behavior modification are the most important for the client and society.
26. What is key to ensuring ethical and effective treatment programs by applied behavior analysts/behavior therapists?

The Structure of This Book

This chapter has introduced the behavioral orientation of this book. Chapter 2 describes major areas of application of behavior modification techniques for improving a wide variety of behaviors of individuals in diverse settings. Chapters 3–30 are presented in six major sections.

Basic Behavioral Principles and Procedures

After the overview in the next chapter, the fourteen chapters in Part II describe the principles and procedures of behavior modification. In essence, principles are procedures that have a consistent effect and are so simple that they cannot be broken down into simpler procedures. Principles are like laws in advanced sciences. Most procedures used in behavior modification are combinations of the principles of behavior modification. In Part II, to better illustrate the individual principles under discussion, we have selected relatively simple lead cases for each chapter. After illustrating the principles involved in such cases, we elaborate on how these principles are used with other types of problems. We also give numerous illustrations of how these principles influence typical behavior in everyday life.

Capitalizing on Antecedent Control Procedures

Many of the chapters in Part II focus on the use of consequences (rewards and punishers) to bring about behavior change. But because of our learning histories, we have all learned to respond to various prompts and antecedent stimuli, such as instructions and goals. The three chapters in Part III describe strategies for capitalizing on these antecedent control procedures.

Dealing with Data

The three chapters in Part IV present detailed procedures for assessing, recording, and graphing behavior, and for evaluating the effects of behavioral treatments. Because some instructors of behavioral courses prefer to present this material at the beginning of the course, we have written the chapters in Part IV so that they can be read independently of the rest of the book.

Putting It all Together to Develop Effective Behavioral Programs

It's one thing to know about behavioral principles and procedures; it's another thing to incorporate them into effective programming strategies. The four chapters in Part V deal with how to accomplish the latter.

Behavior Therapy for Psychological Disorders

The three chapters in Part VI focus on the profession of behavior therapy. These chapters are not intended to teach you how to do behavior therapy, but rather to build your awareness of the field.

A Historical Perspective and Ethical Issues

Some historical highlights and ethical issues of behavior modification were introduced previously. In Part VII we present a more detailed history of behavior modification, and a more detailed discussion of ethical issues in the field.

We hope that after reading this book you will be fully aware that the only justification for behavior modification is its usefulness in serving all humanity in general and its recipients in particular. We hope that this book provides satisfactory answers to teachers, counselors, psychologists, students, teenagers, fathers, mothers, and others who say, "Thank you, Ms. or Mr. Expert, but what can I do about it?" (This is the question asked by the mother in Figure 1.1.) We hope also that the book will give introductory students of behavior modification an understanding of why the procedures are effective.

Application Exercises

In most of the chapters of this book, we provide you with exercises to apply the concepts you learned in the chapters. Generally, we present two types of application exercises: (a) exercises that involve the behavior of others, and (b) self-modification exercises in which you apply the behavior modification concepts you have learned to your own behavior.

A. Exercise Involving Others

Consider someone other than yourself. From your point of view, identify:

1. two behavioral deficits for that person to overcome
2. two behavioral excesses to decrease

For each example, indicate whether you have described:

a. a specific behavior or a general summary label

b. an observable behavior or a covert behavior

c. a behavior or the product of a behavior

B. Self-Modification Exercise

Apply the above exercise to yourself.

Notes for Further Learning

1. Behavioral assessment emerged as an alternative to traditional psychodiagnostic assessment in the 1960s. Psychoanalytic approaches to abnormal behavior originated with Sigmund Freud and others who viewed abnormal behavior as a symptom of an underlying mental disturbance in a personality mechanism. A major purpose of traditional diagnostic assessment was to identify the type of mental disorder assumed to underlie abnormal behavior. To help therapists diagnose clients with different types of presumed mental illness, the American Psychiatric Association developed the *Diagnostic and Statistical Manual of Mental Disorders* (*DSM-I*, 1952). The manual has been revised several times, with the most recent, *DSM-5*, being published in 2013. Because they did not agree with Freud's model of abnormal behavior, and because there was little evidence that diagnoses based on that model were reliable or valid, applied behavior analysts and behavior therapists made little use of the first three *DSMs* (Hersen, 1976). However, the later *DSMs*, beginning in 1987, were improved considerably over their predecessors in several respects. First, they are based primarily on research rather than on Freudian theory. Second, individual disorders (e.g., obsessive-compulsive disorder, generalized anxiety disorder, major depression) are based on categories of problem behaviors. Third, they use a multidimensional recording system that provides extra information for planning treatment, managing a case, and predicting outcomes. With these improvements, applied behavior analysts and behavior therapists have used *DSMs* to classify their clients. They also do so in part because official diagnoses are usually required by clinics, hospitals, schools, and social service agencies before treatment can be provided, and because health insurance companies reimburse practitioners on the basis of a *DSM* diagnosis. However, it is important to remember that because a *DSM-5* diagnosis (such as autistic spectrum disorder) refers to an individual's behaviors, it is likely to result in the individual being labeled (e.g., autistic), which may lead to the disadvantages of labeling mentioned in this chapter. Moreover, in spite of the implication that all individuals with the same label (e.g., autistic) are the same, they are not. To avoid problems associated with labeling, we should use what has come to be referred to as "people first language" when describing individuals with problems. For example, in the case of autism, we should describe the client as a child with autism rather than an autistic child. (As expressed by Malott, 2008, an even better approach would be to refer to the client as a child with autistic behaviors.) In addition to obtaining a *DSM-5* diagnosis for an individual, we should always conduct detailed behavioral assessments in order to obtain the necessary information for designing the most effective, individualized treatment program.

2. If you are interested in behavior analysis, you might visit the website of the Association for Behavior Analysis International (www.abainternational.org), an organization whose mission as stated on their website is "to contribute to the well-being of society by developing, enhancing, and supporting the growth and vitality of the science of behavior analysis through research, education, and practice". You might also visit the Behavior Analyst Online (BAO) website (http://baojournal.com/BAO%20site/BAO-Index.html). BAO is an organization that is dedicated to educating the public about behavior analysis and is a resource for professionals involved in applied behavior analysis. The BAO website also contains links to eight online journals providing research and applications in various sub-areas of behavior analysis.

Questions for Further Learning

1. What is the full title of the *DSM-5*? Describe what it is in a sentence.
2. Give five reasons why many behavior modifiers use the *DSM-5*.
3. What is a potential disadvantage of using the *DSM-5*?
4. What is meant by "people first language" when describing individuals with problems? Illustrate with an example.

CHAPTER 2

Areas of Application: An Overview

LEARNING OBJECTIVES

After studying this chapter, you will be able to describe applications of behavior modification to:

- parenting and child management.
- education.
- developmental disabilities.
- autism.
- schizophrenia.
- behavior therapy.
- self-management.
- medicine and health care.
- gerontology.
- business, industry, and government.
- behavioral sport psychology.
- diverse populations.

The value of behavior modification techniques for improving a wide variety of behaviors has been amply demonstrated in thousands of research reports. Successful applications have been documented with populations ranging from persons with profound learning disabilities to the highly intelligent, from the very young to the very old, and from controlled institutional programs to varied community settings. Modified behaviors range from simple motor skills to complex problem solving. In areas such as education, social work, nursing, clinical psychology, psychiatry, community psychology, medicine, rehabilitation, business, industry, and sports, applications are occurring with ever-increasing frequency. This chapter briefly describes major areas of application in which behavior modification has a solid foundation and a promising future for further development.

Parenting and Child Management

Being a parent is a challenging job. In addition to meeting basic needs, parents are totally responsible for their children's initial behavioral development. That responsibility is shared with teachers and others as the child develops through early childhood, adolescence, and into adulthood. There are numerous books and articles on behavior modification to teach parents ways to improve their child-rearing practices. Behavioral techniques have been applied to help parents teach their children to walk, develop initial language skills, use the toilet, and perform household chores (Dishon, Stormshak, & Kavanagh, 2012). Parents have also been taught behavioral strategies for solving their children's sleep problems (Wirth, 2014) and decreasing problem behaviors, such as nail biting, temper tantrums, aggressive behaviors, disregarding rules, noncompliance with parents' requests, and frequent arguing (Wilder & King-Peery, 2012). Some child and adolescent behavior problems are so complex that, in addition to helping parents work with their children, applied behavior analysts and behavior therapists treat the problems directly (Christner, Stewart, & Freeman, 2007; Gimpel & Holland, 2003; Neef, Perrin, & Madden, 2013; Wahler, 2007). Moreover, a behavioral program referred to as "Triple P" ("Positive Parenting Program") has been demonstrated to be an effective multilevel parenting program to prevent and treat severe behavioral, emotional, and developmental problems in children (Graaf, Speetjens, Smit, Wolff, & Tavecchio, 2008). Behavioral strategies have also been developed for helping communities prevent youth violence (Mattaini & McGuire, 2006).

Education: From Preschool to University

Since the early 1960s, behavior modification applications in classrooms have progressed on several fronts (Martens, Daily III, Begeny, & VanDerHeyden, 2011). Many applications in elementary school were initially designed to change student behaviors that were disruptive or incompatible with academic learning. Out-of-seat behavior, tantrums, aggressive behavior, and excessive socializing have all been successfully dealt with in classroom settings. Other behavioral applications in schools have involved modifying academic behavior directly, including oral reading, reading comprehension, composition, spelling, handwriting, and mastering mathematics and science concepts. Considerable success has also been achieved in applications with individuals with special problems, such as learning disabilities, hyperactivity, and attention deficits (Neef & Northup, 2007). Excellent "how-to" descriptions of behavior modification techniques for teachers have been published by Alberto and Troutman (2012), Cipani (2004), and Schloss and Schloss (1997). See also issues of the *Journal of Applied Behavior Analysis* and the *Journal of Behavioral Education*. Progress has also been made in the use of behavior modification in physical education (Siedentop & Tannehill, 2000; Ward, 2005).

A behavior modification approach to university teaching was developed by Fred S. Keller and his colleagues in the United States and Brazil in the 1960s (Keller, 1968). Since then variations of behavioral approaches to university teaching have been described (Austin, 2000; Bernstein & Chase, 2013; Michael, 1991; Pear, 2012). These approaches have three common features: *(a) the instructional goals for a course are stated in the form of study questions and application exercises, such as those in this book; (b) students are given opportunities to demonstrate their mastery of the course content through frequent tests (based on the study questions) or some combination of tests and assignments; and (c) students are given detailed information at the beginning of a course about what is expected of them on the tests and assignments in order to achieve various letter grades.* Research has indicated that with these features, and with an absolute standard for letter grades and expectations clearly specified, the great majority of students work exceptionally hard and a high percentage typically earn "A's" or "B's" (Bernstein & Chase, 2013; Moran & Mallott, 2004; Pascarella & Terenzini, 1991).

In addition, Keller's (1968) approach, known as the Personalized System of Instruction (PSI), includes several other features, such as mastery criteria where students must perform at a high level on a test or written assignment before proceeding to the next part of the course, and the use of student assistants called proctors to immediately score tests or written assignments. Before the widespread use of computers, PSI courses, as originally conceived by Keller, required a good deal of labor to administer because of the frequent testing and extensive record keeping that PSI requires. With the rise of computer technology, some instructors have automated much of the PSI procedure to make it more efficient. For example, at the University of Manitoba, computer-aided PSI (called CAPSI) was developed by Joseph Pear and his colleagues in the 1980s and used at universities in Canada, the United States, and Brazil. (For reviews of CAPSI, see Pear & Martin, 2004; Pear, Schnerch, Silva, Svenningsen, & Lambert, 2011.) An innovative feature of CAPSI is the use of students in the same course who have mastered a given unit of study material to act as proctors (called "peer reviewers") for that study unit. Research on CAPSI courses has demonstrated measurable feedback accuracy by peer reviewers, and compliance with feedback by students (Martin, Pear, & Martin, 2002a, 2002b). In addition, students in a CAPSI course receive much more substantive feedback than would be possible in a course taught using traditional methods (Pear & Crone-Todd, 2002).

Questions for Learning

1. List four children's behaviors that have been improved by parents' application of behavior modification.
2. List four elementary school students' behaviors that have been modified with behavior modification techniques.
3. Describe three characteristics common to behavioral approaches in university teaching.
4. What is PSI, and who was its founder?
5. What is CAPSI?

Developmental Disabilities

Beginning in the 1960s, some of the most dramatic successes of behavior modification occurred in applications to individuals with severe behavioral limitations due to atypical childhood development. Intellectual disabilities and autism are two types of developmental disabilities that have received particular attention from behavior modifiers. But before discussing these areas, we will provide a brief history of the use of several closely related terms that can be somewhat confusing.

During the latter half of the 20th century, it was common to use the term *mental retardation* to refer to individuals with intellectual impairments (Conyers, Martin, Martin, & Yu, 2002). During the 1990s, a frequently proposed alternative to the term *mental retardation* was the term *developmental disability* (Warren, 2000), which is commonly used by many professionals today. However, according to the Developmental Disabilities Act in the USA (Public Law 98-517, 1984), the term *developmental disability* is broader in meaning than the term *mental retardation*. In part because of this consideration, the American Association on Intellectual and Developmental Disabilities (AAIDD), formerly the American Association on Mental Retardation, indicated in 2007 that the term *intellectual disability* is the preferred term for the disability historically referred to as mental retardation. In consideration of this history, we view developmental disabilities as a broad area that includes the sub-areas of intellectual disabilities and autism.

Intellectual Disabilities

The AAIDD defines "intellectual disability" as a disability that originates before age 18 and that is characterized by significant limitations both in adaptive behavior and intellectual functioning. The latter limitation is defined as a score of approximately 70 to 75 or below on standardized IQ tests. This comprises approximately 2.3% of the population.

Many studies have demonstrated the effectiveness of behavioral techniques for teaching persons with intellectual disabilities behaviors such as toileting, self-help skills (e.g., feeding, dressing, and personal hygiene), social skills, communication skills, vocational skills, leisure-time activities, and a variety of community survival behaviors. Reviews of the literature can be found in sources such as Cuvo and Davis (2000), Didden (2007), Kurtz and Lind (2013), and Williams (2004); see also issues of the *Journal of Applied Behavior Analysis*.

Autism

In the *Diagnostic and Statistical Manual of Mental Disorders* (*DSM-5*, American Psychiatric Association, 2013), children diagnosed with autism spectrum disorders (ASDs) are likely to show some combination of impaired social behavior (e.g., not responding to parents' playful gestures), impaired communication (e.g., meaningless repetition of words or phrases), and repetitive self-stimulatory behaviors (e.g., fluttering their fingers in front of their eyes). They are also likely to show some behaviors similar to children diagnosed with intellectual disabilities in that they may score far below average on a variety of self-care tasks, such as dressing, grooming, and feeding. For reasons that are not well understood, the prevalence of ASDs seems to be increasing. According to the U.S. Centers for Disease Control and Prevention (2014), approximately 1 in 68 children in the United States has an ASD.

In the 1960s and 1970s, Ivar Lovaas developed behavioral treatments for children with autism. Using an approach he called early intensive behavioral intervention (EIBI), Lovaas (1966, 1977) focused on strategies to teach social and play behaviors, eliminate self-stimulatory behaviors, and develop language skills. When EIBI was applied to children with autism younger than 30 months old and continued till they reached school age, 50% of those children were able to enter a regular classroom at the normal school age (Lovaas, 1987). Moreover, the behavioral treatment produced long-lasting gains (McEachin, Smith, & Lovaas, 1993). Although some reviewers have criticized the experimental design of the Lovaas study (e.g., Gresham & MacMillan, 1997; Tews, 2007), subsequent research has established EIBI as the treatment of choice for children with autism in terms of both cost and effectiveness (Ahearn & Tiger, 2013; **NOTE 1** Kodak & Grow, 2011; Matson & Smith, 2008; Matson & Sturmey, 2011). There are now an increasing number of government-funded EIBI programs for children with autism. In Canada, for example, EIBI programs are currently available in all 10 provinces.

Schizophrenia

According to the United States National Institute of Mental Health (NIMH), "[s]chizophrenia is a chronic, severe, and disabling brain disorder that has affected people throughout history. About 1 percent of Americans have this illness. People with the disorder may hear voices other people don't hear. They may believe other people are reading their minds, controlling their thoughts, or plotting to harm them. This can terrify people with the illness and make them withdrawn or extremely agitated. People with schizophrenia may not make sense when they talk. They may sit for hours without moving or talking. Sometimes people with schizophrenia seem perfectly fine until they talk about what they are really thinking." (Retrieved April 17, 2014, from www.nimh.nih.gov/health/publications/schizophrenia/what-is-schizophrenia.shtml.)

Beginning with a few case studies in the 1950s, major attention was directed toward schizophrenia by applied behavior analysts and therapists in the 1960s and early 1970s (Kazdin, 1978). In the late 1970s and early 1980s, however, interest in this area decreased and only a small number of articles on behavior modification were published (Bellack, 1986). There is, nevertheless, clear evidence of the success of behavior modification treatments with this population. Because inadequate social relationships are a prime contributor to the poor quality of life experienced by people with schizophrenia, social skills have been one of the behaviors targeted for change. Available research indicates considerable success in teaching people with schizophrenia positive social interactions, communication skills, assertiveness skills, and job-finding skills (Bellack & Hersen, 1993; Bellack & Muser, 1990; Bellack, Muser, Gingerich, & Agresta, 1997). Cognitive-behavioral techniques have also been used effectively to reduce or eliminate hallucinations or delusions in persons with schizophrenia (Bouchard, Vallieres, Roy, & Maziade, 1996). These and other studies strongly indicate that behavior therapy can make a significant contribution to the treatment, management, and rehabilitation of persons with schizophrenia (Beck, Rector, Stolar, & Grant, 2008; McKinney & Fiedler, 2004; Wilder & Wong, 2007).

Behavior Therapy in Clinical Settings

Many studies have demonstrated that there are psychological problems (e.g., anxiety disorders, obsessive-compulsive disorders, stress-related problems, depression, obesity, marital problems, sexual dysfunction, habit disorders) for which specific behavioral procedures are demonstrably superior to other forms of psychotherapy (Barlow, 2008). But what about the use of pharmaceuticals? In a provocative book titled "Taking America off Drugs," Stephen Ray Flora (2007) argues that Americans have been deceived into believing that, whatever one's psychological problem, there is a drug to cure it. In contrast, he argues that most psychological problems, including eating disorders, phobias, obsessive-compulsive disorder, attention deficit hyperactive disorder, depression, schizophrenia, sleep disorders, and sexual disorders, are behavior-based, not "neurochemical" or "brain-based." He argues further that, for such problems, behavior therapy is more effective than drug treatment, although he does acknowledge that, in a minority of cases for a minority of behavioral difficulties, the treatment of choice may be a combination of behavior therapy and drug treatment.

As mentioned in the previous chapter, behavior therapy is a form of behavior modification of dysfunctional behaviors usually carried out in a clinical setting (e.g., a therapist's office). Chapters 27 and 28 provide a detailed discussion of behavioral treatment of a variety of psychological problems. Detailed discussion of behavioral treatment of psychological disorders can also be found in Beck (2011), Clark and Beck (2010), Guinther and Dougher (2013), Hayes, Strosahl, and Wilson (2011), Grant, Townend, Mulhern, and Short (2010), Leahy, Holland, and McGinn (2011), and Zweig and Leahy (2012).

Questions for Learning

6. What is currently the preferred term for the disability previously referred to as "mental retardation"?
7. List four behaviors of persons with intellectual disabilities that have been modified using behavior modification.
8. List four behaviors of children with autism that have been modified using behavior modification.
9. List four behaviors of people with schizophrenia that have been modified using behavior modification.
10. List four psychological problems that have been effectively treated with behavior therapy.

Self-Management of Personal Problems

Recall some of the problems described in Chapter 1. Sam had difficulty studying and finishing his term papers on time. Karen experienced extreme nervousness just before having to perform her gymnastics routine. Mary frequently experienced irrational thinking about her performance on her college exams. Many people would like to change their behavior. How about you? Would you like to eat healthier? Get into an exercise program? Become more assertive? Are there skills you can learn to help you to modify your behavior? A great deal of progress has been made in the area referred to as self-management, self-control, self-adjustment, self-regulation, self-direction, or self-modification. Successful self-modification requires a set of skills that can be learned. These skills involve ways of rearranging your environment to control your subsequent behavior. Hundreds of successful self-modification projects directed at behaviors such as saving money, exercising, engaging in good study habits, and controlling gambling have been reported in the behavioral literature. Self-modification for personal adjustment is described in more detail in Chapter 26. Discussion of this topic can also be found in Choi and Chung (2012), and Watson and Tharp (2007).

Medical and Health Care

Traditionally, a person who suffered from chronic headaches, a respiratory disorder, or hypertension would never have seen a psychologist for help with any of these problems. In the late 1960s, however, psychologists collaborating with physicians began using behavior modification techniques to treat these and other medical problems (Doleys, Meredith, & Ciminero, 1982). This launched *behavioral medicine,* a broad interdisciplinary field concerned with the links between health, illness, and behavior (Searight, 1998). Within behavioral medicine, *health psychology* considers how psychological factors can influence or cause illness, and how people can be encouraged to practice healthy behavior so as to prevent health problems (Taylor, 2011). Health psychologists have applied behavioral modification in five major areas. In addition to the following five areas, Nisbet and Gick (2008) suggested that health psychology could help to save the planet.

   1. *Direct Treatment of Medical Problems.* Health psychologists are continuing the trend of the late 1960s of developing behavioral techniques to treat symptoms such as migraine headaches, backaches, hypertension, seizures, irregular heartbeat, and stomach problems (DiTomasso, Golden, & Morris, 2011; Taylor, 2011). One such technique is called *biofeedback,* which consists of providing immediate information to an individual about that person's physiological processes, such as heart rate, blood pressure, muscle tension, and brain waves. Such information helps the individual to gain control over the physiological process that is monitored (Schwartz & Andrasic, 2003; Strack, Linden, & Wilson, 2011; Taylor, 2011).

   2. *Establishing Treatment Compliance.* Do you always keep your dental appointments? Do you always take medication exactly as prescribed by your doctor? Many do not. Because it is behavior, compliance with medical regimens is a natural target for behavior modification. Thus, an important part of health psychology is promoting treatment compliance (DiTomasso et al., 2011; Taylor, 2011).

   3. *Promotion of Healthy Living.* Do you exercise at least three times per week? Do you eat healthy foods and minimize your consumption of saturated fat, cholesterol, and salt? Do you limit your consumption of alcohol? Do you say no to nicotine and other addictive drugs? If you can answer yes to these questions, and if you can continue to answer yes as the years go by, then you can considerably lengthen your life span (see Figure 2.1). An important area of behavior modification involves the application of

FIGURE 2.1

Behavioral strategies have been used effectively to help people persist in physical fitness programs.

techniques to help people manage their own behaviors to stay healthy, such as by eating moderate-size well-balanced meals and exercising frequently (see Chapter 26, Sanderson, 2012; Taylor, 2011).

4. *Management of Caregivers.* Health psychologists are concerned not only with the behavior of the client or patient, but also with the behavior of those who have an impact on the medical condition of the client. Thus, health psychologists deal with changing the behavior of the client's family and friends, physicians, nurses, psychiatric nurses, occupational therapists, and other medical personnel to improve service provided to patients (see, e.g., Clarke & Wilson, 2008; DiTomasso et al., 2011; Nyp et al., 2011).

5. *Stress Management.* Like death and taxes, stress is one of the things that you can be sure of encountering in life. Stressors are conditions or events (e.g., being stuck in traffic, lack of sleep, smog, pending examinations, debts, marital breakdown, and serious illness or death in the family) that present coping difficulties. Stress reactions are physiological and behavioral responses, such as fatigue, hypertension, and ulcers. An important area of health psychology concerns the study of stressors, their effects on behavior, and the development of behavioral strategies for coping with stressors (e.g., Lehrer, Woolfolk, & Sime, 2007; Sanderson, 2012; Taylor, 2011). Some of these strategies are described in later chapters.

The broad interdisciplinary field of behavioral medicine and the subfield of health psychology have the potential to make a profound contribution to the efficiency and effectiveness of modern medicine and health care. For additional reading in this area, see issues of the *Journal of Behavioral Medicine,* and the books by Baum, Revenson, and Singer (2011), DiTomasso et al. (2011), Sanderson (2012), and Taylor (2011).

Gerontology

Do you want to know what it's like to be old? Then "you should smear dirt on your glasses, stuff cotton in your ears, put on heavy shoes that are too big for you, and wear gloves, and then try to spend the day in a normal way" (Skinner & Vaughan, 1983, p. 38). As the elderly are an increasing percentage of the population, more and more individuals must deal daily with the loss of skills and abilities to function independently that occurs with old age or chronic illness. Again, behavior modification can make a positive contribution here. For example, prior habitual ways of performing daily routines may no longer be possible and new routines must be developed and learned. Anxiety or fear about the possibility of failing to cope also might have to be dealt with. Disruptive behaviors in nursing homes may become a serious concern and new relationships might need to be developed with professional care staff. Behavioral techniques are being used increasingly to help the elderly and chronic-care patients to solve these problems (see the Special Issue on Geriatric Behavior Therapy in *Behavior Therapy,* 2011, Vol. 42, No.1; LeBlanc, Raetz, & Feliciano, 2011; Spira & Edelstein, 2006; and Turner & Mathews, 2013).

Questions for Learning

11. List four behaviors in the area of self-management of personal problems that have been modified by behavior modification techniques.
12. What is health psychology?
13. List five areas of application within health psychology.
14. List three behaviors of elderly persons that have been improved with behavior modification techniques.

Community Behavioral Analysis

As further discussed in Chapter 29, the bulk of the early (1950s) behavioral applications focused on individuals (such as persons with developmental disabilities and psychiatric patients) with severe problems, and took place in institutional or highly controlled settings. By the 1970s, however, important behavior modification projects were directed toward such broad community objectives as controlling littering in public campgrounds, increasing recycling of returnable soft drink containers, helping community boards to use problem-solving techniques, promoting energy conservation by increasing bus ridership, encouraging welfare recipients to attend self-help meetings, and helping college students live together in a cooperative housing project (for reviews of the early research in these areas, see Geller,

Winett, & Everett, 1982; Martin & Osborne, 1980). The scope of behavior modification had clearly expanded from individual problems to community concerns. One of the early studies in this area defined *behavioral community psychology* as "applications to socially significant problems in unstructured community settings where the behavior of individuals is not considered deviant in the traditional sense" (Briscoe, Hoffman, & Bailey, 1975, p. 57). For additional readings in behavioral community psychology, see issues of the *Journal of Applied Behavior Analysis*—for example, O'Connor, Lerman, Fritz, and Hodde (2010). For a discussion of how applications of behavioral analysis can lead to "population-wide improvements in human well-being," see Biglan and Glenn (2013).

Business, Industry, and Government

Behavior modification has also been applied to improve the performance of individuals in a wide variety of organizational settings ranging from small businesses to large corporations and from small community centers (note the overlap with behavioral community psychology) to large state hospitals. This general area is referred to as *organizational behavior management* (OBM), which has been defined as the application of behavioral principles and methods to the study and control of individual or group behavior within organizational settings (Frederiksen & Lovett, 1980). Other labels used interchangeably with organizational behavior management include *performance management, industrial behavior modification, organizational behavior modification, organizational behavior technology,* and *organizational behavior analysis.* Organizational behavior management emphasizes: (a) specific staff activities that characterize successful performances or produce successful results, and (b) frequent feedback and rewards for employees who show desirable behaviors.

One of the earliest studies in OBM was carried out at the Emery Air Freight Company. According to an article titled "Conversations with B. F. Skinner" in the 1973 issue of *Organizational Dynamics,* the desired behavior—employees' placement of packages in special containers—was increased from 45% to 95% through the use of positive reinforcement in the form of praise from supervisors.

Later studies in OBM have used behavioral techniques to change behavior in ways that improve productivity, decrease tardiness and absenteeism, increase sales volume, create new business, improve worker safety, reduce theft by employees, reduce shoplifting, and improve management-employee relations. For additional reading in this area, see Abernathy (2013), Daniels and Daniels (2005), Moorhead and Griffin (2010), Reid, O'Kane, and Macurik (2011), and issues of the *Journal of Organizational Behavior Management.*

Behavioral Sport Psychology

Since the early 1970s, there has been a growing desire on the part of coaches and athletes for more applied sport science research, particularly in the area of sport psychology, and applied behavior analysts have made a number of contributions to this area (Martin & Thomson, 2011). *Behavioral sport psychology* has been defined as the use of behavior analysis principles and techniques to enhance the performance and satisfaction of athletes and others associated with sports (Martin & Tkachuk, 2000). Areas of application include motivating practice and fitness training, teaching new athletic skills, controlling troublesome emotions that interfere with athletic performance, helping athletes to cope with pressure at major competitions, and helping coaches function more effectively as behavior modifiers with respect to athletic performance. For information on research and applications in this area, see Luiselli and Reed (2011), Martin (2015), and Virues-Ortega and Martin (2010).

Behavior Modification with Diverse Populations

During the past three decades applied behavior analysts/behavior therapists have given increased attention to issues of culture, gender, ethnicity, and sexual orientation as variables that can influence the effectiveness of treatment (see, e.g., Borrego, Ibanez, Spendlove, & Pemberton, 2007; Hatch, Friedman, & Paradis, 1996; Iwamasa, 1999; Iwamasa & Smith, 1996; Paradis, Friedman, Hatch, & Ackerman, 1996; Purcell, Campos, & Perilla, 1996). It is helpful, for example, for therapists to know that many clients with Asian cultural backgrounds prefer to be told specifically what to do by the therapist (as opposed to a more nondirective approach) (Chen, 1995). Many clients with Hispanic cultural backgrounds are more likely to comply with specific goal-directed suggestions if those suggestions are preceded by a period of familiarizing "small talk" (Tanaka-Matsumi & Higginbotham, 1994; also see the special series on behavior therapy with Latino Families, *Cognitive Behavioral Practice*, 2010, Vol. 17, No. 2).

A particularly striking example of the importance of understanding the cultural backgrounds of one's clients comes from the Lakota Sioux reservation near the Badlands in South Dakota. Dr. Tawa Witko, a psychologist on the reservation, described the case of an individual who had been diagnosed by another psychologist as schizophrenic. The reason for the diagnosis was that the man heard voices, especially around ceremony times. Dr. Witko explained that if the therapist had dug deeper, she would have found that this phenomenon is common among Native Americans, has spiritual meaning, and does not by itself indicate mental illness (Winerman, 2004).

Some cultural factors might weigh against teaching a particular behavior. For example, increased eye contact as a target behavior for a social skills training program for some Native Americans might be inappropriate. For the Navajo culture prolonged eye contact is typically considered to be aggressive (Tanaka-Matsumi, Higginbotham, & Chang, 2002). Readers interested in behavioral treatment with culturally diverse clients are encouraged to examine the special issues on cultural diversity in *Cognitive and Behavioral Practice* (1996, Vol. 3, No. 1) and in *The Behavior Therapist* (2013, Vol. 36, No. 5), and issues of the *Journal of Muslim Mental Health* and the *International Journal of Culture and Mental Health*.

Although information about clients' cultural backgrounds can be helpful for applied behavior analysts and therapists, we must also be sensitive to the dangers of overgeneralizing about any particular cultural group. (Cautions similar to those made in Chapter 1 about the dangers of labeling are relevant here.) For example, as Iwamasa (1999) pointed out, the Asian American population is comprised of over 30 different cultural and ethnic groups, and each has its own primary language, values, lifestyles, and patterns of adaptation to the United States.

Questions for Learning

15. Define behavioral community psychology.
16. List four behaviors in the area of behavioral community psychology that have been modified by behavior modification.
17. Define organizational behavior management (OBM).
18. List four behaviors in business, industry, or government that have been modified by behavior modification.
19. Define behavioral sport psychology.
20. List four areas of application of behavioral sport psychology related to athletes.
21. Describe how knowledge of a cultural characteristic might be helpful for applied behavior analysts/behavior therapists working with individuals from different cultures. Give an example.

Conclusion

The rise of behavior modification as a successful approach for dealing with a wide range of human problems has been remarkable. Books and journal articles describe behavioral procedures and research ranging from child rearing to coping with old age, from work to leisure activities, and from self-improvement to preserving the environment. It has been used with individuals ranging from those with profound disabilities to those who are gifted. Several thousand books have been published dealing with basic, applied, and theoretical issues in behavior modification. At least 31 journals are predominantly behavioral in their orientation. Examples of applications in many of these areas are described and illustrated in the following chapters.

Application Exercise

Self-Modification Exercise

In the subsections on "Self-Management of Personal Problems," "Medical and Health Care," "Community Behavioral Analysis," and "Behavioral Sport Psychology," we list many behaviors that have been successfully modified. Review each of those sections and prepare a list of ten of those behaviors that you or a friend would like to improve. For each behavior, indicate whether it is a deficit or an excess, and whether it is one of your behaviors or a friend's.

Note for Further Learning

1. A common strategy for delivering EIBI with children with autism is called discrete-trials teaching (DTT). DTT is made up of a series of individual teaching trials that typically last approximately 5 to 20 seconds each. On each trial, a teacher provides an antecedent (an instruction plus prompts to encourage a correct response), the child typically responds, and the teacher provides an immediate and appropriate consequence, such as a reward for correct behavior or saying "no" following an error. Repetitive DTT trials are typically separated by brief inter-trial intervals and presented in blocks of 12 to 20 trials. Researchers have investigated a variety of strategies for teaching staff and parents to implement DTT in EIBI programs (for a review of the teaching strategies, see Thomson, Martin, Arnal, Fazzio, & Yu, 2009). Considering the millions of dollars that are spent on public programs to fund EIBI treatment of children with autism, reviewers of outcome literature (e.g., Matson & Smith, 2008; Perry, Pritchard, & Penn, 2006) have identified several important requirements that must be met to ensure that resources are being allocated efficiently. Two of these requirements are: (a) the development of quality assessment systems to evaluate specific components of EIBI interventions, and (b) the development of research-based, economical, rapid training procedures for teaching parents and instructors to conduct DTT. A step toward meeting the first need is the development and field testing of the Discrete-Trials Teaching Evaluation Form (Babel, Martin, Fazzio, Arnal, & Thomson, 2008; Jeanson et al., 2010), and a step toward meeting the second need is the field-testing of a self-instructional manual (Fazzio & Martin, 2012) for teaching DTT to instructors of children with autism (Boris et al., 2012; Fazzio, Martin, Arnal, & Yu, 2009; Thiessen et al., 2009; Thomson et al., 2012; Young, Boris, Thomson, Martin, & Yu, 2012).

Questions for Further Learning

1. Describe the characteristics of discrete-trials teaching.
2. What are two important research needs in EIBI programs for children with autism?

CHAPTER 3

Respondent (Classical, Pavlovian) Conditioning of Reflexive Behavior

LEARNING OBJECTIVES

After studying this chapter, you will be able to:

- Define *respondent conditioning, higher-order conditioning, respondent extinction,* and *counter-conditioning.*
- Explain how respondent conditioning is involved in digestion, circulation, and respiration.

- Describe generalization and discrimination of respondent behavior.
- Discuss several applications of respondent conditioning principles.
- Distinguish between reflexes and operant behavior, and between respondent conditioning and operant conditioning.

That word makes me feel uncomfortable!

Making Words "Unpleasant"[1]

Sue was a student in first-year psychology at Arizona State University. As a participant in an experiment, she had been asked to memorize a list of words presented to her one at a time. Sitting as comfortably as one can be with electrical wires attached to one's ankle, and wearing headphones, Sue read the words as they were presented: "chair," "these," "radio," "large"—ZAP! CLANG! Sue was startled by the feeling of a mild electric shock to her ankle, and a loud "clang" through the headphones. Sue continued to memorize the words on the list. All the words appeared several times in different orders, and each time the word "large" occurred it was paired with the mild shock and the loud sound. During the experiment the shock and the sound caused Sue to feel anxious as measured by her galvanic skin response (GSR), an increase in the electrical conductivity of the skin that occurs during a sweat gland reaction. As a result of pairing the word "large" with the mild shock and the loud sound, hearing the word "large" by itself now caused Sue to feel anxious. Afterward, when Sue was asked to rate the pleasantness of the words on the list, she rated "large" as more unpleasant than the other words.

Note: *During a debriefing session, Sue learned the purposes of the experiment. She also discovered that by saying the word "large" many times without pairing it with the mild shock and the loud "clang" the word gradually lost its unpleasantness.*

---

[1] This example is based on an experiment by Staats, Staats, and Crawford (1962).

Behavioral Principles and Procedures

Behavioral principles and procedures are essentially ways of manipulating stimuli in order to influence behavior. As we stated in Chapter 1, principles are procedures that have a consistent effect and are so simple that they cannot be broken down into simpler procedures, while behavioral procedures are combinations of behavioral principles. In this chapter, we describe basic principles and procedures of *respondent conditioning*, also called *Pavlovian conditioning* (after Ivan Pavlov, the Russian physiologist who studied it), or *classical conditioning* (because it was the first type of conditioning to be identified). We use these three terms interchangeably.

Principle of Respondent Conditioning

Some of our behaviors, like Sue's anxious feelings to the mild shock and loud "clang," seem to be reflexive, and are called **respondent behaviors**, which are behaviors elicited by prior stimuli and are not affected by their consequences. Examples include salivating when smelling dinner cooking, feeling frightened when watching a scary movie, blushing when told that your fly or blouse is undone, and becoming sexually aroused when watching X-rated movies. Respondent behaviors are influenced by respondent conditioning, defined later, which is based on *unconditioned reflexes*. An **unconditioned reflex** is a stimulus–response relationship in which a stimulus automatically elicits a response apart from any prior learning. In other words, unconditioned reflexes are "hard wired" or inborn. A stimulus that elicits a response without prior learning or conditioning is called an **unconditioned stimulus (US)**. A response elicited by an unconditioned stimulus is called an **unconditioned response (UR)**. In other words, an unconditioned reflex consists of a US and a UR. In the experiment with Sue, the mild shock and loud "clang" were USs, and Sue's anxious feeling and GSR to the shock were URs. Examples of unconditioned reflexes are listed in Table 3.1.

For each of the responses in Table 3.1, there are stimuli that do not elicit them. In that sense, such stimuli are considered neutral. For example, assume that a particular stimulus (such as the opening motif of Beethoven's Fifth Symphony) is a neutral stimulus (NS) with respect to the response of salivation in the sense that it does not elicit salivation in a particular individual. The principle of **respondent conditioning** states that if an NS (the opening motif of Beethoven's Fifth Symphony) is followed closely in time by a US (food in the mouth) that elicits a UR (salivation), then the previous NS (the opening motif of Beethoven's Fifth Symphony) will also tend to elicit the response of salivation in the future. Of course, it may take more than just one pairing of the opening motif of Beethoven's Fifth Symphony with food before it would elicit any noticeable amount of salivation. Figure 3.1 illustrates respondent conditioning.

A **conditioned reflex** is a stimulus–response relationship in which a stimulus elicits a response because of prior respondent conditioning. If a salivation response is in fact conditioned to the opening motif of Beethoven's Fifth Symphony, that stimulus–response relationship would be referred to as a *conditioned reflex*. The stimulus in a conditioned reflex is called a **conditioned stimulus (CS**; e.g., the opening motif of Beethoven's Fifth Symphony), defined as a stimulus that elicits a response because that stimulus has been paired with another stimulus that elicits that response. The response in a conditioned reflex is referred to as a **conditioned response (CR**; e.g., salivation to the opening motif of Beethoven's Fifth Symphony), defined as a response elicited by a conditioned stimulus. In the experiment with Sue, the word "large" became a CS eliciting an anxious feeling and a GSR as CRs. You can see how respondent conditioning

TABLE 3.1   Examples of Unconditioned Reflexes

Unconditioned Stimulus ⟶	Unconditioned Response
Food	Salivation
Bright light	Squinting, pupil constriction
High temperature	Sweating
Low temperature	Shivering
Loss of support (falling)	Catching of breath, pounding heart
Finger in throat	Gagging, vomiting
Loud sounds	Catching of breath, pounding heart
Genital stimulation	Vaginal lubrication or penile erection

Respondent Conditioning

Procedure: Pair neutral stimulus and unconditioned stimulus.

Many
pairings
{ NS (sound of classical music)
{ US (food in mouth) ——→ UR (salivation)

Result: Neutral stimulus acquires ability to elicit response.

CS (sound of classical music) ——→ CR (salivation)

Note: NS = neutral stimulus
US = unconditioned stimulus
UR = unconditioned response
CS = conditioned stimulus
CR = conditioned response

FIGURE 3.1
Model for respondent conditioning

might explain your reactions to certain words (such as cancer) or even to a single letter (such as "F" on an exam). As indicated by Sue's rating of the word "large" as unpleasant, such pairings contribute to the meaning of words on a personal level (Staats, 1996; Tyron & Cicero, 1989). (For a review of research on the mechanisms that underlie Pavlovian conditioning, see Lattal, 2013.)

Factors Influencing Respondent Conditioning

There are several variables that influence the development of a conditioned reflex.

First, *the greater the number of pairings of a CS with a US, the greater is the ability of the CS to elicit the CR*, until a maximum strength of the conditioned reflex has been reached. If a child was frightened several times by seeing a loudly barking dog, the sight of the dog will elicit a stronger fear than if the child had been scared by seeing a loudly barking dog only once.

Second, *stronger conditioning occurs if the CS precedes the US by about half a second, rather than by a longer time or rather than following the US*. Conditioning in the latter case, called *backward conditioning*, is difficult to attain. If a child sees a dog and the dog immediately barks loudly, the sight of the dog is likely to become a CS with fear as a CR for the child. If, however, the child hears the loud barking of a dog hidden from view and a few seconds later sees a dog trot around the corner of a building, the fear caused by the loud barking is not likely to be conditioned to the sight of the dog.

Third, *a CS acquires greater ability to elicit a CR if the CS is always paired with the US than if it is only occasionally paired with the US*. If a couple consistently lights a candle in the bedroom just before having sex and not at other times, then the candlelight is likely to become a CS eliciting sexual arousal. If they light a candle in the bedroom every night but have sex there only one or two nights each week, then the candlelight will be a weaker CS for sexual arousal.

Fourth, *when several neutral stimuli precede a US, the stimulus that is most consistently associated with the US is the one most likely to become a strong CS*. A child may experience thunderstorms in which dark clouds and lightning are followed by loud claps of thunder, which cause fear. On other occasions, the child sees dark clouds but there is no lightning and no thunder. The child will acquire a stronger fear of lightning than of the dark clouds because lightning is paired with thunder but dark clouds alone are not.

Fifth, *respondent conditioning will develop more quickly and strongly when the CS or US or both are intense rather than weak* (Lutz, 1994; Polenchar, Romano, Steinmetz, & Patterson, 1984). A child will acquire a stronger fear of lightning if the lightning is exceptionally bright and the thunder is exceptionally loud than if either or both are relatively weak.

Questions for Learning

1. What are two other names for respondent conditioning?
2. What are respondent behaviors? Give three examples.
3. Define *unconditioned reflex*. Give three examples.

4. State the principle of respondent conditioning. Clearly diagram an example of respondent conditioning that is not in the text.
5. Define *conditioned reflex*, and give an example.
6. Define and give an example of the following: *unconditioned stimulus, unconditioned response, conditioned stimulus,* and *conditioned response*.
7. Briefly, in a sentence each, describe five variables that influence the development of a conditioned reflex.

Higher-Order Conditioning

Suppose that someone is conditioned to salivate to the opening motif of Beethoven's Fifth Symphony by following it with food many times. The opening motif of Beethoven's Fifth Symphony will thus have become a CS for salivation. Now let's suppose that, over several trials, just before presenting the opening motif of Beethoven's Fifth Symphony by itself (i.e., without following it with food), we turn on a yellow light. The light is a neutral stimulus for salivation, and is never paired with food. However, after a number of pairings of the light with the music (an established CS for the response of salivation), the light itself will come to elicit salivation. The procedure in which a neutral stimulus becomes a conditioned stimulus by being paired with another conditioned stimulus, instead of with an unconditioned stimulus, is known as **higher-order conditioning.** The pairing of the music with the food is referred to as conditioning of the *first order*. Pairing the light with the music is referred to as conditioning of the *second order*. Although third-order conditioning has been reported (Pavlov, 1927), higher-order conditioning beyond the second order appears to be difficult. The model for higher-order conditioning is presented in Figure 3.2.

Let's see how higher-order conditioning might apply in everyday life. Suppose that a child experiences painful stimuli several times, such as from touching a hot stove on one occasion and a sharp thorn on another. Each painful stimulus can be considered a US causing fear as a UR. Let's suppose further that, each time just as each painful experience occurred, a parent yelled, "Watch out! You'll hurt yourself!" This warning from the parent is likely to become a CS eliciting fear. Suppose, also, that the parent later utters the same warning when the child climbs on a ladder, stands on a chair, or climbs onto the kitchen counter. Pairings of the warning with these other activities might influence the child to develop a general fear of heights through higher-order conditioning. The conditioning stages were as follows: First, warnings were paired with painful stimuli; second, being in high places was paired with warnings. Result: Being in a high place now elicits a response (fear) similar to that elicited by painful stimuli.

Common Respondently Conditioned Responses

Through evolution, humans are born with numerous unconditioned reflexes, such as those listed in Table 3.1. Such reflexes are important to our survival, reproduction, and day-to-day biological functioning. We also evolved with a susceptibility to Pavlovian conditioning. The fact that reflexive responses

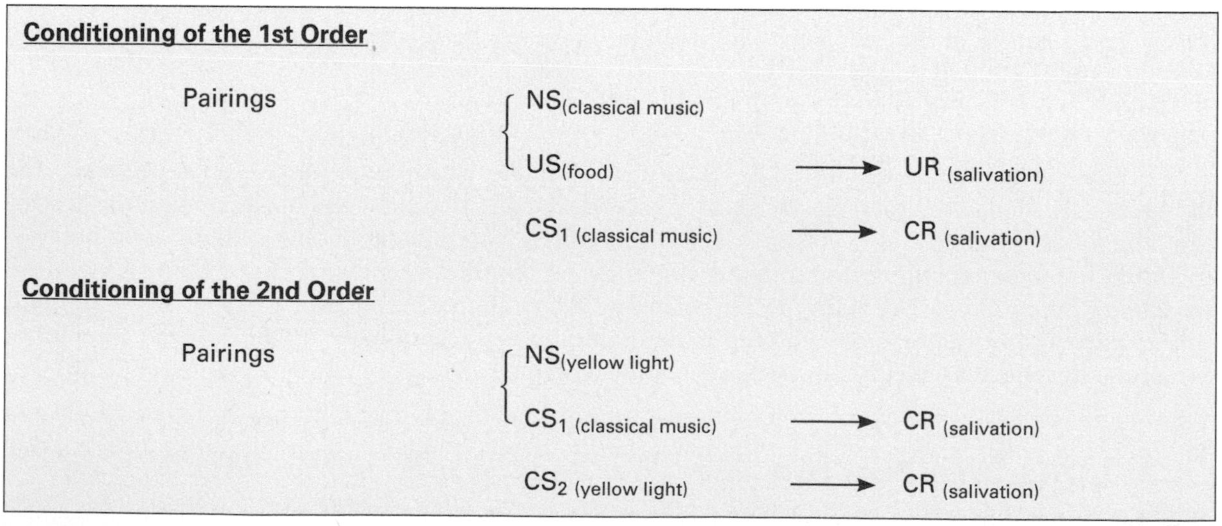

Conditioning of the 1st Order

Pairings $\left\{ \begin{array}{l} NS_{(classical\ music)} \\ US_{(food)} \end{array} \right.$ $\longrightarrow$ UR $_{(salivation)}$

CS$_1$ $_{(classical\ music)}$ $\longrightarrow$ CR $_{(salivation)}$

Conditioning of the 2nd Order

Pairings $\left\{ \begin{array}{l} NS_{(yellow\ light)} \\ CS_1\ {(classical\ music)} \end{array} \right.$ $\longrightarrow$ CR $_{(salivation)}$

CS$_2$ $_{(yellow\ light)}$ $\longrightarrow$ CR $_{(salivation)}$

FIGURE 3.2
Model for higher-order conditioning

can be conditioned to previously neutral stimuli is biologically adaptive. Our capability of being conditioned to secrete saliva (and other gastric juices) at the sight of food, for example, prepares us to digest our food more rapidly than would occur if there were no such thing as Pavlovian conditioning. Let's consider in more detail some major categories of conditioned reflexes.

Digestive System

The salivation reflex is only one of the digestive reflexes that are susceptible to Pavlovian conditioning. A student experiences butterflies in the stomach before giving a talk in class. After experiencing chemotherapy, some patients feel nauseous while waiting in the treatment room for therapy to begin. An extremely frightening experience, such as being threatened by a knife-wielding intruder, can cause anxiety defecation.

When one of the authors was 16 years old, he had an encounter with lemon gin at a party. Except for the occasional bottle of beer, he was an inexperienced drinker of alcohol. The first few sips of lemon gin were quite enjoyable, and produced no immediate reaction of drunkenness. In approximately 15 minutes, he had drunk several ounces of lemon gin. Approximately an hour later, he became violently ill. Since that time the smell or taste of lemon gin causes instant nausea. Even the thought of it causes his stomach to start complaining. In this example, the large amount of lemon gin in the stomach was a US causing nausea as a UR. Even though the smell and taste of lemon gin were paired with the reflexive responses of nausea and vomiting just once, and even though there was a long delay between the previously neutral stimuli (the taste and smell of lemon gin) and the experience of nausea, Pavlovian conditioning occurred. The taste and smell of lemon gin became a CS for the nausea reflex, and a *conditioned taste aversion*, a dislike for lemon gin, was established. The phenomenon of conditioned taste aversion is an exception to the rule that respondent conditioning is ineffective if there is a long delay between the CS and the US. Evolution has apparently provided for a long delay between the CS and US to be effective in this case because of the time toxic substances take to have an effect on the body. It is also an exception to the need for there to be many conditioning trials in order for a strong conditioned reflex to be formed. Evolution has apparently provided for just one conditioning trial to be effective in this case because just one ingestion of a toxic substance can be extremely harmful or even fatal.

Circulatory System

Increased heart rate and blood flow are involved in many conditioned reflexes. Feeling embarrassed in a social setting, overhearing risqué topics discussed, having socially inappropriate thoughts—are all CSs for blushing in many individuals as blood flows to the outer layers of the skin. The circulatory system is involved when a scary scene in a movie or novel causes your heart to pound, and when nude photographs elicit increased heart rate and increased blood flow to the genitals.

Respiratory System

Pavlovian conditioning has also been implicated in influencing coughing, sneezing, and asthma attacks—reflexes of the respiratory system. Suppose a person's aunt, who visits rarely, happens to visit when that person suffers an asthma attack. The aunt might become a CS for the coughing and wheezing characteristic of an asthmatic reaction. Dekker and Groen (1956) reported that asthmatic responses have been elicited by such CSs as the sight of horses, caged birds, goldfish, and police vans.

Other Systems

Other organ systems of the body—such as the urinary and reproductive systems—are also susceptible to Pavlovian conditioning.

Seligman (1971) coined the term *biological preparedness* to refer to the predisposition of members of a species to be more readily conditioned to some neutral stimuli as CSs than to others. As an example of biological preparedness, humans will more quickly learn fears to stimuli, such as snakes and insects, that posed a threat to our survival than to stimuli, such as pictures of flowers, that were nonthreatening in our distant ancestors' history (Ohman, Dimberg, & Ost, 1984). Conditioned taste aversion is another example of biological preparedness. Having evolved the strong tendency for taste to be conditioned to nausea greatly decreases the chances that one will repeatedly consume food that causes illness and perhaps death.

Procedures for Eliminating a Conditioned Reflex

Once a conditioned reflex is developed, does it stay with us forever? Not necessarily. It may be eliminated through either of two procedures.

Respondent Extinction

The principle of **respondent extinction** involves the procedure of presenting a CS while withholding the US, with the result that the CS gradually loses its capability of eliciting the CR. Suppose that a child reaches out to touch a large dog just as the dog barks loudly, scaring the child. As a function of the pairing of the loud bark with the sight of the big dog, the sight of the dog alone now elicits crying and trembling. This is a Pavlovian conditioned response that we label "fear." Now suppose that the parent takes the child to a dog show. Although there are lots of large dogs around, they have been trained to walk and sit quietly while on display. Repeated contact with these dogs (without them being paired with barking) will help the child overcome the fear of seeing dogs. That is, the sight of dogs loses its capability of functioning as a CS to elicit the fear reaction as a CR. Many of the fears that we acquire during childhood—fears of needles, the dark, lightning, and so on—undergo respondent extinction as we grow older, due to repeated exposure to these things in the absence of dire consequences. Figure 3.3 illustrates respondent extinction. And luckily for Sue, after encountering the word "large" several times without further pairings with the shock and tone, "large" gradually lost its ability to elicit anxiety.

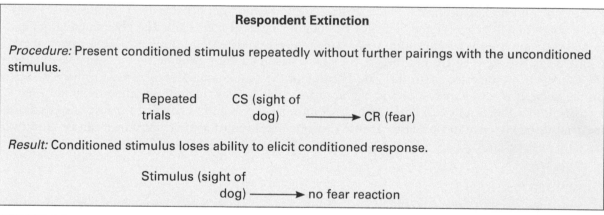

FIGURE 3.3
Model for respondent extinction

Respondent extinction is the reason that higher-order conditioning is difficult to obtain beyond the second order. In the example cited in Figure 3.2, when conditioning of the second order is attempted, CS_1, the opening motif of Beethoven's Fifth Symphony, is no longer paired with food, the US. Thus, the opening motif of Beethoven's Fifth Symphony is undergoing extinction as a CS and the salivation elicited by the opening motif of Beethoven's Fifth Symphony is weaker than the salivation originally elicited by food.

Counterconditioning

A conditioned response may be eliminated more effectively if a new response is conditioned to the conditioned stimulus at the same time that the former conditioned response is being extinguished. This process is called **counterconditioning.** Stated technically, a CS will lose its ability to elicit a CR if that CS is paired with a stimulus that elicits a response that is incompatible with the CR. To illustrate this process, let's reconsider the example of a child who acquired a fear of the sight of dogs. Let's suppose that the child likes playing with a friend who has become a CS eliciting feelings of happiness as a CR, and let's suppose that the friend has a friendly dog that doesn't bark loudly. As the child plays with his or her friend and the friend's dog, some of the positive emotions elicited by the friend will become conditioned to the friend's dog. These positive conditioned emotional responses will help counteract the negative conditioned emotional responses previously elicited by dogs and thus more quickly and more effectively eliminate the negative responses. Figure 3.4 illustrates counterconditioning.

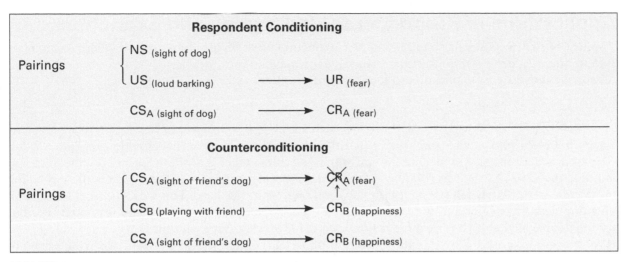

FIGURE 3.4
A diagram of counterconditioning

Questions for Learning

8. Diagram an example of higher-order conditioning.
9. Give three examples of conditioned reflexes, one for each of these categories: digestion, circulation, and respiration.
10. Give an example of a conditioned taste aversion.
11. Why do you suppose that we have evolved so that we are susceptible to conditioned taste aversion?
12. What is biological preparedness? Give an example.
13. Discuss whether all stimuli are equally capable of becoming CSs.
14. State the procedure and result of the principle of respondent extinction. Give an example that is not in this chapter.
15. Describe the process of counterconditioning. Describe or diagram an example of counterconditioning that is not in this chapter.

Generalization and Discrimination of Respondent Behavior

Consider the example given previously in which the sight of a dog became a CS causing a child to feel frightened (a CR) because the sight of that dog had been paired with loud barking. If the child now saw a different dog, would this dog also cause the child to feel fear? Probably yes. **Respondent stimulus generalization** occurs when an organism has been conditioned so that a particular CS elicits a CR, and then a similar stimulus elicits that CR. Suppose, for example, while the dentist is drilling a cavity you have, you experience considerable pain while sitting in the dentist's chair. The sound of the dentist's drill is likely to become a CS causing you to cringe. Later, while visiting the meat market and hearing the sound of the butcher's cutting machine, you feel yourself cringing. You are illustrating an example of respondent stimulus generalization. However, if you were to experience several repeated episodes of the dentist's drill paired with some pain, and several repeated episodes of the butcher's cutting tool never being paired with pain, then you would eventually show **respondent stimulus discrimination**—a stimulus functions as a CS to elicit a CR because that stimulus has been paired with a US that elicits that CR, but a similar stimulus does not function as a CS for that CR because the second stimulus has been paired with extinction trials. We have evolved to show respondent stimulus generalization and respondent stimulus discrimination because such processes have had adaptive survival value for our early ancestors. For example, with respect to respondent stimulus generalization, in the early days of mankind, if being bitten by one snake caused the individual to show fear to other snakes, then that individual was more likely to survive. On the other hand, with respect to respondent stimulus discrimination, if the sight of a wild wolf came to elicit fear in a child, but the sight of a pet dog gradually did not do so, then that also had survival value.

Applications of Respondent Conditioning and Extinction

NOTE 1 Applications of respondent conditioning and extinction have involved controlling allergies, immune system function, drug reactions, sexual arousal, nausea, blood pressure, thoughts, and emotions. In this section we illustrate its application to four types of problems.

Treatment of Fear in a Young Figure Skater[2]

Susan, a 12-year-old novice competitive figure skater, was working on her double axel jump at her skating practice. She skated around the rink, approached the takeoff position for her double axel, and initiated the jump. As she was rotating in the air she suddenly realized that she was on a tilt and falling (a US). She immediately felt strong fear (a UR), and then hit the ice hard. This was Susan's third bad fall on a double axel attempt during the past week. She got up, brushed herself off, and was determined to try the double axel at least once more before leaving for the day. But each time that she approached the takeoff position (now a CS), she experienced strong feelings of fear (CR) and could not bring herself to attempt the jump during the rest of that practice session.

A meeting was arranged for Susan to talk to the figure skating team's sport psychologist. The psychologist taught Susan a relaxation technique referred to as deep center breathing, which involves breathing low down in the stomach rather than high up in the chest. Deep center breathing is a US that produces feelings of relaxation as a UR. Also, each time that Susan practiced deep center breathing and while she was slowly exhaling on each breath, she was encouraged to say "reeeee-laaaaax" slowly to herself. "Reeeee-laaaaax" therefore became a CS for feeling relaxed as a CR. At the next practice, when Susan was getting ready to attempt a double axel, the psychologist called her over to the side of the rink and asked her to practice deep center breathing for several breaths, each time saying to herself "reeeee-laaaaax" while exhaling. The psychologist then prompted Susan to skate around and approach the takeoff position for the double axel. Just before getting to the place where she would normally initiate the jump, she was to tell herself to "reeeee-laaaaax" but not attempt the jump. Susan did this five times in succession. After the fifth time, she told the psychologist that she did not feel nearly as nervous on the fifth trial as she did on the first trial when she was approaching the takeoff position. She felt that she was ready to try another double axel, including repeating the preceding routine while approaching the takeoff position. Susan successfully attempted the jump, and, although she two-footed the landing, she said afterwards that she felt much less fear on the takeoff. She was confident that she could now continue successfully practicing double-axels with only a moderate amount of fear, and this proved to be the case. (Applications of respondent principles to treat anxiety disorders are discussed in Chapter 28.)

Aversion Therapy to Treat Alcoholism

In the early days of behavior therapy, respondent conditioning was used in the treatment of alcoholism. In a clinic or hospital setting, a client was given an alcoholic drink that contained the drug disulfiram. Disulfiram was a US that produced nausea and other extremely unpleasant effects as URs. After several pairings of drinking alcohol with nausea (caused by the disulfiram), the sight, smell, and taste of the drink became CSs causing nausea as a CR. A side effect of this respondent conditioning process was that the client no longer experienced the desire to drink an alcoholic beverage, at least in the treatment setting (Lubetkin, Rivers, & Rosenberg, 1971). The process of pairing something unpleasant (such as nausea) with an undesirable behavior (such as alcohol drinking for someone with alcoholism), with the goal of decreasing the undesirable behavior, is referred to as *aversion* therapy. Although aversion therapy appears to be a valuable component of treatment programs for certain types of problems such as alcoholism (Azrin, Sisson, Meyers, & Godley, 1982) and cigarette smoking (Tiffany, Martin, & Baker, 1986), it is now not commonly used. As Wilson (1991) indicated, its limited use extends from ethical concerns about the use of aversive stimulation in treatment and the fact that there is a fairly high dropout rate of clients from treatment programs using aversion therapy.

---

[2] This case was described in Martin (2015).

Treatment of Chronic Constipation

An example of respondent conditioning of a desirable response is the treatment for chronic constipation developed by Quarti and Renaud (1964). Defecation, the desired response in cases of constipation, can be elicited by administering a laxative. However, reliance on such drugs to achieve regularity is not the healthiest solution because of undesirable side effects. Quarti and Renaud had their clients administer a distinctive electrical stimulus—a mild, nonpainful electric current— to themselves immediately prior to defecating. Defecation (UR) was initially elicited by a laxative (US), and then the amount of the drug was gradually decreased until defecation (CR) was elicited by the electrical stimulus (CS) alone. Then, by applying the electrical stimulus at the same time each day, several of the clients were eventually able to get rid of the electrical stimulus, because the natural environment stimuli characteristically present at that time each day acquired control over the behavior of defecating. Thus, these clients achieved regularity without the continued use of a laxative (see also Rovetto, 1979).

Treatment of Nocturnal Enuresis (Bed-Wetting)

Another example of respondent conditioning of a desirable response is the bell-pad treatment for nocturnal enuresis (bed-wetting; Friman & Piazza, 2011; Scott, Barclay, & Houts, 1992; Williams, Jackson, & Friman, 2007). One possible explanation for bed-wetting, a problem that is rather common in young children, is that pressure on the child's bladder while asleep and needing to urinate does not provide sufficient stimulation to awaken the child. A device that seems to be effective for many enuretic children consists of a bell connected to a special pad under the bottom sheet on the child's bed. The apparatus is wired so that the bell sounds (US) and awakens (UR) the child as soon as the first drop of urine makes contact with the pad. Eventually, in many cases, the child will awake before urinating because the response of waking up (now a CR) has been conditioned to the stimulus of pressure on the bladder (a CS). When that happens, the behavioral sequence of getting up, walking to the bathroom, and urinating in the toilet should be encouraged. But this latter sequence involves a type of learning called operant conditioning, rather than respondent conditioning.

An Introduction to Operant Conditioning: Another Type of Learning

Reflexes! That's what respondent conditioning is all about—automatic responses to prior stimuli. But much of our behavior appears to be voluntary rather than reflexive, behavior that is influenced by its consequences (rewards and punishers) rather than by prior stimuli (CSs and USs). Behavior that is influenced by its consequences is referred to as **operant behavior**—behavior that affects or "operates on" the environment to produce consequences, and which is, in turn, influenced by those consequences. Examples include putting gas in your car, asking for directions, writing an exam, turning on a computer, and making breakfast. **Operant conditioning** is a type of learning in which behavior is modified by its consequences. For example, through operant conditioning, we have learned to turn on a water tap to produce water, and not to touch a hot stove because of the pain following past instances of doing so. Principles and procedures of operant conditioning are discussed in Chapters 4 through 14. In Chapter 15 we compare respondent and operant conditioning, and discuss how, at any given time, we are likely to be influenced by respondent and operant conditioning occurring concurrently. In Chapter 15 we also discuss how both respondent and operant conditioning are important in explaining our "thinking" and "emotions."

Questions for Learning

16. Define respondent stimulus generalization, and give an example.
17. Define respondent stimulus discrimination, and give an example.
18. In the example of Susan learning to fear performing the double axel jump, what was the US, UR, CS, and CR?
19. Describe (or diagram) how counterconditioning was involved to help Susan overcome her fear of attempting a double axel jump.
20. In the respondent conditioning component for treating alcoholism, what is the US, UR, CS, and CR?
21. What is aversion therapy? Give an example.

22. Describe a respondent conditioning procedure for treating constipation. Identify the US, UR, CS, and CR.
23. Describe a respondent conditioning component of a procedure for treating nocturnal enuresis. Identify the US, UR, CS, and CR.
24. What is operant behavior? Give an example.
25. What is operant conditioning? Give an example.

Application Exercises

A. Exercise Involving Others

Interview a relative, friend, or acquaintance regarding something that elicits feelings of fear or nausea in that person, but does not do so in many people. Determine whether that person can recall events that may have led to this unusual reaction. Are these events consistent with the description of respondent conditioning in this chapter? Discuss.

B. Self-Modification Exercise

Describe three examples of conditioned reflexes of yours, one for each of these categories: digestion, circulation, and respiration. Make sure the stimuli in your examples are CSs and not USs.

Note for Further Learning

1. Pavlovian conditioning procedures may affect the functioning of our immune systems. Ader and Cohen (1982) found with rats that pairing saccharine with an immune-suppressive drug established saccharine as a conditioned stimulus that elicits immune suppression. Other studies have also demonstrated classical conditioning of various aspects of immune responses in other species (Ader & Cohen, 1993; Maier, Watkins, & Fleshner, 1994). For a human example, consider that a standard treatment for cancer, chemotherapy, involves chemical agents that are immunosuppressive. In a study in which repeated chemotherapy was done in the same room in the same hospital setting for women suffering from ovarian cancer, the women eventually displayed immunosuppression after simply being brought to that room of the hospital prior to receiving chemotherapy (Bovjberg et al., 1990). Further research may lead to ways of using Pavlovian conditioning to strengthen the immune system. This exciting area of research on the effects of conditioning processes on the functioning of the body's immune system is called psychoimmunology or psychoneuroimmunology (Daruna, 2004).

Questions for Further Learning

1. What conditioned reflex occurred in a study of chemotherapy for ovarian cancer?
2. What is the field of psychoimmunology or psychoneuroimmunology all about?

CHAPTER 4

Increasing a Behavior with Positive Reinforcement

After studying this chapter, you will be able to:

- Define *positive reinforcement*.
- Discuss how we are influenced by positive reinforcement on an almost continuous basis.
- Distinguish between positive reinforcement and negative reinforcement.

- Describe factors that influence the effectiveness of positive reinforcement.
- Explain how positive reinforcement can work against individuals who are unaware of it.

Do you want to sit here, Mommy?

Reinforcing Darren's Cooperative Behavior[1]

Six-year-old Darren was extremely uncooperative with his parents. In the hope of learning how to deal more effectively with his excessive commanding behavior, Darren's parents took him to the Gatzert Child Developmental Clinic at the University of Washington. As his parents described the problem, Darren virtually "ran the show" at home, deciding when he would go to bed, what foods he would eat, when his parents could play with him, and so on. To obtain direct observations of Darren's behavior, both cooperative and uncooperative, Dr. Robert Wahler asked Darren's mother to spend some time with Darren in a playroom at the clinic. The playroom was equipped with adjoining observation rooms for data recording. During the first two 20-minute sessions, called a baseline phase,[2] Darren's mother was instructed: "Just play with Darren as you might at home." Darren's commanding behavior was defined as any verbal or nonverbal instructions to his mother, such as pushing her into a chair or saying such things as "You go over there and I'll stay here," or "No, that's wrong. Do it this way." Cooperative behavior was defined as any noncommanding statements, actions, or questions, such as, "Do you want to sit here?" while pointing to a chair. Darren showed a very low rate of cooperative behavior during the baseline sessions. His commanding behavior, on the other hand, occurred at an extremely high rate. Following the baseline sessions, Darren's mother was asked to be very positive and supportive to any instances of cooperative behavior shown by Darren. At the same time, she was instructed to completely ignore his commanding behavior. Over the next two sessions, Darren's cooperative behavior steadily increased. (During the same time, his commanding behavior decreased to near zero.) Further experimentation was done by Dr. Wahler and his colleagues to demonstrate that Darren's improvement resulted from the positive consequences provided by his mother following instances of Darren's cooperative behavior (in conjunction with her ignoring of commanding behavior).

---

[1] This example is based on an article by Wahler, Winkel, Peterson, and Morrison (1965).
[2] A *baseline phase* (discussed further in Chapters 20, 22, and 23) is a measure of behavior in the absence of a treatment program.

Positive Reinforcement

A **positive reinforcer** is an event that, when presented immediately following a behavior, causes the behavior to increase in frequency. The term *positive reinforcer* is roughly synonymous with the word *reward*. Once an event has been determined to function as a positive reinforcer for a particular individual in a particular situation, that event can be used to increase other behaviors of that individual in other situations. In conjunction with the concept of positive reinforcer, the principle called **positive reinforcement** states that *if someone in a given situation does something that is followed immediately by a positive reinforcer, then that person is more likely to do the same thing the next time he or she encounters a similar situation.* Although everyone has a common-sense notion of rewards, very few people are aware of just how frequently they are influenced by positive reinforcement every minute of their lives. Some examples of reinforcement are shown in Table 4.1.

The individuals in each of the examples in Table 4.1 were not consciously using the principle of positive reinforcement; they were just "doing what comes naturally." In each example, it might take several repetitions before there would be any really obvious increase in the positively reinforced response (i.e., an increase that would be noticeable to a casual observer). Nevertheless, the effect is still there.

Think about some of your behaviors during the past hour. Were any of those behaviors followed immediately by reinforcing consequences? In some cases we may not be aware of these consequences and the effects they have had and are continuously having on our behavior.

As stated at the end of Chapter 3, behaviors that operate on the environment to generate consequences and are in turn influenced by those consequences are called **operant behaviors** (or *operant responses*). Each of the responses listed in Table 4.1 is an example of operant behavior. Operant behaviors that are followed by positive reinforcers are increased, while operant behaviors that are followed by punishers (as will be seen in Chapter 12) are decreased. A different type of behavior—reflexive or respondent behavior—was discussed in Chapter 3.

TABLE 4.1   Examples of Instances of Reinforcement of Desirable Behaviors

Situation	Response	Immediate Consequences	Long-Term Effects
1. While you are waiting in a long line of cars for the light to change at a busy intersection, a car stops in the alley on your right.	You wave to the driver in the alley to pull into the line of traffic in front of you.	The driver nods and waves thanks to you and pulls into the line of traffic.	The pleasant feedback from the driver increases the likelihood that you will be courteous in similar situations in the future.
2. The students in a third-grade class have been given an assignment to complete.	Suzy, who is often quite disruptive, sits quietly at her desk and starts working on the assignment.	The teacher walks over to Suzy and gives a thumbs-up.	In the future, Suzy is more likely to work on the assignments given to her in class.
3. A college student is preparing answers to the study questions in this chapter, and isn't sure about one of the answers.	The student asks her friend, who has already studied this chapter, for some help.	Her friend tells her the correct answer.	If the student can't find answers to questions in the remaining chapters, she's likely to ask her friend for help.
4. Father and child are shopping in a department store on a hot afternoon and both are very tired.	The child (uncharacteristically) follows father around the store quietly and without complaining.	Father turns to the child and says, "Let's go and buy an ice cream cone and sit down for a while."	On future shopping excursions, the child is more likely to follow father quietly.
5. A woman has just tasted a batch of soup she made, and it tasted very bland.	She adds a little Worcestershire sauce and then tastes it again.	"It tastes very tangy, just like minestrone soup," she says to herself.	There is an increased likelihood that, in similar situations in the future, she will add Worcestershire sauce to her soup.

Positive Reinforcement Versus Negative Reinforcement

It is important to keep in mind that positive reinforcers are events that increase a response when they are introduced or added following the response. The removal of an event following a response may also increase that response, but this is not positive reinforcement. For example, a parent might nag a teenager to do the dishes. When the child complies, the nagging stops. Although the cessation of nagging when dishwashing occurs may increase the dishwashing response, it was the nagging's *removal* (not its introduction) following the response that increased it. This is an example of the principle of **negative reinforcement** (also known as **escape conditioning**), which states that the removal of certain stimuli immediately after the occurrence of a response will increase the likelihood of that response. As indicated by the word *reinforcement*, positive and negative reinforcement are similar in that both increase responses. They are different as indicated by the words *positive* and *negative* in that positive reinforcement increases a response because of the presentation of a positive stimulus, whereas negative reinforcement increases a response by the removal or taking away of a negative (or aversive) stimulus. Negative reinforcement is discussed further in Chapter 14. Note: Do not confuse negative reinforcement (which increases behavior) with punishment (which decreases behavior). Punishment is discussed in Chapter 13.

Positive Reinforcement Is a Law of Behavior

It is helpful to think about behavior in the same way that we think about other aspects of nature. What happens when you drop a shoe? It falls toward the earth. What happens to a lake when the temperature drops below 0°C? The water freezes. These are things that we all know about and that physicists have studied extensively and formulated into laws, such as the law of gravity. The principle of positive reinforcement, one of the principles of operant conditioning, is also a law. Scientific psychology has been studying this principle in great detail for over a century (e.g., Thorndike, 1911), and we know that it is an extremely important part of the learning process. We also know of a number of factors that determine the degree of influence the principle of reinforcement has on behavior. (For a review of research on these factors, see DeLeon, Bullock, & Catania, 2013.) These factors have been formulated into guidelines to be followed when using positive reinforcement to increase desirable behavior.

Questions for Learning

1. What is a baseline?
2. Describe the baseline condition for Darren's program.
3. Describe the treatment condition for Darren's program.
4. What is a positive reinforcer?
5. What is the principle of positive reinforcement?
6. Give an example of positive reinforcement of a desirable behavior that you have encountered. Identify the situation, behavior, immediate consequence, and probable long-term effects (as shown in Table 4.1). The example should not be from the text.
7. What is operant behavior? Give an example, and indicate how the example fits the definition of operant behavior.
8. Define negative reinforcement and give an example that is not from this chapter.
9. How are positive and negative reinforcement similar, and how are they different?
10. In what way is positive reinforcement like gravity?

Factors Influencing the Effectiveness of Positive Reinforcement

1. Selecting the Behavior to Be Increased

The behaviors to be reinforced must first be identified specifically. If you start with a general behavior category (e.g., being more friendly), you should then identify specific behaviors (e.g., smiling) that characterize that category. By being specific, you (a) help to ensure the reliability of detecting instances of the behavior and changes in its frequency, which is the measure by which one judges reinforcer effectiveness; and (b) increase the likelihood that the reinforcement program will be applied consistently.

2. Choosing Reinforcers ("Different Strokes for Different Folks")

Some stimuli are positive reinforcers for virtually everyone. Food is a positive reinforcer for almost anyone who has not had anything to eat for several hours. Candy is a reinforcer for most children. A mother's immediate imitation of her infant's babbling (e.g., the child says "dadaba" and the mother says "dadaba") is a reinforcer for most 6-month-old infants (Pelaez, Virues-Ortega, & Gewirtz, 2011). However, different individuals are frequently "turned on" by different things. Consider the case of Dianne, a 6-year-old girl with a developmental disability who was in a project conducted by one of the authors. She was able to mimic a number of words, and was being taught to name pictures. Two commonly used reinforcers in the project were candy and bites of other preferred foods, but these were not effective with Dianne. She spat them out about as often as she ate them. After trying many other potential reinforcers, we finally discovered that allowing her to play with a toy purse for 15 seconds was very reinforcing. As a result, after many hours of training she was able to speak in phrases and complete sentences. For another child, listening to a music box for a few seconds turned out to be an effective reinforcer after other potential reinforcers failed. These stimuli might not have been reinforcing for everyone, but that is not important. The important thing is to use a reinforcer that is effective with the individual with whom you are working.

FIGURE 4.1

Praise is a powerful positive reinforcer for strengthening and maintaining valued behaviors in everyday life.

Most positive reinforcers can be classified under five somewhat overlapping headings: *consumable, activity, manipulative, possessional,* and *social*. Consumable reinforcers are items that one can eat or drink (i.e., consume), such as candy, cookies, fruit, and soft drinks. Examples of activity reinforcers are the opportunities to watch television, look at a picture book, or even stare out of a window. Manipulative reinforcers include the opportunities to play with a favorite toy, color or paint, ride a bicycle, surf the Internet, or tinker with a tape recorder. Possessional reinforcers are the opportunities to sit in one's favorite chair, wear a favorite shirt or dress, have a private room, or enjoy some other item that one can possess (at least temporarily). Social reinforcement includes affectionate pats and hugs, praise, nods, smiles, and even a simple glance or other indication of social attention. Attention from others is a very strong reinforcer for almost everyone (see Figure 4.1). In choosing effective reinforcers for an individual, you might find one of the following strategies to be helpful. (For additional discussion of identifying reinforcers, see Piazza, Roane, & Karsten, 2011.)

Use a Reinforcer Questionnaire or Reinforcer Menu   If the individual can read, it is often helpful to ask them to complete a reinforcer questionnaire (see Table 4.2). Another option is to list specific reinforcers (or pictures of them if the individual cannot read) in the form of a "reinforcer menu," and the preferred reinforcers can be chosen similar to the way one would order a meal at a restaurant.

TABLE 4.2   A Questionnaire to Help Identify Reinforcers for an Individual

Read each question carefully and then fill in the appropriate blanks.

a) Consumable Reinforcers: What do you like to eat or drink?

   1. What do you like to eat most?

   _____

   _____

   2. What do you like to drink most?

   _____

   _____

b) Activity Reinforcers: What things do you like to do?

   1. What do you like to do in your home or residence?

   _____

   _____

   2. What do you like to do in your yard or courtyard?

   _____

   _____

   3. What activities do you like to do in your neighborhood?

   _____

   _____

   4. What passive activities (e.g., watching TV) do you like to do?

   _____

   _____

c) Manipulative Reinforcers: What kinds of games do you like?

   _____

   _____

d) What kinds of things do you like to possess? (e.g., hair clippers, perfume, etc.)?

   _____

   _____

e) What social rewards do you like?

   1. What types of praise statements do you like to receive?

   _____

   _____

   2. What type of physical contact do you enjoy (e.g., hugging, etc.)?

   _____

   _____

Matson and colleagues (1999) described a reinforcer menu that staff in institutional settings might use to select reinforcers for persons with severe and profound developmental disabilities.

Use the Premack Principle   Another method for finding an appropriate reinforcer for a particular individual is simply to observe the individual in everyday activities and note those activities engaged in most often. This method makes use of the **Premack principle** (first formulated by David Premack, 1959), which states that if the opportunity to engage in a behavior that has a high probability of occurring is made contingent on a behavior that has a low probability of occurring, then the behavior that has a low probability of occurring will increase.

For example, let's suppose that parents of a 13-year-old boy observe that, during the school year, their son spends several hours each weekday evening on Facebook or texting friends, but almost never studies or does homework. If the parents were to assume control of their son's cell phone and computer each evening, and if they were to tell their son, "From now on, each school night, for each hour of studying or doing homework, you can have access to your computer and cell phone for the following half hour," then studying and homework would likely increase in frequency. For additional examples of applications of the Premack Principle, see Watson and Tharp (2007). For a discussion of the limitations of the Premack principle, see Timberlake and Farmer-Dougan (1991).

Conduct a preference assessment   It is often quite effective to allow an individual to choose among a number of available reinforcers (DeLeon & Iwata, 1996). Variety is not only the spice of life; it is also a valuable asset to a training program. For example, in a program for a person with developmental disabilities, a tray containing sliced fruits, peanuts, raisins, and diet drinks can be presented as a reinforcer with the instruction to take one item. The advantage of this is that only one of the reinforcers among the selection has to be strong in order for the selection to be a strong reinforcer. For examples of research on preference assessment procedures with persons with developmental disabilities see Davies, Chand, Yu, Martin, and Martin (2013) and Lee, Yu, Martin, and Martin (2010).

When in Doubt, Do a Reinforcer Test   No matter how you have selected a potential reinforcer for an individual, it is always the individual's performance that tells you whether or not you have selected an effective reinforcer. When you are not sure if a particular item is reinforcing, you can always conduct an experimental test that involves *going back to the definition of a reinforcer given at the beginning of this chapter.* Simply choose a behavior that the individual emits occasionally and that does not appear to be followed by any reinforcer, record how often the behavior occurs without obvious reinforcement over several trials, and then present the item immediate following the behavior for a few additional trials and see what happens. If the individual begins to emit that behavior more often, then your item is indeed a reinforcer. If the performance does not increase, then you do not have an effective reinforcer. In our experience, not using an effective reinforcer is a common error of training programs. For example, a teacher may claim that a particular reinforcement program that he is trying to use is failing. Upon examination, the reinforcer used may turn out not to be a reinforcer for the student. You can never really be sure that an item is a reinforcer for someone until it has been demonstrated to function as such for that person. In other words, an object or event *is defined as a reinforcer only by its effect on behavior.*

External Reinforcers and Intrinsic Motivation   At this point, an objection might be raised: If you deliberately use a tangible (or extrinsic) item to reinforce someone's behavior, won't you undermine that person's intrinsic motivation (inner desire or sense of satisfaction) to perform that behavior? Some critics of behavior modification (e.g., Deci, Koestner, & Ryan, 1999) have suggested that you will. Some (e.g., Kohn, 1993) have gone so far as to argue that tangible rewards should never be given because, for example, if a parent gives a child money as a reinforcer for reading, then the child will be less likely to "read for reading's sake." However, a careful review of the experimental literature on this topic (Cameron, Banko, & Pierce, 2001), and two experiments (Flora & Flora, 1999; McGinnis, Friman, & Carlyon, 1999), clearly indicate that this view is wrong. Moreover, the notion that extrinsic reinforcers undermine intrinsic motivation flies in the face of common sense (Flora, 1990). If extrinsic reinforcers undermine intrinsic motivation, then those fortunate people who genuinely enjoy their jobs should refuse to be paid for fear that their paychecks will destroy their enjoyment of their work. It is also worth noting that the extrinsic–intrinsic distinction between reinforcers may not even be valid: All reinforcers involve external (i.e., extrinsic) stimuli and all have internal (i.e., intrinsic) aspects.

Questions for Learning

11. Why is it necessary to be specific when selecting a behavior for a reinforcement program?
12. List the five somewhat overlapping headings under which most positive reinforcers can be classified, and give an example of each that would be a positive reinforcer for you.
13. Describe the Premack principle. Give an example.
14. "It is always the individual's performance that tells you whether or not you have selected an effective reinforcer." Explain what this means.
15. Using the definition of positive reinforcer, describe the steps to test if a particular item is a reinforcer for someone. Illustrate with an example that is not from this chapter.
16. Using the definition of positive reinforcer, how might you conduct a test to determine if the social attention of a particular adult is or is not reinforcing for a withdrawn child?
17. Does extrinsic reinforcement undermine intrinsic motivation? Discuss.

3. Motivating Operations

Most reinforcers will not be effective unless the individual has been deprived of them for some period of time prior to their use. In general, the longer the deprivation period, the more effective the reinforcer will be. Sweets will usually not be reinforcing to a child who has just eaten a large bag of candy. Playing with a purse would not have been an effective reinforcer for Dianne had she been allowed to play with one prior to the training session. We use the term **deprivation** to indicate the time during which an individual does not experience the reinforcer. The term **satiation** refers to that condition in which the individual has experienced the reinforcer to such an extent that it is no longer reinforcing. "Enough's enough," as the saying goes.

Events or conditions—such as deprivation and satiation—that (a) temporarily alter the effectiveness of a reinforcer, and (b) alter the frequency of behavior reinforced by that reinforcer, are called **motivating operations (MOs)** (discussed further in Chapter 19). Thus, food deprivation not only establishes food as an effective reinforcer for the person who is food deprived, it also momentarily increases various behaviors that have been reinforced with food. As another example, feeding a child very salty food would be an MO because (a) it would momentarily increase the effectiveness of water as a reinforcer for that child, and (b) it would also evoke behavior (e.g., turning on a tap, asking for a drink) that had previously been followed by water. Another name for MO is *motivational variable*—a variable that affects the likelihood and direction of behavior. Because food deprivation increases the effectiveness of food as a reinforcer and salt ingestion increases the effectiveness of water as a reinforcer without prior learning, these events are called *unconditioned MOs*. In Chapter 19, we will introduce you to the notion of conditioned MOs. In general terms, MOs might be thought of as motivators. In everyday life, people might say that depriving someone of food motivates that person to eat. Similarly, they might say that giving an individual salted peanuts motivates that individual to drink.

4. Reinforcer Size

The size (amount or magnitude) of a reinforcer is an important determinant of its effectiveness. Consider the following example. Staff at a large mental hospital discovered that only 60% of the female patients brushed their teeth. When the patients were given a token (that could be cashed in later for reinforcing items such as cigarettes, coffee, or snacks) for brushing their teeth, the percent of those who did so increased to 76%. When the patients were given five tokens for brushing their teeth, the percent of those who did so increased to 91% (Fisher, 1979). Now consider an example that is more typical of the everyday lives of many of us. Many teenagers in a northern state like Minnesota would likely be unwilling to shovel snow from a driveway or sidewalk of a house for 25¢, although many would eagerly do so for $25. As we will discuss further in Chapter 8, the optimum size or amount of a reinforcer needed to ensure its effectiveness will depend on additional factors, such as the difficulty of the behavior and the availability of competing behaviors for alternative reinforcers. For now, keep in mind that the size of the reinforcer must be sufficient to increase the behavior that you want to increase. At the same time, if the goal is to conduct a number of trials during a session, such as in teaching basic language skills to a person with developmental disabilities, the reinforcer on each trial should be small enough so as to minimize satiation and thus maximize the number of reinforced trials that can be given per session.

5. Instructions: Make Use of Rules

NOTE 1   For a reinforcer to increase an individual's behavior, it is not necessary that that individual be able to talk about or indicate an understanding of why he or she was reinforced. After all, the principle has been shown to work quite effectively with animals that cannot speak a human-type language. Nevertheless, *instructions should generally be used.*

Instructional influences on behavior will be easier for you to understand after reading Chapters 9 and 17. For now, let's view instructions as specific rules or guidelines that indicate that specific behaviors will pay off in particular situations. For example, your instructor might state, "If you learn the answers to all of the study questions in this book, you will receive an A in the course."

Instructions can facilitate behavioral change in several ways. First, specific instructions will speed up the learning process for individuals who understand them. For example, in a study on teaching tennis (Ziegler, 1987), beginning tennis players practicing backhand shots showed little progress when simply told to "concentrate." However, they showed rapid improvement when told to vocalize the word "ready" when the ball machine was about to present the next ball, the word "ball" when they saw the ball fired from the machine, the word "bounce" as they watched the ball contact the surface of the court, and the word "hit" when they observed the ball contacting their racquet while swinging their backhand. Second, as indicated earlier (and discussed further in Chapter 17), instructions may influence an individual to work for delayed reinforcement. Getting an A in the course for which you are using this book, for example, is delayed several months from the beginning of the course. Daily rehearsing of the rule, "If I learn the answers to the questions at the end of each chapter, I'll likely get an A," may exert some influence over your study behavior. Third (as discussed further in Chapter 9), adding instructions to reinforcement programs may help to teach individuals (such as very young children or persons with developmental disabilities) to learn to follow instructions.

Critics have accused behavior modifiers of using bribery. Suppose that a gambler offered $5,000,000 to a famous baseball player to strike out during each at-bat in the World Series. Clearly, that fits the definition of *bribery*—a reward or a gift offered to induce someone to commit an immoral or illegal act. Now suppose that a parent offers a child $5 for completing a homework assignment within a set period of time. Is that bribery? Of course not. The parent's offer is the use of instructions about a reinforcement program to increase desirable behavior. Similarly, people at most jobs are told ahead of time how much they will be paid for their work, but that is not bribery. Obviously, critics who accuse behavior modifiers of using bribery fail to distinguish between the promise of reinforcers for desirable behaviors versus the promise of reinforcers for immoral or illegal deeds.

6. Reinforcer Immediacy

For maximum effectiveness, a reinforcer should be given immediately after the desired response. Consider the example in Table 4.1 where Suzie uncharacteristically sat quietly at her desk and started working on the assignment, and a teacher immediately gave Suzie a thumbs-up. If the teacher had waited until after recess to do so, when Suzie was once again being disruptive, the thumbs-up would not have strengthened Suzie's working on her assignment. However, in some cases, it may appear that a behavior is influenced by delayed reinforcement. Telling a child that if she cleans up her room in the morning her father will bring her a toy in the evening is sometimes effective. Moreover, people do work toward long-delayed goals, such as college degrees. However, it is a mistake to attribute such results just to the effects of the principle of positive reinforcement. It has been found with animals that a reinforcer is unlikely to have much direct effect on a behavior that precedes it by much longer than 30 seconds (Chung, 1965; Lattal & Metzger, 1994; Perin, 1943), and we have no reason to believe that humans are essentially different in this respect (Michael, 1986; Okouchi, 2009).

How is it, then, that a long-delayed reinforcer might be effective with humans? The answer is that there must be certain events that mediate or "bridge the gap" between the response and the long-delayed reinforcer (see Pear, 2001, pp. 246–249). Consider the example above where a child was told in the morning that if she cleaned up her room her father would bring her a toy in the evening. Perhaps while cleaning up her room in the morning, and frequently during the day, the child reminded herself that she was going to get a toy in the evening, and these self-statements may have influenced the critical behavior. Although the positive effects of the program were due to the treatment, the treatment was more complex than that of a positive reinforcer increasing the frequency of a response that immediately preceded it.

The direct-acting effect of the principle of positive reinforcement is the increased frequency of a **NOTE 2** response because of its immediate reinforcing consequences. The indirect-acting effect of positive reinforcement is the strengthening of a response (such as the child cleaning up her room in the morning) that is followed by a reinforcer (getting a toy in the evening) even though the reinforcer is delayed. Delayed reinforcers may have an effect on behavior because of instructions about the behavior leading to the reinforcer, and/or because of self-statements (or "thoughts") that intervene between that behavior and the delayed reinforcer. During the day, for example, the child may have been making self-statements (i.e., "thinking") about what kind of toy her father would bring. (Other explanations of indirect-acting effects of positive reinforcement are presented in Chapter 17.)

The distinction between direct- and indirect-acting effects of reinforcement has important implica- **NOTE 3** tions for practitioners. If you can't present a reinforcer immediately following the desired behavior, then provide instructions concerning the delay of reinforcement.

Questions for Learning

18. What do behavior modifiers mean by the term *deprivation*? Give an example.
19. What do behavior modifiers mean by the term *satiation*? Give an example.
20. What is a motivating operation? Give two examples, one of which should not be from this chapter.
21. Should you tell an individual with whom you are using reinforcement about the reinforcement program before putting it into effect? Why or why not?
22. If you instruct someone about a positive reinforcement program for his or her behavior, is that bribery? Why or why not?
23. Distinguish between the direct- and indirect-acting effects of reinforcement.

7. Contingent versus Noncontingent Reinforcers

We say that a reinforcer is **contingent** when a specific behavior must occur before that reinforcer will be presented. We say that a reinforcer is **non-contingent** if that reinforcer is presented at a particular time regardless of the preceding behavior. To illustrate the importance of this distinction, consider the following example.[3] Coach Keedwell watched her young swimmers swim a set during a regular practice at the Marlin Youth Swim Club. (A set is several lengths of a particular stroke to be swum within a specified time.) She had frequently tried to impress on them the importance of practicing their racing turns at each end of the pool and swimming the sets without stopping in the middle. Following the suggestion of one of the other coaches, she had even added a reward to her practices. During the last 10 minutes of each practice, the swimmers were allowed to participate in a fun activity of their choice (swimming relays, playing water polo, etc.). However, the results were still the same: The young swimmers continued to show a high frequency of improper turns and unscheduled stops during sets.

The mistake made by Coach Keedwell is common among novice behavior modifiers. Incorporating a noncontingent fun activity into practices might increase attendance, but it's not likely to have much effect on practice behaviors. Educators frequently make the same mistake as Coach Keedwell. They assume that creating a pleasant environment will improve the learning of the students in that environment. However, reinforcers must be contingent on specific behaviors in order for those behaviors to improve. When this was pointed out to Coach Keedwell, she made the fun activity contingent on desirable practice behaviors. For the next few practices, the swimmers had to meet a goal of practicing a minimum number of racing turns at each end of the pool and swimming their sets without stopping in order to earn the reinforcer at the end of practice. As a result, the swimmers showed approximately 150% improvement. Thus, to maximize the effectiveness of a reinforcement program, be sure that the reinforcers are contingent on specific behaviors that you want to improve.

---

[3] This example is based on a study by Cracklen and Martin (1983).

In addition to not increasing a desirable behavior, a noncontingent reinforcer may increase an undesirable behavior that it happens to follow. Suppose, for example, that, unbeknown to a parent, little Johnny is in his bedroom drawing on the walls with a crayon when the parent calls out, "Johnny, let's go get some ice cream." This accidental contingency might increase Johnny's tendency to draw on his walls. That is, behavior that is "accidentally" followed by a reinforcer may be increased even if it did not actually produce the reinforcer. This is called **adventitious reinforcement**, and behavior increased in this way is called **superstitious behavior** (Skinner, 1948a). As another example, suppose a man playing a slot machine tends to cross his fingers because, in the past, doing so was accidentally followed by winning a jackpot. Such behavior would be considered superstitious.

8. Weaning the Learner from the Program and Changing to Natural Reinforcers

The factors described above influence the effectiveness of positive reinforcement while it is being applied in a program. But what happens to the behavior when the reinforcement program terminates and the individual returns to his or her everyday life? Most everyday behaviors are followed by reinforcers that no one has specifically or deliberately programmed to increase or maintain those behaviors. Reading signs is frequently reinforced by finding desired objects or directions. Eating is reinforced by the taste of food. Flipping on a light switch is reinforced by increased illumination. Turning on a water tap is reinforced by the flow of water. Verbal and other social behaviors are reinforced by the reactions of other people. A setting in which an individual carries out normal, everyday functions (i.e., not a situation explicitly designed for training) is referred to as the **natural environment**. Reinforcers that follow behavior in the course of everyday living (i.e., that occur in the natural environment), are called **natural reinforcers**. Reinforcers that are arranged systematically by psychologists, teachers, and others in behavior modification programs are referred to as *arbitrary*, *contrived*, or **programmed reinforcers**.

After we have increased a behavior through proper use of positive reinforcement, it may then be possible for a reinforcer in the individual's natural environment to take over the maintenance of that behavior. For example, sometimes it is necessary to use reinforcers such as edibles to increase object naming in children with developmental disabilities. However, when the children leave the classroom and return to their homes, they often say the words that they have learned and receive a great deal of attention from their parents. Eventually, the edibles may no longer be needed to reinforce the children for saying the names of objects. This, of course, is the ultimate goal of any training program. The behavior modifier should always try to ensure that the behavior established in a training program will be reinforced and maintained in the natural environment. One thing that you can count on is that if a behavior that has been increased in a reinforcement program is no longer reinforced at least occasionally (either by arbitrary or natural reinforcers), then that behavior will return to its original level. Because the problem of maintaining desirable behaviors is so important, it is discussed in greater detail in Chapters 8 and 16.

Questions for Learning

24. When Coach Keedwell required young swimmers to show improved performance in order to earn a fun activity at the end of practice, their performance improved dramatically. Was this a direct-acting or an indirect-acting effect of reinforcement? Justify your choice.
25. Give an example of contingent reinforcement that is not in this chapter.
26. Give an example of noncontingent reinforcement that is not in this chapter.
27. What is adventitious reinforcement? What is a superstitious behavior? Give an example of each that are not in this chapter.
28. What do we mean by the *natural environment*? By *natural reinforcers*? By *programmed reinforcers*?
29. Describe three behavioral episodes in this chapter that involved natural reinforcers. Justify your choices.
30. Briefly describe, in a sentence each, eight factors that influence the effectiveness of reinforcement.

Pitfalls of Positive Reinforcement

Those who are well versed in behavior principles, like positive reinforcement, can use them to bring about desirable changes in behavior. There are four distinct ways in which lack of knowledge of a principle or procedure can be problematic. In a "Pitfalls" section for each of Chapters 4–16 we will consider one or more of these four different types of pitfalls. We will now illustrate these pitfalls with respect to the principle of positive reinforcement.

Unaware-Misapplication Pitfall

Unfortunately, those who are not aware of positive reinforcement are apt to use it unknowingly to strengthen undesirable behavior, as illustrated in Table 4.3. Many undesirable behaviors are due to the social attention that such behavior evokes from aides, nurses, peers, teachers, parents, doctors, and others. This may be true even in cases where one would least expect it. Consider, for example, children who exhibit extreme social withdrawal. One behavioral characteristic of such children is that they avoid looking at someone who is talking to them. Frequently, they move away from adults. We might conclude that they don't want our attention. Actually, the withdrawn child's behavior probably evokes more social attention than would have been obtained by looking at the adult. In such cases it is only natural for adults to persist in attempting to get a child to look at them when they speak. Unfortunately, this attention is likely to reinforce the child's withdrawal behavior. The tendency to shower attention is sometimes maintained by the theory that social interaction is needed to "bring the child out of his or her withdrawn state." In reality, an appropriate treatment might involve withholding social attention for withdrawal behavior and presenting it only when the child engages in some sort of social-interaction behavior—such as looking in the direction of the adult who is attempting the interaction. The hard work of one behavior modifier using appropriate behavior techniques can be greatly hindered, or completely undone, by others who reinforce the wrong behavior. For example, an aide who attempts to reinforce eye contact in a withdrawn child is probably not going to have much effect if other people who interact with the child consistently reinforce looking-away behavior. In Chapter 23 we discuss methods for assessing whether a problem behavior is being maintained by positive reinforcement and how to treat it if it is.

Partial-Knowledge-Misapplication Pitfall

A person may know a behavioral principle but not realize some ramification that interferes with applying it effectively. "A little knowledge can be a dangerous thing," as the saying goes. For example, novice behavior modifiers often assume that simply presenting reinforcers noncontingently will strengthen a specific behavior. Coach Keedwell, as described earlier in this chapter, assumed that providing a fun activity at the end of each swimming practice would strengthen desirable swimming behaviors. That didn't occur, however, because the fun activity was not contingent on specific practice behaviors.

TABLE 4.3   Examples of Positive Reinforcement Following Undesirable Behavior

Situation	Response	Immediate Consequences	Long-Term Effects
1. While getting ready for work in the morning, a man cannot find his clean shirt.	He hollers loudly, "Where in the hell is my shirt?"	His wife immediately finds the husband's shirt.	In the future, the husband is more likely to holler and swear when he can't find his clothes.
2. Two college students, Bill and Fred, are having coffee and talking.	Bill says, "I probably shouldn't tell you this, but you won't believe what I heard about Mary!"	Fred responds, "Hey, what did you hear? I won't tell anyone."	In the future Bill is more likely to share gossip with Fred.
3. Mother and child are shopping in a department store.	Child begins to whine, "I want to go home; I want to go home; I want to go home."	Mother is embarrassed and leaves the store immediately with the child, before making her purchases.	The child is more likely to whine in a similar situation in the future.
4. Father is watching a Stanley Cup playoff hockey game on TV.	Two of his children are playing in the same room and are being extremely noisy.	Father gives them each some money so that they will go to the store and not interfere with his TV watching.	The children are more likely to play noisily when father is watching TV in similar situations in the future.
5. At a party, a husband becomes sullen when his wife is dancing flirtatiously with another man.	The husband shows signs of jealousy and angrily leaves the party.	The wife immediately follows him, and showers him with attention.	The husband is more likely to leave parties in similar situations in the future.

Failure-to-Apply Pitfall

Some behavioral procedures aren't applied because they are quite complex and require specialized knowledge or training. For example, a parent who is unfamiliar with the principle of positive reinforcement may fail to reinforce a rare instance of a normally inconsiderate child showing polite behavior, thereby missing an opportunity to strengthen that behavior.

Inaccurate-Explanation-of-Behavior Pitfall

There are two common ways that individuals inaccurately explain behavior. First, a principle can be inaccurately used as an oversimplified explanation of a change in behavior. Suppose that a college student studies for 3 hours on Monday evening for an exam, writes the exam on Tuesday, and receives an "A" on Thursday. If someone were to say that the college student studied for 3 hours because the student was reinforced by getting a good grade, then that would be an overly simplistic explanation. There was a long gap in time between the studying and receiving the "A." When explaining a behavior, we should always look for immediate consequences that may have strengthened that behavior in the past. With respect to the student's studying behavior, perhaps the night before the exam the student worried about failing, which caused the student to feel anxious. Perhaps the immediate consequence of studying was the removal of anxiety (an instance of negative reinforcement, as discussed further in Chapters 14 and 17). Or perhaps immediately after studying the student thought about the likelihood of getting an "A," which helped "bridge the gap" between the behavior and the reinforcer. As discussed in Chapter 26, reminding oneself of a delayed natural reinforcer for a behavior immediately after it occurs can strengthen that behavior. Remember, when you are attempting to explain the strengthening of a behavior by positive reinforcement, always look for an immediate consequence of that behavior. If a reinforcer is delayed by (as a rule of thumb) more than 30 seconds following a behavior, then offering just positive reinforcement as an explanation of the increase in that behavior may be overly simplistic. (It should be noted, however, that there is research showing that, under certain conditions, delayed positive reinforcement can be effective with no apparent stimuli that "bridge the gap" between the behavior and the reinforcer—e.g., see Stromer, McComas, & Rehfeldt, 2000.)

The second common way that behavior is inaccurately explained is that individuals without behavioral knowledge sometimes attempt to "explain" behavior or the lack of it by inappropriately giving people a label. Suppose that a teenager consistently leaves his room in a mess, never makes his bed, never cleans up in the kitchen after making a snack, rarely studies, and spends many hours each week watching TV or on Facebook. His parents "explain" his behavior by saying, "He's just lazy." A more accurate explanation of his behavior would be that his friends provide frequent reinforcement for his interactions on Facebook, he frequently observes enjoyable scenes while watching TV, and he has not received much reinforcement from his parents for helping around the house or from his teachers for studying.

Guidelines for the Effective Application of Positive Reinforcement

These summary guidelines are offered to ensure the effective use of positive reinforcement.

1. *Selecting the behavior to be increased.*   As indicated earlier in this chapter, the target behavior should be a specific behavior (such as smiling) rather than a general category (such as socializing). Also, if possible, select a behavior that will come under the control of natural reinforcers after it has been increased in frequency. Finally, as shown in Darren's case at the beginning of this chapter, to judge the effectiveness of your reinforcer accurately it is important to keep track of how often the behavior occurs prior to your program.
2. *Selecting a reinforcer.*
   a. Select strong reinforcers that
      (1) are readily available.
      (2) can be presented immediately following the desired behavior.
      (3) can be used over and over again without causing rapid satiation.
      (4) do not require a great deal of time to consume (if it takes a half-hour to consume the reinforcer, this minimizes the training time).

   b. Use as many reinforcers as feasible, and, where appropriate, use a reinforcer tray or menu.
3. *Applying positive reinforcement.*
   a. Tell the individual about the plan before starting.
   b. Reinforce *immediately* following the desired behavior.
   c. Describe the desired behavior to the individual while the reinforcer is being given. (For example say, "You cleaned your room very nicely.")
   d. Use lots of praise and physical contact (if appropriate and if these are reinforcing to the individual) when dispensing reinforcers. However, to avoid satiation, vary the phrases you use as social reinforcers. Don't always say "Good for you." (Some sample phrases are "Very nice," "That's great," "Super," "Tremendous.")
4. *Weaning the student from the program* (discussed more fully in Chapter 16).
   a. If, during a dozen or so opportunities, a behavior has been occurring at a desirable rate, you might try to gradually eliminate tangible reinforcers (such as treats and toys) and maintain the behavior with social reinforcement.
   b. Look for other natural reinforcers in the environment that might also maintain the behavior once it has been increased in frequency.
   c. To ensure that the behavior is being reinforced occasionally and that the desired frequency is being maintained, plan periodic assessments of the behavior after the program has terminated.

Questions for Learning

31. Is it correct to conclude that a withdrawn child necessarily does not like attention from other people? Explain.
32. Describe an example of the Pitfall that involves a person unknowingly applying positive reinforcement to strengthen an undesirable behavior.
33. State the Partial-Knowledge Misapplication Pitfall. How was this pitfall exemplified by Coach Keedwell?
34. Consider this statement: "A college student was reinforced for studying for 3 hours on the weekend by getting a good grade on the test the following week." How does this statement exemplify the Inaccurate-Explanation-of-Behavior Pitfall?
35. State the second type of Inaccurate-Explanation-of-Behavior Pitfall, and give an example.
36. Ideally, what four qualities should a reinforcer have (besides the necessary quality of functioning as a reinforcer)? (See p. 42.)

Application Exercises

A. Exercises Involving Others

1. During an hour that you spend with children, how many times do you dispense social approval (nods, smiles, or kind words)? How many times do you dispense social disapproval (frowns, harsh words, etc.)? Ideally, your social approval total at the end of the hour will be four or five times the social disapproval total. We encourage you to continue this exercise until you have achieved this ratio. Several studies have shown this ratio of reinforcers to reprimands to be beneficial (e.g., Madsen & Madsen, 1974; Stuart, 1971; also see Flora, 2000).
2. List 10 different phrases that you might use to express your enthusiastic approval to an individual. Practice varying these phrases until they come naturally to you.
3. Are you aware of how your gestures, expressions, posture, and body language in general affect those around you? Briefly describe five different examples of such behaviors that you might show when expressing your approval to an individual.

B. Self-Modification Exercises

1. Be aware of your own behavior for five 1-minute periods while behaving naturally. At the end of each minute, describe a situation, a specific behavior, and the immediate consequences of that behavior. Choose behaviors whose consequences seemed pleasant (rather than neutral or unpleasant).
2. Complete the reinforcer questionnaire (Table 4.2) for yourself.
3. Assume that someone close to you (your spouse, friend, etc.) is going to reinforce one of your behaviors (such as making your bed daily, talking in conversation without swearing, or reading pages of this book). Select the two reinforcers from your completed questionnaire that best satisfy the guidelines given previously for *selecting a reinforcer* (p. 42). Indicate how the guidelines have been satisfied.

Notes for Further Learning

1. Although it may seem strange to think of people learning without understanding, or being reinforced for emitting a certain behavior without being aware of it, this is much easier to understand when we consider the following observations: First, from everyday experience as well as from basic experiments, it is obvious that animals can learn even though they are not able to verbalize an understanding or an awareness of their behavioral changes. Similarly, the behavior of persons with profound developmental disabilities who cannot speak has been shown experimentally to be strengthened by reinforcement (see Fuller, 1949). Finally, a number of experiments have demonstrated that normal adult humans can be influenced by reinforcement to show behavioral changes even if they are unable to verbalize them. For example, university students in an experiment were instructed to say individual words. When the experimenter nodded and said "Mmm-hmm" following particular types of words (such as plural nouns), the students showed an increased frequency of saying that particular type of word. And yet, when questioned after the experiment, the students were unaware (i.e., were unable to verbalize) that their behavior had been influenced (Greenspoon, 1951).

2. Michael (1986) identified three indicators that a behavior change is due to indirect-acting vs. direct-acting effects of a consequence: (a) the consequence follows the reinforcer by more than 30 seconds (such as in the case of the child who cleaned her room in the morning and her father didn't bring her a toy until the evening); (b) the behavior that is measured shows some increase in strength prior to the first occurrence of the consequence (such as the child cleaning up her room the very first time her father offered to bring a toy for her in the evening if she cleaned up her room in the morning); and (c) a single occurrence of a consequence produces a large change in behavior (such as the child doing a lot of room-cleaning immediately after her father gives her a toy for doing so). In Chapter 17, we discuss in detail strategies that teachers can use to increase the chances of obtaining indirect-acting effects with procedures that involve positive reinforcers.

3. Suppose that you are trying to teach an individual with a severe intellectual disability to open containers. In one condition, on each trial, you give a container to the individual and ask the individual to "open it"; if he or she does so, you hand an edible to the individual as a reinforcer. In the second condition, everything is the same, except that the edible is hidden inside the container and will be discovered if the individual opens it. Research indicates that individuals with severe intellectual disability or autism learn better under the second condition (Koegel & Williams, 1980; Thompson & Iwata, 2000). The authors of these studies describe the first arrangement as an indirect reinforcement contingency, and the second arrangement as a direct reinforcement contingency. To avoid confusion with what we call direct- and indirect-acting effects of reinforcement, we suggest that an instance where a response reveals the reinforcer (such as opening the container revealing the edible hidden within it) be described as a *reinforcer-discovery contingency.*

Questions for Further Learning

1. Discuss evidence that people's behavior can be modified without their being aware of it.
2. What are three indicators that a behavior change is due to indirect-acting versus direct-acting effects?
3. How do some authors use the terms *direct* and *indirect contingencies of reinforcement*? What suggestions do the authors of this text make regarding that usage, and why?

CHAPTER 5

Increasing Behavior with Conditioned Reinforcement

LEARNING OBJECTIVES

After studying this chapter, you will be able to:
- Discuss the differences between conditioned reinforcers, unconditioned reinforcers, generalized conditioned reinforcers, backup reinforcers, and token reinforcers.
- Describe factors that influence the effectiveness of conditioned reinforcement in behavior modification programs.

- Explain how those who are unfamiliar with the principle of conditioned reinforcement may unknowingly misapply it.

Don't be so rude! Be nice!

Erin's Points[1] Program

"Erin, don't be so rude," exclaimed Erin's friend, Carly. "You're so unpleasant to everybody, even your friends. Why don't you try being nice for a change?" As Carly walked away, Erin decided that she had to modify her behavior. She wanted to be nicer to her friends, instead of always making smart comments. But being rude was such a habit that she knew she needed some extra motivation to change. After reading about self-management strategies in her psychology course, she decided to put herself on a points program. She really liked spending time on Facebook after doing her homework, but from now on she would have to earn the opportunity to do so. Every time she left her house in the morning, she carried an index card and a pen with her. Each time she said something nice to her friends, she gave herself a point on the card. Then after finishing her homework that evening, she allowed herself time on Facebook according to her "points menu." Her menu looked like this:

2 points	20 minutes of time
4 points	40 minutes of time
6 points	60 minutes of time
More than 6 points	As much time as I want

A week later when Carly and Erin were having lunch, Carly said, "I can't believe how nice you've been lately. It's like you are a different person." Erin replied jokingly, "Yeah, it's that personality operation I had."

---

[1] Based on a case described by Watson and Tharp (2007).

Unconditioned and Conditioned Reinforcers

We have inherited the capacity to be reinforced by some stimuli without prior learning. Such stimuli or events are important for our biological functioning or survival as a species and are called **unconditioned reinforcers**, which are stimuli that are reinforcing without prior learning or conditioning. (They are also called *primary* or *unlearned reinforcers*.) Examples include food for a hungry person, water for a thirsty person, warmth for someone who is cold, and sexual contact for someone who has been deprived of such contact. Other stimuli become reinforcers because of particular learning experiences. These stimuli, called **conditioned reinforcers**, are stimuli that were not originally reinforcing but have become reinforcers by

NOTE 1   being paired or associated with other reinforcers. (They are also called *secondary* or *learned reinforcers*.) Examples of conditioned reinforcers include praise, a picture of a loved one, books that we like to read, our favorite television programs, and clothes that make us look good. Most of the reinforcers that influence us on a daily basis are conditioned reinforcers.

When a stimulus becomes a conditioned reinforcer through deliberate association with other reinforcers, the other reinforcers are called **backup reinforcers**. Consider, for example, the type of training conducted with dolphins at Sea World. Early on, the trainer pairs the sound from a hand-held clicker with the delivery of fish to a dolphin. A fish is a backup reinforcer, and after a number of pairings, the clicking sound becomes a conditioned reinforcer. Later, when teaching a dolphin to perform a trick, the sound of the clicker is presented as an immediate conditioned reinforcer, and the clicker sound continues to be intermittently paired with fish.

In this example of training the dolphins, the backup reinforcer—the fish—was an unconditioned reinforcer. However, backup reinforcers for a conditioned reinforcer could also be other conditioned reinforcers. To illustrate, consider Erin's program. The points that she awarded herself were not primary reinforcers. We doubt that she would have worked very hard, if at all, just to obtain them for their own sake. The points were conditioned reinforcers because they were paired with the backup reinforcer, the opportunity to go on Facebook. In this example, the backup reinforcer for the points was also a conditioned reinforcer. Erin was not born with the stimuli provided by Facebook being unconditioned reinforcers for her. Rather, these stimuli would have become conditioned reinforcers by being paired with other things such as attention from adults and friends. Thus, backup reinforcers that give a conditioned reinforcer its strength can be either unconditioned reinforcers (such as the fish with the dolphins) or other conditioned reinforcers (such as the stimuli provided by Facebook).

A category of stimuli that are not commonly recognized as conditioned reinforcers includes stimuli that have been paired with addictive drugs. These conditioned reinforcers include such things as the

NOTE 2   smell or taste of substances containing the drug (e.g., tobacco) or the sight of the paraphernalia used to prepare or administer the drug.

Questions for Learning

1. Explain what an unconditioned reinforcer is. Give two examples.
2. Explain what a conditioned reinforcer is. Give and explain two examples.
3. Explain what a backup reinforcer is. Give and explain two examples.
4. What were the backup reinforcers in Erin's program?
5. Describe a target behavior of yours that you would like to improve that might be amenable to a points program like Erin's. What would you use as backup reinforcers for the points?

Tokens as Conditioned Reinforcers

Tokens are conditioned reinforcers that can be accumulated and exchanged for backup reinforcers. A behavior modification program in which individuals can earn tokens for specific behaviors and can cash in their tokens for backup reinforcers is called a **token economy** or a **token system**. For example, a first-grade teacher might implement a token economy in which the children could earn stamped happy faces for various behaviors, such as one stamped happy face per child for playing cooperatively during recess and one stamped happy face per correct answer given in class. At the end of the day, the children might be allowed to cash in their stamped happy faces for backup reinforcers, such as five stamped happy faces per child to play a computer game or three stamped happy faces per child for the class to have an extra 5 minutes of story time. Just about anything that can be accumulated can be used as the medium of exchange in a token economy or system. In some token economies, individuals earn plastic discs (like poker chips), which they can retain until they are ready to cash them in for backup reinforcers. In other token economies, people receive payment as "paper money" on which is written (to control use and facilitate record keeping) the amount earned, the individual's name, the name of the employee who paid the individual, the date, and the task the individual performed to earn the token. In still others, as in Erin's program, individuals receive points, which are recorded on a chart, on an index card, or in a notebook. (Token economies are discussed further in Chapter 25. Also see Boerke & Reitman, 2011; Hackenberg, 2009.)

The main advantage of using tokens or other conditioned reinforcers in a behavior modification program is that they can usually be delivered more immediately than the backup reinforcer can. Hence, they help to bridge delays between behavior and more powerful reinforcers.

Related to the concept of conditioned reinforcement is the concept of *conditioned punishment*. Just as a stimulus that is paired with reinforcement becomes reinforcing itself, so a stimulus that is paired with punishment becomes punishing itself. "No!" and "Stop that!" are examples of stimuli that become conditioned punishers because they are often followed by punishment if the individual continues to engage in the behavior that provoked them. Moreover, punishing tokens as well as reinforcing ones are possible. The demerit system used in the military is an example of a punishment token system. There are, however, problems with the use of punishment (see Chapter 13).

Simple Versus Generalized Conditioned Reinforcers

A stimulus can become a conditioned reinforcer because of pairings with a single backup reinforcer. In the days when ice cream vendors drove through a neighborhood and rang a bell to attract people's attention, the sound of the ice cream vendor's bell became a conditioned reinforcer for the children in the neighborhood. After a few pairings of the bell with receiving ice cream, a child's probability of making similar sounds—such as ringing a bicycle bell—increased, at least for awhile (see the section "Loss of Value of a Conditioned Reinforcer," page 49). A conditioned reinforcer that is paired with a single backup reinforcer is called a **simple conditioned reinforcer**. The sound of the ice cream vendor's bell in the above example was a simple conditioned reinforcer. In contrast, a stimulus that is paired with more than one kind of backup reinforcer is referred to as a **generalized conditioned reinforcer**. A common example is praise. A mother who expresses pleasure at her child's good behavior is disposed to smile at, hug, or play with the child. Sometimes a treat, toy, or other things the child enjoys may accompany the mother's praise. Normally, praise is established as a generalized conditioned reinforcer during childhood, but it continues to be maintained as one for adults. When people praise us, they are generally more likely to favor us in various ways than when they do not praise us. Therefore, we are highly likely to engage in behaviors that are followed by praise, even when not deprived of any specific reinforcer.

Examples of simple and generalized conditioned reinforcers are given in Table 5.1.

Questions for Learning

6. What are tokens?
7. Explain in two or three sentences what a token economy is.
8. Is money a token? Justify your answer.

TABLE 5.1   Examples of Conditioned and Unconditioned Reinforcers

Examples of Simple Conditioned Reinforcers	Examples of Generalized Conditioned Reinforcers	Examples of Unconditioned Reinforcers
Air miles	Money	Food
Being told in a restaurant, "A waiter is coming to take your order."	Praise	Water
A subway token	A gift certificate for food and beverages at a restaurant	Sex
A coupon for a free hamburger		Physical comfort
		Sleep
		Novelty

9. Give two examples of stimuli that are conditioned reinforcers but not tokens. Explain why they are conditioned reinforcers, and why they are not tokens.
10. Explain what a conditioned punisher is. Give and explain two examples.
11. Distinguish between a simple conditioned reinforcer and a generalized conditioned reinforcer. Explain why a generalized conditioned reinforcer is more effective than a simple conditioned reinforcer.
12. Is praise a generalized conditioned reinforcer? Defend your answer.
13. Were the points in Erin's program a generalized conditioned reinforcer? Defend your answer.

Factors Influencing the Effectiveness of Conditioned Reinforcement

1. The Strength of Backup Reinforcers

The reinforcing power of a conditioned reinforcer depends in part on the reinforcing power of the backup reinforcer(s) on which it is based. For example, because Facebook was a strong backup reinforcer for Erin, the points functioned as effective conditioned reinforcers.

2. The Variety of Backup Reinforcers

The reinforcing power of a conditioned reinforcer depends in part on the number of different backup reinforcers with which it has been paired. Money is a powerful generalized reinforcer for us because of its pairings with many backup reinforcers such as food, clothing, shelter, transportation, entertainment, and other reinforcers (see Figure 5.1). This factor is related to the preceding one in that, if many different backup reinforcers are available, then at any given time, at least one of them will probably be strong enough to maintain the conditioned reinforcer at a high reinforcing strength for the individual in the program.

3. The Number of Pairings with a Backup Reinforcer

A conditioned reinforcer is likely to be stronger if it is paired with a backup reinforcer many times. For example, the expression "good girl" or "good boy" spoken to a very young child immediately following a desirable behavior is likely to be a stronger conditioned reinforcer if that expression has been paired with a hug from a parent many times as opposed to having been paired with a hug from a parent just once (assuming that other backup reinforcers were not involved).

FIGURE 5.1
Why is money a generalized conditioned reinforcer?

4. Loss of Value of a Conditioned Reinforcer

For a conditioned reinforcer to remain effective, it must, at least occasionally, continue to be associated with a suitable backup reinforcer. In the example of the token program described previously, in which the children could earn stamped happy faces from their teacher, if the teacher discontinued the backup reinforcers, the children may have eventually stopped engaging in the behavior for which they received the stamped happy faces.

Pitfalls of Conditioned Reinforcement

In Chapter 4, we introduced four types of pitfalls that work against those who have little or no knowledge of behavioral principles, and we showed how those pitfalls apply to the principle of positive reinforcement. Here we consider two of those pitfall types with regard to conditioned reinforcement.

Unaware-Misapplication Pitfall

People who are unfamiliar with the principle of conditioned reinforcement may unknowingly misapply it in various ways. One misapplication is the unknown pairing of conditioned reinforcers with stimuli that are meant to be punishing. An example of this misapplication is when an adult frequently reprimands a child for behaving inappropriately but (a) never provides any type of "backup punisher" (see Chapter 13), and (b) the reprimand is accompanied by other aspects of adult attention (e.g., being close by, being spoken to) that are likely to have acquired conditioned reinforcing value because of previous pairings with reinforcers. The attention that accompanies such negative verbal stimuli may even be highly reinforcing, especially for children or individuals with developmental handicaps who may not receive much attention from adults. Thus, in some situations, reprimands and other negative verbal stimuli (such as "No!") might come to function as conditioned reinforcers, and the individual will behave inappropriately to obtain them.

Indeed, even stimuli that are normally punishing can become conditioned reinforcers through association with powerful primary reinforcers. The classic example is the parent who scolds a child for misbehavior and then, feeling guilty from the ensuing crying, immediately hugs the child and provides a treat. The possible outcome of this unthinking procedure is that scolding could become a conditioned reinforcer that would maintain, not eliminate, the behavior it follows.

Partial-Knowledge-Misapplication Pitfall

Ceasing to pair a conditioned reinforcer with a backup reinforcer can have unfortunate results for those who are not aware that this will cause a conditioned reinforcer to lose its value. An example of this is a teacher who awards stamped happy faces as tokens for good behavior but fails to use effective backup reinforcers. The result is that the stamped happy faces eventually lose whatever reinforcing power they may have had when they were first introduced.

Guidelines for the Effective Use of Conditioned Reinforcement

The following guidelines should be observed in applying conditioned reinforcement.

1. A conditioned reinforcer should be a stimulus that can be managed and administered easily in the situations in which you plan to use it. For example, points were ideally suited for Erin's program.
2. As much as possible, use the same conditioned reinforcers that the individual will encounter in the natural environment. For example, it is desirable in training programs to transfer control from artificial tokens to the monetary economy of the natural environment or to naturally receive praise and attention from others.
3. In the early stages of establishing a conditioned reinforcer, a backup reinforcer should be presented as quickly as possible after the presentation of the conditioned reinforcer. Later, the delay between the conditioned reinforcer and the backup reinforcer can be increased gradually if desired.
4. Use generalized conditioned reinforcers whenever possible; that is, use many different types of backup reinforcers, not just one. In this way, at least one of the backup reinforcers will probably be strong enough at any given time to maintain the power of the conditioned reinforcer.

5. When the program involves more than one individual (such as a class of students), avoid destructive competition for conditioned and backup reinforcers. Giving one person reinforcement to the detriment of another may evoke aggressive behavior in the second individual or cause that individual's desirable behavior to extinguish. One should therefore avoid drawing attention to the fact that one individual is earning more conditioned and backup reinforcement than another. Of course, people differ in their abilities, but designing programs in which individuals earn sufficient reinforcement for performing at their own levels can minimize any difficulties that these differences might cause.

6. In addition to the preceding five rules, one should follow the same rules for conditioned reinforcers that apply to any positive reinforcer (Chapter 4). Additional details for establishing token economies are described in Chapter 25.

Questions for Learning

14. List three factors that influence the effectiveness of conditioned reinforcers.
15. Explain what causes a conditioned reinforcer to lose its value.
16. Describe two pitfalls of conditioned reinforcement, and give an example of each.

Application Exercises

A. Exercise Involving Others

1. What is the probable reinforcer and what behavior does it strengthen in each of the following situations? Are these reinforcers unconditioned or conditioned? Justify your choice in each case.
   a. An individual walks through a park in autumn and admires the beautifully colored leaves on the trees.
   b. A person finishes jogging 3 miles and experiences the runner's "high" (caused by the release of endorphins in the brain).
   c. A teenager finishes mowing the lawn and is allowed to use the family car.
   d. A thirsty child holds a glass of milk and drinks several swallows.

B. Self-Modification Exercise

Identify a behavioral deficiency of yours that you would like to overcome. Next, describe the details of a plausible token system that might be applied by a friend or a relative to help you overcome your behavioral deficiency.

Notes for Further Learning

1. How is it that infants appear to learn new words when those words are not immediately followed by an observable reinforcer? A part of the answer lies with automatic conditioned reinforcement—a reinforcing effect produced by a response due to the resemblance of that response to a conditioned reinforcer (Skinner, 1957). Suppose that a parent says, "Say 'ma ma'" to an infant while providing reinforcement (tickling, touching, feeding, etc.). After several such trials, the sounds "ma ma" will become a conditioned reinforcer. Later, when in the crib alone, the infant may begin saying "ma ma" because of the automatic conditioned reinforcement received from reproducing the same sound. More generally, vocal responses of infants may increase in frequency because the sounds that those vocal responses produce have become conditioned reinforcers and thus automatically strengthen their production responses. Studies have clearly confirmed this role of automatic conditioned reinforcement in early language acquisition (Sundberg, Michael, Partington, & Sundberg, 1996; Smith, Michael, & Sundberg, 1996). Automatic reinforcement appears to be important in not only language acquisition but also the strengthening of a variety of practical and artistic behaviors (Skinner, 1957; Vaughan & Michael, 1982).

2. As is commonly known, what gives cigarettes their reinforcing power is the addictive drug nicotine that is concentrated in tobacco. It is doubtful that anyone would smoke just to experience the smell, taste, and sensations that come from cigarette smoke in the mouth, lungs, and nose. What is perhaps not so well known is that because these stimuli are paired with the reinforcing effects of nicotine in the bloodstream, they become strong conditioned reinforcers, and for regular smokers the conditioned reinforcing effects of the stimuli associated with nicotine appear to be comparable to the unconditioned reinforcing effects of

nicotine (Juliano, Donny, Houtsmuller, & Stitzer, 2006; Shahan, Bickel, Madden, & Badger, 1999). This underscores the point that when treating smoking and other addictions, therapists need to attend to the effects that conditioned reinforcement can have on the progress of the treatment.

Questions for Further Learning

1. How is conditioned reinforcement involved in influencing babies to babble sounds in their native language, even when no adults are around to reinforce this behavior?
2. Discuss how conditioned reinforcement is involved in an addiction such as to nicotine and in making it difficult for people to quit their addiction.

CHAPTER 6

Decreasing a Behavior with Operant Extinction

LEARNING OBJECTIVES

After studying this chapter, you will be able to:

- Define *operant extinction*.
- Describe factors that influence the effectiveness of operant extinction.

- Explain how individuals who are not aware of operant extinction are apt to apply it unknowingly to the behavior of friends, acquaintances, family, and others.

Louise, let's get rid of your migraines.

Louise's Case[1]

When Louise was 13 years old, she began complaining about headaches. Over the next few years, she received inordinate amounts of parental, social, and professional attention for her headaches, including comments such as, "You poor dear, that must really hurt," "Let me give you a hug; that might make you feel better," and "I'm so sorry about your headaches—is there anything I can do to help?" In addition, Louise's complaints about headaches often led to her being allowed to stay home from school. These consequences may have reinforced the problem. At 26 years of age, Louise experienced debilitating headaches almost daily. These headaches had typical migraine characteristics—some visual effects (seeing "silver specks") followed by throbbing pain over her temples, nausea, and occasional vomiting. Various treatments had been tried unsuccessfully, including medication, acupuncture, chiropractic, psychotherapy, and electroconvulsive shock. Demerol injections, which she received from her physician approximately three times per week, appeared to provide temporary relief.

Several medical examinations failed to identify an organic basis for Louise's headaches. Following extensive assessment by behavior therapist Dr. Peter Aubuchon, Louise agreed that her migraines might be due to their being reinforced and said she would try a behavioral treatment program. During a baseline assessment, Louise understood that her physician would no longer provide Demerol. Also, Louise and her husband agreed that he would record her pain behaviors which were identified as complaints, going to bed, and putting cold compresses on her head. During 2 weeks of baseline assessment her pain behaviors averaged eight per day. Then, during treatment, Louise's parents, husband, physician, and nurses at the clinic that she regularly visited all agreed to completely ignore all pain behaviors Louise exhibited. Moreover, these same individuals provided praise and other reinforcers for "well" behaviors such as exercising and performing domestic duties. To ensure her commitment, Louise signed a statement indicating her agreement with this program (such a written statement is called a behavioral contract, which is discussed further in Chapters 24 and 26). Her pain behaviors (recorded by her husband) dropped to approximately one per day by the third week, and eventually were totally eliminated.

---

[1] This case is based on one reported by Aubuchon, Haber, and Adams (1985).

Operant Extinction

The principle of **operant extinction** states that (a) if an individual, in a given situation, emits a previously reinforced behavior and that behavior is not followed by a reinforcer, (b) then that person is less likely to do the same thing again when next encountering a similar situation. Stated differently, if a response has been increased in frequency through reinforcement, then completely ceasing to reinforce the response will cause it to decrease in frequency. Note that operant extinction is similar to respondent extinction, which we discussed in Chapter 3. However, there are also important differences. Specifically, respondent extinction is a decrease in a conditioned response due to a CS no longer being followed by a US, whereas, extinction is a decrease in an operant response due to it no longer being reinforced. In this book when we use the term *extinction* by itself without qualification, we are referring to operant extinction.

Discussions with Louise had indicated that she received a lot of attention for showing overt symptoms of and talking about her headaches. It is possible that this attention was a positive reinforcer in maintaining the high frequency of her pain behaviors. When Louise's pain behaviors no longer received attention, their frequency decreased to a low level. Although operant extinction was an effective treatment for Louise, we are not implying that all pain behaviors are maintained by attention from others. For an evaluation of other factors that may influence behaviors of patients with chronic pain, see Turk and Okifuji (1997). **NOTE 1**

As with other behavior principles, very few of us are aware of how frequently we are influenced by operant extinction every day of our lives. Some examples appear in Table 6.1. In each example, the individuals are simply doing their daily activities. It might take several repetitions of the behavior occurring and not being reinforced before any really obvious decrease in its frequency occurs. Nevertheless, the effect is still there. Over a number of trials, behaviors that no longer "pay off" gradually decrease. Of course, this is highly desirable in general, for if we persisted in useless behavior, we would soon disappear as a species. Put another way, if any organism's useless behavior did not extinguish, its species would eventually extinguish.

TABLE 6.1   Examples of Operant Extinction Following Undesirable Behavior

Situation	Response	Immediate Consequences	Long-Term Effects
1. A 4-year-old child is lying in bed at night while the parents are sitting in the living room talking to guests.	The child begins to make loud animal noises while lying in bed.	The parents and guests ignore the child and continue to talk quietly.	The child is less likely to make animal noises in future situations of that sort.
2. The next evening, the same child and parents are having dinner at the dining room table. The child has just finished the main course.	The child holds up her empty plate and yells, "Dessert! Dessert! Dessert!"	The parents continue talking and ignore the child's loud demands.	The behavior of demanding dessert is less likely to occur in similar situations in the future.
3. A husband and wife are standing in the kitchen just after the husband comes home from work.	The husband complains about the traffic.	The wife goes about preparing supper and does not pay attention to his comments about the traffic.	Unproductive complaining by the husband is less likely to occur in that situation in the future.
4. A child in a third-grade classroom has just finished an assignment and raised his hand.	The child begins to snap his fingers.	The teacher ignores the child and responds to those children who raised their hands and are not snapping their fingers.	The child is less likely to snap his fingers in similar situations in the future.
5. At a store, five people are waiting in the checkout line to pay for their goods.	An aggressive customer pushes his way to the front of the line and demands service.	The store clerk says coldly, "Please go to the back of the line," and continues to serve the previous customer.	The customer who pushed ahead is less likely to do so in similar situations in the future.

Keep in mind that operant extinction is just one of several possible causes of decreases in operant behavior. Suppose, for example, that the parents of a child who swears a lot decide to implement a program to decrease swearing. Suppose that, over several days, each time the child swears, the parents immediately yell "Stop that!" As a result, swearing is eliminated. In this case, swearing decreased because it was followed by a *punisher* (a reprimand). Now consider another possibility. Suppose that rather than reprimanding the child following instances of swearing, the parents said to the child, "You have just lost 25¢ of your weekly allowance" and that this procedure eliminated swearing. In this case, the removal of the child's allowance contingent on swearing is referred to as *response-cost punishment* (both reprimands and response-cost punishment are discussed in Chapter 13). Behavior can also decrease because of forgetting. In *forgetting,* a behavior is weakened as a function of time following its last occurrence. (For behavioral interpretations of remembering and forgetting, see Pear, 2001, pp. 207–236; White, 2013.) Operant extinction differs from each of these in that extinction weakens behavior as a result of being emitted without being reinforced. For a review of research on operant extinction see Lattal, St. Peter, and Escobar (2013).

Questions for Learning

1. What are the two parts to the principle of operant extinction?
2. Is telling someone to stop eating candies and the person stops an example of operant extinction? Explain why or why not on the basis of the definition of operant extinction.
3. Is a parent ignoring a child's behavior an example of operant extinction? Explain why or why not on the basis of the definition of operant extinction.
4. Suppose that, immediately after an instance of swearing, parents remove a portion of the child's weekly allowance and the result is that swearing decreases. Is this an example of operant extinction? Explain why or why not.
5. What is the difference between forgetting and operant extinction?
6. Explain the difference, in terms of procedure and results, between the loss of value of a conditioned reinforcer (see Chapter 5) and the operant extinction of a positively reinforced behavior.

Factors Influencing the Effectiveness of Operant Extinction

1. Control of Reinforcers for the Behavior That Is to Be Decreased

Consider the case of a 4-year-old girl, Susie, who has developed a great deal of whining behavior, especially in situations where she wants something. Her mother has decided to ignore this behavior in the hope that it will go away. On three occasions during an afternoon, Mother ignored the behavior until it ceased, and then, following a brief period of no whining, provided Susie with the item she desired. Things seemed to be progressing well until early evening when Father came home. While Mother was in the kitchen, Susie approached her and in a whiny tone asked for some popcorn to eat while watching TV. Although Mother completely ignored Susie, Father entered the room and said, "Can't you hear Susie? Come here, Susie, I'll get your popcorn." We are sure that you can now predict the effect this episode will have on Susie's future whining behavior.

Eliminating (or at least reducing) reinforcers following a behavior to be decreased has been used as a component in an effective treatment for bullying, which is a problem of growing concern in schools. Considering that bullying is frequently reinforced by peer attention (Salmivalli, 2002), Ross and Horner (2009) developed and tested a program that taught teachers to teach elementary grade students to withhold reinforcement (e.g., complaining, or whining on the part of the victim, and cheering or laughing on the part of bystanders) following *disrespectful behavior* (the word "bullying" was not used because of the difficulty of obtaining a reliable behavioral definition of it—see Chapter 1, pages 2–3). After teacher training, the teachers taught the students who received disrespect to: (a) recognize instances of disrespect; (b) say "Stop" while holding up a hand to gesture stop following an instance of disrespect; and (c) walk away. Students were also encouraged to follow the same routine if they saw another student receiving "disrespect," except that Step c involved helping the victim to walk away. The bullying (disrespectful) behavior of six students at three schools was monitored before and after the program, and bullying (disrespectful) behavior significantly decreased for all six students. Bystander support of bullying also decreased significantly. It should be noted that this treatment was part of a larger school-wide program called *Positive Behavior Support* (Horner, Sugai, Todd, & Lewis-Palmer, 2005).

NOTE 2   Reinforcers presented by other people or by the physical environment can undo your good efforts at applying operant extinction. Unfortunately, it is often difficult to convince others of this if they are not familiar with the principles of positive reinforcement and extinction. For example, if several nursery school staff are ignoring a child's tantrumming behavior and another staff member enters and says, "Oh, I can get this child to stop crying—here, Tommy, have a candy," then Tommy is likely to stop crying at that moment. But in the long run, his crying may increase in frequency because of that reinforced trial. Because Tommy did stop crying temporarily, however, it would probably be difficult to convince that staff member of the importance of operant extinction. In such cases, it is necessary either to control the behavior of individuals who might sabotage an extinction procedure or to carry out the procedure in their absence.

It is also important during the application of extinction to ensure that the reinforcers that you are withholding are the ones that were actually maintaining the undesirable behavior. Failure to do this would not meet the definition of extinction, and the undesirable behavior would not likely decrease, as shown in Figure 6.1.

FIGURE 6.1
An extreme example of why attempts to apply extinction often fail. The actual reinforcer for the behavior must always be withheld.

2. Combining Extinction with Positive Reinforcement for an Alternative Behavior

Operant extinction is most effective when combined with positive reinforcement for some desirable alternative behavior (Lerman & Iwata, 1996). (Note: This is referred to as differential reinforcement of alternative behavior, and is discussed further in Chapter 12.) Thus, not only were Louise's pain behaviors ignored (operant extinction), alternative behaviors (exercising, performing domestic duties, etc.) were reinforced as well. The combination of the two procedures probably decreased the frequency of the undesirable behavior much faster (and possibly to a lower level) than would have been the case had the extinction procedure been used alone.

Suppose that a parent wanted to combine extinction of a child's inappropriate crying with positive reinforcement for a desirable alternative behavior. It is often impractical to reinforce a child every few seconds for engaging in some desirable behavior (such as playing quietly) rather than disruptive behavior. It is possible, however, to begin with short intervals of desirable behavior and gradually increase them to longer, more manageable intervals. For example, the child who is engaging in inappropriate crying could be ignored until he stopped crying and was playing quietly for a period of 10 seconds. At the end of the 10-second interval, he could be reinforced with praise. On subsequent trials, the parent could require successively longer periods of playing quietly—15 seconds, then 25, then a minute, and so on—before presenting reinforcement. It is important that the increase in the requirement of the desirable behavior be very gradual; otherwise, the undesirable behavior is likely to reoccur. Also, care must be taken not to present the reinforcer immediately after the undesirable behavior (e.g., crying) ceases because this would tend to reinforce the undesirable behavior, thereby increasing rather than reducing it.

The use of operant extinction is sometimes criticized on the grounds that it is cruel to deprive people of social attention during their time of need (this criticism usually assumes that an individual who is crying, whining, or showing various other behaviors that commonly evoke attention is in a "time of need"). In some cases, this might be a valid criticism. Crying often indicates injury, emotional distress, and other forms of discomfort. Any behavior you are thinking of decreasing must be examined closely in terms of the desirability of decreasing it. If a decrease is desired, extinction frequently is the right procedure.

3. The Setting in Which Extinction Is Carried Out

As indicated previously, one reason for changing the setting in which operant extinction is carried out is to minimize the possibility that other people will reinforce the behavior you are trying to decrease. Another reason is that it may be socially difficult or even impossible to carry out operant extinction in certain situations. It would be unwise, for example, for a mother to initiate extinction of her child's temper tantrums in a department store. The nasty stares from other shoppers and store clerks would decrease the chances that the mother would carry through effectively with the procedure. It is important to consider the setting in which operant extinction will be carried out to (a) minimize the influence of alternative reinforcers on the undesirable behavior to be extinguished and (b) maximize the chances of the behavior modifier persisting with the program.

4. Instructions or Rules

Although an individual may not understand the principles behind operant extinction, it will still decrease the individual's behavior. However, it would help speed up the decrease in behavior if the person is initially told something like this: "If you do X [the undesirable behavior], then Y [the reinforcing item] will no longer occur." Consider, for example, the third case described in Table 6.1. Upon arriving home from work each day, the husband complains excessively about the slow traffic. His wife would be adding instructional control to extinction if she said something like, "George, the traffic is the same each day, and it doesn't do any good complaining about it. I love to talk to you about other things. But each time that you come home and complain excessively about the traffic, I'm just going to ignore it." This should cause George's complaining to decrease rapidly, although it may take a few trials. However, keep in mind that this procedure is more complex than simple operant extinction. (Instructional control is discussed further in Chapter 17.)

5. The Schedule of Reinforcement before Extinction Is Carried Out

Let's take another look at the case of Susie's whining behavior. Before Mother decided to implement operant extinction, what happened when Susie was whining? Sometimes nothing would happen because Mother was busy with other things, such as talking on the telephone. But at other times (often after five or six instances of whining), Mother would attend to Susie and give her what she wanted. This is typical of many reinforcement situations in that Susie's whining was not reinforced following each instance. Rather, her whining was reinforced occasionally, following several instances of it. This is an example of *intermittent reinforcement,* which is discussed in detail in Chapters 8 and 12. It is necessary to mention continuous and intermittent reinforcement here because they can influence the effectiveness of extinction. **Continuous reinforcement** is an arrangement or schedule in which each instance of a particular response is reinforced. **Intermittent reinforcement** is an arrangement or schedule in which a response is reinforced only occasionally (i.e., intermittently) rather than each time it occurs.

The influence of reinforcement schedules on subsequent operant extinction can easily be imagined if you consider a little problem that you may have encountered. Suppose you are writing with a pen that suddenly stops. What do you do? You probably shake it up and down a couple of times and try to write with it a few more times. If it still doesn't write, you get another pen. Now suppose that you are writing with the second pen and it occasionally skips. You shake it a few times and write some more, and then it misses some more. Each time you shake it, it writes a little more. Now suppose the second pen stops writing altogether. In which situation are you likely to persist longer in shaking and attempting to use the pen? Obviously, the second because the pen occasionally quits but it usually writes again.

When a behavior has always been reinforced and then abruptly is never reinforced, that behavior extinguishes quickly. When intermittent reinforcement has maintained a behavior (such as a pen writing again each time after shaking it), that behavior (pen shaking) is likely to extinguish slowly (Kazdin & Polster, 1973). This seemingly simple phenomenon is complex and depends in part on how one measures behavior during extinction (Lerman, Iwata, Shore, & Kahng, 1996; Nevin, 1988). For our purposes, it is sufficient to note that, in general, behavior that has been intermittently reinforced extinguishes more slowly than behavior that has been continuously reinforced. Behavior that extinguishes slowly is said to be *resistant to extinction*.

Now let's look closely at Susie's whining. It will likely take longer for operant extinction to eliminate her whining completely if it sometimes pays off and sometimes does not than if it always paid off before being ignored completely. In other words, extinction is typically quicker after *continuous reinforcement* than after *intermittent reinforcement*. If you try to extinguish a behavior that has been reinforced intermittently, you must be prepared for extinction to take longer.

Questions for Learning

7. If a behavior that was maintained by positive reinforcement is not reinforced at least once in a while, what will happen to the behavior?
8. Why did the mother's attempt to extinguish the child's cookie eating fail (refer to Figure 6.1)?
9. Examine Table 6.1. Which one of those examples involved positive reinforcement for an alternative response? For those that do not, indicate how positive reinforcement for an alternative response might be introduced.
10. Why is it necessary to consider the setting as a factor influencing your operant extinction program?
11. Describe a particular behavior you would like to decrease in a child with whom you have contact. Would your extinction program require a special setting? Why or why not?
12. Define *continuous reinforcement* and give an example that is not in this chapter.
13. Define *intermittent reinforcement* and give an example that is not in this chapter.
14. What is the effect of continuous versus intermittent reinforcement on the resistance to extinction of an operant behavior?

6. Behavior Being Extinguished May Get Worse before It Gets Better

During operant extinction, behavior may increase before it begins to decrease. That is, things may get worse before they get better. An increase in responding during extinction is commonly referred to as an **extinction burst**. Suppose a child in a classroom is constantly raising her or his hand and snapping her or his fingers to gain the teacher's attention. A teacher who keeps track of the frequency of finger snapping for a while and then introduces operant extinction (i.e., ignores the finger snapping) would probably observe an increase in finger snapping during the first few minutes of extinction before the behavior gradually began to taper off. Why? Most of us have learned that if something is no longer paying off, a slight increase in the behavior may be sufficient to again bring the payoff. Well documented in basic research, extinction bursts have also been reported in applied research (Lerman & Iwata, 1995; Lerman, Iwata, & Wallace, 1999). Thus, extinction bursting is something that everyone who attempts to apply an operant extinction procedure should know about. A teacher who decided to introduce extinction following finger snapping and then observed an increase in this behavior during the next few minutes might erroneously conclude that extinction wasn't working and give up too early in the program. The effect of this action would be to reinforce the behavior when it gets worse. The rule to follow here is this:

> If you introduce operant extinction, keep with it. Things usually get worse before they get better, but hang in there; doing so will pay off in the long run.

Exceptions to this rule are situations in which an extinction burst may be harmful. If you can anticipate that possibility, you should take preventive steps. For example, before implementing an extinction program to decrease head banging of a young girl with developmental disabilities, Brian Iwata and his colleagues put a helmet on the girl during extinction sessions so that she would not harm herself during an extinction burst (Iwata, Pace, Cowdery, & Miltenberger, 1994). Alternatively, if you predict that an extinction burst might cause harm, then don't use extinction. Other strategies for decreasing problem behaviors are described in later chapters.

7. Extinction May Produce Aggression That Interferes with the Program

Another difficulty of operant extinction is that the procedure may produce aggression. We have all experienced this. Probably all of us have had the desire to pound and kick a vending machine that took our money and did not deliver the merchandise. If we reconsider the finger-snapping example, we might at first see some mild aggression. If a teacher ignores a child's finger snapping, the child might start snapping his or her fingers louder and louder and perhaps banging on the desk and yelling "Hey!" This aspect of operant extinction, which is sometimes called *elicited aggression*, has been studied extensively in laboratory situations (Pear, 2001, pp. 320–321, 332–333) and has also been reported in applied research (Lerman & Iwata, 1996; Lerman et al., 1999). In studies of operant extinction of self-injurious behavior, aggression was observed in nearly half of the cases in which extinction was the sole intervention. However, the prevalence of aggression was substantially lower when extinction was implemented as part of a treatment package that included positive reinforcement for an alternative desirable behavior. It is important to minimize aggression not only because it is undesirable but also because it could lead to giving up too soon. This might not only reinforce the undesirable behavior on an intermittent schedule but also reinforce aggression.

Another option would be to conduct an operant extinction program in a setting in which a certain amount of aggression can be tolerated. If parents decide to apply extinction to decrease a child's tantrumming, for example, they might do so at home after removing any breakable objects. As another example, in an extinction program to decrease aggressive behaviors (scratching, hitting, kicking, and biting) of a boy with a severe developmental disability, Edward Carr and his colleagues had teachers wear protective clothing that consisted of a thick corduroy coat and rubber gloves (Carr, Newsom, & Binkoff, 1980).

8. Spontaneous Recovery: Reappearance of an Extinguished Behavior after a Delay

Another difficulty of operant extinction is that a behavior that has disappeared during an extinction session may reappear at the next opportunity after some time has passed. The reappearance of an extinguished behavior following a break is called **spontaneous recovery**. Let's reconsider the finger-snapping example. Suppose that the teacher initiated an extinction program for finger snapping when the student returned to school after lunch. During the first hour, 10 instances of finger snapping occurred, and the teacher and the other students ignored each. Let's suppose further that there were no instances of finger snapping during the remainder of the afternoon and that the teacher assumed that finger snapping had been successfully extinguished. When the teacher returned to class the next morning, however, another five instances of finger snapping occurred during the first hour of school. This would be spontaneous recovery of finger snapping. Typically, the amount of behavior that recovers spontaneously following a break is less than the amount that occurred during the previous extinction session. After several additional extinction sessions, spontaneous recovery is usually not a problem. Although these characteristics of spontaneous recovery are well documented in basic research (Pear, 2001, pp. 61–63), it has not been formally studied in applied research, and very few anecdotal (i.e., informal) reports of spontaneous recovery occurring in applications of operant extinction (Lerman & Iwata, 1996) have been reported. We strongly recommend that the teacher be prepared to continue with the extinction program despite the occurrence of spontaneous recovery.

To review, in this chapter and Chapters 4 and 5, we suggest that if you want behavior to happen more often, reinforce it; if you want behavior to happen less often, ignore it. But beware: There is much **NOTE 3** more to positive reinforcement and operant extinction than first meets the eye.

Pitfalls of Operant Extinction

In Chapter 4, we introduced four types of pitfalls that can work against the unwary. Here we consider two of these pitfall types with regard to extinction.

Unaware-Misapplication Pitfall

As with many natural laws, such as the law of gravity and the principle of positive reinforcement, the principle of operant extinction operates whether or not we are aware of it. Unfortunately, those who are not aware of extinction are apt to apply it unknowingly to the desirable behavior of friends, acquaintances, family, and others. See Table 6.2 for some examples of how operant extinction may, in the long run, work to decrease desirable behavior.

TABLE 6.2 Examples of Operant Extinction Following Desirable Behavior

Situation	Responses	Immediate Consequences	Long-Term Effects
1. You ask a friend to call you on your cell phone on a particular evening.	Your friend dials your number several times.	Each time the phone rings, you ignore it and continue reading your novel.	Your friend is less likely to attempt to call you when requested to do so.
2. Two staff members are talking to each other in a special education classroom, and a student approaches.	The student stands and waits patiently beside the two staff members for several minutes. Finally, the student interrupts.	The staff members continued talking while the student waited patiently and stopped talking and listened after the student interrupted.	In the future the response of standing beside the staff and waiting patiently is less likely to occur, and the response of interrupting staff is more likely to occur.
3. A man carrying several parcels is walking toward the exit door of a department store. A woman standing by the door sees the man coming.	The woman opens the door for the man.	The man rushes out without saying a word.	The chances of the woman opening the door in similar situations in the future are decreased.
4. A 3-month-old baby is lying quietly in the crib just before feeding time.	The baby begins making cooing sounds (which might be interpreted by eager parents as "mama" or "dada").	The mother, busy preparing a bottle, ignores the child. When the child is picked up later, she is again quiet (or, more likely, crying).	The mother has just missed an opportunity to reinforce noise making that approximates speech. Instead, she reinforced lying quietly (or crying). Therefore, cooing is less likely to occur in the future.

Partial-Knowledge Pitfall

Even when some individuals are knowledgeably applying behavior modification in an effort to help behaviorally deficient individuals, others who are less knowledgeable about operant extinction may undo their good work. Suppose, for example, that a child in a program for persons with developmental disabilities has been reinforced by an aide for dressing himself. Suppose also that this aide has been transferred or has gone on vacation and is replaced by an aide who is less familiar with the principles of positive reinforcement and extinction. Confronted with one child who dresses himself and many children who cannot, the new aide will likely spend a great deal of time helping the latter children but give little attention to the one child. It is a common human tendency to give plenty of attention to problems and to ignore situations in which things seem to be going well. It is easy to rationalize this selective attention. "After all," the aide may say, "why should I reinforce Johnny for doing something that he already knows how to do?" However, if the child's self-dressing behavior is to be maintained after it has been established, it must be reinforced at least occasionally. Strategies to maintain desirable behavior and thereby prevent unwanted operant extinction are described in Chapter 16.

Guidelines for the Effective Application of Operant Extinction

The following rules are offered as a checklist for effectively using operant extinction to decrease a particular behavior. As with the guidelines for positive reinforcement in Chapter 4, assume that the user is a parent, teacher, or some other person working with individuals with behavior problems.

1. *Selecting the Behavior to Be Decreased*
   a. In choosing the behavior, be specific. Don't expect a major character improvement to take place all at once. For example, do not try to extinguish all of Johnny's troublemaking behavior in a classroom. Rather, choose a particular behavior, such as Johnny's finger snapping.
   b. Remember that the behavior often gets worse before it gets better and that aggressive behavior is sometimes produced during the extinction process. Therefore, make sure that the circumstances are such that you can follow through with your extinction procedure. For example, be very careful if the target behavior is destructive to the individual or others. Will it be harmful for you to persist in your extinction program if the behavior gets worse? You should also consider the setting in which the target behavior is likely to occur. It may be impractical to extinguish temper tantrums in a restaurant because of obvious social pressures that you may be unable to resist. If you are concerned with decreasing a particular behavior but you cannot apply extinction because of these considerations, do not despair. We will describe other procedures for decreasing behavior in Chapters 12, 13, 17, 18, and 23.
   c. Select a behavior for which you can control the reinforcers that are currently maintaining it.
2. *Preliminary Considerations*
   a. If possible, keep track of how often the target behavior occurs prior to your extinction program. During this recording phase, do not attempt to withhold the reinforcer for the undesirable behavior.
   b. Try to identify what is currently reinforcing the undesirable behavior so that you can withhold the reinforcer during treatment. (If this is not possible, then, technically, the program does not have an extinction component.) The reinforcement history of the undesirable behavior might provide some idea of just how long extinction will take.
   c. Identify some desirable alternative behavior in which the individual can engage.
   d. Identify effective reinforcers that can be used for desirable alternative behavior by the individual.
   e. Try to select a setting in which extinction can be carried out successfully.
   f. Be sure that all relevant individuals know before the program starts just which behavior is being extinguished and which behavior is being reinforced. Be sure that all who will be coming in contact with the individual have been prompted to ignore the undesirable behavior and to reinforce the desirable alternative behavior.
3. *Implementing the Plan*
   a. Tell the individual about the plan before starting.
   b. Regarding the positive reinforcement for the desirable alternative behavior, be sure to follow the rules in Chapter 4 for putting the plan into effect.
   c. After initiating the program, be completely consistent in withholding reinforcement after all instances of the undesirable behavior and reinforcing all instances of the desirable alternative behavior.
4. *Weaning the Student from the Program*   (discussed in more detail in Chapter 16)
   a. After the undesirable behavior has decreased to zero, occasional relapses may occur, so be prepared.
   b. Three possible reasons for the failure of your operant extinction procedure are
      (1) the attention you are withholding following the undesirable behavior is not the reinforcer that was maintaining the behavior
      (2) the undesirable behavior is receiving intermittent reinforcement from another source
      (3) the desired alternative behavior has not been strengthened sufficiently
      Examine these reasons carefully if it is taking a long time to complete the extinction procedure successfully.
   c. Regarding the reinforcement of the desirable alternative behavior, try to follow the rules in Chapter 4 for weaning the child from the program.

Questions for Learning

15. What is an extinction burst? Describe an example.
16. What is spontaneous recovery? Describe an example.
17. In a sentence for each, describe eight general factors influencing the effectiveness of operant extinction.
18. Describe two examples of operant extinction that you have encountered, one involving a desirable behavior and one involving an undesirable behavior. For each example, identify the situation, behavior, immediate consequence, and probable long-term effects as is done in Tables 6.1 and 6.2. (Your examples should not be from the text.)

19. Briefly describe an example of a pitfall of operant extinction. Which type of Pitfall does your example illustrate?
20. Operant extinction should not be applied to certain behaviors or in certain situations. What types of behaviors and situations would these be? Give an example of a behavior to which operant extinction should not be applied. Give an example of a situation in which operant extinction should not be applied.
21. What are three possible reasons for the failure of an operant extinction program?

Application Exercises

A. Exercise Involving Others

Choose a situation in which you can observe an adult interact with one or more children for approximately half an hour. During this period, write the number of times that the adult pays attention to desirable behaviors of the children and the number of times the adult ignores specific desirable behaviors. This will give you some idea of how often we miss opportunities to reinforce the desirable behaviors of those around us.

B. Self-Modification Exercises

1. Think of something you did today that did not pay off. Give a specific, complete description of the situation and behavior following the examples in Tables 6.1 and 6.2.
2. Select one of your behavioral excesses (perhaps one that you listed at the end of Chapter 1). Outline a complete operant extinction program that you (with a little help from your friends) might apply to decrease that behavior. Make sure that you select a behavior for which the reinforcer that maintains it can be withheld. Make sure that your plan follows the guidelines given for the effective application of operant extinction.

Notes for Further Learning

1. Louise's case raises some intriguing questions. Was it simply her reports of pain that decreased? Did her "feelings" of pain—the actual headaches—also decrease? Although she did not self-monitor headache frequency, Louise reported at a 12-month follow-up that she had experienced only two headaches over the previous several months. Her other behaviors tended to support this: She was able to perform a variety of activities (domestic chores, work, etc.) that she had not been able to do in the past, and she and her husband reported that their marital relationship had greatly improved. As discussed further in Chapters 15, 26, and 27, private behaviors are assumed to be affected by behavioral techniques in the same way as are public behaviors. Perhaps in Louise's case, both public complaints about pain and private pain behavior were decreased as a function of the operant extinction procedure.

2. One of the greatest hazards an operant extinction program faces is reinforcement from a well-intentioned person who does not understand the program or its rationale. This obstacle was encountered in one of the earliest reports on the application of extinction to a child's temper tantrums. C. D. Williams (1959) reported the case of a 21-month-old infant who screamed and cried if his parents left the bedroom after putting him to bed at night. A program was initiated in which the parent left the room after bedtime pleasantries and did not reenter it, no matter how much the infant screamed and raged. The first time the child was put to bed under this extinction procedure, he screamed for 45 minutes. By the 10th night, however, he no longer cried but smiled as the parent left the room. About a week later, when the parents were enjoying a much-needed evening out, he screamed and fussed after his aunt, the babysitter, had put him to bed. The aunt reinforced the behavior by returning to the bedroom and remaining there until he went to sleep. It was then necessary to extinguish the behavior a second time, which took almost as long as the first time. Ayllon and Michael (1959) observed the undesirable effect of unwanted reinforcement in operant extinction, which they called *bootleg reinforcement*. A patient in a psychiatric hospital engaged in such annoying psychotic talk (of the type referred to as *delusional*) that other patients had on several occasions beaten her in an effort to keep her quiet. To decrease her psychotic talk, the doctors instructed the nurses to ignore it and to pay attention only to sensible talk. As a result, the proportion of her speech that was psychotic decreased from 0.91 to 0.25. Later, though, it increased to a high level again, probably because of bootleg reinforcement from a social worker. This came to light when the patient remarked to one of the nurses, "Well, you're not listening to me. I'll have to go and see [the social worker] again, cause she told me that if she listens to my past she could help me."

3. An alternative to operant extinction for reducing undesirable behavior in persons with developmental disabilities is *noncontingent reinforcement*. For example, suppose that in a treatment center for children with developmental disabilities, Suzy appears to display frequent tantrums because tantrumming usually leads to adult attention. A noncontingent reinforcement program might involve giving Suzy adult attention once every 30 seconds regardless of the behavior that is occurring. If such a procedure causes Suzy to satiate on adult attention as a reinforcer, then she is less likely to tantrum in order to get attention. In a number of

studies, this type of treatment has proven to be effective in decreasing challenging behavior (for a review of such studies, see Smith, 2011; Tucker, Sigafoos, & Bushell, 1998). A potential criticism of this strategy to decrease behavior is that it might reduce the client's motivation to participate in teaching sessions (considering that a reinforcer is received frequently for essentially doing nothing). In addition, because it acts indiscriminately on any behavior that occurs at a high rate, it can also reduce desirable behavior.

Questions for Further Learning

1. Discuss whether the operant extinction program with Louise decreased her "feelings" of pain.
2. What is bootleg reinforcement? Give an example.
3. Describe how noncontingent reinforcement might be used to decrease challenging behavior. What is a potential limitation of this approach?

CHAPTER 7

Getting a New Behavior
to Occur with Shaping

Frank, did you do your jogging?

Improving Frank's Exercising[1]

After taking early retirement at the age of 55, Frank decided to make some changes in his life. But he wasn't sure where to start. Knowing that he needed to change some long-standing habits, he enrolled in a behavior modification course at the local community college. Next, on the advice of his doctor, he resolved to begin a regular exercise program. Frank had been a "couch potato" all his adult life. He typically came home from work, grabbed a can of beer, and parked himself in front of the television set. Frank launched his exercise program with a pledge to his wife that he would jog a quarter of a mile each day. But after a couple of attempts, he returned to his couch-potato routine. He had expected too much too soon. He then decided to try a procedure called shaping that he had studied in his behavior modification course. The following three stages summarize that procedure.

1. *Specify the final target behavior.*   Frank's goal was to jog a quarter of a mile each day. However, for a chronic nonexerciser, this was more than could be expected.
2. *Identify a response that could be used as a starting point in working toward the final target behavior.*   Frank decided that he would put on his sneakers and walk around the outside of the house once (approximately 30 yards). Although this was a long way from a quarter of a mile, it was a start.
3. *Reinforce the starting behavior; then reinforce closer and closer approximations until eventually the final target behavior occurs.*   Frank decided to use the opportunity to drink a beer as a reinforcer. He explained his program to his wife and asked her to remind him that he had to complete his exercise before he could have a beer. After the first approximation of 30 yards occurred on several successive afternoons, Frank increased the requirement to walking around the house twice

---

[1] This case is based on one described by Watson and Tharp (1997).

(approximately 60 yards). A few days later, the distance was increased to walking around the house four times (approximately 120 yards), then six times (180 yards), then farther and farther until the distance was approximately a quarter of a mile, and then finally to jogging that distance. By reinforcing successive approximations to his goal, Frank reached the point where he jogged a quarter of a mile regularly.

Shaping

In Chapters 4 and 5, we described how positive reinforcement could be used to increase the frequency of a behavior provided that the behavior occurred occasionally. But what if a desired behavior never occurs? In that case, it is not possible to increase its frequency simply by waiting until it occurs and then reinforcing it. However, a procedure called *shaping* can be used to establish a behavior that the individual never performs. The behavior modifier begins by reinforcing a response that occurs with a frequency greater than zero and that at least remotely resembles the final target behavior. Frank, for example, was first reinforced for walking once around his house because this behavior occurred occasionally and remotely approximated his nonexistent behavior of jogging a quarter of a mile. When this initial response is occurring at a high frequency, the behavior modifier stops reinforcing it and begins reinforcing a slightly closer approximation of the final target behavior. In this way, the final target behavior is eventually established by reinforcing successive approximations to it. **Shaping** can be defined as the development of a new operant behavior by the reinforcement of successive approximations of that behavior and the extinction of earlier approximations of that behavior until the new behavior occurs. Shaping is sometimes referred to as the *method of successive approximations*.

The behaviors that an individual acquires during a lifetime develop from a variety of sources and influences. Sometimes a new behavior develops when an individual performs some initial behavior and the environment then reinforces slight variations in that behavior across a number of trials. Eventually, that initial behavior may be shaped so that the final form no longer resembles it. For example, most parents use shaping in teaching their children to talk. An infant first beginning to babble makes some sounds that remotely approximate words in the parents' native language. When this happens, the parents usually reinforce the behavior with hugs, caresses, kisses, and smiles. The sounds "mmm" and "daa" typically receive exceptionally large doses of reinforcement from English-speaking parents. Eventually "ma-ma" and "da-da" occur and are strongly reinforced, and the more primitive "mmm" and daa are subjected to operant extinction. At a later stage, reinforcement is given after the child says "mommy" and "daddy," and "ma-ma" and "da-da" are extinguished.

The same process occurs with other words. First, the child passes through a stage in which very remote approximations of words in the parents' native language are reinforced. Then the child enters a stage in which "baby talk" is reinforced. Finally, the parents and others require the child to pronounce words in accordance with the practices of the verbal community before reinforcement is given. For example, a child who says "wa-wa" at an early stage is given a glass of water, and if she is thirsty this action reinforces the response. At a later stage "watah" rather than wa-wa is reinforced with water. Finally, the child must say "water" before water reinforcement will be given.

Of course, this description greatly oversimplifies the way in which a child learns to talk. However, it serves to illustrate the importance of shaping in the process by which typically developing children gradually progress from babbling to baby talk and finally to speaking in accordance with prevailing social conventions. Other processes that play important roles in speech development are discussed elsewhere in this book.

There are five aspects or dimensions of behavior that can be shaped. These are topography, frequency, duration, latency, and intensity (or force). *Topography* is the spatial configuration or form of a particular response (i.e., the specific movements involved). Printing a word and writing the same word are examples of the same response made with two different topographies. Topography shaping occurs, for example, when teaching a child to switch from a printing response to a writing response, teaching a child to say, "Mommy" instead of "Mama," learning to ice skate with longer and longer strides rather than short choppy steps, and learning the proper finger movements for eating with chopsticks. Stokes, Luiselli, and Reed (2010) used topography shaping to improve tackling skills of two high school football players. The coach first identified the components of effective tackling (head up, wrap arms around ball carrier's thighs, etc.). Then, in a tackling drill, a player tried to tackle a ball carrier who tried to elude or run around the tackler. Ten instances of the drill were completed in each practice. Across practices the coach reinforced the player with a colorful helmet sticker if the player showed an improved topography of tackling by demonstrating more components of effective tackling than in the previous practice. The two players' tackling improved across practices, and the improved tackling transferred to games.

We sometimes refer to the frequency or duration of a particular behavior as the *amount* of that behavior. The *frequency* of a behavior is the number of instances that occur in a given period of time. Examples of frequency shaping include increasing the number of steps (the distance) that Frank walked in his exercise program and increasing the number of repetitions that a golfer practices a particular golf shot. The frequency of a response may also be reduced by shaping as in a behavior modification program in which a patient with multiple sclerosis learned through shaping to gradually increase the time between and thus decrease the frequency of bathroom visits (O'Neill & Gardner, 1983). The *duration* of a response is the length of time that it lasts. Examples of duration shaping include lengthening the time spent studying before taking a break and gradually adjusting the duration of stirring pancake batter until it achieves just the right consistency. Duration shaping was used by Athens, Vollmer, and St. Peter Pipkin (2007) to increase academic behavior of students with learning disabilities.

Latency is the time between the occurrence of a stimulus and the response evoked by that stimulus. A common term for latency is *reaction time*. On the popular TV quiz show *Jeopardy!* the time from the presentation of the host's verbal stimulus until a contestant presses a button is the contestant's latency of responding to that particular stimulus. In a race, the time between firing the starter's pistol and the runner leaving the blocks is the latency of the runner's response to the firing of the starting pistol. Latency shaping might enable the runner to react more quickly or the *Jeopardy!* contestant to press the button faster.

The *intensity* or force of a response refers to the physical effect the response has or potentially has on the environment. For an example of shaping force, consider a farm boy whose job is to pump water out of a well with an old-fashioned hand pump. When the pump was first installed, it was freshly oiled, and when the boy applied a certain amount of force to the handle, it moved up and down very easily and water flowed. Suppose, however, that with lack of regular oiling, the pump has gradually acquired a little rust. Each day the boy applies approximately the amount of force he applied on the first day. When applying that force is no longer reinforced by the flow of water because the addition of rust has made the pump handle more difficult to move, the boy will likely apply a little more force and find that it pays off. Over several months, the boy's behavior is gradually shaped so that he presses very hard on the first trial, a terminal behavior quite different from the initial behavior. Other examples of intensity shaping include learning to shake hands with a firmer grip and learning to apply the right amount of force when scratching to relieve an itch without damaging one's skin. An example of intensity shaping in a behavior modification program involved teaching a socially withdrawn girl whose speech was barely audible to speak louder and louder until she was speaking at normal voice volume (Jackson & Wallace, 1974). See Table 7.1 for a summary of the dimensions of behavior.

TABLE 7.1 Dimensions of Behavior That Can Be Shaped

Dimension	Definition	Example
Topography (form)	Physical movements involved in the behavior	Extent of follow through on a tennis serve
Amount: frequency	Number of instances of the behavior in a given time	Number of dishes washed in 5 minutes
Amount: duration	Continuous amount of time that the behavior lasts	Length of time treading water
Latency	Time between the controlling stimulus and the behavior	Time between the question "What time is it?" and the response of looking at your watch
Intensity (force)	Amount of energy expended on the behavior	Force of a punch in boxing

Shaping is so common in everyday life that people are seldom aware of it. Sometimes the shaping procedure is applied systematically as in Frank's case, sometimes unsystematically as when parents shape correct pronunciation of words spoken by their children; and sometimes shaping occurs from consequences in the natural environment as when a cook gradually perfects the method for flipping pancakes.

Questions for Learning

1. Identify the three basic stages in any shaping procedure as presented at the beginning of this chapter, and describe them with an example (either Frank's case or an example of your own).
2. Define *shaping*.
3. What is another name for shaping?
4. Explain how shaping involves successive applications of the principles of positive reinforcement and operant extinction.
5. Why bother with shaping? Why not just learn about the use of straightforward positive reinforcement to increase a behavior?
6. In terms of the three stages in a shaping procedure, describe how parents might shape their child to say a particular word.
7. List five dimensions of behavior that can be shaped. Give two examples of each.
8. Describe a behavior of yours that was shaped by consequences in the natural environment, and state several of the initial approximations.

Factors Influencing the Effectiveness of Shaping

1. Specifying the Final Target Behavior

NOTE 1 The first stage in shaping is to identify clearly the final target behavior. In Frank's case, the final target behavior was jogging a quarter of a mile each day. With a definition as specific as this, there was little possibility that Frank or his wife would develop different expectations regarding his performance. If different people working with the individual expect different things, or if one person is not consistent from one training session or situation to the next, progress is likely to be delayed. A precise statement of the final target behavior increases the chances for consistent reinforcement of successive approximations of that behavior. The final target behavior should be stated in such a way that all of the relevant characteristics of the behavior (its topography, duration, frequency, latency, and intensity) are identified. In addition, the conditions under which the behavior is or is not to occur should be stated, and any other guidelines that appear to be necessary for consistency should be provided.

2. Choosing the Starting Behavior

Because the final target behavior does not occur initially and because it is necessary to reinforce some behavior that approximates it, you must identify a *starting behavior*. This should be a behavior that occurs often enough to be reinforced within the session time, and it should approximate the final target behavior. For example, Frank's behavior of walking around the house once is something that he did periodically. This was the closest approximation that he regularly made with respect to the goal of jogging a quarter of a mile.

In a shaping program, it is crucial to know not only where you are going (the final target behavior) but also the starting behavior at which the individual is currently performing. The purpose of the shaping program is to get from one to the other by reinforcing successive approximations from the starting behavior to the final target behavior even though they might be very dissimilar. For example, in a classic study, Isaacs, Thomas, and Goldiamond (1960) applied shaping to redevelop verbal behavior in a man with catatonic schizophrenia. The man had been mute for 19 years. Using chewing gum as a reinforcer, the experimenter took the patient through the shaping steps of eye movement toward the gum, facial movement, mouth movements, lip movements, vocalizations, word utterance, and, finally, understandable speech.

3. Choosing the Shaping Steps

Before initiating the shaping program, it is helpful to outline the successive approximations through which the person will be moved in the attempt to approximate the final target behavior. For example, suppose that the final target behavior in a shaping program for a child is saying *daddy*. It has been determined that the child says *daa*, and this response is set as the starting behavior. Let's suppose that we decide to go from the initial behavior of saying daa through the following steps: saying *da-da, dad, dad-ee,* and *daddy*. To begin, reinforcement is given on a number of occasions for emitting the initial behavior (daa). When this behavior is occurring repetitively, the trainer moves to step 2 (da-da) and reinforces that approximation for several trials. This step-by-step procedure continues until the child finally says *daddy*.

How many successive approximations should there be? In other words, what is a reasonable step size?   **NOTE 2** Unfortunately, there are no specific guidelines for identifying the ideal step size. In attempting to specify the behavioral steps from the starting behavior to the final target behavior, behavior modifiers might imagine what steps they would go through. Also it is sometimes helpful to observe others who can already perform the final target behavior and to ask them to perform an initial and some subsequent approximations. Whatever guidelines or guesses are used, it is important to try to stick to them yet be flexible if the trainee does not proceed quickly enough or is learning more quickly than had been expected. Some guidelines for moving through the behavioral program are offered in the following section.

4. The Pace of Movement through the Shaping Steps

How many times should each approximation be reinforced before proceeding to the next approximation? Again, there are no specific guidelines for answering this question. However, there are several rules of thumb to follow in reinforcing successive approximations of a final target response:

a. Reinforce an approximation at least several times before proceeding to the next step. In other words, avoid underreinforcement of a shaping step. Trying to go to a new step before the previous approximation has been well established can result in losing the previous approximation through extinction without achieving the new approximation.

b. Avoid reinforcing too many times at any shaping step. Item *a* cautions against going too fast. It is also important not to progress too slowly. If one approximation is reinforced for so long that it becomes extremely strong, new approximations are less likely to appear.

c. If you lose a behavior because you are moving too fast or taking too large a step, return to an earlier approximation where you can pick up the behavior again. You also may need to insert an extra step or two.

These guidelines may not seem very helpful. On the one hand, it is advisable not to move too fast from one approximation to another; on the other hand, it is advisable not to move too slowly. If we could accompany these guidelines with a mathematical formula for calculating the exact size of the steps that should be taken in any situation and exactly how many reinforcements should be given at each step, the guidelines would be much more useful. Unfortunately, the experiments necessary for providing this information have not yet been conducted. The behavior modifier should observe the behavior carefully and be prepared to make changes in the procedure—changing the size of the steps, slowing down, speeding up, or retracing steps—whenever the behavior does not seem to be developing properly. Shaping requires a good deal of practice and skill if it is to be performed with maximum effectiveness.

Questions for Learning

9. What is meant by the term *final target behavior* in a shaping program? Give an example.
10. What is meant by the term *starting behavior* in a shaping program? Give an example.
11. How do you know you have enough successive approximations or shaping steps of the right size?
12. Why is it necessary to avoid underreinforcement at any shaping step?
13. Why is it necessary to avoid reinforcing too many times at any shaping step?

Pitfalls of Shaping

Unaware-Misapplication Pitfall

As with other procedures and natural processes, shaping operates whether we are aware of it or not. Unfortunately, those who are not aware of shaping may unknowingly apply it to develop undesirable behavior of friends, acquaintances, family members, and others. See Figure 7.1 for an example of this.   **NOTE 3** Consider another example of this pitfall. Suppose a small child receives very little social attention from family members when he performs appropriate behavior. Perhaps 1 day the child accidentally

FIGURE 7.1
A misapplication of shaping.

falls and strikes his head lightly against a hard floor. Even if the child is not injured seriously, a parent may come running quickly and make a big fuss over the incident. Because of this reinforcement and because anything else the child does that is appropriate seldom evokes attention, he is likely to repeat the response of striking his head lightly against the floor. The first few times this occurs, the parent may continue to reinforce the response. Eventually, however, seeing that the child is not really hurting himself, the parent may stop reinforcing it. Because the behavior has now been placed on operant extinction, the *intensity* of the behavior may increase (see Chapter 6). That is, the child may begin to hit his head more forcefully, and the slightly louder thud will cause the parent to come running again. If this shaping process continues, the child will eventually hit his head with sufficient force to cause physical injury. It is extremely difficult, if not impossible, to use operant extinction to eliminate such violently self-destructive behavior. It would have been best never to have let the behavior develop to the point at which the child's parents were forced to continue reinforcing it and increasing its strength.

Many undesirable behaviors commonly seen in children with special needs—for example, violent temper tantrums, constant fidgeting, injuring other children, voluntary vomiting—are often products of the inadvertent application of shaping. It is possible that these behaviors can be eliminated by a combination of operant extinction of the undesirable behavior and positive reinforcement of the desirable behavior. Unfortunately, this is often difficult to do because (a) the behavior is sometimes so harmful that it cannot be allowed to occur even once during the period in which extinction is to take place and (b) adults who are ignorant of behavior principles sometimes unknowingly foil the efforts of those who are conscientiously attempting to apply these principles.

In Chapter 23, we describe how to diagnose and treat problem behaviors that may have been developed inadvertently through shaping. As in medicine, however, the best cure is prevention. Ideally, all persons responsible for the care of other persons will be so thoroughly versed in behavior principles that they will refrain from shaping undesirable behavior.

Failure-to-Apply Pitfall

Another type of pitfall is the failure to apply shaping to develop desirable behavior. Some parents, for example, may not be responsive enough to their child's babbling behavior. Perhaps they expect too much at the beginning and do not reinforce extremely remote approximations of normal speech. Some parents, for example, seem to expect their tiny infant to say "Father!" right off the bat and are not impressed when the child says "da-da." The opposite type of problem also exists. Instead of not giving enough reinforcement for babbling, some parents may overreinforce babbling. This could result in a child whose speech consists entirely of baby talk at an age when most children have mastered their culture's speech patterns.

Inaccurate-Explanation-of-Behavior Pitfall

If a child has not learned to speak by a certain age, some people might try to explain the deficit by labeling the child as intellectually disabled or autistic. It is possible that there are individuals with intellectual disabilities or autism whose deficiency exists not because of any genetic or physical defect but simply because they were never exposed to effective shaping procedures. Many variables can prevent a physically normal child from receiving the shaping that is necessary to establish normal behaviors. For an excellent discussion of how delays in acquiring age-appropriate language skills develop in preschool children with no known genetic or physical defects that might cause the delayed behavior, see Drash and Tudor (1993).

Guidelines for the Effective Application of Shaping

1. *Select the Final Target Behavior*
   a. Choose a specific behavior (such as working quietly at a desk for 10 minutes) rather than a general category (e.g., "good" classroom behavior). Shaping is appropriate for changing amount, latency, and intensity of behavior, as well as for developing new behavior of a different topography (form). If the final target behavior is a complex sequence of activities (such as making a bed) that can be broken down into sequential steps, and if the program amounts to linking the steps together in a particular order, it is not a shaping program. Rather, the final target behavior needs to be developed by chaining (see Chapter 11).
   b. If possible, select a behavior that will come under the control of natural reinforcers after it has been shaped.
2. *Select an Appropriate Reinforcer*   See Table 4.2 and the "Guidelines for the Effective Application of Positive Reinforcement," pp. 42–43.
3. *The Initial Plan*
   a. List successive approximations to the final target behavior, beginning with the starting behavior. To choose the starting behavior, find a behavior already in the learner's repertoire that resembles the final target behavior most closely and that occurs at least once during an observation period.
   b. Your initial steps or successive approximations are usually "educated guesses." During your program, you can modify these according to the learner's performance.
4. *Implementing the Plan*
   a. Tell the learner about the plan before starting.
   b. Begin reinforcing immediately following each occurrence of the starting behavior.
   c. Never move to a new approximation until the learner has mastered the previous one.
   d. If you are not sure when to move the learner to a new approximation, use the following rule. Move to the next step when the learner performs the current step correctly in 6 of 10 trials, usually with 1 or 2 trials less perfect than desired and one or two trials in which the behavior is better than the current step.
   e. Do not reinforce too many times at any one step, and avoid underreinforcement at any one step.
   f. If the learner stops working, you may have moved up the steps too quickly, the steps may not be the right size, or the reinforcer may be ineffective.
      (1) First, check the effectiveness of your reinforcer.
      (2) If the learner becomes inattentive or shows signs of boredom, the steps may be too small.
      (3) Inattention or boredom may also mean you have progressed too rapidly. If so, return to the previous step for a few more trials and then try the present step again.
      (4) If the learner continues to have difficulty, despite retraining at previous steps, add more steps at the point of difficulty.

Questions for Learning

14. Give an example of the Unaware-Misapplication Pitfall in which shaping might be accidentally applied to develop an undesirable behavior. Describe some of the shaping steps in your example.
15. Give an example of the Pitfall in which the failure to apply shaping might have an undesirable result.
16. Give an example from your own experience of a final target behavior that might best be developed through a procedure other than shaping (see Guideline 1a, p. 69).
17. State a rule for deciding when to move the learner to a new approximation (see p. 69).
18. Why do we refer to positive reinforcement and operant extinction as principles but to shaping as a procedure? (*Hint:* See Chapter 1, p. 10.)

Application Exercises

A. Exercise Involving Others

Think of a normal child between the ages of 2 and 7 with whom you have had contact (e.g., a sister, brother, or neighbor). Specify a realistic final target behavior of that child that you might try to develop by using a shaping procedure. Identify the starting point you would choose, the reinforcer, and the successive approximations you would go through.

B. Self-Modification Exercises

1. Take a close look at many of your own skills—for example, personal interaction, lovemaking, and studying. Identify two specific skills that were probably shaped by others, either knowingly or unknowingly. Identify two specific behaviors that were probably shaped by the natural environment. For each example, identify the reinforcer and at least three approximations that you likely performed during the shaping process.
2. Select one of your behavioral deficits, perhaps one that you listed at the end of Chapter 2. Outline a complete shaping program that with a little help from your friends you might use to overcome that deficit. Make sure that your plan follows the guidelines for the effective application of shaping discussed in this chapter.

Notes for Further Learning

1. Shaping appears to be useful in modifying not only external behavior but also internal behavior. For example, R. W. Scott and colleagues (1973) demonstrated that shaping could be used to modify heart rate. In this study, the device monitoring heart rate was hooked up to the video portion of a TV set that the individual watched. Although the sound portion of the TV was on continuously, the video portion appeared only when the individual's heart rate changed by a few beats per minute from its previous level. When the subject's heart rate remained at a new level for three consecutive sessions, the video portion was used to reinforce a further change in heart rate. In one case involving a psychiatric patient suffering from chronic anxiety and manifesting a moderately elevated heart rate, the investigators shaped several decreases in the individual's heart rate. Interestingly, when the individual's heart rate had been decreased to a lower level, reports from his ward indicated that "he seemed less 'tense' and 'anxious'" and that "he made fewer requests for medication."
2. How fast should you move from one step to the next? How large should step size be? One reason there are no specific answers to these questions is the difficulty of measuring specific step sizes and consistently reinforcing responses that satisfy a given step size. Human judgment is simply not fast enough or accurate enough to ensure that any given shaping procedure is being applied consistently in order to make comparisons between it and other consistently applied shaping procedures. This is particularly true when topography is the aspect of behavior that is being shaped. Computers, however, are both more accurate and faster and may therefore be useful in answering fundamental questions concerning which shaping procedures are most effective (Midgley, Lea, & Kirby, 1989; Pear & Legris, 1987). For example, using two video cameras that were connected to a microcomputer programmed to detect the position of a pigeon's head within a test chamber, Pear and Legris demonstrated that a computer can shape where the pigeon moves its head.

   In addition to providing a methodology for studying shaping, these studies suggest that computers may be able to shape some kinds of behavior as effectively as humans. For example, a device that shapes movements may help a person regain the use of a limb that has been paralyzed by a stroke or accident (e.g., see Taub et al., 1994).

   Such a device would have the advantage over a human shaper in its precision, its ability to provide extremely rapid and systematic feedback, and its patience (i.e., computers are nonjudgmental and untiring).

3. Rasey and Iversen (1993) provided a good laboratory demonstration of a potential maladaptive effect of shaping. They reinforced rats with food for extending their noses over the edge of a platform on which the rats were standing. Over trials, the rats were required to extend their noses farther and farther over the edge before receiving reinforcement. Eventually, each rat extended its nose so far over the edge that it actually fell off the platform. A net under the platform kept the rat from being injured; however, this experiment demonstrates that animals, and probably humans as well, can be shaped to engage in behavior that is harmful to them.

Questions for Further Learning

1. Describe how Scott and colleagues used shaping to decrease the heart rate of a man suffering from chronic anxiety.
2. Describe how computer technology might be used to shape specific limb movements in a paralyzed person.
3. Describe how computer technology might be used to study shaping more accurately than can be done with the usual noncomputerized shaping procedures.
4. Describe an experiment demonstrating that maladaptive behavior can be shaped.

CHAPTER 8

Developing Behavioral Persistence with Schedules of Reinforcement

LEARNING OBJECTIVES

After studying this chapter, you will be able to:

- Define *intermittent reinforcement*.
- Compare intermittent with continuous reinforcement.
- Define ratio schedules, interval schedules, limited hold, duration schedules, and concurrent schedules.

- Explain how a common pitfall of intermittent reinforcement often traps not only the uninitiated but also those with some knowledge of behavior modification.

Jan, let's see how many math problems you can do.

Improving Jan's Work Rate in Math Class[1]

Jan was a 13-year-old seventh-grade student of average intelligence. During math classes, she exhibited a great deal of inattentive behavior and made frequent errors. With the support of her teacher, two behavior modifiers introduced a strategy for improving Jan's work rate. One of them worked with Jan every day during math class, giving Jan a worksheet containing math problems. During the first 2 days, when Jan completed two problems correctly, the behavior modifier responded with "Good work" or "Excellent job," or some similar positive reaction. During the next 2 days, the number of problems to be completed before praise was given increased to four. Two days after that, Jan had to complete eight problems correctly before receiving praise. During the final 2 days, no praise was given until Jan had completed 16 problems.

The praise schedule had a positive effect on Jan's work rate. From the beginning to the end of the study, her rate of correct problem solving tripled, with the highest work rate occurring when Jan was praised following each of 16 problems solved. Moreover, by the end of the study, Jan was attending to the task 100% of the time.

---

[1] This case is based on a report by Kirby and Shields (1972).

Some Definitions

As stated in Chapter 6, *intermittent reinforcement* is an arrangement in which a behavior is positively reinforced only occasionally (i.e., intermittently) rather than every time it occurs. Jan's problem-solving behavior was not reinforced after each math problem that she solved. Instead, she received reinforcement after a fixed number of problem-solving responses had occurred. On this reinforcement schedule, Jan worked at a very steady rate.

Response rate refers to the number of instances of a behavior that occur in a given period of time. It is synomous with the term *response frequency*, which was used in the earlier chapters of this book; however, *response rate* is more commonly used when talking about schedules of reinforcement, so that is the term we use in this chapter.

A *schedule of reinforcement* is a rule specifying which occurrences of a given behavior, if any, will be reinforced. The simplest schedule of reinforcement is *continuous reinforcement (CRF)*, which is an arrangement in which each instance of a particular response is reinforced. Had Jan received reinforcement for each problem solved, we would say that she was on a CRF schedule. Many behaviors in everyday life are reinforced on a CRF schedule. Each time you turn the tap, your behavior is reinforced by water. Each time that you insert and turn the key in the front door of your home or apartment, your behavior is reinforced by the door opening.

The opposite of CRF is called *operant extinction*. As discussed in Chapter 6, on an extinction schedule no instance of a given behavior is reinforced. The effect is that the behavior eventually decreases to a very low level or ceases altogether.

Between these two extremes—CRF and operant extinction—lies intermittent reinforcement. Many activities in the natural environment are not reinforced continuously. You may not always get a good grade after studying. You have to work for a week before you get your weekly paycheck. Experiments on the effects of various strategies for positively reinforcing behaviors have been studied under the topic of schedules of reinforcement. The number of such schedules is unlimited. Because each produces its own characteristic behavior pattern, different schedules are suitable for different types of applications. In addition, certain schedules are more practical than others (e.g., some require more time or **NOTE 1** effort to apply than others).

While a behavior is being conditioned or learned, it is said to be in the *acquisition* phase. After it has become well learned, it is said to be in the *maintenance* phase. It is best to provide CRF during acquisition and then switch to intermittent reinforcement during maintenance. Intermittent schedules of reinforcement have several advantages over CRF for maintaining behavior: (a) The reinforcer remains effective longer because satiation takes place more slowly; (b) behavior that has been reinforced intermittently tends to take longer to extinguish (see Chapter 6); (c) individuals work more consistently on certain intermittent schedules; and (d) behavior that has been reinforced intermittently is more likely to persist after being transferred to reinforcers in the natural environment. In this chapter, we discuss four types of intermittent schedules for increasing and maintaining behavior: ratio, simple interval, schedules with limited hold, and duration. (Basic research on these schedules is described in Pear, 2001; for a more recent discussion of reinforcement schedules see Lattal, 2012; Nevin & Wacker, 2013.)

Questions for Learning

1. Define and give an example of *intermittent reinforcement*.
2. Define and give an example of *response rate*.
3. Define and give an example of *schedule of reinforcement*.
4. Define CRF and give an example that is not in this chapter.
5. Describe four advantages of intermittent reinforcement over CRF for maintaining behavior.

Ratio Schedules

In a **fixed-ratio (FR) schedule**, a reinforcer occurs each time a fixed number of responses of a particular type are emitted. The reinforcement schedules for Jan were FR schedules. Recall that early in her program, she had to complete two math problems for each reinforcement, which is abbreviated FR 2. Later she had to solve four problems for reinforcement, which is abbreviated FR 4. Finally, she had to make 16 correct responses, abbreviated FR 16. Note that the schedule was increased in steps. If Jan's responses had been put on FR 16 immediately (i.e., without the intervening FR values), her behavior might have deteriorated and appeared as though it were on extinction. This deterioration of responding from increasing an FR schedule too rapidly is sometimes referred to as *ratio strain*. The optimal response requirement differs for different individuals and for different tasks. For example, Jan increased her response rate even when the FR increased to 16. Other students may have shown a decrease before reaching FR 16. In general, the higher the ratio at which an individual is expected to perform, the more important it is to approach it gradually through exposure to lower ratios. The optimal ratio value or response requirement that will maintain a high rate of response without producing ratio strain must be found by trial and error.

When considering the effects of schedules of reinforcement on response rate, we need to distinguish between free-operant procedures and discrete-trials procedures. A *free-operant procedure* is one in which the individual is "free" to respond at various rates in the sense that there are no constraints on successive responses. For example, if Jan had been given a worksheet containing 12 math problems to solve, she could have worked at a rate of one problem per minute, or a rate of three per minute, or at some other rate. In a *discrete-trials procedure*, the individual is "not free" to respond at whatever rate he or she chooses because the environment places limits on the availability of response opportunities. For example, if a parent told a teenage child, "You can use the family car after you have helped do the dishes following three evening meals," then that would be a discrete-trials procedure. The teenager cannot do the dishes for three quick meals in an hour, but has to wait and respond at a maximum rate of doing the dishes once per day. When we talk about the characteristic effects of schedules of reinforcement on response rate, we are referring to free-operant procedures unless otherwise specified. (For discussion of a procedure called discrete-trials teaching, see p. 20.)

When introduced gradually, FR schedules produce a high steady rate until reinforcement, followed by a postreinforcement pause. The length of the postreinforcement pause depends on the value of the FR—the higher the value, the longer the pause (Schlinger, Derenne, & Baron, 2008). FR schedules also produce high resistance to extinction (see Chapter 6, p. 56–57).

NOTE 2   There are many examples of FR schedules in everyday life. If a football coach were to say to the team, "Everybody do 20 push-ups before taking a break," that would be an FR 20. Another example is paying an industrial worker for a specified number of parts completed or a farm worker for a specified amount of fruit or vegetables picked (called *piece-rate pay*).

With a **variable-ratio (VR) schedule**, a reinforcer occurs after a certain number of a particular response, and the number of responses required for each reinforcer changes unpredictably from one reinforcer to the next. The number of responses required for each reinforcement in a VR schedule varies around some mean value, and this value is specified in the designation of that particular VR schedule. Suppose, for example, that over a period of several months, a door-to-door salesperson averages one sale for every 10 houses called on. This does not mean that the salesperson makes a sale at exactly every 10th house. Sometimes a sale might have been made after calling on five houses in a row. Sometimes sales might occur at two houses in a row. And sometimes the salesperson might call on a large number of houses before making a sale. Over several months, however, a mean of 10 house calls is required to produce reinforcement. A VR schedule that requires an average of 10 responses is abbreviated VR 10. VR, like FR, produces a high steady rate of responding. However, it also produces no or a minimal postreinforcement pause (Schlinger et al., 2008). The salesperson can never predict exactly when a sale will occur and is likely to continue making house calls right after a sale. Three additional differences between the effects of VR and FR schedules are that the VR schedule can be increased somewhat more abruptly than an FR schedule without producing ratio strain, the values of VR that can maintain responding are somewhat higher than FR, and VR produces a higher resistance to extinction than FR schedules of the same value.

The natural environment contains many examples of VR schedules. Asking someone for a date is an example because even the most popular people often have to ask an unpredictable number of different people to obtain an acceptance. Slot machines are programmed on VR schedules: The gambler has no way of predicting how many times he or she must play to hit a payoff. Similarly, casting for fish is also reinforced on a VR schedule: One must cast an unpredictable number of times to get a bite.

Ratio schedules—both FR and VR—are used when one wants to generate a high rate of responding and can monitor each response (because it is necessary to count the responses to know when to deliver reinforcement on a ratio schedule). FR is more commonly used than VR in behavioral programs because it is simpler to administer.

A type of reinforcement schedule that is becoming increasingly popular in applied settings is *progressive ratio (PR)*. In fact, the *Journal of Applied Behavior Analysis* devoted its summer 2008 issue to this topic. A PR schedule is like an FR schedule, but the ratio requirement increases by a specified amount after each reinforcement. At the beginning of each session, the ratio requirement starts back at its original value. After a number of sessions, the ratio requirement reaches a level—called the *break point* or *breaking point*—at which the individual stops responding completely. The typical effect of a PR schedule is an increasingly longer pause after each successive reinforcement and an indefinitely long pause at the break point (Schlinger et al., 2008). The main application of PR is to determine how potent, powerful, or effective a particular reinforcer is for a particular individual. The higher the reinforcer's break point is for an individual, the more effective that reinforcer is likely to be in a treatment program for that individual (Roane, 2008). However, it has been argued that because PR does not correlate with easier-to-apply and less-aversive measures of reinforcer effectiveness, they should not be used in applied settings with members of protected populations such as individuals with autism (Poling, 2010).

Although the preceding discussion pertains to ratio schedules in a free-operant procedure, ratio schedules have also been studied in discrete-trials procedures. An example of the use of a ratio schedule in a discrete-trials procedure involves a task designed to teach children with developmental disabilities to name pictures of objects. The procedure involves presenting a carefully designed sequence of trials in which the teacher sometimes speaks the name of the picture for the child to imitate and sometimes requires that the child name the picture correctly. Correct responses are reinforced with praise (e.g., "Good!") and a treat. Children make more correct responses and learn to name more pictures when correct responses are reinforced with a treat on a ratio schedule than when they are continuously reinforced with a treat. However, this is true only if the ratio schedule does not require too many correct responses per reinforcement. As the response requirement increases, performance improves at first but then begins to show ratio strain (see Stephens, Pear, Wray, & Jackson, 1975).

Questions for Learning

6. Explain what an FR schedule is. Illustrate with two examples of FR schedules in everyday life (at least one of which is not in this chapter).
7. What is a free-operant procedure? Give an example.
8. What is a discrete-trials procedure? Give an example.
9. What are three characteristic effects of an FR schedule?
10. What is ratio strain?
11. Explain what a VR schedule is. Illustrate with two examples of VR schedules in everyday life (at least one of which is not in this chapter). Do your examples involve a free-operant procedure or a discrete-trials procedure?
12. Describe how a VR schedule is similar procedurally to an FR schedule. Describe how it is different procedurally.
13. What are three characteristic effects of a VR schedule?
14. Illustrate with two examples of how FR or VR might be applied in training programs. (By *training program*, we refer to any situation in which someone deliberately uses behavior principles to increase and maintain someone else's behavior, such as parents to influence a child's behavior, a teacher to influence students' behavior, a coach to influence athletes' behavior, and an employer to influence employees' behavior.) Do your examples involve a free-operant or a discrete-trials procedure?
15. Explain what a PR schedule is and how PR has been mainly used in applied settings.

Simple Interval Schedules

In a **fixed-interval (FI) schedule**, a reinforcer is presented following the first instance of a specific response after a fixed period of time (see Figure 8.1). The only requirement for a reinforcer to occur is that the individual engage in the behavior after reinforcement has become available because of the passage of time. The size of the FI schedule is the amount of time that must elapse before reinforcement becomes available. For example, let's suppose that your favorite TV show occurs at 7:00 pm every Thursday, and your video recorder is set up to record the show each time it occurs. Because 1 week must elapse before you can be reinforced for watching your favorite show, we would call the schedule an *FI 1-week schedule*. Note from Figure 8.1 that although the passage of a certain amount of time is necessary for reinforcement to occur, a response must occur sometime after the specified time interval (e.g., anytime after the week is up you must watch your recorded show to be entertained). Note also that there is no limit on how long after the end of the interval a response can occur in order to be reinforced (e.g., you can watch your recorded show anytime after Thursday). Finally, note that a response occurring before the specified interval ends has absolutely no effect on the occurrence of the reinforcer (e.g., if you try to watch your favorite show on Monday, Tuesday, or Wednesday, you won't see it because it doesn't come on until Thursday).

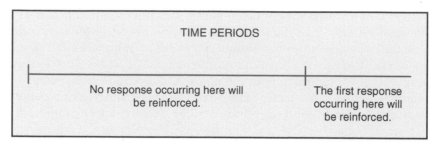

FIGURE 8.1

Diagram of a fixed-interval schedule. The horizontal line represents a period of time

Most of us rely on clocks to tell us when to do things that are reinforced on an FI schedule. We usually wait until the reinforcer is available and then make one response and receive it. For children who have not yet learned to tell time, however, the typical effects of an FI schedule are somewhat different. For example, suppose that two young children who can't tell the time play together each morning. About 2 hours after breakfast, a parent has a midmorning snack prepared for them; approximately 2 hours after that, lunch is prepared for them. As the time draws to a close in each 2-hour period, the children begin making more and more frequent trips to the kitchen, each time asking, "Is it time to eat yet?" Finally, after 2 hours, it's ready. After eating, they return to their play, and there's a fairly lengthy passage of time before they start to make trips to the kitchen again. The children's behavior of going to the kitchen is characteristic of behavior reinforced on an FI schedule for individuals who don't have access to clocks or others who will tell them the time. In such cases FI schedules produce: (a) a rate of responding that increases gradually near the end of the interval until reinforcement occurs; and (b) a postreinforcement pause. Note that the word *pause* simply means that the behavior of interest, such as the trip to the kitchen, does not occur. The length of the postreinforcement pause depends on the value of the FI—the higher the value (i.e., the more time between reinforcers), the longer the pause.

When judging whether a behavior is reinforced on an FI schedule, you should ask yourself two questions: (a) Does reinforcement require only one response after a fixed interval of time? (b) Does responding during the interval affect anything? If you can answer yes to the first question and no to the second question, your example is an FI. Consider, for example, a college class in which students have a test on the same day of the week. The students' pattern of studying likely resembles the characteristic pattern of responding on an FI schedule in that little or no studying occurs immediately after a test and studying increases as the test day draws near. However, consider the preceding two questions. Can the students wait around until a week has passed, make "one" study response, and receive a good grade? No, a good grade is contingent on studying during the 1-week interval. Does responding before the interval ends affect anything? Yes, it contributes to a good grade. Therefore, this is not an example of FI, although it may resemble it in some ways.

A job that pays by the hour is often erroneously cited as an example of an FI schedule. A little thought shows that it is incorrect because hourly pay assumes that the individual works throughout each hour. But an FI schedule requires only one response at the end of the interval (see Figure 8.1). Checking one's bank account to see if the employer has deposited one's pay, however, is an example of behavior reinforced on an FI schedule. An employer depositing pay into an employee's account occurs only after a certain period of time, and checking one's bank account earlier does not make it appear there any sooner.

In a **variable-interval (VI) schedule**, a reinforcer is presented following the first instance of a specific response after an interval of time, and the length of the interval changes unpredictably from one reinforcer to the next. Stated more simply, on a VI schedule, a response is reinforced after unpredictable intervals of time. Because messages on one's telephone answering machine or e-mail messages on one's computer can be left at unpredictable times, checking one's answering machine for messages, and one's computer for e-mail are examples of VI schedules in the natural environment. The lengths of the intervals in a VI schedule vary around some mean value, which is specified in the designation of that particular VI schedule. For example, if a mean of 25 minutes is required before reinforcement (e.g., receiving an e-mail) becomes available, the schedule is abbreviated VI 25 minutes. VI produces a moderate steady rate of responding and no (or at most a very small) postreinforcement pause. Like the intermittent schedules discussed previously, VI produces a high resistance to extinction relative to continuous reinforcement. However, responding is lower during extinction after VI than it is after FR or VR.

Simple interval schedules are not often used in behavior modification programs for several reasons: (a) FI produces long postreinforcement pauses; (b) although VI does not produce long postreinforcement pauses, it does generate lower response rates than ratio schedules do; and (c) simple interval schedules require continuous monitoring of behavior after the end of each interval until a response occurs.

Questions for Learning

16. What is an FI schedule?
17. What are two questions to ask when judging whether a behavior is reinforced on an FI schedule? What answers to those questions would indicate that the behavior is reinforced on an FI schedule?
18. Suppose that a professor gives an exam to students every Friday. The students' studying behavior would likely resemble the characteristic pattern of an FI schedule in that studying would gradually increase as Friday approaches, and the students would show a break in studying (similar to a lengthy postreinforcement pause) after each exam. But this is not an example of an FI schedule for studying. Explain why.
19. What is a VI schedule?
20. Explain why simple interval schedules are not often used in training programs.

Schedules with a Limited Hold

A **limited hold** is a deadline for meeting the response requirement of a schedule of reinforcement. A limited hold can be added to any of the ratio or interval schedules.

Fixed-Ratio Schedules with a Limited Hold

Suppose that a fitness instructor says to a person who is exercising, "If you do 30 sit-ups, then you can get a drink of water." That would be an FR 30 schedule. Now suppose that the fitness instructor says to the person, "If you do 30 sit-ups in 2 minutes, then you can get a drink of water." That would be an example of an FR 30 schedule with a limited hold of 2 minutes. The addition of a limited hold to a schedule is indicated by writing the abbreviation of the schedule followed by "/LH" and the value of the limited hold. The previous example would be written as an FR 30/LH 2 minutes. Because ratio schedules already generate high rates of response, it is not common for a limited hold to be added to ratio schedules.

Fixed-Interval Schedules with a Limited Hold

Most FI schedules that you encounter in everyday life have a limited hold attached to them (see Figure 8.2). In the natural environment, a good approximation of an FI/LH schedule is waiting for a bus. Buses usually run on a regular schedule (e.g., one every 20 minutes). An individual may arrive at the bus stop early, just before the bus is due, or as it is arriving—it makes no difference, for that person will still catch the bus. So

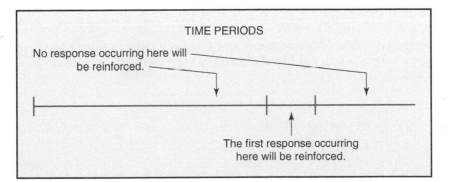

FIGURE 8.2

Diagram of a fixed-interval schedule with a limited hold. The horizontal line represents a period of time

far, this is just like a simple FI schedule. However, the bus will wait only a limited time—perhaps 1 minute. If the individual is not at the bus stop within this limited period of time, the bus goes on and the person must wait for the next one.

Variable-Interval Schedules with a Limited Hold

Like FI schedules, most VI schedules in everyday life have a limited hold attached to them. We'll explain how a VI/LH works by describing an effective strategy for managing the behavior of kids on a family car trip. It's based on *The Timer Game*,[2] also known as *The Good Behavior Game* (Donaldson, Vollmer, Krous, Downs, & Berard, 2011; Kleinman & Saigh, 2011; Tingstrom, Sterling-Turner, & Wilczynski, 2006). When one of the authors' two boys were children, family car trips were trying. With Mom and Dad in the front seat and the boys in the backseat, nonstop bickering between the boys seemed to rule the day ("You're on my side," "Give me that," "Don't touch me," etc.). After several unpleasant car trips, Mom and Dad decided to try a variation of *The Timer Game*. First, they purchased a timer that could be set at values up to 30 minutes and produced a "ding" when the set time ran out. At the beginning of the car trip, they announced the new rules to the boys: "Here's the deal. Every time this timer goes 'ding,' if you're playing nicely, you can earn 5 extra minutes for watching late-night TV in the motel room [a powerful reinforcer for the boys in the days before there were DVD players in vehicles]. But if you're bickering, you lose those 5 minutes. We'll play the game until we get there." Thereafter, a parent set the timer ranging from 1 to 30 minute intervals for the duration of the trip. Because, on average, the timer was set for 15 minutes, this was a VI 15 minute schedule. Because the boys had to be cooperative the instant that a "ding" occurred, the limited hold was zero seconds and, this was a VI 30 minutes/LH 0 seconds schedule. The results seemed miraculous. From nonstop bickering, the boys switched to mainly cooperative play. Although it required only an instant of cooperative play to earn a reinforcer, the boys never knew when that opportunity might occur. The result: continuous cooperation.

A good approximation of behavior on a VI/LH schedule occurs when we are telephoning a friend whose line is busy. Note that as long as the line is busy, we will not get through to our friend no matter how many times we dial, and we have no way of predicting how long the line will be busy. However, after finishing the call, our friend may receive another call. In either case, if we do not call during one of the limited periods in which the line is free, we miss the reinforcement of talking to our friend and must wait another unpredictable period before we again have an opportunity to gain this particular reinforcement.

Interval schedules with short limited holds produce effects similar to those caused by ratio schedules (including strain if large increases in interval size are introduced abruptly). For small FIs, FI/LH produces effects similar to those produced by FR schedules (Schoenfeld & Farmer, 1970). VI/LH produces effects similar to those produced by VR schedules. Thus, interval schedules with short limited holds are sometimes used when a teacher wants to produce ratio-like behavior but is unable to count each instance of the behavior, such as when the teacher can monitor the behavior only periodically or at irregular intervals.

Interval schedules with short limited holds are common in behavior modification programs. For example, a teacher might use a variation of *The Timer Game*, such as a VI 30 minutes/LH 0 seconds schedule to reinforce the students' in-seat behavior. That is, if the children are working quietly at their seats whenever the timer rings after a variable 30-minute interval, they would receive some desirable item such as points that could be accumulated toward extra free time.

Note that interval schedules with limited holds are also more common in nature than are interval schedules without limited holds. For example, if you go to the grocery store to pick your favorite fruit before it is ripe, your behavior will not be reinforced by the taste of the fruit, nor will waiting too long after it has ripened reinforce your behavior.

Questions for Learning

21. Explain what an FR/LH schedule is, and illustrate with an example from everyday life that is not in this chapter.
22. Explain what an FI/LH schedule is, and illustrate with an example that is not in this chapter. (*Hint:* Think of behaviors that occur at certain fixed times, such as arriving for meals, plane departures, and cooking.)

---

[2] This procedure was developed on the basis of a study by Wolf, Hanley, King, Lachowicz, and Giles (1970).

23. Describe how an FI/LH schedule is procedurally similar to a simple FI schedule. Describe how it procedurally differs.
24. Explain what a VI/LH schedule is. Illustrate with two examples from everyday life (at least one of which is not in this chapter).
25. Give two examples of how VI/LH might be applied in training programs.
26. For each of the photos in Figure 8.3, identify the schedule of reinforcement that appears to be operating.

Response: Watching for one's luggage at an airport
Reinforcer: Getting the luggage

Contingency arrangement: After an unpredictable time, luggage appears on the conveyor.

Response: Stacking pieces on a pegboard
Reinforcer: Getting all the pieces stacked
Contingency arrangement: After a fixed number of responses, all the pieces will be stacked.

iStock © JerryPDX

Response: Taking clothes out of dryer
Reinforcer: Clothes are dry

Contingency arrangement: After a fixed period of time, the first response will pay off.

Response: Watching TV
Reinforcer: Viewing an enjoyable scene
Contingency arrangement: Enjoyable scene occurs unpredictably, and lasts briefly.

FIGURE 8.3
Examples of people responding on intermittent reinforcement schedules

Duration Schedules

In a **fixed-duration (FD) schedule**, a reinforcer is presented only if a behavior occurs continuously for a fixed period of time (e.g., Stevenson & Clayton, 1970; see Figure 8.4). The value of the FD schedule is the amount of time that the behavior must be engaged in continuously before reinforcement occurs (e.g., if it is 1 minute, we call the schedule an FD 1-minute schedule). A number of examples of fixed-duration schedules occur in the natural environment. For instance, a worker who is paid by the hour might be considered to be on an FD schedule. Melting solder might also be an example of behavior on an FD schedule. To melt the solder, one must hold the tip of the soldering iron on the solder for a continuous fixed period of time. If the tip is removed, the solder cools quickly and the person has to

NOTE 3   re-apply heat for the same continuous period.

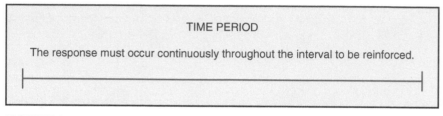

FIGURE 8.4
Diagram of a fixed-duration schedule. The horizontal line represents a period of time

In a **variable-duration (VD) schedule**, a reinforcer is presented only if a behavior occurs continuously for a fixed period of time, and the interval of time from reinforcer to reinforcer changes unpredictably. The mean interval is specified in the designation of the VD schedule. For example, if the mean is 1 minute, the schedule is abbreviated VD 1-minute. An example of a VD schedule might be rubbing two sticks together to produce fire because the amount of time this takes varies as a function of factors such as the size, shape, and dryness of the sticks. Another example of a VD schedule is waiting for traffic to clear before crossing a busy street.

Both FD and VD schedules produce long periods of continuous behavior. The FD schedule, however, produces a postreinforcement pause, whereas the VD schedule does not.

Behavior modification programs use duration schedules only when the target behavior can be measured continuously and reinforced on the basis of its duration. One should not assume, however, that this is the case for any target behavior. Presenting reinforcement contingent on a child studying or practicing the piano for an hour may work. However, it may also reinforce only sitting at the desk or in front of the piano. This is particularly true of something like studying, for which it is difficult for the parent or teacher to observe whether the desired behavior is occurring as the child could be daydreaming, texting, or reading a book instead of studying. Practicing the piano is easier to monitor because the parent or teacher can hear whether the child is doing the lesson.

Eye contact is a behavior that is commonly reinforced on duration schedules in training programs for children with developmental disabilities. Many such children do not make eye contact with others, and any attempt by an adult to initiate this behavior causes the child to quickly avert her or his eyes from the adult. It is generally agreed that eye contact is important as a prerequisite to further social development (e.g., Kleinke, 1986; Baron-Cohen, 1995).

Questions for Learning

27. Explain what an FD schedule is. Illustrate with two examples of FD schedules that occur in everyday life (at least one of which is not in this chapter).
28. Suppose that each time that you put bread in a toaster and press the lever, 30 seconds passes before your toast is ready. Is this an example of an FD schedule? Why or why not? Would it be an FD schedule if (a) the catch that keeps the lever down doesn't work? or (b) the timer that releases it doesn't work? Explain in each case.
29. Explain why FD might not be a very good schedule for reinforcing study behavior.
30. Give two examples of how FD might be applied in training programs.
31. Explain what a VD schedule is, and illustrate with an example of one from everyday life (that is not in this chapter).

Overview of Six Commonly Used Intermittent Schedules for Increasing and Maintaining Behavior

Refer to Table 8.1 for six commonly used intermittent schedules we have discussed in this chapter and their characteristic effects. To summarize, the six schedules are: FR, VR, FI/LH, VI/LH, FD, and VD. NOTE 4 *Ratio schedules* (FR and VR) make reinforcement contingent on a certain number of responses being completed; *interval schedules with limited hold* (FI/LH and VI/LH) make reinforcement contingent on a response occurring within a limited period of time after reinforcement becomes available; and *duration schedules* (FD and VD) make reinforcement contingent on a response being made for a certain continuous period of time.

TABLE 8.1   Characteristic Effects and Applications of Six Common Intermittent Reinforcement Schedules for Increasing and Maintaining Behavior

Schedule	Fixed	Variable	Application
Ratio	High steady rate; short postreinforcement pause; high RTE*	High steady rate; no postreinforcement pause; very high RTE	To increase and maintain rate of specific responses that can be easily counted, such as solving addition or subtraction problems correctly or correct repetitions of a sport skill
Interval with limited hold	High steady rate (with small intervals); short postreinforcement pause; moderate RTE	High steady rate; no postreinforcement pause; high RTE	To increase and maintain duration or steady rate of behaviors such as on-task behavior of children in a classroom, cooperative behavior of children on a family car trip, or treading water by persons in a swimming class
Duration	Continuous behavior; moderate RTE	Continuous behavior; high RTE	To increase and maintain behaviors that can be monitored continuously and that should persist throughout a period of time, such as practicing the piano

*RTE = resistance to extinction.

Concurrent Schedules of Reinforcement

In most situations, we have the option of performing more than just one type of behavior. At home during a particular evening, for example, a student might have the choice of watching a TV show, watching an online movie, surfing the Net, texting, doing homework, or talking on the phone. When each of two or more behaviors is reinforced on different schedules at the same time, the schedules of reinforcement that are in effect are called *concurrent schedules of reinforcement*. Considering the concurrent schedules of reinforcement for the same student, in which option is the student likely to engage? In 1961, Richard Herrnstein proposed that choice is governed by a mathematical equation called the *matching law*, which states that the response rate or the time devoted to an activity schedule is proportional to the rate of reinforcement of that activity relative to the rates of reinforcement on other, concurrently available activities. Research has indicated, in addition to reinforcement rate, factors that are likely to influence one's choice when several schedules are available are: (a) the types of schedules that are operating; (b) the immediacy of reinforcement; (c) the magnitude of reinforcement (e.g., a student might choose to study for an exam worth 50% of the final grade over watching a boring TV show); and (d) the response effort involved in the different options (Friman & Poling, 1995; Mazur, 1991; Myerson & Hale, 1984; Neef, Mace, & Shade, 1993; Neef, Mace, Shea, & Shade, 1992; Neef, Shade, & Miller, 1994). Attempts have been made to extend or modify the matching law to incorporate these other factors influencing choice (e.g., Baum, 2012).

An understanding of the research on concurrent schedules is valuable when designing a behavior modification program. Suppose, for example, that you are attempting to decrease an undesirable behavior by reinforcing a desirable alternative behavior. You should ensure that the schedule of reinforcement for the desirable alternative behavior involves more immediate reinforcers, more frequent reinforcement, more powerful reinforcers, and less response effort than that for the undesirable behavior.

Pitfalls of Intermittent Reinforcement

Unaware-Misapplication Pitfall

The most common pitfall of intermittent reinforcement often traps not only the unwary but also those with some knowledge of behavior modification. It involves what may be described as inconsistent use of extinction. For example, a parent may at first attempt to ignore a child's tantrums. But the child persists, and in despair, the parent finally gives in to the child's demands. Thus, the child obtains reinforcement on a VR or VD schedule, and this leads to further persistent tantrumming in the future. Many times, parents and staff say that they had to give in to the child's demands because "extinction was not working." However, the resulting intermittent reinforcement produces behavior that occurs at a higher rate and is more resistant to extinction than behavior that has been continuously reinforced.

Guidelines for the Effective Use of Intermittent Reinforcement

To use intermittent schedules effectively in generating and maintaining desired behaviors, observing the following rules is important:

1. Choose a schedule that is appropriate to the behavior you wish to strengthen and maintain.
2. Choose a schedule that is convenient to administer.
3. Use appropriate instruments and materials to determine accurately and conveniently when the behavior should be reinforced. For example, if you are using a ratio schedule, make sure that you have a counter of some sort—a wrist counter, a calculator, a string of beads, or simply pencil and paper. Similarly, if you are using an interval or duration schedule, make sure that you have an accurate timer appropriate for your schedule. If you are using a variable schedule, make sure that you have arranged to follow a sequence of random numbers that vary around the mean you have chosen.
4. The frequency of reinforcement should initially be high enough to maintain the desired behavior and should then be decreased gradually until the final desired amount of behavior per reinforcement is being maintained. (Recall that for Jan, the FR was at first very small and was then increased.) Always remain at each stage long enough to ensure that the behavior is strong. This is similar to the shaping procedure described in Chapter 7. If you increase the requirement too rapidly, the behavior will deteriorate, and you will have to return to an earlier stage (possibly continuous reinforcement) to recapture it.
5. In language that he or she can understand, inform the individual of the schedule you are using. A number of studies (Pouthas, Droit, Jacquet, & Wearden, 1990; Shimoff, Matthews, & Catania, 1986; Wearden, 1988) indicate that people perform more efficiently if they have specific rules to follow regarding the schedule in effect (see discussion of rule-governed behavior in Chapter 17).

Questions for Learning

32. What are concurrent schedules of reinforcement? Give an example.
33. If an individual has an option of engaging in two or more behaviors that are reinforced on different schedules by different reinforcers, what four factors in combination are likely to determine the response that the person will make?
34. Describe how intermittent reinforcement works against those who are ignorant of its effects. Give an example.
35. Name six schedules of reinforcement commonly used to develop behavior persistence (i.e., the ones described in Table 8.1).
36. In general, which schedules tend to produce higher resistance to extinction (RTE), the fixed or the variable schedules (see Table 8.1)?

Application Exercises

A. Exercise Involving Others

Assume that the following behaviors have been established:
1. dishwashing behavior of roommate or spouse
2. dusting behavior of son or daughter
3. doing mathematics assignments by a student

You now face the task of maintaining them. Following the guidelines for the effective use of intermittent reinforcement, describe in detail the best schedules of reinforcement and how you might apply them for each of these behaviors.

B. Self-Modification Exercise

1. Assume that you have been assigned a 200-page book to read in the next few days. Select an appropriate reinforcer for yourself, and identify the best schedule on which to dispense the reinforcer. Describe the reasons for your selections (characteristic effects, ease of application, etc.), and outline the mechanics of how you might implement the program and complete it successfully.

Notes for Further Learning

1. The effects of the various schedules of reinforcement have been worked out mainly with animals. The classic authoritative work on this topic written by Ferster and Skinner (1957) deals mostly with pigeons pecking on a response key to obtain reinforcement in the form of access to grain for a few seconds. A number of experiments have been conducted to determine whether humans show the same patterns of responding that other animals do when exposed to basic schedules of reinforcement. In one common procedure, for example, a human volunteer presses a lever to produce points that can be exchanged for money or some other reinforcing item. In many cases, however, humans responding under these conditions do not show the behavior patterns described in this chapter (e.g., see Pear, 2001, pp. 74–75). One possible reason for these differences between humans and animals has to do with the complex verbal behavior humans have typically been conditioned to emit and to respond to—that is, humans can verbalize rules (as described in Chapter 17) that may influence them to show different behavior patterns than animals show when exposed to various reinforcement schedules (Michael, 1987). Thus, humans may make statements to themselves about the schedule of reinforcement in effect and respond to those statements rather than to the actual schedule itself. Evidence for this view comes from data indicating that the patterns shown by preverbal infants are similar to those shown by animals (Lowe, Beasty, & Bentall, 1983) and gradually become less similar as children become increasingly verbal (Bentall, Lowe, & Beasty, 1985). In addition, instructions can very strongly influence rate and patterns of responding on various schedules of reinforcement (Otto, Torgrud, & Holborn, 1999; Torgrud & Holborn, 1990).

2. An analysis of records kept by novelist Irving Wallace suggests that novel writing follows a fixed-ratio pattern (Wallace & Pear, 1977). Wallace typically stopped writing immediately after completing each chapter of a book he was working on. After a brief pause of a day or so, he resumed writing at a high rate, which he maintained until the next chapter was completed. In addition, longer pauses typically occurred after a draft of a manuscript was completed. Thus, one might reasonably argue that completed chapters and completed drafts of manuscripts are reinforcements for novel writing and that these reinforcements occur according to FR schedules. Of course, it should be recognized that novel writing is a complex behavior and that other factors are also involved.

3. Evidence supports the position that, when FR and FD both appear to be applicable, the former is preferable. Semb and Semb (1975) compared two methods of scheduling workbook assignments for elementary school children. In one method, which they called "fixed-page assignment," the children were instructed to work until they had finished 15 pages. In the other method, "fixed-time assignment," the children were instructed to work until the teacher told them to stop. The amount of time the children were required to work was equal to the average amount of time they spent working during the fixed-page condition. In both methods, each child who answered correctly at least 18 of 20 randomly selected workbook frames received free time; otherwise, the child(ren) had to redo the entire assignment. On the whole, the children completed more work and made more correct responses under the fixed-page condition than under the fixed-time condition.

4. Schedules of reinforcement can help us understand behavior that has frequently been attributed to inner motivational states. For example, consider the pathological gambler. Because this individual is acting against his or her own best interests, it is sometimes said that the individual has an inner motive of masochism—a need for self-punishment. However, the pathological gambler may be a victim of an accidental adjustment

to a high VR schedule. Perhaps when first introduced to gambling, this individual won several large sums in a row. Over time, however, the gambler won bets less frequently and now maintains the gambling at a high rate of very infrequent reinforcers. Similar adjustment to a high VR schedule with a low reinforcement rate can account for highly persistent desirable behavior as well—for example, that of the dedicated student, businessperson, or scientist.

Questions for Further Learning

1. Who wrote the classic authoritative work on schedules of reinforcement, and what is the title of that book?
2. What may account for the failures to obtain the schedule effects in basic research with humans that are typically found in basic research with animals?
3. Describe how FR schedules may be involved in writing a novel.
4. Might it be better to reinforce a child for dusting the living room furniture for a fixed period of time or for a fixed number of items dusted? Explain your answer.
5. Briefly describe how schedules of reinforcement can help us understand behavior that has frequently been attributed to inner motivational states.

CHAPTER 9

Responding at the Right Time and Place: Stimulus Discrimination and Stimulus Generalization

LEARNING OBJECTIVES

After studying this chapter, you will be able to:

- Define *stimulus control, discriminative stimulus,* and *stimulus discrimination training.*
- Compare and contrast stimulus discrimination with stimulus generalization.
- Discuss the characteristics of concepts and stimulus equivalence and their relation to language.

- Describe factors determining the effectiveness of stimulus discrimination training.
- Explain how ignorance of stimulus discrimination training may lead parents or other caregivers to develop undesirable behavior in individuals under their care.

Children, please work at your desks.

Learning to Follow Teacher's Instructions[1]

The teacher in a regular third-grade class in an Auckland suburban elementary school had a problem. When she was giving instructions to the class, she wanted the children to listen attentively from their seats. At other times she wanted them to work quietly on their own. But 9 of the 34 children posed special problems of inattention and poor in-seat behavior. These youngsters frequently argued, shouted, hit and kicked other youngsters, banged on furniture, and left the classroom without permission. They did listen attentively and work quietly occasionally but not often and usually not when the teacher wanted them to. This was clearly a situation in which the desired behavior (listening attentively or working quietly) occasionally occurred, but it did not occur at all the desired times.

On several mornings, observers recorded the on-task behavior of the nine problem children during teacher instruction when they were to sit silently in their seats and listen to their teacher and during work period when they were to write a story, draw a picture, or perform other activities prescribed by the teacher. The problem children were typically on task less than 50% of the time. The teacher then introduced a procedure for getting the desired behavior to occur at the desired time during an oral and written language lesson from 9:30 to 10:20 every morning. She made a large chart, on one side of which was printed in red letters:

LOOK AT THE TEACHER
STAY IN YOUR SEAT
BE QUIET

---

[1] This example is based on a study by Glynn and Thomas (1974).

On the other side, in green letters, was

WORK AT YOUR PLACE
WRITE IN YOUR BOOKS
READ INSTRUCTIONS ON THE BLACKBOARD

At various times, one side of the chart or the other was showing. The children were each given a 10 × 12-inch card with several rows of squares on it, one row for each day of the week. The children were told that a "beep" would sound several times throughout the lesson, and they were to mark themselves on task by placing a check mark in one of the squares if they were "doing what the chart says" when a beep occurred. The beeps occurred an average of once every 2 minutes. The children were also told that at the end of the lesson, they would be able to cash in each check mark for 1 minute of free play time in a nearby room that contained a variety of games and toys. The program was introduced for all of the children in the class, although data were taken only on the nine problem children. In very short order, the sign telling them what to do exerted strong control over their behavior, influencing them to perform the desired behavior at the desired times. The program increased the on-task behavior of the nine problem children to approximately 91%.

Learning to Respond at the Right Time and Place

As you have seen in previous chapters, behavior is strongly affected by its consequences. Behavior that is reinforced increases. Behavior that is not reinforced decreases. However, any behavior is valuable only if it occurs at the right times and in appropriate situations. For instance, at an intersection, it is desirable to stop the car when the light is red, not when the light is green. Executing a perfect double back flip will earn you valuable points in a gymnastics routine, but it probably won't have the same effect in your first corporate-level job interview. As we acquire new behaviors, we also learn to produce those behaviors at the right time and place. How do we learn to do this successfully?

To understand the process, we must first recognize that there are always other people, places, or things that are around when behavior is reinforced or extinguished. For example, when Johnny is playing outside with his friends, laughter and attention are likely to reinforce his swearing. When Johnny is sitting at the dinner table at Grandpa and Grandma's on Sunday, his swearing is not likely to be reinforced and may even be punished. After several such experiences, the people and things that were around during reinforcement and extinction come to cue the behavior. Johnny's swearing becomes highly probable in the presence of the kids on the street and very improbable in his grandparents' house.

Any situation in which behavior occurs can be analyzed in terms of three sets of events: (a) the stimuli that exist just prior to the occurrence of the behavior, called *antecedent stimuli* (such as the presence of friends or the dinner table at Grandma and Grandpa's house just before Johnny swore), (b) the behavior itself (Johnny's swearing), and (c) the consequences of the behavior (either approval from Johnny's friends or disapproval from Grandma and Grandpa). Recall from Chapter 1 that *stimuli* are the people, objects, and events currently present in one's immediate surroundings that impinge on one's sense receptors and that can affect behavior. Visual objects, such as books, clothing, furniture, lights, people, pets, and trees, are all potential stimuli as are all types of sounds, smells, tastes, and physical contacts with the body. Any stimulus can be an antecedent or a consequence of a behavior. Identifying the antecedents and consequences of a behavior is sometimes referred to as an *ABC (antecedents, behavior, and consequences) assessment.*

When a behavior is reinforced in the presence of a particular stimulus but not others, that antecedent stimulus begins to exert control over the occurrence of that behavior. For example, at the end of the program at the Auckland elementary school, when the children saw the signs saying LOOK AT THE TEACHER and so on in big red letters, they listened carefully to what the teacher had to say because doing so had been reinforced in the presence of that antecedent stimulus. We say that the stimulus had come to exert control over the behavior. When a particular behavior is more likely to occur in the presence of a particular stimulus but not others, we say that the behavior is under the control of that stimulus.

We use the term **stimulus control** to refer to the degree of correlation between the occurrence of a particular antecedent stimulus and the occurrence of a subsequent response. *Good, strong,* or *effective stimulus control* refers to a strong correlation between the occurrence of a particular stimulus and a particular response; that is, when the stimulus occurs, the response is likely to follow. For example, suppose that you have just put money into a vending machine and are looking for your favorite candy bar. You see the name of that bar beside a particular button, and you press that button. The sign exerted good stimulus control over your button-pressing behavior. Similarly, at the end of the program in the lead example for this chapter, the signs LOOK AT THE TEACHER and so on exerted good stimulus control over the children's behavior of paying attention.

While some stimuli are consistent predictors that a particular behavior will be reinforced, other stimuli are consistent predictors that a particular behavior will not be reinforced. An "Out of Order" sign on a vending machine is a cue that the behavior of inserting money into the machine will not be reinforced. The appearance of an empty cup is a cue that raising the cup to your lips will not result in a drink. Through experience, we learn to refrain from performing certain behaviors in the presence of certain stimuli because we have learned that those behaviors will go unreinforced. Thus, there are two types of controlling stimuli, which are described next.

Types of Controlling Stimuli: S^{D}s and S$^\Delta$s

A **discriminative stimulus** or S^D (pronounced "ess-dee") is a stimulus in the presence of which a response will be reinforced. Loosely speaking, an S^D is a cue that a particular response will pay off. An S$^\Delta$ (pronounced "ess-delta") is a stimulus in the presence of which a response will not be reinforced. Loosely speaking, an S$^\Delta$ is a cue that a particular response will *not* pay off. An S^D might be called a *discriminative stimulus for the availability of reinforcement for responding,* and an S$^\Delta$ might be called a *discriminative stimulus for the non-availability of reinforcement for responding* (i.e., extinction). "Δ" or "delta" is "D" in ancient Greek.

In our example of Johnny's swearing, the stimulus of the other kids is an S^D for the response of swearing because their laughter and attention reinforced that response. The stimulus of Grandpa and Grandma is an S$^\Delta$ for the response of swearing because it was not reinforced in their presence. This can be diagrammed as follows:

(an instance of positive reinforcement)

1. S^D ──────────→   Response ──────────→   Reinforcer
   (other kids)   (swearing)   (approval of kids)

(an instance of extinction)

2. S$^\Delta$ ──────────→   Response ──────────→   No reinforcer
   (Grandma and Grandpa)   (swearing)   (no positive attention)

A stimulus can simultaneously be an S^D for one response and an S$^\Delta$ for another, that is, in the presence of a particular stimulus, one response may be reinforced while another may not be. For instance, if you are eating dinner with friends and someone asks you, "Please pass the pepper," that statement is an S^D for your response of passing the pepper, and it is an S$^\Delta$ for you to pass the salt.

Questions for Learning

1. What is a stimulus? Give two examples that are not from the text.
2. What is an ABC assessment?
3. Define *stimulus control*.
4. What is good stimulus control? Give an example that is not in this chapter.
5. Define S^D and give an example that is not in this chapter. Identify both the S^D and the response in the example.
6. Define S$^\Delta$ and give an example that is not in this chapter. Identify both the S$^\Delta$ and the response in the example.
7. What is the difference between a stimulus and a discriminative stimulus?
8. Give an example (not from this chapter) of a stimulus that is an S^D for one behavior and an S$^\Delta$ for a different behavior.

Stimulus Discrimination

Stimulus discrimination training refers to the *procedure* of reinforcing a response in the presence of an S^D and extinguishing that response in the presence of an S$^\Delta$. After sufficient stimulus discrimination training, the *effects* can be described as (1) **good stimulus control**—a strong correlation between the occurrence of a particular stimulus and a particular response, or (2) a **stimulus discrimination**—a response occurs to an

S^D, not to an S$^\Delta$. In the example of Johnny's swearing described previously, Johnny received discrimination training as diagrammed on p. 87. The result was good stimulus control (in the presence and not in the absence of other kids Johnny would swear), and a stimulus discrimination (Johnny swore when with other kids but not when with Grandma and Grandpa).

Stimulus Generalization

Stimulus generalization refers to the *procedure* of reinforcing a response in the presence of a stimulus or situation and the *effect* of the response becoming more probable in the presence of another stimulus or situation. In other words, instead of discriminating between two stimuli and responding differentially to them, an individual responds in the same way to two different stimuli. Thus, stimulus generalization is the opposite of stimulus discrimination. There are several reasons for the occurrence of stimulus generalization.

Unlearned Stimulus Generalization Due to Strong Physical Similarity

People and animals are likely to perform a behavior in a new situation if that situation is very similar to the one in which they learned the behavior. Consider a case that is familiar to many parents: an infant learns to say "doggie" to a large, hairy, four-legged creature with floppy ears and a friendly bark. Later, the infant sees a different kind of large dog and says "doggie." It is fortunate that we have evolved in this way. Imagine what life would be like if you could not perform a newly learned skill in a new situation that was somewhat different from the circumstances in which you originally learned the skill. You would have to relearn how to cook in each new kitchen; you would have to relearn to ski on each new slope; you would have to relearn to dance to each new song. Fortunately, we have evolved so that the more physically similar two stimuli are, the more stimulus generalization will occur between them.

Learned Stimulus Generalization Involving Limited Physical Similarity

Suppose a child learns to say "dog" to a large German shepherd. Would the child also spontaneously say "dog" to a tiny Chihuahua? Probably not. Although these two types of dogs have some limited physical similarity, they are very different in many respects. Stimulus generalization is not likely to occur in the latter case until the child has learned the concept *dog*. A more technical name for concept is *stimulus class*.

A **common-element stimulus class** is a set of stimuli, all of which have one or more physical characteristics in common. For example, cars typically have four wheels, windows, a steering wheel, and so forth. When a child learns to say the word *car* when seeing a particular car, the child is likely to show unlearned stimulus generalization and be able to identify other cars. For other concepts, however, their members have only limited physical characteristics in common, and some learning is required for stimulus generalization to occur. To teach a child the concept red, you might reinforce the response *red* to many different red-colored objects and extinguish that response to objects that are not red. Eventually, the child would learn to recognize a red pencil and a red automobile as both being red, even though the pencil and the automobile are very different in other respects. As another example, to teach the concept of wetness, you would reinforce the response *wet* to many different wet objects and extinguish that response (and reinforce the response *dry*) to dry objects.

When an individual emits an appropriate response to all members of a common-element stimulus class and does not emit that response to stimuli that do not belong to the class, we say that the individual generalizes to all members within a common-element stimulus class or concept, such as recognizing red objects as red, and discriminating between common-element stimulus classes such as between red objects and blue objects. When an individual responds in this way, such as to the concept red, we say that the individual is showing *conceptual behavior*.

It is important to note that verbal behavior is not necessarily involved in conceptual behavior. Pigeons, although nonverbal, can readily learn a surprising range of concepts. By presenting slides to them and reinforcing pecks at slides that are exemplars of a particular concept while withholding reinforcement for pecks at slides that are not exemplars of that concept, researchers have taught pigeons the concepts such as person and tree as well as some number concepts such as 16 versus 20 (Herrnstein & deVilliers, 1980; Herrnstein, Loveland, & Cable, 1976; Honig & Stewart, 1988; Lubow, 1974; Vaughan & Herrnstein, 1987). The proof that the pigeons have learned a concept (identifying fish) is that they respond correctly to types of fish that they have never seen before.

Learned Stimulus Generalization in Spite of No Physical Similarity

Suppose that you are shown a number of items such as a carrot, a calculator, a pea, a pencil, and a glass of milk. You are asked to identify the food items. Obviously, you will be able to do so. You would be showing conceptual behavior with respect to the concept food, yet nothing about a carrot, a pea, and milk is physically similar.

A **stimulus equivalence class** is a set of completely dissimilar stimuli (i.e., have no common stimulus element) that an individual has learned to group or match together or respond to in the same way. (*Stimulus equivalence classes* are sometimes referred to simply as *equivalence classes,* although the former term is preferred because of the potential confusion of the latter with the mathematical meaning of the term *equivalence class.*) Behavioral researchers have often studied the formation of stimulus equivalence classes during match-to-sample training. Consider the following experiment for teaching the stimulus equivalence class of 3, ∴, and III to a young child. In Phase I, the child is given a number of trials with Training Panel 1 (see Figure 9.1). Using appropriate prompting and reinforcement, the child is taught to match 3 to ∴ even though the positions of ∴, IV, and 7 are randomly alternated across trials. Then Phase II proceeds similarly, but with Training Panel 2, and the child is taught to match ∴ to III. Now comes a test to see whether the child has learned the stimulus equivalence class. The child is shown the Test Panel and asked to match III to either 4, 6, or 3. In this experiment, the child will likely match III to 3. The III and the 3 have become members of a stimulus equivalence class, even though those two stimuli were never previously paired. The members of this stimulus equivalence class are functionally equivalent in the sense that they all control the same behavior. (For examples of the use of stimulus equivalence procedures to teach course material to college students, see Critchfield & Fienup, 2010; Walker & Rehfeldt, 2012; Walker, Rehfeldt, & Ninness, 2010. For reviews on research on discrimination learning, stimulus control, and stimulus class formation, see McIlvane, 2013; Urcuioli, 2013.)   **NOTE 1**

As we grow up, we acquire many stimulus equivalence classes in which all members of a class control the same response but in which the members of the class are physically very different. When a new behavior becomes conditioned to one member of a stimulus equivalence class, we are likely to generalize that behavior to other members of that class because we have previously learned to respond to all the class members in the same way. In everyday speech, we would say that the members of a stimulus equivalence

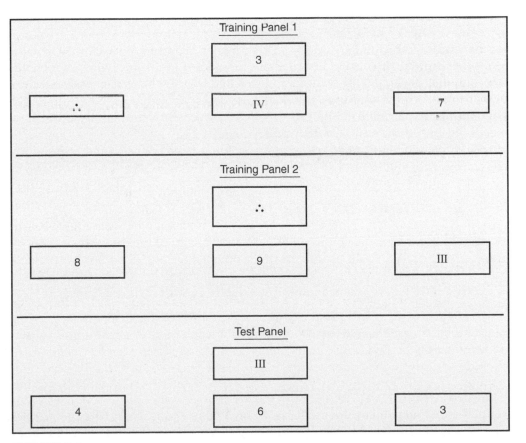

FIGURE 9.1

Visual displays in a stimulus equivalence experiment

class mean the same thing or share a common meaning (as when we learn the different representations for the number 3, the different words for drinking utensil, that *mammal* indicates animals such as cows, whales, and bats, and that *fruit* indicates plants such as apples, pears, and strawberries). Like common-element stimulus classes, a stimulus equivalence class is also a *concept*.

NOTE 2

In summary, if a response that has been reinforced to one stimulus occurs to a different stimulus (due to unlearned generalization, the learning of a common-element stimulus class, or the learning of a stimulus equivalence class), we say that *stimulus generalization* has occurred. But note that not all instances of stimulus generalization are favorable. For example, a child might learn to say "doggie" to a hairy four-legged creature and later say "doggie" when seeing a cat. In these and thousands of other instances, it is necessary to teach discriminations as described in the next section. (Strategies for improving generalization are discussed further in Chapter 16. Also see Spradlin & Simon, 2011.)

Questions for Learning

9. Describe the stimulus discrimination training procedure, and give an example that is not in this chapter.
10. State the two effects of stimulus discrimination training.
11. Define *stimulus generalization,* and give an example that is not in this chapter.
12. In a sentence, state the difference between an instance of stimulus discrimination and an instance of stimulus generalization.
13. What do we mean by *common-element stimulus class*? By *conceptual behavior*? Give an example of each that are not in this chapter.
14. Describe how you might teach the concept of honest to a child. Would your program teach a child to be honest? Why or why not?
15. What do we mean by *stimulus equivalence class*? Give an example that is not in this chapter.
16. What is a primary distinction between stimulus generalization involving common-element stimulus classes and stimulus generalization involving stimulus equivalence classes?

Factors Determining the Effectiveness of Stimulus Discrimination Training

1. Choosing Distinct Signals

If it is important to develop stimulus control of a particular behavior, it is often desirable to identify controlling S^Ds that are very distinctive. For example, the teacher in the Auckland school used large, red letters for the sign that prompted the students to listen and look at the teacher and large, green letters for the sign that prompted the students to work at their desks. As another example, to remind chronic nail-biters of their resolve to quit nail biting, the nail-biters wore distinctive non-removable wristbands, which proved to be quite successful (Koritzky & Yechiam, 2011).

When considering a stimulus to be set up as an S^D for the behavior of another person, you might ask yourself the following questions.

NOTE 3

1. Is the stimulus different from other stimuli along more than one dimension? That is, is it different in location, size, color, and sensory modality (vision, hearing, touch, etc.)?
2. Is the stimulus one that can be presented only or at least mainly on occasions when the desired response should occur to avoid confusion with the occurrence of the stimulus on other occasions?
3. Is the stimulus of the type that the probability of the person attending to it when it is presented is high?
4. Are there any undesirable responses that might be controlled by the chosen stimulus? (If some undesirable response follows the stimulus, it will interfere with the development of new stimulus control of the desired response.)

Careful attention to these questions will increase the chances that your stimulus discrimination training will be effective.

2. Minimizing the Opportunities for Error

During discrimination training, a response to an S^Δ or a failure to respond to an S^D is referred to as an *error*. Consider the example of a child learning to pick up a phone when it rings but not when it is silent. The responses of picking up the phone if it is silent or failure to pick up the phone when it rings are, as defined above, errors. Stimulus control can be developed most effectively when the behavior modifier minimizes the possibility of errors. For example, a parent who is teaching a child to answer the phone might move the phone out of reach if it is not ringing and add verbal prompts of this sort: "Now remember, we don't pick up telephones when they are not ringing. We only answer them when they ring." Then, as soon as the phone rings (a call made specifically for training purposes), the parent might immediately place the phone in front of the child and say, "The phone is ringing. Now you should answer it."

At this point, you might say, "But often we want to teach people to respond to subtle cues. Why should we then maximize distinctive signals?" Let's simply reply that choosing distinctive cues and minimizing errors will lead to more rapid stimulus control than might otherwise occur. In Chapter 10, we discuss techniques for gradually introducing discriminations involving subtle cues. For the moment, it is important to keep in mind that efforts to choose distinctive signals and to minimize errors will lead to the development of effective stimulus control more quickly and with less frustration than attempting to develop discriminations that involve subtle cues.

3. Maximizing the Number of Trials

In general, it is well accepted that a number of reinforced trials are necessary to develop consistent behaviors in persons with developmental disabilities and other individuals who are behaviorally deficient. What many people forget is that this is often true for all of us when we are acquiring new discriminations. Suppose, for example, that, after a couple of months of marriage, one of the partners presents subtle cues that he or she is not in the mood for lovemaking. What that partner must realize is that the other person may not yet have learned to respond to subtle cues, or even obvious cues, with just one or two trials. After a number of instances of reinforcement for correct responding to the S^Ds and extinction for responses to the S^Δs, those S^Ds and S^Δs will likely control the response on subsequent trials.

4. Using Rules: Describe the Contingencies

In Chapter 4, we introduced you to contingent versus noncontingent reinforcement. In general, a *contingency* is an if-then type of arrangement. For example, *if* you press the button on the water fountain, *then* a stream of water will appear. We say that the appearance of the water is contingent upon the button-pressing response. This would be an example of a two-term (behavior-consequence) contingency. If we describe both the antecedents and the consequences of a behavior, then we would be identifying a three-term contingency (Skinner, 1969).

The development of stimulus control often involves trial and error with three-term contingencies—several trials of positive reinforcement for a behavior in the presence of an S^D and several trials of that behavior going unreinforced in the presence of an S^Δ. Johnny's swearing, for example, came under the control of other kids as S^Ds (and came to not occur in the presence of Grandma and Grandpa as S^Δs) through trial and error. Behavior that develops because of its immediate consequences through trial and error is referred to as **contingency-shaped behavior**. Thus, Johnny's swearing illustrates contingency-shaped behavior. However, the children in the Auckland classroom did not take a few trials to show evidence of stimulus control. During the very first session after the teacher had explained the new set of classroom rules, the children showed an immediate increase in on task behavior in the presence of the appropriate signs (LOOK AT THE TEACHER and so on). Thus, the behavior of the children in the Auckland school illustrates what is called *rule-governed behavior*. A **rule** (from a behavioral perspective) describes a *situation* in which a *behavior* will lead to a *consequence*. Thus, a rule describes a three-term contingency of reinforcement. **Rule-governed behavior** is behavior that is controlled by the statement of a rule. When you wish to develop good stimulus control over a particular behavior, you should always provide the individual with a rule or set of rules stating what behaviors in what situations will lead to what consequences. Because of our complex conditioning histories for following instructions, the addition of a set of rules to a stimulus discrimination program may lead to instantaneous stimulus control. For example, if a father were to tell his 16-year-old son, "You can use the family car each Saturday night, but only if you mow the lawn each Friday," then the son is likely to comply with the rule on the first opportunity. (Use of rules is discussed further in Chapter 17.)

Pitfalls of Stimulus Discrimination Training

Unaware-Misapplication Pitfall

Any effective method can be misapplied inadvertently by the unwary, and stimulus discrimination training is no exception. Behavioral episodes of the following sort are common in many households with young children. Terri, a 3-year-old girl, is playing with the TV remote, causing annoying channel changes, volume increases and decreases, etc. Mother says quietly, "Terri, please leave the remote alone." Terri continues to fiddle with the remote. A few minutes later, Mother says a little louder and less politely, "Terri, put the remote down." Terri continues to fiddle with the remote, rapidly changing channels, which is a reinforcer for her. A minute or two later, Mother says, this time loudly and with a threatening tone, "Terri, for the last time, leave the remote alone or else!!!" Terri finally puts the remote down and Mother says, "Now, that's better, Terri. Mommy likes it when you do what I tell you; why didn't you do that in the first place?" It is probably obvious to you that Mother has just reinforced Terri for responding to her third-level threat. The discrimination Terri is learning is that of waiting until Mother is really angry and threatening before attending to her requests.

If you feel that you have to tell an individual something many times before the person responds, or that nobody listens to you, or that others are not doing the right thing at the right time and place, you should closely examine your interactions with these individuals for instances of misapplication of stimulus discrimination training.

Guidelines for Effective Stimulus Discrimination Training

1. *Choose Distinct Signals*   Specify the S^Ds and at least one S^Δ. (In other words, specify conditions under which the behavior should and should not occur.)
2. *Select an Appropriate Reinforcer*   See Chapter 4.
3. *Develop the Discrimination*
   a. Arrange for several reinforced responses in the presence of the S^D.
      (1) Specify clearly in a rule the S^D–desirable response–reinforcer sequence. Help identify the cues that indicate that the behavior will be reinforced versus the cues that indicate that the behavior will not be reinforced, and use instructions when appropriate to teach the person to act in a particular way under one set of circumstances but not under another.
      (2) Initially keep verbal cues constant.
      (3) Post the rules in a conspicuous place, and review them regularly.
      (4) Recognize that stimulus control over the behavior will not develop if the individual is not attending to the cues; therefore, use prompts (discussed further in Chapter 10) to emphasize the cues.
      (5) To teach the individual to act at a specific time, present prompts for correct performance just before the action is to occur.
   b. When the S^Δ is presented, make the change from the S^D very obvious and follow the rules for extinction for the behavior of concern. Stimuli that can acquire control over behavior include such things as location of training place; physical characteristics and location of furniture, equipment, and people in the training room; time of day of training; and sequence of events that precede and accompany training. A change in any of these may disrupt stimulus control.
4. *Weaning the Individual from the Program*   (discussed in more detail in Chapter 16).
   a. If the behavior occurs in the right place at the right time at a desirable rate during a dozen or so of the opportunities for the behavior and if it is not occurring in the presence of the S^Δ situations, it might be possible to gradually eliminate contrived reinforcers and maintain the behavior with natural reinforcers.
   b. Look for other natural reinforcers in the environment that might maintain the behavior once it is occurring in the presence of S^Ds, and not in the presence of S^Δs.
   c. After the program is terminated, plan periodic assessments of the behavior to ensure that it is occasionally being reinforced and that the desired frequency of the behavior is being maintained in the presence of the S^Ds.

Questions for Learning

17. When you are considering the selection of a stimulus to be set up as an S^D, what four questions might you ask yourself about that stimulus? (See p. 90.)
18. Describe a stimulus that you would like to establish as an S^D for a behavior of yourself or a friend, and describe the behavior. Then, for that stimulus, answer the four questions that you asked yourself in Question 17.
19. What do we mean by an error in stimulus discrimination training?
20. In general, what is a contingency? Give an example that is not in this chapter.
21. What is a three-term contingency of reinforcement? Give an example that is not in this chapter.
22. From a behavioral perspective, what is a rule?
23. With examples that are not in this chapter, distinguish between rule-governed and contingency-shaped behavior.
24. Was the children's high on task behavior to the posted rule in the Auckland classroom likely rule governed or contingency shaped? Justify your choice.
25. Give an example of how ignorance of stimulus discrimination training may lead parents or other caregivers to develop an undesirable behavior in a child or adult in their care.

Application Exercises

A. Exercises Involving Others

1. Identify five situations in which you presented an S^D that controlled the behavior of another person. Clearly identify the general situations, the controlling S^Ds, the behaviors controlled, and the reinforcers.
2. Describe five situations in which you presented an S^Δ to some other person. Clearly identify the general situations, the S^Δs, the behaviors for which your stimuli were S^Δs, and the consequences. Indicate whether the S^Δs controlled the behaviors appropriately.

B. Self-Modification Exercises

1. Describe a recent situation in which you generalized in a desirable way. Clearly identify the behavior, the situation in which the behavior was initially reinforced (the training situation), and the situation to which the behavior generalized (target situation).
2. Describe a recent situation in which you generalized in an undesirable way (in other words, had an undesirable outcome). Again, identify the behavior, training situation, and target situation.
3. Choose an excessive behavior of yours that you might like to decrease. Carefully monitor those situations in which the behavior occurs and does not occur over a two- or three-day period. Clearly identify some controlling S^Ds and some controlling S^Δs for the behavior.

Notes for Further Learning

1. Technically, stimulus equivalence requires the demonstration of three relationships: reflexivity, symmetry, and transitivity (Dymond & Rehfeldt, 2000; Sidman, 1994). Reflexivity simply involves recognizing instances of a stimulus. In other words, a child is able to match 3 to 3, ∴ to ∴, and III to III. Symmetry involves being able to recognize the equality of two different stimuli, so that if A = B then B = A. For example, consider the top panel in Figure 9.1. Suppose that, after training, the child has learned to correctly press the panel ∴ when shown 3. Now we will exchange the locations of ∴ and 3 by placing ∴ in the top panel and then randomly placing 3 with the other two choices. The child will demonstrate symmetry by choosing 3 when shown ∴. Transitivity is demonstrated when the child passes the test in the third panel shown in Figure 9.1. In other words, as a result of learning to match A to B and B to C, an individual now matches C to A without specific training to do so.
2. Following Skinner's (1957) publication of a behavioral account of language, some psycholinguists have argued that operant conditioning is inadequate to explain a child's acquisition of her or his native language (Brown, 1973; Chomsky, 1959; Pinker, 1994). Their argument is based largely on the view that children learn more about language than is directly trained or directly reinforced. However, through automatic conditioned reinforcement (described in Note 1 of Chapter 5), infants are able to emit vocal behaviors that have not been directly reinforced. And through stimulus equivalence training, children learn that physically different sounds that are members of the same stimulus equivalence class "mean" the same thing as other sounds. Such factors can explain how individuals can produce a new sentence they have never heard before, and experimental analysis of these factors can provide empirical support for a behavioral view of language development (Stromer, Mackay, & Remington, 1996).

3. Some forms of stimulus control are more complex than a single stimulus (such as a green light or a sign in a window) controlling a single response (such as crossing a street or going into a shop to buy something). One complex type of stimulus control, called *contextual control,* occurs when the general setting or context may alter the manner in which an individual responds to particular stimuli. For example, when you drive in Great Britain, the highway dividing line is an S^D to steer to the left of it, whereas when you drive in Canada, it is an S^D to steer to the right of it. In this example, the country in which you are driving is the context that determines how a particular stimulus controls your behavior. Knowledge of contextual control can be important in designing effective behavioral treatments. For example, Haring and Kennedy (1990) found a procedure that was effective in reducing the self-stimulating behavior of a girl with autism in the classroom was not effective in a recreational setting; and, conversely, a procedure that was effective in reducing her self-stimulatory behavior when she was doing leisure activities was not effective in reducing it when she was performing classroom tasks.

Questions for Further Learning

1. Using examples, explain what is meant by *reflexivity, symmetry,* and *transitivity.*
2. How have studies of stimulus equivalence provided support for a behavioral view of language development?
3. What is meant by the term *contextual control*? Illustrate with an example.
4. Just before starting to cross a street, a pedestrian from England visiting Canada observed that the street was clear to the right, stepped into the street, and was struck by a car. Explain how lack of contextual control was involved in this accident.

CHAPTER 10

Changing the Stimulus Control of a Behavior with Fading

LEARNING OBJECTIVES

After studying this chapter, you will be able to:

- Define *fading*.
- Identify dimensions of stimuli along which fading can occur.
- Describe factors influencing the effectiveness of fading.

- Distinguish between fading and shaping.
- Explain how fading works to the disadvantage of those who are ignorant of it.

Peter, what's your name?

Teaching Peter His Name[1]

Peter, diagnosed with autism, possessed an extensive vocal mimicking repertoire. He could repeat many of the words other people said but had little other verbal behavior. He would imitate many words, even when it was not appropriate. For example, when asked, "What's your name?" he would reply, "Name." Sometimes he would repeat the entire question, "What's your name?" This was a problem of stimulus control in that questions (stimuli) evoked mimicking responses rather than appropriate answers.

A university student named Veronica taught Peter to respond appropriately to the question, "What's your name?" as follows. First, Veronica identified an effective reinforcer. Because Peter had been taught to work for tokens (poker chips) that could be exchanged for treats such as candy and popcorn, Veronica decided to use the tokens as reinforcers.

Peter sat at a small table in a quiet room, and Veronica sat across from him. In a very soft whisper, Veronica asked, "What's your name?" Then very loudly and quickly, before Peter could respond, she shouted, "PETER!" Of course, Peter mimicked the word "Peter," and Veronica reinforced this with "Good boy!" and a token. You may wonder how this could represent any progress because the boy was still only mimicking. However, over several trials, Veronica began asking the question "What's your name?" more loudly and supplying the answer "Peter" more quietly. On each trial, she continued to reinforce the correct response—"Peter." Eventually, Veronica asked loudly, "What's your name?" and simply mouthed the word "Peter." Nevertheless, the boy responded with the correct answer, "Peter." Over several trials, Veronica ceased mouthing the correct answer, but Peter still responded correctly to the question "What's your name?"

---

[1] This case was adapted from Martin, England, Kaprowy, Kilgour, and Pilek (1968).

Fading

Fading is the gradual change over successive trials of an antecedent stimulus that controls a response so that the response eventually occurs to a partially changed or completely new antecedent stimulus.

Peter would at first say his name only when it was said to him. Through a fading process, the stimulus control over the response "Peter" was gradually transferred from the antecedent stimulus "Peter" to the antecedent stimulus "What's your name?" One might ask whether Peter knew that he was saying his own name. To phrase this question more behaviorally, would Peter have consistently responded correctly when asked other questions involving his name? For example, would he have consistently answered "Peter" when shown his reflection in the mirror and asked, "Who's that?" Probably not. However, teaching him to respond appropriately to "What's your name?" was an important start to teaching him to answer other questions involving his name and to his knowing that he was saying his name.

Fading is involved in many everyday situations in which one person teaches a behavior to another person. Parents are likely to fade out their help and support when a child is learning to walk or to ride a bicycle. A dance instructor might use less and less hand pressure to guide a student through new dance steps. And as a teenager progresses in drivers' education, the driving instructor is likely to provide fewer and fewer hints regarding traffic regulations.

In any situation in which a stimulus exerts strong control over a response, fading can be a very useful procedure for transferring the control of that response to some other stimulus. *Errorless discrimination training*, sometimes referred to as *errorless learning*, is the use of a fading procedure to establish a stimulus discrimination so that no errors occur. The discovery and development of fading techniques have led to some changes in educators' views regarding the learning process. At one time, it was believed that people had to make mistakes while learning in order to know what *not* to do. However, errorless transfer of a discrimination can occur, and it has at least three advantages over procedures involving trial and error. First, errors consume valuable time. Second, if an error occurs once, it tends to occur many times, even though it is being extinguished. (Remember from Chapter 6 that during extinction, things may get worse before they get better.) Third, the nonreinforcement that occurs when errors are being extinguished often produces emotional side effects such as tantrums, aggressive behavior, and attempts to escape from the situation.

Fading procedures can be used in many learning situations with very young children and with persons with developmental disabilities including autism (e.g., see Groff, Piazza, Zeleny, & Dempsey, 2011). In teaching a young child to name a shirt, for example, you might proceed according to the following steps:

1. *Point to your shirt and say "shirt."*   Keep doing this until the child consistently mimics "shirt" a number of times, and immediately reinforce each correct response.
2. *When the child consistently mimics "shirt," insert the question and at the same time gradually fade out saying "shirt."*   That is, you might say, "What's this? Shirt" while pointing to the shirt. In response, the child usually mimics "shirt." Over several trials, gradually decrease the intensity of saying "shirt" to zero so that the child eventually responds with the answer "shirt" to the stimulus of you pointing at a shirt and asking, "What's this?" Again, each appropriate response is to be reinforced.

Script-fading procedures have been used to teach children with autism to initiate interactions with others. For example, Reagon and Higbee (2009) taught parents of children with autism to use script-fading to promote play-based verbal initiations by their children. With a child who liked to play with toy cars, the mother first taught the child to imitate, "Mom, let's play cars," following which the mother and child would play with toy cars. After the child would imitate the complete statement, the script was faded from "Mom, let's play cars," to "Mom, let's play," to "Mom, let's," to "Mom," to nothing being said. Following script-fading, the child continued to emit the complete phrase, and also generalized the verbal imitation to other items (e.g., novel blocks).

Fading can also be used to teach tracing, copying, and drawing shapes (e.g., circles, lines, squares, and triangles), numerals, and letters of the alphabet. To teach a child to trace a circle, the teacher might begin with a large number of sheets with a heavily dotted circle on each of them. The teacher places a pencil in the child's hand, says "Trace the circle," and then guides the child's hand so that the pencil traces the circle by connecting the dots. Immediately after this, the child receives a reinforcer. After several trials, the teacher fades out the pressure of her hand as a cue controlling the child's tracing by

1. lightly holding the child's hand for several trials
2. touching her fingertips to the back of the child's hand for several trials

3. pointing to the item to be traced
4. finally, simply giving the instruction, "Trace the circle." (Steps 1, 2, and 3 are always accompanied by this instruction.)

Once the teacher has taught the child to trace, the child can be taught to draw or copy by the teacher fading out the dotted cues that guide the tracing. For example, the teacher might use a sheet on which there are several dotted circles. The circles progress from a heavily dotted circle on the left to a circle with very few dots on the right. The teacher points to the most heavily dotted circle and instructs the child, "Trace the circle here." The desired response is reinforced, and the procedure is repeated with the more lightly dotted circles. On subsequent steps, the dots can be faded out completely so that the child will draw a circle in their absence. It is then a simple matter to fade in the instruction "Draw a circle" to this newly acquired response. The instruction "Copy a circle" said while the teacher points to a circle can also be faded in and come to control the response. Learning to copy many different shapes in this fashion will eventually enable the child to copy shapes not previously copied.

Dimensions of Stimuli for Fading

In general, a **dimension** of a stimulus is any characteristic that can be measured on some continuum. As illustrated by the preceding examples, fading occurs along dimensions of stimuli, such as the loudness of the question that Veronica presented to Peter, the pressure of a teacher's hand that guides a child's printing, and the clarity of dots that a child might be expected to trace. Thus far, we have talked of fading across very specific stimulus dimensions, but fading can also occur across changes in a general situation or setting. In one of the authors' programs with children with autism, a group of children was expected to respond appropriately in a classroom setting (Martin et al., 1968). However, the children were very disruptive, especially in a group situation, and could not be placed directly into a classroom setting. So, the desired behavior for each child was obtained in an individual situation that was then faded into the classroom setting.

The initial training sessions were conducted in a small room in which there were several chairs and tablet-arm desks. Each day two or three university students worked individually with two or three children on a one-to-one basis. The procedures involved eliminating tantrums through extinction and reinforcing sitting attentively, exhibiting appropriate verbal behavior, drawing, copying, and displaying other desirable behaviors. Each child's desk was placed against the wall in such a fashion that it was difficult for the child to leave the situation.

Within 1 week, the children learned to sit quietly, attend to the university students, and imitate words. Stimulus control was established between the general training situation and the children's attentiveness. But the goal was to teach the children to function appropriately in a regular classroom situation with one teacher. If the classroom situation had been switched to after the first week, much inattentiveness and disruptive behavior would no doubt have occurred. Over a period of 4 weeks, the training situation was gradually changed from one small room with three children and three university students to a standard-sized classroom with seven students and one teacher.

One dimension was the physical structure of the room. The children were moved from the small room to the regular large classroom. This was done by first placing the three tablet-arm desks against the wall of the regular classroom, just as we had done in the small room. The three chairs that the university students sat in were also moved to the regular classroom. The rest of the classroom was empty. Over several days, the tablet-arm desks were gradually moved away from the wall and toward the center of the room until, finally, the three desks were side by side. Additional desks and furnishings were added one at a time until the children were finally sitting in desks in a normally furnished classroom.

The second dimension was the number of children per teacher. Fading along this dimension was carried out at the same time that fading along the first dimension took place. At first, one university student worked with one student for several sessions. The university student then worked with two students, alternating questions between them for several sessions. In this fashion, the student–teacher ratio was increased gradually until only one teacher worked with the seven children in a classroom situation.

Questions for Learning

1. Define *fading* and give an example of it.
2. Define *errorless discrimination training*.
3. Why is establishing a stimulus discrimination without errors advantageous?

4. What is meant by a dimension of a stimulus? Give an example.
5. Identify three stimulus dimensions along which fading occurred in the examples cited in the first 2 sections of this chapter.
6. Give an example from this chapter in which the training situation remained constant but a specific stimulus dimension was faded.
7. Give an example from this chapter in which the general training situation was faded.
8. Describe how one might use fading to teach a pet to perform a trick.
9. Assume that you have an 18-month-old child who imitates the word *chip*. Describe in detail how you might use fading to teach your child to correctly identify a chip (e.g., a potato chip) when you point to it and ask, "What's that?"

Factors Influencing the Effectiveness of Fading

1. The Final Target Stimulus

The *final target stimulus* should be chosen carefully. It is important to select it so that the occurrence of the response to that particular stimulus is likely to be maintained in the natural environment. Some fading programs make the error of stopping with a stimulus that does not include some aspect of the situation that the learner will frequently encounter in the natural environment. In Peter's case, it would have been easy for Veronica to stop training at the second to last step, at which Veronica asked loudly, "What's your name?" and then mouthed the word "Peter." However, when others approached Peter in his natural environment and asked "What's your name?" they would not likely mouth "Peter." Therefore, Veronica conducted the last step of the program, in which Peter responded correctly to the question "What's your name?" completely on his own.

2. The Starting Stimulus: A Prompt

At the beginning of a fading program, it is important to select a *starting stimulus* that reliably evokes the desired behavior. In the task of teaching Peter his name, Veronica knew that Peter would mimic the last word of a question when that word was spoken loudly. Therefore, the starting stimulus with Peter was the question, "What's your name?" said very softly and followed quickly by the shouted word, "Peter!" The shouted word "Peter" prompted him to give the correct answer. A **prompt** is a supplemental antecedent stimulus provided to increase the likelihood that a desired behavior will occur, but that is not the final target stimulus to control that behavior.

Instructor Behaviors as Prompts   It is helpful to distinguish between several types of instructor behaviors that can be used as prompts. *Physical prompts* (also called *physical guidance*) consist of guiding the learning through touch. Parents frequently use physical guidance to help their children learn **NOTE 1** new behavior, such as holding their hands while teaching them to walk. Beginning dancers, martial arts students, and novice golfers often find a guiding hand to be helpful. *Gestural prompts* are certain motions that a teacher makes, such as pointing to the correct cue or making signals directed to the learner without touching him or her. A teacher, for example, might extend a hand in a palm-downward motion as a prompt for children to talk softly. *Modeling prompts* occur when the correct behavior is demonstrated (modeling is discussed further in Chapter 18). A swimming coach might model the correct arm movements for the freestyle stroke for young swimmers. A golfing instructor might model the correct way to grip a golf club for a group of beginning golfers. *Verbal prompts* are verbal hints or cues. A driving instructor might use verbal prompts by telling a student driver to "check over your left shoulder before pulling out." Parents frequently use verbal prompts when teaching their children how to dress themselves (e.g., "Now pull the sweater over your head.").

Environmental Alterations as Prompts   *Environmental prompts* consist of alterations of the physical environment in a manner that will evoke the desired behavior. Someone attempting to eat healthily, for example, might put a bowl of fresh fruit in easy reach while keeping junk food out of sight in a difficult-to-reach cupboard. As another example, a student might ensure that a study area contains only objects and materials related to studying.

Technically speaking, all of the categories of prompts are parts of the environment for a learner. However, to distinguish instructor-behavior prompts from other aspects of the physical environment, we define each category of the prompts as described earlier.

Extra-Stimulus Versus Within-Stimulus Prompts   Instructor-behavior prompts and environmental prompts can be further subdivided into extra-stimulus prompts and within-stimulus prompts. An *extra-stimulus prompt* is something that is added to the environment to make a correct response more likely. Suppose that a parent wanted to teach a child to place a knife, fork, and spoon appropriately when setting a table for dinner. One option would be for the parent to point to the appropriate location of each utensil as it was named and placed. Pointing would be an extra-stimulus instructor-behavior prompt, and it would be faded out over trials. Alternatively, the parent might draw a knife, fork, and a spoon in their appropriate locations on a placemat and require the child to place the utensils appropriately. The line drawings would be an extra-stimulus environmental prompt and could gradually be erased over trials. A *within-stimulus prompt* is a variation of the S^D or the S^Δ to make their characteristics more noticeable and therefore easier to discriminate. In the table-setting example, training might be initiated with a normal fork and knife in their normal positions with a large wooden spoon as the training item. This would be a within-stimulus environmental prompt. The initial focus would be on teaching the child to place the spoon in the correct position. Over trials, the size of the spoon could be faded back to normal. This process could then be repeated with the knife and the fork until the child sets the table correctly. A within-stimulus prompt could also involve teacher behavior. A teacher trying to teach a child to respond appropriately to two words that sound similar, such as pen and pencil (both include the "pen" sound), might initially exaggerate differences in the sounds of the words when asking for either a pen ("PEN!") or a pencil ("pen-CIL!") and then gradually fade the sounds to their normal pitch and loudness. The different types of prompts are listed in Table 10.1. Several studies have indicated that within-stimulus prompt fading is more effective than extra-stimulus prompt fading with children with developmental disabilities including autism (Schreibman, 1975; Witt & Wacker, 1981; Wolfe & Cuvo, 1978).

A behavior analyst may provide any or all of these types of prompts to ensure the correct response. Suppose a teacher wishes to develop appropriate stimulus control by the instruction "Touch your head" over the response of a learner touching her head. The behavior analyst might initiate training by saying "Touch your head. Raise your hand and put it on your head like this" while touching his own head. In this example, "Raise your hand and put it on your head like this" is a verbal prompt, and the teacher's action of putting his hand on his head is a modeling prompt. Selecting several kinds of prompts that together reliably produce the desired response will minimize errors and maximize the success of the fading program.

3. The Fading Steps

When the desired response is occurring reliably to the prompts given at the onset of the training program, the prompts can then be gradually removed over trials. As with shaping steps (see Chapter 7), the steps through which prompts are to be eliminated should be carefully chosen. Also similar to shaping, **NOTE 2**

TABLE 10.1   Types of Prompts
Instructor-Behavior Prompts
Physical guidance—physically assisting the learner
Gestures—pointing or motioning
Modeling—demonstrating the correct behavior
Verbal—using words as hints or cues, giving instructions
Environmental Prompts
Environmental—rearranging the physical surroundings
Extra-Stimulus Versus Within-Stimulus Prompts
Extra-stimulus—adding another stimulus to make a correct response more likely
Within-stimulus—making the S^D or the S^Δ more noticeable and easier to discriminate

effective use of fading is somewhat of an art. It is very important to monitor the learner's performance closely to determine the speed at which fading should be carried out. Fading should be neither too fast nor too slow. If the learner begins to make errors, the prompts may have been faded too quickly or through too few fading steps. It is then necessary to backtrack until the behavior is again well established before continuing with fading. However, if too many steps are introduced or too many prompts are provided over a number of trials, the learner might become overly dependent on the prompts. Consider the example of teaching a child to touch her head when asked to do so. If the teacher spends a great many trials providing the prompt of touching his own head, the child may become dependent on it and attend much less to the instruction, "Touch your head."

Fading Versus Shaping

Care should be taken to avoid confusing fading with shaping. Both are procedures of gradual change. However, as described in Chapter 7, shaping involves reinforcement of slight changes in a behavior so that it gradually comes to resemble the target behavior. Thus, *fading involves the gradual change of a stimulus while the response stays about the same; shaping involves the gradual change of a response while the stimulus stays about the same.*

Pitfalls of Fading

Unaware-Misapplication Pitfall

Just as other behavior principles and procedures can be applied unknowingly by those who are not familiar with them, so can fading be misused. However, it appears to be more difficult to misuse fading inadvertently because the necessary gradual change in cues rarely occurs by chance.

The case of a child who banged his head on hard surfaces might be an example of the effects of the misuse of fading. Suppose that the child began attracting attention initially by hitting his head on soft surfaces, such as grass. At first, this behavior may have caused adults to come running to see whether the child had injured himself. When they eventually learned that no injury resulted from this behavior, they ceased providing him attention. The child may then have progressed to hitting his head with the same force but on slightly harder surfaces, such as carpeted floors. For a while, this perhaps increased the amount of attention elicited from adults, but this amount may eventually have decreased when the adults learned that the child did not injure himself in this way. Only when the child graduated to hitting his head on surfaces such as hard floors and even concrete, which caused real and serious self-injury, did the adults give him continued attention. Note that throughout this example, a gradual change occurred in the stimulus (the type of surface), evoking the undesired behavior; eventually, the behavior was evoked by the most undesirable stimulus possible. Thus, this example fits the technical definition of fading.

Guidelines for the Effective Application of Fading

1. *Choose the Final Target Stimulus*
   Specify very clearly the stimuli in the presence of which the target behavior should eventually occur.
2. *Select an Appropriate Reinforcer*
   See Chapter 4.
3. *Choose the Starting Stimulus and Fading Steps*
   a. Specify clearly the conditions under which the desired behavior now occurs—that is, what people, words, physical guidance, and so forth, presently are necessary to evoke the desired behavior.
   b. Specify specific prompts that will evoke the desired behavior.
   c. Specify clearly the dimensions (such as color, people, and room size) that you will fade to reach the final target stimulus control.
   d. Outline the specific fading steps to be followed and the rules for moving from one step to the next.
4. *Put the Plan Into Effect*
   a. Present the starting stimulus and reinforce the correct behavior.

b. Across trials, the fading of cues should be so gradual that there are as few errors as possible. However, if an error occurs, move back to the previous step for several trials and provide additional prompts.

c. When control by the final target stimulus is obtained, review the guidelines in previous chapters for weaning the learner from the program (a topic that is discussed in more detail in Chapter 16).

Questions for Learning

10. What do we mean by *final target stimulus*? Give an example.
11. What do we mean by *starting stimulus*? Give an example.
12. Define *prompt*. Give an example that is not from this chapter.
13. Define the four major categories of teacher-behavior prompts. Give an example of each.
14. Define *environmental prompt*, and give an example that is not from this chapter.
15. Define *within-stimulus prompt*, and give an example that is not from this chapter. Does your example involve a teacher-behavior prompt or an environmental prompt?
16. Define *extra-stimulus prompt*, and give an example that is not from this chapter. Does your example involve a teacher-behavior prompt or an environmental prompt?
17. How many reinforced trials should occur at any given fading step before the stimuli of that particular step are changed? (*Hint:* What suggestions were made in the examples in this chapter?)
18. Distinguish between fading and shaping.

Application Exercises

A. Exercises Involving Others

1. Suppose that a 3-year-old child has already learned some speech, and you wish to teach her to answer the question, "Where do you live?" Outline a fading program you could use to teach the answer to this question; indicate what you would use as a reinforcer, the number of trials you would have at each fading step, and so forth.

2. You want to instruct a child with severe developmental disabilities or a very young normal child to eat with a spoon. Name and describe the categories of prompts that you would use. Describe how each of the prompts would be faded.

B. Self-Modification Exercise

Suppose that you detest certain vegetables from the cabbage family—such as broccoli—but research studies have convinced you that you can reduce your chances of heart disease and cancer by eating more of these vegetables. Outline a fading program that you could use to increase the amount of broccoli or other such vegetables that you eat. (*Hint:* Your program should not—at least in the long run—increase your fat intake because that would defeat its purpose.)

Notes for Further Learning

1. The use of physical guidance raises a potential ethical issue. Suppose that in a program for persons with developmental disabilities, a teacher decides to use physical guidance. Suppose further that an individual client resists being guided. Physical guidance in that instance would therefore be viewed as somewhat intrusive or restrictive. However, as indicated in the discussion of ethical guidelines in Chapter 30, the least intrusive and restrictive interventions possible should be chosen. The teacher applying physical guidance in this instance should ensure that doing so meets appropriate ethical guidelines and accreditation standards. This issue is discussed further in Chapter 30.

2. The four methods of removing prompts gradually are (a) decreasing assistance, (b) increasing assistance, (c) graduated guidance, and (d) time delay. All of the examples of this chapter illustrate decreasing assistance in which a starting stimulus that evokes the response is gradually removed or changed until the response is evoked by the final target stimulus. Increasing assistance takes the opposite approach. The teacher begins with the final target stimulus and introduces prompts only if the learner fails to respond appropriately to the final target stimulus. The level of the prompts gradually increases during a trial in which the learner failed to respond at the preceding level until eventually the learner responds to the prompt. Graduated guidance is similar to the method of decreasing assistance except that the teacher's physical guidance is gradually

adjusted from moment to moment within a trial as needed and then is faded across trials. For example, the teacher may grasp the learner's hand firmly at the beginning of the trial and gradually reduce the force on the learner's hand as the trial progresses. With time delay, the final target stimulus and the starting stimulus are presented together at first; then, rather than change the starting stimulus, the time interval between the final target stimulus and the starting stimulus is gradually increased until eventually the individual is responding only to the final target stimulus. Many studies have indicated little or no difference in the effectiveness of these different prompt-removal methods (for a review, see Demchak, 1990).

Questions for Further Learning

1. Describe a plausible example in which use of physical guidance in a teaching program might require ethical approval. Why would ethical approval be required?
2. Which of the prompt-removal procedures fit the definition of fading given at the beginning of this chapter, and which do not? Explain.

CHAPTER 11

Getting a New Sequence of Behaviors to Occur with Behavior Chaining

Steve, your preputt routine is inconsistent.

Teaching Steve to Follow a Consistent Preputt Routine[1]

Steve was a young professional golfer on the Canadian PGA Tour who, although playing well, had not yet won a professional tournament due in part to inconsistent putting. He knew that professional golfers have a more consistent preputt routine than skilled amateur golfers, and that skilled amateur golfers have a more consistent preputt routine than less skilled amateur golfers. Steve realized that his own preputt routine was not as consistent as it might be. He did not always check the slope of the putting green from both sides of the ball before putting. If it was an especially important putt, he tended to stand over the ball for a longer period of time than usual before stroking it toward the hole. Other inconsistencies also occurred from one instance of putting to the next during a competitive round. He concluded that his inconsistent preputt routine could be contributing to inconsistent putting.

The first step to establishing a consistent sequence of responses during his preputt routine was to list the specific steps that he wanted to follow on each occasion. They were as follows:

1. When approaching the ball, forget about the score and think only about the putt at hand.
2. Go behind the hole, look back at the ball, and check the slope of the green in order to estimate the speed and path of the putt.
3. Move behind the ball, look toward the hole, and recheck the slope.
4. While standing behind the ball, pick a spot to aim at, take two practice strokes, and visualize the ball rolling in the hole.
5. Move beside the ball, set the putter down behind the ball, and adjust it so that it is aiming at the desired spot.
6. Adjust your feet so that they are parallel to the putting line, grip the putter in the usual way, and say, "Stroke it smooth."
7. Look at the hole, look at the ball, look at the spot, look at the ball, and stroke the putt.

---

[1] This example is based on a consultation with G. Martin (1999).

The training procedure involved 10 trials. On each trial, Steve performed all seven steps of the preputt routine while practicing a short putt on the practice green. The reason he practiced the routine on short putts rather than long ones was that he wanted each sequence to be followed by the reinforcer of making the putt. On each trial, a friend checked off the steps as they were performed. If he missed a step, his friend prompted him to perform it before continuing to the next step. After completing the 10 trials, Steve and his friend played a practice round of golf during which his friend prompted him to complete the preputt routine on every putt. During subsequent tournament rounds, Steve asked his caddy to remind him to follow his preputt routine. Three weeks later Steve won his first tour event. While a number of factors undoubtedly contributed to his win, Steve felt that one of them was his improved putting as the result of his more consistent preputt routine.

Behavior Chaining

A **behavior chain,** also called a **stimulus-response chain,** is a consistent sequence of stimuli and responses that occur closely to each other in time and in which the last response is typically followed by a reinforcer. In a behavior chain, each response produces a stimulus that serves as an S^D for the next response (and, as will be discussed later, a conditioned reinforcer for the previous response). What Steve acquired in learning to follow a consistent preputt routine was a behavior chain. The first stimulus (S^D_1) for the entire sequence was the sight of his ball on the putting green as he walked toward it. The response (R_1) to that stimulus was "I'm going to focus just on this putt." This statement was the cue (S^D_2) to go behind the hole, look back at the ball, and check the slope of the green in order to estimate the speed and path of the putt (R_2). The resulting visual stimuli (and perhaps certain internal stimuli we might call "an image of the putt and speed of the ball") was the cue (S^D_3) to walk behind the ball and look toward the hole to observe the slope of the green from that angle (R_3). In this way, each response produced the cue or stimulus for the next response until the entire chain was completed and Steve experienced the reinforcement of making the putt. The reason for calling this sequence a *stimulus-response chain* can be seen by writing it out as follows:

$$S^D_1 \rightarrow R_1 \rightarrow S^D_2 \rightarrow R_2 \rightarrow S^D_3 \rightarrow R_3 \ldots S^D_7 \rightarrow R_7 \rightarrow S^+$$

The stimulus–response connections are the "links" that hold the chain together. As the saying goes, "A chain is only as strong as its weakest link." Similarly, if any response is so weak that it fails to be evoked by the S^D preceding it, the rest of the chain will not occur. The chain will be broken at the point of its weakest link. The only way to repair the chain is to strengthen the weak stimulus–response connection by means of an effective training procedure.

The symbol S^+ at the far right of the diagram symbolizes the positive reinforcer that follows the last response in the chain. It designates the "oil" that one must apply regularly to keep the chain rust free and strong. The reinforcer at the end of a chain maintains the stimuli in the chain as effective S^Ds for the responses that follow them (and as will be described later, as effective conditioned reinforcers for the responses that precede them).

Not All Behavior Sequences Are Behavior Chains

Many behavior sequences that you perform in everyday life are behavior chains. Playing a particular song on a musical instrument, brushing your teeth, lacing and tying your shoes, and making a sandwich are all behavior chains. However, not all behavior sequences are behavior chains. Studying for an exam, writing an exam, and attending the next class to get a grade represent a sequence of behavior that a college student performs. But this general sequence consists of a variety of activities (reading, memorizing, writing, etc.) with many breaks in the action (studying, then sleeping, then going to class, etc.). It is not made up of a consistent series of stimuli and responses that occur closely in time and for which each stimulus (except the last) is an S^D for the next response.

Questions for Learning

1. Briefly describe the chaining procedure used to teach Steve to perform a consistent preputt routine.
2. Describe or define *behavior chain,* and give an example other than those in this chapter.

3. Why do you suppose a behavior chain is called a *chain*?
4. Distinguish between a behavior sequence that is a chain and one that is not a chain.
5. Give an example of a behavior sequence (that is not in this chapter) that is not a chain, and explain why it is not one.

Methods for Teaching a Behavior Chain

The three major methods of teaching a behavior chain are the total-task presentation method, the backward-chaining method, and the forward-chaining method. With the **total-task presentation** method, an individual attempts all of the steps from the beginning to the end of the chain on each trial and continues with total task trials until that person learns the chain (see Figure 11.1). Prompting is provided at each step as needed, and a reinforcer follows the correct completion of the last step. Using this strategy, Steve learned to follow a consistent preputt routine. As another example, Horner and Keilitz (1975) used total-task presentation to teach adolescents with developmental disabilities to brush their teeth.

With the **backward-chaining** method, the last step is taught first, then the next-to-last step is taught and linked to the last step, then the third-from-last step is taught and linked to the last two steps, and so on, progressing backward toward the beginning of the chain (see Figure 11.1). Backward chaining gradually constructs the chain in a reverse order from that in which the chain is performed. Backward chaining has been used in numerous programs, including teaching various dressing, grooming, work, and verbal behaviors to individuals with developmental disabilities (e.g., Martin, England, & England, 1971). To teach Craig, a boy with a developmental disability, to put on a pair of slacks, for example, the instructor broke down the task into the seven steps illustrated in Figure 11.2. The instructor then conducted a baseline assessment to determine the type of prompt needed for Craig to perform each step correctly. Training began with the last step (Step 7). Craig's instructor helped him put on the slacks except for the response at Step 7. Several training trials were then conducted to teach Craig the response at Step 7. As Figure 11.2 documents, over several trials, prompts were faded until Craig could do up the zipper by himself. When Craig had learned this, his instructor then started him from Step 6 and taught him to finish from there. When Craig could perform the last two steps without errors, training trials began at Step 5. With the slacks down around his ankles, he was taught to pull them all the

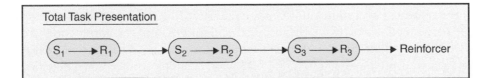

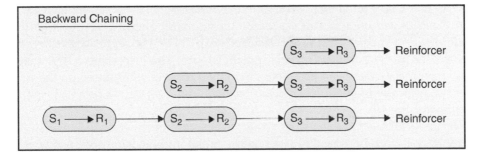

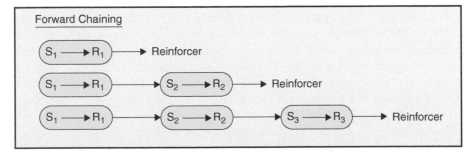

FIGURE 11.1
A diagram of the three major chaining methods

TASK	Putting on slacks	Scoring System
CLIENT	Craig	3 = without prompts
REINFORCERS	praise & edible	2 = verbal prompt
		1 = gestural/imitative prompts
		0 = physical guidance

S^{D}s	Responses	Baseline	Training Trials									
1. "Put on your slacks."	Taking slacks from dresser drawer	2										
2. Slacks in hands	Hold slacks upright with front facing away from client	1										
3. Slacks held upright	Put one leg in slacks	1										
4. One leg in slacks	Put other leg in slacks	1										
5. Both legs in slacks	Pull slacks all the way up	2									2	3
6. Slacks all the way up	Do up the snap	0					0	1	2	3	3	3
7. Snap done up	Do up the zipper	0	0	1	2	3	3	3	3	3	3	3

FIGURE 11.2

A simple task analysis and data sheet for teaching a person with a developmental disability to put on slacks

way up (Step 5), which was the S^D for him to perform Step 6. Performing Step 6 provided the S^D to perform Step 7. On each trial, Craig completed all of the steps learned previously. Training proceeded in this way, one step added at a time, until Craig could perform all seven steps. Throughout training, individual steps performed correctly were reinforced with praise, and the completion of Step 7 on each trial was followed by an edible treat as an unconditioned or primary reinforcer (see Chapter 5).

Students of behavior modification often find backward chaining strange when they first read about it, apparently because the name suggests that an individual learns to perform the chain backward. Naturally, this is not true. There is a very good theoretical rationale for using backward chaining. Consider the example of teaching Craig to put on a pair of slacks. By starting with Step 7, the response of "doing up the zipper" was reinforced in the presence of the fastened snap above the zipper. Therefore, the sight of the snap fastened became an S^D for Step 7, doing up the zipper. Also, the sight of the snap fastened was paired with the reinforcers (praise and an edible) that Craig received after doing up the zipper. Therefore, on the basis of the principle of conditioned reinforcement, the sight of the fastened snap also became a conditioned reinforcer for whatever preceded it. After several trials at Step 7, Craig's instructor went on to Step 6. The behavior of fastening the snap produced the sight-of-the-fastened-snap stimulus. The sight of the fastened snap had become a conditioned reinforcer, and it immediately followed performing Step 6. Thus, when one uses backward chaining, the reinforcement of the last step in the presence of the appropriate stimulus, over trials, establishes that stimulus as a discriminative stimulus for the last step and as a conditioned reinforcer for the next-to-last step. When the step before the last is added, the S^D in that step also becomes a conditioned reinforcer, and so on. Thus, the power of the positive reinforcer that is presented at the end of the chain is transferred up the line to each S^D as it is added to the chain. In this way, backward chaining has a theoretical advantage of always having a built-in conditioned reinforcer to strengthen each new response that is added to the sequence. In chains taught by total-task presentation and forward chaining (described next), each stimulus (after the first) also eventually functions as an S^D for the next response **NOTE 1** and as a conditioned reinforcer for the previous response. In backward chaining, as described, however, these two functions are developed very systematically.

The **forward-chaining** method teaches the initial step of the sequence first, then teaches and links together the first and second steps, then the first three steps, and so on until the entire chain is acquired (see Figure 11.1). For example, Mahoney, VanWagenen, and Meyerson (1971) used forward chaining to toilet-train typically developing children and other children who were developmentally disabled. The components of the chain included walking to the toilet, lowering the pants, sitting on or standing facing the toilet (as appropriate), urinating, and pulling up the pants. Training began with the first step, and after a step was mastered, the next step was introduced. Each step was reinforced until the next step was introduced.

At least partly because backward chaining resembles a reversal of the natural order of things, forward chaining and total-task presentation are used more often in everyday situations by individuals not trained in behavior modification. Among the many examples that can be cited to illustrate forward chaining, consider the way in which a child might be taught to pronounce a word such as *milk*. She or he might be first taught to say "mm," then "mi," then "mil," and finally "milk." A variation of a similar forward chaining procedure was used for teaching children with autism to imitate words (Tarbox, Madrid, Aguilar, Jacobo, & Schiff, 2009).

The three major chaining methods are outlined in Table 11.1. Which is most effective? A number of studies (e.g., Ash & Holding, 1990; Hur & Osborne, 1993; Slocom & Tiger, 2011; Smith, 1999; Spooner & Spooner, 1984; Walls, Zane, & Ellis, 1981; Weiss, 1978) have compared forward and backward chaining with different categories of individuals and behaviors. Overall, no clear difference in effectiveness between these two procedures has been found. In one tightly controlled study, Slocom and Tiger (2011) found both forward and backward chaining to be about equally effective for teaching children with learning and developmental disabilities to perform specific arbitrary motor sequences (e.g., touch head, clap, touch nose) of different lengths. Moreover, neither procedure was consistently preferred by the children.

There has been considerably less research comparing total task presentation with other chaining methods. However, several studies have demonstrated that total-task presentation is at least as good as, or better than, either backward or forward chaining for teaching various tasks to persons with developmental disabilities (Martin, Koop, Turner, & Hanel, 1981; Spooner, 1984; Yu, Martin, Suthons, Koop, & Pallotta-Cornick, 1980). Moreover, Bellamy, Horner, and Inman (1979) suggested that total-task presentation has several practical advantages over the other chaining formats for teaching persons with developmental disabilities. Total-task presentation requires the instructor to spend less time in partial assembly or disassembly to prepare the task for training; it focuses on teaching response topography and response sequence simultaneously and, therefore, intuitively should produce results more quickly; and it also appears to maximize the learner's independence early in training, especially if some steps are already familiar to him or her.

TABLE 11.1   An Outline of the Three Major Chaining Methods

For All Methods

- Do a task analysis.

Total-Task Presentation

- The learner attempts every step on each trial, so that all unmastered steps are taught concurrently.
- The instructor provides prompts and praise for all unmastered steps.
- A reinforcer is presented following the last step.
- Training continues in this way until all steps are mastered.

Forward Chaining

- Starting with the first one, the step must be mastered before proceeding to the next one.
- The instructor provides prompts and a reinforcer for the step that is being taught.
- On each trial, all previously mastered steps are required.
- In this way, one step is learned at a time, progressing forward to the last step.

Backward Chaining

- Starting with the last step, it must be mastered before proceeding to the next-to-last step.
- The instructor provides prompts for the step that is being taught.
- On each trial, all previously mastered steps are required, and the last step is followed by a reinforcer.
- In this way, one step is learned at a time, progressing backward to the first step.

Which is the method of choice for individuals who do not have developmental disabilities? For tasks with a small number of steps that can be completed in a short period of time (within a few minutes or less), total task presentation is probably the method of choice. There are many examples of such tasks in sports, such as the preputt routine for Steve, or the overhand float-serve in volleyball (e.g., Velentzas, Heinen, & Schack, 2011). For more complex tasks, however, either backward or forward chaining is likely to be more effective. For example, in teaching a complex sequence of dive bombing to pilots, Bailey, Hughes, and Jones (1980) found backward chaining to be more effective than total-task presentation. In an experiment to teach introductory psychology students to perform a musical task on a keyboard for which they were scored for both melodic and timing errors, backward chaining and forward chaining were both more effective than total-task presentation, and forward chaining was more effective than backward chaining on most measures (Ash & Holding, 1990). Also, using backward chaining to teach certain tasks may be more practical. When giving driving instructions, for example, it is highly advisable to teach the use of the brake before teaching the use of the accelerator.

Questions for Learning

6. Briefly describe the total-task presentation chaining method.
7. Briefly describe the backward-chaining method.
8. Briefly describe the forward-chaining method.
9. Describe how each of the three major chaining methods could be used to teach bed making.
10. In a chain, a given stimulus is both an S^D and a conditioned reinforcer. How can this be? Explain with an example.
11. Which of the major chaining methods do the authors recommend for teaching persons with developmental disabilities, and for what four reasons?

Chaining Compared with Fading and Shaping

Behavior chaining, fading, and shaping are sometimes called *gradual change* procedures because each involves progressing gradually through a series of steps to produce a new behavior, new stimulus control over a behavior, or a new sequence of stimulus–response steps. Clearly understanding the distinctions among the three gradual change procedures is important. Table 11.2 summarizes some of the similarities and differences of the three procedures as they are typically applied.

TABLE 11.2	**Similarities and Differences among Shaping, Fading, and Chaining**		
	Shaping	**Fading**	**Chaining**
Target behavior	New behavior along some physical dimension such as topography, amount, or intensity	New stimulus control of a particular behavior	New consistent sequence of stimuli and responses
General training environment	Often involves an unstructured environment in which the learner has the opportunity to emit a variety of behaviors	Typically involves a structured environment because the stimuli must be controlled precisely	Typically involves a structured environment because the stimuli and responses must be sequenced precisely
Other procedural considerations	Involves successive applications of reinforcement and extinction	Involves successive applications of reinforcement; if extinction has to be used, fading has not proceeded optimally	Frequently involves verbal and physical prompts and/or physical guidance combined with fading and/or shaping at some of the steps

Factors Influencing the Effectiveness of Behavior Chaining

1. The Task Analysis

For maximum effectiveness of behavior chaining, the behavior sequence must be broken down into manageable components, and the proper order of the components must be maintained. The process of breaking down a task into smaller steps or component responses to facilitate training is called a **task analysis.** Some examples of complex skills that have had task analyses performed on them are apartment-upkeep skills (Williams & Cuvo, 1986), menstrual care skills (Richman, Reiss, Bauman, & Bailey, 1984), tennis skills (Buzas & Ayllon, 1981), play execution of the offensive backfield on a youth football team (Komaki & Barnett, 1977), leisure skills (Schleien, Wehman, & Kiernan, 1981), and pedestrian skills for walking safely through traffic (Page, Iwata, & Neef, 1976).

As with the selection of shaping steps (discussed in Chapter 7), the selection of chaining steps or components is somewhat subjective. The components should be simple enough to be learned without great difficulty. If you want a child to learn proper toothbrushing, it would be a mistake to consider the task to be learned as putting toothpaste on the brush, brushing, and rinsing. For the child to master the chain, each of these components should be subdivided into smaller components. The components should also be selected so that there is a clear-cut stimulus signaling the completion of each component. These stimuli will then become conditioned reinforcers for the responses preceding them and S^Ds for the subsequent responses in the chain. For example, in teaching proper hand washing, you might select putting water in the sink as one of the components. It would be important to specify a particular level of water in the sink and perhaps even make a mark (at least temporarily) at that level to provide a very clear stimulus that terminates the end of this particular component (which you might define as holding the water taps on until the water reaches the desired level).

After completing your task analysis, review each of the controlling stimuli or S^Ds for each response in the sequence. Ideally, each S^D should be clearly distinct from the other S^Ds. Having similar stimuli control different responses increases the chance for the learner's error and confusion. If, in your task analysis, two of the controlling stimuli are quite similar and there appears to be nothing you can do about it, then consider artificially coding one of the stimuli in some way to make acquisition of the chain easier.

2. Independent Use of Prompts by Learners

As with Steve, many individuals can use prompts independently to guide the mastery of a chain of behaviors. For learners able to read, a *written task analysis* might effectively prompt them to appropriately complete behavior chains (see, e.g., Cuvo, Davis, O'Reilly, Mooney, & Crowley, 1992). If the learners are unable to read, a series of *picture prompts* might guide them. For example, Thierman and Martin (1989) prepared a picture-prompt album to guide adults with severe intellectual disabilities to complete behavior chains that improved the quality of their household cleaning. The learners were taught to look at the picture of an appropriate step, perform that step, and then transfer a self-monitoring adhesive dot to indicate that the step had been completed. The strategy proved to be effective. Another strategy that involves independent use of prompts to guide completion of behavior chains involves reciting *self-instructions.* Individuals with developmental disabilities have been taught to recite self-instructions to prompt correct completion of vocational tasks (Salend, Ellis, & Reynolds, 1989), completion of math problems correctly (Albion & Salzburg, 1982), and sorting letters into boxes correctly (Whitman, Spence, & Maxwell, 1987).

3. A Preliminary Modeling Trial

In some cases, such as with persons with developmental disabilities or young children, it may be desirable to model the entire sequence while verbally describing the performance of each step (see, e.g., Griffen, Wolery, & Schuster, 1992). (Guidelines for modeling are described in Chapter 18.) If only one sample of the training task is available, the task must be disassembled after the modeling trial and the components rearranged for the learner to perform the task. Otherwise, the learner can be taught using alternative samples of the task.

4. Training the Behavior Chain

Training should start with a request to begin work and to complete the step(s) of the task. The step or steps to begin depend on whether you use total-task presentation, backward chaining, or forward chaining. If at any step the learner stops responding or appears distracted, you should first provide a pacing prompt such as "What's next?" or "Carry on." If the learner performs a response incorrectly or fails to begin responding at any step within a reasonable period of time, you should proceed with error correction. Provide the necessary instruction or physical guidance to help the learner perform that step correctly. After an error is corrected, go on to the next step.

5. Ample Social and Other Reinforcers

Sometimes a natural reinforcer that follows the completion of a chain will be sufficient to maintain it. This was the case with Steve. When teaching behavior chains to persons with developmental disabilities or young children, however, it is often desirable to immediately praise the correct completion of each step during early training trials (see, e.g., Koop, Martin, Yu, & Suthons, 1980). In addition, providing a primary or unconditioned reinforcer (such as an edible) contingent upon successful completion of the last step in the chain is often desirable. As the learner becomes more skillful in performing the steps, praise and other reinforcers can be gradually eliminated. Additional strategies for maintaining behavior chains that have been mastered are described in Chapter 16.

6. Assistance at Individual Steps

Depending on the details of the task analysis, providing some additional instruction or physical assistance in correcting errors may be necessary. Across successive trials, this extra assistance should be faded as quickly as possible. Don't provide assistance to the point of creating a dependency in the learner. That is, be careful not to reinforce errors or waiting for your help at particular steps.

Questions for Learning

12. Distinguish among the types of target behavior typically established by shaping, fading, and chaining.
13. Suppose that you want to teach someone to change a tire on a car. Would you use shaping or chaining? Justify your choice.
14. What is meant by the term *task analysis*? Describe a plausible task analysis appropriate for teaching a 3-year-old child the chain of tying a knot in a shoelace.
15. Briefly describe three strategies to help individuals use prompts independently to guide the mastery of a chain of behaviors.

Pitfalls of Behavior Chaining

Unaware-Misapplication Pitfall

In a manner similar to the way in which superstitious behavior can develop through adventitious reinforcement, as discussed in Chapter 4, chains with one or more undesirable component can develop without anyone being aware of or noticing this happening. A behavior chain that has some components that are functional in producing the reinforcer and at least one component (called a *superstitious component*) that is not functional is called an **adventitious chain**.

A common kind of undesirable adventitious chaining occurs when an inappropriate and nonfunctional response precedes one or more appropriate responses that are reinforced; both the inappropriate and appropriate responses are thereby strengthened. An example of this type of chaining is the distracting habit of frequently saying "like" or "uh" while talking. A similar, although somewhat more serious, example is making bizarre facial expressions prior to each utterance.

Other examples of the Unaware-Misapplication Pitfall involve self-control problems that plague many people. The undesirable behavior chains that characterize such problems are not adventitious chains because all of the components are functional in producing reinforcement. However, they are inadvertent or unintentional in that one or more of the components of the chain are undesirable. Consider the problem of overeating. Although undoubtedly a variety of possible reasons for overeating exists, one of the more frequent causes may be the unintentional development of undesirable behavior chains. For example, it has been observed that some overweight people eat very rapidly (e.g., Spiegel, Wadden, & Foster, 1991). An examination of the behavior sequence involved suggests the following chain: loading food onto the utensil, placing food in the mouth, reloading the utensil while chewing the food, simultaneously swallowing the food while raising the next load of food to the mouth, and so forth. This behavior chain can be broken successfully by extending the chain and introducing delays (Stuart, 1967). A more desirable chain might be the following: loading food onto the utensil, placing food in the mouth, putting down the utensil, chewing the food, swallowing, waiting 3 seconds, reloading the utensil, and so on. In other words, in the undesirable chain, the person gets ready to consume the next mouthful before even finishing the present one. A more desirable chain separates these components and introduces brief delays. Later these delays might be faded out without the individual returning to the previous rapid rate of eating.

Another undesirable behavior chain that is manifested by some overweight people consists of watching TV until a commercial comes on, going to the kitchen during the commercial, getting a snack, and returning to the TV program (which, along with the taste of the food, reinforces getting the snack). A variety of procedures can solve such self-control problems, and these are discussed more fully in Chapter 26. The point to remember here is that undesirable behaviors are frequently components of unintentionally developed behavior chains.

Partial-Knowledge-Misapplication Pitfall

Some seemingly sound behavior modification procedures can promote undesirable chaining if the behavior modifier is not careful. A project by Olenick and Pear (1980) to teach names of pictures to children with developmental disabilities illustrated this. The children were given a question trial in which they were shown a picture to be named and were asked, "What's this?" Correct responses were reinforced. If the children made an error, they were then given an imitation trial in which the instructor presented the question and then immediately modeled the answer (e.g., "What's this? Cat."). Olenick and Pear observed that some children made a large number of errors even when it appeared that they could name the pictures appropriately. The researchers suggested that for these youngsters, a chain had developed in which errors on question trials were reinforced by imitation trials because an easier response (imitation) was reinforced on these trials. Olenick and Pear solved this problem by lowering the reinforcement rate for correct responses on imitation trials while maintaining a high reinforcement rate for correct responses on question trials.

Guidelines for the Effective Use of Behavior Chaining

Observe the following rules when teaching behavior chains.

1. *Do a Task Analysis.* Identify the units of the chain that are simple enough for the learner to learn without great difficulty.
2. *Consider Strategies (e.g., Pictures) for Independent Use of Prompts by Learners.*
3. *If Necessary, Do a Preliminary Modeling Trial.*
4. *Decide on the chaining method (total-task presentation, backward chaining, or forward chaining) and Teach the Units in the Proper Sequence.*
5. *To Expedite Learning, Use a Fading Procedure to Decrease Extra Help That the Learner May Need to Perform Some of the Steps.*
6. *When Using Backward or Forward Chaining, Make Sure That on Each Trial, the Individual Performs the Entire Set of Components Learned up to That Point.*
7. *Early in Training, Use Ample Reinforcement for Correct Performance of Individual Steps.* Gradually decrease this reinforcement as the learner becomes more skillful.
8. *Make Sure That the Reinforcement Provided at the End of the Chain Conforms to the Guidelines for the Effective Application of Positive Reinforcement Given in Chapter 4.* The more effective this terminal reinforcement, the more stable is the chain of responses. This does not mean, however, that once a chain is developed, it must be reinforced each time it occurs in order to be maintained. After a chain has been taught, it can be viewed as a single response, which could, if desired, be put on any intermittent reinforcement schedule.

Questions for Learning

16. What is an adventitious chain?
17. Give an example of an adventitious chain that is not from this chapter. Clearly identify the superstitious component.
18. Give an example of an Unaware-Misapplication Pitfall of chaining other than an adventitious chain. Explain how this pitfall could be avoided.

Application Exercises

A. Exercises Involving Others

1. Describe how you might use behavior chaining to teach a child to lace his or her shoes.
2. Describe how you might use behavior chaining to teach a child to tie a knot.
3. Describe how you might use behavior chaining to teach a child to tie a bow.
4. Try out your chaining programs in Application Exercises 1, 2, and 3, and see how they work.

B. Self-Modification Exercise

Identify a behavior deficit of yours that might be amenable to a chaining procedure. Describe in detail how you might use the guidelines for the effective use of chaining to overcome this deficit.

Note for Further Learning

1. The theory that the stimuli in a chain function as conditioned reinforcers for the preceding responses and as S^Ds for the subsequent response has appealed to many behavior analysts because of its elegant simplicity. However, basic research with animals over the past 50 plus years has shown this theory to be an oversimplification (see, e.g., Fantino, 2008). The earlier stimuli in a long behavior chain take on another function besides that of being conditioned reinforcers and S^Ds. Indeed, if the conditioned reinforcers occur a long enough time before the primary or unconditioned reinforcer (see Chapter 5) at the end of the chain, they actually become S^Δs. To be more precise, as the temporal distance (i.e., the distance in time) of the stimuli in a behavior chain from the primary reinforcer increases, the more their quality of being S^Ds decreases and the more they begin to take on the property of S^Δs. This is so because as their distance in time from primary reinforcement increases, the more they become associated with the absence of primary reinforcement. In other words, in considering the strength of an S^D on the basis of the conditioned reinforcer that follows it, one also has to consider its weakness as an S^D—or, more technically, its inhibitory potential—as a function of its distance in time from primary reinforcement. This inhibitory function may offset whatever advantage backward chaining may have in providing conditioned reinforcement, which may be why applied studies have typically found no superiority of backward chaining over forward chaining (e.g., Ash & Holding, 1990; Batra & Batra, 2005/2006; Hur & Osborne, 1993; Walls et al., 1981).

Question for Further Learning

1. Explain how the theory that the stimuli in a behavior chain are conditioned reinforcers for the preceding responses and S^Ds for the subsequent responses is an oversimplification.

CHAPTER 12

Differential Reinforcement Procedures to Decrease Behavior

LEARNING OBJECTIVES

After studying this chapter, you will be able to:

- Define *differential reinforcement*.
- Compare and contrast differential reinforcement of: (a) low rates; (b) zero responding; (c) incompatible behavior; and (d) alternative behavior.

- Explain how differential reinforcement can work to the disadvantage of those who are ignorant of it.

Tommy, a little less talking out, please!

Decreasing Tommy's Talking Out[1]

Tommy, an 11-year-old boy with a developmental disability, was judged by his teacher to be the most disruptive student in his classroom. He frequently engaged in inappropriate talking and other vocalizations during class. The behavior was troublesome not so much because of its nature but because of the high rate at which it occurred. A program was therefore undertaken to reduce his vocalizations to a less bothersome level.

The undesirable behavior, "talking out," was given the following precise behavioral definition: "talking to the teacher or classmates without the teacher's permission; talking, singing, or humming to himself; and making statements not related to the ongoing class discussion." A teacher's assistant located in the back of the room recorded Tommy's talk-outs during one 50-minute session per day. A second trained observer also recorded Tommy's talk-outs to ensure the accuracy of the observations.

In phase 1 of the program, the behavior was recorded for 10 sessions. It was found that Tommy averaged about one talk-out every 9 minutes (or about 0.11 per minute). In phase 2, Tommy was told the definition of a talk-out and instructed that he would be allowed 5 minutes of free play time at or near the end of the day if at the end of the 50-minute session he had made three or fewer talk-outs (i.e., fewer than about one every 17 minutes). At the end of each session, the teacher told Tommy whether he had met the requirement, but during the session, he was never told the number of talk-outs recorded.

This differential reinforcement procedure was quite effective. During phase 2, which lasted 15 sessions, Tommy averaged about one talk-out every 54 minutes (0.02 per minute). Moreover, he never exceeded the upper limit of three per session.

---

[1] This case is based on Deitz and Repp (1973).

In the third and final phase, the differential reinforcement schedule was removed, and Tommy was told that he would no longer receive free time for low rates of talk-outs. Over the eight sessions of this phase for which data were taken, his rate of talking out increased to an average of one every 33 minutes (0.03 per minute). Although this rate was higher than the rate during the treatment procedure (phase 2), it was still a great deal lower than the rate before the procedure was introduced (phase 1). Thus, the treatment had a beneficial effect even after it was terminated.

Decreasing Operant Behavior

Differential reinforcement schedules or procedures are schedules that reinforce specific rates of responding. They may be used to reinforce high or low response rates. This chapter describes differential reinforcement procedures for decreasing response rates.

Procedures presented in earlier chapters that can be used to *increase and maintain operant behavior* include positive reinforcement, shaping, fading, chaining, stimulus discrimination training, generalization, and the schedules of reinforcement described in Chapter 8. Procedures that can be used to *decrease operant behavior* include operant extinction (Chapter 6), punishment (Chapter 13), the antecedent control procedures described in Part III (Chapters 17, 18, and 19), and the differential reinforcement procedures described in this chapter.

Differential Reinforcement of Low Rates

Differential reinforcement of low (DRL) rates is a schedule of reinforcement in which a reinforcer is presented *only* if a particular response occurs at a low rate. One type of DRL, called **limited-responding DRL**, specifies a maximum allowable number of responses during a certain time interval in order for a reinforcer to occur. This was the type of schedule used with Tommy. In that case, an interval (50 minutes) **NOTE 1** was specified and a reinforcer occurred at the end of the interval if it contained three or fewer talk-outs.

The maximum allowable number of responses in limited-responding DRL for reinforcement to occur can be specified for an entire session or for separate intervals throughout a session. An example of this would be to divide Tommy's 50-minute session into three intervals, each approximately 17 minutes long, and to give Tommy reinforcement at the end of each interval in which no more than one talk-out occurred.

Limited-responding DRL is useful when two conditions hold: (a) some of the behavior is tolerable but (b) less of it is better. For example, Austin and Bevan (2011) used a limited-responding DRL (which they called a "full-session DRL") with 3 primary school children to decrease to acceptable levels their rates of requesting attention from their teacher. In Tommy's case, the teacher believed that three talk-outs per session would not be too disruptive and she did not wish to impose too stringent a requirement on Tommy. Therefore, Tommy would hear that he had earned his 5 minutes of free time by making three or less talk-outs during any given session.

A second type of DRL, called **spaced-responding DRL**, requires that a specified behavior not occur during a specified interval, and after the interval has passed, an instance of that behavior must then occur in order for a reinforcer to occur. In other words, instances of a specific behavior must be spaced out over time. Spaced-responding DRL is useful when the behavior to be reduced is actually desirable provided that it does not occur at too high a rate. For example, a student who always calls out the correct answer deprives classmates of the chance to respond to the teacher's questions. Naturally, we would not wish to eliminate this child's correct answering. We would hope, however, to reduce the calling out behavior. We might do this by placing the behavior on the following type of DRL schedule: Any target response that occurs after 15 minutes of the previous target response is immediately reinforced; any target response that occurs within 15 minutes of the previous target response is not reinforced. Note that a target response before the interval has passed causes the timing of the interval to start over again. This procedure is called a *spaced-responding DRL 1-response/15-minute schedule*. This type of schedule requires that responses be emitted for reinforcement to occur. On the limited-responding schedule used with Tommy, the individual need not respond at all to obtain reinforcement.

Another example of the use of spaced-responding DRL is the reinforcement of slow speech in a student who speaks too rapidly. The student would be asked questions such as "How are you?" or "Where do you live?" for which standard responses are reinforced—but only if they encompass a certain minimum time period whose length is determined by what the teacher regards as a normally acceptable rate of speech. Thus, the sequence of respond–wait–respond is reinforced (provided that the wait is long enough). As another example, Lennox, Miltenberger, and Donnelly (1987) used a spaced-responding DRL to decrease the eating rate of three individuals with profound developmental disabilities who ate their meals at such a rapid rate that it was considered unhealthy.

Questions for Learning

1. What is the difference in the use of the schedules of reinforcement in Chapter 8 compared to the differential reinforcement procedures in this chapter?
2. Describe briefly, point by point, how Tommy's talking out in class was reduced.
3. Explain, in general, what a DRL schedule is. Give an example of one that occurs in everyday life, and that is not in this chapter.
4. Define *limited-responding DRL,* and give an example.
5. Define *spaced-responding DRL,* and give an example.
6. How is a spaced-responding DRL procedurally similar to and different from an FI schedule?
7. What is a procedural difference between a spaced-responding DRL and an FD schedule?
8. Give in some detail an example, which is not in this chapter, of how DRL would be useful in treating a behavior problem. Indicate which type of DRL is to be used.

Differential Reinforcement of Zero Responding

Tommy's teacher was willing to put up with a certain amount of talking out. But consider the case of Gerry, a 9-year-old boy who scratched and rubbed his skin so severely that he produced open sores all over his body. Because of this problem, he had spent most of his time in hospitals and had never attended school. A DRL procedure would not have been appropriate because none of Gerry's skin scratching and rubbing behavior was tolerable. The procedure that was used is referred to as DRO (pronounced "dee-arr-oh"). **Differential reinforcement of zero responding (DRO)** is a schedule in which a reinforcer is presented *only* if a specified response does *not* occur during a specified period of time. Note that a target response before the interval has passed causes the timing of the interval to start over again. Working with the nurses in the hospital, researchers (Cowdery, Iwata, & Pace, 1990) began with a schedule referred to as *DRO 2 minutes.* If scratching occurred during the 2-minute interval, the interval started again. However, if scratching did not occur (i.e., was at a zero rate), Gerry was given tokens that he could later exchange for access to TV, snacks, video games, and various play materials. Over several days, the DRO interval was increased to 4 minutes, then to 8 minutes, then to 15 minutes, and eventually to 30 minutes. Although DRO was initially applied in brief sessions, it was subsequently extended to the entire day. Eventually, Gerry was discharged from the hospital, and his parents continued to use the procedure at home.

Technically, when Gerry was reinforced on DRO 30 minutes, he would have received a token for doing anything other than scratching. For this reason, a DRO is sometimes referred to as *differential reinforcement of other responding.* Practically, however, we're sure that Gerry would not have been allowed to do "anything" other than scratching. If, for example, he began breaking windows instead of scratching, the behavior modifiers would have intervened. DRO schedules have been used successfully to decrease a variety of target behaviors, such as inappropriate classroom behaviors (Repp, Deitz, & Deitz, 1976), thumbsucking (Knight & McKenzie, 1974), skin-picking (Toussaint & Tiger, 2012), motor and vocal tics (i.e., sudden, rapid, repetitive movements or vocalizations) such as occur in Tourette Syndrome (Capriotti, Brandt, Ricketts, Espil, & Woods, 2012; Himle, Woods, & Bunaciu, 2008), and self-injurious behavior (Mazaleski, Iwata, Vollmer, Zarcone, & Smith, 1993).

If an undesirable behavior occurs often and for long intervals, beginning with a DRO of short duration would be wise. For example, DRO 5 minutes might be used to eliminate tantrum behavior. This procedure could be carried out by resetting a stopwatch to zero each time a tantrum occurred and allowing it to "tick off" seconds when the tantrum stopped. Reinforcement would occur when a continuous 5 minutes had elapsed with no tantrumming. When the nonoccurrence of the behavior is under good control of this contingency, the schedule should be increased—for example, to DRO 10 minutes. The size of DRO should continue to be increased in this fashion until (a) the behavior is occurring very rarely or not at all and (b) a minimum amount of reinforcement is being given for its nonoccurrence.

Differential Reinforcement of Incompatible Behavior

When applying a DRO, some behavior is occurring when the reinforcer is received. Even though Gerry wasn't scratching, for example, he was doing something when the 30-minute interval passed and he was given a token. Whatever that behavior was, it would be reinforced when the reinforcer occurred. Rather than leave that behavior to chance or unknown factors, however, one might specify an incompatible response that is to be reinforced in eliminating a particular target response. By an incompatible response, we mean a response that cannot be emitted at the same time as the target response. For example, sitting and standing are incompatible behaviors. If we decide to decrease a target response by withholding reinforcers for it (if we know their source and block them) and by reinforcing an incompatible response, the schedule is referred to as **differential reinforcement of incompatible (DRI) behavior.** Suppose you are a grade school teacher who wants to eliminate the running-around-the-room behavior of one of your students with attention-deficit hyperactivity disorder. One possibility would be to put the behavior on a DRO schedule; however, it might be replaced by an incompatible behavior that is also undesirable—for example, lying on the floor. To avoid this, you might use DRI instead of DRO by specifying the incompatible behavior that is to be reinforced. You might, for example, reinforce sitting quietly. An even better choice would be completing schoolwork because this behavior is more useful to the child. As another example, Allen and Stokes (1987) applied DRI successfully to strengthen the behavior of being still and quiet while children were being treated in a dentist's chair. See Table 12.1 for other examples of potential incompatible behaviors for target behaviors.

TABLE 12.1	Examples of Incompatible Behaviors for Target Behaviors	
Target Behaviors to Decrease	**Incompatible Behaviors to Increase**
Driving after excessive alcohol consumption	Taking a taxi or asking a friend to drive
Biting fingernails	Keeping hands below shoulders
Time on Facebook	Time spent studying
Arriving late to classes	Arriving to classes on time

Questions for Learning

9. Explain what a DRO schedule is. Give an example of one that occurs in everyday life.
10. Give in some detail an example, which is not in this chapter, of how a DRO might be useful in treating a behavior problem.
11. What two words does the O in DRO stand for? Explain your answer.
12. Explain what a DRI schedule is. Give an example that is not in this chapter.
13. Why might a DRI schedule sometimes be chosen instead of a DRO schedule?

Differential Reinforcement of Alternative Behavior

An alternative to DRI is the **differential reinforcement of alternative (DRA) behavior,** which is a procedure that involves the extinction of a problem behavior combined with reinforcing a behavior that is topographically dissimilar to, but not necessarily incompatible with, the problem behavior (Vollmer & Iwata, 1992; Vollmer, Roane, Ringdahl, & Marcus, 1999). Consider the case of Kyle, a 4-year-old boy with severe developmental disabilities. During training sessions, Kyle was frequently aggressive and attempted to hit, scratch, or kick the therapist. To decrease this behavior, Vollmer et al. implemented a DRA. During training sessions, they reinforced compliance with performing various requested tasks and ignored aggressive behavior. Note that this was a DRA instead of a DRI in that Kyle was physically able to be compliant and still show aggression. The DRA nevertheless was effective in decreasing Kyle's aggression as well as increasing his compliance.

The use of DRA to eliminate an undesirable behavior is essentially what we recommended in Chapter 6 when we stated, "Extinction is most effective when combined with positive reinforcement for some desirable alternative behavior." In fact, DRA (and the other schedules discussed in this chapter) will likely be very effective if you use the reinforcer that was maintaining the undesirable behavior; techniques for identifying that reinforcer are described in Chapter 23. The choice of schedule for reinforcing the alternative behavior should be based on considerations discussed in Chapter 8.

Before closing this section, we should point out that there is some question as to whether DRI and DRA really are more effective than simple extinction in reducing or eliminating undesirable behavior (e.g., see Johnston, 2006). Until this issue is resolved, however, we stand by the preceding recommendations as the safer course to follow. In addition, although DRI and DRA have the disadvantage of being more complicated to administer than simple extinction, they have the advantage of developing new or strengthening old desirable behavior.

Pitfalls of Differential Reinforcement Procedures for Decreasing Behavior

Unaware-Misapplication Pitfall

A pitfall that is unique to DRL is the tendency to unknowingly reinforce a desirable behavior on a DRL, thereby causing that desirable behavior to occur at a low rate rather than reinforcing the behavior on a schedule that would maintain that behavior at a high rate. Understanding this pitfall may help us to appreciate how underachievers are frequently generated in our society.

Consider what happens when a child starts performing well in school. At first, the teacher is impressed and enthusiastically reinforces the behavior. However, as the rate of the behavior increases, the teacher gradually becomes less impressed. The teacher thinks that this is "obviously a bright child" and so expects a high rate of good behavior from her. Thus, the rate of reinforcement gradually decreases, perhaps to zero, as the rate of the behavior increases. Eventually, the child learns that more reinforcement occurs when performance is at a low rate because the teacher is more impressed with good behavior when it occurs infrequently than when it occurs frequently. Some children show only occasional flashes of brilliance in school instead of using their full potential. To avoid this type of inadvertent DRL schedule, teachers should define precisely the behavior they want to maintain at a high rate and reinforce it on an appropriate schedule.

Pitfalls of DRO and DRI are similar to the pitfalls already discussed for reinforcement (Chapter 4) and extinction (Chapter 6).

Guidelines for the Effective Use of Differential Reinforcement to Decrease Behavior

1. Decide which type of schedule should be used to reduce the target behavior. Use limited-responding DRL if some of the target behavior is tolerable, but the less the better. Use spaced-responding DRL if the behavior is desirable as long as it does not occur too rapidly or too frequently. Use DRO if the behavior should be eliminated and there is no danger that the DRO procedure might result in the reinforcement of an undesirable alternative behavior. Use DRI or DRA if the behavior should be eliminated and there is a danger that DRO would strengthen undesirable alternative behavior.
2. Decide what reinforcer to use. In general, the procedure will be most effective if the reinforcer is the one maintaining the behavior that you want to reduce and if the reinforcer can be withheld for that behavior (see Chapter 23).
3. Having chosen which procedure to use and a reinforcer, proceed as follows.
   a. If a limited-responding DRL schedule is to be used:
      (1) Record as baseline data the number of target responses per session for several sessions or more to obtain an initial value for the DRL schedule that will ensure frequent reinforcement.
      (2) Gradually decrease the responses allowed on the DRL in such a way that reinforcement occurs frequently enough throughout the procedure to ensure adequate progress by the student.
      (3) Gradually increase the size of the interval to decrease response rate below that obtained with (2).
   b. If a spaced-responding DRL schedule is to be used:
      (1) Record baseline data over several sessions or more, determine the average time between responses, and use this average as the starting value of the DRL schedule.

(2) Gradually increase the value of the DRL schedule in such a way that reinforcement occurs frequently enough throughout the procedure to ensure adequate progress by the student.

c. If DRO is to be used:

(1) Record baseline data over several sessions or more to obtain an initial interval for the DRO.

(2) Use DRO starting values that are approximately equal to the mean value between instances of the target behaviors during baseline.

(3) Gradually increase the size of the interval in such a way that reinforcement occurs frequently enough to ensure adequate progress by the student.

d. If DRI is to be used:

(1) Choose an appropriate behavior to strengthen that is incompatible with the behavior to be eliminated.

(2) Take baseline data of the appropriate behavior over several sessions or more to determine how frequently the appropriate behavior should be reinforced to raise it to a level at which it will replace the inappropriate behavior.

(3) Select a suitable schedule of reinforcement for increasing the appropriate behavior (see Chapter 8).

(4) While strengthening the incompatible behavior, apply the guidelines for the extinction of the problem behavior, as described in Chapter 6.

(5) Gradually increase the schedule requirement for the appropriate behavior in such a manner that it continues to replace the inappropriate behavior as the reinforcement frequency decreases.

e. If DRA is to be used, follow all of the guidelines listed for DRI except that the behavior to be strengthened does not have to be incompatible with the behavior to be eliminated.

4. If possible, inform the individual in a manner that he or she is able to understand of the procedure that you are using.

Questions for Learning

14. What is the difference between DRI and DRA?
15. What happens if the frequency of reinforcement on DRL, DRO, DRI, or DRA is too low or is decreased too rapidly?
16. Describe a pitfall of DRL for people who are ignorant of its effects. Give an example.

Application Exercises

A. Exercises Involving Others

1. For each of the two types of DRL schedules cited in this chapter, describe a possible application in training programs for children with developmental disabilities. Describe in detail how you would program and administer DRL in these situations.
2. Describe two possible applications of DRO in programs of early childhood education. Describe in detail how you would program and administer DRO in these situations.

B. Self-Modification Exercise

Give in some detail how you might use one of the differential reinforcement procedures in this chapter to reduce one of your own behaviors that you would like to occur less frequently.

Note for Further Learning

1. One might think that the 5 minutes of free play that occurred near the end of the day functioned as a reinforcer for decreasing Tommy's talk-outs much earlier in the day. Recall from Chapter 4, however, that the direct effects of reinforcement operate only over very short intervals. Therefore, Tommy's improvement cannot be attributed to the direct effect of the free play near the end of the school day as a reinforcer for the behavior of working quietly in the classroom much earlier. Rather, when Tommy was working quietly earlier in the day, the immediate consequence was probably praise and attention from the teacher, who might have said, "You're doing great, Tommy; keep it up and you'll earn another 5 minutes of free play. Just think of how much fun you're going to have." The praise may have been a reinforcer for Tommy's improved performance.

In addition, immediately after a few minutes of working quietly, Tommy might have told himself how much fun he was going to have during his extra play time. This rehearsal of a rule (as discussed earlier and further explained in Chapter 17) may have helped to bridge the time gap between the occurrence of desirable behavior during the 50-minute session and the extra playtime that occurred on a much-delayed basis. Tommy's saying the rule was eventually reinforced by the occurrence of the free play because the free play confirmed the rule, and confirmation of a rule is typically a reinforcer.

Questions for Further Learning

1. What immediate consequence might account for the effectiveness of the delayed reinforcement contingency applied to Tommy's talk-outs?
2. Describe how saying a rule to himself may have influenced Tommy's decreased talk-outs.

CHAPTER 13

Decreasing Behavior with Punishment

LEARNING OBJECTIVES

After studying this chapter, you will be able to:

- Define *punishment*.
- Define *punisher*.
- Distinguish between four different types of punishers.
- Describe factors influencing the effectiveness of punishment.

- Discuss potentially harmful side effects of the application of punishment.
- Evaluate the ethics of using punishment as opposed to other methods for decreasing unwanted behavior.
- Explain how punishment can work to the disadvantage of those who are ignorant of it.

Ben, don't be so aggressive.

Eliminating Ben's Aggressiveness[1]

Ben, a 7-year-old boy diagnosed as a child with developmental delay, was in a public school program for severely disturbed children. The staff at the school noticed an increase in his frequency of hitting other children and staff members. In fact, during baseline observations over a period of approximately 3 weeks, the frequency of Ben's hits averaged about 30 per day. Something had to be done. The staff decided to examine whether making required exercise contingent on Ben's hitting would decrease it.

A number of precautions were taken to ensure that the contingent exercise would not be detrimental to Ben's health and would be ethically acceptable. The procedures were explained thoroughly to the parents, and parental consent was obtained for Ben's participation in the program. The procedures were also reviewed and approved by the ethical review board of the school district in which the program was conducted.

The program was conducted at Ben's school throughout the school day. On the day that the contingent exercise was introduced, Ben's first hit was followed by the nearest staff member saying, "Ben, no hitting. Stand up and sit down 10 times." The staff member then held Ben's hand and lifted it over his head to prompt standing up and then pulled his upper body forward to prompt sitting down, at the same time saying "Stand up, sit down" each time. Although Ben showed some verbal resistance to the exercise on a few occasions, physical prompting was necessary only on the first few training trials. On subsequent days, only verbal reminders were necessary to prompt the exercise task. From an average of approximately 30 hits per day during baseline, Ben's hits dropped to 11 on the first day of the program, 10 on the second day, 1 on the third day, and either zero or 1 thereafter.

After 2 weeks of the procedure, the staff stopped applying the contingent exercise to see what would happen to Ben's hits. The frequency of hits remained low for 4 days but then began to increase over the next 4 days. The staff reinstituted the contingent exercise and observed an immediate drop in the frequency of hitting to near zero. Ben could run about and interact with other children and no longer showed the troubling aggressiveness characteristic of his past behavior.

---

[1] This example is based on an article by Luce, Delquadri, and Hall (1980).

The Principle of Punishment

A **punisher** is an immediate consequence of an operant behavior that causes that behavior to decrease in frequency. Punishers are sometimes referred to as *aversive stimuli,* or simply *aversives.* Once an event has been determined to function as a punisher for a particular behavior of an individual in a particular situation, that event can be used to decrease other operant behaviors of that individual in other situations. Associated with the concept of a punisher is the **principle of punishment**: If, in a given situation, someone does something that is immediately followed by a punisher, then that person is less likely to do the same thing again when she or he next encounters a similar situation. In Ben's case, contingent exercise was a punisher for his hitting.

Note that the technical meaning of the word *punishment* for behavior modifiers is quite specific and differs in three ways from the common meaning of the word for most people: (1) it occurs immediately after the problem behavior; (2) it is not a form of moral sanction, vengeance, or retribution; (3) it is not used to deter others from engaging in the target behavior. Consider, for example, a common use of the word *punishment* in our culture: Sending a person to prison is seen as punishment for committing a crime. But going to prison is not likely to be an *immediate* consequence of committing the crime. Also, many individuals believe that prison is or should be a form of *retribution* that is given because the individual *deserves* it in some moral sense. Moreover, sending a person to prison is often viewed as a *deterrent* to other potential wrongdoers. For behavior modifiers, however, the word *punishment* does not mean any of these things; it is simply a technical term referring to the application of an immediate consequence following an individual's specific behavior in a specific situation that has the effect of decreasing the likelihood of future instances of that individual engaging in that specific behavior in that specific situation. This is not to deny that some consequences of the legal system may function as punishment in this technical sense, such as when someone immediately receives a traffic ticket for speeding. However, legal consequences for crimes often do not function as punishment in the technical sense and are generally not thought of in that limited way by legislators, law enforcement officials, members of the legal professions, and the general public.

Like positive reinforcement, punishment affects our learning throughout life. The immediate consequences of touching a hot stove teach us not to do that again. Early in life, the pain from a few falls helped to teach us better balance. However, it is important to recognize that some controversy regarding the deliberate use of punishment exists within the field of behavior modification. We return to this issue later in this chapter after discussing the different types of punishment and the factors that influence the effects of punishment in suppressing behavior.

Questions for Learning

1. Briefly describe how Ben's aggressive behavior was eliminated.
2. How was stimulus control an important part of the punishment contingency for Ben?
3. What is a punisher? Give an example that you experienced, and identify both the response and the punisher.
4. State the principle of punishment.
5. How does the meaning of the word *punishment* for behavior modifiers differ from three meanings of that word for most people?

Types of Punishers

Many kinds of events, when delivered as immediate consequences for behavior, fit the definition of punisher as given here. Most of these events can be classified in the following categories (see Lerman & Toole, 2011; Van Houten, 1983): (a) pain-inducing punisher, (b) reprimand, (c) timeout, and (d) response cost. Although there is some overlap among these categories, they provide a convenient way in which to organize punishment procedures. We now consider each category in turn.

Physical Punisher

The most common type of *physical punishers* are stimuli that activate pain receptors which are technically called *nociceptors.* These are nerve endings located throughout the body that detect pressure, stretching, and temperature changes strong enough to potentially cause tissue damage, and that, when activated, are experienced as pain. Examples of stimuli that activate these receptors are spankings, slaps, pinches, hair tugging, extreme cold or heat, very loud sounds, and electric shocks. Such stimuli are called *unconditioned punishers*, which are stimuli that are punishing without prior learning. Of course, there are other stimuli that can cause discomfort without prior learning but that do not involve nociceptors (e.g., bad smells and tastes). These are also included as physical punishers.

Reprimand

A *reprimand* is a strong negative verbal stimulus immediately contingent on behavior. An example would be a parent saying, "No! That was bad!" immediately after a child emits an undesirable behavior. Reprimands also often include a fixed stare and, sometimes, a firm grasp. In Chapter 5 we noted that a stimulus that is a punisher as a result of having been paired with another punisher is called a *conditioned punisher*. It is likely that the verbal component of a reprimand is a conditioned punisher. It is possible that other components, such as a firm grasp, are unconditioned punishers. In some cases, the effectiveness of reprimands has been increased by pairing them with other punishers. For example, Dorsey, Iwata, Ong, and McSween (1980) paired reprimands with a water-mist spray to suppress self-injurious behavior in individuals with developmental disabilities. This caused the reprimands to become effective not only in the original setting but also in a setting where the mist had not been used.

Timeout

A *timeout* is a period of time immediately following a particular behavior during which an individual loses the opportunity to earn reinforcers. There are two types of timeout: exclusionary and nonexclusionary. An *exclusionary timeout* consists of removing an individual briefly from a reinforcing situation immediately following a behavior. Often a special room, called a *timeout room*, is used for this purpose. It is bare of anything that might serve as a reinforcer and may be padded to prevent self-injury. The period in the timeout room should not be very long; about 4 to 5 minutes is usually quite effective (Brantner & Doherty, 1983; Donaldson & Vollmer, 2011; Fabiano et al., 2004). Also, ethical considerations—such as whether the ends justify the means; see Chapter 30—and practical considerations (such as avoiding lengthy timeouts that take the individual away from a learning environment) must also be contemplated in selecting a particular timeout duration. A *nonexclusionary timeout* consists of introducing into the situation, immediately following a behavior, a stimulus associated with less reinforcement. Foxx and Shapiro (1978) reported an example of this. Children in a classroom wore a ribbon that was removed for a short time when a child was disruptive. When not wearing the ribbon, the child was not **NOTE 1** allowed to participate in classroom activities and was ignored by the teacher.

Response Cost

Response cost involves the removal of a specified amount of a reinforcer immediately following a behavior (Reynolds & Kelley, 1997). Response cost is sometimes used in behavior modification programs in which learners earn tokens as reinforcers (see Chapter 25; also see Kazdin, 1977). Working in a classroom setting, for example, Sullivan and O'Leary (1990) showed that loss of tokens (each of which could be exchanged for 1 minute of recess) for off-task behavior successfully decreased it. As another example, Capriotti et al. (2012) demonstrated that token loss was an effective response-cost punisher for decreasing tics in children with Tourette's Syndrome. For a third example, Johnson and Dixon (2009) showed that in a contrived gambling experiment with two pathological gamblers engaging in gambling behaviors that involved response chains (see Chapter 11) charging poker chips to engage in certain components of the chains decreased responding in those components. Note that response cost differs from a timeout in that when response cost is administered, the individual does not temporarily lose the opportunity to earn reinforcers. Response cost is also not to be confused with extinction (see Chapter 6). In an extinction procedure, a reinforcer is withheld following a previously reinforced response, whereas in response cost, a reinforcer is taken away following an undesirable response.

Examples of response cost in everyday life are library fines, traffic tickets, and charges for overdrawn bank accounts. However, these punishers are not typically applied immediately following the offending behavior. Just as we distinguished between the direct-acting effect and the indirect-acting effect of positive reinforcement in Chapter 4, we make a similar distinction with respect to punishment. The *direct-acting effect* of punishment is the decreased frequency of a response because of its immediate punishing consequences. The *indirect-acting effect* of punishment is the weakening of a response that is followed by a punisher even though the punisher is delayed. Suppose that a person speeds through an intersection, is caught by photo radar, and receives a ticket in the mail a week later. Although that procedure may reduce the person's future speeding, it involves much more than the principle of punishment. Delayed punishers may have an effect on behavior because of instructions about the behavior leading to the punisher, because of self-statements ("thoughts") that intervene between that behavior and the delayed punisher, or because of immediate conditioned punishers that intervene between the behavior and the delayed backup punisher. It is a mistake to offer punishment as an overly simplistic explanation of a decrease in behavior when the punisher does not follow the behavior immediately. Explanations of the indirect-acting effect of punishment are discussed further in Chapter 17.

Questions for Learning

6. Define *unconditioned punisher,* and give an example that illustrates the complete definition.
7. Describe or define four different types of punishers, and give an example of each.
8. Under which of the four categories of punishment would you put the type of punishment used with Ben? Justify your choice.
9. Define *conditioned punisher,* and give an example that is not in this chapter.
10. Distinguish between an exclusionary and nonexclusionary timeout.
11. What is an example of response-cost punishment that parents commonly apply to their children?
12. State the procedures for extinction, response cost, and exclusionary timeout.
13. Distinguish between the direct-acting and indirect-acting effects of punishment. Give an example of each.
14. What are three reasons that could explain the effectiveness of a delayed punisher in decreasing a behavior?

Factors Influencing the Effectiveness of Punishment

1. The Conditions for a Desirable Alternative Response

To decrease an undesirable response, it is generally considered to be maximally effective to increase some desirable alternative response that will compete with the undesirable behavior to be eliminated (see, e.g., Thompson, Iwata, Conners, & Roscoe, 1999; for an alternative view, see Johnston, 2006).

You should attempt to identify S^Ds that control the desirable behavior and present these to increase the likelihood that the desirable behavior will occur. To maintain the desirable behavior, you should also have effective positive reinforcers that can be presented on an effective schedule (see, e.g., Figure 13.1).

2. The Cause of the Undesirable Behavior

To maximize the opportunity for the desirable alternative behavior to occur, anyone attempting a punishment procedure should also minimize the causes of the undesirable behavior. This implies two things: First, the person should try to identify and eliminate the current S^Ds for the undesirable behavior. Second,

FIGURE 13.1
An example of the reinforcement of a desirable alternative behavior

the person should try to identify and eliminate existing reinforcers that are maintaining the undesirable behavior. Identifying the antecedents and consequences of a behavior is referred to as a *functional assessment* and is discussed in more detail in Chapter 23.

It is important to emphasize that punishment may often not be necessary to eliminate or reduce an undersirable behavior. Minimizing the causes of the undesirable behavior while maximizing the conditions for a desirable alternative behavior may cause the desirable behavior to compete so strongly with the undesirable behavior that it is greatly reduced or completely suppressed without the use of punishment.

3. The Punishing Stimulus

If punishment is to be used, it is important to be sure that the punisher is effective. In general, the more intense or strong the punishing stimulus, the more effective it will be in decreasing the undesirable behavior. However, the intensity of the punisher that is needed to be effective depends on the success in minimizing the causes of the undesirable behavior while maximizing the conditions for a desirable alternative behavior. Even a mild punisher, such as a reprimand, can be effective if the reinforcer for the undesirable behavior is withheld following instances of the behavior and if a desirable alternative behavior is reinforced with a strong reinforcer. For example, Thompson et al. (1999) evaluated the effects of reprimands and brief manual restraint as mild punishers contingent on the self-injurious behavior of four individuals who had been diagnosed with developmental disabilities. In all cases, the mild punishers produced greater response suppression when access to a reinforcer for desirable alternative behavior (manipulation of leisure materials) was available.

Contingent exercise turned out to be a suitable punisher for Ben. It was highly effective, could be presented immediately following the undesirable behavior, and could be presented in a manner so that it was in no way paired with positive reinforcement. The care and attention that the staff gave to choosing the actual exercise task obviously paid off. The staff chose the task because it could be prompted by a voice command from a staff member, it could be carried out in a variety of settings, and it appeared to tire Ben quickly without causing any unnecessary strain.

Rather than selecting just one punisher, it may be more effective to select several that vary over successive instances of the undesirable behavior. For example, Charlop, Burgio, Iwata, and Ivancic (1988) applied a reprimand, physical restriction, timeout, or loud noise as a punisher following aggression and self-stimulation by children with developmental disabilities. In some sessions, only one of the punishers was applied. In other sessions, the four punishers were varied while still administering just one at a time. The children showed less aggression and self-stimulation during sessions when the teacher varied the punishers.

4. The Antecedents (Including Verbal Rules) for Punishment

You will recall from Chapter 9 that an S^D is a stimulus in the presence of which a response will be reinforced. Similarly, an S^{Dp} is a stimulus in the presence of which a response will be punished.[2] Children quickly learn that asking parents for something when they are in a bad mood often leads to a reprimand. Parental behaviors characteristic of "being in a bad mood" constitute an S^{Dp}. Research on the effects of S^{Dp}s has shown that if in the presence of an S^{Dp} a punisher is consistently applied following a response, then that response is less likely to occur when the S^{Dp} is encountered (e.g., O'Donnell, Crosbie, Williams, & Saunders, 2000).

Beginning students of behavior analysis often confuse an S^{Dp} with an S^Δ. Suppose, for example, that for each time a child swore, the parents deducted 25 cents from the child's allowance and that, as a result of this response-cost contingency, the swearing decreased. In this example, the sight of the parents would be an S^{Dp} for swearing. If, on the other hand, the parents simply ignored the child when swearing (i.e., withheld their attention as a reinforcer), and the swearing decreased as a result of this extinction contingency, then the sight of the parents would be an S^Δ for swearing. In both scenarios, the presence of the parents would eliminate the swearing. However, the causes of the behavior change are different.

---

[2] We acknowledge Jennifer O'Donnell (2001) for introducing the symbol S^{Dp}.

As we described for positive reinforcement and extinction, adding rules to a punishment procedure often helps to decrease the undesirable behavior and increase the desirable alternative behavior more quickly (see, e.g., Bierman, Miller, & Stabb, 1987). Also, as stressed in Chapter 4, emphasizing the behav*ior,* not the behav*er,* is very important. The behav*ior,* not the individual, is undesirable. Appropriate use of rules is discussed further in Chapter 17.

5. The Delivery of the Punisher

To increase the effectiveness of punishment when delivering it, several guidelines should be followed.

1. The punisher should be presented immediately following the undesirable behavior   If the punisher is delayed, a more desirable behavior may occur prior to the use of the punisher, and this behavior may be suppressed to a much greater extent than the undesirable behavior. The classic example of this is the mother who asks her husband after he returns home from work to punish their child, who has misbehaved earlier in the day. This request is doubly disastrous. First, the child receives the punisher even though she or he may now be engaging in good behavior. Second, the father is punished for coming home from work. We do not mean to imply that delayed punishment is completely ineffective. As we point out in our discussion of rule-governed behavior in Chapter 17, most humans are adept at bridging rather large time gaps between their behavior and its consequences. Even so, immediate punishment is more effective than delayed punishment.

2. The punisher should be presented following every instance of the undesirable behavior   Occasional punishment is not as effective as punishment after every instance of the undesirable behavior (see, e.g., Kircher, Pear, & Martin, 1971; Lerman, Iwata, Shore, & DeLeon, 1997). If behavior modifiers are unable to detect most instances of the behavior to be punished, they should have serious doubts about the value of implementing a punishment procedure for two reasons. First, occasions in which a behavior modifier is unable to detect instances of the undesirable behavior may be occasions in which the undesirable behavior is positively reinforced, which would maintain its strength. Second, punishment procedures have negative side effects (to be discussed later), and it may be unethical to implement a procedure that may not be effective when that procedure also has negative side effects.

3. The delivery of the punisher should not be paired with positive reinforcement   This requirement often presents difficulties when the punisher is delivered by an adult and the individual being punished receives very little adult attention. If a child has received a lot of loving attention from an adult during a period of time prior to the occurrence of the undesired behavior and the adult immediately presents a strong verbal reprimand following the undesirable behavior, the verbal reprimand is likely to be punishing. However, if that reprimand is the only adult attention that the child has received for an extended period of time, such attention may reinforce the undesirable behavior.

4. The person administering the punisher should remain calm when doing so   Anger and frustration on the part of the person administering the punisher may reinforce the undesirable behavior or inappropriately alter the consistency or intensity of the punisher. A calm, matter-of-fact approach helps ensure that a punishment program will be followed consistently and appropriately. This also makes clear to the recipient that punishment is not being administered out of anger or for other irrelevant reasons. For reviews of research on factors affecting the effectiveness of punishment, see Hineline and Rosales-Ruiz (2013), Lerman and Vorndran (2002), and Lerman and Toole (2011).

Questions for Learning

15. If you do a good job of attending to the first two factors influencing the effectiveness of punishment, you may not have to apply punishment. Discuss.
16. What are two conditions under which a mild punisher can be effective?
17. What steps might you follow to experimentally determine whether a verbal reprimand is a punisher for a particular child?
18. Compare S^D to S^{Dp}. Give an example of each from your own experience.
19. Compare S^Δ to S^{Dp}. Give an example of each from your own experience.
20. What are four guidelines in regard to delivering a punisher?
21. We suggested that if behavior modifiers are unable to detect most instances of a behavior to be punished, they should have serious doubts about the value of implementing a punishment procedure.
    a. Give two reasons to support this suggestion.
    b. What alternative means for decreasing behavior are available to the behavior modifier (see Chapters 6 and 12)?

Some Examples of Therapeutic Punishment

Behavioral journals describe numerous reports of the use of punishment as a treatment strategy, sometimes referred to as *therapeutic punishment,* with individuals who have severe behavioral challenges. We will describe several examples.

An example of possibly life-saving therapeutic punishment is the treatment of a 6-month-old baby who was admitted to a hospital because of a failure to gain weight (Sajwaj, Libet, & Agras, 1974). Sandra was underweight and undernourished, and death was a distinct possibility. Preliminary observations indicated that, a few minutes after being given milk, Sandra would begin ruminating, or bringing up the milk and reswallowing it, and would continue this for about 20–40 minutes. Because some of the regurgitated milk would spill out of her mouth, she apparently lost most of the milk she had ingested. Sajwaj and his colleagues decided to administer lemon juice as a punisher of Sandra's ruminating behavior. During treatment, her mouth was filled with lemon juice immediately after staff members detected the vigorous tongue movements that reliably preceded her rumination. After 16 feedings with lemon juice punishment, the rumination had decreased to a very low level. To ensure that the improvement was due to the treatment program, Sajwaj and his colleagues suspended the use of lemon juice for two feedings. The result was a dramatic increase in rumination. Following additional treatment, Sandra was discharged to foster parents, who maintained the treatment until it was no longer necessary.

Another example involves a severe case of bruxism—the constant grinding of one's teeth. Gerri was a 16-year-old girl with profound intellectual disability who had been grinding her teeth almost ever since her permanent teeth had grown in. Her teeth were severely worn and were in danger of being lost. Behavior modifiers were consulted about the problem (Blount, Drabman, Wilson, & Stewart, 1982). After considering a variety of reinforcement procedures and rejecting them for various reasons, they settled on a mild pain-inducing punishment procedure. Each time Gerri audibly ground her teeth, a staff member touched her face with an ice cube for a few seconds. Gerri's teeth grinding decreased considerably within the first few days of treatment, and after 2 months of this procedure, her bruxism had almost completely ceased.

As another example, consider Tom, a 15-year-old with profound intellectual disability who suffered from pica, which is eating inedible or non-nutritive substances. Tom had a tendency to eat whatever he could get his hands on, including cigarette butts, plastic objects, pieces of hair, paint chips, dirt, sand, and bits of paper. Pica has been associated with lead poisoning, intestinal blockage, intestinal perforation, and intestinal parasites. To treat Tom's pica, Johnson, Hunt, and Siebert (1994) taught him to eat only items that were placed on a bright yellow plastic placemat. Each time that Tom complied, he experienced the natural reinforcement of the good taste of the items on the placemat and was enthusiastically praised by the staff at the institution where he lived. Ingesting items that were not on the placemat was immediately followed by a punisher—Tom's face was washed with a cool damp cloth for 15 seconds. The procedure effectively eliminated Tom's pica.

Some individuals with intellectual disabilities or autism repeatedly engage in severe self-injurious behavior—damaging their vision by gouging their eyes, damaging their hearing by clapping their hands against their ears, causing tissue damage and bleeding by banging their heads on hard objects or tearing at their flesh, and becoming malnourished by inducing vomiting after eating—that places them in great danger of disabling or killing themselves. A number of studies demonstrate that these behaviors can be suppressed by pain-inducing punishment (see, e.g., Favell et al., 1982; Linscheid, Iwata, Ricketts, Williams, & Griffin, 1990; Linscheid, Pejeau, Cohen, & Footo-Lenz, 1994). Once the self-injurious behavior is suppressed, positive reinforcement is then used to maintain the desirable alternative behavior, but this cannot be done until the self-injurious behavior has been controlled.

The preceding examples involve pain-inducing punishers. There are also many reports of therapeutic punishment with children involving response cost, timeout, and reprimand punishers. For example, in a preschool classroom, children could earn tokens (stars) for a variety of desirable behaviors, and the tokens could be cashed in at the end of each session for various reinforcers such as gummi bears and jelly beans (Conyers et al., 2004). In some sessions, there were no consequences for disruptive behaviors, but in other sessions disruptive behaviors were followed by token loss (response-cost punishment). The response-cost procedure was effective for decreasing disruptive behavior. As another example, Mathews et al. (1987) taught mothers to use a reprimand combined with a timeout to decrease dangerous behaviors (e.g., touching an electrical cord outlet) of their 1-year-old children. A mother would praise her child for playing appropriately, and say "No" and place the child in a playpen for a brief period immediately contingent upon the occurrence of a dangerous behavior. The intervention effectively decreased the dangerous behavior for all of the children.

As these and other examples illustrate, in some situations applications of punishment by parents, teachers, and others appear to be in the best interests of the persons who receive it. Nevertheless, because of the potential harmful side effects of punishment, considerable controversy exists over whether behavior modifiers should design and implement therapeutic punishment programs. Before discussing the controversy, we review the potential harmful side effects of punishment.

Potential Harmful Side Effects of Punishment

1. *Aggressive Behavior*   Punishment, especially physical punishment, tends to elicit aggressive behavior. Experiments with animals show that painful stimuli cause them to attack other animals—even though these other animals had nothing to do with inflicting these stimuli (Azrin, 1967). A recent review of 20 years of studies of physical punishment with children found that physical punishment was associated with higher levels of aggression against parents, siblings, and peers (Durrant & Ensom, 2012). However, this side effect of physical punishment was not reported for reprimands, timeout, or response cost.

2. *Emotional Behavior*   Punishment, especially physical punishment, can produce undesirable emotional side effects, such as crying and general fearfulness. These side effects not only are unpleasant for all concerned but also frequently interfere with desirable behavior—especially if it is of a complex **NOTE 2** nature.

3. *Escape and Avoidance Behavior*   Punishment may cause the situation and people associated with the aversive stimulus to become conditioned punishers. For example, if, while teaching a child to read, you punish him or her whenever he or she makes a mistake, anything associated with this situation—such as printed words, books, the person who delivers the punishment, the type of room in which the punishment occurs—will tend to become punishing. The child may then attempt to escape or avoid these stimuli (see Chapter 14). Thus, instead of helping the individual to learn, punishment may drive him or her away from everything having to do with the learning situation.

The punisher need not be particularly strong to have the undesirable effects just mentioned. For example, a teacher we know used a timeout chair as a punisher for students in her first-grade class. For some unknown reason—perhaps it had something to do with the fact that the chair was black and the teacher told rowdy children to go sit in the "black chair"—the chair became frightening to the students. Years later, former students who came back to visit the teacher mentioned how fearful they had been of the "black chair," even though nothing bad ever happened to them when they sat there. When the teacher discovered the problem with the chair, she changed her procedure. The chair is no longer black, and she now calls it the "calming-down chair" and periodically demonstrates its benign qualities to her students by sitting in it herself when she feels the need to calm down![3]

4. *No New Behavior*   Punishment does not establish any new behavior; it only suppresses old behavior. In other words, punishment does not teach an individual what to do; at best, it teaches only what *not* to do. For example, the main defining characteristic of persons with developmental disabilities is that they lack some behavior that the majority of people have. The primary emphasis for these individuals, then, should be on establishing new behavior rather than on merely eliminating old behavior. Reinforcement is required to accomplish this.

5. *Modeling of Punishment*   Children often model or imitate adults. If adults apply punishment to children, the children are apt to do the same to others. Thus, in punishing children, we may inadvertently be providing a model for them to follow in presenting aversive stimuli toward others (Bandura, 1965, 1969). For example, children who were taught a game in which they were fined for incorrect behavior fined other children to whom they taught the game (Gelfand et al., 1974).

6. *Overuse of Punishment*   Because punishment often results in rapid suppression of undesirable behavior, it can tempt the user to rely heavily on it and neglect the use of positive reinforcement for desirable behavior. However, the undesirable behavior may return after only a temporary suppression, or some other undesirable behavior could occur. The person administering punishment may then resort to progressively heavier doses, thereby creating a vicious circle with disastrous effects.

---

[3] We thank Fran Falzarano for this example.

Questions for Learning

22. In two or three sentences, describe either the case of the lemon juice therapy with Sandra or the ice cube therapy with Gerri.
23. What is pica? What factors influencing the effectiveness of punishment did Johnston et al. incorporate into their treatment for pica?
24. Briefly describe the procedure that Mathews et al. taught mothers to decrease dangerous behaviors of their 1-year-old children. Was the timeout component exclusionary or nonexclusionary? Justify your choice.
25. Cite six potential harmful side effects of the application of punishment.

Should Punishment Be Used?

The deliberate use of physical punishment, especially with children or persons with developmental disabilities, has always been highly controversial, even before the advent of behavior modification, but the controversy intensified during the 1980s and 1990s. As reviewed by Feldman (1990) and by Vause, Regehr, Feldman, Griffiths, and Owen (2009), two opposing positions emerged. On the one hand, the right-to-effective-treatment position is that a client's right to effective treatment might in some cases dictate the use of quicker-acting punishment procedures rather than slower-acting procedures involving positive reinforcement of alternative behavior (see Van Houten et al., 1988). On the other hand, the freedom-from-harm position is that nonaversive methods for eliminating unacceptable behavior are always at least as effective as punishment and that, therefore, using pain-inducing punishment is never justified (see Guess, Helmstetter, Turnbull, & Knowlton, 1986). During the 1980s and 1990s, advocates of this latter position described a variety of alternatives to punishment for treating challenging behavior. For example, Carr and Durand (1985) observed that some children with developmental disabilities emitted self-injurious behavior to obtain caregiver attention. They developed a procedure called *functional communication training* in which the children were taught a simple communicative response (e.g., ringing a bell) as an alternative to self-abuse to obtain staff attention. The self-injurious behavior was effectively eliminated. Another example of this approach was reported by Kuhn, Chirighin, and Zelenka (2010) who taught two children with developmental disabilities to use a vocal communication response (e.g., "Excuse me") instead of a variety of problem behaviors (e.g., headbanging, throwing objects) to get staff attention. They also taught the children to discriminate when staff were "busy" (e.g., talking on the phone) or "nonbusy" (e.g., reading a magazine), and to request attention primarily when staff were "nonbusy." Nevertheless, some research has indicated that functional communication training combined with punishment of a problem behavior is more effective than functional communication training alone (Hagopian et al., 1998; Hanley, Piazza, Fisher, & Maglieri, 2005).

As another example of alternatives to punishment, Horner et al. (1990) described an approach called *positive behavior support* (PBS) that emphasized nonaversive approaches for treating individuals who exhibit challenging behavior. PBS has gathered a number of adherents and now includes an organization that holds an annual conference and produces the *Journal of Positive Behavior Interventions* and a number of other publications. (For a discussion of PBS, see Anderson & Freeman, 2000; Bambara & Kern, 2005; Carr & Sidener, 2002; Filter, 2007; Johnston, Foxx, Jacobson, Green, & Mulick, 2006.)

An important effect of the controversy is that use of physical punishment with children has become increasingly unacceptable. Thirty countries have banned corporal punishment of children; and in the United States the District of Columbia and 28 states have banned corporal punishment in schools (Global Initiative to End All Corporal Punishment of Children, 2010). Associations like the American Association on Intellectual and Developmental Disabilities and the Association of Behavior Analysis International also have specific policies recommending limits on use of harsh punishment (see their respective websites).

Now let's reconsider the question of whether punishment of any type should be deliberately used. Before doing so, we reemphasize a point made earlier in this chapter: We are not talking about the concept of punishment as many people think of it. That is, we are *not* talking about punishment of an individual as retribution, as a deterrent to others, or as a delayed consequence for misbehavior. Also, we are not talking about a harsh physical punishment such as slapping and spanking, which should not be used. Rather, we are talking about consistently presenting some type of mild physical punishment (such as the therapeutic punishers described previously), reprimands, response-cost, or timeout immediately following a problem behavior and doing so in full consideration of the factors influencing the effectiveness of punishment and its potentially harmful side effects as discussed previously. Because punishment can have a number of potentially harmful side effects, *we recommend that behavior modifiers consider designing punishment programs only when:*

- The behavior is very maladaptive, and it is in the client's best interest to bring about rapid behavior change.
- Clear steps are taken to maximize the conditions for a desirable alternative response and to minimize the causes of the response to be punished before resorting to punishment.
- The client or the client's parent or guardian provides informed consent (see Chapter 30).
- The intervention meets ethical standards (see Chapter 30).
- Punishment is applied according to clear guidelines (see page 125).
- The program includes safeguards to protect the client (see Chapter 30).

Pitfalls of Punishment

Unaware-Misapplication Pitfall

People who are not aware that they are doing so often apply punishment. A common example is criticizing or ridiculing a person for inadequate behavior. Criticism and ridicule are punishing, and will likely suppress future instances of that behavior. Yet the inadequate behavior that is criticized and ridiculed may be an approximation of more adequate behavior. Suppressing it could destroy the individual's opportunity to obtain the more desired behavior through the use of shaping. In everyday language, the individual becomes discouraged and gives up in his or her attempt to develop adequate behavior. In addition, because he or she may attempt to escape from and avoid the person administering the criticism and ridicule (see Chapter 14), that person will lose a great deal of potential reinforcing effectiveness.

Another example of someone applying punishment without being aware of it is the person who says "That was good, but...." Suppose a teenager helps a parent with the dishes and the parent replies, "Thanks for helping, but next time don't be so slow." We are sure that, based on the foregoing discussion, you can describe a much more effective and pleasant way for the parent to react.

Partial-Knowledge-Misapplication Pitfall

Sometimes an individual thinks that she or he is applying a punisher but in fact is applying a reinforcer. For example, an adult may say "No! Naughty child! Stop that!" to a child who is engaging in an undesirable behavior. The child may immediately cease the undesirable behavior, and the adult might then conclude that the reprimand was an effective punisher. However, someone who tracked the frequency of that undesirable behavior might find that the reprimand was not a punisher but in fact a reinforcer. The child may have stopped temporarily because, having obtained the attention of the adult, he or she can then engage in other behavior that will maintain the adult's attention. Several studies indicate that reprimands can function as positive reinforcers and that the long-term frequency of the undesirable behavior that evoked the reprimand is therefore likely to increase (e.g., Madsen, Becker, Thomas, Koser, & Plager, 1970). This is not to say that reprimands are never punishing. As in our previous discussion of reprimands, they can be effective punishers. Situations in which they are most effective, however, seem to be those in which they are consistently backed up by another punisher, the causes of the undesirable behavior have been minimized, and the conditions for a desirable alternative behavior have been maximized (Van Houten & Doleys, 1983).

Guidelines for the Effective Application of Punishment

The rules for the effective use of punishment are probably violated more than those for other principles. Therefore, extra care must be taken when designing a behavior modification program involving punishment. The conditions under which it is to be applied must be stated clearly, written down, and followed consistently.

1. *Select a Response*   Punishment is most effective with a specific behavior, such as jumping on the arm of the chair, rather than a general category of behavior (such as wrecking furniture).

2. *Maximize the Conditions for a Desirable (Nonpunished) Alternative Response*
   a. Select a desirable alternative behavior that competes with the behavior to be punished so that the alternative behavior can be reinforced. If possible, select a behavior that the natural environment will maintain after the termination of your reinforcement program.
   b. Provide strong prompts to increase the likelihood that the desirable alternative behavior will occur.
   c. Reinforce the desirable behavior with a powerful reinforcer on an appropriate schedule.
3. *Minimize the Causes of the Response to Be Punished*
   a. Try to identify and eliminate as many as possible of the S^Ds for the undesirable behavior early in the training program.
   b. Try to eliminate any possible reinforcement for the undesirable behavior.
4. *Select an Effective Punisher*
   a. Choose an effective punisher that can be presented immediately following the undesirable behavior.
   b. The punisher should be one that will not be paired with positive reinforcement following the undesirable behavior.
   c. Select a punisher that can be presented following every instance of the undesirable behavior.
5. *Present Clear S^{Dp}s*
   a. Tell the learner about the plan before starting.
   b. Give a clear "warning" or "reminder" (e.g., "Wait for mommy before crossing").
6. *Deliver the Punisher*
   a. Present the punisher *immediately* following the response to be decreased.
   b. Present the punisher following *every* instance of the response to be decreased.
   c. Take care not to pair punishment of the undesirable behavior with reinforcement for that behavior.
   d. Administer the punisher in a calm and matter-of-fact manner.
7. *Take Data*   In all programs involving punishment, careful data should be taken on the effects of the program.

Questions for Learning

26. Briefly describe the right-to-effective-treatment and freedom-from-harm positions in regard to the deliberate use of punishment treatment procedures.
27. Give an example of functional communication training.
28. List six conditions that should be met for behavior modifiers to design punishment programs.
29. In view of the controversy regarding the use of punishment, do you agree with the way punishment was used with Ben? Defend your answer.
30. Give an example of how punishment is applied by people who are not aware that they are doing so.

Application Exercises

A. Exercises Involving Others

1. Consider the behavior of speeding (driving a car in excess of the speed limit) in our culture.
   • Briefly outline the current reinforcement and punishment contingencies with respect to speeding.
   • Compare the current punishment contingencies for speeding with the Guidelines for the Effective Application of Punishment (pages 129–130). Identify those guidelines that lawmakers and law enforcers typically ignore.
2. Consider the behavior of littering the highways in your area. Answer the questions for this behavior that you answered for speeding in Application Exercise 1.

B. Self-Modification Exercise

Choose a behavior of yours that you would like to decrease. Describe in detail a punishment program that, with the help of a friend, would likely decrease that behavior. (Make the program as realistic as possible, but do not apply it.) Your punishment program should be consistent with all of the guidelines for the effective application of punishment.

Notes for Further Learning

1. In a recent review of trends in timeout research, Warzak, Floress, Kellen, Kazmerski, and Chopko (2012) analyzed 26 years of published abstracts on timeout research. They concluded that more research was needed to: (a) evaluate the relative efficacy of exclusionary versus nonexclusionary timeout; (b) examine how to best teach children how to comply with timeout when it is applied to them; and (c) examine how to best teach parents and treatment staff to implement timeout effectively and within acceptable ethical guidelines.

2. The issue of spankings by parents has made headlines in many newspapers, including the *New York Times* and *USA Today*. For example, popular press reported on a study by Afifi et al. (2012) that was reported in *Pediatrics*, the official journal of the American Academy of Pediatrics. The researchers reported on a U.S. adult population sample that had been asked if they had experienced harsh physical punishment (e.g., pushing, grabbing, shoving, slapping, hitting) as a child. "Sometimes" was the answer by 5.9% of the sample, and such individuals were 2% to 7% more likely to experience some type of mental disorder (mood disorders, anxiety disorders, alcohol or drug abuse/dependence, or severe personality disorders), in comparison to individuals who did not report experiencing harsh physical punishment during childhood. We hasten to point out, however, that discussion of the use of punishment by parents need not imply corporal punishment (for a review of corporal punishment by parents, see Gershoff, 2002). Rather, punishment can involve timeout, response cost, or reprimands. Also, we want to reemphasize that any discussion of punishment should be done with full consideration of the behavioral approach to punishment used in this chapter. In that sense, there are situations in which application of punishment by parents would likely be in the best interests of their children, as in the case of a child who frequently runs into a busy street, sticks metal objects into electrical outlets, or eats paint chips off walls. However, before applying punishment, parents should become knowledgeable concerning the factors that influence the effectiveness of punishment. An excellent source for parents is the book by Cipani (2004) that describes myths about punishment, basic principles of punishment, and guidelines for responsible use of punishment by parents.

Questions for Further Learning

1. Identify three areas where more research is needed on the use of timeout with children.
2. Do you think parents should use punishment? Discuss.

CHAPTER 14

Establishing Behavior by Escape and Avoidance Conditioning

LEARNING OBJECTIVES

After studying this chapter, you will be able to:

- Define *escape conditioning* and *avoidance conditioning*.
- Compare and contrast escape conditioning, avoidance conditioning, punishment, and positive reinforcement in terms of the antecedents and consequences involved in each.

- Identify and produce examples of escape and avoidance conditioning in everyday life.
- Explain how escape and avoidance conditioning can work to the disadvantage of those who are ignorant of them.

Joanne, that's bad for your health!

Curing Joanne's Slouching[1]

Joanne was a model employee. An attendant at the Anna State Hospital, she was hardworking, punctual, and well liked by the patients. Unfortunately, Joanne constantly slouched while she worked. While slouching might not seem to be a serious problem, slouching by staff presented an inappropriate role model for the psychiatric patients at the hospital. Poor posture by such individuals frequently discourages social acceptability when they return to the community. Moreover, many medical authorities believe that good posture benefits health.

Fortunately for Joanne, some psychologists at the hospital were conducting research on behavioral engineering—the use of an apparatus to manage contingencies to change behavior. Joanne agreed to participate in the experiment which involved a specially designed elastic cord taped to her back under her blouse. The elastic cord contained sensors that were wired to a small programmable device that contained a tone generator and a clicker. The programmable device was supported by a cloth necklace that she wore under her blouse and that fitted comfortably in her brassiere. Thus the entire apparatus was completely concealed. The procedure of the experiment had three components. First, when Joanne slouched, the elastic cord stretched activating the sensors which caused the programmable device to produce a clicking sound and 3 seconds later a loud aversive tone. This was an instance of punishment for slouching. Second, while the aversive tone was on, if Joanne exhibited good posture she would escape the sound of the tone because it would turn off. Third, when the clicker sounded, if Joanne showed good posture during the next 3 seconds, the aversive tone would not occur, and if she continued to display good posture, she would avoid the clicking sound and the tone altogether. The results were dramatic. Before Joanne wore the apparatus, she slouched almost 60% of the time, but when she wore it, she slouched only 1% of the time. When Joanne removed the apparatus, her slouching did

---

[1] This case is based on Azrin, Rubin, O'Brien, Ayllon, and Roll (1968).

recover somewhat (to approximately 11%), but the clear demonstration of the effects of the apparatus gave her hope that she could cure her slouching habit.

Three behavioral principles were used in Joanne's case: punishment, escape conditioning, and avoidance conditioning. We described punishment in Chapter 13 and we now describe escape and avoidance conditioning.

Escape Conditioning (Negative Reinforcement)

The principle of **escape conditioning** (also called **negative reinforcement**) states that the removal of certain stimuli (called *aversive stimuli*) immediately after the occurrence of a behavior will increase the likelihood of that behavior. In the second component of the treatment used with Joanne, the removal of the loud tone following the response of showing good posture was an escape procedure that increased the probability that she would show good posture as an escape response in the presence of the tone.

Escape conditioning is similar to punishment in that both involve the use of an aversive stimulus. While escape conditioning and punishment are therefore similar, they differ procedurally in terms of both the antecedents and the consequences of behavior. With regard to punishment, as illustrated by the first component of the treatment procedure with Joanne, the aversive stimulus (the loud tone) is not present before the response (Joanne's slouching); rather it is presented after the response. With regard to escape conditioning, as illustrated by the second component of Joanne's treatment, the aversive stimulus (the loud tone) must be present prior to an escape response, and the aversive stimulus is removed immediately following the escape response. In terms of results, the punishment procedure *decreases* the likelihood of the target response of slouching, whereas the escape conditioning procedure *increases* the likelihood of the target response of exhibiting good posture.

As stated in Chapter 4, another name for escape conditioning is *negative reinforcement* (Skinner, 1953). The word *reinforcement* indicates that it is analogous to positive reinforcement in that both strengthen responses. The word *negative* indicates that the strengthening effect occurs because the response leads to the removal (taking away) of an aversive stimulus.

Escape conditioning is common in everyday living. In the presence of a bright light, we have learned to escape the intensity of the light by closing our eyes or squinting. When a room is too cold, we escape the chill by putting on an extra sweater (see Figure 14.1). When it is too hot, we escape the heat by

FIGURE 14.1
Escape conditioning is strengthened by dressing warmly in the winter

turning on a fan or air conditioner. If a street crew is repairing the street outside your room, you might close the window to escape the noise. See Table 14.1 for other examples of escape conditioning.

TABLE 14.1   Examples of Escape Conditioning

Aversive Situation	Escape Response by Individual	Removal of Aversive Situation	Long-Term Effect
1. A child sees an adult with a bag of candies. The child begins to scream, "Candy, candy, candy."	To terminate the screaming, the adult gives the screaming child a candy.	The child stops screaming.	In the future, the adult is more likely to give in to the screaming child to escape the screaming (and the child is likely to scream to get candy, a positive reinforcer).
2. A teacher presents prompts every 30 seconds to a child with developmental disabilities.	The child begins to tantrum.	The teacher gives the child a break from the training program.	The child is likely to tantrum when presented with frequent prompts from the teacher.
3. A nonverbal child has had shoes put on her that are too tight and are pinching her toes.	The child makes loud noises in the presence of an adult and points to her toes.	The adult removes the shoes (and perhaps puts on larger shoes).	The child is likely to make loud noises and point to her feet (or other areas of pain) more quickly in the future.
4. A jogger experiences a sensation of sore lips while jogging.	The jogger puts lip balm on his lips.	The sensation of soreness ceases.	The jogger is likely to use lip balm while jogging to soothe his lips.
5. A zookeeper encounters a pile of smelly dung on the floor of a monkey cage.	The zookeeper walks away without cleaning it up.	The zookeeper escapes the aversive smell.	In the future, the zookeeper will likely walk away from smelly dung on the floor of the monkey cage.

Questions for Learning

1. Define *escape conditioning*, and describe how it was used with Joanne.
2. How is escape conditioning similar to punishment? In what two procedural ways do they differ? How do their effects differ?
3. Describe two examples of escape conditioning in everyday life, one of which is not in this chapter.
4. What is another name for escape conditioning, and why is it called that?
5. In what two procedural ways is negative reinforcement different from positive reinforcement? How are their effects similar?

In Chapter 6 we described the principle of operant extinction which states that (a) if any individual, in a given situation, emits a previously reinforced behavior and that behavior is not followed by a reinforcer, then (b) that person is less likely to do the same thing again when encountering a similar situation. Extinction can also occur following escape conditioning (negative reinforcement), which we will refer to as *escape extinction*. For example, after Joanne had learned good posture to escape the loud tone, if the apparatus had been adjusted so that good posture was no longer followed by the removal of the loud tone, then Joanne would likely have shown a decrease of good posture in the presence of the tone. LaRue et al. (2011) used escape extinction to treat feeding problems of five children. In some cases of children with feeding disorders, when a parent attempts to feed the child with a spoon the child might exhibit refusal behavior (e.g., crying, batting at the spoon). If, in such situations, the parents tend to terminate feeding or postpone bite presentations, then they are strengthening the child's food refusal through escape conditioning. In five cases of children whose parents had strengthened food refusal through escape conditioning, LaRue et al. taught the parents to use escape extinction by holding the spoon at the child's lips until the child's mouth opened, and then placing the food in the child's mouth. If the child expelled the food instead of swallowing, then the procedure was immediately repeated. The escape extinction procedure was effective with all five children.

Avoidance Conditioning

Escape conditioning has the disadvantage that the aversive stimulus must be present for the desired response to occur. In the escape procedure used with Joanne, the loud tone was on before she showed good posture. Therefore, escape conditioning is generally not a final contingency for maintaining behavior but is preparatory training for avoidance conditioning. Thus, Joanne was influenced by avoidance conditioning after she had demonstrated escape behavior.

The **principle of avoidance conditioning** is a contingency in which a behavior prevents an aversive stimulus from occurring thereby resulting in an increase in the frequency of that behavior. During the avoidance procedure used with Joanne, good posture prevented the tone from occurring. Note that both escape conditioning and avoidance conditioning involve the use of an aversive stimulus. And with both, the likelihood of a behavior increases. However, one difference between escape and avoidance conditioning is that an escape response removes an aversive stimulus that has already occurred while an avoidance response prevents an aversive stimulus from occurring at all. Keeping this in mind will help you to distinguish between instances of escape versus instances of avoidance. Suppose you are walking down the aisle of a shopping mall and someone whom you dislike steps in front of you and begins talking. You make an excuse that you are late for an appointment and must leave and you walk away. That is an instance of escape conditioning because the aversive stimulus was there and you responded to escape from it. Now suppose that the next day, you are once again walking in that shopping mall and you see the person whom you dislike come out of a store some distance away, but that person hasn't yet seen you. You duck into a store to avoid that person. That is an instance of avoidance conditioning.

A second difference between escape and avoidance conditioning is that the latter often iinvolves a **warning stimulus** (also called *conditioned aversive stimulus*), which is a stimulus that signals a forth- **NOTE 1** coming aversive stimulus. In the example at the shopping mall, the sight of the person you dislike some distance away was a warning stimulus, and you ducked into the store to avoid that person. The clicking of the apparatus when Joanne slouched was a warning stimulus—it signaled the occurrence of the tone 3 seconds later. Joanne quickly learned to show good posture at the sound of the clicker to avoid the backup aversive stimulus, the loud tone. This type of avoidance conditioning, which includes a warning signal that enables the individual to discriminate a forthcoming aversive stimulus, is called *discriminated avoidance conditioning*.

Like escape conditioning, avoidance conditioning is also common in everyday living. Students learn to give the right answers on tests to avoid poor grades. Our legal system is based largely on avoidance conditioning. We pay our taxes to avoid going to prison. We put money in parking meters to avoid getting a ticket. We pay our parking fines to avoid a court summons. Researchers have demonstrated the effectiveness of avoidance conditioning procedures by drivers. In one study, Clayton and Helms (2009) monitored seatbelt usage by drivers of automobiles who drove through a one-way exit from a medium-sized university campus. In a baseline condition, one student at the exit held up a sign stating "Have a nice day," and another student recorded whether or not the driver was wearing a seatbelt. In a second phase of the study, the student held up a sign stating either "Please buckle up—I Care" or "Click It or Ticket" (implying a monetary fine if the seatbelt was not done up). Seatbelt use increased by 20% over baseline in the "Click It or Ticket" condition compared to only 14% in the "Please buckle up—I Care" condition. In another study (Van Houten et al., 2010), 101 commercial drivers from the United States and Canada agreed to have a device installed in their vehicle that presented a chime and prevented drivers from shifting into gear for up to 8 seconds unless seatbelts were buckled. The driver could avoid the delay (and the chime) by fastening his/her seatbelt before shifting out of park. Once the 8 seconds (and the chime) started timing, the driver could escape the remaining delay (and the chime) by buckling up. The procedure increased seatbelt usage for 84% of the drivers.

Behavioral theoreticians have debated the theoretical explanation for avoidance responding. The increase in positively reinforced responses and escape responses and the decrease in punished responses are all explained by their immediate stimulus consequences. However, the consequence of an avoidance response is the nonoccurrence of a stimulus. How can the nonoccurrence of something cause a behavior? Because theoreticians tend to dislike paradoxes such as this, behavioral theoreticians have asked themselves the following question: Are there immediate consequences that perhaps are easily overlooked by the casual observer but that might nevertheless maintain avoidance responses?

There appear to be several possibilities. One possibility in discriminated avoidance conditioning is that the avoidance response is strengthened because it immediately terminates the warning stimulus. For example, recall that in Joanne's case, the loud tone was the backup aversive stimulus. Because clicking was paired with the tone, clicking became an aversive stimulus. When Joanne showed good posture in the presence of the clicking, the immediate result was that the clicking ceased. Although Joanne's good posture was an avoidance response with respect to the tone, it was an escape response with respect to the clicking. This type of explanation might enable us to account for the first example of avoidance conditioning in Table 14.2.

TABLE 14.2   Examples of Avoidance Conditioning

Situation	Warning Stimulus	Avoidance Response	Immediate Consequence	Aversive Consequence Avoided
1. While driving, you are exceeding the speed limit.	You notice a police car just ahead.	You immediately turn down a side street.	You no longer see the police car.	You avoid receiving a speeding ticket.
2. A child playing in her front yard hears the neighbor's dog barking (the dog had previously scared the child by barking loudly).	The child feels anxious.	The child goes into her house.	The child feels less anxious.	The child avoids hearing the loud barking.
3. One of the authors is about to leave his office to go home.	He remembers that his son is practicing his drumming at home.	He phones home to ask his son to stop practicing.	Thoughts of encountering loud drumming cease.	He avoids experiencing extremely loud drumming when he enters his house.

A second possible explanation of discriminated avoidance conditioning is that, in some cases, the avoidance response enables a person to immediately escape from anxious feelings. This is illustrated by the second example in Table 14.2. Hearing the dog's barking caused the child to feel anxious. Immediately following the avoidance response, she felt less anxious. The possibility that avoidance responses occur because they enable us to escape from anxiety is discussed further in Chapter 15.

A third possible explanation is that in some cases, the avoidance response enables a person to immediately escape from unpleasant thoughts. This might explain the avoidance response in the third example in Table 14.2. Perhaps thoughts of experiencing his son's loud drumming were aversive to the author and these thoughts immediately ceased following the phone call. Or perhaps the explanation of that example may involve rule-governed control over behavior, discussed in Chapter 17. While such explanations are plausible, they are speculative. You can see why behavior modifiers are puzzled about how to explain avoidance responding in terms of immediate stimulus consequences. (For a review of research on escape and avoidance conditioning, see Hineline & Rosales-Ruiz, 2013.)

Questions for Learning

6. Define *avoidance conditioning,* and describe how it was used with Joanne.
7. Give another name for warning stimulus.
8. What is the name of the type of avoidance conditioning that involves a warning stimulus?
9. How is a warning stimulus different than an S^{Dp} (see Chapter 13)?
10. What are two procedural differences between escape conditioning and avoidance conditioning?
11. Describe two examples of avoidance conditioning in everyday life, one of which is not in this chapter.
12. Describe three types of immediate consequences that might maintain avoidance responses.

Pitfalls of Escape and Avoidance Conditioning

Unaware-Misapplication Pitfall

People often unknowingly strengthen others' undesirable behavior by allowing such behavior to lead to escape or avoidance of aversive stimuli. This is illustrated by Example 2 in Table 14.1. Addison and Lerman (2009) observed this pitfall when they studied three special education teachers who conducted training sessions with children with autism. The teachers had been taught that if a child emitted problem behavior during the teaching trial, the teacher should ignore the problem behavior and continue with the prompting sequence. What they observed, however, was that, following a problem behavior of a child, the teacher would often stop all instructions and prompts for at least 10 seconds. As another example, observations of family interactions by Snyder, Schrepferman, and St. Peter (1997) indicated that parents of children labeled as antisocial frequently strengthened aggressive behavior in their children by backing off or giving in when the aggressive behavior occurred. Parents may inadvertently establish inappropriate verbal behavior with a child who desperately promises, "I'll be good; I won't do it again," to escape or avoid punishment for some infraction of parental authority. When such pleas are successful, the pleading behavior is strengthened and thus increased in frequency under similar circumstances, but the undesirable behavior the parent meant to decrease may have been affected very little or not at all. Verbal behavior having little relation to reality may be increased while the undesirable target response may persist in strength.

Another example of this pitfall sometimes can be seen when prisoners learn to make the "right" verbal statements to obtain early parole. Parole boards often have difficulty determining when it is only the verbal behavior of prisoners that has been modified, not their antisocial behaviors (e.g., assaults). Apologies, confessions, and the "guilty look" characteristic of transgressors in all walks of life can be traced to similar contingencies. Lying or misrepresenting the facts is a way of avoiding punishment if one can get away with it. (Other examples of undesirable behavior maintained by escape conditioning are presented in Chapter 23.)

A second variety of the Unaware-Misapplication Pitfall is the inadvertent establishment of conditioned aversive stimuli to which an individual then responds in such a way as to escape or avoid them. For example, if a coach yells at, criticizes, and ridicules athletes, the athletes may show improved skills primarily to avoid or escape the coach's wrath. But in the process, the coach has become a conditioned aversive stimulus for the athletes, so that they are now likely to avoid the coach. If the coaching tactics become too aversive, everything associated with the sport will become aversive, and some team members might even quit it entirely.

A third variety of this Pitfall is that in some situations, a person might be inadvertently influenced by escape and avoidance conditioning to positively reinforce the undesirable behavior of others. An example with regard to escape conditioning is the first example in Table 14.1. An example with regard to avoidance conditioning is the reinforcement of a threat because it prevents the more aversive behavior that might follow, such as when a parent gives a child a candy because the child threatens to cry if candy is not forthcoming.

Guidelines for the Effective Application of Escape and Avoidance Conditioning

Any person who applies escape and avoidance conditioning should observe the following rules:

1. *Given a Choice Between Maintaining Behavior on an Escape or an Avoidance Procedure, the Latter Is to Be Preferred*   There are two reasons for this. First, in escape conditioning, the backup aversive stimulus must be present prior to the target response, whereas in avoidance conditioning, the backup aversive stimulus occurs only when the target response fails to occur. Second, in escape conditioning, the target response does not occur when the backup aversive stimulus is not present, whereas in avoidance conditioning, responding decreases very slowly when the backup aversive stimulus may no longer be forthcoming.
2. *The Target Behavior Should Be Established by Escape Conditioning Before It Is Put on an Avoidance Procedure*   In the case at the beginning of this chapter, Joanne learned how to escape the loud noise prior to learning how to avoid it.
3. *During Avoidance Conditioning, a Warning Stimulus Should Signal the Impending Aversive Stimulus*   This enhances conditioning by providing a warning that failure to respond will result in aversive stimulation. An example is the printed word "VIOLATION" on a parking meter's time indicator, which indicates that the motorist may receive a parking ticket if he or she does not put a coin in the meter (or pay at the paystation or by phone for the fully electrical parking meters). The clicker served a similar function for Joanne, indicating that the loud tone would occur 3 seconds later unless she showed good posture. And if Joanne showed good posture during the 3 seconds, she could avoid the loud tone. Similarly, paying at a parking meter or paystation removes the VIOLATION sign and prevents getting a ticket.

4. *Escape and Avoidance Conditioning, Like Punishment, Should Be Used Cautiously* Because these procedures involve aversive stimuli, they can result in harmful side effects, such as aggression, fearfulness, and a tendency to avoid or escape any person or thing associated with the procedure.

5. *Positive Reinforcement for the Target Response Should Be Used in Conjunction with Escape and Avoidance Conditioning* This will not only help to strengthen the desired behavior but will also tend to counteract the undesirable side effects mentioned. The procedure used with Joanne would probably have worked even better if positive reinforcement for good posture had been added to it. (This was not done because the experimenters were interested only in the escape and avoidance procedures.)

6. *As with All Procedures Described in This Text, the Individual Concerned Should Be Told—to the Best of His or Her Understanding—About the Contingencies in Effect* Again, as with all of these

NOTE 2 procedures, however, instructions are not necessary for escape and avoidance conditioning to work.

Questions for Learning

13. Briefly illustrate how people unknowingly strengthen others' undesirable behavior by allowing such behavior to lead to escape or avoidance of aversive stimuli.

14. Give an example of the inadvertent establishment of conditioned aversive stimuli, which then causes individuals to avoid or escape those stimuli.

15. Explain with an example of your own why an individual might unknowingly positively reinforce the undesirable behavior of another individual. (*Hint*: See the first example in Table 14.1.) Clearly identify the behavior principles involved.

16. Explain how escape conditioning might influence an adult to unknowingly positively reinforce a child's extreme social withdrawal.

Application Exercises

A. Exercise Involving Others

Successful avoidance behavior means that an individual probably has been conditioned to respond to a warning signal in such a way as to avoid the occurrence of a backup aversive stimulus. This means that the avoidance behavior might persist even if the environment has changed so that the backup aversive stimulus will no longer be presented regardless of the individual's behavior. Give an example you have observed in someone other than yourself that illustrates this effect.

B. Self-Modification Exercise

Construct a table similar to Table 14.1 in which you present five examples of escape conditioning that have influenced your behavior. Present each example in terms of the categories of aversive situation, escape response, removal of aversive stimulus, and probable long-term effects on the escape response.

Notes for Further Learning

1. Not all types of avoidance conditioning involve a warning stimulus. One type that does not is known as *Sidman avoidance* (named for Murray Sidman, who studied this type of avoidance extensively with lower organisms; e.g., Sidman, 1953). In a typical Sidman avoidance conditioning experiment with a laboratory rat, a brief electric shock is presented every 30 seconds without a preceding warning stimulus. If the rat makes a designated response, the shock will be postponed for 30 seconds. Under these conditions, the rat will learn to make the appropriate avoidance response on a regular basis and will be relatively shock free. Sidman avoidance conditioning is also referred to as *nondiscriminated, noncued,* or *free-operant avoidance conditioning.* Sidman avoidance has been demonstrated with humans (Hefferline, Keenan, & Harford, 1959) and appears to underlie some everyday preventive behaviors. For example, many older model cars have no warning light to indicate when the windshield wiper fluid container is almost empty. Nevertheless, to avoid running out of fluid, many drivers of these cars regularly refill the container before it is empty. However, as discussed in Chapter 17, this behavior in the case of humans might also be explained as rule-governed behavior. There is still much debate regarding how Sidman avoidance can be explained more generally when rule-governed behavior is not involved, such as for animals that do not possess verbal behavior (e.g., see Baum, 2012).

2. Even animals whose nervous systems are quite different from ours show escape and avoidance conditioning. For example, the hermit crab—an animal that carries around or "wears" a discarded sea shell it has found— will leave its shell and tend to select another shell rather than returning to its original shell if it has received a small electric shock in the original shell (Elwood & Appel, 2009).

Questions for Further Learning

1. What is Sidman avoidance conditioning?
2. Explain how applying sunscreen or insect repellent might be an example of Sidman avoidance. Give another example from everyday life. (*Hint:* Some common computer applications have built-in timers that fit the definition of Sidman avoidance conditioning.)
3. Describe how avoidance conditioning has been demonstrated in the hermit crab. Did this study also demonstrate escape conditioning? Explain.

CHAPTER 15

Respondent and Operant Conditioning Together

LEARNING OBJECTIVES

After studying this chapter, you will be able to:

- Discuss operant–respondent interactions that occur in the normal course of everyday life.
- Describe how respondent and operant conditioning are involved in our emotions.
- Identify respondent and operant components of emotions.
- Identify respondent and operant components of thinking.

I have to finish my term paper!

Responding to Meet Deadlines

Janice was a student at the University of Manitoba. At the beginning of a course Janice was taking, students were assigned a paper that was due by midterm. Like many students, Janice liked to party. A week before the paper was due, Janice still hadn't started to work on it. Five days before the due date, she started to get a little concerned. But when her friends asked her to go to a bar, she thought, "What the heck, I've got 5 days left." At the bar she told her friends, "Don't call me for the next 4 days. I have to finish a major paper." Although Janice started on her paper the next day, the deadline was fast approaching. As each day passed, she felt increasingly nervous about the likelihood of finishing it on time. After working three late nights in a row, Janice finally finished the paper and felt a huge weight lifted from her shoulders.

Respondent and Operant Conditioning Compared

As we have seen, the principles of respondent and operant conditioning form the basis of behavior modification. In Chapter 3 we described principles and procedures of respondent conditioning. In Chapters 4–14, we described principles and procedures of operant conditioning. Before continuing with Janice's and other cases we will briefly review an example of respondent conditioning, and will then compare respondent and operant conditioning. In Chapter 3 we described the case of Susan, a young competitive figure skater who acquired a fear of attempting her double axel jump. Examine Figure 15.1, which presents a diagram of the respondent conditioning of Susan's fear. As illustrated by Susan's case, and as we stated in a Chapter 3, respondent behaviors are elicited by prior stimuli and are not affected by their consequences. Examples include feeling anxious when walking into a final exam, salivating when you smell the food placed in front of you, or blushing when you walk out of a restroom and someone points out that your zipper is undone. Operant behavior, on the other hand, is behavior that affects the environment to produce consequences, and which is, in turn, influenced by

Example of Respondent Conditioning

Several Pairings {

NS (approaching takeoff position for double axel)

US (bad fall) ⟶ UR (feelings of fear)

Result: CS (approaching takeoff ⟶ CR (fear)
position for double axel)

NS = neutral stimulus
US = unconditioned stimulus
UR = unconditioned response
CS = conditioned stimulus
CR = conditioned response

FIGURE 15.1
An illustration of respondent conditioning of fear in a figure skater (reprinted with permission from Martin, 2015)

those consequences. Examples include turning on your cell phone or asking someone to pass you the salt. Before reading the rest of this chapter we encourage you to carefully study Table 15.1 which summarizes some major differences between respondent and operant conditioning.

Questions for Learning

1. Diagram an example of respondent conditioning that is not in this chapter.
2. Describe three differences between operant responses and respondent responses.
3. Describe the conditioning procedures and the results of conditioning for operant conditioning (positive reinforcement only) and respondent conditioning.
4. Describe the extinction procedure and the results of extinction for operant conditioning and respondent conditioning.

TABLE 15.1   Respondent and Operant Conditioning Compared*

	Operant	Respondent
Type of Behavior	- controlled by consequences - referred to as voluntary behavior - usually involves skeletal muscles - is said to be *emitted by an individual*	- automatic responses to prior stimuli - referred to as reflexive or involuntary - usually involves smooth muscles and glands that control our gastrointestinal tract and blood vessels - is said to be *elicited by prior stimuli*
Conditioning Procedure	- in the presence of a stimulus, a response is *followed by* a reinforcer**	- pairing of a neutral stimulus with an eliciting stimulus *prior to* a response
Results of Conditioning	- response is more likely to occur to prior stimulus, now called an S^D	- response is more likely to occur to the neutral stimulus, now called *a CS*
Extinction Procedure	- a response is no longer followed *by* a reinforcer	- the CS is no longer *paired with* the US
Results of Extinction	- response is less likely to occur to the former S^D	- the CS loses the ability to elicit the CR

*This table was adapted, with permission, from Martin (2015).

**Positive reinforcement is only one of the operant conditioning procedures. Others, as seen in previous chapters, are escape conditioning, avoidance conditioning, and punishment.

Operant–Respondent Interactions

Any given experience is likely to include both respondent and operant conditioning occurring concurrently. Let's consider Janice's case. Like all of us, Janice probably had a history of being punished for failing to meet deadlines. Punishment elicits feelings of anxiety, a respondent reaction. As a consequence of prior pairings with punishment, stimuli associated with missing a deadline were likely CSs eliciting anxiety as a CR in Janice. The closer to the deadline, the stronger would be the CSs associated with missing the deadline, and hence the stronger would be the CR of anxiety. What about working on the term paper—how does it fit into this picture? The relevant responses (looking up references, reading background material, taking notes, making an outline, and finally writing the paper) are operant responses. As these responses occurred and Janice began to see that she would meet the deadline, the anxiety decreased. Thus, stimuli associated with the deadline likely caused Janice to feel anxious, a respondent response, and responding to meet the deadline, operant responses, were maintained by the negative reinforcement of the decrease in Janice's anxiety. While other factors were undoubtedly influencing Janice's behavior, the preceding analysis illustrates how both operant and respondent conditioning may have occurred concurrently and interacted.

Here is another example of a behavioral sequence that involves both respondent and operant conditioning. A small child runs to pet a large dog. Never having had any reason to fear dogs, the child shows no fear now. Suppose, however, that the dog playfully jumps and knocks the child down. Quite naturally, the child will begin crying because of the pain and surprise of this rough treatment. With respect to this behavioral sequence, illustrated in Figure 15.2, first consider how it is an instance of respondent conditioning. A stimulus (sight of dog) that was previously not a CS for a particular response (crying and other types of fear behavior) has come to be one because it was paired with a US (suddenly being knocked down) that did elicit that response.

Now let's consider how that behavioral sequence involved an instance of operant conditioning. The operant response of the child approaching the dog was followed by a punisher (the child was knocked

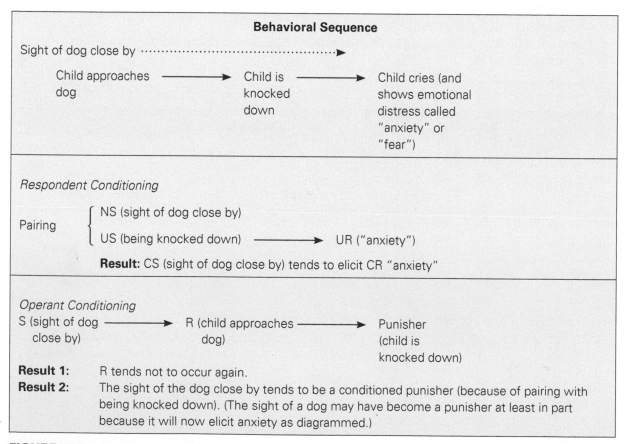

FIGURE 15.2

A behavioral sequence that involves both respondent and operant conditioning, and that leads to the development of a stimulus as a conditioned punisher

down). Consistent with the principle of punishment, the child is less likely to approach large dogs in the future. Moreover, the sight of a large dog nearby is likely to be a conditioned punisher (because of a pairing with being knocked down).

A result of this operant and respondent conditioning interaction is that it will likely cause the child to escape (in the technical sense described in Chapter 14) or avoid large dogs in the future. That is, if the child sees a large dog nearby, it will likely be a CS eliciting anxiety. If the child runs away, the anxiety is likely to decrease. Thus, running away from large dogs is likely to be maintained by negative reinforcement or escape conditioning in that the child will escape both the sight of the dog close by (a conditioned aversive stimulus) and the feelings of anxiety.

Both operant and respondent conditioning also occur in behavioral sequences involving positive reinforcers. As you can see in the behavioral sequence illustrated in Figure 15.3, the sound of the bell will become both a CS for a respondent response and an S^D for an operant response.

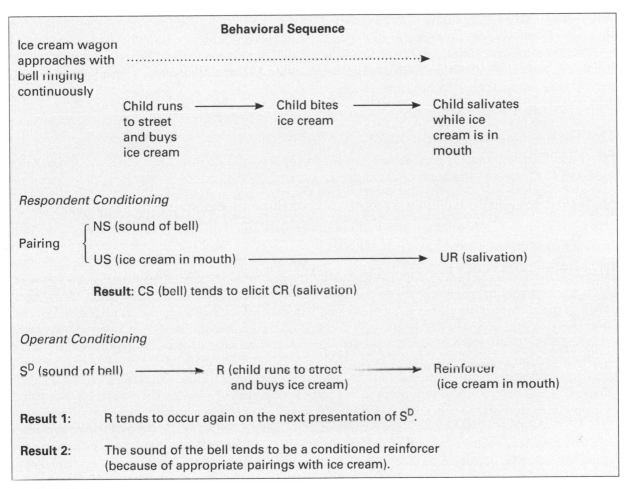

FIGURE 15.3

A behavioral sequence that includes both operant and respondent conditioning, and that leads to the development of a stimulus as a conditioned reinforcer

Questions for Learning

5. Explain why, for most of us, an approaching deadline likely functions as a CS eliciting anxiety as a CR.
6. Describe how respondent and operant conditioning interacted to influence Janice to get her term paper done by the deadline.
7. Describe a behavior sequence that involves an aversive stimulus and that includes both respondent conditioning and operant conditioning. Diagram the respondent conditioning and the operant conditioning components.
8. Describe a behavioral sequence that involves a positive reinforcer and that includes both respondent and operant conditioning. Diagram the respondent conditioning and the operant conditioning components.

In the lead case in Chapter 3, we focused on respondent behavior. In the lead cases in Chapters 4–15, we focused on operant behavior. However, each of the individuals in those cases likely experienced both respondent and operant conditioning in those situations. Although we, as behavior modifiers, chose to focus on one or the other, we should not lose sight of the fact that both are involved in most situations, and complete behavioral explanations sometimes necessitate consideration of both (see Pear & Eldridge, 1984). One area in which it is necessary to consider both respondent and operant conditioning is in the study of emotions.

Respondent and Operant Components of Emotions

Emotion researchers recognize that there are several sides or components to any emotion. There is (a) the feeling component, which is internal, private, and subjective; and, there is (b) an overt, public, and objective component (e.g., see Damasio, 2000; Hoeksm, Oosterlaan, & Schipper, 2004; Scherer, 2000). Emotions play an important role in our lives. To fully understand this important topic, we examine the role of respondent and operant conditioning in four areas: (a) the reaction that one feels during the experience of an emotion (such as "queasiness" in the pit of one's stomach before an important job interview); (b) the way that one learns to outwardly express or disguise an emotion (such as hugging a friend to show affection or clasping one's hands tightly to hide nervousness); (c) how one becomes aware of and describes one's emotions (such as saying to oneself or others, "I'm nervous" as opposed to "I'm angry"); and (d) some causes of emotions.

The Respondent Component: Our Feelings

The respondent component of emotions involves primarily the three major classes of respondents discussed in Chapter 3—reflexes of the digestive system, the circulatory system, and the respiratory system. These reflexes are controlled by the part of our nervous system referred to as the *autonomic nervous system*. What happens inside you in a moment of great fear? Your adrenal glands secrete adrenaline into your bloodstream, which physically arouses and mobilizes your body for action. Your heart rate increases dramatically (circulatory system). At the same time, you breathe more rapidly (respiratory system), providing an increased supply of oxygen to the blood. This oxygen surges through your body with the increased heart rate, supplying more oxygen to your muscles. You may begin to sweat, which acts as a cooling mechanism in preparation for increased energy output of the body. At the same time that these changes are occurring, you may get a queasy feeling in your stomach (digestive system). Blood vessels to the stomach and intestines constrict, and the process of digestion is interrupted, diverting blood from your internal organs to your muscles. Your mouth becomes dry as the action of the salivary glands is impeded. You might even temporarily lose bowel or bladder control (a reaction that for our primative ancestors lightened their bodies in preparation for flight and tended to distract their pursuers). These internal reactions prepare the body for fighting or fleeing. They clearly had survival value in our evolutionary history, but they may not always be useful in modern society.

The autonomic nervous system is not involved in all respondent behaviors. Some respondent behaviors are a part of skeletal reflexes (also called motor reflexes). Some skeletal reflexes that have been identified in normally developing newborns include a sucking reflex, which involves sucking in response to stimulating the area around the mouth; a grasp reflex, which involves squeezing a finger or similar object placed in the palm; the Moro reflex, which involves a startled look and flinging out the arms sideways in response to support being momentarily withdrawn; a startle reflex, which involves flinging out the arms sideways in response to a loud noise; a stepping reflex, which involves a stepping motion in response to the feet contacting a hard surface; a swimming reflex, which involves swimming motions when placed in a prone position in water; a blink reflex, which involves blinking in response to the eyes being touched or a bright light; a cough reflex, which involves coughing when the airway to the lungs is stimulated; a gag reflex, which involves gagging when the throat or back of the mouth is touched; a sneeze reflex, which involves sneezing when the nasal passage is irritated; and a yawn reflex, which involves yawning when there is a decrease in oxygen intake (Goldenring, 2011; Woody, 2012, pp. 427–430). Except for the last five, the rest of the reflexes normally disappear as the child grows older, usually within a few months. The last five continue throughout the lifetime of the individual.

It appears that skeletal reflexes may not be as easily conditioned by respondent conditioning as autonomic reflexes are. Nearly every organ and gland controlled by the autonomic nervous system is susceptible to respondent conditioning (Airapetyantz & Bykov, 1966). Moreover, it is the autonomic system that appears to be primarily involved in the feeling component of emotions.

Emotion researchers distinguish between primary and secondary emotions. The list of primary emotions advanced by emotion researchers typically includes fear, anger, joy, happiness, sadness, interest, anticipation, and excitement. The list of secondary emotions typically includes envy, jealousy, anxiety, guilt, shame, relief, hope, depression, pride, love, gratitude, and compassion (Lazarus, 2007). The secondary emotions develop after the primary emotions and are thought by some emotion researchers to stem from the primary emotions (e.g., Plutchik, 2001; Walsh, 2012, pp. 120–121).

We have seen that the feeling of fear in Susan's case, as illustrated in Figure 15.1, was influenced by respondent conditioning. A great deal of research has focused on demonstrating that respondent conditioning can produce feelings of fear and anxiety to specific stimuli (see Craske, Hermans, & Vansteenwegen, 2006; Mineka & Oehlberg, 2008; Mineka & Zinbarg, 2006).

Nevertheless, the feelings associated with other emotions are also influenced by respondent conditioning. At a family reunion, for example, family members experience many happy moments. A few weeks later, when viewing the photos taken at the reunion, the pictures will likely be CSs eliciting "happy" feelings. But there is more to emotions than the autonomic responses that we feel. Let's see how operant conditioning is also involved.

An Operant Component: Our Actions

When you experience an emotion-causing event, your body responds with an immediate physiological reaction and accompanying facial expression (the respondent component). Then what happens? That depends on your operant learning experiences. In a situation that causes anger, one person might clench her fists and swear (see Figure 15.4), while another person in that same situation might count to ten and walk away. Because the operant component of emotions depends on each individual's conditioning

FIGURE 15.4

Withholding reinforcers following a previously reinforced response can cause anger. What are some operant and respondent components of anger?

history, these secondary displays of emotion vary from person to person and from culture to culture. Fans at a sporting event in North America are likely to show their displeasure for unsportsmanlike play by booing, while fans in Europe do so by whistling. We learn to operantly display our emotions in ways that have been modeled and reinforced in the past.

Another Operant Component: Our Awareness and Descriptions

Operant conditioning is also involved when we are taught to be aware of and describe our emotions. As we grow up, people around us teach us to label our emotions. Depending on our behavior, moms and dads ask questions such as, "Why are you so angry?" or "Aren't you having fun?" or "How are you feeling?" From such experiences, we learn about "being angry," "feeling happy," and "feeling sad." By age 9, most children have learned to recognize a large number of emotional expressions in themselves and others (Izard, 1991). Nevertheless, many emotions are not easily described or defined. We can account for this difficulty to some extent by considering the multiple sources of control over the naming of our emotions. Suppose you see a girl's brother grab her toy train and the girl run after him screaming. You might conclude that the girl is angry. The next day, when coming out of your house, you see the same girl screaming and running after her brother. You might again conclude that she is angry. However, in the second instance, the children could simply be enjoying a game of tag. Thus, when labeling emotions, we don't always have access to the emotion-causing events, the inner feelings, and the relevant operant behaviors. This contributes to inconsistencies in the way that we talk about emotions.

Some Causes of Emotions

Presentation and withdrawal of reinforcers and presentation and withdrawal of aversive stimuli produce four major emotions. Presentation of reinforcers produces the emotion called *joy*. Getting an "A+" on an exam, receiving a compliment, cashing your paycheck, and watching a funny movie all involve the presentation of positive reinforcers. Withholding or withdrawing reinforcers produces the emotion called *anger*. All of us have experienced such anger-causing events as putting our money in a vending machine that takes it but fails to produce the goods, using a pen that stops writing in the middle of a quiz, and having a ticket office close just before you get to the window to buy a ticket. The presentation of aversive stimuli produces the emotion called *anxiety*. Approaching scary-looking strangers in a dark alley, seeing a car drive directly toward you at a high speed, or hearing a dog bark right behind you are all likely to cause you to feel anxious. Finally, withdrawal of aversive stimuli produces an emotion that is called *relief*. When a woman receives the results from a test of a lump on her breast or a man receives the results of an assessment of an enlarged prostate, each is likely to feel relief if she or he is told that the problem is not cancer.

Emotions can occur on a continuum from very mild to very strong. Presentation of reinforcers, for example, can cause emotions ranging from mild pleasure to ecstasy. Withdrawal of reinforcers can cause emotions ranging from mild annoyance to rage. Presentation of aversive events can cause emotions ranging from mild apprehension to stark terror. And the effects of withdrawal of aversive stimuli might range from mild relief to intense relief verging on an emotional collapse. Other emotions might represent a mix of some of these basic emotions (see, e.g., Martin & Osborne, 1993; Mason & Capitanio, 2012; Plutchik, 2001).

To summarize, many of our emotions are caused by either the presentation or withdrawal of reinforcers or aversive stimuli. Our emotions have three important components: (a) the autonomic reaction that you feel during the experience of an emotion (typically accompanied by visible signs, such as frowns or smiles), which is influenced by respondent conditioning; (b) the way that you learn to express an emotion overtly (such as shouting, jumping up and down), which is influenced by operant conditioning; and (c) the way that you become aware of and describe your emotions, which is also influenced by operant conditioning. In Chapters 27 and 28, we discuss examples of how respondent and operant conditioning have been used to change troublesome emotions.

Questions for Learning

9. Describe several physiological activities that we experience in a moment of great fear.
10. Describe three unconditioned reflexes that are shown by newborn infants, and that normally do not disappear as the child grows older.

11. Describe the procedures that are major causes for each of the emotions of joy, anger, anxiety, and relief.
12. In a sentence for each, summarize three important components that make up our emotions, and name the type of conditioning involved in each component.

Respondent and Operant Components of Thinking

Like emotions, much of what we call "thinking" in everyday language involves both respondent and operant conditioning.

A Respondent Component: Our Imagery

Try the following exercise. Close your eyes and imagine that you are looking at the flag of your country. **NOTE 1** Chances are that you will be able to form a clear image of the flag. Thus, one type of thinking appears to consist of imagining in response to words—imagining so vividly that it can sometimes seem like the real thing. This probably comes about through respondent conditioning. If you actually look at your country's flag, the sight of the flag elicits activity in the visual system much as food elicited salivation in Pavlov's dogs. If you grew up in an English-speaking country, you experienced many trials in which the words "our flag" were paired with actually looking at the flag. As a consequence, when you close your eyes and imagine the flag, the words likely elicit activity in the visual part of your brain so that you experience the behavior of "seeing" the actual flag. This has been referred to as *conditioned seeing* (Skinner, 1953; see Figure 15.5).

In a broader sense, we might think of conditioned sensing. That is, just as we acquire conditioned seeing through experience, we also acquire conditioned hearing, conditioned smelling, and conditioned feeling. Consider the example described by Martin and Osborne (1993) in which an individual experienced numerous passionate sexual encounters with a partner who consistently used a distinctive perfume. One day when someone wearing that same perfume walked past that individual in a department store, he immediately imagined seeing the partner (conditioned seeing), felt "tingly" all over (conditioned feeling, an emotional response), and even imagined that he heard the partner's voice (conditioned hearing). This sort of thing is also a part of what goes on during fantasy (Malott & Whaley, 1983). To experience a fantasy or to read or listen to a story is, in some sense, to be there. It's as though you can see what the people in the story see, feel what they feel, and hear what they hear. We are able to do this because of many instances of conditioned sensing. Our long histories of associating words with actual sights, sounds, smells, and feelings enable us to experience the scenes that an author's words describe. The internal actions that occur when we're thinking are real—we're really seeing, feeling, or hearing when we respond to the words (Malott & Whaley, 1983; Pear, 2001, pp. 108–109). This is not to say that everyone experiences the same conditioned sensory responses; they are undoubtedly unique to each individual.

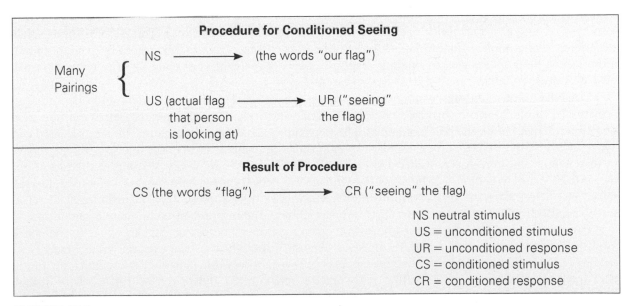

FIGURE 15.5
An example of conditioned seeing (or conditioned imagining)

An Operant Component: Our Self-Talk

Imagining (conditioned seeing) constitutes one type of thinking. Another type of thinking is self-directed verbal behavior, or self-talk. As we indicated in earlier chapters, our verbal behavior is taught to us by others through operant conditioning. We learn to speak because of effective consequences for doing so. As children, we learn to ask for such things as our favorite foods and the opportunity to watch our favorite cartoons. We also learn to say things that please our parents and other adults. Much of our thinking is private verbal behavior. We learn to think out loud as children because it helps us to perform tasks more efficiently (Roberts, 1979). When children first start attending school, they often say rules out loud to themselves to adjust to difficult tasks (Roberts & Tharp, 1980). When they are about 5 or 6 years old, however, they also begin to engage in subvocal speech in the sense that their self-talk begins to occur below the spoken level (Vygotsky, 1978).

We learn to talk silently to ourselves at a very early age largely because we encounter punishers when we think out loud (Skinner, 1957). For example, teachers in school request children to think quietly because thinking out loud disturbs the other students. Naturally distressed reactions from others teach us to keep certain thoughts to ourselves. When you are introduced to the hostess at a party, your first reaction might be, "Wow, what an ugly dress!" But you probably won't say it out loud; instead, you'll just "say it to yourself" or "think" it. (Other reasons for silent self-talk are that it requires less effort and can occur more rapidly than overt self-talk.)

Private Thoughts and Feelings: More Respondent–Operant Interactions

Much of what we call "thinking" and "feeling" in everyday life goes on at a level that is not observable by others. As indicated in Chapter 1, we refer to such activity as *covert* or *private*. Although private behavior is more difficult to "get at," behavior modifiers assume that in other respects it is the same as public behavior; that is, that the principles and procedures of operant and respondent conditioning apply to private behavior.

Often an instance of what we would refer to as private behavior includes both respondent and operant components of thinking and emotions. To illustrate, consider the following example (described by Martin & Osborne, 1993). One of the authors grew up on a farm just outside a small town in Manitoba, Canada. He attended school in the town, and it was very important to him to be accepted by the town children. Wilf, one of the town kids, frequently teased him about being a "farmer." "Hey, gang," Wilf would say, "Here comes Garry the farmer. Hey, Garry, do you have cow dung on your boots?" Now imagine that it's Saturday afternoon and Garry and his family are getting ready to go to town. Garry is going to the afternoon matinee at the Roxy Theatre with his friends, which is a big deal because they didn't have TV on the farm. Garry says to himself, "I wonder if Wilf will be there" (operant thinking). Garry can picture Wilf clearly (conditioned seeing) and can imagine Wilf teasing him about being a farmer (both operant thinking and conditioned hearing). Thoughts of the aversive experience elicit unpleasant feelings (a reflexively learned response). Garry reacts by paying special attention to his appearance (an operant response) in the hope that appearing like the town kids will give Wilf nothing to say.

Consider some additional examples of private behavior that involve respondent and operant components of thinking and emotions. Imagine a lineman in football preparing to go after the opposing quarterback just before the ball is snapped. The lineman thinks, "I'm all over him! I'll tear his head off! This guy is history!" That kind of self-talk (operant thinking) is likely to help the lineman feel aggressive (a respondent emotion). Or consider a sprinter who thinks "explode" while waiting in the blocks for the starter's pistol to sound; or a figure skater who says to herself during her program, "Graceful, feel the music" to help create the proper mood for the music and the choreography. In instances like these, the operant self-talk serves as a CS to elicit certain feelings—the respondent component of emotions.

You can see that, contrary to the impression given by some introductory psychology texts, behavior modifiers do not ignore what goes on inside a person. Although it is true that the great majority of studies in behavior modification have been concerned with observable behavior, many behavior modifiers have taken an interest in dealing with private behavior. As illustrated by the work of Joseph Cautela and his colleagues, thinking and feeling as private behaviors are proper subject matter for behavior modifiers and can be readily dealt with in terms of operant and respondent conditioning principles (e.g., Cautela & Kearney, 1993). In Chapters 27 and 28, we'll describe behavioral strategies for overcoming troublesome thoughts and feelings. (For a debate on the role of private events in a science of behavior, see *The Behavior Analyst*, 2011, Number 2.—which can be freely downloaded from http://www.ncbi.nlm.nih.gov/pmc/issues/202234/)

Questions for Learning

13. Give an example of respondent thinking involving visual imagery that is not in this chapter.
14. Give an example of operant thinking that is not in this chapter.
15. When behavior modifiers speak of private behavior, to what are they referring?
16. What basic assumption do the authors of this text make about public and private behavior?
17. Give an example, which is not discussed in this chapter, that illustrates how operant thinking might function as a CS to elicit the respondent component of an emotion.
18. Discuss whether behavior modifiers deny the existence and importance of thoughts and feelings.

Application Exercises

A. Exercise Involving Others

Pick an emotion (e.g., anger), and observe the operant displays of that emotion in two people you know. Are their operant components of that emotion similar or different?

B. Self-Modification Exercise

Consider an emotion that you frequently experience. Describe how experiencing that emotion includes both respondent and operant responses.

Note for Further Learning

1. A number of behavioral techniques rely on imagery. One such technique is called *covert sensitization* (Cautela, 1966), which is essentially a form of aversion therapy in which a troublesome reinforcer is paired repeatedly with an aversive stimulus. Recall from Chapter 3 that aversion therapy is based on counterconditioning—it is assumed that the troublesome reinforcer will become less reinforcing because it will come to elicit a response similar to that elicited by the aversive stimulus. In covert sensitization, the client imagines both the troublesome reinforcer and the aversive stimulus. This procedure is so named because the pairing of the stimuli occurs only in the client's imagination (in other words, it is covert) and the anticipated result of this covert pairing process is that the undesirable reinforcer becomes aversive (i.e., the client becomes sensitized to it).

   The procedure has been used with clients who wish to give up smoking, as described by Irey (1972). During a particular trial, the client might be instructed to vividly imagine lighting a cigarette after dinner in a restaurant, inhaling, and then suddenly becoming so violently ill that he vomits all over his hands, his clothes, the tablecloth, and the other people at the table. He continues to vomit and then, when his stomach is empty, to gag while the other people in the restaurant stare at him in disgust. In short, the scene is made extremely realistic and aversive. When the client feels the maximum degree of aversiveness, he is instructed to imagine turning away from his cigarette and immediately beginning to feel better. The scene concludes with the client washing up in the bathroom without his cigarettes and feeling tremendous relief. Research on covert sensitization can be found in Cautela and Kearney (1993).

Questions for Further Learning

1. What is the rationale of covert sensitization?
2. Describe in some detail a plausible example of covert sensitization.

CHAPTER 16

Transferring Behavior to New Settings and Making It Last: Generality of Behavioral Change

LEARNING OBJECTIVES

After studying this chapter, you will be able to:

- Identify the different types of generality.
- Summarize guidelines for programming generality of behavior change.

- Explain how generality can work to the disadvantage of those who are ignorant of it.

My orals are in two weeks. How should I prepare?

Helping Carole Have a Successful Class Presentation[1]

Carole was in the last year of her BA Honors degree in psychology at the University of Manitoba. Like all such students, she had to give an oral presentation of her honors thesis research to the Honors Seminar Instructor and to the rest of the class. Carole had already prepared a detailed outline of her 15-minute presentation, including PowerPoint slides, and had timed it while giving a mock presentation in front of the mirror in her bedroom. However, because she had received a low mark on the oral presentation of her thesis proposal earlier in the year, she was stressed about the possibility of receiving another low mark. She asked her thesis advisor for some preparation suggestions.

After some discussion, Carole, who had previously taken a course in sport psychology, decided to use a practice strategy commonly used by athletes when practicing to prepare for an important competition. The strategy involves using imagery at practices to simulate aspects of the environment that will be encountered at the competition. A golfer, for example, while on the driving range, might imagine all 18 holes of a course that she will play in a golf tournament. Assuming that the golfer is familiar with the course layout, she could pretend to play each hole at the driving range. For each shot on a hole, she could visualize the trees, sand traps, and so forth for that hole, and then hit the shot (at the driving range) that she wants to play on that particular hole. This type of simulation strategy has been used by athletes to increase the chances that successful practice performance will transfer to the setting of the competition.

In order to implement the above strategy, Carole booked the classroom where her presentation would occur so that she could practice it by doing some run-throughs. Before each run-through she sat in a chair in the classroom and visualized other students from the class and the Honors Seminar Instructor sitting in the room. She imagined the instructor calling her name and stating the title of her

---

[1] This case is based on a report from a student of one of the authors.

presentation. She then walked to the podium on which she had previously placed the laptop containing her PowerPoint slides, faced the imaginary audience, imagined making eye contact with the instructor, and then began the practice of her presentation. While practicing her presentation she made frequent imaginary eye contact with the members of the audience, appropriately used the laser pointer to guide the attention of the audience to aspects of her slides, talked at a reasonable rate, and imagined support-ive head nods from her classmates who were also her friends. When she said "thank you" at the end of her presentation, she imagined the audience giving her enthusiastic applause.

During the 2 weeks leading up to Carole's presentation she did three of the above practice sessions. By the end of the third practice session, her confidence had improved considerably. On the day of her presentation she behaved very similarly to her last practice session, received enthusiastic applause from the audience, and obtained a high mark.

Generality

In discussing cases like that of Carole we are concerned with two types of situations: (a) the *train-ing* situation(s)—the setting(s) in which the behavior is initially strengthened; and (b) the *target* situation(s)—the setting(s) in which we want the behavior to occur. For Carole, the training situations were her bedroom in front of a mirror and the empty classroom. The target situation was the classroom with the audience consisting of the instructor and the other students. A behavior change is said to have *generality* to the extent that the following occur:

(a) *stimulus generalization*: the trained behavior transfers from the training situation(s) to the target situation(s) (which is usually the natural environment)
(b) *response generalization*: training leads to the development of new behavior that has not been specifi-cally trained
(c) *behavior maintenance*: the trained behavior persists in the target situation(s) over time (Baer, Wolf, & Risley, 1968).

It should be noted that the term *situation* in "training situation" and "target situation" may refer to particular stimuli or to particular settings, or to both. For example, in teaching reading, after a child learns to read one passage (a training situation) we would want him or her to be able to read untrained passages (test situations). Similarly, after a child has learned to read in a classroom (a training situation) we would want him or her to be able to read at home (a target situation).

Because programming for generality is somewhat different for operant and respondent behavior, we shall consider each separately.

Programming Generality of Operant Behavior

Programming for generality of operant behavior change includes strategies of programming for stimulus generalization, response generalization, and behavior maintenance.

Programming Operant Stimulus Generalization

As discussed in Chapter 9, *stimulus generalization* refers to the *procedure* of reinforcing a response in the presence of a stimulus or situation, and the *effect* of the response becoming more probable **NOTE 1** in the presence of another stimulus or situation. The more similar the training and target situations are, the more stimulus generalization there will be between them. There are four main strategies for programming operant stimulus generalization.

Train in the Target Situation   The first effort of the behavior modifier attempting to program stimulus generalization should be to make the final stages of the training situation similar to the target situation in as many ways as possible. Other things being equal, the best way in which to do this is to train in the target situation itself. In the lead case in this chapter, Carole was able to practice her speech in an approximation of the target situation by practicing in the same room where her presentation was to be held, and by imagining the audience and conditions that would occur.

For another example, Koegel, Kuriakose, Singh, and Koegel (2012) wanted to teach children with autism to engage in appropriate social play during recess on a school playground with typically developing children. Therefore, the behavior modifier conducted training during recess on the playground and initiated the interactions of the children and reinforced social play. During the target situation, the behavior modifier was not present on the playground. Nevertheless, the children with autism continued to initiate social play with the normally developing children. Although there is evidence that the children with autism generalized social play with the other children to the recess periods when the behavior modifier was not present, the researchers did not examine if long-term maintenance of this behavior occurred.

Vary the Training Conditions   If behaviors are brought under the control of a wide variety of stimuli during training, then the probability of some of those stimuli being present in the target situation, and therefore the probability of generalization, increases. For example, a golfer who practices making putts when it is cold, windy, hot, calm, or noisy is more likely to make putts during an actual competition if one or more of those conditions are encountered.

Program Common Stimuli   A third tactic is to program common stimuli deliberately by developing the behavior to specific stimuli that are present in the training settings, and then ensuring that those stimuli are in the target settings. For example, Walker and Buckley (1972) described a program in which social and academic classroom behaviors were taught to children in a remedial classroom. Stimulus generalization to the regular academic classroom was ensured by using the same academic materials in both classrooms. As another example, Bergstrom, Najdowski, and Tarbox (2012) developed a training package for teaching children with autism to seek help from store employees (the common stimuli) when lost in a retail store. During training, the children learned to seek help from employees in one or more actual retail stores—Target, Walmart, and Best Buy. Results showed that the children's' help-seeking behavior generalized to employees in stores in which they were not trained to seek help.

A useful strategy for programming common stimuli is to bring the desired behavior under the control of instructions or rules that an individual can rehearse in novel situations (Guevremont, Osnes, & Stokes, 1986; Lima & Abreu-Rodrigues, 2010; Stokes & Osnes, 1989). When this occurs, the individual is said to be using a self-mediated physical or verbal stimulus. For example, Lima and Abreu-Rodrigues (2010) showed that reinforcing self-mediated verbal-stimuli can be used successfully with 3- to 5-year-old children in what is called *correspondence training*. In this training, the children were taught to do what they said they were going to do (e.g., play with a specific toy) at a later time. Lima and Abreu-Rodrigues found that the children learned to do this more effectively if they repeated saying what they were going to do during the interval before they were to perform the behavior. In addition, the behavior of repeated statements to themselves about what they were going to do and doing it generalized to other statements that the children made regarding what they were going to do at a later time. As another example, Martin (2015) described how a young figure skater used a self-mediated verbal stimulus to transfer skilled skating performance from practices to competitions. The young skater was able to land her double axel consistently at practices but often missed it at competitions because the jump was rushed in the excitement of the moment. To solve the problem, she inserted into her routine the word *easy* (said very slowly and stretched out) just before stepping onto her takeoff foot as a prompt to control the speed of the takeoff. Using this key word consistently at practices and then at competitions improved her execution during competitions. (Rule control over behavior is discussed further in Chapter 17.)

Train Sufficient Stimulus Exemplars   As discussed in Chapter 9, a common-element stimulus class is a set of stimuli that have some physical characteristic in common. A common-element stimulus class (e.g., dogs) is likely to have many members (e.g., many varieties of dogs). The members of a common-element stimulus class are often referred to as exemplars of that class. A generalization tactic which Stokes and Baer (1977) considered to be one of the most valuable for programming generality is called *training sufficient stimulus exemplars*. For example, if a child is taught to say "dog" when viewing several exemplars of dogs, then the child is likely to generalize and refer to any variety of dog as a "dog." Another example is teaching children with autism to share some desirable items within a given category (e.g., art, snacks, toys) and finding that the children will share other items within the same category. Thus, children who are taught to share crayons, dot paint, and markers will more likely share colored pencils (e.g., Marzullo-Kerth, Reeve, Reeve, & Townsend, 2011). A further example comes from teaching children to read. Silber and Martens (2010) obtained evidence that an efficient way to teach children a long passage with a high degree of accuracy is to teach them to read a number of short passages that, in total, contain the same words as the larger passage.

Horner and colleagues described a variation of training sufficient stimulus exemplars that they referred to as *general case programming* (Horner, 2005; Horner, Sprague, & Wilcox, 1982). With this approach, the teacher begins by identifying the range of relevant stimulus situations to which a learner will be expected to respond and the response variations that might be required. Then, during training, the learner's behavior and acceptable variations are brought under the control of samples of the range of relevant stimuli. Sprague and Horner (1984) used this approach to teach adolescents with developmental disabilities to use vending machines by introducing them to a variety of different machines and the responses needed to use them. This approach was effective in producing generalization to enable the learners to subsequently operate any available vending machine with which they came in contact.

Questions for Learning

1. When discussing programming of generality of behavior, what do we mean by the training situation versus the target situation?
2. When is a behavior change said to have generality?
3. Briefly describe how Carole's honors presentation demonstrated behavioral generality.
4. Define stimulus generalization, and give an example that is not in this chapter.
5. List four tactics for programming operant stimulus generalization. Give an example of each.
6. How might the teaching of a rule facilitate operant stimulus generalization? State the general factor for programming for generalization that seems to be operating, and illustrate with an example.
7. Describe the example of a self-generated mediator of generalization involving the figure skater.
8. Describe the generalization strategy referred to as *general case programming*. Give an example.

Programming Operant Response Generalization

Response generalization refers to the *procedure* of reinforcing a response in the presence of a stimulus or situation, and the *effect* of another response becoming more probable in the presence of that or similar stimuli or situations.

An example of response generalization in an applied setting was described by DeRiso and Ludwig (2012). The employees in a restaurant were shown a poster for performing cleaning and restocking tasks in the dining and kitchen areas, and when they performed those tasks they were reinforced by seeing check marks by their names on a performance feedback chart. This resulted in a substantial increase in the targeted behaviors. Bathroom cleaning and restocking were not targeted in this study. Nevertheless, these behaviors also increased when the targeted behaviors increased (DeRiso and Ludwig, 2012).

Response generalization occurs for several reasons. First, the more physically similar two responses are, the more unlearned response generalization will occur between them. If you learn a forehand shot in racquetball, chances are that you would be able to perform a forehand shot in squash or tennis. The responses involved are very similar.

Second, learned response generalization can occur if widely different responses share a common characteristic. For example, a child who has learned to add *s* to the ends of words pertaining to more than one object or event may show response generalization even when it is grammatically incorrect (e.g., saying "foots" instead of "feet" while looking at a picture of two feet).   **NOTE 2**

Third, an individual might show response generalization because he or she has learned functionally equivalent responses to a stimulus (i.e., responses that produce the same consequences). If you are asked to start a fire, you might use a match or a cigarette lighter, lite a stick from an existing fire, or perhaps even rub two sticks together. As another example, a child who learns to "be honest" might tell the truth, return articles left or dropped by others, and refrain from copying another student's answers. All of these "honest" responses are functionally equivalent in the sense that they are likely to bring praise from various members of the child's community.

It appears that there has been less concern in the literature for programming response generalization than for programming stimulus generalization. Nevertheless, there are some strategies for programming response generalization, three of which are described next.

Train Sufficient Response Exemplars   A strategy for programming response generalization is similar to that of training sufficient stimulus exemplars to establish stimulus generalization. This is referred to as *training sufficient response exemplars* (Stokes & Baer, 1977). Guess, Sailor, Rutherford, and Baer (1968) taught a girl with a developmental disability to use plural nouns correctly in speech with this technique. With prompting and reinforcement, they first taught the girl to name objects correctly in the singular and the plural when presented with one object (e.g., cup) and two objects (e.g., cups). They continued in this way until, after a number of exemplars of the correct singular and plural labels had been taught, the girl appropriately named new objects in the plural even though only the singular labels for these objects had been taught. Thus, the girl showed response generalization. As another example, in the study described previously on teaching children with autism to share, each child was taught several verbal responses (exemplars) to use when initiating sharing. As a result, the children also responded with verbal sharing responses that they had not been taught. Thus, a child who was taught to say "Do you want to try this?" "Would you like to try?" and "Here, you try it" when offering to share items such as colored pencils would occasionally say "Would you like to draw," which he had not been taught to say (Marzullo-Kerth et al., 2011).

Vary the Acceptable Responses During Training   Another strategy is to vary the responses that are acceptable during training. For example, in developing creativity, Goetz and Baer (1973) reinforced children during block building in a nursery school setting for any response that was different from prior block-building responses. This tactic led to an increase in the children's creative block building. Since Goetz and Baer's study, others (e.g., Esch, Esch, & Love, 2009, Miller & Neuringer, 2000) have shown that reinforcing variability in children can lead to new responses that are then available for reinforcement if they should turn out to be useful (i.e., "creative"). In addition, a number of studies have shown that simply reinforcing behavior on certain intermittent reinforcement schedules (e.g., FR or FI schedules, as opposed to CRF) can lead to variability in responding (i.e., increased response generalization), which in turn can potentially give rise to creativity (see Lee, Sturmey, & Fields, 2007).

Capitalize on Behavioral Momentum   A third strategy for programming response generalization is to capitalize on *behavioral momentum,* which is analogous to the concept of momentum in physics (e.g., Dube, Ahearn, Lionello-DeNolf, & McIlvane, 2009; Nevin & Grace, 2000; Nevin & Shahan, 2011; Nevin & Wacker, 2013). Essentially, the theory of behavioral momentum states that once a behavior is initiated in the presence of a specific stimulus and is occurring at a high rate in the presence of that stimulus, that behavior and similar behaviors will tend to occur at a high rate in the presence of that stimulus unless some disrupting influence (e.g., a distracting stimulus, the onset of extinction) occurs. Consider the problem of overcoming noncompliance with children. Compliance with instructions can include a variety of functionally equivalent or similar responses. To increase the probability that a child will follow instructions that the he or she normally does not follow, it is often effective to start by repeatedly giving instructions that the child is likely to follow and to reinforce compliance with those instructions. This gets compliance started, whereas it may not have started if the teacher had begun with instructions that the child was less likely to follow. If instructions that the child is less likely to follow are then given soon after this, the chances are greatly increased that the child will follow them (Mace & Belfiore, 1990; Mace et al., 1988; Singer, Singer, & Horner, 1987). In other words, like a stalled car that is being pushed, once the compliance behavior gets going, it becomes easier and easier to keep it going and even to increase it with instructions that the child probably would not have followed if the teacher had started with them.

Questions for Learning

9. Define response generalization.
10. Describe an example of unlearned response generalization that is not in this chapter.
11. Give an example of learned response generalization that occurs when different responses share a common characteristic.
12. Give an example of learned response generalization due to functionally equivalent responses.
13. List three tactics for programming operant response generalization. Give an example of each.
14. What is the meaning of the term *behavioral momentum*? Give an example.

Programming Operant Behavior Maintenance

It is one thing to program stimulus generalization to a new setting or response generalization for new behaviors. It's another thing for a therapeutic behavioral change to last in those new settings or with those new behaviors. Maintenance depends critically on whether the behavior will continue to be reinforced. There are four general approaches to the problem of achieving behavior maintenance.

Use Behavioral Trapping: Allow Natural Contingencies of Reinforcement to Take Effect   A *behavioral trap* is a contingency in which a behavior that has been developed by programmed reinforcers is "trapped" or maintained by natural reinforcers (Baer & Wolf, 1970; Kohler & Greenwood, 1986). Using a behavioral trap can be a very effective way to program behavior maintenance. This approach requires the behavior modifier to realistically identify contingencies in the natural environment and then to tailor the target behavior so that it will be trapped by those contingencies. Talking is an obvious example of behavior that is heavily reinforced in most social environments. After speech has been established in a training situation, it may continue unabated in the natural environment because of the natural contingencies of reinforcement for it there. Indeed, it often seems necessary only to establish vocal imitation and a few object-naming responses for the natural contingencies of reinforcement to take over and develop functional speech behavior. Behavioral trapping might be involved in overcoming a child's shyness. Playing with other children is a behavior that might gradually be shaped in a shy child. Once this behavior is strongly established, however, the behavior modifier probably will not have to worry about reinforcing it further. The other children will take care of that in the course of their play, for, indeed, that is what social play is all about. Reading is a behavior that, once established, is clearly trapped because of the many reinforcers that it makes available to the individual who can read. Exercising is another example of a behavior that, once established, can be maintained because of the positive benefits an exerciser gains from exercising, providing that the exerciser experiences those benefits. See Figure 16.1 for another example of behavioral trapping.

Behavioral trapping is highly important from an ethical or moral perspective. It has been argued that a major indicator of the social validity—that is, the importance to society—of a specific behavioral treatment is the extent to which the desirable behaviors established by that treatment are maintained in the natural environment (Kennedy, 2002a, 2002b, 2005, pp. 220–221; also see Carter, 2010, pp. 31-32, 199-200, and, Chapters 24 and 30 of this book).

Change the Behavior of People in the Natural Environment   A second approach to the problem of achieving lasting generality is usually more difficult than the first. It involves actually changing the behavior of people in the target situation so that they will maintain a learner's behavior that has generalized from the training situation. In following this approach, it is necessary to work with people in the target situation—parents, teachers, neighbors, and others—who have contact with the target behavior. The behavior modifier must teach these individuals how to reinforce the learner's behavior if it is desirable or how to extinguish it if it is undesirable. The behavior modifier must also occasionally reinforce the appropriate behavior of these individuals—at least until there is contact with the learner's improved target behavior, which will then ideally reinforce their continued application of the appropriate procedures.

An example of this approach for achieving lasting generality was described by Rice, Austin, and Gravina (2009). They worked with the manager and employees to improve customer service at a grocery store. First, the manager was taught to follow a script to teach employees correct greetings of customers and correct closings (thanking customers for their purchases). The experimenter then trained the manager to watch for a correct greeting or closing and to inconspicuously approach the employee and provide praise (e.g., "Great job on your greeting," or "That was great customer service"). Correct greetings and closings by staff greatly increased following training, and follow-up data indicated that the manager continued to maintain the desirable behavior of the staff 48 weeks following the initial training.

Use Intermittent Schedules of Reinforcement in the Target Situation   After a behavior has generalized to a target situation, it may be desirable to reinforce the behavior deliberately in the target situation on an intermittent schedule for at least a few reinforced trials. The intermittent schedule should make that behavior more persistent in the target situation and thereby increase the probability of the behavior lasting until it can come under the control of natural reinforcers. You might recall an example of this approach described in Chapter 8 involving the use of the Timer Game (also called the

FIGURE 16.1

An example of behavioral trapping

Good Behavior Game) to maintain desirable play behavior of one of the author's two boys during family car trips. On a VI/LH the timer would ring, and if the boys were playing quietly in the backseat of the car, they would earn extra TV time that evening when they arrived at the hotel. VI/LH schedules can be used effectively to maintain a variety of desirable behaviors of individuals in a variety of situations.

Give the Control to the Individual　An area within behavior modification concerns helping individuals to apply behavior modification to their own behavior. This area, which has been referred to as *self-management, self-modification,* or *behavioral self-control,* has produced many books containing easy-to-follow "how-to" procedures that help individuals manage their own behavior. This area is discussed more fully in Chapter 26. Giving control to the individual to maintain behavior in the target situation might occur in one of two major ways. First, it might be possible to teach an individual to assess and record instances of his or her own generalized behavior and apply a specific reinforcement procedure to that behavior. Second, as Stokes and Baer (1977) suggested, it might be possible to teach an individual to emit a desirable behavior and then tell someone about it in order to *recruit reinforcement* to maintain the generalized responding. For example, Hildebrand, Martin, Furer, and Hazen (1990) taught workers with developmental disabilities in a sheltered workshop to meet a productivity goal and then to call a staff member's attention to their good work. This led to increased reinforcement for the workers from the staff, which in turn helped to maintain the workers' higher level of productivity.

Questions for Learning

15. Define *behavioral trap*, and give an example.
16. Briefly describe four tactics for programming operant behavior maintenance. Give an example of each.
17. Suppose a manager at a local fast-food restaurant has encouraged staff to show frequent desirable customer service behaviors. Describe the details of a plausible VI/LH schedule that the manager might use to maintain the desirable service behaviors at a high rate.
18. What is meant by "recruitment of reinforcement"? Illustrate with an example that is not in this chapter.

Programming Generality of Respondent Behavior

Recall that in respondent conditioning, by being paired with another stimulus a neutral stimulus comes to elicit the response of that stimulus. In this way, a conditioned reflex is established in which the former neutral stimulus becomes a CS elicits the same response as the stimulus it was paired with. However, not only does the CS elicit the response; stimuli that are similar to the CS also elicit the response. For example, if a picture of a face is paired with an electric shock which elicits a fear response (a blink startle and skin conductance response), then pictures of that face will also elicit a fear response. In addition, pictures of faces similar to that face will also elicit the fear response, although not so strongly as pictures of the original face but more strongly than nonface pictures (Haddad, Pritchett, Lissek, & Lau, 2012).

As indicated previously, programming for generality of operant behavior involves strategies to bring about stimulus generalization, response generalization, and behavior maintenance. When dealing with respondent behavior, stimulus generalization is also important. When extinguishing a phobia, for example, one would not want to decrease the fear to only one specific stimulus (see Figure 16.2). For many treatments involving respondent conditioning, however, we are typically concerned primarily with maintaining the conditioned reflex over time. To see why this is so, let's review a couple of examples of respondent conditioning from Chapter 3. In that chapter, the results of a respondent conditioning program for constipation was a conditioned reflex in which a particular time of day became a CS causing a bowel movement as a CR. In each case, having the adults experience a bowel movement upon arising in the morning was desirable. Would they have wanted stimulus generalization to occur so that bowel movements were elicited at other times during the day? No, that would have been very inconvenient. Was it important to program response generalization so that a wide variety of bowel movements were elicited by the CS of a specific time of day? No, that would not have been adaptive.

Let's consider another example from Chapter 3 in which, after conditioning, pressure on a child's bladder in the middle of the night became a CS causing awakening as a CR so that the child could subsequently go to the bathroom to urinate rather than wetting the bed. Would it have been desirable for stimulus generalization to occur so that only a slight amount of pressure would cause awakening? No—the amount of pressure just before having to urinate was the ideal CS, and that's what was trained. Was it necessary to program response generalization of awakening? No, as long as awakening occurred at the right time, the manner in which it occurred did not seem to be important. As these examples illustrate, programming stimulus and response generalization is often not of concern in behavior management programs involving conditioned reflexes.

It is important, however, that desirable conditioned reflexes be maintained over time. If a CS is presented without further pairings with a US, the CS will lose its ability to elicit the CR. Thus, in programs involving respondent conditioning, it is sometimes necessary to periodically pair the CS with the US so that the CS will continue to elicit the desired response over time.

Pitfalls of Generality

Unaware-Misapplication Pitfall

A behavior learned in a situation in which it is appropriate may show stimulus generalization to a situation in which it is inappropriate. A conspicuous example of this can often be seen among individuals with developmental disabilities involving greetings and displays of affection. Of course, it is highly desirable for these behaviors to occur under appropriate circumstances, but when an individual walks up to and hugs a total stranger, the results can be less than favorable. The solution to this problem is to teach the individual to discriminate between situations in which different forms of greetings and expressions of affection are appropriate and situations in which they are inappropriate.

FIGURE 16.2
An example of a failure to program stimulus generalization of a respondent behavior

Another example of inappropriate stimulus generalization of a desirable behavior may be the destructive competitiveness demonstrated frequently by some individuals and occasionally by all of us. Such behavior may stem in part from the strong reinforcement given in our culture for winning in sports. As the saying goes, "It may be true that wars have been won on the playing fields of Eton, but they have also been started there."

A second variety of Pitfall Type 1 is the stimulus generalization of an undesirable behavior from the situation in which it developed to a new situation for which it is also undesirable. Suppose that an overly protective grandparent while supervising a grandchild who is learning how to walk provides a great deal of attention each time the child falls. As a result, falling increases in frequency. When the child returns to the parents, the excessive falling might generalize to their presence as well.

A third variety of Pitfall Type 1 involves response generalization, the strengthening of an undesirable response that can lead to an increased frequency of similar undesirable responses. An example can be seen when a child is reinforced for emitting a swear word, perhaps by an adult who is amused by this "cute" behavior, and that child emits subsequent variations of that word.

Failure-to-Apply Pitfall

As stated in Chapter 4, some behavioral procedures aren't applied because they are complex and require specialized knowledge or training, and this is a reason why some individuals fail to program for desirable generalization. An illustration of this can be seen in the study habits of students who cram the night before an examination. They memorize certain verbal chains in response to certain prompts and questions. What they frequently fail to consider is the importance of bringing their knowledge of the material under broader stimulus control than just one or two questions. Many people have had the same experience with learning a second language. Both authors took a second language during 4 years of high school but at the end of that time were still incapable of speaking the second language. They had a certain repertoire for answering questions on exams, translating English articles into the second language, and translating articles in the second language into English, but these repertoires had not been brought under the stimulus control of a typical conversational setting.

Another example of lack of programming for stimulus generalization of desirable behaviors can be seen in the interaction between some parents and their children. In various social situations, such as restaurants, some parents do not present the same stimuli to their children, or provide the same contingencies of reinforcement, that they present at mealtimes in the home situation. Consequently, the children do not generalize table manners and good behaviors that occur at home to the restaurant or other social settings. It is not uncommon to hear a parent lament, "I thought I taught you how act appropriately at the table." We hope that after reading this book and performing the study questions and study exercises, the same parents would do a much better job of programming stimulus generalization. If not, you would hear us lament, "We thought we taught you how to be a good behavior modifier!"

The pitfalls for programming maintenance of behavior change concerning schedules of reinforcement were described in Chapters 8 and 12.

Guidelines for Programming Generality of Operant Behavior

To ensure stimulus and response generalization from the training situation to the natural environment and to ensure behavior maintenance, the behavior modifier should observe the following rules as closely as possible:

1. Choose target behaviors that are clearly useful to the learner because these are the behaviors that are most likely to be reinforced in the natural environment.
2. Teach the target behavior in a situation that is as similar as possible to the environment in which you want the behavior to occur.
3. Vary the training conditions to maximally sample relevant stimulus dimensions for transfer to other situations and to reinforce various forms of the desirable behavior.
4. Establish the target behavior successively in as many situations as is feasible, starting with the easiest and progressing to the most difficult.
5. Program common stimuli (such as rules) that might facilitate transfer to novel environments.
6. Vary the acceptable responses in the training settings.
7. Gradually reduce the frequency of reinforcement in the training situation until it is less than that occurring in the natural environment.
8. When changing to a new situation, increase the frequency of reinforcement in that situation to offset the tendency of the learner to discriminate the new situation from the training situation.
9. Ensure sufficient reinforcement for maintaining the target behavior in the natural environment. This rule requires especially close attention in the early stages of transferring the target behavior from the training situation to the natural environment. Add reinforcement as necessary, including reinforcement to those (such as parents and teachers) who are responsible for maintaining the target behavior in the natural environment, and then decrease this reinforcement slowly enough to prevent the target behavior from deteriorating.

Questions for Learning

19. Briefly explain why considerations regarding generality of respondent behavior differ from those regarding operant behavior.

20. Give two examples of the Unaware-Misapplication Pitfall involving stimulus generalization; (a) one of which involves generalization of a desirable behavior to an inappropriate situation; and (b) the other of which involves generalization of an undesirable behavior.
21. Give an example of the Unaware-Misapplication Pitfall involving response generalization.
22. State the Failure-to-Apply Pitfall, and give an example of it that involves failure to program for desirable generalization.

Application Exercises

A. Exercise Involving Others

Choose one of the cases described in the previous chapters in which there was no effort to program generality. Outline a specific plausible program for producing generality in that case.

B. Self-Modification Exercises

1. Describe a recent situation in which you generalized in a desirable way. Clearly identify the behavior, the training situation (in which the behavior was initially reinforced), and the test situation (to which the behavior generalized).
2. Describe a recent situation in which you generalized in an undesirable way (in other words, the outcome was undesirable). Again, identify the behavior, training situation, and test situation.
3. Consider the behavior deficit for which you outlined a shaping program at the end of Chapter 7. Assuming that your shaping program will be successful, discuss what you might do to program generality. (See the factors influencing the effectiveness of generality that were discussed in this chapter.)

Notes for Further Learning

1. In a study by Welch and Pear (1980), objects, pictures of the objects, and photographs of the objects were compared as training stimuli for naming responses in four children with severe developmental disabilities in a special training room. It was found that three of the four children displayed considerably more generalization to the objects in their natural environment when they were trained with the objects rather than the pictures or photographs of the objects. The fourth child, who was also the most proficient linguistically, displayed substantial generalization regardless of the type of training stimulus used. A follow-up study by Salmon, Pear, and Kuhn (1986) indicates that training with objects also produces more generalization to untrained objects in the same stimulus class than does training with pictures. The results suggest that parents and teachers of children with severe developmental disabilities should use objects as training stimuli as much as possible whenever generalization to those objects is desired.
2. This instance of response generalization is somewhat more complex than our straightforward definition given at the beginning of this chapter. It does appear, in this example, that the reinforcement of a specific response has increased the probability of similar responses. The new form of the response (the plural for a new object), however, is also occurring to a new stimulus (the plurality of the new object itself). Thus, stimulus generalization is also involved. For a discussion of difficulties in defining response generalization, see the *Journal of Organizational Behavior Management,* 2001, 21(4).

Question for Further Learning

1. What rule for programming stimulus generalization is exemplified by the study in which object and picture names were taught to children with developmental disabilities? Explain.

CHAPTER 17

Antecedent Control:
Rules and Goals

LEARNING OBJECTIVES

After studying this chapter, you will be able to:

- Define *contingency-shaped behavior* and *rule-governed behavior*.
- Describe the differences between rule-governed and contingency-shaped behavior.
- Summarize strategies for effectively using rules to influence behavior.

- Discuss how goals capitalize on rule-governed behavior.
- Summarize strategies for effectively using goal setting to influence behavior.

What if I don't skate well?

Helping Susan to Skate Well[1]

Susan, a 12-year-old figure skater competing in the novice category, was standing beside her sport psychologist and coach just off the ice surface, waiting for her turn to skate her short program in the Provincial Figure Skating Championship. Showing signs of extreme nervousness, Susan turned to her sport psychologist and expressed her concerns: "I hope I don't fall on my double axel. I hope I don't come in last. What if I don't skate well?" Her sport psychologist could see that Susan's negative self-talk was causing her to feel anxious, and her anxiety was likely to interfere with her skating well. But there was no time to go through a lengthy behavior modification program. The psychologist said to Susan, "I want you to repeat after me, and focus on what it is that you are saying: 'I've landed all of my jumps in practice and I can land them all here.'" Susan repeated the words. "If I take it one step at a time, and if I focus on the things that I do when I'm skating well at practices, I will skate well here." Again, Susan repeated the words. "I'll smile, have fun, and play to the judges." After Susan repeated the last statement, her psychologist asked her to practice a relaxation technique called deep-center breathing, in which she breathed low down in her abdomen, and quietly said "r-e-l-a-x" each time she exhaled. The combination of positive self-talk and deep-center breathing helped Susan to feel considerably calmer and more confident. At that moment, the skater before her finished skating her program. Shortly thereafter Susan stepped on the ice, skated to her start position, and performed well.

---

[1] This case is based on Martin and Toogood (1997).

Antecedent Control

Because our behavior of responding to various antecedent stimuli (people, places, words, smells, sounds, etc.) has been reinforced, punished, or extinguished, those stimuli exert control over our behavior whenever they occur. Before designing a lengthy behavior modification program involving procedures like shaping and chaining, it's important to ask, "Can I capitalize on existing forms of stimulus control?" Susan's sport psychologist did not go through a lengthy shaping process. Instead, the psychologist capitalized on Susan's reinforcement history of responding to instructions. Treatment packages that focus on the manipulation of antecedent stimuli—also called *antecedents*—fall into the categories of rules, goals, modeling, physical guidance, situational inducement, and motivation. We discuss the first two categories in this chapter and the others in the next two chapters. (For additional discussion of antecedent interventions for problem behavior, see Smith, 2011.)

Rules

In behavioral terminology, a **rule** describes a *situation* in which a *behavior* will lead to a *consequence*. Speaking loosely, it is a statement that a specific behavior will "pay off" or have a bad outcome in a particular situation. When we were infants, rules were meaningless. As we grew older, we learned that following rules often led to rewards (e.g., "If you eat all your vegetables, you can have dessert.") or enabled us to avoid punishers (e.g., "If you're not quiet, I'll send you to your room."). Thus, a rule can function as an S^D—a cue that emitting the behavior specified by the rule will lead to the reinforcer identified in the rule, or a cue that not following the rule will lead to a punisher (Skinner, 1969; Tarbox, Zuckerman, Bishop, Olive, & O'Hora, 2011; Vaughan, 1989). (As described in the next section and in Chapter 19, rules can also function as motivating operations.)

Sometimes rules clearly identify reinforcers or punishers associated with the rules, as illustrated in the foregoing examples. In other cases, consequences are implied. A parent saying to a child in an excited voice, "Wow! Look at that!" looking in the indicated direction will likely enable the child to see something interesting. Reinforcers are also implied for rules stated in the form of advice. For example, the advice "You should get a good education" typically implies that doing so will lead to favorable consequences such as a well-paying job. On the other hand, rules given in the form of a command or a threat imply that noncompliance will be punished. For example, the command "Don't touch that vase" implies that touching it will lead to an unpleasantness such as a reprimand.

Rules that do not identify all three aspects of a contingency of reinforcement are referred to as *partial rules*. The examples of partial rules in the preceding paragraph focused on the behavior. Other partial rules identify the antecedent (school zone sign) while the behavior (drive slowly) and the consequence (avoid hitting a child or getting a ticket) are implied. In other instances, partial rules identify the consequences (e.g., "98% payout") while the antecedent ("at this casino") and the behavior (put money in the slot machines) are implied. Because of our various learning experiences, partial rules also control our behavior.

Contingency-Shaped Versus Rule-Governed Behavior

As stated in the above discussion, in behavioral terminology, rules are verbal stimuli that control behavior because they specify consequences of specific behavior in specific situations. However, not all consequnces of behavior in specific situations have descriptive verbal stimuli associated with them. While attending church with his parents, Bobby whispers funny comments to his sister. She ignores him and his mom gives him a firm look. In the future, Bobby is less likely to whisper comments in church, even though no one taught him the rule "Don't whisper comments in church or Mom will give you a firm look." Now suppose that Bobby whispers funny comments to his teammates on the pee-wee hockey team while his coach is trying to explain how to execute a play. Bobby's teammates laugh, and his whispering is strengthened in that setting, even though no one taught him the rule "If I whisper funny comments to my teammates while the coach is talking they will laugh." In these examples, we would refer to Bobby's whispering as **contingency-shaped behavior**—behavior that develops because of its immediate consequences rather than because of a specific statement or rule. Suppose at the start of the next practice, Bobby's coach says, "Bobby, if you listen carefully and don't whisper when I'm talking to the team, we'll have an extra 5 minutes of scrimmage at the end of practice." During the practice, Bobby frequently repeats the rule, makes it through the practice without whispering, and earns the reinforcer. In this example, listening attentively without whispering while the coach is talking to the team is **rule-governed behavior**—behavior controlled by the statement of a rule.

Contingency-shaped behavior involves immediate consequences and is typically strengthened gradually through "trial and error"—or, to be more precise, through immediate reinforcement and nonreinforcement. Bobby's whispering initially came under the control of his teammates as S^D s through several trials involving immediate reinforcement for whispering and nonreinforcement for other behavior. His whispering in church gradually decreased in the presence of his sister and parents as S^Δ s after several trials of extinction in their presence. Rule-governed behavior, in contrast, often involves delayed consequences and frequently leads to immediate behavior change. When Bobby's coach gave him a rule concerning not whispering at practices, Bobby's behavior improved immediately. It did not take a few trials to show evidence of stimulus control, even though the reinforcer for following the rule was delayed until the end of practice.

Knowledge of rule-governed behavior enables us to more fully explain some applications we presented earlier that involved indirect effects of reinforcers. Recall the case of Tommy's classroom talk-outs at the beginning of Chapter 12. When Tommy was told that he would be allowed 5 minutes of free play time near the end of the day if he had made three or fewer talk-outs at the end of the 50-minute class, he never again exceeded the upper limit of three talk-outs per class. This was not an example of the direct effects of reinforcement because the reinforcer of extra playtime occurred well after the behavior of working quietly and not talking out. Instead, it was likely Tommy's reversal of a rule (e.g., "If I don't talk out, I am going to have lots of fun with my extra play time") that controlled his behavior of working quietly during the class.

In the discussion of correspondence training in Chapter 16, we noted that studies showed that children who said what they were going to do at a later time were more likely to do it if they said what they were going to do during the delay. Similarly, a number of studies have found that children will choose a delayed large reinforcer over an immediate small reinforcer if they are trained to make repeat rules to themselves regarding the value of waiting during the delay, such as "It is good if I wait" (e.g., Anderson, 1978; Binder, Dixon, & Ghezzi, 2000; Grey, Healy, Leader, & Hayes, 2009; Hanley, Heal, Tiger, & Ingvarsson, 2007; Vollmer, Borrero, Lalli, & Daniel, 1999). In one study that did not obtain this result, the children may not have repeated the rule sufficiently during the delay (Newquist, Dozier, & Neidert, 2012).

Often behavior that might seem to be strengthened by the direct effects of reinforcement is also the result of rule-governed behavior. For example, the child who has just cleaned her room and is told, "Good girl for cleaning your room," might tend to engage in this behavior more frequently. The stimulus "Good girl for cleaning your room" seems to be acting as a reinforcer in this instance. But the child has also been given a rule—namely, "If I clean my room, I'll be a good girl"—which tends to exert rule-governed control over the room-cleaning behavior in the future quite apart from the reinforcing effect of praise. This is one of the reasons that *descriptive praise* ("Good girl for cleaning your room")—that is, praise that describes the specific behavior receiving the praise, also called *behavior-specific praise*—is often recommended over *general praise* ("Good girl"). However, the few studies that have compared descriptive and general praise found little or no difference in the effectiveness of these two types of praise (Polick, Carr, & Hanney, 2012; Stevens, Sidener, Reeve, & Sidener, 2011). For example, Polick et al. (2012) taught two children with autism to respond to questions such as "What animal do you get milk from?" and provided either general praise (such as "Good job!" or "Great job!") or descriptive praise (such as "Great job saying 'cow'!"). Teaching efficiency was slightly better with descriptive praise, but the difference was small and there was no difference in the maintenance of responses developed by the two types of praise. Similar results were found by Stevens et al. (2011). It is possible that the children in these studies did not benefit more from descriptive praise than from general praise because they did not have the verbal skills necessary to formulate effective rules.

Questions for Learning

1. Define *rule* behaviorally and give an example that is not in this chapter.
2. Give an example of a rule that was stated by the figure skater just before competing.
3. A teacher complains to you, "When I tell the children to stay at their desks and work, they never listen to me." Describe the contingencies that are likely operating with respect to that rule given by the teacher to the kids in the class.
4. Give an example of a partial rule that is not in this chapter. What aspects of the three-term contingency does your partial rule identify? What are the missing parts that the partial rule implied?

5. Define *contingency-shaped behavior*, and give an example that is not in this chapter.
6. Define *rule-governed behavior*, and give an example that is not in this chapter.
7. Describe two common differences between rule-governed and contingency-shaped behavior.
8. Give an example of an indirect effect of a reinforcer for your behavior.

When Rules Are Especially Helpful

In several chapters, we have asserted that behavior modification programs should always include instructions in the form of rules, even with individuals with limited verbal skills. And in Chapter 30, we discuss ethical reasons why behavior modification programs should be clearly explained to all clients. However, including rules in a behavior modification program in the following situations with verbal people is especially effective (Baldwin & Baldwin, 2000; Skinner, 1969, 1974).

When Rapid Behavior Change is Desirable   Correct use of rules can often produce behavior change much more rapidly than shaping, chaining, or trial and error. The sport psychologist helping Susan at the figure skating competition essentially gave her a rule: "If I focus on the things that I think about when I'm skating well at a practice, then I'll land all the elements in my program, just like I do at practice." Rehearsing the rule helped Susan focus on the cues that normally enabled her to land her jumps. The rule might also have functioned as a CS to elicit the relaxed feelings that were typically experienced at practices and that might have been part of the contextual stimuli that controlled good skating.

When Consequences are Delayed   Suppose that a parent wants to encourage a child to study for an hour or so each evening during the week. A suitable reinforcer might be allowing the child to stay up late on the weekend to watch a movie. However, movie watching on Friday night is long delayed from studying for an hour on Monday. By adding the rule, "If you study for an hour each night this week, you can watch the late movie on Friday night," the parent has increased the chances of the delayed reinforcer having an effect on the desired behavior.

When Natural Reinforcers are Highly Intermittent   Suppose that salespeople in a department store are working on a commission during times when sales are slow. Making a sale is immediately reinforced because it is associated with more money for the salesperson who makes it. However, the salespeople must approach many customers before a sale is made. In other words, the schedule of reinforcement is very lean, so ratio strain might occur. The store manager might increase their persistence by encouraging the salespeople to rehearse the rule, "Be persistent! The very next customer might mean a sale."

When Behavior Will Lead to Immediate and Severe Punishment   Rules can help people learn appropriate behavior when learning "the hard way" could be costly. For example, surprising though it might seem, some students are genuinely unaware that copying parts of a textbook word for word on a term paper without acknowledging the source is unacceptable. All students should be taught, long before they ever reach college, the rule, "Copying from a source without giving credit is plagiarism and can lead to serious academic penalty." As another example, driving under the influence of alcohol (DUI) is a source of serious traffic accidents and can lead to serious penalties for individuals convicted of DUI. Yet few people who frequent bars ensure that one of them is a designated driver (DD) who doesn't drink for the evening. In an attempt to increase the occurrence of DDs at a bar that was popular with students attending Florida State University, Kazbour and Bailey (2010) advertised the following rule in the local newspaper, on the local radio, and on posters near the bar: "DESIGNATED DRIVERS GET FREE GAS & PASSENGERS ENJOY FREE PIZZA AT [bar name] THURSDAY AND FRIDAY NIGHTS NOW THROUGH NOVEMBER 21ST!" The percentage of bar patrons functioning as or riding with a designated driver from 12 AM until 2 AM at that bar increased an average of 12% in comparison to days during which the program was not in effect.

Why Rules Control Our Behavior

It's easy to understand why people would learn to follow rules that describe direct-acting consequences. Following the rule "Try this new flavor of ice cream; I think you'll like it" will be reinforced immediately by the taste of the ice cream. Failure to follow the rule "Move back from the campfire or you might get burned" could lead to an immediate punisher. But why do we follow rules that identify very delayed consequences? There are several possibilities.

First, although the reinforcer identified in a rule might be delayed for an individual, other people might provide other immediate consequences if the individual follows or does not follow the rule. In the example of the parent who provides the rule, "If you study for an hour each night this week, you can watch the late movie on Friday night," the parent might also say, immediately after an instance of studying on Monday night, "Good for you. Keep it up and you'll be able to stay up late on Friday."

Second, an individual might follow a rule and then immediately make reinforcing statements. As we expressed previously, in the case of Tommy's classroom talk-outs, after complying with the rule of working quietly with three or fewer talk-outs during a 50-minute class, Tommy likely speculated about how he was going to spend the extra play time at the end of the day. (Self-reinforcement is discussed further in Chapter 26.) Alternatively, failure to comply with a rule might lead to immediate self-punishment.

A third possibility is that our operant–respondent interactions (see Chapter 15) give us a reinforcement history so that following rules is automatically strengthened and failure to follow rules is automatically punished. Suppose you give yourself the rule, "I'd better start studying my behavior modification text now or I'll fail the exam tomorrow." Perhaps because of your history of being punished for failing to meet deadlines, such a statement might increase the aversiveness of stimuli associated with not studying for the exam, which would elicit some anxiety. When you comply with the rule, your anxiety decreases and your rule following is maintained by escape conditioning. In everyday language, rehearsal of the deadline causes you to feel anxious, but responding to the rule to meet the deadline then makes you feel a lot better (Malott, 1989). Of course, whether such automatic consequences will continue to influence your rule following will depend on the extent to which you continue to experience punishment for noncompliance with rules and failure to meet deadlines.

Although we have given many examples illustrating how rules generally enhance the development and maintenance of behavior, it is important to realize that exceptions to this generalization exist. Rules introduce extra stimuli and responses that, in some circumstances, can have the net effect of interfering with contingency-shaped behavior. A person trying to verbalize and follow rules might, in these circumstances, become somewhat like the proverbial centipede that tied itself in knots trying to think about how it walked.

Effective and Ineffective Rules

We have said that a rule is a cue that behaving as specified in the rule will lead to a reinforcer or escape from or avoidance of an aversive stimulus. But all rules are not created equal. Some rules are more likely to be followed than others. Let's look at five conditions that affect the likelihood of rule-following behavior.

Specific Versus Vague Descriptions of Behavior   A rule that describes behavior specifically is more likely to be followed than a rule that describes a behavior vaguely. Telling yourself, for example, that you need to study this book more to get a better grade in your behavior modification course is less effective than telling yourself, "For every 20 study questions for which I learn the answers, I will allow myself an hour on Facebook."

Specific Versus Vague Descriptions of Circumstances   A rule that describes specific circumstances in which the behavior should occur is more likely to be followed than a rule that describes the circumstances vaguely or not at all. Telling a young child, for example, "Remember to say 'please' " is less effective than telling the child, "Remember to say 'please' when you ask for something."

Probable Versus Improbable Consequences   Rules are likely to be followed if they identify behavior for which the consequences are highly probable even though they might be delayed. Suppose that a parent tells a teenage child, "Mow the lawn on Monday and I'll give you $20 on Saturday." Assuming that the parent always follows up on such rules, we can then assume that it is highly likely that the teenager will mow the lawn on Monday. If the teenager does so, receiving the $20 the following Saturday is a certainty. Conversely, rules are likely to be ineffective if they describe low-probability outcomes for behavior even if those outcomes are immediate when they occur (Malott, 1989, 1992). To illustrate this point, most people know that wearing a helmet when bike riding could prevent brain damage from a serious accident. So, why do many people go bike riding without a helmet? One reason (that does not necessarily involve rules) might be that desirable safety behavior in such instances leads to immediate punishment—(the helmet is hot and uncomfortable). Another reason is that the rule to wear a helmet while bike riding involves low-probability consequences. Having never experienced a serious bicycle accident, many bike riders think that an accident that would cause brain damage is unlikely. We are not suggesting that rules should not be used in such situations. All bike riders should be encouraged to rehearse before getting on a bike, "If I wear my helmet, I reduce the possibility of serious injury." However, for a rule to be effective when it describes improbable or low-frequency consequences, it might need to be supplemented by other behavior management strategies, such as modeling (see Chapter 18), self-monitoring (see Chapter 26), or behavioral contracting (see Chapter 26). Governments often supplement low-probability natural consequences with laws that specify high-probability consequences, such as fines, for not using protective equipment. This is because health-care costs and disability payments due to accidents lead to higher taxes that result in punishment for politicians in the form of bad public relations and lost elections.

Sizeable Consequences Versus Small but Cumulatively Significant Consequences
Rules that describe sizeable consequences are likely to be effective. In the lawn-mowing example just cited, $20 was a sizeable consequence for that teenager. However, a rule is less likely to be effective if the consequence is small after each instance of following the rule. Suppose an individual resolves, "I'm going to stop eating desserts" and "I'm going to exercise three times a week." Why are such rules often ineffective? One reason that does not necessarily involve rules is that there are direct-acting consequences that support behavior that is incompatible with following the rule. Eating a dessert is immediately reinforced by the delicious taste. And exercising often involves fairly immediate punishers (boredom, discomfort, and tiredness). Another reason that such rules are ineffective is that the supportive consequences of a single instance of following such a rule are too small to be noticeable and are only cumulatively significant (Malott, 1989, 1992). (Other possibilities are discussed in Chapter 26.) That is, it's not the excess weight from the single extra dessert that's a problem; it's the increased weight that occurs when you have the extra dessert on many occasions (see Figure 17.1). Likewise, a single instance of exercising won't produce observable benefits. It's the accumulation of the benefits of exercising on many occasions that is eventually noticeable. Rules that describe small consequences that are harmful or beneficial only after they have accumulated, and therefore only after a long delay, are likely to be ineffective unless complemented by some of the self-management strategies described in Chapter 26.

Deadlines Versus No Deadlines
Suppose that a preschool teacher says to a child, "If you put all the toys away, I'll bring you a treat next week." Is the child likely to put the toys away for such a delayed reinforcer? What if the teacher says to the child, "If you put all the toys away *right now,* I'll bring you a treat next week." Would specifying "right now" make a difference? Surprisingly, it would. Braam and Malott (1990) found that giving 4-year-old children rules to perform behavior with no

FIGURE 17.1
Why are some rules (such as resisting extra dessert) so difficult to follow?

deadline and a 1-week delay of the reinforcer were relatively ineffective, while giving the children rules to perform behavior *with a deadline* and a 1-week delay of a reinforcer were quite effective. Very early in life we learn that meeting deadlines is likely to be reinforced and failing to meet them leads to unpleasantness.

To summarize, rules that describe *specific circumstances* and *deadlines* for *specific behavior* that will lead to *sizeable* and *probable outcomes* are often effective even when the outcomes are delayed. **NOTE 1** Conversely, rules that describe the behavior and the circumstances for it vaguely, that do not identify a deadline for the behavior, and that lead to small or improbable consequences for the behavior are often weak or ineffective.

Guidelines for Using Rules Effectively

Here are some general guidelines for the effective use of rules.

1. The rules should be within the understanding of the individual to whom they are applied.
2. Rules should clearly identify:
   a. the circumstances in which the behavior should occur
   b. the specific behavior in which the individual is to engage
   c. a deadline for performing the behavior
   d. the specific consequences involved in complying with the rule, and/or
   e. the specific consequences for not complying with the rule.
3. Rules should describe probable and sizeable outcomes rather than improbable and small outcomes. (Rules that describe improbable and/or small consequences might need to be supplemented by some of the procedures described in Chapter 26.)
4. Complex rules should be broken into easy-to-follow steps.
5. Rules should be delivered in a pleasant, courteous, unemotional manner.
6. Fading of rules should be used as necessary to allow other stimuli that are present to take control of the behavior.

Questions for Learning

9. Briefly describe four situations in which the addition of rules to a behavior modification program might be especially helpful. Give an example of each.
10. Describe, using examples, three explanations for why we might follow rules that identify very delayed consequences.
11. Explain (in terms of contextual stimulus control, as described in Note 3 of Chapter 9) why the tone of voice of someone giving you instructions might determine whether you will follow the instructions.
12. How might we explain the behavior of someone who fails to wear a helmet when riding a bicycle even though that person knows that wearing a helmet could prevent brain damage from an accident?
13. How might we account for the relative ineffectiveness of such rules as "I'm going to stop eating sweets"?
14. In a couple of sentences, distinguish between rules that are often effective versus rules that are often weak or ineffective in controlling behavior.

Goals

A *goal* is a level of performance or outcome that an individual or group attempts to achieve. *Goal setting* is the process of making goals for oneself or one or more other people. An example would be a salesperson setting the goal of making a certain number of sales per week. In industrial and organizational settings, goal-setting programs have led to improved performance in such areas as productivity, truck loading, safety behavior, customer service, and typing (Latham & Arshoff, 2013; Locke & Latham, 2002; Pritchard, Young, Koenig, Schmerling, & Dixon, 2013; Saari, 2013; Schmidt, 2013). Goal setting has been used to increase physical activity in obese preschool children (Hustyi, Normand, & Larson, 2011), to increase the following headway of young drivers talking on cell phones in a driving simulator (Arnold & Van Houten, 2011), and to increase the percentage of sharp instruments passed safely in surgery units (Cunningham & Austin, 2007). It has been used to improve academic performance (Morisano, 2013), promote health behavior (Shilts, Townsend, & Dishman, 2013), and promote personal development (Travers, 2013). In sports, goal-setting programs have led to improvements in such areas as laps completed in running, foul shots in basketball, serves in tennis, correct positioning and tackling in football, and accuracy in archery (Gould, 2010; Ward, 2011; Williams, 2013).

Goals are motivational (discussed further in Chapter 19). From a behavioral perspective, a goal is a rule that acts as a motivating operation to achieve some specific desired objective. If a basketball player says, "I'll go to the gym and practice shooting foul shots until I can make 10 in a row," that player has identified the circumstances (at the gym), the behavior (practicing foul shots), and the reinforcer or desired objective (making 10 in a row, plus the implied reinforcer of scoring a higher percentage of foul shots in games). And like the rules discussed in the previous section, goals are often used to influence individuals to improve performance when reinforcers are delayed (e.g., a bonus in a work setting is received well after the work has been completed) or are immediate but highly intermittent (e.g., the basketball player initially making only 1 of every 30 foul shots).

The circumstances in which one might apply goal setting are different from those described in the previous section on rules. In that section we said that it is possible to capitalize on stimulus control by using rules to bring about instant behavior change. The sport psychologist, for example, was concerned with helping Susan "on the spot" rather than giving her a long-term objective to work toward. Goal setting, in contrast, is often used to influence individuals to work toward some objective over a period of time or during a number of practice opportunities. We wouldn't expect the basketball player to immediately meet the goal of making 10 foul shots in a row. Nevertheless, setting a practice goal in that type of situation is likely to lead to faster performance improvement than if the player just practiced shooting foul shots without a particular goal in mind.

Effective and Ineffective Goal Setting

The efficacy of goal setting is well established provided that a number of conditions are met (Gould, 2010; Locke & Latham, 2013). We can distinguish two types of goals: (a) goals for behavior and (b) goals for the products or outcomes of behavior. Examples of the former are eating a healthier diet and exercising more. An example of the latter is losing 10 pounds.

Specific Goals are More Effective Than Vague Goals   Rather than a goal of having a better relationship, a couple might agree to spend half an hour of quality time together or to tell each other daily at least three things that they appreciate about their relationship. It would be more effective for an individual considering dieting to have as a goal to lose 10 pounds rather than saying that the goal is to lose some weight. Similarly, saying that you want to save a specific percentage of your take-home pay would likely be more effective than the goal of wanting to save some money.

Goals with Respect to Learning Specific Skills should Include Mastery Criteria A **mastery criterion** is a specific guideline for performing a skill so that if the guideline is met, the skill is likely to be mastered. This means that an individual who has met a mastery criterion for a skill has learned it well enough to perform it correctly upon demand or when it is necessary to do so. Examples of mastery criteria for learning athletic skills might include making six 4-foot putts in a row in golf, hitting 10 backhands in a row down the line in tennis, or making 10 foul shots in a row in basketball. Examples of mastery criteria for academic skills are reciting the periodic table or a Shakespearean sonnet three times in a row without making a mistake. When confronted with a complex task, it is usually efficient to set learning goals before setting performance goals. For example, if one's ultimate goal is to start a business, unless one is already skilled in doing that, it would be most effective to begin by setting a goal to master the knowledge needed to start a business (J. R. Baum, 2013; Saari, 2013; Seijts, Latham, & Woodwark, 2013).

Goals Should Identify the Circumstances Under Which the Desirable Behavior Should Occur   A goal for a wrestler to practice takedowns is somewhat vague. A goal to practice arm-drag take downs until three in a row occur adds a quantity dimension but still does not indicate the circumstances under which the behavior should occur. A goal to practice arm-drag takedowns until three in a row occur on an opponent offering moderate resistance identifies the circumstances surrounding the performance. Similarly, a goal to give a talk to an audience of 30 strangers is different from a goal to give the same talk to two friends.

Realistic, Challenging Goals are More Effective Than Do-Your-Best Goals   The phrase *just do your best* is often said by coaches to young athletes just before a competition, by parents to their children who are about to perform in a concert, by teachers to students before taking tests, and by employers to employees doing their jobs. A number of studies, however, have demonstrated that do-your-best goals are not nearly as effective as are specific goals for improving performance. Perhaps do-your-best goals are ineffective because they are vague. Or perhaps individuals who are instructed to simply do your best set relatively easy goals, and, as Locke and Latham (2002, 2013) suggested, difficult or challenging goals might produce better performance. From a behavioral perspective, an instructor who identifies a specific goal for a learner is more likely to consistently provide reinforcement for meeting the goal than is an instructor who simply gives the learner a do-your-best goal. The reason for this is that the instructor and the learner might disagree as to whether or not the learner did his or her best. After all, the judgment of whether a goal is easy or difficult is somewhat subjective because our information about someone's physiological and behavioral capabilities is always incomplete. The accuracy of that judgment might be maximized, however, by considering the individual's current level of performance and the range of performance on similar tasks by others of similar ability.

Exactly how difficult or challenging goals should be is an issue that is receiving considerable research (Locke & Latham, 2013). It has even been suggested that under certain circumstances, so-called "stretch goals"—that is, goals that are impossible to achieve—can be effective in improving performance, even though by definition the goal is never reached. However, stretch goals, or even very difficult goals, can lead to considerable frustration and should be used only with great caution (Kerr & LePelley, 2013).

Public Goals Are More Effective Than Private Goals Consider the following experiment with three groups of college students who were all given the same booklet of material to study. The first group of students participated in a public goal-setting program. Each student set a goal concerning the amount of time he or she would study and the score that he or she hoped to receive on a test to be given at the end of the program. These students announced their goals to other members of their group. The second group of students practiced private goal setting. They were treated the same as the first group except that they kept their goals to themselves. The third group of students was not asked to set any goals; it was a control group. These students were simply given the material to study for the same amount of time as the first group with the knowledge that they would receive a test at the end of the experiment. The results: The public goal-setting group scored an average of 17 percentage points higher on the test than either of the other two groups, who performed at about the same level (Hayes et al., 1985). Similar results on the effects of public goals versus private goals were found by Seigts, Meertens, and Kok (1997). Hayes and colleagues theorized that setting a public goal results in a public standard against which performance can be evaluated and that it also implies social consequences for achieving or not achieving the goal (see also Klein, Cooper, & Monahan, 2013, p. 75).

Although goals that someone else knows about might be more likely to be met than private goals that nobody knows about, the public component must be practiced with some caution. Suppose that you recommend goal setting as a part of a behavior modification program to help someone exercise consistently. If you recommend that the exerciser share the goals with another person, that person should be someone who is likely to prompt the exerciser with gentle reminders when goals are not met and who will offer encouragement when progress is satisfactory. That person should not be someone who will send the exerciser on a heavy guilt trip for not meeting the goals. (This issue is discussed further in Chapter 30.)

Goal Setting Is More Effective If Deadlines Are Included Each of us has a history of positive reinforcement for meeting various deadlines and for encountering aversive consequences when we don't meet them. Capitalizing on this history increases the effectiveness of goal setting. Suppose that you set a goal for yourself during the coming year of emailing friends and relatives more often. You are more likely to meet that goal if you resolve that by February 1 you'll have emailed a specific number of individuals, by March 1 you'll have emailed so many more, and so on.

Goal Setting Plus Feedback Is More Effective Than Goal Setting Alone Goals are more likely to be met if feedback indicates the degree of progress toward the goal (Ashford and De Stobbeleir, 2013). One way of providing feedback is to chart the progress being made. As discussed in Chapter 20, individuals who chart their progress toward a goal are likely to find improvements in the chart to be reinforcing. Another way to provide feedback is to break long-term goals into a number of short-term goals and to congratulate oneself each time a short-term goal is met. Suppose that a couple decides to repaint their entire house, inside and out. Short-term goals might include painting the bedroom by the end of February, then the living room by the end of March, and so on, and admiring each room as it is completed.

Goal Setting Is Most Effective When Individuals Are Committed to the Goals   Goals are likely to be effective only if the individuals involved have a continuing commitment to them. Although there are problems defining and measuring commitment in the goal-setting literature (Klein et al., 2013), by *commitment,* we mean statements or actions by the learner indicating that the goal is important, the learner will work toward it, and the learner recognizes the benefits of doing so. One way of gaining commitment is to have the learner participate in the goal-setting process. Research indicates that self-selected goals are at least as effective as those that are externally imposed (Fellner & Sulzer-Azaroff, 1984). Also individuals should be provided with frequent reminders of their commitment to their goals (Watson & Tharp, 2007).

Guidelines for Goal Setting

Many individuals attempt to capitalize on goal setting with New Year's resolutions. However, this is not necessarily the best time for setting goals due to competing festive activities. In addition, the stimuli present on January 1 are likely to be quite different from stimuli present during other times of the year. This would be unlikely to result in good generalization. Also, if goal setting occurs only on New Year's Day, then by definition, it occurs only once a year, whereas goal setting is more effective when it can be practiced a number of times throughout the year. Moreover, there are clearly ways of setting goals that are more effective than the kinds of New Year's resolutions that people typically make. If your goals are vague or do-your-best goals with no deadlines or timelines for meeting them and without a feedback mechanism for monitoring progress, they are not likely to have much effect on behavior. If, however, you practice goal setting according to the following guidelines, your goals are more likely to be effective in modifying your behavior.

1. Set goals that are specific, realistic, and challenging.
2. Identify the specific behaviors and the circumstances in which those behaviors should occur in order for the goals to have been met.
3. Be clear about the specific consequences that might occur for meeting or not meeting the goal.
4. Break long-term goals into several short-term goals.
5. If the goal is complex, devise an action plan for meeting it.
6. Set deadlines for goal attainment.
7. Ensure that individuals involved are committed to the goals.
8. Encourage the learner to share the goals with a friendly supporter.
9. Design a system for monitoring progress toward goals.
10. Provide positive feedback as progress toward goals is achieved.

Questions for Learning

15. In general, what do we mean by the word *goal*? Give an example of a behavioral goal that is not in this chapter. Give an example of an outcome goal that is not in this chapter.
16. Is goal setting different from using rules? Discuss.
17. Briefly list six of the eight conditions that summarize effective versus ineffective goal setting as a behavior modification strategy.
18. What is a mastery criterion? Give an example that is not in this chapter.
19. From a behavioral perspective, why might realistic, challenging goals be more effective than do-your-best goals?
20. From a behavioral perspective, why might public goals be more effective than private goals?
21. What do the authors mean by *commitment* in the context of goal setting?

Application Exercises

A. Exercises Involving Others

1. Choose a behavior that a parent might want to change in a child such that there is no obvious immediate, natural reinforcer for that behavior. Describe how the parent, following the guidelines for using rules effectively, might capitalize on rule-governed behavior to bring about a desired outcome.
2. Consider a practice setting for a youth sport with which you are familiar. Describe how a coach might use goal setting to influence desirable practice behavior of an athlete in that setting. Indicate how the coach has followed the guidelines for goal setting.

B. Self-Modification Exercises

1. Consider the guidelines for using rules effectively. Now consider a behavior that you could physically perform. Identify a rule with respect to that behavior, and describe how you would structure the contingencies according to the guidelines for using rules effectively.

2. Identify a behavior of yours that was probably contingency shaped. It might be something like riding a bicycle, balancing on one foot, eating with chopsticks, whistling a short tune, or flipping flapjacks. Devise a measure (e.g., number of errors) of how well you perform the behavior. Then, using the measure, record your performance of the behavior on several trials. Next write out a set of rules for performing the behavior, and again perform and record the behavior on several occasions, carefully following the rules. According to your measure, how did the addition of rules affect your performance? Interpret your finding.

Note for Further Learning

1. For persons who suffer from insomnia, one option is to treat the problem with drugs. Another option, which has been shown to be at least equally as effective, is an approach that is based on behavioral principles and relies partly on rule-governed behavior (Blampied & Bootzin, 2013; Carney & Edinger, 2010; Edinger & Carney, 2008; Perlis, 2012; Perlis, Jungquist, Smith, & Posner, 2008; Smith et al., 2002). Some of the recommendations or rules in this treatment are: (1) Exercise regularly, but not in the late evening; (2) relax before bedtime; (3) don't consume caffeine or alcohol late in the evening; (4) go to bed only when you are feeling sleepy; (5) if sleep has not occurred within 10 minutes, leave the bedroom and read a book until you feel sleepy; (6) avoid nonsleep activities in bed; (7) get up at the same time each morning, regardless of the time that you go to bed. In a review of 21 studies of a total of 470 participants with insomnia, behavioral sleep therapy was more effective than pharmacological treatment on all measures. This indicates that behavior therapy should be a first-line treatment for chronic insomnia. For an excellent book on managing and preventing children's sleep problems see Wirth (2014). More detailed discussions of behavioral clinical treatments are presented in Chapters 27 and 28.

Question for Further Learning

1. List five rules that are a part of a behavioral treatment for insomnia.

CHAPTER 18

Antecedent Control: Modeling, Physical Guidance, and Situational Inducement

James, feel the soles of your feet.

A Mindfulness-Based Intervention for Aggression[1]

James, a 27-year-old man with mild intellectual disability, had alternated between group home placement and a psychiatric hospital for many years. He preferred to live in a group home, but his aggressive behavior resulted in regular readmissions to a psychiatric hospital. Although a variety of aggression management treatments had been tried, none had been successful. As a last resort, after spending 12 months as an inpatient without achieving much control over his verbal and physical aggression, James agreed to try a mindfulness-based self-control strategy. Mindfulness (discussed further in Chapter 27) involves becoming fully aware of one's sensations, thoughts, feelings, and observable behavior on a moment-to-moment basis.

Following a procedure called *Soles of the Feet*, James learned to divert his attention from whatever was making him angry at a particular moment by focusing on the soles of his feet. Doing so enabled James to feel calm, smile, and walk away from the anger-causing situation. To teach James to practice this strategy, the therapist used modeling and role-playing. During therapy sessions, James would be standing or sitting but always with his feet flat on the floor. The therapist would then remind James of an incident in which he was angry and verbally or physically aggressive toward a person who made him angry. When James showed signs of anger, such as rapid breathing, the therapist would say, while modeling the behavior being described, "Feel the soles of your feet. Slowly, move your toes, and feel your socks. Can you feel them? Now move the heels of your feet against the back of your shoes. Feel your heels rubbing your shoes. Keep breathing slowly, and pay attention to the soles of your feet until you feel calm. Now smile, and walk away from the situation, like I'm doing." The therapist and James would then walk away from each other smiling. The therapist provided this type of training

---

[1] This case is based on a report by Singh, Wahler, Adkins, and Myers (2003).

during 30-minute role-playing sessions held twice a day for 5 days. This was followed by homework practice assignments for another week. Then James was instructed to use the procedure to control his verbal and physical aggression in actual situations. The procedure was very effective. Before treatment, James had averaged approximately 10 instances of serious verbal aggression and 15 instances of physical aggression per month. Following treatment, James met the requirement of 6 months of aggression-free behavior in the psychiatric hospital before being returned to the group home. He then successfully lived in the group home with no aggressive behavior during a 1-year follow-up.

Capitalizing on Existing Stimulus Control

As we indicated in the previous chapter, behavior modification programs should include instructions in the form of rules that can be followed easily. Sometimes, however, instructions are not enough so it is necessary to introduce other types of antecedent stimuli, as was done with James. This chapter describes these additional strategies for capitalizing on existing forms of stimulus control.

Modeling

Modeling is a procedure by which a sample of a given behavior is demonstrated to an individual to induce that individual to engage in a similar behavior. As is true for rules, modeling can be quite powerful. You may convince yourself of this by performing the following simple experiments:

1. For an entire day, speak only in a whisper and note how often people around you also whisper.
2. Yawn conspicuously in the presence of other people and note their frequency of yawning.
3. Stand on the corner of a street where there are lots of pedestrians and look at the sky for 30 minutes, and note how many people stop and also look at the sky.

In each case, compare the data obtained with data gathered under comparable circumstances when the behavior is not being modeled.

As with rules, the general public so commonly uses modeling that few people think of it as a behavior modification procedure. Parents use it rather unsystematically, but in general effectively, to teach politeness, caring, language, and many other behaviors to their children. When a dog walks by a parent and a 2-year-old child, the parent, while looking at the dog, might say, "Look at the dog. Can you say 'dog'?" When showing a child how to make a sandwich, a parent might say "Do it like this" while modeling the desired behavior. Modeling affects the behavior of individuals of all ages, not just young children. When teenagers first enter high school, they see how the older students dress and talk, and they soon dress the same way and use the same expressions. All of us in our daily lives have frequent opportunities to observe the actions of others, and we frequently imitate their behaviors.

What determines whether we will imitate the behavior of a model? Although several possible explanations exist, clearly our history of reinforcement and punishment for imitating others is an important factor. Also, because each of us has had different experiences, the specific variables that **NOTE 1** determine who we imitate vary somewhat from person to person. Nevertheless, several general factors influence the effectiveness of modeling as a behavior modification technique for most people (Bandura, 1986, pp. 53–55). The following rules capitalize on these factors.

Arrange for Peers to be Models

People are more likely to imitate those who are similar to them in various ways (age, socioeconomic status, physical appearance, etc.). Friends and peers are more likely to be imitated than are strangers or individuals outside one's peer group. Thus, whenever possible, use peers as models in your behavior modification programs. Consider the case of an extremely withdrawn nursery school child who almost never interacts with other children. You might arrange for the child to observe several instances of another child joining in the activities of a group of children (see Prendeville, Prelock, & Unwin, 2006). The group should be responding to the model in a reinforcing manner such as by offering her play material, talking to her, or smiling. To ensure that the modeling occurs under optimal circumstances and in a suitable fashion, it may be necessary to instruct certain children to perform as models and to instruct the children in the group to behave in a conspicuously reinforcing manner to the models. Another approach that has shown promise is one that encourages normally developing siblings to act as models for developing play behavior in children with autism (Walton, & Ingersoll, 2012).

Video modeling, which involves showing video-recorded displays of a typically developing child or children emitting target responses, is an effective strategy for teaching a child with autism to emit those target responses (Ganz, Earles-Vollrath, & Cook, 2011). Examples of target responses taught using video modeling include social and vocational skills (Rayner, Denholm, & Sigafoos, 2009), play behaviors (MacDonald et al., 2009), and language skills (Plavnick & Ferreri, 2011).

Research indicates that video modeling to teach social skills to children with autism is as effective as peer-mediated modeling (Wang, Cui, & Parrila, 2011). An interesting aspect of video modeling is that the individual being worked with may be his or her own model by being shown video recordings of him or herself performing the target behavior correctly. Both video modeling and video self-modeling can be used effectively to teach skills to children and adolescents with autism (Bellini & Akullian, 2007).

Arrange for the Modeled Behavior to Be Seen to Be Effective

Suppose that you want to improve your debating skills. Are you more likely to imitate the discussion strategies of friends who consistently get their points across or friends who consistently lose arguments? Clearly, you are more likely to initiate someone whose behavior produces desired consequences (Bandura, 1986, p. 53). Even with children, peers who are more proficient at obtaining consequences for various behaviors are more likely to be imitated (Schunk, 1987). Therefore, to capitalize on this factor when using modeling in your behavior modification program, arrange for the learner to observe the model emit the desired behavior and receive reinforcement.

Social psychologists have long known that high-status and prestigious persons are more likely to be imitated than individuals of lower status or prestige (e.g., Asch, 1948; Henrich & Gil-White, 2001). This is likely because individuals of high status frequently emit effective behaviors. A high-status teenager, for example, is likely to be imitated by peers who frequently observe that the popular teenager receives many positive consequences for his or her behaviors.

Use Multiple Models

Sarah, a 35-year-old real estate salesperson and part-time student, drank beer regularly with six other women at a local bar on Friday afternoons. All of them were taking a course on behavior modification, but Sarah was unaware that her own drinking behavior was being studied. Over several sessions of baseline, it was established that Sarah invariably drank about 72 ounces of beer in an hour. Then the experimental phases of the study began. During the first experimental phase, one of the other women modeled a drinking rate of half of Sarah's. Sarah's drinking was not affected. During the second experimental phase, her drinking was also not affected when two of the other women modeled drinking rates half of hers. However, when in the third experimental phase, four other women modeled drinking rates that were half of Sarah's, her drinking rate reduced by half (DeRicco & Niemann, 1980). This study illustrates that the number of people modeling a particular behavior is a factor in determining whether that behavior will be imitated. In addition, an increase in the number of models is, by definition, an increase in the number of stimulus exemplars which, as discussed in Chapter 16, increases stimulus generalization of the behavior (Pierce & Schreibman, 1997).

Combine Modeling with Rules

Modeling is likely to be most effective when combined with rules and other behavioral strategies. The following based on an excerpt from a therapy session illustrates this (Masters, Burrish, Hollon, & Rimm, 1987, pp. 100–101). The client was being treated for having difficulty asking for a date. In the excerpt, the client is rehearsing effective date-asking behavior. Note how the therapist combines instruction and shaping with modeling.

CLIENT: By the way (*pause*) I don't suppose you want to go out Saturday night?
THERAPIST: Up to actually asking for the date, you were very good. However, if I were the woman, I think I might have been a bit offended when you said, "By the way." It's like your asking her out is pretty casual. Also, the way you phrased the question, you are kind

of suggesting to her that she doesn't want to go out with you. Pretend for the moment I'm you. Now, how does this sound: "There's a play this Saturday that I want to see. If you don't have other plans, I'd very much like you to go with me."

CLIENT: That sounded good. Like you were sure of yourself and liked the woman too.

THERAPIST: Why don't you try it?

CLIENT: There's a play I'd like to see, and I'd like you to go with me on Saturday, if you don't have anything better to do.

THERAPIST: Well, that certainly was better. Your tone of voice was especially good. But the last line, "if you don't have anything better to do," sounded like you don't think you have much to offer. Why not run through it one more time?

CLIENT: There's a play I'd like to see on Saturday, and, if you haven't made other plans, I'd like you to go with me.

THERAPIST: Much better. Excellent, in fact. You were confident, forceful, and sincere.

This example also illustrates a technique referred to as **behavioral rehearsal** or **role-playing** in which a client rehearses particular behaviors (plays a role) in a practice setting to increase the likelihood that the client will follow those behaviors appropriately in the real world. In the preceding example, the client rehearsed asking for a date. Role-playing was also used with James to teach him to focus on the soles of his feet as an alternative to aggression. A combination of instructions, modeling, behavioral rehearsal, and consequence management has been used to enhance performance in a variety of areas, such as social skills training (Huang & Cuvo, 1997), anger management training (Larkin & Zayfert, 1996), teaching parents of children with autism to increase the diet variety for their children (Seiverling, Williams, Sturmey, & Hart, 2012), and training staff to appropriately ambulate children with multiple physical disabilities in their care (Nabeyama & Sturmey, 2010).

Guidelines for Using Modeling

The following are some general guidelines for the effective use of modeling. It may not be possible to follow all of them in every situation, but the more that are followed, the more effective the modeling is likely to be.

1. Select models who are friends or peers of the learner and who are seen by the learner as competent individuals with status or prestige.
2. Use more than one model.
3. The complexity of the modeled behavior should be suitable for the behavioral level of the learner.
4. Combine rules with modeling.
5. Have the learner watch the model perform the behavior and receive reinforcement (preferably by natural reinforcers).
6. Design the training so that correct imitation of the modeled behavior will lead to a natural reinforcer for the learner. If this is not possible, arrange for reinforcement for correct imitation of the modeled behavior.
7. If the behavior is quite complex, then the modeling episode should be sequenced from very easy to more difficult approximations for the learner.
8. To enhance stimulus generalization, the modeling scenes should be as realistic as possible.
9. Use fading as necessary so that stimuli other than the model can take control over the desired behavior.

Questions for Learning

1. Define *modeling*. How was it incorporated into the therapy sessions with James?
2. List four strategies that you might follow to influence the effectiveness of modeling as a behavior modification technique.
3. Describe two recent situations in which you were influenced by modeling to emit a behavior. For each instance, describe which of the four factors that influence the effectiveness of modeling were present.
4. Describe the specific steps you might go through in using modeling to overcome the extreme withdrawal behavior of a nursery school child who never interacts with other children. Identify the basic principles and procedures being applied in your program.

5. In the dialogue between the client and the therapist concerning the client's difficulty in asking for a date, briefly describe
   a. how modeling was involved
   b. how instructions were involved
   c. how shaping was involved
6. Define or describe behavioral rehearsal (or role-playing), and give an example.

Physical Guidance

Physical guidance is the application of physical contact to induce an individual to go through the motions of a desired behavior. Some familiar examples are a dance instructor leading a pupil through a new dance step, a golf instructor holding a novice's arms and moving the novice through a proper swing, and a parent holding a child's hand while teaching the child to cross the street safely. Physical guidance is typically only one component of a teaching procedure. Both the dance instructor and the golf instructor will also use instruction (telling the student what to do and giving pointers), modeling (demonstrating the appropriate physical postures and motions), and reinforcement for correct responses or approximations to them (such as "Much better!" or "Excellent!"). Likewise, the parent teaching safe street crossing will use rules (e.g., by saying, "Look both ways") and modeling (looking both ways in an exaggerated manner).

Physical guidance is often used as an aid for teaching individuals to follow instructions or imitate a modeled behavior so that instruction or modeling can then be used without physical guidance to establish other behaviors. In one procedure for teaching instruction following, a child is placed in a chair opposite the teacher. At the beginning of a trial, the teacher says, "Johnny, stand up," and then guides the child to his feet. Reinforcement is then presented immediately, as though the child himself had performed the response. Next, the teacher says, "Johnny, sit down," and gently presses him back on the chair. Again, immediate reinforcement is presented. The process is repeated over trials while physical guidance is faded out (see Kazdin & Erickson, 1975). After this set of instructions is learned, another set (such as "Come here" and "Go there") is taught using a similar procedure. Less and less physical guidance may be required to teach successive instruction following until eventually even fairly complex instruction following can be taught with little or no physical guidance.

As in teaching instruction following, the teacher who uses physical guidance to teach a child to imitate a model starts with a few simple imitations (such as touching one's head, clapping one's hands, tapping the table, standing up, and sitting down) and adds new imitations as the previous ones are learned. At the beginning of each trial, the teacher says, "Do this" while modeling the response and guiding the child to perform the response. Correct responses are reinforced and physical guidance is faded out over trials. This facilitates the development of **generalized imitation** by which an individual, after learning to imitate a number of behaviors (perhaps with some shaping, fading, physical guidance, and reinforcement), learns to imitate a new response on the first trial without reinforcement (Baer, Peterson, & Sherman, 1967; Ledford & Wolery, 2011).

Physical guidance may also be used as a transition to other types of prompting. For example, a child may be asked to point to a picture of a dog where a picture of a dog and three other pictures are laid out on a table. The teacher may use various prompts, such as pointing to the correct picture or showing the child a picture identical to the correct picture. If the child does not respond correctly to one of these prompts, the teacher may gently take the child's hand and move it to the correct picture. Over trials the teacher asks the child to point to different pictures, and fades out the physical guidance so that the child is responding correctly to nonphysical prompts. Eventually the child learns to respond to the correct pictures without being prompted (Carp, Peterson, Arkel, Petursdottir, & Ingvarsson, 2012).

Another common application of physical guidance is in helping individuals to overcome fears. Helping an individual who is terrified of water might involve gradually leading the individual by the hand into the shallow end of a swimming pool and providing support while the individual floats. The least fear-provoking aspects of a situation should be introduced first and the more fear-provoking aspects added later in a gradual manner. One should never try to force an individual to do more than the individual feels comfortable doing. The more fearful the individual is, the more gradual the process should be. In the case of a very fearful individual, one may have to spend several sessions simply sitting with the individual on the edge of the pool. (Use of modeling and other procedures to help a client overcome extreme fears is discussed further in Chapter 28.)

Guidelines for Using Physical Guidance

Some general guidelines for the effective use of physical guidance follow.

1. Ensure that the learner is comfortable and relaxed while being touched and guided. Some initial relaxation training may be necessary to accomplish this.
2. Determine the stimuli that you want to control the behavior and ensure that they are conspicuously present during physical guidance.
3. Consider using rules or cue words during physical guidance so that they may eventually control the behavior. For example, when teaching a novice right-handed golfer the proper shoulder turn during a golf swing, the instructor might say the cue words, "Left shoulder to chin, right shoulder to chin," while guiding the novice through the backswing and the downswing.
4. Reinforcement should be given immediately after the successful completion of the guided response.
5. Physical guidance should be sequenced gradually from very easy to more difficult behavior for the learner.
6. Use fading so that other stimuli can take control over the behavior.

Questions for Learning

7. What does the term *physical guidance* mean? How does it differ from gestural prompting (see page 98)?
8. Identify a behavior that you were influenced to perform as a result of physical guidance. Describe how physical guidance was involved.
9. What is generalized imitation? Describe an example.

Situational Inducement

Largely because of our similar histories of reinforcement and punishment, numerous situations and occasions in society control similar behavior in many of us. The interiors of certain public buildings, such as churches, museums, and libraries, tend to suppress loud talking. Parties tend to evoke socializing and jovial behavior. Catchy melodies prompt humming and singing. Audience laughter, real or artificial, induces many people to continue watching TV sitcoms.

The term **situational inducement** refers to the influence of a behavior by using situations and occasions that already exert control over the behavior. Such techniques no doubt predate recorded history. Gatherings involving singing and dancing probably served to strengthen a sense of community in ancient tribes, just as they do today in many cultures. Monasteries and convents have been used for centuries to promote spiritual behavior by providing an environment conducive to reading religious texts and meditating. Supermarkets and department stores use many situational features to induce buying. Among these are the ways in which the products or pictures of the products are prominently and attractively displayed. Fine restaurants provide relaxing atmospheres to induce leisurely enjoyment of a full-course meal. Fast-food restaurants where many people are waiting for tables play fast music to induce rapid eating.

Examples of situational inducement can also be found in the home. Many people prominently display items such as interesting *objets d'art* to stimulate conversation when guests arrive. If a guest seems about to mishandle one of these conversation pieces, the host may use situational inducement by handing the potential offender a drink.

Situational inducement has been used in a number of imaginative and effective ways in behavior modification programs to help increase or decrease target behaviors or to bring them under appropriate stimulus control. Examples can be discussed under four somewhat overlapping categories: (a) rearranging the existing surroundings, (b) moving the activity to a new location, (c) relocating the people, and (d) changing the time of the activity.

Rearranging the Surroundings

An interesting example of rearranging the surroundings occurred in a case reported by the pioneering behaviorist Israel Goldiamond (1965). He was consulted by a couple having a problem in their relationship.[2] When they were at home together, the husband could not refrain from screaming at his wife

---

[2] For additional discussion of behavior therapy for couples, see Chapter 28.

about her once having gone to bed with his best friend. One of the therapy goals decided on was to replace the screaming with civilized conversational behavior. Goldiamond reasoned that the husband's screaming had probably come under the control of the S^Ds in the home environment and that one way to weaken the behavior in that situation would be to change those S^Ds. He therefore instructed the couple to rearrange the rooms and furniture in the house to make it appear considerably different. The wife went one step further and bought herself a new outfit. Goldiamond then provided for the reinforcement of civilized conversation in the presence of these new cues that were not associated so strongly with screaming. (How he did this is explained in the next section.) It was important to make these changes as quickly as possible because if screaming occurred in the presence of these new stimuli, they might become S^Ds for screaming just as the old stimuli had.

Another example of rearranging the surroundings is altering the items in one's room to promote better and more persistent studying behavior. A student might turn on more lights, use a brighter light bulb, clear the desk of irrelevant material, move the bed as far as possible from the desk, or have the desk facing away from the bed. Better yet, the bed should not be in the same room as the desk because the bed is an S^D for sleeping. To prevent nonstudy behaviors from being conditioned to the new stimuli, the student should engage only in studying behavior in the rearranged environment (see Goldiamond, 1965). Other examples of rearranging the surroundings include placing potato chips on the middle shelf rather than the high or the low shelves in a store to increase sales of the potato chips (Sigurdsson, Saevarsson, & Foxall, 2009), wearing nonremovable wristbands as a reminder to quit nail biting (Koritzky & Yechiam, 2011), and placing recycling bins in classrooms on a university campus to increase recycling of plastic bottles (O'Connor, Lerman, Fritz, & Hodde, 2010).

Moving the Activity to a New Location

In the case reported by Goldiamond, rearranging the furniture eliminated some but not all of the S^Ds that evoked the husband's screaming. Goldiamond therefore arranged for the interaction between the spouses to initially be moved to a new location. He instructed the couple that, after rearranging the furniture in their home, they were to immediately go to a place that would induce civilized conversation. It was hoped that this behavior would continue until they returned home and then would come under the control of the new stimuli in the home.

To quote from Goldiamond's report (1965, p. 856),

> Since it was impossible for [the husband] to converse in a civilized manner with his wife, we discussed a program of going to one evening spot on Monday, another on Tuesday, and another on Wednesday.
> "Oh," he said, "you want us to be together. We'll go bowling on Thursday."
> "On the contrary," I said, "I am interested in your subjecting yourself to an environment where civilized chit-chat is maintained. Such is not the case at a bowling alley."
> I also asked if there was any topic of conversation which once started would maintain itself. He commented on his mother-in-law's crazy ideas about farming. He was then given an index card and instructed to write "farm" on it and to attach some money to that card. The money was to be used to pay the waitress on Thursday, at which point he was to start the "farm" discussion which hopefully would continue into the taxi and home.

Changing the location of the activity is one approach to improving studying (see Figure 18.1). A student using this approach should select a place that is conducive to studying and has distinctive stimuli that are not associated with texting friends, going on Facebook, or any behavior other than studying. A reserved carrel in a university library is ideal for this, although other well-lit, quiet areas with adequate working space would be suitable. Depending on how deficient the student's study behavior is, it may be necessary to combine relocating the activity with some of the basic procedures discussed in Part II of this text. For severe deficiencies, behavior incorporating good study skills should first be shaped and then placed on either a low-duration or a low-ratio schedule in the special studying area. The value of the schedule should then be increased gradually so that the behavior will eventually be maintained at the desired level. Appropriate reinforcement such as coffee with a friend should be arranged to occur immediately after the schedule requirement has been met. A student who experiences a tendency to daydream or to engage in other nonstudy behavior while in the studying area should do a little more productive studying and then leave immediately so that daydreaming does not become conditioned to the stimuli in the studying area. Similarly, the husband in the case reported by Goldiamond was instructed to go to the garage and sit on a specially designated "sulking" stool whenever he felt a

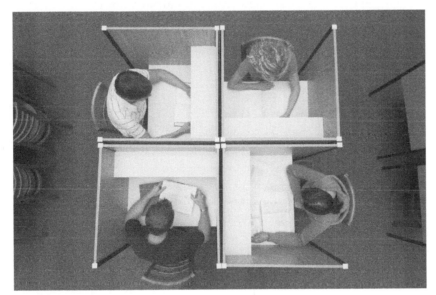

FIGURE 18.1
Examples of situational inducement

tendency to sulk—this being a behavior that was threatening the recently strengthened conversational behavior after screaming had been eliminated.

Stimulus control training has been effectively used to help chronic worriers decrease their worrying behavior. McGowan and Behar (2013) got worriers to identify their worrisome thoughts and also to identify a specific location where they could go each day to engage in worrying. The worriers picked a time and place that was at least 3 hours prior to their bedtimes so that the worrying would be less likely to interfere with sleep. Each day the worriers would go to their worrying location and worry as intensely as possible for 30 minutes. They also tried to postpone spontaneous worrying during the day to the worry period, and instead to focus on present moment experiences. The procedure produced clinically significant decreases in the worrying and anxiety of the participants.

Relocating People

The third category of situational inducement, relocating people, was not illustrated in Goldiamond's case study. Although relocating the participants is generally a measure of last resort when dealing with individuals who wish to maintain their respective relationships, it is sometimes the most practical tactic in other circumstances. If you cannot get along with someone with whom you have no particular reason to associate, then why make the effort to be more compatible? Both of you would probably be happier respecting each other from a distance. Relocating people can also be used to bring about the opposite effect, that is, to bring people together. For example, getting dates is a problem for many college students. To deal with this problem, therapists often recommend that clients increase their non-dating contacts with others who may be candidates for dating. Teachers often change seating arrangements to relocate students whose close proximity leads to various types of disruptions. This is usually much easier than designing and carrying out reinforcement or punishment programs to eliminate undesirable interactions. For example, Bicard, Ervin, Bicard, and Baylot-Casey (2012) found that disruptive behavior of fifth-grade students occurred more than three times as often when the students chose their own seats as compared to when teachers arranged where the students sat.

Changing the Time of the Activity

The final category of situational inducement involves taking advantage of the fact that certain stimuli and behavioral tendencies change predictably with the passage of time. For example, couples may find that sexual activity is better for them in the morning than at night. Changing the time of an activity has been used effectively in weight-control programs. People who cook for their families sometimes put on excess weight by "nibbling" while preparing meals and then sitting down for a full-course dinner. Rather than forgoing dinner with one's family, a partial solution to this problem is to do the preparation shortly after having eaten the previous meal while the tendency to eat is still relatively weak (see LeBow, 1989, 2013).

Guidelines for Using Situational Inducement

Situational inducement covers a broad set of procedures. Its use, therefore, is considerably less straightforward than is that of the other methods discussed in this chapter. In short, a good deal of imagination is typically required if it is to be used effectively. We suggest the following guidelines.

1. Clearly identify the desired behavior to be strengthened and, if appropriate, the undesirable behavior to be decreased.
2. Brainstorm all possible environmental arrangements in the presence of which the desired behavior has occurred in the past or is likely to occur. Remember, situations and controlling stimuli can be anything—people, places, times, days, events, objects, and so on.
3. From the list of stimuli that have controlled the target behavior in the past, identify those that could be easily introduced to control the target behavior.
4. Arrange for the learner to be exposed to the stimuli that control the target behavior in the desired way and to avoid locations and arrangements that do not have this control.
5. Make sure that undesirable behavior never occurs in the presence of situations introduced to strengthen desirable behavior.
6. When the desirable behavior occurs in the presence of the new arrangement, be sure that it is reinforced.
7. Use fading to bring the behavior under desired stimulus control.

Questions for Learning

10. What do we mean by the term *situational inducement*? Which term given previously in this book has essentially the same meaning (see page 98)?
11. Describe each of the four categories of situational inducement.
12. Give an example from your own experience of each of the four categories of situational inducement.
13. For each of the following examples, identify the category of situational inducement in which it might best be placed and indicate why.
    a. On Saturday afternoon, an exercise buff can't seem to get the energy to lift weights. To increase the likelihood of weight lifting, the exercise buff places the weights in the center of the exercise room, turns on the TV to a sporting event, and opens a copy of *Muscle Beach* magazine to the centerfold showing a famous bodybuilder.
    b. It is said that Victor Hugo, a renowned writer, controlled his work habits in his study by having his servant take his clothes away and not bring them back until the end of the day (Wallace, 1971, pp. 68–69).
    c. To stop drinking, an alcoholic surrounds herself or himself with members of Alcoholics Anonymous and stops seeing her or his old drinking buddies.

d. A couch potato has decided to jog a mile every night before going to bed. Alas, "the road to hell [or perhaps to heart attack] is paved with good intentions." Late nights, good TV, wine with dinner, and other delights take their toll. Three months later, the couch potato is still overweight and out of shape because of many missed jogging nights. The couch potato takes a friend's advice to change the routine and begins jogging each day immediately upon arriving home and before eating dinner.

e. After many interruptions while working on this book at the university, the authors began working at one of their homes.

14. According to the proposed guidelines for the use of rules, modeling, and physical guidance,
   a. what behavior principle is used with all three procedures?
   b. what two other behavioral procedures are likely to be used with all three procedures?

Application Exercises

A. Exercise Involving Others

Outline a program that a parent might follow to teach a 2-year-old child to respond consistently to the instruction, "Please bring me your shoes." Indicate how your program might use rules, modeling, and physical guidance, and how it follows the guidelines for the effective application of each.

B. Self-Modification Exercise

Select two of your behaviors from the following list:

1. doing the dishes or putting them in the dishwasher immediately after a meal
2. getting up when the alarm sounds
3. feeling happy
4. cleaning up your bedroom twice per week
5. doing some exercises daily
6. increasing your studying

Describe how you might influence each behavior by combining at least four of the following tactics: rules, modeling, physical guidance, rearranging the existing surroundings, moving the activity to a new location, relocating people, and changing the time of the activity. Make your suggestions highly plausible in regard to the situation.

Note for Further Learning

1. Many neuroscientists have speculated that the discovery of mirror neuron system (MNS) in the brains of primates has shown that neurons play a critical role in social behavior. The MNS is seen as being especially important for imitation because specific neurons in it are activated both when an individual sees someone perform a given action and when the individual him/herself performs an identical action. It is as though a specific behavior related to the activation of certain mirror neurons in individual A's brain activates the corresponding mirror neurons in individual B's brain when individual B sees individual A perform that behavior. Some cognitive neuroscientists argue that this indicates that there is an innate imitation module in our brain, and hence that imitation does not depend on learning (e.g., Keyers & Gazzola, 2009). Other cognitive neuroscientists argue that the data suggest that rather than imitation mirror neurons being responsible for imitation, imitative behavior is learned and mirror neurons are a by-product of learning (e.g., Heyes, 2010; Ray & Heyes, 2011). The former group of cognitive neuroscientists maintains that there must be an innate imitation module in the brain because the stimuli present in an individual's environment contain insufficient information for imitation to be acquired through learning (poverty of the stimulus argument), whereas the latter group asserts that the stimuli in an individual's environment contain ample information for imitation to be learned (wealth of the stimulus argument). Many behavioral psychologists agree with the latter cognitive neuroscientists. Furthermore, many behavioral psychologists believe that the learning principles described in Part II (Chapters 3–16) of this book can fully account for how imitative behavior is learned.

   There are several processes by which imitative behavior can be learned. First, an individual is frequently reinforced after emitting behavior that is similar to behavior that another individual has emitted. Other people's actions tend to become S^Ds for engaging in similar actions. For example, a child who watches someone open a door to go outside receives the reinforcement of going outside after performing the same action. Second, to the extent that other people are reinforcing to us, their actions acquire conditioned reinforcing properties. We receive conditioned reinforcement when we perform the same actions. A third possibility is that once we have learned to imitate simple responses, we can then imitate more complex behaviors, provided that these are composed of the simpler responses. For example, once a child has learned to imitate "al," "li," "ga," and "tor" as single syllables, or as units of various words, the child can then imitate the word *alligator* upon hearing it for the first time (Skinner, 1957). A fourth possibility is that we imitate because, as infants, our mothers and others imitated us, creating an association between our behavior and similar behavior in them (the possibility is particularly cogent in explaining how we can imitate behavior when our own matching behavior is not visible to us, such as facial expressions when there is no mirror present). A fifth possibility is that imitative behavior is not just a set of separate stimulus–response relationships but is itself an operant class of responses. In other words, it is possible that once a child is reinforced for imitating some behaviors, the child will then tend to imitate other behaviors even though they contain no elements in common with the imitative behaviors that were reinforced. As indicated earlier in this chapter, this is referred to as *generalized imitation*. For more detailed interpretations of vicarious or observational or imitative learning from a behavioral approach, see Masia and Chase (1997), Pear (2001, pp. 95–100), or Taylor and DeQuinzio (2012).

Question for Further Learning

1. Describe five processes by which imitative behavior might be learned, and give an example of each.

CHAPTER 19

Antecedent Control: Motivation

OK, team! Here's how you can earn an Eagle Effort award.

Coach Dawson's Motivation Program[1]

"Let's see a little concentration out there. You should hardly ever miss layups in drills!" shouted Jim Dawson at a basketball practice. Jim was coach of the Clinton Junior High basketball team in Columbus, Ohio. He was concerned about the players' performance during a series of drills that he used to open each practice. There was also an attitude problem. "Some of them just aren't team players," he thought to himself. "Some of them really have a bad attitude."

With the help of Daryl Siedentop of the Ohio State University, he worked out a motivational system in which players could earn points for performance in layup drills, jump-shooting drills, and free throw drills at daily practice. In addition, they could earn points for being a "team player" by making supportive comments to teammates. Points were deducted if Coach Dawson saw a lack of hustle or a bad attitude. Student volunteers who served as managers for the team recorded the points. This motivational system was explained in detail to the players beforehand. At the end of a practice, the coach praised players who earned more points than they had in the previous practice as well as players who earned a large number of points. In addition, players who earned a sufficient number of points had their names posted conspicuously on an "Eagle Effort" board in the hall leading to the gymnasium. These players were also honored with an "Eagle Effort" award at a postseason banquet. Overall, the program was highly effective. Performance in layup drills improved from an average of 68% to an average of 80%. Jump-shooting performance improved from 37% to 51%. Free throw shooting at practices improved from 59% to 67%. However, the most dramatic improvement was in the "team player" category. The number of supportive comments made by the players to teammates increased to such an extent that the managers could not monitor them all. In addition, at first most of the supportive comments sounded "pretty phony," according to Coach Dawson, but over the season, they became increasingly sincere. By the end of the season, the players were exhibiting behavior meeting the definition of a positive attitude to a remarkable extent. In Coach Dawson's words, "We were more together than I ever could have imagined."

[1] This example is based on a report by Siedentop (1978).

A Traditional View of Motivation

Consider the behavior of Susie and Jack, two children in third grade. Susie consistently completes homework assignments, works hard during various classroom activities, listens attentively to the teacher, and is polite with the other children. According to Susie's teacher, "Susie is a good student *because* she's highly motivated." Jack, on the other hand, is the opposite. Jack rarely completes homework assignments, fools around while the teacher is talking, and doesn't appear to apply himself. Jack's teacher believes that Jack lacks motivation. As illustrated by these examples, many people conceptualize motivation as some "thing" within us that causes our actions. Many introductory psychology texts describe motivation as the study of inner drives, needs, and wants that cause our actions.

A conceptual or logical problem with the traditional view of motivation is that it involves circular reasoning. Why does Susie work hard? Because she is highly motivated. How do we know she's highly motivated? Because she works hard. In addition to this circularity, conceptualizing motivation as an internal cause of behavior has several practical problems. First, the suggestion that the causes of behavior are inside of us rather than in the environment might influence some to ignore the principles for changing behavior described in the earlier chapters of this book and the enormous amount of data demonstrating that application of those principles can effectively modify behavior. Second, conceptualizing motivation as an internal cause of behavior may influence some to blame the individual for substandard performance by attributing this to a lack of motivation, or laziness, rather than trying to help such individuals to improve their performance. Third, conceptualizing motivation as an internal cause of behavior may influence some to blame themselves for failures to emit various behaviors (e.g., "I just can't get motivated to go on a diet") rather than examining potential self-management strategies (see Chapter 26).

Questions for Learning

1. How do many people who are not behaviorists or behavior modifiers conceptualize motivation? Illustrate with an example.
2. What is a conceptual problem with the traditional view of motivation? Illustrate with an example.
3. Describe three practical problems with conceptualizing motivation as an internal cause of behavior.
4. If by "motivating someone to do something" we mean nothing more than manipulating antecedent conditions to influence that person to behave in a certain way, list each of the strategies presented in Chapters 17 and 18 to accomplish that task.

A Behavioral View of Motivation

It's one thing for a person to *know how* to emit a given behavior; it's another thing for that person to *want* to emit that behavior. Traditional psychological theories of motivation have addressed the "processes of wanting" by postulating inner drives. However, rather than taking this approach, behavioral psychologists have adopted the concept of a motivating operation, as introduced and developed by the pioneering behaviorist Jack Michael (1982, 1993, 2000, 2007). We touched on the concept of motivating operation in Chapter 4, but now we discuss it more in depth. (For a detailed discussion of the history of the treatment of motivation in behavior analysis, see Sundberg, 2004.)

A **motivating operation (MO)** is an event or operation that (a) temporarily alters the effectiveness of a reinforcer or punisher (a value-altering effect) and (b) influences behavior that normally leads to that reinforcer or punisher (a behavior-altering effect) (Laraway, Snycerski, Michael, & Poling, 2003). Let's first examine MOs involving reinforcers. Consider, for example, the unconditioned reinforcer of food. When we are food deprived, food is a powerful reinforcer, and we are likely to engage in various food-seeking behaviors. Just after eating a big meal, however, food temporarily loses its effectiveness as **NOTE 1** a reinforcer, and we are less likely to engage in food-seeking behaviors. Thus, deprivation and satiation of food are MOs.

MOs also affect punishers. Consider the punisher of timeout as discussed in Chapter 13. Suppose that at Little League baseball practices, a coach typically required a player to sit in the dugout alone for 5 minutes as a timeout contingent for swearing, throwing bats, and other misbehavior. Suppose also that at one particular practice, the coach announced that players would earn points for performing well (catching the ball, getting a hit, etc.), and that the five players with the most points would each be awarded a ticket to attend a major league baseball game. This announcement immediately made points a reinforcer for the players. In addition, it increased the effectiveness of the timeout as a punisher because the players could not earn points if they were sitting in the dugout for misbehavior.

You can see from these examples that there are two main types of mos: motivating establishing operations and motivating abolishing operations. A *motivating establishing operation (MEO)* is an event or operation that temporarily increases the effectiveness of a reinforcer or punisher and that increases the likelihood of behaviors that lead to that reinforcer or decreases the likelihood of behaviors that lead to that punisher. Food deprivation is an MEO. The announcement of the coach's points program was an MEO for points because it increased their reinforcing effectiveness. A *motivating abolishing operation (MAO)* is an event or operation that temporarily decreases the effectiveness of a reinforcer or punisher and decreases the likelihood of behaviors that normally lead to that reinforcer or increases the likelihood of behaviors that normally lead to that punisher. Food satiation is an MAO. Lang et al. (2009) used an MAO to temporarily decrease a problem behavior that interfered with teaching an appropriate play behavior to a child with autism. The problem behavior that was frequently displayed by the child was stereotyped spinning of toys on a flat surface so that a toy rotated in rapid circles. When the child was allowed to engage in a stereotyped behavior freely prior to a training session for functional play, this acted as an MAO to decrease the reinforcing value of stereotypy, so that it was much lower during the functional play session.

Unconditioned Versus Conditioned Motivating Operations

In addition to distinguishing between MEOs and MAOs, we also distinguish between unconditioned and conditioned motivating operations (Michael, 1993); see Figure 19.1. With *unconditioned motivating operations (UMOs)*, the value-altering effect is innate. Thus, deprivation of food is an *unconditioned motivating establishing operation (UMEO)* because it increases the effectiveness of food as a reinforcer without prior learning. Satiation is an *unconditioned motivating abolishing operation (UMAO)* because it decreases the effectiveness of food as a reinforcer without prior learning. The behavior-altering effect of UMOs, however, is learned. For example, when someone is hungry, the behaviors of looking in the refrigerator or going to a fast-food outlet are learned behaviors. Other UMEOs include deprivation of **NOTE 2** water, sleep, activity, oxygen, and sexual stimulation. Satiation of each of these are UMAOs

Some MOs alter the effectiveness of consequences as reinforcers or punishers because of prior learning. Such MOs are called *conditioned motivating operations (CMOs)*. Coach Dawson's announcement of the program with the basketball players was an MEO because it established the points as reinforcers for the players and it increased the likelihood of desirable practice behaviors to earn those reinforcers. More specifically, his announcement of the program was a conditioned motivating establishing operation (CMEO) because it established points as conditioned reinforcers from prior learning. The announcement would not have worked as a motivating operation if the players had not previously learned to respond to such announcements.

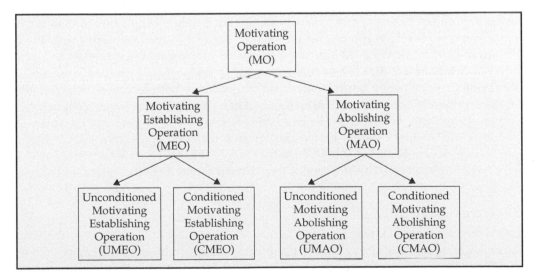

FIGURE 19.1
Types of motivating operations

Martin (2015) described the strategy that a young competitive golfer used to motivate himself to practice putting. The golfer used imagery to create pressure games. When practicing putting, the golfer would frequently imagine that he was leading the tournament on the final day of the U.S. Open. For each of 18 practice putts, he would pretend that he needed the putt to maintain the lead. In this example, by using the imaginary pressure game, the golfer was administering a CMEO to himself. The pressure game increased the conditioned reinforcing value of making a putt and increased the likelihood of focusing appropriately to make the putt.

As indicated previously, the value-altering effect of a UMO is innate, while the behavior-altering effect is learned. However, with CMOs, both the value-altering and the behavior-altering effects are due to learning. As Sundberg (2004) pointed out, many of the topics discussed under motivation in introductory psychology books, such as "acquired drives" or "social motives," involve CMOs.

CMEOs and S^Ds

When considering stimulus control over behavior, it is easy to confuse the concept of discriminative stimulus, or S^D, and the concept of CMEO. Knowledge of both is important in being able to reliably and effectively use either as antecedent variables to influence behavior. An S^D is a stimulus that has been correlated with the availability of a reinforcer for a particular behavior. To influence an individual's behavior by presenting an S^D, that individual must have been deprived of the reinforcer associated with responding to that S^D. In everyday language, an S^D is a cue that tells you what to do to get what you already want. Suppose that a family is camping on a cold fall evening. A parent might say to a shivering child, "Move your sleeping bag closer to the campfire and you'll feel warmer." This statement would be an S^D for the child to move the sleeping bag closer to the campfire. Warmth was obviously a reinforcer for the shivering child. A CMEO is a motivator that momentarily increases the value of a conditioned reinforcer and increases the likelihood of behavior that has led to that reinforcer in the past. In everyday language, a CMEO is a cue that makes you want something and tells you what to do to get it. Suppose a parent says to his teenage daughter, "Each time that you mow the lawn, you can earn 3 points, and each time that you trim the hedges you can earn 2 points. When you accumulate 20 points, you can use the family car for a weekend." In this example, the rule given by the parent is a CMEO. The rule established points as conditioned reinforcers for the teenager and told her how to earn them.

CMAOs and S^Δs

The distinction between S^Δ and conditioned motivating abolishing operation (CMAO) is analogous to the distinction between S^D and CMEO. An S^Δ is a stimulus in the presence of which a response has not been reinforced. It is also assumed that the individual has been deprived of that particular reinforcer. In everyday language, an S^Δ is a cue that tells you that emitting a particular behavior will not lead to something that you want. Suppose that while shopping with their child in the past, parents had purchased candy when the child screamed, "I want candy." Suppose further that, at the beginning of a shopping excursion, the same parents tell their child, "We're not going to buy you candy when you scream." If the parents stick to this rule, this instruction would be an S^Δ for screaming. In contrast, a CMAO is a stimulus that momentarily decreases the value of a conditioned reinforcer and decreases the likelihood of behavior that has led to that reinforcer in the past. In everyday language, a CMAO influences someone to no longer want a particular consequence and decreases behavior that would lead to that consequence. Suppose that Charlie shopped at a particular grocery store because purchases were accompanied by coupons that could be cashed in for movie tickets. One day the store announced that in the future, the coupons would be exchanged only for country-western CDs. Charlie, who is not a country-western fan, begins to shop at another store. The store's announcement was a CMAO for Charlie, decreasing the value of the coupons and decreasing the behavior that had led to obtaining those coupons.

Questions for Learning

5. Define *motivating operation*. Give an example that illustrates both aspects of the definition.
6. In what two ways are motivating establishing operations and motivating abolishing operations different?
7. Are the value-altering and behavior-alternating effects of unconditioned motivating operations learned or innate? Discuss with reference to an example.

8. Are the value-altering and behavior-alternating effects of CMOs learned or innate? Discuss with reference to an example.
9. Would you describe Coach Dawson's explanation of the points program to the basketball players as a UMEO or a CMEO? Justify your choice.
10. Suppose that a football team has been practicing for an hour in the hot sun without water. The coach says to one of the players, "Here are the keys to my car. Get the bottles of water from the trunk." Would this request be classified as an S^D or a CMEO for getting the water? Justify your choice.
11. Suppose that a pianist sets a goal for practicing a piece: "Before I can stop practicing, I have to play this piece through 10 times in a row without making a mistake." Is that goal best conceptualized as an S^D or a CMEO? Justify your choice.

Some Applications of Motivating Operations
Teaching Mands to Children with Autism

Considerable success has been achieved in a number of language intervention programs for typically developing children and children with autism and other developmental disabilities by combining intensive behavioral interventions with Skinner's (1957) analysis of verbal behavior (Carr & Miguel, 2013; Sundberg & Michael, 2001; Sundberg & Partington, 1998; Verbeke, Martin, Thorsteinsson, Murphy, & Yu, 2009). Skinner was interested in studying the verbal behavior of individual speakers rather than the grammatical practices of a verbal community. He defined *verbal behavior* as behavior that is reinforced through the mediation of another person when the person providing the reinforcement was specifically trained to provide such reinforcement. Verbal behavior is contrasted with nonverbal behavior, which is behavior that is reinforced through contact with the physical environment. Skinner distinguished among several types of basic verbal responses, three of which were echoics, tacts, and mands. Skinner's definitions are technical, but roughly, an **echoic** is a vocal imitative response that is developed and maintained by social reinforcement. If a parent says, "Say 'water,'" and the child says "water" and receives praise, the child's response "water" is an echoic. A **tact** is a naming response that is developed and maintained by social reinforcement. If the parent points to a glass of water and asks, "What's that?" and the child says "water" and receives praise, the child's response "water" is a tact. A **mand** is a verbal response that is under the control of a motivating operation and is reinforced by the corresponding reinforcer or removal of the corresponding aversive stimulus. If a child is thirsty NOTE 3 and asks a parent for "water," the child's response "water" is a mand. The same spoken word, *water*, is considered to be a different verbal response (e.g., an echoic, a tact, or a mand) depending on its controlling variables.

Observations suggest that a mand is the first type of verbal behavior acquired by a child (Bijou & Baer, 1965; Skinner, 1957). Therefore, it is natural to start with mands when training verbal behavior. MOs have been used effectively in mand training programs for children with autism and developmental disabilities (Sundberg & Michael, 2001). Structured mand training typically begins by teaching a child to mand a reinforcer (such as a specific food or a favorite toy) that has high motivational value. To teach the child to mand for juice, the parent might give the child a sip of juice on the first trial. Next, in full view of the child, the parent might hide the juice under the table and ask the child, "What do you want? Say 'juice.'" If the child responds correctly, the child would be given another sip of juice. At this point, as you probably have discerned, the child is showing echoic behavior. On subsequent trials while hiding the juice, the parent would simply say, "What do you want?" and would reinforce asking for juice. After a certain amount of this type of training, the child is likely to generalize the behavior of saying "juice" to other situations when motivated for juice. Sundberg and Partington (1998) and Sundberg (2004) described additional strategies for using MOs for mand training.

Researchers have used contrived CMEOs to teach children with autism to mand for information. For example, in what was referred to as a *hide-and-seek* CMEO, a child and experimenter played with some toys and the toy that the child seemed to prefer was hidden when the child was not looking (Roy-Wsiaki, Marion, Martin, & Yu, 2010). The experimenter would then say, "I hid something," and the child would be prompted to as "What?" The experimenter then stated the item (e.g., the train) and gave the item to the child. Over several trials the prompt was faded and the child continued to appropriately ask "What?" when the experimenter said, "I hid something." Also, the child generalized the use of the mand "What" across three different settings, to a novel activity, with novel scripts, and over time. Similar procedures have been used to teach children with autism to appropriately mand "Where" (Marion, Martin, Yu, Buhler, & Kerr, 2012) and "Which" (Marion et al., 2012).

Motivating Seat Belt Use among Senior Drivers

Pleasant Oaks is a residential senior community in Virginia. The seniors living there have an enjoyable lifestyle including frequent car trips to nearby Charlottesville. Many of those at Pleasant Oaks were acutely aware that automobile accidents are the leading cause of accidental death among individuals between the ages of 65 and 74. Although injuries, hospitalizations, and deaths are significantly fewer among drivers who wear safety belts, 30% of the drivers and passengers entering and leaving Pleasant Oaks did not buckle up. Brian, Amanda, and Daniel Cox of the University of Virginia Health Sciences Center decided to implement a simple procedure to try to encourage more residents of Pleasant Oaks to wear their seat belts. On stop signs located at the exits of the community scattered around Pleasant Oaks, these researchers placed the message, "BUCKLE UP, STAY SAFE" on permanent, aluminum vinyl-lettered signs. Because feeling safe is an important concern for seniors, the researchers hypothesized that the signs would function as a CMEO to increase the reinforcing value of wearing a fastened seat belt and therefore would increase the behavior of buckling up. They were right. Following installation of the signs, the percentage of seniors who buckled up increased from 70% to 94%. Six months after installation of the signs, 88% of the seniors continued to use seat belts appropriately (Cox, Cox, & Cox, 2000). (For a description of the use of CMEOs to increase seat belt use of drivers at a medium sized university campus, see Clayton & Helms, 2009; and to increase seat belt usage of commercial drivers from the United States and Canada, see VanHouten et al., 2010.)

Decreasing Self-Injurious Behavior Maintained by Attention

MOs are frequently manipulated to decrease problem behavior, usually to prevent the behavior from interfering with an ongoing program or as a first step toward using other procedures (e.g., extinction) to reduce the behavior further (see Simó-Pinatella, Font-Roura, Planella-Morató, McGill, Alomar-Kurz, & Giné, 2013). This is illustrated by the following case. Brenda was a 42-year-old woman with profound intellectual disability who lived in a public residential facility for persons with developmental disabilities. She had a long history of self-injurious behavior (SIB), including severe head banging and head hitting. Observations indicated that her SIB was maintained by reactions of well-meaning staff. After an instance of SIB, a staff member might say, "Brenda, don't do that, you'll hurt yourself." To treat Brenda's SIB, Timothy Vollmer and colleagues introduced a program that included an MAO for staff attention. During treatment sessions, a schedule of noncontingent reinforcement in which attention was initially provided every 10 seconds was arranged. This satiated Brenda on attention, and her SIB that had been previously reinforced by attention immediately dropped to a very low level. Extinction was also a part of the treatment in that the SIB was no longer followed by attention. Over several sessions, the frequency of noncontingent attention gradually decreased from its initial rate of six instances per minute to a final rate of one instance every 5 minutes. SIB remained at a very low level. Similar results were obtained with two other individuals (Vollmer, Iwata, Zarcone, Smith, & Mazaleski, 1993). In order to manipulate MOs to decrease problem behavior it is necessary to identify MOs that control the problem behavior and determine exactly how they control it (Simó-Pinatella et al., 2013). This is discussed further in Chapter 23. For a review of manipulated MOs during interventions to treat problem behaviors of school-age participants with intellectual disabilities, see Simó-Pinatella et al. (2013).

Motivating Operations and Behavior Modification

In this chapter, we discussed an antecedent variable—MOs—that temporarily alter the effectiveness of consequences as reinforcers or punishers and that thereby temporarily alter the occurrence of behavior influenced by such consequences. Consideration of MOs in the design of behavior modification programs is likely to enhance their effectiveness.

Questions for Learning

12. Define *echoic*, and give an example that is not in the book.
13. Define *tact*, and give an example that is not in the book .
14. Define *mand*, and give an example that is not in the book .

15. Using an example, describe how a motivating operation might be incorporated into mand training with a child.
16. How was a CMEO used to motivate seat belt use among senior drivers?
17. How was an MAO applied to decrease the self-injurious behavior of a woman with profound intellectual disability?

Application Exercise

Self-Modification Exercise

Suppose that you want to increase the frequency of your studying. Several strategies might help motivate you to master the answers to the study questions in this book. (a) Post the dates beginning now and ending with the final exam for the course, and cross off each day as it passes. (b) Arrange to study with a friend on a regular basis. (c) Sign a contract with a friend or relative that stipulates that you will be given certain reinforcers if you meet certain study objectives. (d) Rearrange your study environment to present cues for studying and to eliminate cues for incompatible behaviors (such as watching TV). Pick three strategies and briefly describe each of them. Indicate whether each of the strategies involves presentation of an S^D, S^Δ, CMEO, or CMAO. In each case, justify your choice.

Notes for Further Learning

1. As Poling (2001) has pointed out, it is important to keep in mind that a given MO is likely to affect many behaviors, and a given behavior is likely to be affected by many MOs. Consider, for example, the MEO of food deprivation. Food deprivation not only increases the reinforcing value of food and leads to various food-seeking behaviors but also increases the reinforcing value of a broad range of abused drugs and could lead to increased drug use. It also increases the reinforcing value of water and thus increases water intake (Poling). Thus, for the MO concept to be maximally useful as a behavior management tool, researchers must examine ways for isolating MOs that affect important behaviors in predictable ways.

2. Ingestion or injection of drugs also functions as a motivating operation (Pear, 2001, p. 281). Amphetamines, for example, function as a UMAO to decrease the reinforcing effectiveness of food; aphrodisiacs function as a UMEO to increase the reinforcing effectiveness of sexual stimulation. In this book, however, we focus on motivational variables that are located in the individual's external environment.

3. According to Skinner's (1957) analysis of verbal behavior, a child's response "juice" to a parent's question "What do you want?" fits the definition of an *intraverbal*—because it is a verbal response under the control of a preceding verbal stimulus with no point-to-point correspondence between the stimulus and the response. The child's response "juice" is, however, at least partly a mand because it is under the control of a specific deprivation state. Thus, overlap among the different categories of verbal behavior can occur. When training mands, some intraverbal training may be necessary to begin. Ideally, the child will eventually learn to make requests without requiring an antecedent verbal stimulus to prompt the request. At that point, the child will be emitting pure mands.

Questions for Further Learning

1. Give an example illustrating that a given MO may affect the value of more than one reinforcer and may influence the occurrence of many behaviors.
2. Give an example that illustrates how a drug might function as an MO. What subtype of MO would it be (see Figure 19.1)? Justify your answer.
3. Distinguish between a mand and an intraverbal. Illustrate each with an example that is not in the text.

CHAPTER 20

Behavioral Assessment: Initial Considerations

LEARNING OBJECTIVES

After studying this chapter, you will be able to:

- Describe the minimal phases of a behavior modification program.
- Compare and contrast indirect and direct behavioral assessment procedures.

- Explain why it is important to record accurate data during a baseline and throughout a program.

Throughout this book, numerous examples illustrate the effectiveness of behavior modification procedures. Many of these examples are accompanied by graphs showing the changes (increases or decreases) that occurred in behavior when particular procedures were applied. Some of the graphs also include follow-up observations indicating that the improvements were maintained after the programs had terminated. The graphs were presented not just to make it easier for you to understand the material; precise records of behavior represent an inseparable part of behavior modification procedures. Indeed, some have gone so far as to say that the major contribution of behavior modification has been the insistence on accurately recording specific behaviors and making decisions on the basis of recorded data rather than merely on the basis of subjective impressions.

As indicated in Chapter 1, the behaviors to be improved in a behavior modification program are frequently called target behaviors. **Behavioral assessment** involves the collection and analysis of information and data in order to (a) identify and describe target behavior; (b) identify possible causes of the behavior; (c) select appropriate treatment strategies to modify the behavior; and (d) evaluate treatment outcome.

Minimal Phases of a Program

A successful behavior modification program typically involves four phases during which the target behavior is identified, defined, and recorded: (a) a screening or intake phase, (b) a preprogram or baseline assessment phase, (c) a treatment phase, and (d) a follow-up phase. In this section, we give a brief overview of these phases.

Screening or Intake Phase

The initial interactions between a client and a practitioner or an agency constitute the *intake phase.* During this phase, a client typically completes an *intake form,* which requests general information: the client's name, address, date of birth, marital status, and so forth. It also asks the client to state the reason for seeking service from that agency or practitioner.

One function of the screening phase is to determine whether a particular agency, behavior therapist, or applied behavior analyst is appropriate to deal with a potential client's behavior (Hawkins, 1979). If not, the results of this phase should indicate the agency or practitioner who should work with the client. For example, a center for children with learning difficulties might screen a child to determine whether the child's academic skills are unusual enough to require some sort of program not ordinarily provided by the school. A second function is to inform the client about the agency's or practitioner's policies and procedures related to service provision. A third function is to screen for the presence of a crisis condition (child abuse, suicide risk, etc.) that might require immediate intervention. A fourth function of the screening phase is to gather sufficient information through client interview and psychological tests (such as intelligence tests) to diagnose the client according to the standardized categories of mental disorder, such as those listed in the *Diagnostic and Statistical Manual of Mental Disorders, 5th ed.* (American Psychiatric Association, 2013), also known as the *DSM-5*. As indicated in Note 1 of Chapter 1, clinics, hospitals, schools, and other agencies might require such diagnoses before treatment can be offered, and health insurance companies might require them before treatment can be paid for. A fifth function of the screening phase is to provide specific information about which behavior(s) should be assessed. To achieve this initial assessment, applied behavior analysts and behavior therapists use all of the above information plus other information such as teachers' reports, various traditional test results, and other assessment devices to aid in pinpointing specific target behaviors to address.

Preprogram Assessment or Baseline Phase

During the *assessment or baseline* phase, the behavior modifier assesses the target behavior to determine its level prior to the introduction of the program or treatment and analyzes the individual's current environment to identify possible controlling variables of the behavior to be changed.

The need for a preprogram assessment phase follows from the importance that applied behavior analysts and behavior therapists place on directly measuring the behavior of concern and using changes in the measure as the best indicator that the problem is being helped as explained in Chapter 1. If a child is having difficulty in school, for example, the behavior modifier would be especially interested in obtaining a baseline of specific behavioral excesses or deficits that constitute the problem (e.g., a reading deficiency or disruptive behavior). Further details about the sources of information for the preprogram assessment phase are given later in this chapter.

Treatment Phase

After making a precise preprogram assessment, an applied behavior analyst or behavior therapist will design a program to bring about the desired behavior change. In educational settings, such a program is typically referred to as a *training* or *teaching program*. In community and clinical settings, the program is referred to more often as an *intervention strategy* or a *therapy program*.

Behavior modification programs typically provide for frequent observation and monitoring of the target behavior during training or treatment. In some cases, the difference between behavior modification and other approaches on this point is primarily a matter of degree. Traditional educational practices typically involve periodic assessment during the teaching program for the purpose of monitoring the students' performance. Clinical treatment programs typically involve client assessment at various intervals. Moreover, some programs that have been labeled behavior modification have consisted primarily of before-and-after measures and have lacked precise, ongoing recording during treatment. Nevertheless, behavior modifiers emphasize and practice, to a degree rarely found in other approaches, frequent monitoring of the behavior throughout the application of the specific treatment or intervention strategies. In addition, applied behavior analysts and behavior therapists strongly emphasize changing the program if the measurements taken indicate that the desired change in behavior is not occurring within a reasonable period of time.

Follow-Up Phase

Finally, the *follow-up phase* is conducted to determine whether the improvements achieved during treatment are maintained after the program's termination. When feasible, this will consist of precise observation or assessment in the natural environment or under circumstances in which the behavior is expected to occur.

Questions for Learning

1. What does the term *target behavior* mean? Illustrate with an example from an earlier chapter.
2. Define *behavioral assessment*.
3. List the four phases of a behavior modification program.
4. What are the five functions of the intake phase of a behavior modification program?
5. What two things typically occur during the assessment phase of a behavior modification program?

6. In what types of settings are the terms *training program*, and *intervention strategy* or *therapy program* typically used?

7. What is the purpose of the follow-up phase of a behavior modification program?

Sources of Information for Preprogram Assessment

Defining target behaviors clearly, completely, and in measurable terms is an important prerequisite to the design and implementation of behavior modification programs. Behavioral assessment procedures for collecting information to define and monitor target behaviors fall into three categories: indirect, direct, and experimental.

Indirect Assessment Procedures

In many situations in which a behavior modification program might be applied, the behavior modifier can directly observe the behavior of interest. However, suppose that you are a behavior therapist who, like other professional therapists, sees clients in your office at regularly scheduled appointment times. It might be impractical for you to observe clients regularly in the situations in which the target behaviors occur. Moreover, what if some of your clients wanted to change some of their thoughts and feelings that others couldn't observe? As discussed in Chapters 15 and 27, most applied behavior analysts and behavior therapists regard thoughts and feelings as private or covert behaviors (for exceptions see Baum, 2011 and Rachlin, 2011; for counter arguments to their views, see, e.g., Schlinger, 2011). For such changes, behavior therapists have made considerable use of indirect assessment procedures. The most common are interviews with the client and significant others, questionnaires, role-playing, information obtained from consulting professionals, and client self-monitoring. Indirect assessment procedures have the advantages of being convenient, not requiring an inordinate amount of time, and potentially providing information about covert behaviors. However, they suffer from the disadvantages that those providing information might not remember relevant observations accurately or have biases that would influence them to provide inaccurate data.

Interviews with the Client and Significant Others   In interviewing the client and significant others (spouse, parents, or anyone else directly concerned with the client's welfare), behavior therapists attempt to establish and maintain rapport with the client and the significant others. The therapist might begin by briefly describing the types of problems that he or she typically works with and the general approach that he or she uses. The therapist might then ask a number of simple questions concerning the client's background or might ask the client to complete a simple demographic referral form. The therapist is attentive to the client's description of the problem while refraining from expressing personal values that might unduly influence the client, showing empathy by communicating understanding of the client's feelings, and emphasizing the confidentiality of the client–therapist relationship.

During initial interviews, behavior therapists and traditional therapists typically use similar techniques such as being a good listener, asking open-ended questions, requesting clarification, and acknowledging the validity of the client's feelings and problems. In addition to using the initial interview to build rapport with the client, the behavior therapist attempts to obtain information that will be helpful in identifying the target behavior and the variables that currently control it (Sarwer & Sayers, 1998; Spiegler & Guevremont, 2010, pp. 84–85). Table 20.1 shows the types of questions that the behavior therapist typically asks in the initial interview.

Questionnaires   A well-designed questionnaire provides information that might be useful in assessing a client's problem and developing a behavioral program tailored to the client. A large number of such questionnaires are available. Many of these, including questionnaires for couples, families, children, and adults, can be found in a two-volume compendium complied by Fischer and Corcoran (2007a, 2007b). Several types of questionnaires are popular with behavior therapists.

Life history questionnaires provide demographic data such as marital status, vocational status, and religious affiliation, and background data such as sexual, health, and educational histories. A notable example is *The Multimodal Life History Inventory* (Lazarus & Lazarus, 2005).

Self-report problem checklists have the client indicate from a detailed list those problem(s) that apply to him or her. Such questionnaires are particularly useful in helping the therapist completely specify the problem or problems for which the client is seeking therapy. An example of a self-report behavioral checklist was developed by Martin and Thomson (2010) for helping young figure skaters

TABLE 20.1   Examples of Questions a Behavior Therapist Typically Asks During an Intake Interview

1. What seems to be the problem?
2. Can you describe what you typically say or do when you experience the problem?
3. How often does the problem occur?
4. For how long has the problem been occurring?
5. In what situations does the problem typically occur? In other words, what sets it off?
6. What tends to occur immediately after you experience the problem?
7. What are you typically thinking and feeling when the problem occurs?
8. How have you tried to deal with the problem thus far?

identify problems that might require sport psychology consultation (see Figure 20.1). Asher, Gordon, Selbst, and Cooperberg (2010) developed a variety of checklists for clinical work with children and adolescents experiencing a wide range of diagnoses, including ADHD and mood disorders.   NOTE 1

Name _____   Date _____

Would you say you need help or need to improve:	Check here if not sure	Definitely no		To some extent		Definitely yes

Regarding Free Skating Practices, to:

1. Set specific goals for every practice?	_____	1	2	3	4	5
2. Arrive at every practice totally committed to do your best?	_____	1	2	3	4	5
3. Consistently be stretched and warmed up before stepping on the ice at practice?	_____	1	2	3	4	5
4. Be more focused when doing your jumps and spins? (Answer "yes" if you often just do the jumps or spins in a haphazard way without trying to do your best.)	_____	1	2	3	4	5
5. Stay positive and not get down on yourself when you're having a bad practice?	_____	1	2	3	4	5
6. Make better use of full practice time?	_____	1	2	3	4	5
7. Overcome fear of doing difficult jumps?	_____	1	2	3	4	5
8. Improve consistency of jumps you can already land?	_____	1	2	3	4	5
9. Feel more confident about your ability to do difficult jumps?	_____	1	2	3	4	5
10. Not worry about what other skaters are doing?	_____	1	2	3	4	5
11. Figure out how to monitor progress on a new jump that you are learning, so that you don't get discouraged when progress seems slow?	_____	1	2	3	4	5
12. Do more complete program run-throughs (where you try everything in your program)?	_____	1	2	3	4	5
13. Keep track of your % landed during program run-throughs?	_____	1	2	3	4	5
14. Make better use of video feedback when learning a new jump?	_____	1	2	3	4	5
15. Push harder while stroking, in order to get in better shape?	_____	1	2	3	4	5
16. Keep a written record of your progress in meeting your goal?	_____	1	2	3	4	5

FIGURE 20.1

A questionnaire to assess areas in need of help during a seasonal sport psychology program for figure skaters

Source: Reprinted with permission from Martin and Thomson (2010)

Would you say you need help or need to improve:	Check here if not sure	Definitely no		To some extent		Definitely yes
Regarding Free Skating at a Competition, to:						
1. Stay confident at practices when you see what the other skaters are doing?	_____	1	2	3	4	5
2. At practices, forget about other skaters and just focus on your own skating?	_____	1	2	3	4	5
3. Avoid putting extra pressure on yourself when you see what other skaters are doing at practices?	_____	1	2	3	4	5
4. Learn how not to worry about other skaters?	_____	1	2	3	4	5
5. Learn how not to worry about where you will place?	_____	1	2	3	4	5
6. Have a better time management plan for the entire competition so you are well organized, eat healthy, and get lots of rest?	_____	1	2	3	4	5
7. Skate as well during a competition as during the last 2 or 3 weeks before the competition (in other words, skate up to your potential)?	_____	1	2	3	4	5
8. Stay loose (not too tense) during the last ½-hour or so before the 6' warmup?	_____	1	2	3	4	5
9. Stay loose (not too tense) during the 6' warmup?	_____	1	2	3	4	5
10. Stay loose (not too tense) after the 6' warmup while waiting for your turn?	_____	1	2	3	4	5
11. Stay loose (not too tense) when you go on the ice for your turn?	_____	1	2	3	4	5
12. Feel confident about your skating while stretching before the 6' warmup?	_____	1	2	3	4	5
13. Not be psyched out by other skaters?	_____	1	2	3	4	5
14. Feel confident about your skating during the 6' warmup?	_____	1	2	3	4	5
15. Feel confident about your skating after the 6' warmup, while waiting for your turn to skate?	_____	1	2	3	4	5
16. Take it one element at a time during your program (& not get ahead of yourself or think only about difficult elements)?	_____	1	2	3	4	5
17. Concentrate on easy elements as well as hard ones?	_____	1	2	3	4	5
18. Stay positive and skate well for the rest of your program, even if you fall?	_____	1	2	3	4	5

FIGURE 20.1
Continued

Survey schedules provide the therapist information needed to conduct a particular therapeutic technique with the client. The questionnaire shown in Table 4.2 provides information useful in applying positive reinforcement procedures. Other types of survey schedules are designed to provide information preparatory to using other behavioral procedures (e.g., see Asher et al., 2010).

Third-party behavioral checklists or *rating scales* permit significant others and professionals to subjectively assess the frequency and quality of certain client behaviors. An example of such a checklist is the Discrete-Trials Teaching Evaluation Form (Fazzio, Arnal, & Martin, 2010), which can be used to reliably evaluate the quality of one-on-one training sessions conducted by a behavior modifier with a child with autism (Jeanson et al., 2010).

Role-Playing   If it is not feasible for the therapist to observe the client in the actual situation in which the problem occurs, an alternative is to re-create that situation or at least certain crucial aspects of it in the therapist's office. That, essentially, is the rationale behind role-playing—the client and therapist enact interpersonal interactions related to the client's problem (as described in Chapter 18). For example, the client might enact being interviewed for a job with the therapist playing the role of the interviewer. Role-playing is frequently used both in assessing a problem and in treating it (see, e.g., Answer: page 175; also see Spiegler & Guevremont, 2010, pp. 77–80).

Information from Consulting Professionals   If other professionals (physicians, physiotherapists, teachers, nurses, social workers) have been dealing with the client in any way related to the problem, the therapist should obtain relevant information from them. A client's problem might be related to a medical factor about which his or her physician could provide important information for dealing with it. Before requesting such information, the client must give permission.

Client Self-Monitoring   Self-monitoring—the direct observation by the client of his or her own behavior—is the next best thing to the therapist's direct observation. We mention it under indirect assessment procedures because the therapist does not observe the behavior directly. Thus, as with the other indirect assessment procedures, the therapist cannot have as much confidence in the observations as would be the case if a trained observer had made them.

Except for covert behavior, behaviors that might be self-monitored are the same as those that a trained observer would observe directly. These are described in Chapter 21. Self-monitoring might also aid the discovery of the causes of the problem behavior, as discussed in Chapter 23. Additional examples of self-monitoring are provided in Chapter 26.

Direct Assessment Procedures

In each of the case histories at the beginning of Chapters 4–14, the target behavior was directly observable by other individuals. Observation of a person's behavior by another individual constitutes a direct assessment procedure. The main advantage of direct assessment procedures is that they are more accurate than indirect assessment procedures. Disadvantages of direct assessment procedures are that they are time consuming, require that observers be appropriately trained, and cannot be used to monitor covert behaviors. Chapter 21 is devoted to a discussion of direct assessment procedures.

Experimental Assessment Procedures

Experimental assessment procedures are used to clearly reveal the antecedent and consequent events that control and maintain problem behavior. Such procedures are referred to as *experimental functional analyses* or more simply as *functional analyses*. They are used to demonstrate that the occurrence of a behavior is a function of certain controlling variables. Functional analysis is discussed in detail in Chapter 23.

Computer-Assisted Data Collection

Starting around the early 1990s, computer technology in the form of devices such as personal computers, laptops, personal digital assistants (PDAs), smartphones, and tablet computers has become available for direct observational recording (Farrell, 1991; Haynes, 1998; Ice, 2004; Kahng, Ingvarsson, Quigg, Seckinger, & Teichman, 2011, pp. 117–118; Thompson, Felce, & Symons, 2000; Whiting & Dixon, 2012). Applications (apps) for handheld devices used to collect direct observational data from single or multiple clients can be found online or custom-made. The data are directly transferred to a computer for analysis.

Examples of computerized observation systems for direct assessment procedures have been described by Brown et al. (2006), Bush and Ciocco (1992), Hile (1991), McIver, Brown, Pfeiffer, Dowda, and Pate (2009), Raiff and Dallery (2010), and Richard and Bobicz (2003). Brown et al. and McIver et al. described a handheld system in which an observer moves a light pen over various bar codes to enter the occurrence of different categories of children's physical activity in real time. For an overview of a number of computerized systems that have been used to collect observational data, see Ice (2004) and Kahng and Iwata (2000). Handheld devices have also been used to facilitate client self-monitoring. For example, in a study by Taylor, Fried, and Kenardy (1990), clients recorded panic and anxiety symptoms, cognitive factors, and settings, while, in a study by Agras, Taylor, Feldman, Losch, and Burnett (1990), obese clients monitored their weight, caloric intake, exercise, daily goals, and goal attainment using hand held devices.

Devices that automatically record behavior are also being developed and used in applied settings. For example, devices have been developed to automatically record physical activity (e.g., see Loprinzi & Cardinal, 2011; Sirard & Pate, 2001), facial movements (e.g., Lancioni et al., 2011), and seat belt use (Van Houten, Malenfant, Austin, & Lebbon, 2005).

Questions for Learning

8. What is prerequisite to the design and implementation of a behavior modification program?
9. Briefly distinguish between direct and indirect assessment procedures.
10. Describe two circumstances that might lead to the use of indirect assessment procedures.
11. Briefly describe the advantages and disadvantages of indirect assessment procedures.
12. List the five main types of indirect assessment procedures.
13. List and describe briefly four types of questionnaires used in behavioral assessments.
14. Briefly describe the advantages and disadvantages of direct assessment procedures.

Data! Data! Data! Why Bother?

Accurate data are recorded for a number of reasons. One reason is that, as indicated at the beginning of this chapter, an accurate behavioral preprogram assessment helps the behavior modifier to decide whether he or she is the appropriate one to design a treatment program. Considerations relevant to this are described in more detail in Chapter 24.

A second reason is that an accurate baseline will sometimes indicate that what someone thought to be a problem is actually not one. For example, a teacher might say, "I don't know what to do with Johnny; he's always hitting the other kids." But after taking a baseline, the teacher might discover that the behavior actually occurs so rarely that it does not merit a special program. Both of the authors have experienced this phenomenon more than once. Others have, too, as illustrated by the following example from Greenspoon (1976):

> The reliance on casual observation led a woman to complain to a psychologist that her husband rarely talked to her during mealtime. She said that his failure to talk to her was becoming an increasing source of annoyance to her and she wanted to do something about it. The psychologist suggested that she prepare a chart and record on the chart the number of times that he initiated a conversation or responded to the verbal behavior that she emitted. She agreed to the suggestion. At the end of a week, she called back to inform the psychologist that she was surprised and pleased to report that she had been in error. It turned out that her husband both initiated conversation and responded to her verbal emissions at a very high rate. (p. 177)

A third reason is that data collected during the preprogram assessment phase often helps the behavior modifier identify both the causes of a behavior and the best treatment strategy. For example, determining whether a behavioral excess of an individual is reinforced by the attention of others, whether it enables the individual to escape from the demands of an unpleasant task, or whether some other variable controls it can be helpful for discovering potential reinforcers and designing an effective intervention program. As mentioned, using information from a baseline to analyze the causes of behavior is referred to as a *functional assessment*; it is discussed further in Chapter 23.

A fourth reason for collecting accurate data throughout a program is that it provides a means for clearly determining whether the program is producing the desired change in behavior. Sometimes people claim that they do not need to record data to know whether a desirable change in behavior has occurred. No doubt this is often true. A mother obviously needs no data sheet or graphs to tell her that her child is completely toilet trained. But not all cases are so clear-cut—at least not immediately. Suppose that a child is acquiring toileting behavior very slowly. The parent might think that the program is not working and abandon it prematurely. With accurate data, this type of mistake can be avoided. This point is well illustrated by the following case.[1] Dr. Lynn Caldwell was consulted by a

---

[1] This case was described by Lynn Caldwell at the first Manitoba Behavior Change Conference, Portage la Prairie, Manitoba, Canada, 1971.

woman whose 6-year-old son was, in her words, "driving me up a wall with his constant slamming of the kitchen door every time he goes out of the kitchen." Dr. Caldwell asked the mother to obtain a baseline of the target behavior, by tallying each instance of it on a sheet of paper attached to the refrigerator. Over a 3-day period, the total number of door slams was 123. Dr. Caldwell then instructed the mother to provide approval each time the boy went through the door without slamming it. However, she was to administer a brief timeout each time he slammed the door. He was to go back and remain for 3 minutes in whichever room he had just left, and the mother was to ignore him during that time and then require him to proceed through the door without slamming it. After applying this procedure for 3 days, the mother brought the tally sheet to Dr. Caldwell. "This behavior modification stuff doesn't work," she complained, pointing to the large number of tally marks on the data sheet. "He's just as bad as he ever was." When the tally marks were counted, however, there were only 87 of them over the 3 days of treatment, compared with the 123 that were entered over the 3 days of baseline. Encouraged by this observation, the mother continued the program, and the behavior quickly dropped to an acceptable level of about five per day.

Without accurate data, one might also make the opposite type of error. One might conclude that a procedure is working and continue it when in fact it is ineffective and should be abandoned or modified. For example, Harris, Wolf, and Baer (1964) described the case of a boy in a laboratory preschool who had the annoying habit of pinching adults. His teachers decided to use a behavior modification procedure to encourage him to pat rather than pinch. After the procedure had been in effect for some time, the teachers agreed that they had succeeded in reducing pinching by substituting patting. When they looked at the data recorded by an outside observer, however, they saw clearly that, although patting was considerably above the level it had been during the baseline recordings, pinching had not decreased from its baseline level. Perhaps concentrating on the procedure or the patting so diverted the teachers that they had failed to notice the pinching as much as they had before introducing the procedure. In any case, had it not been for the recorded data, the teachers probably would have wasted a great deal more time and effort than they did on an ineffective procedure.

A fifth reason for accurately recording behavior is that publicly posted results—preferably in the form of a graph or a chart—can prompt and reinforce behavior modifiers for carrying out a program. In training centers for persons with developmental disabilities, for example, staff often become more conscientious in applying procedures when up-to-date charts or graphs clearly showing the effects of the procedures are posted conspicuously (e.g., see Hrydowy & Martin, 1994). Parents and teachers alike might find that their efforts to modify children's behavior are strengthened by graphic representation of the behavior.

A final reason for recording data is that the displayed data might lead to improvements by the learner separately from any further treatment program. This is an example of a phenomenon known as *reactivity* (Tyron, 1998): When people know that their behavior is being observed either by others or by self-recording, their observed behaviors might change. For example, students who graph their own study behavior by daily recording the number of paragraphs or pages studied or the amount of time spent studying might find increases in the graph to be reinforcing (see Figure 20.2). Data that are presented appropriately can be reinforcing even to young children. For example, an occupational therapist working in a school consulted one of the authors concerning a 7-year-old girl who each morning took an excessive amount of time taking off her outside garments and hanging them up. It appeared that the teachers could not be persuaded to stop attending to the child when she was in the coatroom. The author suggested that the therapist somehow attempt to influence the child with a graph of the amount of time she spent in the coatroom each morning. The procedure that the therapist devised proved to be as effective as it was ingenious.[2] A large chart was hung on the wall. The chart was colored green to represent grass, and a carrot patch was depicted near the bottom of it. Days were indicated along the bottom of the chart and the amount of time in the coatroom was indicated along the side. Each day, a circle was marked on the chart to indicate the amount of time spent in the coatroom in the morning, and a small paper rabbit was attached to the most recent circle. Using simple language, the therapist explained the procedure to the child and concluded by saying, "Now let's see if you can get the bunny down to eat the carrots." When the rabbit was down to the level of the carrots, the child was encouraged to keep it there. "Remember, the longer the bunny stays in the carrot patch, the more it can eat." A follow-up showed that the improved behavior persisted over a period of 1 year.

---

[2] We are grateful to Nancy Staisey for providing us with the details of this procedure.

FIGURE 20.2
Monitoring and charting performance can serve at least six functions. Can you name them?

Behavior modifiers were not the first to discover the usefulness of recording one's behavior to help modify it. As with many other supposedly "new" psychological discoveries, the real credit should perhaps go to the writers of great literature. For example, novelist Ernest Hemingway used self-recording to help maintain his literary output. One of his interviewers reported the following (Plimpton, 1965, p. 219):

> He keeps track of his daily progress—"so as not to kid myself"—on a large chart made out of the side of a cardboard packing case and set up against the wall under the nose of a mounted gazelle head. The numbers on the chart showing the daily output of words differ from 450, 575, 462, 1250, back to 512, the higher figures on days Hemingway puts in extra work so he won't feel guilty spending the following day fishing on the gulf stream.

Author Irving Wallace also used self-recording even before he was aware that others had done the same. In a book touching on his writing methods (1971, pp. 65–66), he made the following comment.

> I kept a work chart when I wrote my first book—which remains unpublished—at the age of nineteen. I maintained work charts while writing my first four published books. These charts showed the date I started each chapter, the date I finished it, and number of pages written in that period. With my fifth book, I started keeping a more detailed chart which also showed how many pages I had written by the end of every working day. I am not sure why I started keeping such records. I suspect that it was because, as a free-lance writer, entirely on my own, without employer or deadline, I wanted to create disciplines for myself, ones that were guilt-making when ignored. A chart on the wall served as such a discipline, its figures scolding me or encouraging me.

See Wallace and Pear (1977) for examples of his charts.

Questions for Learning

15. Give six reasons for collecting accurate data during an assessment or baseline phase and throughout a program.
16. What error does the case of Dr. Caldwell and the door slammer's mother exemplify? Explain how accurately recorded data counteracted this error.
17. What error does the case of the boy who went around pinching adults exemplify? Explain how accurately recorded data counteracted this error.
18. What does *reactivity* mean in behavioral assessment? Illustrate with an example.
19. Briefly describe the details of the clever graphing system devised for the child who got the rabbit to the carrot patch.
20. Briefly describe how Ernest Hemingway and Irving Wallace used self-recording to help them maintain their writing behavior.

Behavioral Assessment Compared to Traditional Assessment

As indicated in Note 1 of Chapter 1, a major purpose of traditional psychodiagnostic assessment is to identify the type of mental disorder presumed to underlie abnormal behavior. Behavioral assessment began to emerge during the 1960s and 1970s in response to criticisms made by behaviorally oriented psychologists against the underlying assumptions of traditional psychodiagnostic assessment approaches (Nelson, 1983). Barrios and Hartmann (1986) described some differences in the aims, assumptions, and applications of the behavioral and traditional approaches to assessment (see the summary in Table 20.2).

TABLE 20.2 Some Differences Between Behavioral and Psychodiagnostic Approaches to Assessment	
Behavioral Approach	**Psychodiagnostic Approach**
Basic Assumptions	
—Performance on a checklist is a sample of a person's response to specific stimuli	—Test performance is viewed as a sign of an enduring, intrapsychic trait, or person variable
—Covert behaviors (thoughts and feelings) are like overt behaviors (in terms of their controlling variables) and are not accorded special status	—Covert behaviors (e.g., cognitions) are viewed as fundamentally different from overt behaviors
Goals of Assessment	
—To identify behavioral excesses or deficits	—To diagnose or classify individuals
—To identify environmental causes of current problem behaviors	—To identify intrapsychic or trait causes of behavior
Methods of Assessment	
—Preference for direct observation of specific Behaviors	—Direct assessment of intrapsychic factors and underlying traits is impossible (by definition)
Frequency of Assessment	
—Preference for continuous assessments before, during, and after application of intervention	—Typically pre- and posttreatment assessments based on standardized tests

Questions for Learning

21. How does a behavioral approach differ from a traditional approach to assessment in terms of a basic assumption about performance on a test or a checklist?
22. Describe two differences in the goals of a behavioral approach to assessment compared to a traditional approach.
23. Describe a difference between the method of a behavioral approach compared to a traditional approach to assessment.

Application Exercise

Self-Modification Exercise

Pick a behavioral excess of yours that you would like to decrease. Design a self-monitoring data sheet that you could use to record instances of the behavior over a 1-week period to serve as a baseline. On your data sheet, set it up so that you can record antecedents of each instance of the behavior, the behavior itself, and consequences of each instance of the behavior.

Note for Further Learning

1. Martin, Toogood, and Tkachuk (1997) developed a manual of self-report problem checklists for sport psychology consultation. For example, the sport psychology checklist for basketball players asks such questions as: "Would you say that you need to improve at tuning out negative thoughts, staying relaxed, and not getting too nervous just before or during a game?" and "Do you need to improve at identifying and reacting to your opponents' weaknesses and making adjustments as the game progresses?" The manual

includes self-report problem checklists for 21 sports. Each checklist contains 20 items to identify areas in which an athlete might need to improve before or during competitions, 5 items to identify areas in which an athlete might need to improve on postcompetition evaluations, and 17 items to identify areas in which an athlete might need to improve at practices. These behavioral checklists are not like traditional psychological tests such as the Wexler Adult Intelligence Scale (Wexler, 1981) or the 16-Personality Factor Inventory (Cattell, Eber, & Tatsuoka, 1970). Behavioral checklists do not have norms, nor are they designed to measure character or personality traits. Rather, such behavioral assessment tools provide information necessary to design effective interventions for remediating deficits or excesses in specific situations with individual athletes. Although formal research on these tools has been limited, those checklists that have been formally researched have shown high test–retest reliability and high face validity (Leslie-Toogood & Martin, 2003; Lines, Schwartzman, Tkachuk, Leslie-Toogood, & Martin, 1999). Feedback from athletes and sport psychology consultants who have used various checklists in the manual mentioned here has been uniformly positive concerning their value in obtaining useful behavioral assessment information.

Questions for Further Learning

1. What is the major purpose of sport-specific behavioral checklists?
2. What are two differences between behavioral checklists and traditional psychological tests?

CHAPTER 21

Direct Behavioral Assessment: What to Record and How

After studying this chapter, you will be able to:

- Describe behavioral characteristics that you can record.

- Summarize strategies for recording behavior.
- Explain procedures for assessing the accuracy of observations.

Suppose that you have chosen a particular behavior to modify. How do you directly measure, assess, or evaluate that behavior? As mentioned in Chapter 20, behavior analysts prefer direct to indirect measurement. In measuring behavior directly, six general characteristics should be considered: topography, amount, intensity, stimulus control, latency, and quality.

Characteristics of Behavior to Be Recorded

Topography of Behavior

As indicated in Chapter 7, the *topography* of a response is the specific movements involved in making the **NOTE 1** response. For example, Stokes, Luiselli, and Reed (2010) divided the movements of effective tackling in high school football into 10 components (head up, wrap arms around ball carrier's thighs, etc.).

Picture prompts are sometimes useful for helping observers to identify variations in the topography of a response. One of the authors developed detailed checklists with picture prompts for evaluating swimming strokes of young competitive swimmers. See Figure 21.1 for the backstroke checklist.

Amount of Behavior

Two measures of the amount of a given behavior are frequency and duration.

Frequency of Behavior *Frequency (or rate) of behavior* refers to the number of instances of a behavior that occur in a given period of time. If you wanted to improve the practice performance of figure skaters, for example, you might examine the frequency with which they performed various jumps and spins. That was the approach taken by Michelle Hume, a figure skating coach at St. Anne's Figure Skating Club in Manitoba (Hume, Martin, Gonzales, Cracklen, & Genthon, 1985). Coach Hume first defined jumps and spins in such a way that student observers could decide when either of those responses occurred. A *jump* was defined as any occasion when a skater jumped in the air so that both skates left the ice, a minimum of one complete revolution occurred in the air, and the skater landed on one foot, facing in the opposite direction without falling. A *spin* was defined as spinning on one skate for a minimum of three revolutions while maintaining a balanced, stationary position. When the observers knew

Hands: Fingers together
Arms: Roll shoulder into your ear
(Recovery) Arm comes over straight
Arm comes over close to ear
Little finger enters water first

Arms: Lower arm bends to almost 90 degrees under shoulder
(Pull) As arm straightens underwater, snap wrist at thigh and down

Legs: Leg action begins at the hips
Knees move up and down very little
Knees don't break the surface
Toes point down at bottom of kick
Toes just break surface at top of kick

Body: Hips kept high in the water
Hips kept as flat as possible
Head: Tilted up slightly, ears in water
Head kept stationary, don't rock

FIGURE 21.1
Checklist for the backstroke

what behaviors to look for, Coach Hume's next step was to take a baseline of the number of jumps and spins each individual skater performed during several practices. The observers used the data sheet shown in Figure 21.2.

In many situations, an observer does not have the time or helpers to take data using paper and pencil. Fortunately, other ways of measuring the amount of behavior require minimal time. One simple method is a golf counter. With these counters, you can count up to 99 simply by pressing a button for each instance of the behavior. You could also use a calculator and press +1 each time the behavior occurs. As described in the previous chapter, devices such as PDAs, smartphones, and tablet computers, with appropriate apps obtained online or custom-made, can be used to record (a) more than one behavior, (b) the behavior of more than one individual, and (c) the times at which each instance of behavior occurs (Brown et al., 2006; Kahng, Ingvarsson, Quigg, Seckinger, & Teichman, 2011; McIver, Brown, Pfeiffer, Dowda, & Pate, 2009; Paggeot, Kvale, Mace, & Sharkey, 1988; Repp, Karsh, Felce, & Ludewig, 1989).

Date: January 3 Student: Kathy	Observation Observer: Bill K.			
	Instances	**Total**	**Time**	**Additional Comments**
Jumps:	╫╫╫ ╫╫╫ ╫╫╫ ╫╫╫ ╫╫╫ ╫╫╫ ╫╫╫ ╫	35	25 min	Kathy spent 5 minutes chatting with other skaters
Spins:	╫╫╫ ╫╫╫ ╫╫╫	15	20 min	

FIGURE 21.2

A sample data sheet for recording jumps and spins at figure skating practices

The baseline performance of one of the figure skaters in Coach Hume's program can be seen in Figure 21.3. This type of graph is called a *frequency graph*. Each data point represents the total number of elements (jumps plus spins) completed by a skater during a practice session. Following baseline, a chart prepared for each skater contained a checklist of all jumps and spins that he or she should be practicing. These charts were posted at the side of the rink. Pointing to the charts, Coach Hume said to the skaters: "Each practice session, do the first three elements on your chart and then record them here. Then practice the next three elements and record them. Continue in this way until you've practiced all the elements. Then go through the whole routine again until the end of practice. At the end of practice, I will check your charts to see how you are doing." The self-charting program combined with positive feedback from Coach Hume at the end of each practice was effective in improving the number of jumps and spins performed (see Figure 21.3). Interestingly, when charting and coach feedback were discontinued, performance decreased to near baseline levels. When charting and coach feedback were reinstated, performance again improved.

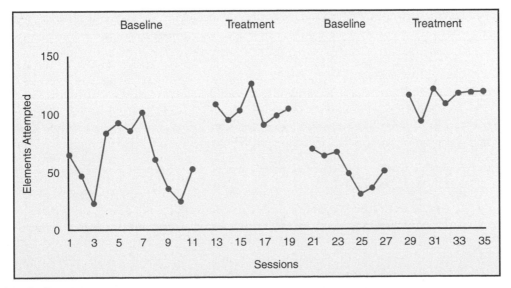

FIGURE 21.3

Frequency graph of the number of elements (jumps and spins) per session performed by a figure skater during baseline and treatment (self-recording)

Sometimes a frequency graph is not the most informative way to present data. Consider a study by Mulaire-Cloutier, Vause, Martin, and Yu (2000). These researchers examined the effects of giving persons with severe intellectual disabilities choice (preferred) and no-choice (less preferred) work tasks. During the first of three daily sessions, each participant was given a choice of which of two tasks to work on. In the remaining two daily sessions, the participants were randomly given either the task they had preferred on the first session or the less preferred task. Because the participants were nonverbal and could not describe how they felt about the different tasks, one dependent measure was a happiness indicator. This consisted of behaviors such as smiling, laughing, and yelling while smiling. A frequency graph of the happiness indicators displayed by one of the participants in the three conditions is shown in Figure 21.4A. Because of the small and somewhat inconsistent effects of the three conditions, it's difficult to see clear differences between the conditions in that figure.

Now look at Figure 21.4B. This figure is based on the same data as the frequency graph in Figure 21.4A. However, Figure 21.4B is a *cumulative graph*. In this type of graph, each response for a condition during a session is cumulated or added to the total responses of all previous sessions for that condition. Consider, for example, the happiness indicators during the no-choice less preferred task (the bottom line). The first three sessions had no happiness indicators, and the cumulative

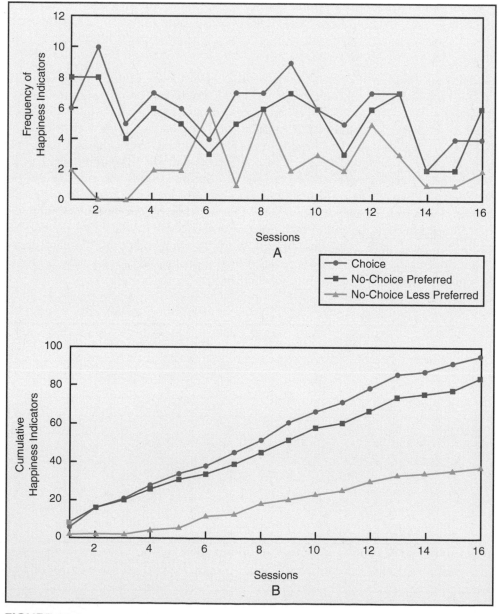

FIGURE 21.4

A frequency graph (A) and a cumulative graph (B) of the same data total of zero was therefore plotted corresponding to sessions 1, 2, and 3. The fourth session had 3 happiness indicators, yielding a cumulative total of 3 plotted for session 4. The fifth session had 2 happiness indicators, which, added to the previous total of 3, made a total of 5 happiness indicators, and that cumulative total was plotted for session 5. During session 6, 5 happiness indicators were added, yielding a cumulative total across the first six sessions of 10 happiness indicators, and a data point was therefore placed at 10 for session 6. In this way, the performance during any one session of a condition was added to the total performance during all previous sessions of that condition and then represented on the cumulative graph.

Note that on a cumulative graph, the average slope of the line over an interval indicates how many responses occurred during that period of time. In other words, the slope of the line in a cumulative graph indicates the rate of the response. The low slope of the line during the no-choice condition indicates a low rate of happiness indicators. The highest slope during the choice condition indicates the highest rate of happiness indicators. Another feature of a cumulative graph should be noted: The line can never decrease. If a participant is not performing at all as during the first three sessions of the no-choice condition, no response is cumulated with what is already there, and the line is flat. In short, a steep line indicates a high rate of responding; a flat line indicates zero responding.

A cumulative graph is usually preferred over a frequency graph when comparing two or more behaviors or conditions and when the differences are small. You can see that differences in the frequency of happiness indicators between the choice, no-choice preferred, and no-choice less preferred tasks are difficult to detect when plotted as frequency graphs in Figure 21.4A. However, when those same data are plotted cumulatively in Figure 21.4B, the gradual spread of the cumulative results shows clear differences between the three conditions. Requiring the workers to function at the less preferred task produced the lowest overall rate of happiness indicators while allowing the workers to choose among tasks produced the highest rate of happiness indicators.

It is sometimes convenient to design a recording sheet that also serves as a final graph. Consider the case of a child who frequently swore at the teacher and teacher's aides in the classroom. The teacher decided to record this behavior using the chart shown in Figure 21.5. Each time the teacher or teacher's aides observed an instance of swearing, they were to ignore the child and go to the front desk and place an X in the appropriate place on the chart.

FIGURE 21.5
Jackie's swearing behavior. Each X represents one swear word

The instances of swearing were recorded up the side of the graph and the days of the program were recorded across the bottom (see Figure 21.5). Each time an instance of swearing occurred, the staff would simply add an X for the appropriate day to the number of Xs that were already on the chart for that particular day. The graph shows clearly that many instances of swearing occurred during the first 10 days. Apparently, something other than attention from the teacher or teacher's aides was maintaining the behavior. On day 11, as the double vertical line in the chart indicates, the child was placed on the following differential reinforcement of other behavior (DRO) schedule: Reinforcement occurred at the end of each 15-minute period in which swearing did not occur. The result can be clearly seen: Swearing showed an immediate drop and eventually decreased to zero. (*Note:* These data are hypothetical and are presented to illustrate the plotting procedure.) This type of graph is useful for those who do not have the time to rechart their behavior tallies from their data sheet to a graph.

Each instance of a behavior that is recorded in terms of frequency, such as jumping or spinning as defined for the figure skaters, is a separate, individually distinct behavior that is easy to tally in a given period of time. Behavior modifiers have recorded the frequency of such behaviors as saying a particular word, swearing, throwing objects, completing arithmetic problems, chewing mouthfuls of food, taking puffs on a cigarette, and exhibiting nervous twitches. Each of these behaviors has characteristics so that successive occurrences of the given behavior are relatively brief and the amount of time that it takes to perform the behavior is about the same from one occasion to the next.

Relative Duration of Behavior   While frequency or rate is a common measure of the amount of behavior, the relative duration of a behavior or, more precisely, the sum of its durations divided by total time, is also sometimes important in measuring amount. The *relative duration of behavior* is the length of time that the behavior occurs within some period. In dealing with a behavior such as temper tantrumming, you may be more concerned with its duration than with its frequency. In fact, frequency can be ambiguous when trying to apply it to something like temper tantrums (Pear, 2004). What should we count as a separate response? Each cry, scream, or kick on the floor? Or should we count each episode of tantrumming as a separate response? Because it's usually difficult to answer these questions, we can generally avoid them by focusing on the duration of tantrumming. Other examples of behaviors for which duration may be more appropriate than frequency are listening attentively, sitting in one's seat in a classroom, watching television, talking on the telephone, and taking coffee breaks.

If you are concerned with keeping track of the relative duration of some activity over successive sessions or days, you might easily tabulate and present these data for effective visual display on a combined data sheet/graph. For example, an individual concerned with monitoring TV watching might prepare a chart showing cumulative minutes of TV watching up the side and days across the bottom. The slope of this graph would indicate the relative duration of the person's TV watching, just as the slope of a cumulative frequency graph indicates response rate. Duration of behavior is measured using timers, stopwatches, or clocks.

Questions for Learning

1. What does the *topography* of a behavior mean? Give an example that is not in this chapter.
2. Name two common measures of the overall amount of a given behavior.
3. What does the *frequency* of a behavior mean? Give an example that is not in this chapter.
4. Describe three ways to keep track of the number of times a certain response occurs during a day.
5. Make a frequency graph and a cumulative graph of the following instances of a behavior that were observed during successive sessions: 3, 7, 19, 0, 0, 0, 27, 12, 12, 6.
6. Describe at least four ways in which a cumulative graph of a set of data differs from a frequency graph of the same data.
7. On a cumulative graph, what can you infer from the following?
   a. a high or steep slope
   b. a low slope
   c. a flat line
8. What two characteristics do behaviors recorded in terms of frequency usually show?
9. What do we mean by the *relative duration* of a behavior? Give and explain an example in which relative duration might be more appropriate than frequency.

Intensity of Behavior

Sometimes we are concerned with measuring the intensity, magnitude, or force of a response. Assessments of intensity often utilize instrumentation. For example, when voice loudness is the behavior of concern, decibel level can be measured by a device called a *voice meter*. To measure the strength of grip pressure (such as during a handshake), a device called a *dynamometer* can be used. Measures of force are common in the skills involved in various sports. Machines are now available that assess how hard a pitcher can throw a baseball or a hockey player can shoot a hockey puck. The speed of an object as determined with such devices is used to infer the force with which it was propelled.

Stimulus Control of Behavior

We often assess a behavior in terms of the conditions under which it might be observed to occur. As we pointed out in Chapter 9, the term *stimulus control* refers to the degree of correlation between a stimulus and a response. An example of an assessment instrument that evaluates stimulus control is the Assessment of Basic Learning Abilities Revised (ABLA-R) (DeWiele, Martin, Martin, Yu, & Thomson, 2012), a revision of the ABLA first developed by pioneering behaviorists Nancy Kerr and Lee Meyerson. The ABLA-R assesses the ease with which persons with intellectual disabilities are able to learn six stimulus-discrimination levels: *Level 1, imitation,* a tester puts an object into a container and asks a client to do likewise; *Level 2, position discrimination,* a tester presents a red box and a yellow can in fixed left-right positions and requires a client to consistently place an object in the container on the left; *Level 3, visual discrimination,* when the red box and the yellow can are presented in randomized left-right positions, a client is required to consistently place a neutral nonmatching object in the yellow can independent of its position when the teacher says, "Put it in"; *Level 4, visual identity match-to-sample discrimination,* a client demonstrates visual match-to-sample behavior if, when she or he is allowed to view the yellow can and the red box in randomized left-right positions and is then presented with a yellow cylinder or a red cube sequentially, she or he consistently places the yellow cylinder in the yellow can and the red cube in the red box; *Level 5, visual nonidentity match-to-sample discrimination,* a client demonstrates this type of discrimination when he or she is allowed to view the yellow can and the red box in randomized left-right positions and then is presented with a purple-colored piece of wood shaped like the word *Can* or a piece of silver-colored wood shaped like the word *BOX,* he or she consistently places the word *Can* into the yellow can and the word *BOX* into the red box; and *Level 6, auditory-visual combined discrimination,* the client correctly puts a nonmatching object into the yellow can or the red box when the position of the containers are randomly alternated and the tester randomly says, "red box" or "yellow can." Level 6 is an auditory-visual discrimination because the client must first hear the words ("red box" or "yellow can"), then look at the position of the containers, and subsequently put the object in the correct container.

During the assessment of each ABLA-R level, correct responses are reinforced, and incorrect responses are followed by an error-correction procedure. Testing at a level continues until a client meets a pass criterion of eight consecutive correct responses or a failure criterion of eight cumulative errors. Research on the original ABLA and the ABLA-R indicates that the six levels are ordered in difficulty from Levels 1 (easiest) to 6 (most difficult) and that it is a valuable tool for teachers and rehabilitation workers for selecting and sequencing training and work tasks for persons with profound, severe, and moderate intellectual disabilities and children with autism (Martin, Thorsteinsson, Yu, Martin, & Vause, 2008; Sakko, Martin, Vause, Martin, & Yu, 2004; Vause, Yu, & Martin, 2007; Yu, Martin, Vause, & Martin, 2013). An example of this would be a client who in passing ABLA-R Level 4 is able to readily learn socially useful identity matching tasks such as sorting socks into pairs or restocking a salad bar at a fast-food restaurant.

Behavior modification programs concerned with the development of preverbal and verbal skills are typically preceded by behavior assessments of the stimulus control of the client's verbal behavior. Tests are available to determine the conditions under which clients will emit appropriate requesting, vocal imitation, or object identification (i.e., mands, echoics, or tacts, as described in Chapter 19; also see Marion et al., 2003). In many training programs, the critical measure of behavior is whether the client identifies some pictorial or printed stimulus correctly (see, e.g., Verbeke, Martin, Yu, & Martin, 2007). In such cases, the client's identification response is said to be controlled by the stimulus that the client is identifying. For that matter, any kind of test in which a person answers questions is a test of the stimulus control of behavior. Such tests assess whether the correct answers are under the control of the questions.

Latency of Behavior

The *latency* of a behavior is the time between the occurrence of a stimulus and the beginning of that behavior. For example, although a child in a classroom might work effectively once started, when first given a task the child seems to fool around forever before starting. This child has a long latency getting started. Like duration, latency is assessed using timers, stopwatches, or clocks.

Quality of Behavior

Concern about the quality of a behavior is frequently encountered in everyday life. Teachers might describe the quality of a child's handwriting as good, average, or poor. In judgmental sports such as diving, gymnastics, and figure skating, athletes receive points based on the quality of their performances. We all make resolutions to do various activities "better." But quality is not a characteristic additional to those mentioned previously. Rather, it is a refinement of one or more of them. Sometimes differences in judgments of quality are based on topography, as when a figure skating jump that is landed on one foot is considered better than one that lands on two feet. Sometimes it is a combination of frequency and stimulus control. For example, someone who is a good student is most likely to show a high frequency of studying and answering test questions correctly. A child who is said to be "good" shows a high frequency of following instructions from parents and teachers. In terms of latency, a runner who leaves the blocks very quickly after the firing of the starter's pistol might be considered to have a "good" start, while a runner who shows a longer latency had a "poor" start. Thus, quality of response is essentially an arbitrary designation of one or more of the previously mentioned characteristics of behavior that has some functional or social value.

Questions for Learning

10. What is another word for the *intensity* of a response? Give an example in which it would be important to measure the intensity of a behavior.
11. Define *stimulus control,* and give an example.
12. Name the six levels that the ABLA-R assesses.
13. Describe the details of the stimulus control assessed by ABLA-R Level 4, visual identity match-to-sample discrimination.
14. Describe the details of the stimulus control that the ABLA-R test assesses with Level 6, auditory-visual combined discrimination.
15. What do we mean by the *latency* of a response? Give an example that is not in this chapter.
16. Using an example, explain how the quality of a behavior is a refinement of one or more of the other dimensions of behavior.

Strategies for Recording Behavior

One could attempt to observe and record any given target behavior whenever it occurs. In most cases, this is simply impractical. A more practical alternative is to designate a specific period of time in which to observe and record the behavior. Of course, the period in which observations may be made should be chosen because the behavior is particularly likely to occur or is of particular concern during that period, such as a training session, a mealtime, or a recess time. The three basic techniques for recording behavior during a specific observation period are continuous recording, interval recording, and time-sampling recording.

Continuous (also called event-frequency) recording is the recording of every instance of a behavior during a designated observation period. A continuous recording system is commonly used when successive responses are quite similar in duration, such as the number of cigarettes smoked, instances of a child pinching another child, or frequency of saying *you know*. But what if successive responses are of variable duration, such as time spent watching TV, on Facebook, or exhibiting off-task behavior in a classroom? In such cases, interval recording is commonly used.

Interval recording logs the behavior as either occurring or not occurring during short intervals of equal duration (e.g., intervals of 10 seconds) during the specified observation period (such as 30 minutes). The two types of interval recording procedures are partial interval and whole interval. *Partial-interval recording* records the target behavior a maximum of once per interval regardless

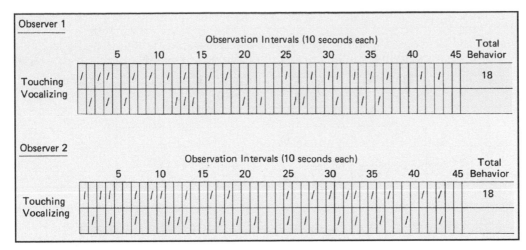

FIGURE 21.6
Sample data sheet for interval recording

of how many times the behavior occurs during each interval and regardless of the behavior's duration. An observer might use a device or application that presents an audible signal such as a beep to indicate the end of one interval and the start of the next. (Such devices or applications can be found on the Web using the search terms "repeating interval timer" or "loop timer.") Suppose that two behaviors of a nursery school child that are of concern are the child's frequent inappropriate touching and loud vocalizations. The two behaviors are to be recorded independently. For each behavior, if an instance occurs once during a 10-second interval, a tally is made on the data sheet (for a sample data sheet, see Figure 21.6). If several instances of a behavior occur during a 10-second interval, the observer still makes only one tally. As soon as the beep sounds indicating the start of the next 10-second interval, the behavior is recorded in that interval if it occurs before the next interval starts. *Whole-interval recording* denotes the target behavior as occurring during an interval only if the behavior persists throughout the entire interval. This type of interval recording is less commonly used than partial-interval recording. Behavior recorded with either a partial-interval or a whole-interval recording procedure is typically graphed in terms of the percentage of observation intervals in which the behavior is recorded as occurring.

Time-sampling recording scores a behavior as occurring or not occurring during very brief observation intervals that are separated from each other by a much longer period of time. For example, a parent of a preschool child might be concerned about the frequency of the child's rocking back and forth (a self-stimulation behavior) while sitting. It might be useful to have records of when this behavior occurs and for how long it occurs throughout the child's waking hours, but usually this is not realistic. An alternative is for the parent to seek out the child once every hour and make a note of whether the child shows any rocking behavior while sitting during a 15-second observation interval. Each observation interval is separated from the next by approximately 1 hour. This type of observational technique enables one observer to record one or more behaviors of one or more individuals even though the observer has many other commitments during the day. An example of a data sheet for time sampling appears in Figure 21.7. A special case of time sampling is referred to as *momentary time sampling* in which a behavior is recorded as occurring or not occurring at specific points in time, such as every hour on the hour rather than during specific brief intervals (e.g., see McIver, Brown, Pfeiffer, Dowda, & Pate, 2009). (For a comparison of momentary time-sampling and partial- interval recording, see Meany-Daboul, Roscoe, Bourret, & Ahearn, 2007.)

Often observers use a recording procedure with features of both interval recording and time-sampling recording. For example, an observer might watch the learner for a specified interval (say, 10 seconds) and then record the behavior during the next 10 seconds. This strategy of *observe* (for 10 seconds) and *record* (for 10 seconds) would continue over a given period of time (for instance, half an hour). In this way, one observer may record the behavior of several learners. In such a case, the observer might watch one learner for 10 seconds and then record a behavior as occurring or not occurring, watch another learner for 10 seconds and record a behavior as occurring or not occurring, and so forth, until all learners have been observed once. All the learners would then be observed a second time, a third time, and so forth,

DATE _____							
	Behavior			Location			Comments
Time	Sitting	Standing	Rocking	Kitchen	Living Room	Bedroom	
8:00 AM							
9:00							
10:00							
11:00							
12:00 PM							
1:00							
2:00							
3:00							
4:00							
5:00							
6:00							
7:00							
8:00							
9:00 PM							

FIGURE 21-7
A time-sampling data sheet for recording behavior of a child who frequently sits and rocks

throughout the observation period. Such a procedure would likely be referred to as an *interval-recording procedure,* although, strictly speaking, it could also be described as time sampling with a very brief time between observation intervals.

Himle, Chang, Woods, Pearlman, Buzzella, Bunaciu, and Piacentini (2006) conducted an interesting study involving continuous recording and partial-interval recording. The researchers videotaped 43 children with chronic tic disorders during several 30-minute periods in two outpatient specialty clinics and the children's respective homes. Observations were made by viewing the video recordings on a television rather than viewing the children directly. This counts as direct observation because all essential aspects of the target behavior were recorded directly. Using continuous recording an observer pressed a designated key to record a tic on a laptop computer that contained a program designed to record and total designated key presses. Observers then viewed the videotapes using partial-interval recording. The results showed a high correlation between the scores obtained by continuous recording and partial-interval recording, indicating that partial-interval recording can be as effective as continuous recording. The results also showed a high correlation between the recordings made in the clinic and in the home, indicating that accurate direct recording can be conducted effectively in naturalistic environments such as the home. Interestingly, there was no correlation between the data obtained by direct recording and the data obtained using an indirect tic assessment tool called the *Yale Global Tic Severity Scale (YGTSS)*, thus supporting the superiority of direct over indirect assessment as discussed in the previous chapter.

For a summary of the various recording strategies discussed above, see Table 21.1.

Questions for Learning

17. Define *continuous recording*. Give an example that is not in this chapter.
18. Define *interval recording*. Distinguish between the partial-interval recording system and the whole-interval recording system.
19. When would one likely select a continuous recording system?
20. When would one likely select an interval-recording system over a continuous recording system?
21. Define *time-sampling recording*. Give an example that is not in this chapter.
22. Briefly describe momentary time-sampling recording.

TABLE 21.1	Summary of Types of Recording Strategies	
Type	**Observation Intervals**	**Criteria for Recording**
Continuous	Equal to the observation period	Record every instance of the behavior.
Partial interval	Short and of equal lengths within an observation period	Record behavior as having occurred once in an interval if it occurred at least once during the interval.
Whole interval	Short and of equal lengths within an observation period	Record behavior as having occurred once in an interval if it occurred throughout that interval.
Time sampling	A short interval within a much larger observation period (which typically is repeated)	Record behavior as having occurred once in an interval if it occurred at least once during the interval.
Momentary time sampling	The observation interval reduced to a single point in time	Record behavior as having occurred during the observation period if it was occurring at the momentary observation point.
Combined interval time sampling	Small intervals of equal length within an observation period	Record behavior only during some portion of the intervals (e.g., once every 4 intervals).

Assessment of the Accuracy of Observations

Hawkins and Dotson (1975) identified three categories of error that can affect the accuracy of observations. First, the *response definition* might be vague, subjective, or incomplete, so that the observer has problems in making accurate observations. Second, the *observational situation* might be such that an observer has difficulty detecting the behavior because of distractions or other obstructions to the observing process or because the behavior is too subtle or complex to be observed accurately in that situation. Third, the *observer* might be poorly trained, unmotivated, or biased. We might add two other possible categories of error: poorly designed *data sheets* and cumbersome *recording procedures*. Kazdin (2011, pp. 114–120) detailed five sources of bias and artifact that can influence an observer: reactivity, observer drift, observer expectancy, feedback, and complexity of the observations. *Reactivity* refers to the fact that accuracy of the observations is a direction function of the observer's belief that he or she is being monitored (and hence is less accurate if the observer believes that he or she is not being monitored). *Observer drift* is the tendency for an observer's definition of the target behavior to gradually shift away from the definition the observer was originally given. *Observer expectancy* refers to the tendency for the observations to inaccurately show improvement in the target behavior as a function of the observer expecting the behavior to improve. *Feedback* refers to the tendency of the observations to be influenced by positive or negative feedback inadvertently provided to the observer by his or her supervisor. Finally, *complexity of the observations* refers to the tendency for observations to be less accurate if the definition of the target response has many parts or the observer is required to observe multiple behaviors at the same time.

Because any one or combination of the above categories and sources of error might be present in any behavior modification project, behavior modifiers frequently conduct **interobserver reliability (IOR)** estimates (also called **interobserver agreement, or IOA**, estimates). Two independent observers might record observations of the same behavior of the same individual during a given session. They are careful not to influence or signal each other while they are recording. The question is, given their best efforts while using the available behavior definitions and recording procedures and considering their training, how closely will their scores compare? Several IOR procedures can evaluate this, but two are more common than the others.

To illustrate one common IOR procedure, we return to the example of the observer recording the number of elements (jumps plus spins) of figure skaters. Suppose that a second observer stands on the opposite side of the ice rink from the first observer. The second observer is familiar with the definitions of jumps and spins and uses a data-recording sheet identical to that used by the first observer. At the end of the session, the first observer recorded 20 elements and the second observer recorded 22 elements. This is converted to an IOR by dividing the smaller number by the larger number and multiplying by 100%: IOR equals 20 divided by 22 times 100% equals 91%. This IOR score means that the two observers agreed quite closely on the total *number* of elements. It does not mean that they agreed on 20 specific elements; the second observer counted 2 extra to make 22. It is quite possible that one observer recorded an element that the second observer missed. The second observer could then have counted an element that the first observer missed. This could have gone on throughout the session, in which case the two observers would have disagreed completely on specific individual responses. Nevertheless, their close agreement on the total gives us confidence that the actual total was close to the number that each observer tallied despite the possible disagreements on individual cases. This approach of counting two totals and then dividing the smaller by the larger and multiplying by 100% is common when two observers are counting the frequency of a particular response over a period of time. However, this approach has been criticized. Some writers advocate for attempting to obtain point-by-point agreement measures in order to better ensure that the agreements and disagreements being measured are about specific instances of the behavior. For discussions on point-by-point agreement and ways to measure it, see Kazdin, (2011, pp. 103–105) and Yoder and Symons (2010, pp. 141–182).

Another IOR procedure is used with interval recording. Recall that interval-recording procedures can record one and only one response during each brief period of time (usually 5 or 10 seconds) over an extended observation period (see Table 21.1). If we have two independent observers recording the same behavior and each is using an interval-recording procedure, then the question is how their corresponding intervals compare with regard to those that contain a response versus those that do not. Let's suppose that two observers are recording two types of social interaction for one child. The behaviors are defined as touching another child and vocalizing in the direction of the other child. Their interval scores are shown in Figure 21.6.

As you can see, both observers counted the same number of instances of touching: 18. However, the two observers agreed on only 16 of these 18 instances. Each counted two instances that the other missed, yielding a total of four disagreements. If we used the procedure described previously, we would obtain an IOR of 100%. However, in the second procedure, the IOR is obtained by dividing the number of intervals on which the two observers agree that the behavior occurred by the total number of intervals on which either recorded a behavior (agreements divided by agreements plus disagreements on the occurrence of a behavior)

NOTE 2   and multiplying by 100%. Thus, in this instance, the second procedure would yield an IOR of 80%.

Typically, by convention, IOR scores between 80% and 100% are considered acceptable in behavior modification programs. Potential variation in computational procedures, however, renders the final IOR value potentially misleading when considered by itself. We suggest that readers of behavior modification literature consider the response definitions, observer-training procedures, recording system, method of calculating IOR, and the final IOR value as a total package when judging the reliability of reported data. Defects in any of these might make the results suspect.

Questions for Learning

23. Describe five categories of error that can affect the accuracy of observations.
24. List and briefly describe five sources of bias and artifact that can influence an observer.
25. In a sentence or two, explain what we mean by *interobserver reliability*. (Describe the process, but don't give the procedures for calculating IORs.)
26. Using the procedure described in the text for computing IORs with interval data, compute an IOR for the data of vocalizing as recorded by observers 1 and 2 (Figure 21.6). Show all of your computations.
27. According to convention, what is an acceptable IOR in a behavior modification program? What does *convention* mean?

Application Exercises

A. Exercise Involving Others

Select a behavioral deficit or excess that was modified successfully (e.g., Peter's tantrums) as described in one of the other chapters. For that behavior:

1. Design a plausible data sheet, including a column for sessions and a column for the instances of behavior per session.

2. Prepare some representative data (real or hypothesized) collected for 6 sessions, and write it in your data sheet.
3. Graph your data in a frequency graph.
4. Graph your data in a cumulative graph.

B. Self-Modification Exercise

Select one of your own behavioral excesses or deficits. For that behavior, answer Items 1 to 4 in the previous exercise.

Notes for Further Learning

1. Researchers using direct observational methods generally attempt to make *unobtrusive observations*. When the observational method affects the behaviors being observed, we say that the observation is *obtrusive*. To record observations *unobtrusively* means that the observations do not cause those being observed to deviate from their typical behavior. You can ensure that your observations are unobtrusive in several ways. One possibility is to observe the behavior from behind a one-way window, as illustrated in the case of Darren in Chapter 4. Another possibility is to inconspicuously observe individuals from a distance, such as that used to study the drinking habits of patrons in bars (Sommer, 1977). Still another method is to have a confederate (a co-observer) make observations while working side by side with a client in a normal work setting (Rae, Martin, & Smyk, 1990). Other alternatives include recording the behavior with a hidden camera and evaluating products of the client's behavior (such as items littered in a public campground; Osborne & Powers, 1980). However, such tactics raise a moral question: Is it ethical to observe individuals without their consent? The American Psychological Association in its *Ethical Principles of Psychologists and Code of Conduct, Including 2010 Amendments,* has developed a set of ethical guidelines governing all types of experiments by psychological researchers (see http://www.apa.org/ethics/code/index.aspx?item=11#803). Of particular relevance to this note, Standard 8.03, titled *Informed Consent for Recording Voices and Images in Research,* states, "Psychologists [must] obtain informed consent from research participants prior to recording their voices or images for data collection unless (1) the research consists solely of naturalistic observations in public places, and it is not anticipated that the recording will be used in a manner that could cause personal identification or harm, or (2) the research design includes deception, and consent for the use of the recording is obtained during debriefing." Anyone contemplating recording the behavior of another person should consult the ethical guidelines of his or her professional organization and the applicable laws pertaining to privacy and confidentiality. (See also Chapter 30 of this text.)

2. The procedure that we have suggested for computing IOR during interval recording is that of dividing the number of intervals on which observers agree that the behavior occurred by the total number of intervals on which either observer recorded the occurrence of the behavior (agreements plus disagreements on the occurrence of the behavior) and multiplying by 100%. Some researchers include instances in which the observers agreed that the behavior did not occur in the measure of agreements—in other words, agreements on blank intervals. When very few behaviors have been recorded, however, this can greatly inflate a reliability score. For example, consider the 45 observation intervals given in Figure 21.6. Let's suppose that observer 1 recorded an instance of touching during interval 5 and that observer 2 recorded an instance of touching during interval 6. No other instances of touching were recorded. In such a case, the two observers would disagree completely on the occurrence of the behavior, and the IOR would be zero if computed as agreement only on instances in which the behavior occurred. However, if agreements on blank intervals are included, the IOR equals 43 agreements divided by 43 agreements plus 2 disagreements times 100%, which equals 95.6%. Because of this distortion, many researchers do not count agreements on blank intervals. In other words, intervals in which neither observer scores the behavior as having occurred are ignored. An acceptable exception to this would be when one is concerned with decreasing a behavior and it is important to have agreement that the behavior did not occur. However, this requires making a decision that could in many cases be subjective and arbitrary. Perhaps the best solution would be to routinely report IOR for both occurrences and non-occurrences of the target behavior separately. See Bailey and Burch (2002, pp. 127–128) regarding the above points and other comments on the complexity of computing IOR.

Questions for Further Learning

1. What is the difference between obtrusive and unobtrusive observations?
2. When is it especially misleading to include agreement on blank intervals in computing the IOR? Give an example.
3. When might it be acceptable to include agreement on blank intervals in your computation of an IOR? Why would this be acceptable?

CHAPTER 22

Doing Behavior Modification Research

LEARNING OBJECTIVES

After studying this chapter, you will be able to:

- Outline research designs commonly used when doing research in behavior modification.
- Describe scientific criteria behavior analysts typically use to evaluate whether a treatment has produced a change in behavior.

- Discuss ways to evaluate the acceptability of a behavioral treatment to the recipients of it.

As described in Chapter 20, a minimal behavior modification program has four phases: a *screening phase* for clarifying the problem and determining who should treat it, an *assessment or baseline phase* for determining the causes of the problem behavior and its initial level prior to the program, a *treatment phase* in which the intervention strategy is initiated, and a *follow-up phase* for evaluating the persistence of the desirable behavioral changes following termination of the program. Many behavior modification projects go beyond these phases and demonstrate convincingly that it was indeed the treatment that caused a particular change in behavior. The value of such demonstrations might be illustrated best with the following hypothetical example.

Kelly, a second-grade student, performed at a much lower level in completing addition and subtraction problems than any of the other students in her daily math classes. In addition, she was disruptive during the class. The teacher reasoned that increasing Kelly's performance in solving the assigned math problems might make it more pleasurable for Kelly to work at the problems and might also decrease the disruptive interactions with nearby students. During a 1-week baseline, the teacher assigned a certain number of problems to the class and recorded the number that Kelly completed successfully during each half-hour period. Kelly averaged seven successfully completed math problems per half hour, less than half the class average of 16 problems in the same amount of time. The teacher next introduced a reinforcement program, telling Kelly that each successfully completed math problem would add an extra minute of recess for the whole class on Friday afternoon. Kelly's performance improved during the first week of the program. During the second week, Kelly exceeded the class average of 16 correct math problems per half-hour class.

Can the teacher attribute the improvement in Kelly's performance to the treatment? Our initial tendency might be to say yes because the performance is much better now than it was during the original baseline. Consider, however, that the improvement might have been the result of other factors. For example, a bad cold could have depressed Kelly's baseline performance, and the recovery from the cold may have improved the mathematical performance after the program began. The problems assigned during the treatment phase might have been easier than those assigned during baseline. Or perhaps something that the teacher could not possibly have been aware of was responsible for the improved performance. Behavior modification research attempts to demonstrate convincingly that it was the treatment, not some uncontrolled variable, that was responsible for any change in the target behavior.

The Reversal-Replication (ABAB) Design

Suppose the teacher would like to demonstrate convincingly that the treatment program was indeed responsible for Kelly's improvement. Besides satisfying the teacher's curiosity, there are several practical reasons why such a demonstration might be desirable. Such a demonstration could indicate whether to try a similar procedure with another problem Kelly might have, whether to try similar procedures with other students in the class, or even whether the teacher should recommend a similar procedure to other teachers. Therefore, at the end of the second week of the reinforcement program, the teacher decided to eliminate the reinforcement and return to the baseline condition. Suppose that the hypothetical results of this manipulation by the teacher are those shown in Figure 22.1.

By the end of the second week of return to the baseline conditions, Kelly was performing at approximately her baseline level. The teacher then reintroduced the treatment phase and Kelly's performance improved (see Figure 22.1). The teacher had replicated both the original baseline and the original treatment effects. If some uncontrolled variable were operating, we must hypothesize that it was occurring mysteriously at exactly the same time the treatment program was operative and was not occurring when the treatment program was removed. This becomes much less plausible with each successful replication of the effect. We are now confident that it was indeed the teacher's procedure that produced the desired behavioral change. Thus, the teacher demonstrated a cause–effect relationship between a particular behavior and the treatment program.

In research terminology, the measure of behavior is referred to as the **dependent variable;** the treatment or the intervention is referred to as the **independent variable.** In the preceding example, correctly completing math problems was the dependent variable and the teacher's program for Kelly was the independent variable. Two considerations in evaluating a possible cause–effect relationship are internal validity and external validity. A study or experiment is said to have **internal validity** if it convincingly demonstrated that the independent variable caused the observed change in the dependent variable. A study or experiment is said to have **external validity** to the extent that the finding can be generalized to other behaviors, individuals, settings, or treatments.

The type of research strategy that Kelly's teacher employed is called a **reversal-replication design,** which is an experimental design consisting of a baseline phase followed by a treatment phase, followed by a reversal back to baseline conditions, and followed by a replication of the treatment phase. The baseline is often represented as A and the treatment noted as B. Hence, this research design is also called an *ABAB design.* It has also been called a *withdrawal* design because the treatment is withdrawn during the second baseline phase (Poling, Methot, & LeSage, 1995). For an example of the use of this design in an actual research study, see Kadey and Roane (2012).

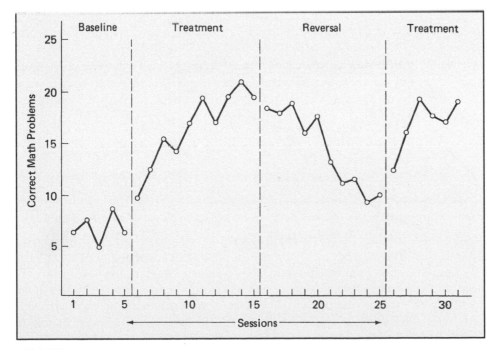

FIGURE 22.1

Hypothetical data showing a reversal-replication (ABAB) design for Kelly

Although the reversal-replication design appears simple at first glance, beginning students doing behavior modification research quickly have several questions that are not easy to answer. Assuming that problems of response definition, observer accuracy, and data recording (discussed in Chapter 21) have been solved, the first question is: How long should the baseline phase last? The difficulties of answering this question might be appreciated best by viewing Figure 22.2. Which of the baselines in this figure do you consider to be the most adequate? If you selected baselines 4 and 5, we agree. Baseline 4 is acceptable because the pattern of behavior appears stable and predictable. Baseline 5 is acceptable because the trend observed is in a direction opposite to the effect predicted for the independent variable acting on the dependent variable. Ideally, then, a baseline phase should continue until the pattern of performance is stable or until it shows a trend in the direction opposite to that predicted when the independent variable is introduced.

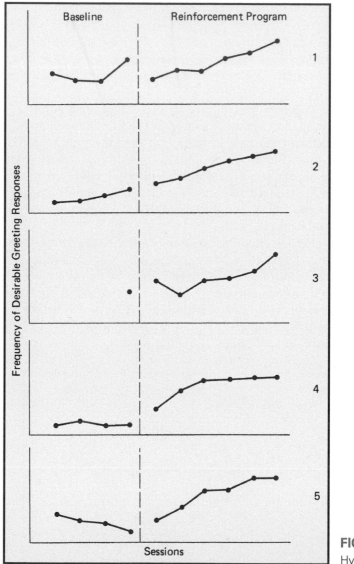

FIGURE 22.2
Hypothetical data for five children

Other considerations might lead to shortening or lengthening a baseline in an applied research project. First, scientific considerations related to the newness of the independent and dependent variables should be reviewed. We might be more comfortable conducting a shorter baseline in a new study of behavior that has already been well researched than in a study of a less explored area. Second, practical considerations might limit the length of baseline observations. The researcher's available time, the observers' availability, the students' restrictions for completing projects on time, and any number of other factors might lead us to limit or extend the baseline for nonscientific reasons. Finally, ethical considerations often affect baseline length. For example, an extended baseline phase is ethically unacceptable when attempting to manage the self-abusive behavior of a child with a developmental disability.

Another question that a beginning student in behavior modification research has pertains to how many reversals and replications are necessary. Again, this question has no easy answer. If we observe a very large effect when the independent variable is introduced and if the area is one that has been explored before, one replication might be sufficient. Other combinations of factors might lead us to conduct several replications to convincingly demonstrate a cause–effect relationship.

Although the reversal-replication design is a common behavior modification research strategy, it has limitations that make it inappropriate in certain situations. First, it might be undesirable to reverse to baseline conditions following a treatment phase. When treating a child's self-abusive behavior, for example, reversing to baseline following a successful treatment to prove that the treatment was responsible for the change in behavior would be ethically unacceptable.

Second, it might be impossible to obtain a reversal due to behavioral trapping. In Chapter 16, we described how improved behavior might become "trapped." Once a shy child has been taught to interact with peers, this interactive behavior might be maintained by attention from the peers. Once a golf pro has taught a novice to hit a golf ball over 200 yards, it is unlikely that the novice golfer will return to a swing that produced a 150-yard drive.

Questions for Learning

1. Briefly name and describe the four minimal components of a behavior modification program.
2. In two or three sentences, explain why we cannot necessarily claim that a change in behavior during a minimal behavior modification program was due to the treatment.
3. In two or three sentences, distinguish between a minimal behavior modification program and behavior modification research.
4. Define *dependent variable,* and give an example.
5. Define *independent variable,* and give an example.
6. Define *internal validity.*
7. Define *external validity.*
8. With reference to an example, briefly describe the four components of the reversal-replication design. What is another name for this design?
9. Ideally, how long should the baseline phase of the reversal-replication design continue?
10. In a sentence or two each, describe why Baselines 1, 2, and 3 from Figure 22.2 are inadequate.
11. What scientific, practical, and ethical considerations might lead someone to lengthen or shorten a baseline?
12. How many reversals and replications are necessary in a reversal-replication design?
13. Identify two limitations of the reversal-replication design, and give an example of each.

Multiple-Baseline Designs

Returning a behavior to baseline sometimes might be impossible and reversing an improvement in behavior even for a short time is often undesirable. Multiple-baseline designs are used to demonstrate the effectiveness of a particular treatment without reversing to baseline conditions.

A Multiple-Baseline-Across-Behaviors Design

Suppose Kelly's teacher wanted to demonstrate the effects of the reinforcement procedure on the child's academic performance but did not want to do a reversal and risk losing the improvement Kelly showed. The teacher might demonstrate the treatment's effect by using a **multiple-baseline-across-behaviors design** which involves establishing baselines for two or more of an individual's behaviors followed by introducing the treatment sequentially across those behaviors. The first step for Kelly's teacher to apply this design might be to record Kelly's performance in solving math problems during math class as well as in spelling and sentence writing during language arts. The resulting baselines might have been those shown in Figure 22.3. The treatment of an extra minute of recess per correct problem might have been introduced in math class while the other baseline conditions might have been continued during language arts. If the results were those shown in Figure 22.3, the teacher might next have introduced the treatment for the second behavior by allowing an extra minute of recess for each word Kelly spelled correctly. Finally, the teacher might have introduced the treatment for the third behavior—sentence writing. If performance was as indicated in Figure 22.3, the behavior changed only when the treatment was introduced. This hypothetical example illustrates the control of a treatment over several behaviors. For examples of this design in research studies, see Gena, Krantz, McClannahan, and Poulson (1996), and Axe and Sainato (2010).

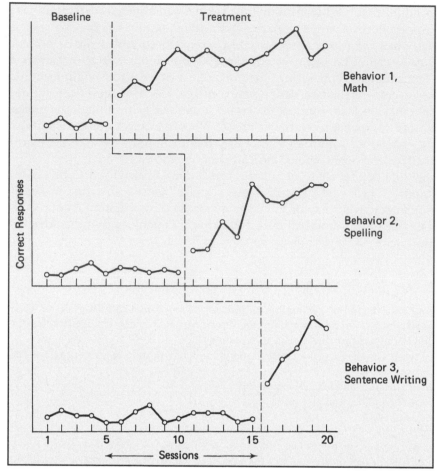

FIGURE 22.3

Hypothetical data illustrating a multiple-baseline-across-behaviors design for Kelly

A potential problem with this design is that the behaviors might not be independent (e.g., Nordquist, 1971). If Kelly's teacher had applied the treatment program to one behavior while the other two behaviors were kept at baseline conditions and if an improvement had been observed in all three behaviors concurrently, the teacher could not have confidently attributed the improvement to the treatment because two of the three behaviors that improved did not receive the treatment. Other limitations are that it might not be possible to find two or more suitable behaviors or sufficient observers to gather the necessary data on several behaviors. In addition, if the procedure is used with only one individual, we can conclude only that the treatment was internally valid with that individual. We must be cautious in extrapolating the results to other individuals.

A Multiple-Baseline-Across-Situations Design

A **multiple-baseline-across-situations design** involves establishing baselines for a behavior of an individual across two or more situations concurrently followed by the introduction of the treatment to the behavior sequentially across those situations. For example, Allen (1973) was concerned with decreasing bizarre verbalizations of an 8-year-old boy with minimal brain damage. While attending a sleep-away summer camp, the boy fantasized for hours about his imaginary pet penguins that he called Tug Tug and Junior Polka Dot. These verbalizations interfered with the boy's interactions with his peers and the camp counselors. During an initial baseline phase, data on the verbalizations were collected in four situations: during trail walks in the evening, in the dining hall, in the boy's cabin, and during classes. The treatment, an extinction program that ignored verbalizations, was then introduced in the first situation (trail walking) while the remaining three situations continued on baseline. Following the successful reduction of the verbalizations during trail walking, treatment was introduced to the second situation, the dining hall, and the remaining two situations continued on baseline. Eventually, the treatment was introduced sequentially across the remaining two situations. The daily number of bizarre verbalizations decreased to near zero in each situation following the introduction of treatment to that situation. For another example of the use of this design in research, see Graff and Karsten (2012).

Similar to the potential problem with the multiple-baseline-across-behaviors design, in a multiple-baseline-across-situations design, when the treatment is applied to the behavior in the first situation, it might cause subsequent improvement in all situations (i.e., stimulus generalization across situations). When this happens, the researcher is not able to conclude that the improvement was necessarily the result of the treatment. Other potential limitations are that the behavior might occur in only one situation, or there might not be sufficient observers to gather the necessary data. In addition, if the procedure is used with only one individual, we can conclude only that the treatment is effective with that individual. We must be cautious in extrapolating the result to other individuals.

A Multiple-Baseline-Across-People Design

A **multiple-baseline-across-people design** involves establishing baselines for a specific behavior across two or more people concurrently followed by the introduction of the treatment sequentially to each person. For example, Wanlin, Hrycaiko, Martin, and Mahon (1997) used a multiple-baseline-across-people design to demonstrate the effectiveness of a combination of procedures (called a *treatment package*) designed to improve the practice performance of four female speed skaters. The average number of skating laps completed per practice of the four skaters was recorded during initial practices. The first skater was then given the treatment package while the others continued on baseline. Exposure to the treatment package improved the practice performance of the first skater. Across practices, the treatment package was introduced sequentially to the second skater, then to the third skater, and then to the fourth skater, and each time it led to an improvement in the number of laps skated per practice. This demonstration of improvement in individuals who receive treatment sequentially across time is a convincing demonstration of a treatment program's effectiveness. For a recent application of this design, see Kraus, Hanley, Cesana, Eisenberg, and Jarvie (2012).

A potential problem with the multiple-baseline-across-people design is that the first individual might explain the treatment or model the desirable behavior to the other individuals, causing them to improve in the absence of treatment (see, e.g., Kazdin, 1973). Also, it is not always possible to find either two or more individuals with the same problem or the additional observers necessary to gather the data. Note that successfully replicating the effect across individuals demonstrates both internal validity and a degree of external validity, in that we can extrapolate the effects with some confidence to other individuals.

Questions for Learning

14. State an advantage of a multiple-baseline design over a reversal-replication design.
15. With reference to an example, briefly describe a multiple-baseline-across-behaviors design.
16. What are three potential limitations of a multiple-baseline-across-behaviors design?
17. With reference to an example, briefly describe a multiple-baseline-across-situations design.
18. What are three potential limitations of a multiple-baseline-across-situations design?
19. With reference to an example, briefly describe a multiple-baseline-across-people design.
20. What are three potential limitations of a multiple-baseline-across-people design?

The Changing-Criterion Design

With a **changing-criterion design,** the control that a treatment exerts on an individual's behavior is evaluated by introducing successive changes in the behavioral criterion for application of the treatment. If the behavior consistently changes in the same direction each time a change is made in the criterion for application of the treatment, we can conclude that the treatment was responsible for the change in behavior.

DeLuca and Holborn (1992) used a changing-criterion design to demonstrate the effects of a token reinforcement system on exercising by 11-year-old boys, some of whom were obese and others of whom were not. First, during Phase 1 (baseline), consisting of several 30-minute exercise sessions, they assessed each boy's pedaling rate on a stationary bicycle. Based on these data, they set a criterion for reinforcement for each boy that was approximately 15% above his average baseline rate of pedaling. In Phase 2, when a boy met the criterion, he earned points (signaled by a bell ringing and a light going

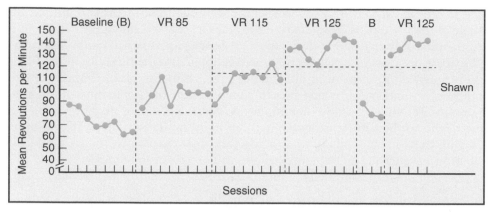

FIGURE 22.4

Mean number of revolutions per minute pedaled on a stationary bicycle by a boy. After a baseline phase, token reinforcement was given at increasingly larger levels of variable ratio (VR) reinforcement (that is, the mean response requirement became increasingly larger)

Source: Figure 1 in "Effects of a Variable Ratio Reinforcement Schedule with Changing Criteria on Exercise in Obese and Non-Obese Boys" by R. V. DeLuca and S. W. Holborn, *Journal of Applied Behavior Analysis, 25,* 1992. Copyright ©1992. Reprinted by permission of Dr. Rayleen DeLuca, University of Manitoba.

on) that could be exchanged later for backup reinforcers. After a boy's performance stabilized at this new higher level of pedaling, Phase 3 was initiated; its criterion for reinforcement was changed to approximately 15% above the average rate of performance in Phase 2. Similarly, each subsequent phase increased the criterion for reinforcement to 15% higher than the average pedaling rate of the preceding phase. As in Figure 22.4, which shows the data for one of the boys, performance improved with each subsequent change in the criterion for reinforcement. This pattern was demonstrated for both the three boys who were obese and the three boys who were not. To further demonstrate the experimental control of the reinforcement program, as indicated in Figure 22.4, a reversal to baseline phase was included in this study. Although the reversal provided confirming information, such reversals are not a defining feature of the changing-criterion design.

Alternating-Treatments (Or Multielement) Design

The preceding experimental designs are ideally suited for demonstrating that a particular treatment was indeed responsible for a specific behavioral change. However, what if we wanted to compare the effects of different treatments for a single behavior of a single individual? Multiple-baseline designs are not well suited for this purpose. An alternative design for such a concern, first proposed by Barlow and Hayes (1979), is known as an **alternating-treatments design,** also called a **multielement design,** which involves alternating two or more treatment conditions, one condition per session, to assess their effects on a single behavior of a single individual. For example, Wolko, Hrycaiko, and Martin (1993) were concerned with comparing three treatments for improving young gymnasts' frequency of completed skills during practice on a balance beam. One treatment was the standard coaching typically applied by the gymnastics coach. The second condition was standard coaching plus public goal setting, monitoring, and coach feedback. In this condition, the coach posted written goals for a gymnast who recorded her practice performance, placed it on a graph in the gymnasium, and received feedback from the coach at the end of each practice. The third condition was standard coaching and private self-management involving a gymnast setting her own goals and keeping track of her performance in a private notebook. The three conditions were randomly alternated across practices. The results with one of the gymnasts were plotted as three cumulative graphs (see Figure 22.5). As the results for this gymnast indicate, standard coaching plus private self-management was consistently more effective than standard coaching plus public self-management and standard coaching alone (the baseline condition). For another example of the alternating-treatments design, see Shayne, Fogel, Miltenberger, and Koehler (2012).

As Sidman (1960, p. 326) suggested, it is possible to use the alternating-treatments design to study the effects of a particular independent variable on different topographies of behavior. For example Ming and Martin (1996) used an alternating-treatments design to study the effects of self-talk on two different figure-skating topographies.

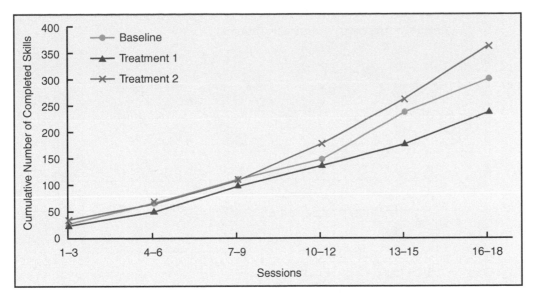

FIGURE 22.5

Frequency of completed beam skills for a gymnast under conditions of standard coaching (baseline), standard coaching plus public self-management (Treatment 1) versus standard coaching plus private self-management (Treatment 2). Each condition was in effect for six sessions with the conditions randomly alternated across a total of 18 sessions

Source: Adapted from data from K. L. Wolko, D. W. Hrycaiko, and G. L. Martin, "A Comparison of Two Self-Management Packages to Standard Coaching for Improving Practice Performance of Gymnasts," *Behavior Modification, 17* (1993), pp. 209–223.

A potential problem with the alternating-treatments design is that the treatments might interact; that is, one of the treatments might produce an effect because of either its contrast to the other treatments in alternating sessions or stimulus generalization across treatments. And in many studies using an alternating-treatments design, interactions have occurred (e.g., Hains & Baer, 1989).

Data Analysis and Interpretation

Researchers who employ the behavior modification experimental designs described in this chapter typi- **NOTE 1** cally analyze their data without using control groups and statistical techniques that are more common in other areas of psychology. This is not to say that behavior analysts never use group averages and test the statistical significance of differences between groups. In general, however, behavior analysts are more interested in understanding and improving the behavior of individuals rather than group averages (see Blampied, 2013; Sidman, 1960, for the classic justification and elaboration of this approach). The evaluation of the effect of a particular treatment is typically made on the basis of two major sets of criteria: scientific and practical. Scientific criteria are the guidelines a researcher uses to evaluate whether there has been a convincing demonstration that the treatment was responsible for producing a reliable effect on the dependent variable. This judgment is commonly made by visually inspecting the graph of the results. Problems in deciding whether a treatment produced a reliable effect on a dependent variable might best be appreciated by examining Figure 22.6. Most observers of the five graphs would probably agree that there is a clear, large effect in Graph 1, a reliable although small effect in Graph 2, and questionable effects in the remaining graphs.

Seven criteria are commonly used for increasing our confidence that the treatment had an effect on the dependent variable. Confidence in the effect is increased:

(1) the more times it has been replicated or repeated,
(2) the fewer the overlapping points between the baseline and treatment phases,
(3) the sooner the effect is observed following the treatment's introduction,
(4) the larger the effect is,
(5) the more precisely the treatment procedures are specified,
(6) the more reliable the response measures are, and
(7) the more consistent the findings are with existing data and accepted behavioral theory.

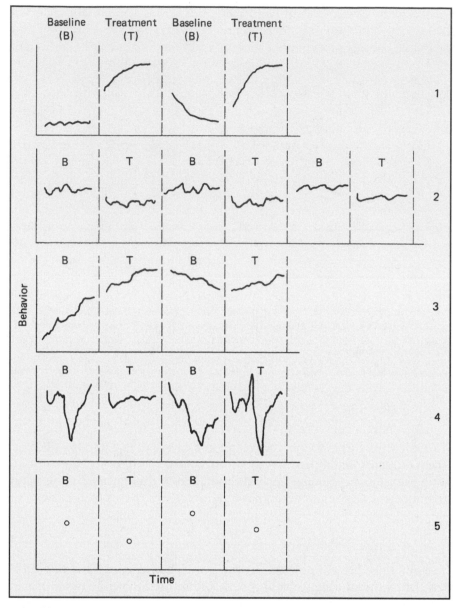

FIGURE 22.6

Some hypothetical data

For a more detailed discussion of visual inspection procedures, see Bourret and Pietras (2013). For discussion of a problem of visual inspection of data, see Fisch (1998). For a description of a visual aid and a staff training program for improving the reliability and validity of visual inspection of single-case designs, see Fisher, Kelley, and Lomas (2003).

Judging whether an effect has been demonstrated from a scientific point of view is one thing; evaluating the practical importance of behavior change to the client, other significant individuals in the client's life, and society in general is something else. In evaluating the practical impact of the treatment, we must consider more than the scientific criteria for judging the treatment's effect on behavior. If Graph 2 in Figure 22.6 were a graph of self-abusive behavior, a reliable cause–effect relationship has been demonstrated but might be of little clinical significance. If the individual is still self-abusive during the treatment phases, those responsible for caring for that individual would not be satisfied. Judgments about the practical importance of behavioral change are referred to as *judgments of clinical effectiveness or social importance.*

A concept related to practical importance is that of *social validity.* Wolf (1978) suggested that behavior modifiers need to socially validate their work on at least three levels: (1) the extent to which the target behaviors are really the most important ones for the client and society, (2) the acceptability to the client of the particular procedures used, especially when alternative procedures can accomplish approximately the same results, and (3) the satisfaction of the consumers (the clients or their caregivers) with the results. One social validation procedure involves subjective evaluation in which clients or other significant individuals are asked about their satisfaction with the goals, procedures, and results. Another social validation procedure is to conduct tests to determine which of two or more alternatives clients prefer. In a third procedure, the goals as well as the results of treatment are validated socially by comparing results with clients to the average performance of some comparison group, such as normal peers. Kennedy (2002a) proposed that social validation methods, such as those listed above, be supplemented with information regarding the maintenance of the change produced by the treatment. He reasoned that (1) this method of measuring social validity is more objective than many other methods that have been proposed, and (2) a behavior change that is not maintained can hardly be said to be socially valid, regardless of how highly people in the client's environment subjectively rate it, whereas maintenance of a behavior change in a client's physical and social environment is a good indicator that the behavior change is functional to the client and society. Kennedy (2002b) also proposed a number of other indicators of social validly with regard to decreasing problem behavior. Social validation helps behavior modifiers do the best job that they can in helping individuals function fully in society. Other strategies to ensure accountability of treatment specialists are discussed in Chapter 30.

Questions for Learning

21. With reference to an example, briefly describe the changing-criterion design.
22. With reference to an example, briefly describe an alternating-treatments design. What is another name for this design? Explain when and why that name might be preferred.
23. Briefly describe a potential problem with the alternating-treatments design.
24. In a sentence or two each, explain the scientific and practical criteria for evaluating the effects of a particular treatment. Be sure to distinguish between the two in your answer.
25. Describe why it is difficult to draw conclusions about the effects of the treatments in Graphs 3, 4, and 5 in Figure 22.6.
26. What seven criteria would give you maximum confidence that the treatment in an ABAB design had produced an effect on the dependent variable?
27. What are the three levels of social validation, and why are they important?

Application Exercises

A. Exercise Involving Others

Suppose you are teaching some students about doing research that utilizes reversal-replication and multiple-baseline designs. Your students must do a research project in which they select a dependent variable and evaluate the effects of some treatment on that dependent variable. Your task as the teacher is to analyze the material in this chapter to prepare a guide that will help the students select the appropriate experimental design. Your guide should take the form of a series of if–then statements that would lead to a particular design. For example, if (a) and (b), then choose a reversal design; but if (c), (d), and (e), then choose a multiple-baseline design, and so forth.

B. Self-Modification Exercise

As described in Chapter 20, self-recording without any additional behavioral procedures sometimes causes reactivity—that is, the self-recording alone leads to behavioral change. Suppose you have decided to describe a self-recording procedure and then to investigate that as a treatment in a self-modification program. Describe a plausible multiple-baseline design that would enable you to assess self-recording as an effective self-control treatment.

Note for Further Learning

1. The experimental designs described in this chapter are referred to as *single-case, single-subject,* or *within-subject experimental designs.* In most of these designs, an individual serves as his or her own control in the sense that performance of that individual in the absence of treatment is compared to that individual's performance during treatment. More common designs in many areas of psychology are control-group or between-subjects designs. A control-group design typically involves at least two groups, one that receives the treatment and one that does not. The average performance of the two groups is then compared according to appropriate statistical procedures. Single-case designs are more popular than control-group designs among behavior modifiers for a number of reasons (Hrycaiko & Martin, 1996). First, they focus on repeated

measurement of an individual's performance across a number of sessions and therefore provide potentially valuable information on individual variation in performance. Group designs, with their emphasis on the average performance of groups, typically gather data at a single point in time rather than continuously monitoring individuals over time. Second, researchers using single-case designs typically need to locate only a few individuals with the same performance problem in order to evaluate an intervention. Researchers using group designs often find locating enough individuals with the same performance problem to form the different groups to be difficult. Third, because all individuals in a single-case design receive the intervention at one time or another, these designs are less vulnerable to the ethical problem of withholding treatment, and the researcher does not face resistance from clients (or their significant others) to participate in a no-treatment control group. Fourth, because single-case designs rely on replication logic rather than the sampling logic of the group designs (Smith, 1988), they are not hampered by the statistical assumptions required of group designs. Often in research using group designs these assumptions are either not assessed or not met (Hoekstra, Kiers, & Johnson, 2012). For these and other reasons, behavior modifiers favor single-case designs. A number of excellent books on single-case designs are available, including Bailey and Burch (2002), Barlow, Nock, and Hersen (2009), Johnston and Pennypacker (2009), Kazdin (2011), Morgan and Morgan (2009), and Richards, Taylor, and Ramasamy (2014). See Martin, Thompson, and Regehr (2004) and Barker, Mellalieu, McCarthy, Jones, and Moran (2013) for reviews of research and Virues-Ortega and Martin (2010) for guidelines for using single-case designs in sport psychology. For a discussion of some common misunderstandings about single-case designs, see Hrycaiko and Martin (1996). For a discussion of reasons for using between-subjects designs, see Poling, Methot, and LeSage (1995). See Brossart, Parker, Olson, and Mahadevan (2006), Ma (2006), Parker (2006), and Parker and Hagan-Burke (2007) for a discussion on statistical techniques that can be used to interpret single-case research. For a discussion of the pros and cons of using statistical inference procedures in behavior analysis research, see *The Behavior Analyst*, 2000, Vol. 22, No. 2. For a discussion of meta-analysis of single-case design research, see the special issue of the *Journal of Behavioral Education*, 2012, Vol. 21, No. 3.

Question for Further Learning

1. List four reasons why many behavior modifiers prefer single-case designs to group designs.

CHAPTER 23

Functional Assessment
of Problem Behavior

LEARNING OBJECTIVES

After studying this chapter, you will be able to:

- Describe approaches to functional assessment of the causes of problem behaviors.

- Discuss major causes of problem behaviors.
- Summarize guidelines for conducting a functional assessment of problem behavior.

Throughout Part II of this book, especially in the "pitfalls" sections, we have repeatedly pointed out how misapplication of behavior principles can cause problem behavior. In other words, if the principles are not working for you, they will be working against you. Increasingly, applied behavior analysts and behavior therapists are attempting to understand the causes of problem behaviors in order to treat them more effectively.

A functional assessment of a problem behavior involves asking two questions: (a) what are the antecedents of the behavior, and (b) what are the immediate consequences of the behavior? More specifically, we ask: Is the behavior being evoked or elicited by particular stimuli? Is it being reinforced? And if so, what is the reinforcement? Does the behavior lead to escape from aversive events? From the client's point of view, what function does the behavior serve? The answers to such questions have important implications for planning effective treatment.

Functional Assessment Procedures

The term *functional assessment* refers to a variety of approaches that attempt to identify the antecedents and consequences for problem behaviors. In this section we consider procedures for identifying variables that control specific problem behaviors, and discuss how knowledge of these variables can help in designing effective treatment programs. The information presented here follows logically from the basic principles and procedures discussed in earlier chapters of this book.

Functional Analysis of Problem Behavior

Functional analysis is the systematic manipulation of environmental events to experimentally test their role as antecedents or consequences in controlling or maintaining specific problem behaviors. In this procedure—which is also called an *experimental functional assessment*—one directly assesses the effects of potential controlling variables on the problem behavior. In the early days of behavior modification, regardless of what was causing or maintaining a problem behavior, it was often assumed that appropriate scheduling of positive reinforcers and/or punishers would overcome whatever might have been causing or maintaining it. This strategy often worked well. However, finding positive reinforcers powerful enough to overcome extremely severe problem behaviors was often difficult. This seemed especially true for self-injurious behavior emitted by individuals with developmental disabilities. And many of those behaviors—for example, eye gouging, head banging, self-biting—were so harmful to the individuals engaging in them that there was no question that those behaviors had to be eliminated. If extremely harmful self-injurious behaviors were to be controlled, behavior modifiers often seemed to have no choice other than to resort

NOTE 1   to strong punishment, such as electric shock punishment.

Then, in 1982, Brian Iwata and his colleagues published a paper that came to be so influential that in 1994 it was reprinted (Iwata, Dorsey, Slifer, Bauman, & Richman, 1982, 1994), and it is still being widely cited. These researchers decided to take a functional analytic approach to get at the causes of self-injurious behavior of children with developmental disabilities. They used a multielement design such as described in the previous chapter.

Nine children with some degree of developmental delay and who engaged in self-injurious behavior were included in the study. Because the study required allowing the children to emit self-injurious behavior, the children were carefully screened by medical personnel to insure that any self-injuries would not be more extensive than minor cuts or scrapes the children would typically incur in their usual daily activities. In addition, throughout the study medical personnel were on hand to treat any self-injuries. Moreover, in consultation with medical personnel, strict criteria were put in place to terminate a session if the self-injuries exceeded a specified small amount. The study lasted an average of about eight days for each child.

There were four conditions in their study. Each condition was carried out twice daily in random order for 15 minutes for each child in a room normally used for therapy. In an *attention condition*, to see if the self-injurious behavior was being maintained by adult attention, a variety of toys were placed in the room and the child and the behavior modifier went into the room together. However, the behavior modifier pretended to do paper work and only interacted with the child when he/she engaged in the problem behavior. Each time the child engaged in self-injurious behavior, the behavior modifier would look at the child and express concern such as, "Don't do that, you're going to hurt yourself." In a *demand condition*, to see if the self-injurious behavior was maintained by escape from demands, the behavior modifier and child went into the room together and the behavior modifier prompted the child to perform some task that the child found difficult. If the child engaged in the problem behavior, the behavior modifier stopped making demands on the child for 30 seconds. In an *alone condition*, to see if the self-injurious behavior was a form of sensory reinforcement when the child was alone, there were no toys in the room and the child was in the room by him/herself, although observed through a one-way window. In a *control condition*, to test whether self-injurious behavior occurred in the absence of the three previous conditions, the child and the behavior modifier were in the room together, a variety of toys were present, and the behavior modifier reinforced the child's appropriate play behavior.

Results indicated clearly that different types of reinforcers were controlling the self-injurious behavior of six of the nine children. Two children showed more self-injurious behavior during condition A, indicating that social attention, social positive reinforcement, was maintaining their self-injurious behavior. Two children showed more self-injurious behavior during condition B, indicating that escape from demand, social negative reinforcement, was maintaining their self-injurious behavior. Two children showed more self-injurious behavior during condition C, suggesting that non-social reinforcement was maintaining their self-injurious behavior. This could be some sort of *internal sensory reinforcement* from the self-injurious behavior. *Internal sensory reinforcement* means reinforcement that is produced simply by the sensations that a response produces, such as the flashes of light one might experience when pressing on one's eyeball. None of the children showed more self-injurious behavior in condition D. The results indicated: (a) for four children self-injurious behavior was relatively high during the self-reinforcement (alone) condition; (b) for two children self-injury was highest during the demand condition; and (c) for three children, self-injurious behavior was relatively high across all stimulus conditions.

Implications of a Functional Analysis for Treatment   Iwata et al.'s (1982, 1994) results indicated that even though the form of self-injurious behavior may be very similar from one individual to another, the function can be quite different. This finding implied that *treatment should be based on the function of the behavior, not on its form.* Suppose, for example, that Iwata et al.'s four conditions were conducted with each of two children who showed self-injurious behavior, with five sessions per condition per child. Suppose further that the results of the multi-element design with the two children were those shown in Figure 23.1. Because the results with Child A indicate that that child's problem behavior is maintained by adult attention, the recommended treatment would be withholding attention for the problem behavior and providing it for a desirable behavior. On the other hand, because Child B's results in Figure 23.1 indicate that that child's problem behavior is maintained by escape from

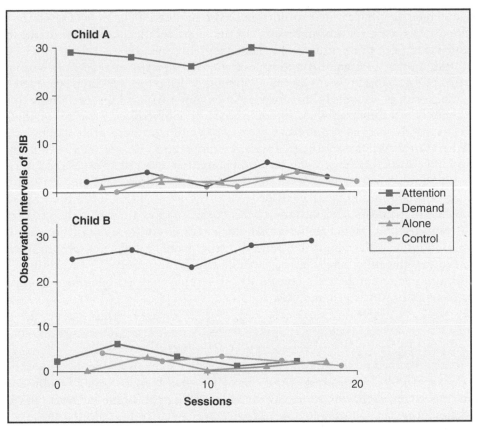

FIGURE 23.1
Hypothetical data of self-injurious behavior (SIB) of two children, each observed in four conditions.

demands, the recommended treatment would be to include more or longer non-demand periods when working with that child, and perhaps persisting with demands if a problem behavior occurred right after a demand (extinction of escape behavior). Although the data in Figure 23.1 is hypothetical, you will see by some examples presented later in this chapter that a functional analysis of the causes of a problem behavior is often combined with the application of an effective treatment based on the results of the functional analysis.

Following the landmark study by Iwata et al. (1982, 1994), over 2,000 articles and book chapters have discussed and extended the functional analysis procedure they originally developed (Beavers, Iwata, & Lerman, 2013). Functional analysis has been used in a number of different settings, with different types of problem behavior, and with different types of individuals (for examples, see Cipani & Schock, 2007; Steege & Watson, 2009; Sturmey, 2007). It is often referred to as the "gold standard" of functional assessment because other functional assessment procedures (described later) have not been as effective in identifying the variables maintaining problem behavior.

Limitations of Functional Analyses   Although functional analysis can convincingly demonstrate the controlling variables of problem behaviors, it has also some limitations. First, the amount of time required to carry out a functional analysis may put a large strain on available staff. For example, in a summary of 152 functional analyses, Iwata et al. (1994) reported that the length of assessments of individual clients ranged from 8 to 66 sessions or 2 to 16.5 hours (Iwata et al., 1994), which is substantial time for trained staff to take from their other duties. Second, functional analysis cannot be applied to extremely dangerous behaviors. Third, many behavior problems occur at frequencies of less than one per day or per week. Functional analyses of such low-frequency behaviors require a great deal of time before sufficient data can be obtained to draw valid conclusions. In an attempt to minimize the first limitation, the time required for a functional analysis, researchers have found that only one or two repetitions of some of the conditions and a decrease in session length to 5 minutes can often give meaningful results (Northup et al., 1991; Tincani, Gastrogiavanni, & Axelrod, 1999). Another way to reduce the amount of time required in a functional analysis is to use the alone condition as a screening phase when internal sensory reinforcement is suspected. If the problem behavior does not decrease over several sessions of the alone condition, this is a strong (although not perfect) indication that the problem behavior is being maintained by internal sensory reinforcement and further testing may be omitted if necessary to save time (Querim et al., 2013). With regard to the second limitation, some dangerous or extremely disruptive behaviors are often preceded by behaviors that are not dangerous or extremely disruptive. An example would be screaming before becoming aggressive. Research has indicated that, in some cases, if a functional analysis of these precursors is carried out and if the results are used to treat and eliminate these precursors, the more severe behavior will be eliminated as well (Fritz, Iwata, Hammond, & Bloom, 2013). With regard to the third limitation, increasing the length of a functional analysis sessions to weeks, days, or even hours is not feasible and could even be considered unethical because of the large amount of time the client would be asked to spend in a nontreatment procedure. However, it has been found that waiting for the problem behavior to occur and initiating a functional analysis right at the moment when it is occurring can result in a functional analysis that yields meaningful results (Tarbox, Wallace, Tarbox, Landaburu, & Williams, 2004). Since by definition the problem behavior occurs infrequently, the sessions required for the functional analysis would also be infrequent. Thus, although functional analysis has limitations, researchers are constantly attempting to overcome those limitations because of the proven benefits of functional analysis.

Interview and Questionnaire Functional Assessments

Another way to identify the antecedents and consequences that control problem behavior is to interview the client or people who are familiar with the client. If verbal, the client may be able to say why he/she engages in a particular behavior. If the client is nonverbal, people familiar with the client many be able to provide the necessary information. A more structured way to find out the cause of the problem behavior is to administer a questionnaire in which the client and/or people familiar with the client are asked a standardized series of relevant questions. Examples of questionnaires that have been developed for this purpose are the *Questions About Behavioral Function* (*QABF*; Matson & Vollmer, 1995), the *Motivation Assessment Scale* (*MAS*; Durand & Crimmins, 1988), and the *Functional Analysis Screening Tool* (*FAST*; Iwata, DeLeon, & Roscoe, 2013).

Unfortunately, none of the questionnaires that have been developed show good reliability or validity when compared with conducting a functional analysis (Iwata et al., 2013; Iwata, Kahng, Wallace, & Lindberg, 2000; Sturmey, 1994). This is true even of FAST, a questionnaire Iwata et al. developed based explicitly on functional analysis methodology. This does not mean that questionnaires should be dismissed as useless. Iwata et al. stated that questionnaires such as QABF, MAS, and FAST may have at least three uses: (1) they provide a rapid and consistent way to gather information; (2) the information they provide may serve as a basis for obtaining follow-up information that might be useful if some unique or idiosyncratic fact about the client turns up; and (3) when there is high agreement among several informants on a questionnaire, it may be possible to save time in conducting a functional analysis by ruling out some potential reinforcers of the problem behavior. Unfortunately, despite their limitations, questionnaires are the primary method of functional assessment used by many clinicians and educators (Desrochers, Hile, & Williams-Mosely, 1997; Ellingson, Miltenberger, & Long, 1999; Knoster, 2000; Van Acker, Boreson, Gable, & Potterton, 2005). Some of the possible reasons that have been suggested for the greater use of questionnaires compared to functional analysis are that questionnaires: (1) are easy to administer, (2) do not take a long time to conduct, and (3) do not require direct observation of the behavior of interest (Dixon , Vogel, & Tarbox, 2012, p. 20).

Observational Functional Assessments

Another way to attempt to identify the variables maintaining a problem behavior is to do an observational or descriptive assessment. In this assessment one carefully observes and describes the antecedents and immediate consequences of the problem behavior in its natural settings. (For examples, see Table 4.3 in Chapter 4.) From these descriptions, one forms hypotheses about the antecedent stimuli, motivational variables, and consequences controlling the problem behavior. Then one devises and implements a treatment plan based on these hypotheses. If the treatment is successful, the descriptive analysis is validated. However, like interviews and questionnaires, observational assessment is not as accurate as functional analysis for identifying the causes of problem behavior. One difficulty is that problem behavior usually results in someone paying attention to it. It is therefore easy to conclude that the reinforcement for the behavior is social attention, which is often not the case. (For additional discussion and examples of observational assessment, see Iwata et al., 2000.)

Questions for Learning

1. A functional assessment of the causes of a problem behavior involves asking what two questions?
2. What does the term *functional assessment* refer to?
3. Define the term *functional analysis*.
4. Briefly describe the four conditions in the multielement design that Iwata et al. (Iwata, Dorsey, Slifer, Bauman, & Richman, 1982, 1994) used in the functional analysis they carried out on self-injurious behavior.
5. Briefly discuss, with examples, what the results of Iwata et al.'s research suggest for the treatment of severe self-injurious behavior.
6. Describe three limitations of functional analyses.
7. Briefly describe how each of the three limitations of functional analyses has been addressed in attempts to overcome these limitations.
8. Briefly describe three approaches to functional assessment, that is, three ways of identifying controlling variables of problem behavior.

Major Causes of Problem Behaviors

Having looked at ways to detect the causes of problem behaviors, we now examine the major causes of problem behaviors and examples of the type of treatment that may be indicated for each cause. These causes can be divided into two categories: operant and respondent or elicited. Causes of operant problem behavior can be further subdivided into the categories shown in Figure 23.2. We consider the subcategories of operant problem behavior first, followed by elicited or respondent problem behavior.

Problem Behaviors Maintained by Social Positive Reinforcement

As we have seen in the "pitfalls" sections of earlier chapters, behavioral excesses often are developed and maintained by the social attention they evoke (see A in Figure 23.2). Indicators that the behavior is maintained by attention include: (a) whether attention reliably follows the behavior; (b) whether the individual looks at or approaches a caregiver just before engaging in the behavior; and (c) whether the individual smiles just before engaging in the behavior. Attention from others can also function as an S^D for problem behavior (e.g., Bergen, Holborn, & Scott-Huyghebart, 2002).

If a functional analysis indicates that the behavior is maintained by attention, treatment involving social reinforcement would be recommended, as illustrated by the following study.

A Case of High Frequency of Delusional Statements   Travis and Sturmey (2010) conducted a functional analysis and treatment of the delusional statements of a man with multiple disabilities. Mr. Jones was a 26-year-old man who had suffered a traumatic brain injury during a car accident at the age of 16, and who lived at an inpatient forensic facility. He engaged in frequent delusional statements (e.g., "Britney Spears is coming to see me this weekend") that were obviously false and noncontextual. The high frequency of Mr. Jones' delusional statements led to him being frequently teased by his peers, and the statements prevented him from participating in various community activities. A direct-care staff member under the supervision of Travis and Sturmey conducted a functional analysis of Mr. Jones'

	Social	Self-Stimulation	Nonsocial
Positive reinforcement	A	B	C
Negative reinforcement	D	E	F

FIGURE 23.2
Causes of operant problem behavior. (See text for explanation.)

delusional statements. Four 12-minute sessions were conducted every other day for 1 week in a private treatment room containing a small table, two chairs, a wall clock, and a one-way observation window. In an *alone condition*, Mr. Jones was alone in the room. In an *attention condition*, Mr. Jones and the staff member maintained a conversation and when Mr. Jones made a delusional statement, the staff member provided approximately 10 seconds of attention in the form of disapproving comments (e.g., "That's not an appropriate topic right now"). In a *demand condition*, the staff member presented Mr. Jones with a vocational task that involved gathering and counting combs and placing them in plastic bags. When Mr. Jones emitted a delusional statement, the therapist removed the task for 10 seconds. During a *control condition*, Mr. Jones was given access to favored reading materials, the staff member provided attention noncontingently every 30 seconds, and there were no consequences for delusional or nondelusional statements.

The results indicated that Mr. Jones showed far more delusional statements in the attention condition than in the alone, demand, or control conditions. Based on the functional analysis, treatment sessions involved a combination of attention for appropriate comments and extinction of delusional statements. More specifically, contextually appropriate, nondelusional statements were each followed by the therapist telling Mr. Jones that what he said sounded nice, and Mr. Jones was then asked to elaborate on what he had said. If Mr. Jones made a delusional statement, the therapist ignored him for approximately 10 seconds. During treatment, the delusional statements decreased to a very low level. Moreover, follow-up observations at 6 months, and 1, 2, and 4 years indicated that, with the training of new staff members to maintain the DRA and extinction intervention, the positive treatment results were maintained.

Problem Behaviors Maintained by Internal Self-Stimulatory Positive Reinforcement

As mentioned earlier in this chapter, behaviors are often reinforced by the sensory stimulation they produce internally. This is termed *internal sensory reinforcement* or *self-stimulation*, and is said to be *self-reinforcing* (see B in Figure 23.2). Another name for internal sensory reinforcement is *automatic reinforcement*, because it is assumed that the behavior itself is automatically reinforcing without producing any consequence that another person can control or detect (see Iwata, Pace, Kalsher, Cowdery, & Cataldo, 1990, p.12). For example, massaging one's scalp produces an enjoyable tingling sensation. Unfortunately, in some individuals, this type of consequence might also maintain extreme self-stimulatory behaviors that can even be self-injurious. Reinforcers that maintain such behaviors might consist of sensory or perceptual feedback including vestibular sensations, visual patterns, repetitive sounds, and tactile or kinesthetic sensations (Guess & Carr, 1991; Lovaas, Newsom, & Hickman, 1987). An indicator that the behavior is self-reinforcing is that it continues unabated at a steady rate although it has no apparent effect on other individuals or the external environment. If it appears that self-injurious behavior is maintained by internal sensory reinforcement, then an important component of treatment might be the enrichment of the individual's environment so as to reduce deprivation of sensory stimulation. (Note that this would be an MAO; see Chapter 19.) Alternatively, extinction of a self-stimulatory behavior by altering the sensory consequences that the behavior produces might also be effective, as illustrated by the following case.

A Case of Face Scratching
This case, described by Rincover and Devaney (1982), illustrates an observational assessment and treatment of a problem behavior maintained by internal sensory stimulation. Sarah, a 4 ½ -year-old child with an intellectual disability, constantly scratched her face with her fingernails. Although her nails were cut so short that it was impossible for them to tear her skin, her scratching still resulted in skin irritations and abrasions. Observations during daily 5-hour classes in a treatment center for persons with developmental disabilities indicated that the scratching occurred frequently during the day. She scratched when smiling, when upset, when interacting with others, when alone, and whether or not demands were placed on her. Clearly, the behavior appeared to be maintained by internal self-stimulation reinforcement rather than by social reinforcement. The treatment therefore consisted of extinction of scratching by eliminating the tactile sensations that the scratching produced. Each day her hands were covered with thin rubber gloves that did not prevent her from scratching, but did eliminate the internal sensory stimulation and also prevented her from damaging her skin. The result was an immediate and substantial decrease in the rate of scratching. Within 4 days,

scratching was eliminated. During follow-up sessions the gloves were removed, first for just 10 minutes a day, then for longer and longer intervals, until finally they were no longer needed.

Interestingly, this case—along with two similar cases in the same article—appeared in the same issue of the journal that the Iwata et al. (1982/1994) study on functional analysis appeared. Rincover and Devaney (1982) did not do a formal functional analysis as described by Iwata et al. (1982, 1994). However, as astute applied behavior analysts they informally made all the observations of Sarah (and several other children who engaged in self-injurious behavior) that they would have made had they done a formal functional analysis. They stated, "In each of the present cases, self-injury had persisted over time in situations where social attention was present as well as when it was not, when demands were present as well as when they were not, and therefore did not appear to be correlated (positively or negatively) with any obvious social or environmental events in the natural environment." Rincover and Devaney therefore concluded that the self-injurious behavior of these children was maintained by self-stimulatory reinforcement rather than by escape from demand or social positive reinforcement. This suggests that there are situations in which informal observation, at least by well-trained applied behavior analysts, can lead to correct identification of the reinforcer maintaining problem behavior.

Problem Behaviors Maintained by External Sensory Positive Reinforcement

Reinforcing sights and sounds of a nonsocial external environment might maintain some problem behavior (see C in Figure 23.2). A child who throws toys might enjoy the loud noise when they land. Flushing items down the toilet repeatedly or letting the water run to overflow a sink might be maintained by the sights produced. This is called *external sensory reinforcement* to distinguish it from the sensory reinforcement discussed earlier. For an indicator that a particular problem behavior is being maintained by external sensory reinforcement, note whether the individual continues the behavior undiminished over numerous occasions even though it appears to have no social consequences. If a functional assessment indicates that the behavior is maintained by external sensory reinforcement, then a component of the treatment program might involve sensory reinforcement of a desirable alternative behavior. This is illustrated in the following case.

A Case of Flushing Jewelry Down the Toilet

This case, treated by one of the authors, involved a child with intellectual disabilities who was living at home. It illustrates a problem behavior that may have been maintained by social attention, by sensory stimulation from the nonsocial external environment, or by both. Occasionally during the day, and always when the mother was busy in the kitchen, the child would go to the mother's bedroom, take a piece of jewelry out of the jewelry box, carry it to the bathroom, and flush it down the toilet. She would then tell her mother what she had done. For the purposes of assessment and treatment, the mother's jewelry was replaced with "junk" jewelry. An observational assessment suggested two possible explanations of the problem behavior. First, the appearance of the jewelry swirling around the toilet bowl before disappearing might have functioned as a sensory reinforcer. Second, the entire sequence of activities may have been a behavioral chain that was reinforced by mother's attention after the child emitted the sequence of steps and then told her mother what she had done. The treatment procedure that was used took both possibilities into account. The girl was given several prompted trials during which, when mother and daughter were both in the kitchen, the mother took the daughter by the hand, went into the bedroom, prompted the daughter to take a piece of jewelry out of the box, and guided the daughter to bring the jewelry into the kitchen and drop it in a jar on the kitchen table. It was thought that the tinkling sound of the jewelry as it dropped into the jar might serve as a sensory reinforcer to replace the sight of the jewelry disappearing down the toilet. In addition, the new sequence or behavioral chain was highly reinforced with praise and an occasional treat.

After several guided trials, the mother was able to initiate the new chain by instructing the child while they were both in the kitchen. During the first 2 days of treatment, the child was not given an opportunity to go into the bedroom. On the start of the third day, the child was instructed that any time she wanted when mom was in the kitchen, she could get some jewelry, place it in the jar in the kitchen, and receive praise from Mom. To enhance the likelihood of this new sequence, the mother took a photograph of the daughter putting the jewelry into the jar on the kitchen table and placed the picture beside the jewelry box in the bedroom. During the next 3 weeks, the child continued periodically to bring jewelry to the kitchen and to receive praise and occasional treats for doing so. Not once did she flush jewelry down the toilet. Eventually, she stopped playing with mother's jewelry altogether.

Questions for Learning

9. What are three indicators that a problem behavior is probably maintained by the social attention that follows it?
10. What were the results of the functional analysis of the causes of excessive delusional statements made by Mr. Jones, and what was the treatment of the delusional statements based on the results of the functional analysis?
11. What is another name for "sensory reinforcement," and what assumption is the other name based on?
12. What is an indicator that a problem behavior is being maintained by self-stimulatory reinforcement?
13. Describe how Rincover and Devaney applied extinction to a problem that appeared to be maintained by self-stimulatory reinforcement.
14. What is an indicator that a problem behavior is being reinforced by nonsocial external sensory stimulation? Give an example illustrating this indicator.
15. What were two plausible explanations of the behavior of the child flushing jewelry down the toilet? How did the treatment procedure take both possibilities into account?

Problem Behaviors Maintained by Social Negative Reinforcement

Some problem behaviors are negatively reinforced by escape from demands (see D in Figure 23.2; also see Chapter 14). For example, when asked to answer difficult questions, some children may engage in tantrums that are reinforced by the withdrawal of the request. A strong indicator that a problem behavior is in this category is that the individual engages in the behavior only when certain types of demands or requests are made. If a functional assessment supports this type of interpretation, it may be feasible to persist with requests or demands until the tantrums extinguish and compliance occurs, as illustrated below for a case of self-injurious behavior. Alternatively, with nonverbal persons, as described in Chapter 14, you might teach the individual some other way to indicate (such as by finger tapping or hand raising) that the task is aversive. In this way, the problem behavior can be replaced by an adaptive response that has the same or similar function as the problem behavior but is more acceptable (Mace, Lalli, Lalli, & Shey, 1993). The above case predates the 1982 study by Iwata et al. (1982/1994). It is instructive, however, to consider how a functional analysis might have been used to identify the variables controlling Edward's unwanted Tarzan noises. We would have needed at least four conditions: (A) a condition with Edward in the absence of the class in which Ms. Millan asked Edward difficult questions and allowed him to escape from having to answer them by making Tarzan noises; (B) a condition with Edward in the absence of the class in which Ms. Millan did not ask Edward difficult questions; (C) a condition with Edward in the presence of the class in which Ms. Millan asked Edward difficult questions and allowed him to escape from having to answer them by making Tarzan noises; (D) a condition with Edward in the presence of the class in which Ms. Millan did not ask Edward difficult questions. If the conclusion that Ms. Millan and the behavior analyst had drawn about the variables controlling Edward's unwanted Tarzan noises was correct, he should have made many more Tarzan noises in condition C than in any of the other conditions. The fact that the treatment was effective indicates that their conclusion was correct.

A Case of Self-Injurious behavior Maintained by Escape from Demand   Consider a case described by Iwata, Pace, Kalsher, Cowdery, and Cataldo (1990). Susie, a 5-year-old child with developmental disabilities, had been referred for therapy because of a high frequency of self-injurious behavior that included banging her head and slapping her face. Was this a way for Susie to get positive reinforcement in the form of adult attention (see Chapter 4)? Was it a way for Susie to escape from demands to perform various tasks (Chapter 14)? Or were the injurious behaviors self-reinforcing? To assess these possibilities experimentally, Iwata and his colleagues examined Susie's self-injurious behavior over several sessions in a therapy room. In an *attention condition*, the therapist approached Susie and voiced concern following instances of self-injurious behavior (e.g., "Oh Susie, what's wrong?"). In a *demand condition*, the therapist presented various educational tasks to Susie at a rate of one every 30 seconds. In an *alone condition*, Susie was either left alone in an empty therapy room or was observed when the therapy room contained a number of toys and games. Across several sessions, the results were clear: Susie frequently engaged in self-injurious behavior in the demand condition but rarely in the other two conditions.

Armed with this functional analysis, Iwata and his colleagues designed a treatment program in which the self-injurious escape behavior was extinguished by continuing the demand when Susie engaged in self-injurious behavior. Instead of backing off following instances of self-injurious behavior, the therapist physically guided Susie to complete the various educational activities as they were presented. By the fifth session, Susie's self-injurious behavior had decreased to near zero and she was more compliant in performing the tasks. Because the treatment was successful, we may infer that the therapist had correctly identified the cause of the problem behavior through the functional analysis. In other words, the success of the treatment validated the results of the functional analysis.

As with all studies presented in this book, all ethical principles were adhered to in the above study in which Susie participated. This is particularly important when self-injury or injury of any type is a possibility. In their article the researchers explicitly stated:

> All subjects underwent medical examination prior to the study, and it was determined that they could be allowed to engage in [self-injurious behavior] unrestrained for brief durations with little risk of inflicting further injury. In addition, physicians and nurses routinely monitored the subjects' physical status both during and after sessions to ensure that the risk remained within acceptable levels. (Iwata et al., 1990, p. 13)

Problem Behaviors Maintained by Internal Sensory Negative Reinforcement

Consider the case of Sarah, the child who severely scratched her face. Observation indicated that there was no underlying medical cause for this behavior, such as an allergy, an insect bite, or a toothache. However, if the child was scratching to relieve the unpleasant sensations caused by a physical condition this would be an example of a problem behavior maintained by internal sensory negative reinforcement (see E in Figure 23.2). In such cases the underlying medical condition should be treated by an appropriate health care professional, as discussed later in this chapter. A problem behavior that may, in some cases, be maintained by internal sensory negative reinforcement is binge eating. For example, Stickney and Miltenberger (1999) and Stickney, Miltenberger, and Wolff (1999) provided evidence that, in some cases, binge eating can be maintained because it leads to a decrease (at least temporarily) in unpleasant emotional responses. Such cases can be treated by an appropriately trained behavior therapist (see Chapter 28).

Problem Behaviors Maintained by External Sensory Negative Reinforcement

Many of our behaviors are maintained by nonsocial negative reinforcement or escape from external sensory aversive stimuli. Examples include squinting in the presence of bright light or covering your ears to escape a loud sound. Some problem behaviors might also be maintained by external sensory negative reinforcement (F in Figure 23.2). A child might repeatedly remove her shoes because they squeeze her toes too tightly. Or an individual who is used to loose-fitting clothes but has a job that requires formal attire might frequently loosen his top button and tie. If there is a possibility that an external sensory negative reinforcer is maintaining an undesirable behavior, the arranging for escape extinction might be an effective treatment component. Such a treatment component has been applied to treat feeding disorders of children when a child frequently spits out food and does not eat sufficient quantities of food. Negative reinforcement in the form of escape from eating has been demonstrated to be one of the maintaining variables for such eating disorders in children (Piazza et al., 2003), and escape extinction has been demonstrated to be an effective component of the treatment of food refusal, either by itself (Piazza, Fisher, et al., 2003), or in combination with other treatment components (Bachmeyer et al., 2009; Piazza, Patel, et al., 2003).

Respondent or Elicited Problem Behaviors

Some problem behaviors are respondent or elicited (see Chapter 3) rather than controlled by their consequences. Aggression can be elicited by aversive stimuli (see Chapter 13) or by withholding a reinforcer following a previously reinforced response (i.e., extinction; see Chapter 6). Emotions have elicited components (see Chapters 3 and 15). For example, if a previously neutral stimulus has occurred in close association with an aversive event, that stimulus might come to elicit anxiety. Several behavioral checklists have been published for conducting questionnaire assessments of the conditioned stimuli (CSs) that elicit the respondent components of emotions. Examples include the *Fear Survey Schedule* (Cautela, Kastenbaum, & Wincze, 1972) and the *Fear Survey for Children* (Morris & Kratochwill, 1983). A descriptive functional assessment or a functional analysis could also be conducted to determine the specific stimuli, circumstances, or thoughts that might elicit respondent components of emotions (Emmelkamp, Bouman, & Scholing, 1992). The two main indicators that a problem behavior is elicited are that it consistently occurs in a certain situation or in the presence of certain stimuli and that it is never followed by any clearly identifiable reinforcing consequence. Another indicator, as suggested by the term elicited, is that the behavior seems to be involuntary (i.e., the person seems unable to inhibit it). If a problem behavior appears to be elicited, the treatment might include establishing one or more responses that compete with it so that their occurrence precludes the occurrence of the undesirable response (i.e., counterconditioning; see Chapter 3), as illustrated in the following example.

A Respondent Conditioning Approach to Reducing Anger Responses   Joel—as reported in a case study by Schloss, Smith, Santora, and Bryant (1989)—was a 26-year-old man with a mild intellectual disability who had recently been dismissed from a dishwashing position due to angry outbursts. A questionnaire assessment with Joel's mother and staff members of the Association for Retarded Citizens with whom Joel was associated, and observational assessments with Joel, led to the identification of three categories of CSs for respondent components of emotions. The CSs included "jokes" (humorous anecdotes told to Joel), "criticism" (especially about deficiencies in Joel's conduct or appearance), and "sexual talk" (discussions of dating, marriage, etc.). Within each category, a hierarchy of provoking events was established and ranged from events that caused the least anger to events that caused the most anger. The respondent components of Joel's anger included rapid breathing, facial expressions indicative of anger, and trembling. The operant components of Joel's anger were also monitored, including talking loudly and avoiding eye contact with the person whose comments elicited Joel's anger. Treatment focused primarily on counterconditioning. Joel was first taught how to relax using a process called progressive muscle relaxation (described further in Chapter 28). Then, while in a state of relaxation, a CS for anger from one of the categories was presented. For example, a "joke-related" situation was described to Joel and he was asked to imagine it while remaining relaxed. Across several sessions, more and more of the CSs for anger were introduced, gradually proceeding up each of the hierarchies from situations that caused the least anger to those that caused the most anger. (As described in Chapter 28, this procedure is referred to as systematic desensitization.) In addition to the clinic-based procedures, Joel was requested, while at home, to listen to a tape recording that induced muscle relaxation, and to practice relaxation exercises when CSs for anger were encountered in everyday life. Overall, the program was successful. Anger-related responses decreased to a very low level during training sessions and generalized to natural settings for each of the categories.

Medical Causes of Problem Behaviors

Often the controlling variables with which behavior modifiers are concerned lie in the individual's environment. Sometimes, however, a behavior that appears problematic may have a medical cause. For example, a nonverbal individual may bang his or her head against hard objects to reduce pain from an internal source, such as an ear infection (E in Figure 23.2). A medical cause may be indicated if the problem emerges suddenly and does not seem to be related to any changes in the individual's environment.

In order to encourage behavior modifiers to gather all possible information about the causes of problem behaviors, Jon Bailey and David Pyles developed the concept of *behavioral diagnostics* (Bailey & Pyles, 1989; Pyles & Bailey, 1990). With this approach to behavioral assessment, the therapist diagnoses the problem after examining antecedents, consequences, and medical and nutritional variables as potential causes of problem behaviors. Based on the diagnosis, the therapist develops a treatment plan, tests the plan under controlled conditions, and if the results are successful puts the treatment plan into effect.

With the behavioral diagnostic model, examples of data that might be collected during the diagnosis phase include: health/medical variables (e.g., menstrual cycles or constipation), nutrition variables (e.g., caloric intake or food allergies), medications, and, of course, the information about the kinds of antecedents and consequences of behavior illustrated in this chapter. The concept of behavioral diagnostics is broader than that of a functional assessment. Consistent with this broader view, variables that influence problem behavior of many individuals are listed in Table 23.1. For variables that commonly act as antecedents or consequences for problem behavior with persons with developmental disabilities, see Demchak and Bossert (1996).

TABLE 23.1   Factors to Consider in Assessing Causes of Problem Behavior
General Setting
Low overall level of reinforcement
Conditions that cause discomfort (e.g., hot, noisy, crowded)
Presence or absence of particular people
Organismic Variables
State of health (e.g., flu, headache, allergies)
Motivational state (e.g., hungry, thirsty)
Emotional state (e.g., angry, jealous)
Temporary bodily states (e.g., fatigue, menstrual cramps)
Task Variables
Too difficult
Improper pace (too fast, too slow)
Lack of variety
Lack of choice
Lack of perceived importance
Specific Antecedents
Sudden change in immediate surroundings
Introduction of new tasks
Excessive demands
Unclear instructions
Removal of visible reinforcers
Withholding of reinforcers following previously reinforced responses
Presentation of aversive stimuli
Instruction to wait
Observance of someone else being reinforced
Specific Consequences: Problem Behavior Leads to
Escape from demands
Attention from others
Sympathy
Getting one's way
Tangible reinforcers
Internal sensory feedback
External sensory feedback

If there is any possibility that a behavior problem has a medical cause, an appropriate health care professional should be consulted prior to treating the problem. This is not to say that behavioral techniques cannot be effective if the problem has a medical cause; on the contrary, often they can. For example, hyperactivity is often treated by a combination of behavioral and medical procedures (Barkley, 2005). Such treatment, however, should be carried out in consultation with a physician (see Chapter 2 for a discussion of behavioral approaches to medical problems).

Guidelines for Conducting a Functional Assessment

The following is a summary of important guidelines for conducting a functional assessment.

1. Define the problem behavior in behavioral terms.
2. Identify antecedent events that consistently precede the problem behavior.

3. Identify consequences that immediately (although possibly intermittently) follow the problem behavior.
4. As suggested by behavioral diagnostics, consider health/medical/personal variables that might contribute to the problem.
5. Based on guidelines 2, 3, and 4, form hypotheses about the consequent events that maintain the problem behavior, the antecedent events that elicit it or evoke it, and/or the health/medical/personal variables that exacerbate it.
6. Take data on the behavior, its antecedents and consequences in its natural setting, and health/medical/personal variables to determine which of the hypotheses in guideline 5 are likely to be correct.
7. If possible, do a functional analysis by directly testing the hypotheses developed in guideline 5. *Be sure to recognize the special ethical concerns of a functional analysis. Specifically, recognize that in a functional analysis you are not treating the behavior, you are deliberately trying to produce it and if successful probably even reinforcing it. Sessions of functional analysis should therefore be as short and as few as possible. All procedures used in the functional analysis must be cleared with qualified medical personnel and carried out by or under the direct supervision of a qualified applied behavior analyst or behavior therapist. If there is any possibility of self-injury, medical personnel must be on hand to provide immediate medical treatment. Finally, the client must benefit from the functional analysis by receiving treatment based on an accurate and valid interpretation of the results of the analysis, as described in guidelines 8 and 9 below.*
8. Incorporating the principles discussed in Part II of this text and following the guidelines for designing treatment programs in Chapter 24, develop a treatment program based on the hypothesis that is most likely to be correct, as determined by guidelines 6 and 7.
9. If the treatment is successful, accept the result of the functional assessment as confirmed. If it is not successful, redo the assessment, or attempt a solution based on the principles in Part II of the book and follow the guidelines in Chapter 24.

Questions for Learning

16. What is a strong indicator that a problem behavior is being maintained as a way of escaping from demands? Give an example illustrating this indicator.
17. Suppose that a nonverbal child screams loudly as a way of escaping from demands by adults in various training settings. Describe two alternative strategies that the adults might follow to deal with the problem behavior.
18. Briefly describe how a functional analysis indicated that Susie's self-injurious behavior was likely maintained because it enabled her to escape from demanding adults. How did the treatment condition confirm the functional analysis?
19. Describe how internal sensory negative reinforcement might be a cause of some cases of binge eating.
20. Describe an example of how external sensory negative reinforcement could produce undesirable behavior.
21. What are the two main indicators that a problem behavior is respondent behavior that is elicited by prior stimuli vs. operant behavior being maintained by reinforcing consequences? Give an example illustrating these indicators.
22. Describe the main components in the treatment of Joel's anger.
23. What is behavioral diagnostics? In what sense is this term broader than functional assessment?
24. In a sentence for each, outline the six major causes of operant problem behaviors described in this chapter.

Application Exercises

A. Exercise Involving Others

Identify a behavioral excess of someone you know well. (Do not identify that person.) Try to identify the stimulus control and maintaining consequences for that behavior. Based on your functional assessment, what do you think would be the best treatment procedure to decrease or eliminate that behavior?

B. Self-Modification Exercise

Identify one of your own behavioral excesses. Try to identify the stimulus control and maintaining consequences for that behavior. Based on your functional assessment, what do you think would be the best treatment procedure to decrease or eliminate that behavior?

Note for Further Learning

1. The term *functional analysis of behavior* has a narrow meaning and a broad meaning. The narrow meaning is that functional analysis refers to discovering the specific antecedents and consequences that control a given behavior of an individual. A broader meaning of functional analysis, however, is scientifically finding a functional relationship between examples of two variables—variables that we call an *independent variable* and a *dependent variable*. For example, physicists conducted a functional analysis in the second sense when they demonstrated that there is a functional relationship between the height at which something is dropped (independent variable, IV) and the force with which it hits the ground (dependent variable, DV). Similarly, all of the principles discussed in Part II of this book are functional relationships of IVs and DVs. For example, Pavlov conducted a functional analysis in the second sense when he demonstrated that pairing an NS (ringing a bell) with a US (presenting food to a dog) caused the NS to become a CS that elicited a CR (caused the dog to salivate at the sound of the bell). In the broad sense of functional analysis, Pavlov demonstrated that respondent behaviors (the DV) could be controlled by respondent conditioning (the IV). Usually when behavior modifiers conduct a functional analysis of an operant problem behavior, they are conducting a functional analysis in both senses of the term: (a) in the first sense, they are demonstrating that a given operant behavior of an individual leads to a specific positive reinforcer or escape from a negative reinforcer; and (b) in the second sense, they are demonstrating in general that the consequences for operant behavior (IV) increases or maintains operant behavior (DV).

   It should also be noted that the functional analysis of problem behaviors differs from the methods used by many traditional psychologists and psychiatrists, who often focus on the form or topography of the behavior rather than the cause. The functional analysis approach is advantageous because it identifies the controlling variables of a problem behavior, while the topography of a behavior typically tells us little or nothing about its cause. Thus, for example, two individuals may be exhibiting similar self-injurious behavior and yet the underlying cause is completely different. Conversely, two individuals may show completely dissimilar behavior and yet the cause might be the same in both cases. In the case of the first set of individuals, behavioral treatment would be different even though the topographies of the problem behaviors are the same, whereas for the second set of individuals behavioral treatment would be similar even though the topographies of the problem behaviors are different. For further discussion of these points with regard to the history and meanings of functional analysis, see Dixon, Vogel, and Tarbox (2012); Schlinger and Normand (2013).

Questions for Further Learning

1. State the two meanings of the term *functional analysis of behavior*.
2. Describe a behavior principle other than respondent conditioning that fits the second sense of functional analysis of behavior and explain how it fits the second sense but not the first.
3. Discuss how and why the functional analytic approach of applied behavior analysts and behavior therapists differs from the approach of many traditional psychologists and psychiatrists. Give an example.

CHAPTER 24

Planning, Applying, and Evaluating a Behavioral Program

LEARNING OBJECTIVES

After studying this chapter, you will be able to:

- Describe considerations to help you decide whether you should design a program to solve a particular behavior problem.
- Outline steps for designing and implementing a behavior modification program.

- Evaluate the results of a behavior modification program.
- Summarize steps to help ensure that results of a successful program are maintained.

"I want to stay inside!" Cindy said in a scared voice, "There's a dog out there."

Overcoming Cindy's Fear of Dogs[1]

Cindy, a normal 5-year-old girl, had developed a dog phobia as a result of several experiences of being chased by a dog. Because her fear caused her to avoid visiting friends who had dogs and limited her outside playtime when dogs were present, her parents took her to an applied behavior analyst for treatment. The treatment consisted of a combination of modeling, shaping, and fading. Treatment started with Cindy imitating the behavior analyst who petted a small quiet dog while it was held, and Cindy was reinforced with praise and stickers that could be cashed in for backup prizes. Across 8 sessions, Cindy was gradually introduced to the small dog on a leash and then when it was loose, then to a medium-sized dog, then to a small hyper dog, and then to a larger dog. Sessions 9–12 occurred with dogs at a dog park. At first she showed some hesitancy and requested that her father pick her up when a dog jumped on her. However, by the 13th session, Cindy was able to walk on her own in the dog park, approaching and petting a variety of dogs.

This chapter provides *general* guidelines that should be followed when designing a behavioral program. It assumes knowledge of the principles and procedures presented in the previous chapters. The client might be anyone—a person with autism or intellectual disabilities; a patient with psychiatric problems; a predelinquent or delinquent child or teenager; a typically developing child or teenager at home, in a classroom, or in a community setting; or a normal adult. The situation is one in which you, as a behavior modifier or a mediator (parent, teacher, etc.), would be largely responsible for carrying out a treatment program or intervention. Many of the guidelines will be illustrated with reference to Cindy's case.

---

[1] This example is based on an article by May, Rudy, Davis III, and Matson (2013).

Deciding Whether to Design a Program Following a Referral

Behavioral problems have a variety of causes, come in a variety of forms and types, and differ widely in degree of complexity and severity. The fact that a problem has been referred is not always a sufficient reason for proceeding with program design and implementation. To decide whether and where to begin, answering the following questions during the screening or intake phase of behavioral assessment is helpful (see Chapter 20).

1. *Was the Problem Referred Primarily for the Benefit of the Client?*   If the problem was referred by others, you must determine whether the accomplishment of the goal will be for the benefit of the client, which was obviously true for Cindy. If its accomplishment is for the benefit of others, it should be at least neutral for the client. Ethical considerations may require that some referrals simply stop here.

2. *Is the Problem Important to the Client or to Others?*   You might ask two questions to evaluate the importance of the problem: Will solving the problem lead to less aversiveness or more positive reinforcement for the client or others? Will solving the problem be likely to give rise directly or indirectly to other desirable behaviors? If the answer to either of these questions is no, you should reconsider your involvement with the problem. Solving Cindy's problem not only led to Cindy enjoying interaction with dogs, it also increased the likelihood of Cindy and her family visiting the homes of friends and family who had dogs.

3. *Can the Problem and the Goal Be Specified So That You Are Dealing with a Specific Behavior or Set of Behaviors That Can Be Measured in Some Way?*   Many referrals are vague, subjective, and general, such as, "Chris is a poor student," "My child is driving me up a wall," "I'm really an unorganized person." If the problem is initially vague you must specify a component behavior or behaviors that (a) define the problem and (b) can be measured or assessed objectively. In such cases, however, it is important to ask whether dealing with the defined component behavior(s) will solve the general problem in the eyes of the referring agent or agencies. If it is impossible to agree with the agent on the component behaviors that define the problem, then you should probably stop there. If you do achieve agreement, it should be specified in writing. The specific target behaviors for Cindy included such things as calmly walking in the dog park and then approaching and petting dogs.

4. *Have You Eliminated the Possibility That the Problem Involves Complications That Would Necessitate Referring It to Another Specialist?*   In other words, are you the appropriate person **NOTE 1** to deal with this problem? If there is any chance that the problem has medical complications, serious psychological ramifications such as the danger of suicide, or a *DSM-5* diagnosis (see Note 1 of Chapter 1 for information on the DSM-5) that you are not qualified to treat, the appropriate specialist should be consulted. You should then treat the problem only in a manner that the specialist recommends. In Cindy's case, prior to treatment, Cindy's father had indicated that Cindy did not have any current or previous medical difficulties, and was not on any medications.

5. *Is the Problem One That Would Appear to Be Easily Manageable?*   To answer this question, you should consider the following: If the problem is to decrease an undesirable behavior, has the behavior been occurring for a short time, under narrow stimulus control, and with no intermittent reinforcement? A problem with these characteristics is likely to be easier to solve than an undesirable behavior that has been occurring for a long time, under the control of many situations, and with a history of intermittent reinforcement. Moreover, you should identify desirable behavior that can replace the undesirable behavior. If the problem is to teach a new behavior, you should assess whether the client has the prerequisite skills. If there is more than one problem, you should rank order them according to their priorities for treatment and begin with the problem assigned the highest priority. In Cindy's case her parents indicated that her dog phobia had developed between the ages of 3 and 5 years, which is a lengthy time. However, at the beginning of therapy, Cindy herself expressed a desire to be able to pet dogs, and the applied behavior analyst was confident that the phobia could be managed.

6. *If the Desired Behavior Change Is Obtained, Can It Be Readily Generalized to and Maintained in the Natural Environment?*   To answer this question, you should consider how your training setting can be faded into the natural environment. You should also consider whether the natural environment has contingencies that will maintain the improved behavior, whether you can influence people in the natural environment to help maintain the improved behavior, and whether the client can learn a self-control program (discussed in Chapter 26) that will help the improved behavior persist. In Cindy's case, the applied behavior analyst programmed generalization by conducting the last stages of therapy with a variety of dogs in a dog park.

NOTE 2

7. *Can You Identify Significant Individuals (Relatives, Friends, and Teachers) in the Client's Natural Environment Who Might Help Record Observations and Manage Controlling Stimuli and Reinforcers?* When designing programs for children, you should consider whether the parents can successfully implement and maintain the program. It makes little sense to accept a referral that would require 2 hours per day for a child in a single-parent family if you have only about 1 hour each week to spend on the project, the parent works full-time, there are four other children who require parental attention, and no other adults are available to implement the program.

8. *If There Are Individuals Who Might Hinder the Program, Can You Identify Ways to Minimize Their Potential Interference?* It makes little sense for you to design a program if people are going to sabotage it by, for example, reinforcing undesirable behavior that you are trying to extinguish.

On the basis of your tentative answers to these eight questions, are your training qualifications, daily schedule, and available time adequate for you to participate in the program? You should accept referrals only for which you have the appropriate training and time to carry out an effective program.

When a behavior modifier first enters settings in which interventions are requested, such as a group home for persons with developmental disabilities, the home of a child with problems, or a classroom, the behavioral problems and the number and complexity of potentially disruptive influences are often staggering. For obvious reasons, it is best to start simple in order to succeed in a small way rather than to attempt too much and risk failing gloriously. A careful evaluation of the initial referral in terms of these questions and considerations can often contribute greatly to the success of a behavioral program.

Questions for Learning

1. How does a behavior modifier evaluate the importance of a problem?
2. What does a behavior modifier do when given a vague problem such as "aggression" to work on? Illustrate with an example.
3. How does a behavior modifier evaluate the ease with which a problem might be solved?
4. How does a behavior modifier evaluate the ease with which the desired behavioral change might be generalized to and maintained in the natural environment?
5. Assume that you are a professional applied behavior analyst or behavior therapist. List four possible conditions under which you would not treat a behavior problem that has been referred to you.

Selection and Implementation of a Preprogram Assessment Procedure

Suppose that you have decided to treat a problem that has been referred to you. You might then proceed through the following steps of implementing a preprogram assessment procedure as introduced in Chapter 20 (pages 191–192, 196).

1. For a reliable baseline, define the problem in precise behavioral terms.
2. Select an appropriate baseline procedure (see Chapters 20, 21, and 23) that will enable you to
   a. monitor the problem behavior
   b. identify the current stimulus control of the problem behavior
   c. identify the maintaining consequences of the problem behavior
   d. monitor relevant medical/health/personal variables
   e. identify an alternative desirable behavior
3. Design recording procedures that will enable you to log the amount of time devoted to the project by professionals (such as teachers or group home staff). This will help you to do a cost-effectiveness analysis.
4. Ensure that the observers have received appropriate training in identifying the critical aspects of the behavior, applying the recording procedures, and graphing the data.
5. If the baseline is likely to be prolonged, select a procedure for increasing and maintaining the strength of the record-keeping behavior of the people recording the data.
6. After beginning to collect baseline data, analyze the data carefully to select an appropriate treatment or intervention strategy and decide when to terminate the baseline phase and begin the intervention.

We reviewed the guidelines for behavioral assessment in Chapters 20, 21, and 23, and will not repeat them here. However, you as a behavior modifier should answer some additional questions during the pretreatment assessment phase:

What Daily Times Can the Mediator(s) Schedule for This Project?   If a teacher has about 10 minutes each day just before lunch to devote to the project, there is no sense in (a) designing time-sampling data sheets that require the teacher to assess behavior throughout the day or (b) gathering data that the teacher will never have time to examine.

Will Others in the Situation Help or Hinder Data Collection?   There is no sense in designing a baseline procedure to record the duration of a child's tantrumming in a home situation if a grandparent, aunt, brother, or other relative is going to give the child a candy to stop the tantrums. On the other hand, well-instructed and motivated relatives and friends can often be extremely helpful, either by recording data directly or by reminding others to do so. If the help of others is to be utilized, posting data sheets and a summary of the recording procedures where everyone involved in the project can see them is a good practice.

Will the Surroundings Make Your Assessment Difficult?   If you want to determine a baseline for the frequency and timing of a child's marking on walls throughout the day and the house has many rooms through which the child wanders, it may be difficult to immediately detect instances of the behavior. Or suppose that you want a baseline for someone's smoking behavior, but during the baseline period that person spends time in the home of a friend who doesn't smoke. Obviously, this is not ideal for assessment procedures. If you want to assess a child's basic self-dressing skills by presenting clothing items with appropriate instructions while the child's favorite TV program is blaring in the background, your assessment is not likely to be accurate.

How Frequent Is the Problem Behavior?   Is it a problem that occurs often each day? Or is it one that occurs once every few weeks? In some cases, your answers to these questions might influence you to withdraw from the project. A problem behavior that occurs rarely can be extremely difficult to treat if you have limited time available for the project. Certainly, the perceived frequency of the behavior will dictate the type of recording procedure as described in Chapter 21 to be selected.

How Rapidly Should the Behavior Change?   Does the behavior require immediate attention because of its inherent danger (e.g., self-injury)? Or is the behavior one whose immediate change is merely convenient for those concerned (e.g., parents wanting to toilet train their child just before going on vacation)? If the behavior (e.g., smoking) has been occurring for many months and if another few days or weeks can be tolerated, you might be more diligent to design a detailed data-recording system to reliably assess baseline levels of performance.

Is the Presenting Problem a Behavioral Deficit or Can It Be Reformulated as Such?   Even if the problem is a behavioral excess to decrease, you should try to identify a desirable alternative behavior to increase. In Cindy's case the applied behavior analyst used an anxiety disorders interview schedule and a child-behavior checklist, as part of a detailed preprogram assessment during a semistructured interview with Cindy's parents, which ensured the presence of a diagnosable specific phobia of dogs and the absence of other significant emotional and behavioral problems. Baseline observations were also taken of Cindy's fear of dogs during the first session.

Questions for Learning

6. What five variables should an appropriate baseline procedure enable you to monitor or identify?
7. What six questions should a behavior modifier answer during the pretreatment assessment phase?

Strategies of Program Design and Implementation

Some behavior modifiers are skillful at designing effective programs off the top of their heads—that is, identifying the program details that are critical to success and that produce rapid desirable results. There are no guidelines that will immediately turn you into that kind of behavior modifier. Nor are there any rigid sets of guidelines to which you should adhere for every program you design. Many behaviors can be managed successfully with a minor rearrangement of existing contingencies; others require much creativity. The following guidelines will help you to design an effective program in most instances.

1. Identify the goals for target behaviors and their desired amount and stimulus control. Then answer these questions.
   a. Is the description precise?
   b. On what grounds did you choose the goal, and how is it in the client's best interest?
   c. Has the client been given all possible information about the goal?
   d. Have steps been taken to increase the client's commitment to accomplish the goal? (Commitment was discussed in Chapter 17 and is discussed later in this chapter.)
   e. What are potential side effects of accomplishing the goal for both the client and others?
   f. Do the answers to the foregoing questions suggest that you should proceed? If so, then continue.
2. Identify individuals (friends, relatives, teachers, and others) who might help to manage controlling stimuli and reinforcers. Also identify individuals who might hinder the program.
3. Examine the possibility of capitalizing on antecedent control. Can you use:
   a. rules
   b. goal setting
   c. modeling
   d. physical guidance
   e. situational inducement (rearrange the surroundings, move the activity to a new location, relocate people, or change the time of the activity)
   f. motivating operations
4. If you are developing a new behavior, will you use shaping, fading, or chaining? What MEO will you use (see Chapter 19)?
5. If you are changing the stimulus control of an existing behavior, can you select the controlling S^Ds so that they:
   a. are different from other stimuli on more than one dimension
   b. are encountered mainly in situations in which the desired stimulus control should occur
   c. evoke attending behavior
   d. do not evoke undesirable behavior
6. If you are decreasing a behavioral excess:
   a. can you remove S^Ds for the problem behavior
   b. can you withhold reinforcers that are maintaining the problem behavior or present MAOs for those reinforcers (see Chapter 19)
   c. can you apply DRL to reduce the rate of the behavior to a low but acceptable rate
   d. can you apply DRO, DRI, or DRA (note that each of these will incorporate extinction of the problem behavior assuming that you can identify and withhold maintaining reinforcers for it)
   e. should you use punishment? Remember that punishment, if used at all, is acceptable only (if at all) as a last resort and under appropriate professional supervision with appropriate ethical approval.
7. Specify the details of the reinforcement system by answering these questions.
   a. How will you select reinforcers? (See Chapter 4.)
   b. What reinforcers will you use? Can you use the same reinforcers currently maintaining a problem behavior? (See Chapter 23.)
   c. How will reinforcer effectiveness be continually monitored, and by whom?
   d. How will reinforcers be stored and dispensed, and by whom?
   e. If you use a token system or token economy, what are the details of its implementation (see Chapter 5 and 25)?
8. Specify the training setting. What environmental rearrangement will be necessary to maximize the desired behavior, minimize errors and competing behavior, and maximize proper recording and stimulus management by the mediators who will directly carry out the program?
9. Describe how you will program generality of behavior change (Chapter 16) by:
   a. Programming stimulus generalization. Can you:
      (i) train in the test situation
      (ii) vary the training conditions
      (iii) program common stimuli
      (iv) train sufficient stimulus exemplars
      (v) establish a stimulus equivalence class
   b. Programming response generalization. Can you:
      (i) train sufficient response exemplars

   (**ii**) vary the acceptable responses during training
   (**iii**) use behavioral momentum to increase low probability responses within a response class
   c. Programming behavior maintenance (generality over time). Can you:
      (**i**) use natural contingencies of reinforcement
      (**ii**) train the people in the natural environment
      (**iii**) use schedules of reinforcement in the training environment
      (**iv**) give the control to the individual

10. Specify the details of the daily recording and graphing procedures.
11. Collect the necessary materials (such as reinforcers, data sheets, graphs, and curriculum materials).
12. Make checklists of rules and responsibilities for all participants in the program (staff, teachers, parents, peers, students, the client, and others; see Figure 24.1).
13. Specify the dates for data and program reviews, and identify those who will attend.
14. Identify some contingencies that will reinforce the behavior modifiers and mediators (in addition to feedback related to the data and program reviews).
15. Review the potential cost of the program as designed (cost of materials, teacher time, professional consulting time, etc.), and judge its merit against its cost. Reprogram as necessary or desired on the basis of this review.
16. Sign a behavioral contract. A **behavioral contract** is a written agreement that provides a clear statement of what behaviors of what individuals will produce what reinforcers and who will deliver those reinforcers. Behavioral contracting was described initially as a strategy for scheduling the exchange of reinforcers between two or more individuals, such as between a teacher and students (Homme, Csanyi, Gonzales, & Rechs, 1969) or between parents and children (Dardig & Heward, 1976; DeRisi & Butz, 1975; Miller & Kelley, 1994). Treatment contracts between behavior therapists and clients are also recommended to ensure that the behavior therapist is accountable to the client (Sulzer-Azaroff & Reese, 1982). In general, a **treatment contract** is a written agreement between the client and the applied behavior analyst or behavior therapist that clearly outlines the objectives and methods of treatment, the framework of the service to be provided, and contingencies for remuneration that may be forthcoming to the behavior modifier. When the agreement is signed, both the client and the behavior modifier have secured basic protections of their rights. We recommend that behavior modifiers prepare such a written agreement with the appropriate individual(s) prior to implementing a program.
17. Implement the program. The implementation of your program also requires a great deal of consideration. This might be done in two parts. First, you must be certain that those carrying out the program—the mediators—understand and agree with their roles and responsibilities. This might involve a detailed discussion and review session with the mediators. It may also involve some modeling and demonstration on your part, perhaps some role-playing on the part of the mediators depending on the complexity of the programs, and finally some monitoring and on the spot feedback when the program is actually implemented. This ensures that parents, teachers, and/or others

iStock © Mike Cherim

FIGURE 24.1
Behavior modification places high value on accountability for everyone involved in behavior modification programs

are encouraged to follow the program and receive reinforcement for doing so (see, e.g., Hrydowy & Martin, 1994). The second aspect of program implementation is introducing it to the client in a manner that will enhance his or her *commitment* to the program. It is very important that the client's initial contact with the program be highly reinforcing to increase the probability of further contacts. Questions to consider include: Does the client fully understand and agree with the goals of the program? Is the client aware of how the program will benefit him or her? Has the mediator spent sufficient time with the client and interacted in such a way as to gain his or her trust and confidence (see Chapter 20)? Has the program been designed so that the client is likely to experience some success quickly? Will the client come in contact with reinforcers early in the program? An affirmative answer to each of these questions greatly increases the chances that the program will be successful. An affirmative answer to these questions occurred in Cindy's case. Cindy encountered frequent positive reinforcement during all training sessions; sessions were initially conducted by the applied behavior analyst while the parents observed, and the parents later got involved in modeling each task and reinforcing Cindy's appropriate behavior; Cindy experienced success early in the program; and successful generalization was both programmed and achieved.

Questions for Learning

8. You are about to design a treatment program. After defining the target behavior and identifying its desired level of occurrence and stimulus control, what six questions should you answer before proceeding to the design?
9. If you are thinking of capitalizing on antecedent control, what six categories should you consider?
10. If you are decreasing a behavioral excess, what five questions should you ask?
11. List five considerations for programming stimulus generalization.
12. List three considerations for programming response generalization.
13. List four considerations for programming behavior maintenance.
14. What is a behavioral contract?
15. What is a treatment contract, and what should it clearly outline?
16. What five questions should be answered affirmatively to increase the client's commitment to the program?

Program Maintenance and Evaluation

Is your program having a satisfactory effect? This is not always an easy question to answer. It is also not always easy to decide, according to some criterion or other, what to do if the program is not having a satisfactory effect. We suggest reviewing the following guidelines to assess a program that has been implemented.

1. Monitor your data to determine whether the recorded behaviors are changing in the desired direction.
2. Consult the people who must deal with the problem and determine whether they are satisfied with the progress.
3. Consult the behavioral journals, professional behavior modifiers, or others with experience in using similar procedures on similar problems to determine whether your results are reasonable in terms of the amount of behavior change during the period the program has been in effect.
4. If, on the basis of Guidelines 1, 2, and 3, the results are satisfactory, proceed directly to guideline 8.
5. If, on the basis of Guideline 1, 2, or 3, your results are unsatisfactory, answer the following questions and make the appropriate adjustment for any yes answer.
   a. Have the reinforcers that are being used lost their effectiveness—in other words, has an MAO occurred with regard to the reinforcers being used?
   b. Are competing responses being reinforced?
   c. Are the procedures being applied incorrectly?
   d. Is outside interference disrupting the program?
   e. Are there any subjective variables—staff or client negative attitudes, teacher or client lack of enthusiasm, and so forth—that might be adversely affecting the program?
6. If none of the answers to these five questions is yes, check to see whether additional programming steps need to be added or removed. The data may show excessive error rates, which would suggest the need for additional programming steps. Or they may show very high rates of correct responses, which might indicate that the program is too easy and that satiation of intrinsic reinforcers or "boredom" is occurring. Add, remove, or modify steps as necessary.

7. If the results are now satisfactory, proceed to Guideline 8; otherwise consult with a colleague or consider redesigning a major aspect of the program or redoing a functional assessment to identify the antecedents and consequences controlling the target behavior.
8. Decide how you will provide appropriate program maintenance until the behavioral objective is reached (see Chapter 16).
9. Following attainment of the behavioral goal, outline an appropriate arrangement for assessing performance during follow-up observations and assessing social validity (see Chapter 22).
10. After successful follow-up observations have been obtained, determine the costs in terms of time and finances for the behavior changes that occurred (called a *cost-effectiveness analysis*).
11. When possible and appropriate, analyze your data and communicate your procedures and results to other behavior modifiers and interested professionals. Be sure to conceal the client's identity to maintain confidentiality.

In Cindy's case, following 13 weekly treatment sessions, Cindy's father reported that Cindy was no longer afraid of dogs that she encountered outside of sessions. Seven months post-treatment, when Cindy's father was contacted, he indicated that, although Cindy did not have regular contact with dogs, she nevertheless did not show fear of them when they were encountered.

Questions for Learning

17. After a program has been implemented, what three things should be done to determine whether it is producing satisfactory results? (See Guidelines 1, 2, and 3.)
18. Describe in detail the steps that should be followed if a program is not producing satisfactory results (see Guidelines 5, 6, and 7).
19. If a program is producing satisfactory results, what two things should be done prior to successfully terminating it? (See Guidelines 8 and 9.)

Application Exercise

A. Exercise Involving Others

Suppose that you are an applied behavior analyst. The mother of a 4-year-old child asks for your help in designing a program to overcome the child's extreme disobedience. Construct realistic but hypothetical details of the behavior problem and take it through all steps in each of the following stages of programming:

1. Deciding whether you should design a program to treat the problem.
2. Selecting and implementing an assessment procedure.
3. Developing strategies of program design and implementation.
4. Establishing program maintenance and evaluation.

(*Note:* The problem will have to be fairly complex for you to take it through all the steps in each of these stages.)

Notes for Further Learning

1. Whether you are the appropriate person to deal with a particular problem may be influenced in part by whether you live in an urban or a rural setting. Rodrigue, Banko, Sears, and Evans (1996) identified a number of difficulties associated with providing behavior therapy services in rural areas. While rural regions have a disproportionate number of at-risk populations that are costly to serve (e.g., the elderly, children, minorities), they typically do not offer the full array of needed mental health services and are characterized by lower availability of and accessibility to specialized services. In other words, while you may not be the ideal person to treat the problem, you may be the best person available. Before accepting the responsibility of designing a program in such a case, however, you should consult the relevant literature with regard to the type of setting for which you have been requested to provide care. For example, a study by Perri et al. (2008) is an excellent model for providing weight management programs to rural communities. You should also consult the ethical guidelines for human services of your professional organization. (See also Chapter 30 of this book.)
2. Even if significant others are not necessary to implement a program, their availability can be extremely valuable for programming generality. Consider the problem of developing effective behavioral weight-loss programs for children (see LeBow, 1991). Israel, Stolmaker, and Adrian (1985) introduced two groups of overweight children (from 8 to 12 years of age) to an 8-week intensive, multicomponent, behavioral weight-reduction program.

The parents of one group were also presented a short course on behavioral child-management skills. At the end of the 8-week treatment program, both groups of children had lost approximately the same amount of weight. After a 1-year follow-up, however, maintenance of improved weight status was superior for the children whose parents had been introduced to the behavioral child-management procedures. Similarly, a number of studies have shown that parental and spousal support are highly correlated with establishing and maintaining healthy physical activity (see Biddle & Mutrie, 2008, Table 7.1, p. 141).

Questions for Further Learning

1. How might the geographic setting affect your decision as a behavior modifier to accept a referral?
2. How did Israel and colleagues demonstrate that utilizing significant others in a program can enhance generality?

CHAPTER 25

Token Economies

LEARNING OBJECTIVES

After studying this chapter, you will be able to:

- Outline steps for setting up and managing a token economy.
- Summarize steps to gradually withdraw a token economy in order to program generality to the natural environment.

- Discuss ethical considerations in the design and management of token economies.

Recall "Erin's points program" described at the beginning of Chapter 5. Erin wanted to be nicer to her friends. To motivate herself to do so, she carried an index card and a pen with her and gave herself a point on the card each time that she said something nice to a friend. That evening, she allowed herself to cash in her points with time on Facebook or YouTube. The more points she earned, the more time she could enjoy Facebook or YouTube. Erin's points were called *tokens*—conditioned reinforcers that can be accumulated and exchanged for goods and services (Hackenberg, 2009).

A behavioral program in which individuals can earn tokens for a variety of desirable behaviors and can exchange the earned tokens for backup reinforcers is called a token economy. Our modern society in which people perform a variety of jobs to earn money that they exchange for various items such as food, shelter, clothing, transportation, luxuries, and access to leisure activities is a complex token economy. A system in which people purchase bus or subway tokens that they exchange for access to public transit is a somewhat simpler token economy. Token economies are also used as educational and therapeutic tools in behavior modification programs. According to Hackenberg (2009, p. 280), "Token economies are among the oldest and most successful programs in all of applied psychology." Although a token economy could be set up for an individual, the term *token economies* generally refers to token systems with groups, and the term is used that way in this chapter.

Using token reinforcers has two major advantages. First, they can be given immediately after a desirable behavior occurs and cashed in at a later time for a backup reinforcer. Thus they can be used to "bridge" long delays between the target response and the backup reinforcer, which is especially important when it is impractical or impossible to deliver the backup reinforcer immediately after the behavior. Second, tokens that are paired with many different backup reinforcers are generalized conditioned reinforcers and therefore do not depend on a specific motivating operation for their strength. This makes it easier to administer consistent and effective reinforcers when dealing with a group of individuals who might be in different motivational states.

Token economies as components of behavioral programs have been used in a variety of settings with individuals and with groups. They have been used in psychiatric wards, treatment centers and classrooms for persons with developmental disabilities and autism, classrooms for children and teenagers with attention-deficit hyperactivity disorder (ADHD), normal classroom settings ranging from preschool to college and university, homes for troubled children, prisons, the military, wards for the treatment of persons with drug addiction or alcoholism, nursing homes, and convalescent centers (e.g., see Boniecki & Moore, 2003; Corrigan, 1995; Dickerson, Tenhula, & Green-Paden, 2005; Ferreri, 2013; Filcheck, McNeil, Greco, & Bernard, 2004; Hackenberg, 2009; Higgins, Silverman, & Heil, 2007; Liberman, 2000; Matson & Boisjoli, 2009). A token economy has also been used in a behaviorally managed experimental community of college students (Johnson, Welch, Miller, & Altus, 1991; Thomas & Miller, 1980). **NOTE 1**

Techniques used in token economies have also been extended to various community settings to decrease littering and noise pollution as well as to increase waste recycling, energy conservation, the use of mass transportation, racial integration, behaviors involved in gaining employment, and self-help behaviors in people who are disadvantaged by the economic system. In normal family homes, token economies have been used to control children's behavior and to treat marital discord. In various work settings, token economies have been used to increase safety behavior, decrease absenteeism, and enhance on-the-job performance (Boerke & Reitman, 2011; Kazdin, 1977, 1985).

In this chapter we describe the typical steps used to set up and manage token economies. We will illustrate many of the steps with reference to Achievement Place, a group home in Lawrence, Kansas. **NOTE 2** A very effective token program was developed there for predelinquent youths—boys from 10 to 16 years of age—who were from difficult home environments and were referred by the courts for committing minor crimes such as petty theft and fighting. That program uses what is termed the *Teaching-Family Model* (*TFM*) in which four to eight individuals live with a married couple in a large domestic home. Major features of the TFM include:

1. a token economy in which participants earn points for appropriate social behaviors, academic performance, and daily living skills and exchange them for privileges such as snacks, television, hobbies, games, allowance, and permission to participate in activities away from the home
2. a self-government system in which the youth participate in the development of daily living rules and the management of the program
3. ongoing evaluation of the performance of the participants

Developed in the early 1970s, the TFM has been extended to a variety of settings, such as homes, schools, and the community at large, across the United States and Canada, and to a variety of individuals, such as children who are emotionally disturbed, individuals with autism or developmental disabilities, and youth in treatment foster care due to prior abuse or neglect. Although further research is needed to develop strategies for long-term maintenance of gains achieved by individuals who participate in TFM programs, the model has been demonstrated to be an effective approach for the treatment of a variety of problems (Bernfeld, 2006; Bernfeld, Blase, & Fixsen, 2006; Braukmann & Wolf, 1987; Fixsen, Blasé, Timbers, & Wolf, 2007; Underwood, Talbott, Mosholder, & von Dresner, 2008).

Questions for Learning

1. What are tokens?
2. What is a token economy?
3. What are two major advantages to using tokens as reinforcers?
4. List at least five settings in which token economies have been used.
5. List at least five behaviors that token economies have been designed to develop.
6. In a sentence, describe the type of individual whom Achievement Place was designed to help.

Steps for Setting Up and Managing a Token Economy

Decide on the Target Behaviors

Target behaviors are determined largely by (a) the type of individuals involved, (b) the short- and long-range objectives to be accomplished, and (c) specific behavioral problems that interfere with achieving those objectives. For example, if you are a classroom teacher, your target behaviors for students might include specific aspects of reading, writing, mathematics, or constructive social interaction. Your target behaviors must be clearly defined so that the students know what behaviors are expected of them and so that you can reinforce those behaviors reliably when they occur. Thus, one of your target behaviors might be sitting quietly when the teacher gives instructions. A more advanced target behavior might be correctly completing 10 addition problems.

At the original Achievement Place TFM (Phillips, 1968) described previously, target behaviors for the predelinquent youth were selected in social, self-care, and academic areas that were considered to be important to the youths both while they were at Achievement Place and in future environments when they left the group home. Both desirable and undesirable behaviors were identified. Two examples of desirable behaviors were doing dishes (which earned up to 1000 points per meal), and performing homework (which earned up to 500 points per day). Two examples of undesirable behaviors were disobeying (which cost from 100 to 1000 points per response), and using poor grammar (which cost from 20 to 50 points per response).

Take Baselines and Keep Data

As is done before initiating other procedures, baseline data on the specific target behaviors should be obtained before initiating a token economy. It might be that your group is already performing at a satisfactory level and that the potential benefits to be gained from setting up a token economy do not justify the time, effort, or cost involved in doing so. After the program has been started, continuing to collect data on the target behaviors and comparing the data with the baseline data will enable you to determine the program's effectiveness.

Select the Type of Tokens to Use

Tokens can include play money, marks on a wall chart, poker chips, stickers or stamps, or numerous other possibilities that will suit the needs of your particular token economy. In general, tokens should be attractive, lightweight, portable, durable, easy to handle, and, of course, not easily counterfeited (Figure 25.1). If automatic dispensers of backup reinforcement are used, you should ensure that your tokens will operate those devices. You should also ensure that you have an adequate number of tokens. For example, Stainback, Payne, Stainback, and Payne (1973) suggested that you should have on hand about 100 tokens per child when starting a token economy in a classroom.

You should also acquire the necessary accessories for handling and storing tokens. For example, schoolchildren might need pencil boxes or resealable storage bags in which to store the tokens they

FIGURE 25.1
Tokens should not be easily counterfeited

have earned. At Achievement Place, as indicated previously, points were used as tokens. Throughout each day, points were recorded on 3 × 5-inch index cards that the youths always carried with them. In this way, the points could be dispensed or taken away immediately following desirable or undesirable behavior.

Select Backup Reinforcers

The methods for selecting backup reinforcers are essentially the same as the methods for selecting reinforcers described in Chapter 4. Keep in mind that a token system increases the variety of practical reinforcers that you can use because they are not limited to those that can be delivered immediately following a desired response.

When considering reinforcers that are normally available, take extreme caution to avoid serious ethical problems. Various legislatures have enacted laws affirming the rights of mentally ill patients and residents of treatment centers to have access to meals, comfortable beds, TV, and so on. Furthermore, a number of court decisions have upheld these civil rights. Therefore, never plan a program that might involve depriving individuals of something that legally and morally belongs to them.

At Achievement Place, the backup reinforcers were items and activities that were naturally available in the group home and that appeared to be important to the youths. Their access to the backup reinforcers, referred to as *privileges,* occurred on a weekly basis. At the end of each week, the youths could trade the points they had earned that week for privileges for the next week. For example, permission to stay up past bedtime for a week could be purchased for 1000 points, while access to games for a week cost 500 points.

Possible Response-Cost Punishers The use of tokens provides the possibility of using fines as punishers for inappropriate behavior (see Lippman & Motta, 1993; Sullivan & O'Leary, 1990). As with all forms of punishment, it should be used sparingly and only for clearly defined behaviors (see Chapter 13).

If fines are used in a token economy, it might be necessary to add training contingencies that teach individuals how to accept fines in a relatively nonemotional, nonaggressive manner. Phillips, Phillips, Fixsen, and Wolf (1973) described such contingencies for the token economy at Achievement Place. In that economy, the contingencies related to fines probably taught the youths an important societal skill: how to accept reprimands from law enforcers.

Manage the Backup Reinforcers

After establishing the backup reinforcers you are going to use and how you are going to obtain them, you should next consider the general method of dispensing them. A store or commissary for storing and dispensing backup reinforcers is an essential feature of most token economies. In a small token economy, such as a classroom, the store can be quite simple, say, a box located on the teacher's desk. In a larger token economy, the store is typically much larger, perhaps occupying one or more rooms. Regardless of the size of the store, a precise method of keeping records of purchases must be devised so that an adequate inventory (especially of high-demand items) can be maintained.

How frequently backup reinforcers will be available to be purchased must be determined. In the beginning, the frequency should be high and then decreased gradually. For schoolchildren, Stainback et al. (1973) recommended that store time be held once per day for the first 3 or 4 days and then decreased gradually until it is held only once a week (e.g., Friday afternoon).

It is also necessary to decide on the token price of each backup reinforcer. In addition to the monetary cost, which is the most obvious consideration in assigning token values to backup reinforcers, two other factors should be considered. One is supply and demand. That is, the price should be higher for items whose demand exceeds the supply and less for items whose supply exceeds the demand. This will help to maintain an adequate supply of effective reinforcers and promote optimal utilization of the reinforcing power of each backup reinforcer. The other factor to consider is the therapeutic value of the backup reinforcer. An individual should be charged very little for a backup reinforcer that is beneficial to him or her. This will help to induce the individual to partake of the reinforcer. For example, an individual whose social skills need improving might be charged only a few tokens for admission to a party because this event might help to develop appropriate social behaviors.

Questions for Learning

7. List and briefly describe five initial steps involved in setting up and managing a token economy.
8. Identify four target behaviors for the youths at Achievement Place: two desirable and two undesirable behaviors.
9. What six characteristics should a token have?
10. What is the recommended number of tokens per child for a teacher to have on hand when starting a token economy in a classroom?
11. List two backup reinforcers used at Achievement Place.
12. Explain how a "fine" in a token economy fits the definition of response-cost punishment (you may want to review Chapter 13).
13. What is a token economy store? Give examples.
14. How often should store time be held in a token economy for schoolchildren?
15. What are three considerations for deciding the token price of each backup reinforcer?

Identify Available Help

In a small token economy, such as a classroom, help from other individuals might not be essential, but is certainly useful especially in the initial stages of the program. In a large token economy, such as a psychiatric facility, such help is essential.

Help might be obtained from a number of sources: (a) people already assigned to work with the individuals of concern (e.g., nurse's aides, teaching assistants), (b) volunteers, (c) behaviorally advanced individuals within the institution (e.g., older students assigned to help younger students), and (d) members of the token economy itself. In some cases, individuals have been taught to deliver tokens to themselves contingent on their own appropriate behavior.   **NOTE 3**

After the token economy begins to function smoothly, more of its members will be able to assume responsibility in helping to achieve its goals. For example, at TFMs, some of the youths supervise others in carrying out routine household tasks (see Fixsen & Blase, 1993). The supervisor, or "manager," as the youth is called, has the authority to both administer and remove tokens for peers' performances. Of the several methods that were studied for selecting managers, democratic elections proved to be best in terms of the youths' performances and their effectiveness in accomplishing tasks (Phillips, Phillips, Wolf, & Fixsen, 1973; Wolf, Braukmann, & Ramp, 1987). In another experiment at Achievement Place, some youths earned tokens for serving as therapists for others who had speech problems. The youths performed this function with remarkable effectiveness despite having very little adult supervision and no specific training (Bailey, Timbers, Phillips, & Wolf, 1971).

In some college courses that use PSI (including CAPSI—see Answer: page 13), students who master an assignment assess the performance of other students on that assignment and give immediate feedback concerning their performance. Another method used in college and university PSI classes is to give the students a test on the first several sections of the course material at the beginning of the term. Each student who demonstrates the ability to readily master the course material is put in charge of a small group of students, whom they tutor and supervise throughout the remainder of the course (Johnson & Ruskin, 1977).

Monitor and Train Staff and Helpers

The staff and helpers who manage a token economy are also subject to the laws of behavior. Their target behaviors must also be identified. For example, it is important to decide who will administer the tokens and for what behaviors. Care should be taken to ensure that tokens are always delivered in a positive and conspicuous manner immediately following the desired response. Friendly, smiling approval should be administered by staff along with the token, and the individual receiving the token should be told, at least in the initial stages, why he or she is receiving it.

Staff and helpers must also receive frequent reinforcement for appropriate behavior, and their inappropriate behavior must be corrected if the token economy is to function effectively. The importance of staff training became clear to Montrose Wolf and his colleagues when they failed in their attempt to replicate the first very successful Achievement Place TFM (Wolf, Kirigin, Fixsen, Blase, & Braukmann, 1995). In their initial failed replication attempt a couple who were to manage the new group home completed a behavioral psychology Master's degree, but did not receive much training on the specific behaviors involved in managing an Achievement Place token economy. After the initial failed replication, and in order to facilitate subsequent successful replications, the developers of the program established the Teaching-Family Association (TFA, Wolf et al., 1995). The TFA (www.teaching-family.org), among its many functions, facilitates the development of each new Achievement Place TFM by specifying desirable behavior of the management couple, monitoring their behavior, and providing the necessary skill teaching to ensure the success of the site (Wolf et al., 1995).

Handle Potential Problems

In the design of a token economy, as with any complex procedure, it is wise to plan for potential problems. Some problems that often arise are (a) confusion, especially during the first few days after the initiation of the economy, (b) staff or helper shortages, (c) attempts by individuals to get tokens they have not earned or backup reinforcers for which they do not have enough tokens, (d) individuals playing with tokens and manipulating them in distracting ways, and (e) failure to purchase backup reinforcers. These and other problems that might arise can be managed by careful planning beforehand.

However, as the initial failures in extending the TFM indicate, careful planning beforehand is not always sufficient to prevent problems from occurring. The developers of Achievement Place attribute overcoming various replication problems to the development and use of subjective feedback questionnaires given to consumers of the program and online staff. These helped the developers identify and solve unanticipated problems (Wolf et al., 1995).

Questions for Learning

16. Identify four sources of potential help for managing a token economy.
17. What are two ways help has been obtained to manage PSI courses?
18. How should tokens be delivered?
19. Describe five potential problems that are likely to occur during the initial days of a token economy.

Prepare a Manual

The final stage to complete before implementing the token economy is to prepare a manual or written set of rules describing exactly how the economy will run. This manual should explain in detail what behaviors will be reinforced, how they will be reinforced with tokens and backup reinforcers, the times at which reinforcement will be available, what data will be recorded, how and when they will be recorded, and the responsibilities and duties of every staff member and helper. Each rule should be reasonable and acceptable to all involved. Each person delivering tokens should receive either a copy of the manual or a clear and accurate version of the portions pertaining to his or her specific duties and responsibilities. If the individual is not able to read fluently but can understand the spoken language, a clear explanation of the relevant portions of the manual should be provided. The manual should include definite procedures for assessing whether the rules are being followed adequately and procedures for ensuring that they are. The manual should also include methods for arbitrating disputes concerning the rules, and the opportunity to participate in the arbitration procedures should be provided to the greatest extent that is practical and consistent with the goals of the token economy.

One of the consequences regarding the difficulty in replicating Achievement Place was that the researchers developed explicit and detailed training manuals so that teaching-parents would know exactly what to do under a wide range of circumstances (Braukmann & Blase, 1979; Phillips, Phillips, Fixsen, & Wolf, 1974). These training manuals provide a good model for developing training manuals for establishing and operating token economies in a variety of settings.

Generality Programming to the Natural Environment

While token economies are sometimes regarded only as means to manage problem behavior within institutional or school settings, their more important function is to help individuals adjust to the natural environment. Kazdin (1985) summarized a large amount of data indicating that token economies are effective with diverse populations and that the gains achieved with these economies are often maintained

NOTE 4   for several years following the termination of the program. However, because social reinforcement, not tokens, prevails in the natural environment, a token economy should be designed so that social reinforcement gradually replaces token reinforcement.

There are two general ways of weaning an individual from tokens. The first weaning method is to eliminate tokens gradually, which can be accomplished by gradually (a) making the token delivery schedule more and more intermittent, (b) decreasing the number of behaviors that earn tokens, or (c) increasing the delay between the target behavior and token delivery. The second weaning method is to decrease the value of the tokens gradually, which can be accomplished by (a) gradually decreasing the amount of backup reinforcement that a given number of tokens can purchase, or (b) by gradually increasing the delay between token acquisition and the purchase of backup reinforcers. At present, we cannot say which method or combination of methods produces the best results. In addition, all considerations involved in programming generality (discussed in Chapter 16) should be reviewed.

Gradually transferring control to the individuals so that they plan and administer their own reinforcements is another step in preparing them for the natural environment. An individual who can evaluate her or his own behavior, decide rationally what changes need to be made, and program effectively for these changes is clearly in a good position to cope with almost any environment. Methods for establishing these skills are discussed in Chapter 26.

Ethical Considerations

Token economies involve the systematic application of behavior modification techniques on a relatively large scale. The possibilities of abusing the techniques, even unintentionally, are thereby magnified, and precautions must be taken to avoid such abuse. One such precaution is to make the system completely open to public scrutiny, provided that such openness is subject to the approval of the individuals in the program or their advocates. An important source of ethical control for the TFM, for example, is the TFA's rigorous standards and procedures for certifying programs that claim to use the TFM. Ethical considerations involving all behavior modification programs are discussed extensively in Chapter 30.

A Summary of Considerations Necessary in Designing a Token Economy

1. Review appropriate literature.
2. Identify target behaviors.
   a. List short-range and long-range objectives.
   b. Arrange objectives in order of priority.
   c. Select those objectives that are most important for the individuals in the program and that are prerequisites for later objectives.
   d. Identify several of the priority objectives on which to start, emphasizing those that can be accomplished quickly.
   e. Determine a number of target behaviors for each of the starting objectives.
3. Take a baseline of target behaviors.
4. Select the most appropriate type of token. (They should be attractive, lightweight, portable, durable, easy to handle, and difficult to counterfeit.)
5. Select backup reinforcers.
   a. Use reinforcers that are effective with the population of interest.
   b. Use the Premack principle (see Chapter 4).
   c. Collect verbal information from the individuals in the program concerning their reinforcers.
   d. Give the individuals in the program catalogs that will help them to identify reinforcers.
   e. Ask individuals in the program what they like to do when they have free time away from work or other demands.
   f. Identify natural reinforcers that could be programmed.
   g. Consider ethics and legalities regarding the reinforcers.
   h. Design an appropriate store to keep, display, and dispense backup reinforcers.
6. Identify those who are available to help manage the program:
   a. existing staff
   b. volunteers

    c. university students

    d. residents of the institution

    e. members of the token economy

7. Decide on specific implementation procedures.

    a. Design appropriate data sheets and determine who will take data and how and when it will be recorded.

    b. Decide who is going to administer reinforcement, how it will be administered, and for what behaviors it will be provided.

    c. Decide on the number of tokens that can be earned per day.

    d. Establish "store" procedures and determine the token value of backup reinforcers.

    e. Be wary of punishment contingencies. Use them sparingly: only for clearly defined behaviors and only when it is ethically justifiable to do so.

    f. Ensure that staff and helper duties are clearly defined and that a desirable schedule of monitoring and reinforcement is implemented.

    g. Plan for potential problems.

8. Prepare a token economy manual for the individuals in the program, the staff, and the helpers.

9. Institute the token economy.

10. Plan strategies for obtaining generality to the natural environment.

11. Monitor and practice relevant ethical guidelines at each step.

Questions for Learning

20. State two general methods of weaning individuals from tokens when transferring behavior to the natural environment.

21. If one decides to wean an individual from tokens by eliminating tokens gradually, what are three ways that might be accomplished?

22. If one decides to wean an individual of tokens by decreasing the value of the tokens gradually, what are two ways that might be accomplished?

23. What is one precaution to help ensure high ethical standards for a token economy?

Application Exercises

A. Exercises Involving Others

1. For a group of individuals of your choosing, identify five plausible goals for a token economy.

2. Define precisely two target behaviors for each of the five goals listed in Exercise 1.

3. Describe things you might do to identify backup reinforcers for the group of individuals you chose in Exercise 1.

Notes for Further Learning

1. Token economies in the classroom took a new turn with the rise of classroom mini-economies in which teachers use play money to teach children basic principles of economics and personal finances (e.g., Day & Ballard, 2005). Children in classroom mini-economies earn play money, which they can exchange later for items in a class store, for (a) working at classroom jobs, (b) running classroom businesses, and (c) engaging in desired academic and classroom management behaviors. Classroom jobs include custodian (cleaning bookshelves), attendance officer (taking daily attendance), and horticulture specialist (taking care of classroom plants). Classroom businesses include making things that other children can purchase (e.g., artwork, craft items, class newspaper) and providing services to other children (e.g., peer tutoring, desk cleaning, organizing notebooks). Desired academic and classroom management behaviors include completing assignments on time, showing improvement in schoolwork, and lining up quietly in the hallway. Thus, while standard classroom token economies have focused on desired academic behavior, classroom mini-economies address the broader goal of preparing children to engage in the economy of the natural environment.

2. Much of the material in this chapter is covered in greater detail in the following major works on token economies: Ayllon (1999); Ayllon and Azrin (1968) and Glynn (1990), which deal with token economies for psychiatric patients; Stainback et al. (1973), which discusses token economies in elementary school classrooms; Welch and Gist (1974), which primarily addresses token economies in sheltered workshops; Ayllon and Milan (1979), which describes token programs in prisons; and Kazdin (1977), which presents

a comprehensive review of token-economy research. For more information on token systems for children and teens with ADHD, see Barkley & Murphy (2005). See Keller and Sherman (1982) and Chapter 2 of this book for additional information on the use of token-economy procedures in college and high school courses in which systems incorporating these procedures are sometimes called *Personalized System of Instruction* (*PSI*). For a review and discussion of token reinforcement procedures and concepts in relation to general principles of behavior, see Hackenberg (2009).

3. Rae, Martin, and Smyk (1990) designed a program to pay tokens to individuals with developmental disabilities in a sheltered workshop for improved on-task performance. The tokens could be redeemed for items in the workshop cafeteria. However, the workshop had insufficient staff to reliably keep track of individuals who were on task and those who were not. A solution was to teach the workers to self-monitor their own on task performance. A pencil and a sheet with squares on it were placed in front of each worker. The workers were taught that when a buzzer sounded, they should mark an X on one of the squares if they were on task. The buzzer was set to go off at six random times during half a day. Upon earning six X's, a worker could exchange them for a token. The total program proved to be effective for increasing the on-task behavior of the workers on a variety of workshop tasks.

4. With regard to the TFM's program generality, research shows that it is effective for managing the behavior of predelinquent youth when they are in the program (e.g., Kirigin, Braukmann, Atwater, & Wolf, 1982). Several studies, however, purported to show that there is no difference between recidivism rate of predelinquents who had been in TFM programs and those who had been in traditional programs (e.g., Fonagy, Target, Cottrell, Phillips, & Kurtz, 2002; Jones, Weinrott, & Howard, 1981; Kirigin et al., 1982; Wilson & Herrnstein, 1985). However, Kingsley (2006) argued that these studies were methodologically and statistically flawed. Moreover, he showed that a number of more recent studies indicate that the TFM does meaningfully reduce recidivism (e.g., Friman et al., 1996; Larzelere et al., 2001; Larzelere, Daly, Davis, Chmelka, & Handwerk, 2004; Lipsey, 1992, 1999a, 1999b; Lipsey & Wilson, 1998; Thompson et al., 1996). Clearly, more research is needed on this. More research is needed to determine effective methods for transferring the gains made in the program to the environment where these individuals will live when they graduate from the program.

Questions for Further Learning

1. What is a classroom mini-economy? Describe its features.
2. Would you expect children in a classroom mini-economy to show more or less generalization to the natural environment than if they had not participated in the mini-economy? Explain.
3. Describe a token program in which individuals in a sheltered workshop administered tokens to themselves.

CHAPTER 26

Helping an Individual to Develop Self-Control[1]

Al and Mary have just finished having doughnuts and coffee in the campus cafeteria. "I think I'll have another doughnut," said Al. "They look so delicious! I just don't have the willpower to resist. Besides," he added, while patting his protruding midsection, "one more won't make any difference."

Many problems of self-control involve self-restraint—learning to decrease excessive behaviors that have immediate gratification—such as excessive eating, drinking, TV watching, and time on Facebook. Other problems of self-control require behavioral change in the opposite direction—responses that need to be increased—such as studying, exercising, being assertive, and performing household chores. Many people speak as though some magical force within us—called *willpower*—is responsible for overcoming such problems. People believe this, in part because others say things like, "If you had more willpower, you could get rid of that bad habit," or "If you had more willpower, you could improve yourself." Most of us have heard such advice many times. Unfortunately, it is not very helpful advice because the person offering it typically neglects to tell us how we can get more of this willpower. It is more useful to look at how problems of self-control stem from differences between effective versus ineffective consequences of a behavior. From such a starting point, we proceed to a model for self-control. Finally, we describe how most successful **self-control programs** proceed through five basic steps. Such programs are also called **self-management** or **self-modification**, a strategy for using principles of behavior analysis to change or control one's own behavior.

Causes of Self-Control Problems

"I just *can't* resist having an extra dessert."
"I *really* should get into an exercise program.
"My term paper is due, I have a big midterm, and I have to finish writing up my lab assignment. What am I doing on Facebook? Why am I not studying?"

Do any of these sound familiar? If you're like most people, you've probably said similar things many times. These are the times when we are tempted to talk about not having enough willpower. Let's see how such problems can be explained by examining how immediately significant, delayed, cumulatively significant, and improbable consequences affect or fail to affect behavior.

---

[1] Material in this chapter was described by Martin and Osborne (1993) and is paraphrased with permission.

Problems of Behavioral Excesses

One type of self-control problem consists of behavioral excesses—doing too much of something. Examples are overeating, watching YouTube excessively, and drinking too much coffee. All such behavioral excesses lead to immediate reinforcers (e.g., tasty food, enjoyable scenes on YouTube). Even though the excesses might eventually lead to negative consequences, the latter are often ineffective. Let's see why.

Immediate Reinforcers Versus Delayed Punishers for a Behavior   Suppose that a teenager wants to go out with friends but still has homework. When the parents ask about the homework, the teenager lies and is allowed to leave with friends. Lying is immediately reinforced. The lie is not discovered until later, and the consequent punishment (e.g., being grounded, failing the assignment) is long delayed from the instance of lying. If a behavior leads to immediate reinforcers but delayed punishers, the immediate reinforcers often win out. Many problems of self-control stem from this fact (Brigham, 1989a, 1989b). The immediate backslapping and laughter of friends after someone "chugs" a pitcher of beer may override the delayed punishing consequences of a hangover. The immediate reinforcing consequences from sexual behavior with a friend's spouse may override the delayed hurt and emotional anguish when the friend finds out and is no longer a friend.

Immediate Reinforcers Versus Cumulatively Significant Punishers for a Behavior   Consider the problem of overeating, resulting in obesity and health problems. Eating an extra dessert is immediately reinforced by the taste. Although the negative effects (e.g., excessive sugar, fat, and cholesterol) of the extra dessert are immediate, they are too small to have an effect. Rather, it is the accumulation of overeating on numerous occasions that causes problems (e.g., see Ogden, 2010; Pi-Sunyer, 2009). Consider the problem of smoking. Although harmful chemicals are immediately deposited on the smoker's lungs with each puff, the negative effect of a single cigarette is too small to counteract the immediate highly positively reinforcing effects of nicotine (not only is nicotine itself a positive reinforcer, it is an MEO for other reinforcers—see Donny, Caggiula, Weaver, Levin, & Sved, 2011). Rather, it is the accumulation of the effects of hundreds of cigarettes that eventually results in serious diseases such as COPD, emphysema, and cancer. Alcohol is an example of a substance that can be immediately reinforcing while having both a delayed punishment effect and a long-term cumulative effect when consumed in excess (e.g., see McDonald, Wang, & Camargo, 2004). The delayed punishment effects include alcohol poisoning, physical or verbal fights, and accidents. The cumulatively significant effects include liver cirrhosis, cancer, and other serious diseases. Thus, for many self-control problems, the immediate reinforcement for consumption of harmful substances wins out over the unnoticeable immediate negative effects that are only cumulatively significant (Malott, 1989).

Immediate Reinforcers for Problem Behavior Versus Delayed Reinforcers for Alternative Desirable Behavior   Let's suppose it's a Thursday evening in the middle of a course you're taking. Your roommate just downloaded a movie that you would like to watch but you have an exam tomorrow. Do you watch the movie now and receive a low grade on the exam later, or do you study for 3 hours and receive a higher grade later? Consider the case of a worker who receives a large Christmas bonus from the company. Will the worker spend the bonus on something that is immediately pleasurable, like a ski trip, or invest it in a tax-free retirement fund? Which would you choose? For self-control problems involving a choice between two alternative behaviors, both with positive outcomes, the one that produces the immediate reinforcer often wins out (Brigham, 1989b).

Problems of Behavioral Deficits

Another type of self-control problem consists of responses that need to be increased, such as flossing your teeth, and exercising regularly. Such behaviors usually lead to small, immediate punishers. And even though there might be positive outcomes if the behaviors occur or major negative outcomes if the behaviors don't occur, both of these outcomes are often ineffective. Let's see why.

Immediate Small Punishers for a Behavior Versus Cumulatively Significant Reinforcers   For nonexercisers, an initial exercising session can be quite unpleasant (e.g., time consuming, tiring, stressful). Even though an instance of exercising may have immediate benefits such as increased cardiovascular fitness, increased muscular strength, endurance, flexibility, and better mental health (e.g., see Agarwal,

2012; Biddle & Mutrie, 2008; Bize, Johnson, & Plotnikoff, 2007), such outcomes are generally too small to be noticed. Rather, it is the accumulation of the benefits of exercising on numerous occasions that is eventually noticeable. People often fail to follow desirable health practices such as exercising because doing so leads to immediate small punishers, whereas the positive effects, though immediate, are too small to be effective until they have accumulated over many trials (Malott, 1989).

Immediate Small Punisher for a Behavior Versus Immediate but Improbable Major Punisher If the Behavior Does Not Occur   Most people know that wearing eye protection when playing racquetball can prevent serious eye damage and that wearing a helmet when riding a bicycle could prevent brain damage. Why, then, do many people not wear goggles when playing racquetball or helmets when riding bicycles? First, such precautions usually lead to immediate mild punishers (the goggles and the helmet may be hot and uncomfortable). Second, although the major aversive events that could result from not performing these safety behaviors would be immediate, they are improbable. According to the laws of probability, however, the longer and more often one engages in these behaviors, the more likely these major aversive events become.

Immediate Small Punisher for a Behavior Versus Delayed Major Punisher If the Behavior Does Not Occur   Why do many students avoid exercising, put off going for a dental checkup, or fail to take good lecture notes? This type of self-control problem has immediate weak punishers. Exercising can make you hot and uncomfortable. The noise and pain of the dentist's drill are punishers. Your fingers get tired while taking good lecture notes. Moreover, all of these activities take time from more reinforcing activities. While the delayed consequences such as major dental problems can be extremely aversive, they occur long after many missed preventive opportunities. In such scenarios, the immediate punishing consequences often win out. In other words, by avoiding a weak aversive stimulus now, one eventually receives a strong aversive consequence later.

Questions for Learning

1. What do people mean when they talk about willpower? Is willpower a useful concept? Why or why not?
2. Describe a problem of a behavioral excess in which an immediate reinforcer wins out over a delayed punisher for the behavior.
3. Describe a problem of a behavioral excess in which an immediate reinforcer wins out over a cumulatively significant punisher for the behavior.
4. Describe a problem of a behavioral excess in which an immediate reinforcer (for the problem behavior) wins out over a delayed reinforcer (for an alternative desirable behavior).
5. Describe a problem of a behavioral deficiency that occurs because the behavior leads to immediate small punishers that win out over cumulatively significant reinforcers for the behavior.
6. Describe a problem of a behavioral deficiency that occurs because immediate small punishers for the behavior win out over immediate but highly improbable major punishers if the behavior does not occur.
7. Describe a problem of a behavioral deficiency that occurs because an immediate small punisher for the behavior wins out over a delayed major punisher if the behavior does not occur.

A Behavioral Model for Self-Control

An effective model of self-control must deal satisfactorily with the causes of self-control problems described in the preceding section. The model that we describe here is a behavioral model with two parts. The first part requires clearly specifying the problem as a behavior to be controlled. The second part requires that you apply behavioral techniques to manage the problem. A **behavior model of self-control** is a statement that self-control occurs when an individual behaves in some way that arranges the environment to manage his or her subsequent behavior. This means emitting a *controlling behavior* to effect a change in a *behavior to be controlled* (Skinner, 1953). See Figure 26.1.

In examples in the previous chapters, one person emitted the behavior to be controlled, and one or more other people emitted the controlling behaviors—manipulating antecedents and applying reinforcing or punishing consequences for the behavior. In instances of self-control, however, the same person emits the behavior to be controlled and the controlling behaviors. This raises the problem of *controlling the controlling behavior*. That is, because self-control implies that some behavior of a person controls other behavior of that person, the question arises as to what controls or causes the controlling behavior.

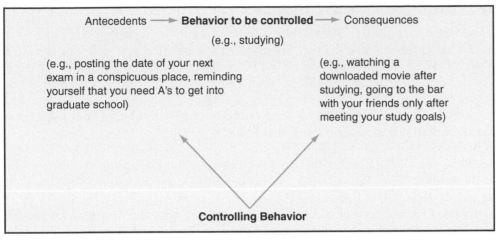

FIGURE 26.1
A model for self-control

The answer is society. The society in which we live teaches us various controlling behaviors (see Skinner, 1953, p. 240). You may have been taught, for example, to emit controlling behaviors such as setting goals for studying, giving yourself reminders for meeting those goals, and keeping track of your progress in doing so. If your efforts in emitting such behaviors are successful and your behaviors to be controlled do in fact occur (e.g., your studying improves), society provides maintaining contingencies for your efforts (e.g., receiving better grades, getting the kind of job that you want, and being able to talk intelligently with other people).

We now turn to self-control strategies that have been successful for many individuals.

Steps in a Self-Control Program

For our discussion of self-control strategies, "you" are anyone who wants to change some aspect of her or his own behavior. Assume that you have decided to use behavior modification to treat one of your self-control problems. We will describe how to do so by using the following steps: (a) specify the problem and set goals, (b) make a commitment to change, (c) take data and assess the causes of the problem, (d) design and implement a treatment plan, and (e) prevent relapse and make your gains last.

1. Specify the Problem and Set Goals

What is it that you would like to change? How will you know if you have succeeded? To answer these questions, you need to try to specify the problem and set some goals in quantitative terms. For Al (at the beginning of this chapter), this was relatively easy. His goal was to lose 30 pounds or 12 kg. Stated more precisely, he wanted to use about 1,000 calories more each day than he consumed to give a weight loss of about 2 pounds or 1 kg each week. Many problems of self-control can be easily specified in quantitative terms. It is relatively easy, for example, to set specific goals in the areas of weight control and exercise. In contrast, other self-improvement goals, such as "having a more positive attitude toward school," "becoming less tense," or "improving a relationship," are more difficult to measure. Mager (1972) referred to such vague abstractions as "fuzzies." A *fuzzy* is an acceptable starting point for identifying a self-control goal; however, you must then "unfuzzify" the abstraction by identifying the performance(s) that would cause you to agree that you have achieved your goal. Mager outlined a number of useful steps for this process.

a. Write out the goal.
b. Make a list of the things that you should say or do that clearly indicates that you have met the goal. That is, what evidence proves that your goal has been achieved?
c. In a group of people with the same goal, how would you decide who has met the goal and who has not?
d. If your goal is a product of behavior —such as achieving a certain weight, saving a certain amount of money, or having a clean room—make a list of specific behaviors that will help you to achieve that product.

2. Make a Commitment to Change

NOTE 1   **Commitment to change** refers to your statements or actions that indicate that it is important to change your behavior, that you recognize the benefits of doing so, and that you will work toward doing so. Perri and Richards (1977) demonstrated that both a commitment to change and knowledge of change techniques were important for successfully accomplishing self-modification projects by undergraduate psychology students. In problem areas such as eating, smoking, studying, or dating, Perri and Richards found that successful self-managers had a stronger commitment to change and used more behavior change techniques than did unsuccessful self-managers.

A high probability of success in changing your behavior requires actions to keep your commitment strong. First, list all the benefits there are for changing your behavior. Write them out and post them in a conspicuous place. Second, make your commitment to change public (Hayes et al., 1985; Seigts, Meertens, & Kok, 1997). Increasing the number of people who can remind you to stick to your program increases your chances of success. Third, rearrange your environment to provide frequent reminders of your commitment and your goal (Watson & Tharp, 2007). You could write your goals on Post-it or sticky notes and leave them in conspicuous places, such as on the door of your fridge or dashboard of your car. Or you might creatively use photographs to remind you of your goal. Also make sure that those reminders are associated with the positive benefits of reaching your goal. Fourth, invest considerable time and energy in initially planning your project (Watson & Tharp, 2007). Prepare a list of statements related to your investment in your project so that you can use those statements to help strengthen and maintain your commitment (e.g., "I've put so much into it, it would be a shame to quit now"). Fifth, because you will undoubtedly encounter temptations to quit your project, plan ahead for various ways to deal with them (Watson & Tharp, 2007).

Questions for Learning

8. Describe the behavioral model of self-control.
9. Consider the model of self-control illustrated in Figure 26.1. In that model, what controls the controlling behavior? Discuss.
10. List the steps that Mager recommends to unfuzzify a vaguely stated problem or self-control goal.
11. How does this book define *commitment*?
12. Describe five steps that you could take to strengthen and maintain your commitment to a program of self-control.

3. Take Data and Analyze Causes

The next step is to take data on the occurrence of the problem behavior—when, where, and how often it occurs. This is especially important when the goal is to decrease excessive behaviors. As indicated in Chapter 20, a number of reasons for keeping track of the problem behavior exist, not the least of which is to provide a reference point or baseline for evaluating progress. For many self-control projects, a Post-it note and a pencil or a tally counter app on a smartphone or other hand-held device can be used to tally instances of the problem as they occur throughout the day. You could use a number of techniques to increase the likelihood of record keeping for a problem behavior. If the problem behavior is smoking, you should record each cigarette before you smoke it so that the behavior will reinforce recording it. You might set external reinforcers that other people control. For example, you might give control of your spending money to someone who can monitor your behavior continuously for extended periods of time and return your money contingent upon consistent data taking. You might also get other people to reinforce your recording behavior by (a) telling friends about your self-modification project, (b) keeping your recording chart or graph in an obvious place to increase the likelihood of feedback from friends, and (c) keeping your friends informed on how the project and results are progressing. Contingencies mediated by other people are important sources of maintenance for your controlling behaviors.

In some cases (as pointed out in Chapter 20), recording and graphing the behavior may be all that is needed to bring about improvement. Maletsky (1974) made a convincing demonstration of this effect. Three of the five cases that he studied were completed successfully, even though he was careful not to introduce any treatment other than the counting and graphing of unwanted behaviors. One successful case concerned repetitive scratching that resulted in unsightly lesions on the arms and legs of a 52-year-old woman; another concerned a 9-year-old boy's repetitive hand raising in class whether or not he knew the answers to the teacher's questions; and the third involved the out-of-seat behavior in school of an 11-year-old girl. In all three cases, the behavior decreased over a 6-week period as a result of daily self-counting and graphing. In some cases, counting each thought, desire, or urge to emit a behavior before the behavior occurs might even be possible. McFall (1970) reported a study in which recording each urge to have a cigarette was sufficient to decrease not only the likelihood of subsequently taking a cigarette but also the number of urges. Additional examples of beneficial effects of self-monitoring can be found in Cone (1999), Latner and Wilson (2002), and Wood, Murdock, and Cronin (2002).

When recording the frequency of the problem during these initial observations, you should take a close look at the antecedents that might be S^Ds or S^Δs for the problem behavior and at the immediate consequences that might be maintaining the problem. Suggestions for successful programming strategies often arise from this exercise.

Recall Al at the beginning of the chapter. When he began examining the circumstances in which he typically snacked, he made a surprising finding. The great majority of instances of eating were followed immediately by some other reinforcing event:

a bite of a doughnut and then a sip of coffee
another potato chip while watching TV—his favorite basketball player just scored another basket
another candy to munch on while in his car—the stoplight turns green and Al drives away

Al ate while drinking coffee, drinking beer, talking to friends, talking on the phone, riding in a car—in other words, while coming into contact with a wide variety of reinforcing events in the natural environment. As we indicated in earlier chapters, the effects of reinforcers are automatic and do not depend on an individual's awareness. Moreover, aspects of the different settings became cues for Al's excessive eating. No wonder Al had trouble with self-control.

Thus, during preliminary observations, it is important to analyze antecedents for the undesired behavior, immediate consequences that might maintain the undesired behavior to be eliminated, and the immediate consequences or lack of them on the behavior that you wish to develop. This information can be very useful in the next step of your program.

4. Design and Implement a Treatment Plan

Throughout your life, in the presence of certain *antecedents,* certain *behaviors* have had certain *consequences.* Each of these three variables provides a fertile area for selecting self-control techniques.

Manage the Antecedents   As indicated in Part III (Chapters 17, 18, and 19), it is helpful to think of major classes of antecedents that control our behavior: instructions, modeling, physical guidance, our immediate surroundings, other people, the time of day, and motivating operations.

Instructions   Meichenbaum (1977) suggested that almost every self-modification program should include some self-instructions. They have been used in formal self-management projects to increase exercise and study behavior (Cohen, DeJames, Nocera, & Ramberger, 1980), reduce fears (Arrick, Voss, & Rimm, 1981), reduce nail biting (Harris & McReynolds, 1977), and improve a variety of other behaviors (Watson & Tharp, 2007). Before planning instructions for your self-control program, we encourage you to review the guidelines for using rules and goals in Chapter 17. We also discuss self-instructional strategies further in Chapter 27.

Modeling   Modeled behavior is another class of stimulus events that is useful in self-control programs. For example, if you want to improve your skills at introducing yourself at social gatherings, find someone who's good at it, observe that person's behavior, and imitate it. A procedure called *participant modeling* (described more fully in Chapter 28) is an especially effective method for reducing fears. With this procedure, the fearful person observes a model interacting with the fear-inducing stimulus and then imitates the model.

Physical Guidance   In Chapter 18, we described how behavior modifiers use physical guidance to induce an individual to go through the motions of the desired behavior. Examples of physically guiding your own behavior are difficult to identify because if you could guide your behavior easily, you would probably not engage in the problem behavior. However, in his classic analysis of self-control, Skinner (1953) described how individuals use physical restraint to control their own behavior. You might, for example, keep your hands in your pockets to avoid nail biting, bite your tongue to avoid making a rude comment, or clasp your hands together to avoid striking someone in a moment of anger.

Our Immediate Surroundings   Do you have trouble studying at home? Try going to the library, where studying is a high-probability behavior (Brigham, 1982). Many people have a particular behavior they would like to decrease that occurs in particular situations. A useful strategy is to rearrange the environment to present cues for the desirable alternative behaviors (see Chapter 18).

Other People   As we said earlier, observing models is one way of providing strong prompts for you to engage in some behavior. Another strategy is simply to change the people around you. You have learned to behave in one way with some people and in other ways with other people. For example, you are less likely to swear when in conversation with a highly religious person but more likely to swear when shooting the breeze with your friends. In some cases, your self-control program will consist of increasing contact with certain people and minimizing it with others.

The Time of Day   Sometimes it is possible to achieve successful self-control by changing the time of the activity. For example, many students are more alert in the evening, but they spend that time socializing. Students might accomplish self-control of studying by moving socializing to mornings and studying to evenings.

Motivating Operations   Recall from Chapter 19 that motivating operations are events that influence the strength of consequences as reinforcers or punishers and that influence behaviors affected by those consequences. In self-control programs, a strategy for increasing desirable behavior is to introduce an MEO for reinforcers that influence that behavior. For example, when one of the authors and his wife were visiting Brazil in the early years of their marriage, he took a picture of his wife jogging on the beach in Rio de Janeiro. In later years, when his wife looked at an enlargement of the photo posted on the closet door in their bedroom, it motivated her to continue her jogging program to maintain her slim figure. MAOs also can be used in self-control programs to decrease the likelihood of undesirable behavior. A strategy that Al could use to decrease his doughnut consumption when having coffee with Mary in the campus cafeteria would be to eat a couple of carrots before going to the cafeteria. This would function as an MAO for food and decrease the likelihood of his purchasing doughnuts with his coffee.

Manage the Behavior   If the behavior of concern is relatively simple, such as swearing, you're likely to focus more on antecedents and consequences. If the behavior is complex, you need to spend some time focusing on the behavior itself. If your goal is to acquire some complex skills, it is helpful to consider task analysis and mastery criteria. A **mastery criterion** is a performance requirement for practicing a skill so that if the criterion is met, the behavior has been learned. Consider, for example, learning to play golf. Simek and O'Brien (1981) task analyzed a golf game into 22 components. They arranged these in a behavioral progression for instructional purposes and identified a mastery criterion for each component. The first component in the progression was a 10-inch putt, and the mastery criterion was four putts consecutively holed. Why did they start with such a simple response? One reason was the general rule to start with the simple and proceed to the complex. Another reason was that it incorporated a powerful natural reinforcer for performing the response correctly—namely, hitting the ball into the hole (note that this is similar to the argument for using backward chaining; see Chapter 11).

Shaping is another procedure for focusing on the behavior, and it is useful for self-improvement projects in which your ultimate goal involves a large behavioral change from your starting point. Important rules of thumb to keep in mind include starting small, meeting a mastery criterion before moving up a step, and keeping progressive steps small. Studies of dieters, for example, have reported that those who set small, gradual shaping steps for reducing calories were more likely to develop self-control of binge eating (Gormally, Black, Daston, & Rardin, 1982; Hawkins & Clement, 1980).

Another manipulation that requires you to focus on the behavior is to consider the energy expenditure needed to perform the behavior, generally referred to as *effort*. One strategy for decreasing a problem behavior is to arrange conditions so that it requires more effort to perform that behavior. For example, Susan typically studies in a carrel in the library. Frequently, she interrupts her studying to call her friends. With her cell phone clearly visible in the study carrel, picking it up and dialing involves very little effort. Leaving her cell phone in a locker at the entrance to the library, however, would greatly increase the effort involved in making a call and would likely decrease the instances of doing so. Altering response requirements to decrease the effort needed to emit a behavior can also be used to increase desirable behavior. David decided that his daily water consumption was too low, and he set a goal of going to a water fountain at least four times a day. However, doing so required considerable effort, and he rarely met his goal. He therefore decided to purchase a water bottle to keep with him. His water consumption increased considerably. Although these examples involve manipulating response effort, note that they might also be described as managing antecedents by manipulating the immediate surroundings.

Questions for Learning

13. Describe two strategies for increasing the likelihood of keeping records of a problem behavior to be changed.
14. Give an example that illustrates how recording and graphing of a problem behavior was all that was needed to bring about improvement.
15. Describe how Al was inadvertently reinforced for eating numerous times throughout the day.
16. List seven major classes of antecedents that you might consider when planning how to manage the situation in a self-control program.
17. Give an example that indicates how the manipulation of a motivating operation was an effective self-control strategy.
18. Define *mastery criterion,* and give an example that is not in the text.
19. Give an example that illustrates how the manipulation of energy expenditure or effort needed to perform a behavior is an effective self-management strategy. Would you say that the example involved the manipulation of a motivating operation? Why or why not?

Manage the Consequences   One strategy for manipulating consequent events is to eliminate certain reinforcers that may inadvertently strengthen a particularly undesirable behavior in a specific situation. When Al analyzed his eating problem, he noticed that, in addition to the taste of food itself, other reinforcers (TV, pleasant conversation) were usually associated with eating. A major feature of Al's dieting control program, therefore, should be to disassociate eating from these other activities. Recommendations by LeBow (2013) to accomplish this include (a) eating only in the kitchen when at home, (b) using the same eating utensils and placemats at each meal, (c) eating only at designated times, and (d) keeping food out of every room but the kitchen.

A second strategy for manipulating consequences is recording and graphing the target behavior (see, e.g., Watson & Tharp, 2007). Seeing a graph that shows gradual improvement can serve as a prompt for positive thoughts about your progress. It can also serve as a prompt for others to give you extra social attention for sticking to the self-control program.

A third strategy for manipulating consequences involves arranging to receive specific reinforcers when you show improvement or even for just sticking to the program (see Watson & Tharp, 2007). This is especially important if your desired behavior will lead to small but cumulatively significant or improbable reinforcers or if failure to perform your desired behavior will lead to small but cumulatively significant or improbable punishers. Three ways of arranging for reinforcers to be received in a self-control program include (a) asking others to manage them for you, (b) reminding yourself of delayed natural reinforcers, and (c) managing reinforcers yourself. This last way may seem the most obvious considering that we are talking about *self*-control; however, there is a problem with it, as you will see.

Asking others to manage reinforcers for you is an effective way to receive reinforcers in self-control programs (Watson & Tharp, 2007). For example, when Mary initiated a jogging program, she decided that she would receive money immediately after jogging. Also, if she jogged every day, she could select and engage in one of several possible social activities with her husband. If she met her goals, Mary's husband dispensed the reinforcers (Kau & Fischer, 1974).

The second way to receive reinforcers—reminding yourself of delayed natural consequences for a behavior immediately after it occurs—can be illustrated by the problem of shopping for holiday presents. Suppose that you set a goal of buying presents early during the year rather than waiting until the last minute. Doing so has sizable natural consequences. You can buy presents on sale, saving a significant amount of money. You can avoid the holiday rush, minimizing the stress and hassles that typically accompany holiday shopping. A better selection of presents is available. And you have more time to select the best present for each person on your gift list. However, the positive consequences of giving the presents, such as the recipients' joyful reactions, are long delayed after the behavior of shopping early. A solution, therefore, is to increase the saliency of such delayed reinforcers right after the behavior to be controlled. Immediately after you purchase a gift during a fall sale, for example, you might record the amount saved and post it in a conspicuous place. You could look at a photograph of the gift's future recipient and imagine how happy that person will be when the present is opened. You could also make a list of nonshopping activities you will enjoy during the holiday rush.

The third way to receive reinforcers in self-control programs is for individuals to manage consequences for their own behavior (Watson & Tharp, 2007). Suppose, for example, that you decide to allow yourself to surf the Internet only after studying for an exam. This seems like an example of self-reinforcement. However, in such circumstances, you can always access the reinforcer without emitting the desired behavior as illustrated in Figure 26.2. What would prevent you from doing so? We suspect that in this and other such examples of self-reinforcement, other contingencies are operating in addition to self-reinforcement. Perhaps just before studying you worried about the likelihood of failing the exam, and studying enabled you to escape from such worrying. Perhaps, immediately after studying, you thought about the likelihood of getting an A. Or perhaps other factors influenced your studying. Thus, while it is certainly possible for you to give yourself a reinforcer only after emitting some behavior, it is not clear that this contingency alone is responsible for the improved behavior. Because of this problem, Catania (2011, pp. 40–41) asserts that "self-reinforcement" is a misnomer and recommends that the term *self-regulation* be used in its place. For further discussion of logical problems involving the concept of self-reinforcement, see Catania (1975, 2011), Goldiamond (1976a, 1976b), and Mace, Belfiore, and Hutchinson (2001).

Some guidelines for incorporating reinforcers into your program include (a) make it possible for you to earn specific reinforcers on a daily basis, (b) set up bonuses that you can earn for progress on a weekly basis, (c) vary the reinforcers from 1 day to the next and 1 week to the next to prevent boredom with the entire system, (d) if possible and desirable, have other individuals dispense the reinforcers to you for meeting your goals, and (e) tell others about your progress.

Recall from Chapter 4 the Premack principle, which states that any activity that you are likely to perform can be used to reinforce a behavior that you are less likely to perform. You can use this strategy in self-control programs. High-frequency behaviors used in documented cases of self-improvement have involved making telephone calls (Todd, 1972), urinating (Johnson, 1971), opening the daily mail at the office (Spinelli & Packard, 1975), and sitting on a particular chair (Horan & Johnson, 1971).

FIGURE 26.2
Does self-reinforcement work?

Questions for Learning

20. List the five steps that characterize many programs of self-control (they start on p. 259).
21. Describe three different strategies for manipulating consequences in self-control programs in a sentence or two for each.
22. Describe three different ways of arranging for reinforcers to be received in a self-control program, in a sentence or two for each.
23. Is self-reinforcement an effective self-control strategy? Discuss.

5. Prevent Relapse and Make Your Gains Last

Suppose you've made good progress on your self-control program: Perhaps you've lost weight, haven't had a cigarette in 3 months, or your studying has paid off and you got an A on your last two exams. Now the question is: Will the changes last? Will you be able to maintain your gains over the long run? Unfortunately, relapses are common in self-control programs (Marlatt & Parks, 1982). By **relapse**, in a self-control program we mean going back to the unwanted behavior at approximately its same level as before you started your program. Just as the three variables of *antecedents, behaviors,* and *consequences* were valuable areas to consider when designing your program, they also provide a useful framework for analyzing causes of relapses and how to prevent them.

Causes of Relapse in Antecedents   A strategy for preventing relapses is to recognize their possible causes and to take steps to minimize them. Let's look at some examples involving antecedents.

Avoidable Setback Antecedents   A common cause of relapses in self-control programs is a failure to anticipate *setback antecedents*—that is, antecedents that increase one's risk for returning to earlier unwanted behavior patterns. Some setback antecedents can simply be avoided until you are better able to cope with them. For example, Carla decided to quit smoking. Initially, she believed that she couldn't resist the temptation to smoke while playing poker with her friends on Friday nights. Her strategy was simply not to play poker for the first month of the program. Fred decided to go on a diet, to eat healthier foods, and to consume fewer calories. But he knew that he couldn't resist the banana splits at the supermarket where he usually bought groceries. His solution: He changed the place where he shopped. If you can successfully avoid setback antecedents until you have achieved some success with your self-control program, you may then be better able to cope with situations that provide strong antecedents for the problem behavior.

Unavoidable Setback Antecedents   Some setback antecedents simply can't be avoided. A strategy to prevent relapse is to anticipate unavoidable setback antecedents and to take steps to cope with them. Consider John's case. He had faithfully followed his exercise program for a month and a half, but he was about to embark on a camping trip. He knew that the complete change in routine and the duties each night around the campground were not conducive to exercising. His solution was to obtain his traveling companions' approval to stop traveling each night half an hour early. While the others relaxed in the campground, John exercised. They then all shared the campground duties. The more you can recognize unavoidable setback antecedents before you encounter them, the better are your chances for planning coping strategies.

Overreaction to Occasional Setbacks   After 2 weeks of sticking faithfully to her schedule for studying, Janice downloaded five movies and watched them for 10 hours straight. Fred, following a month of successful dieting, had a banana split 3 days in a row. Very few people achieve successful self-control without experiencing an occasional setback. However, temporary setbacks are not a problem if you get right back into your program. When you suffer a setback, don't dwell on it. Instead, review the many occasions when you have stuck to your program as a prompt to set new goals and to make a renewed commitment.

Counterproductive Self-Talk   When people attempt to change, they are bound to encounter stumbling blocks. When these happen, counterproductive self-talk can exacerbate the problem and may lead to a relapse. People who have difficulty dieting may say, "I'm too hungry to wait until dinner. I'll have a snack to tide myself over." That type of self-talk is a cue to eat.

What kinds of self-talk in your self-control program might lead to a relapse? For each example that you can think of, identify desirable alternative self-talk that might have the opposite effect. Dieters, for example, might tell themselves, "I feel hungry, but I'm not starving. I'll just focus on something to take my mind off food."

Causes of Relapse in the Specification of the Response   Sometimes relapses occur because individuals do not pay sufficient attention to the response component of their self-control program. Let's look at some examples.

A Fuzzy Target Behavior   Tracy wanted to improve her golf skills. After a month of regular practice at the driving range, however, she wasn't sure she was improving. The problem was that "wanting to improve" was too vague. She had not specified her target behavior precisely enough. If Tracy's goal had been to hit five drives in a row over 175 yards, to hit three 7-irons in a row within 30 feet of the 100-yard marker, or to make four 3-foot putts in a row, she would have been able to evaluate her progress more easily (Martin & Ingram, 2001). As we described earlier, a fuzzy goal is an acceptable starting point, but you must then unfuzzify your target by describing it in such a way that you and others can easily recognize it when it occurs.

A Long-Term Target Behavior   Suppose you set a long-term goal of earning an A in a particular course. Your goal is clear, but it is a long way away. For such projects, you should set short-term goals that provide specific progress checks along the way. With respect to your goal of earning an A, you might set a short-term goal of studying the material for that course for a minimum of 1 hour every day. Another short-term goal might be to answer a certain number of study questions each day. Daily short-term goals should be precisely stated and realistic and should move you in the direction of your long-term goal.

Trying Too Much Too Soon   Some self-control projects never get off the ground because they are too ambitious. Wanting to eat more healthily, exercise more, floss your teeth regularly, manage your money more wisely, and get better grades are admirable goals, but trying to improve in all areas at once is a formula for failure. If you've identified several areas to improve, prioritize them in order of their personal value to you. From the top two or three priority areas, select the easiest one as your focus. Starting small increases your likelihood of success.

Causes of Relapse in Consequences   Recall our model of self-control. It involves emitting a *controlling behavior* to manage a *behavior to be controlled*. Inadequate or poorly scheduled consequences for either of these behaviors can lead to a relapse. Let's look at some examples.

Failure to Incorporate Everyday Rewards into Your Program   Many people begin self-control programs with a great deal of enthusiasm. After awhile, the extra work from recording, graphing, rearranging the environment, and so forth can become burdensome. One way to prevent relapse is to link your self-control program to everyday rewarding activities. One person we know linked his exercise program to watching movies on Netflix. His goal was to exercise a minimum of four times a week. He also downloaded movies about four nights a week. He therefore signed a contract with his wife that he would watch a movie only if he first walked at least 1.5 miles (2.4 km) in the neighborhood. Examine ways that you can incorporate daily rewarding activities into the support of your self-control program.

Consequences That Are Only Cumulatively Significant   Suppose your dieting program has been successful. You decide that your new slim body can easily handle an extra dessert. One dessert is not a problem. Rather, it is the accumulation of extra desserts on numerous occasions that will put the weight back on. As described earlier, for many self-control problems, the immediate reinforcement for consumption of harmful substances is likely to win out over the negative consequences from those substances because the negative effects are noticeable only after they have accumulated over many trials. Individuals with these types of self-control problems are very likely to experience a relapse. One strategy to prevent relapse in such situations is to set specific dates for follow-up checks or postchecks and to list specific strategies to follow if the postchecks are unfavorable. For example, if your self-control program was one of weight reduction, you might agree with a friend that you will weigh yourself in your friend's presence once a week. If your weight increases to a specified level, then you will immediately return to your program.

Additional Strategies to Make It Last   Additional strategies to prevent relapse and maintain your gains over the long term involve all three factors of antecedents, responses, and consequences. One strategy is to practice the self-control steps outlined in this chapter to improve additional behaviors. You are more likely to continue using self-control techniques if you practice them on more than one self-control project (Barone, 1982). Moreover, you are more likely to be able to deal with a relapse if you are skillful in the self-control techniques that brought about the improvement in the first place.

Perhaps the most effective way to make your gains last is to involve supportive others in your program, both in the short term and in the long term. One strategy is to set up a buddy system. When you start your project, you might find a friend or relative with a similar problem and set mutual maintenance goals. Once a month, you could get together and check each other's progress. If your progress has been maintained, you could celebrate in a previously agreed-upon way. In a study of smokers, Karol and Richards (1978) found that those who quit with a buddy and who telephoned encouragement to each other showed more reduction of smoking in an 8-month follow-up than did smokers who tried to quit on their own.

A particularly effective strategy is to sign a behavioral contract with supportive others. Behavioral contracts, which were discussed in Chapter 24, have been used to strengthen desirable target behaviors with children (e.g., Miller & Kelley, 1994) and adults (e.g., Dallery, Meredith, & Glenn, 2008; Leal & Galanter, 1995). A contract usually involves two or more people, although "self-contracts" have also been used (e.g., Seabaugh & Schumaker, 1994). A form that you might use for your contract is presented in Table 26.1.

TABLE 26-1   A Form for a Behavioral Contract

My specific goals for my self-control program are:

_____

_____

_____

Short-term goals for my self-control program include:

_____

_____

_____

To observe, record, and graph my behavior, I will:

_____

_____

_____

To minimize the causes of the problem, I will:

_____

_____

_____

The details of my treatment plan include:
1. Steps to manage the situation:

_____

_____

_____

TABLE 26-1 **Continued**

2. Steps to manage consequences:

_____

_____

_____

3. Steps to deal with or change complex behavior:

_____

_____

_____

4. Rewards that I can earn for sticking to and/or completing my project:

_____

_____

_____

Additional steps that I will take to increase and maintain my commitment to the project and to prevent relapse include:

_____

_____

_____

Schedule for review of progress:

_____

_____

_____

Signatures of all involved and the date of the agreement:

_____	_____	_____
(Date)	(Your signature)	(Supporter's signature)

A contract serves at least four important stimulus control functions:

1. It ensures that all parties involved agree to the goals and procedures and that they do not lose sight of them during the course of the treatment.
2. Because the goals are specified behaviorally, the contract also ensures that throughout the program, all parties will agree on how close they are to reaching the goals.
3. The contract provides the client a realistic estimate of the cost of the program in time, effort, and money.
4. The signatures on the contract help to ensure that all parties will faithfully follow the specified procedures because in our society signing a contract indicates a commitment.

As we have stressed in previous chapters, behavior modification procedures should be revised in appropriate ways when the data indicate that they are not producing satisfactory results. Thus, your contract should be open to renegotiation at any time. If you find that you simply cannot meet some commitment specified in your contract, you should inform the other signatories at your next meeting with them. You can discuss the difficulty and if it seems desirable, you can draft and sign a new contract replacing the previous one. Before doing so, however, you might examine the following troubleshooting guide for behavior contracts.

Troubleshooting Guide[2]

The following questions may help you to spot the problems in your contracting system.

The Contract

1. Was the target behavior specified clearly?
2. If the target behavior was complex, did the contract ask for small approximations to the desired behavior?
3. Were specific deadlines identified for the target behavior?
4. Did the contract clearly identify situations in which the target behavior should occur?
5. Did the contract provide for immediate reinforcement? Are the reinforcers still important and valuable to you?
6. Could reinforcers be earned often (daily or weekly)?
7. Did the contract call for and reward accomplishment rather than obedience?
8. Was the contract phrased in a positive way?
9. Do you consider the contract to be fair and in your best interests?

The Mediator (your cosigner)

1. Did the mediator understand the contract?
2. Did the mediator dispense the kind and amount of reinforcement specified in the contract?
3. Did the mediator meet with you on the dates specified in the contract?
4. Is a new mediator required?

Measurement

1. Are the data accurate?
2. Is your data collection system too complex or too difficult?
3. Does your data collection system clearly reflect your progress in achieving the target behavior?
4. Do you need to improve your data collection system?

Circumvention of the Therapist

Obviously, some personal problems require help from a therapist (as discussed further in Chapters 27 and 28). It should be clear from the preceding sections in this chapter that many people who have mastered some behavioral principles and procedures can use them to control their own behavior. A person who has mastered this book probably does not need a therapist for many behavior problems, such as decreasing smoking, nail biting, or swearing or enhancing studying, exercising, or eating healthy foods. That person knows how to take data, how to plan a program and evaluate its effectiveness, how to apply a large number of behavioral principles and techniques, and how to use a behavioral contract to **NOTE 2** maintain the controlling behavior. In short, many people can be their own behavior modifiers.

Questions for Learning

24. What is the meaning of *relapse* in a self-control program?
25. Briefly describe four possible causes of relapse in situations, and indicate how each might be handled.
26. Briefly describe three possible causes of relapse in the specification of the response, and indicate how each might be handled.
27. Briefly describe two possible causes of relapse in consequences, and indicate how each might be handled.
28. What is a behavioral contract (see pages 243, 267–268)?
29. What important stimulus–control functions does a behavioral contract serve?
30. Is it plausible to suggest that many individuals can become their own behavior therapists? Justify your answer.

---

[2] Adapted from DeRisi and Butz, *Writing Behavioral Contracts: A Case Simulation Practice Manual* (Champaign, IL: Research Press, 1975), pp. 58–60.

Application Exercises

A. Exercise Involving Others

Describe a self-control problem experienced by someone that you know. Is the problem best characterized as a behavioral deficiency or a behavioral excess? What seems to be the cause of the problem?

B. Self-Modification Exercises

Using the information in this and the preceding chapters, describe how you might go about following all five steps of a self-control program for bringing about successful self-adjustment for a behavior of yours that you would like to change.

Notes for Further Learning

1. A verbal commitment to do something is verbal behavior that corresponds to behavior that one later engages in if the commitment is kept. A number of studies have been conducted on training a correspondence between stated intentions (commitments) and later behavior (Lloyd, 2002). For example, Ward and Stare (1990) prompted a group of kindergarten children to state that they were going to play in a certain designated area prior to playing there (*correspondence training*). Specifically, the children were prompted to say, "I'm going to play at the workbench today." The children received a token if they made this statement. After 4 minutes of play, children who played at the workbench received another token for playing there after saying that this is what they would do. Compared to a group of children who simply received tokens for playing in the designated area, the group that received correspondence training showed more instances of following through on stated intentions to engage in another activity (playing with toys) even though they received no tokens for following through on this commitment. The results thus showed that correspondence training on one response can generalize to a new response. This tendency to generalize correspondence training may be what makes it possible for us to keep commitments for behavior change that we have made to ourselves. Correspondence training is one way that humans learn self-awareness or self-knowledge (Dymond & Barnes, 1997).

2. How effective are self-help manuals? Although a review by Rosen (1987) found major limitations to their usefulness, meta-analysis—a statistical procedure for combining the data analysis of many studies—suggests that somewhat more positive conclusions are in order (Den Boer, Wiersma, & Van Den Bosch, 2004; Gould & Clum, 1993; Gregory, Canning, Lee, & Wise, 2004; Hirai & Clum, 2006; Scogin, Bynum, Stephens, & Calhoon, 1990). That does not mean that all self-help books in book stores have been evaluated. However, experiments that examined sophisticated, complex self-help manuals based on behavioral principles indicated that self-administered treatments stand a good chance of success. The most successful targets for improvement involved study habits, depression, parenting skills, social skills, and overcoming anxiety and fears. Less successful self-treatment programs occurred with the control of alcohol drinking, smoking, and overeating (Gould & Clum, 1993; Seligman, 1994; Watkins & Clum, 2008). Also, a number of studies have demonstrated that university students who have read various editions of the self-modification book by David Watson and Ronald Tharp were more successful at completing self-improvement projects than students who have not read the book (Watson & Tharp, 2007). For a list of specific self-help books that have been found to be effective for a specific clinical problem in one or more randomized control studies, see Malouff and Rooke (2007). For a discussion of strategies for integrating self-help formats into psychotherapy, see Norcross (2006).

Questions for Further Learning

1. What is correspondence training? Briefly describe how generalized correspondence was demonstrated in kindergarten children.
2. With which behavior problems are self-help manuals most effective and least effective?

CHAPTER 27

Approaches to Behavior Therapy: Cognitive Restructuring; Self-Directed Coping Methods; and Mindfulness and Acceptance Procedures

LEARNING OBJECTIVES

After studying this chapter, you will be able to:

- Outline three stages in behavioral approaches to psychotherapy.
- Explain the prominent cognitive behavior therapies.
- Explain prominent coping and problem-solving methods.

- Outline the mindfulness and acceptance procedures.
- Critically discuss current research on the effectiveness of cognitive-behavior therapies.

The two chapters in this part (Part VI) of this book deal with the application of behavioral procedures to psychotherapy—in other words, the clinical treatment of psychological disorders. In accordance with the first part of the subtitle of this book, these procedures will be described in some detail; however, no attempt will be made to teach you how to conduct therapy with individuals with clinical problems. Such therapy must only be undertaken by qualified professional therapists.

Behavior modification, as described in the preceding chapters, emerged in the 1950s and 1960s (this early history is discussed further in Chapter 29). During that period, behaviorally oriented therapists began to treat clients who otherwise would have received traditional types of psychotherapy, such as psychoanalysis. Practitioners of this new approach elected to use treatments based on behavior principles (i.e., the principles covered in Part II [Chapters 3–16]). Consequently, this new approach is called *behavior therapy*, and the professionals who apply it are known as *behavior therapists*. The initial focus of behavior therapy was the treatment of clients with fear and anxiety, but soon it was being used to treat a wide variety of clinical problems—anxiety disorders, obsessive-compulsive disorders, stress-related problems, depression, marital problems, and sexual dysfunction—discussed further in Chapter 28. In 1966, the Association for Advancement of Behavior Therapy (AABT) was established.

Publications describing another new approach to psychotherapy, called *cognitive therapy*, appeared in the 1960s and 1970s (Beck, 1970; Ellis, 1962). *Cognitive processes* or *cognitions* are verbalizations or images that are frequently called *believing, thinking, expecting,* or *perceiving*. The basic assumption of cognitive therapy is that problems requiring psychotherapy are caused by dysfunctional cognitions or faulty thinking. Accordingly, cognitive therapists typically help clients to rid themselves of unproductive, debilitating thoughts or beliefs.

Early behavior therapists noted certain similarities between the goals and procedures of cognitive therapists and their own. Cognitive therapists, in turn, adopted some behavior modification methods. Out of this mutual appreciation an area grew that came to be known as *cognitive behavior modification* or *cognitive behavior therapy*. In the 1970s and 1980s the first of these two terms, "cognitive behavior modification," was more commonly used (e.g., Mahoney, 1974; Meichenbaum, 1977, 1986), whereas since then the term cognitive behavior therapy became the more common of the two terms (e.g., Bjorgvinsson & Rosqvist, 2009; Hofmann & Otto, 2008; Lam, 2008). In 2005, AABT was renamed the Association for Behavioral and Cognitive Therapies (ABCT). Both cognitively oriented and behaviorally oriented therapists have learned from each other and agree on many issues (see, e.g., DiGiuseppe, 2008; Dougher, 1997; Hawkins & Forsyth, 1997; Wilson, Hayes, & Gifford, 1997). In addition, practitioners of both approaches are firmly committed to the view that the criterion for judging the effectiveness of any treatment is the amount of measurable improvement that occurs in the client's behavior.

Thus, two stages in behavioral approaches to psychotherapy occurred: (1) behavior therapy and (2) cognitive behavior therapy. These two stages have been followed by a third stage, called the *third wave of behavior therapy* (Hayes, 2004) or *third-generation behavior therapies* by others (Herbert & Forman, 2013). In contrast to the second generation of behavior therapies, the third generation does not try to change the client's cognitions directly but instead attempts to change the clients' reactions to their cognitions.

The purpose of this chapter is to describe briefly procedures referred to as *cognitive behavior therapy* or *cognitive behavior modification* and procedures from the third generation. Two representatives of the third generation are a therapy developed by Steven C. Hayes and his colleagues called *acceptance and commitment therapy* (ACT; Hayes, Strosahl, & Wilson, 1999), and a therapy developed by Marsha Linehan called *dialectical behavior therapy* (DBT; Linehan, 1987).

We have organized the different approaches to behavior therapy discussed in this chapter into three categories: (a) treatments that emphasize cognitive restructuring to decrease maladaptive thoughts that are assumed to cause troublesome emotions and behavior, (b) self-directed strategies to enhance overt coping skills, and (c) treatments of the third generation of behavior therapies that emphasize changing clients' reactions to their maladaptive thoughts rather than the thoughts themselves.

Cognitive Restructuring Methods

Cognitive therapy has two underlying major theoretical assumptions: (1) Individuals interpret and react to events by forming cognitions—beliefs, expectations, attitudes—on the basis of the perceived significance of those events, and (2) defective or maladaptive cognitions can cause emotional and behavioral disorders. It follows from these assumptions that the primary focus of psychotherapy is to fundamentally change a client's cognitions. Stated simply, cognitive therapists believe that faulty thinking is the cause of emotional and behavioral problems, and thus the primary focus of the cognitive approach to therapy is to help clients recognize and change faulty thinking. Strategies for recognizing maladaptive thinking and replacing it with adaptive thinking are often referred to as *cognitive restructuring*. From the point of view of this book, cognitive approaches deal mainly with the client's private verbal behavior and imagery – not with events that occur at some non-behavioral level. (see Chapter 15). This viewpoint is called a *behavioral approach*. However, a person's verbal behavior and imagery can affect his or her emotional and overt behavior, so the differences between cognitive and behavioral approaches are not as great as it might at first appear. (More on this point toward the end of this chapter.) Moreover, therapists who use cognitive techniques generally also include behavior modification components in their treatments.

Questions for Learning

1. What are cognitive processes?
2. What do the letters ABCT stand for?
3. What are the three waves or generations of behavior therapy?
4. What are the two major assumptions of cognitive therapy?
5. Stated simply, what do some cognitive therapists believe to be the cause of emotional and behavioral problems, and what is the primary focus of their approach to therapy?
6. In a sentence, what is cognitive restructuring?

Rational-Emotive Behavior Therapy

Do you ever find yourself saying, "I always screw things up," "I'm such a klutz," or "I never do things right"? The well-known psychotherapist credited with being the founder of cognitive therapy, Albert Ellis, considered such self-statements to be irrational—after all, you don't always screw up, you're not always clumsy, and you do some things right. Ellis believed that such irrational thoughts cause anxiety, sadness, anger, or other troublesome emotions. His approach to therapy was to help people identify such irrational thoughts or beliefs and to replace them with more rational self-statements (e.g., Ellis, 1962; Ellis & Bernard, 1985; Ellis & Dryden, 1997).

The original name for Ellis's approach, *rational-emotive therapy* (RET), was based on the premise that most everyday emotional problems and related overt behaviors stem from irrational interpretations that people make of events in their lives. People tend to think in *absolute terms* such as a student thinking, "I *must* do well in *all* my courses." People tend to *overgeneralize,* such as a student thinking after getting a poor mark on one exam, "I'll *never* be a good student." People also tend to *catastrophize* such as telling themselves that things are so horrible they can't possibly stand it. For example, Jim who slept through his alarm and was going to be late for class, rushed to get ready. He cut himself while shaving and thought, "I'm a walking disaster! I always screw up." Later, he got caught in a traffic jam. "Why does the worst always happen to me?" He felt angry and frustrated. Ellis considered such self-statements like "I'm a walking disaster," and "The worst always happens to me" to be at the root of emotional problems (e.g., Jim's anger and frustration).

Basically, the RET approach is to teach clients to counteract such irrational self-statements with more positive and realistic statements. This is accomplished in three main phases. First, the therapist helps the client identify troublesome thoughts that are based on irrational beliefs, such as Jim's thoughts that he is a walking disaster. Second, in a very confrontational, argumentative way, the RET therapist vigorously challenges the client's irrational beliefs that are thought to be the basis for the problematic self-talk. For example, Jim might be harboring the irrational belief that he *must* never be late for class, a type of irrational thinking that Ellis referred to as "musterbation." To Jim, an RET therapist might say, "Sooner or later everyone living in a city gets caught in a traffic jam and have other events happen that make them late. What makes you so special?" or "What do you mean by you always screw things up? You told me that you got an A on your last computer assignment." Third, the client is taught through modeling and homework assignments to replace the irrational self-statements with statements based on rational beliefs. For example, Jim might be taught to tell himself that there are far worse things than being late for class and that even though things could be better, they could certainly be a lot worse. His situation might be annoying or inconvenient, but it is not catastrophic. (One hopes, however, that Jim would still be able to recognize a real catastrophe, unlike the cartoon character in Figure 27.1.)

Ellis (1993) later added the word *behavior* to the name of his therapy, and it is now called **rational-emotive behavior therapy (REBT)**. He did so because, despite being a cognitive therapist, Ellis frequently used behavioral "homework" assignments. For example, Jim might be told to write down each time he performs a complex action, such as working at his computer, to prove to himself that he is not a walking disaster. The homework assignments are usually designed to help the client challenge irrational beliefs and confront troublesome emotions. (For a practical guide to REBT, see Dryden, DiGiuseppe, & Neenan, 2010.)

Evaluation of REBT   To the extent that Ellis's approach is successful, is it because the therapist disputes the client's irrational beliefs (a "cognitive" component)? Is it because the homework assignments influence the client to confront anxiety-evoking situations in real life, which might lead to extinction of the anxiety ("behavioral" components)? (See Chapter 28.) Or is the improvement the result of a combination of both the correction of faulty thinking and the homework assignments? Examination of studies of REBT that do not include a behavioral component suggests that a big part of the success of REBT might be due to the homework assignments rather than to the disputation of irrational beliefs (Gossette & O'Brien, 1989, 1992; Longmore & Worrell, 2007). For a summary of the empirical support for REBT see Spiegler and Guevremont (2010).

Beck's Cognitive Therapy

Independently of Ellis, Aaron T. Beck (1976) developed a cognitive therapy procedure that is similar to REBT. His cognitive therapy was originally developed for the treatment of depression. However, it has subsequently been applied to a wide variety of other problems, including manic states, anxiety disorders, hysteria, obsessional disorders, psychosomatic disorders, and thinking disorders such as in schizophrenia (Beck, Emery, & Greenberg, 1985; Butler, Chapman, Forman, & Beck, 2006; Spiegler & Guevremont, 2010).

FIGURE 27.1
An exaggerated example of rational-emotive therapy

According to Beck (1976), people with psychological disorders engage excessively in aberrant, fallacious, or dysfunctional thinking, and this is what causes or exacerbates their problems. Among the various types of dysfunctional thinking are the following:

1. *Dichotomous thinking*, which is thinking in absolute terms such as assuming that one is a failure if one gets any grade less than an A.
2. *Arbitrary inference*, which is drawing a conclusion on the basis of inadequate evidence such as misinterpreting a frown on the face of a passerby as the passerby's disapproval.
3. *Overgeneralization*, which is reaching a general conclusion on the basis of a few instances such as assuming that a single failure means that one cannot succeed at anything.
4. *Magnification*, which is exaggerating the meaning or significance of a particular event such as believing that it is terrible or catastrophic not to obtain something that one wants very badly.

Beck's procedure involves three general components. First, clients identify the dysfunctional thoughts and maladaptive assumptions that might be causing debilitating emotions or behavior. This is usually accomplished through a series of visualization exercises and easily answered questions. For example, a client might be encouraged to recall or imagine situations that elicited debilitating emotions and to focus on the thoughts experienced in those situations. Second, once a thought or dysfunctional assumption has been identified, several methods can be used to counteract it. Beck called one such method reality checking or hypothesis testing. After the client has identified the dysfunctional belief or thought and has learned to distinguish it as a hypothesis rather than as a reality, he or she then tests it empirically through homework assignments. For example, if a client believes that everyone he meets turns away from him in disgust, the therapist might help him devise a system for judging other people's facial expressions and body language so that the client can determine objectively whether the thoughts behind the problem are indeed accurate. Or, clients might be encouraged to participate in role-playing sessions. A client who believed that store clerks thought she was inept changed this negative view of herself when she played the role of a salesclerk waiting on her. Third, Beck frequently uses additional homework assignments that contain liberal doses of behavior modification procedures to develop various desirable daily activities. For example, depressed individuals frequently neglect routine tasks such as showering or bathing, bed making, and housecleaning. Homework assignments might be directed toward reestablishing these behaviors. (For a description of procedures for conducting Beck's cognitive therapy, see Beck, 2011; Young, Rygh, Weinberger, & Beck, 2008).

Comparison of the Approaches of Ellis and Beck Some obvious similarities exist between Beck's approach and Ellis's REBT. Both approaches assume the client's difficulty is caused by dysfunctional thought patterns, such as a tendency to exaggerate or catastrophize unpleasant events. Both focus on changing a client's irrational thinking, and both use various behavioral homework assignments. One difference is that Beck does not emphasize the tendency of clients to catastrophize or "awfulize" nearly as much as Ellis did. A second difference is that Beck takes a gentler, less confrontational approach than Ellis did when discussing clients' irrational beliefs. A third difference, related to the second difference, is the way they attempt to change irrational beliefs. Ellis attempted to change them by disputing them aggressively through relentless logical arguments. Beck frequently attempts to change them by helping the client develop homework assignments to test them experimentally.

Evaluation of Beck's Cognitive Therapy There is considerable evidence, from a large number of methodologically sound studies, that Beck's cognitive therapy is effective for treating depression and a number of other psychological disorders (Butler et al., 2006; Dobson, 2012; Spiegler & Guevremont, 2010). Considering the evidence on the overall effectiveness of Beck's cognitive therapy, the question arises as to what are its active ingredients or effective components? As discussed further in Chapter 28, an increasing amount of research suggests that the cognitive restructuring component is not an effective ingredient of Beck's cognitive therapy for treating depression (Dimidjian et al., 2006; Dimidjian, Barrerra, Martell, Munoz, & Lewinsohn, 2011; Jacobson et al., 1996; Latimer & Sweet, 1984; Longmore & Worrell, 2007; Sweet & Loizeaux, 1991); rather the effective ingredient appears to be the homework assignments. Thus, while the addition of cognitive restructuring techniques to behavioral treatments might improve outcomes with some, the studies just cited suggest that it often does not do so. Nevertheless, as discussed in Chapter 28, cognitive behavior therapy has been shown to be effective for a wide variety of disorders.

Questions For Learning

7. What are the three main phases of rational-emotive behavior therapy and who developed it?
8. Why did Ellis change the name of his therapy from RET to REBT?
9. According to Beck, what causes problems for individuals with neuroses? Describe three examples.
10. Describe the three major components of Beck's cognitive therapy.
11. Describe three similarities and three differences between the approaches of Beck and Ellis.
12. Describe the types of homework assignments Beck uses in his cognitive therapy.

Self-Directed Coping Methods

The previous section discussed cognitive restructuring, which focuses on substituting rational thoughts and appraisal of information for irrational or dysfunctional thinking. Other strategies focus on teaching self-instructional and problem-solving strategies to help clients emit overt behaviors to cope with difficult and stressful situations.

Self-Instructional Training

Meichenbaum and Goodman (1971) initially developed self-instructional training to help children control impulsive behavior.

Self-instructional training with children   Self-instructional training with children typically proceeds through five steps:

1. *Adult Demonstrates Self-Instructing*   For example, an adult might say, "My job is to draw a 10. First I'll draw a straight line like this, and then I'll draw an oval beside it" (while drawing a 10). "I did a good job."
2. *Child Performs While Adult Verbalizes*   For example, the adult would give the child the pencil and say, "Draw a 10. First draw a straight line and then draw an oval beside it." The adult gives praise while the child draws a 10.
3. *The Child Performs the Task and Verbalizes Out Loud*   For example, the child would imitate the behavior illustrated by the adult in Step 1.
4. *Overt Self-Instructions Fade*   Over two or three trials, the child is encouraged to repeat the task while saying the instructions and self-praise more and more softly.
5. *Task Performance Is Performed with Covert Self-Instructions*   Finally, the child is prompted to perform the task while saying the instructions and the self-praise silently so that the teacher can't hear them.

An impulsive child receiving self-instructional training would first be encouraged to practice the steps with simple tasks, such as drawing a 10, and then progress to more complex tasks appropriate for the child's developmental level, such as adding and subtracting.

Self-instructional training with adults   Meichenbaum (1986) and others have extended self-instructional training strategies to help adult clients develop coping skills for dealing with stressful situations that are largely out of their control. Often, the emphasis in this approach is more on teaching the client to cope with the negative emotions than on completely eliminating them. For example, following treatment, one phobic client said,

> Self-instructing makes me able to be in the situation, not to be comfortable, but to tolerate it. I don't talk myself out of being afraid, just out of appearing afraid. You immediately react to the things you're afraid of and then start to reason with yourself. I talk myself out of panic. (Meichenbaum, 1986, p. 372)

The first step in Meichenbaum's approach to teach a client to cope with stress is to help the client identify certain internal stimuli produced by the stressful situation and by negative self-statements the client makes such as "I can't deal with this," or "I'm no good". The client learns to use these internal stimuli as S^Ds for engaging in appropriate self-instruction. Next, through modeling and behavioral rehearsal, the client learns self-talk to counteract negative self-statements in the presence of the stressful situation (e.g., "The fact that I'm anxious just before giving a speech doesn't mean I'm going to blow it—my anxiety is just a way of preparing me to be alert and do a good job"). Third, the client is taught to self-instruct the steps for taking appropriate action (e.g., "I'll take three deep breaths, smile, then follow my notes and give my speech"). Finally, the client is instructed to make self-reinforcing statements immediately after he or she has coped successfully with the stressful situation (e.g., "I did it! Wait 'til I tell my therapist about this!").

Stress Inoculations   Meichenbaum (1985) developed a strategy that he called "stress inoculations." It typically proceeds through three phases. In the *reinterpretation phase,* clients are taught that it's not the stressor, such as a student having to give a talk in class, that is the cause of their nervousness or stress reaction; rather, it is the way they view that event. Clients are also taught to verbalize that they are capable of learning to take steps to deal with the situation. In the *coping training phase,* clients learn a variety of appropriate coping strategies, such as relaxation, self-instruction, and self-reinforcement. Finally, in the *application phase,* clients practice self-talk and coping skills to stressful stimuli, such as having an arm immersed in freezing water, watching a gruesome film, or recalling a stressful visit to the dentist. Just prior to and during exposure to such stressful situations, the client practices appropriate coping skills. Research indicates that stress inoculations can be particularly helpful for clients with anxiety or stress problems (Meichenbaum & Deffenbacher, 1988).

Evaluation of Self-Instructional Methods   A large number of studies indicate that self-instructional training strategies are effective for treating a variety of problems including impulsiveness, lack of assertiveness, social withdrawal, anxiety, poor body image, and schizophrenic behaviors (Spiegler & Guevremont, 2010). Self-instructional training appears to rely largely on rule-governed behavior. And as indicated in Chapter 17, rules are often effective when they describe specific circumstances and deadlines for specific behavior that lead to sizable and probable outcomes even when the outcomes are delayed. Rules that are deficient in any of these components are less likely to be effective.

Problem-Solving Therapy

One approach for helping people deal with a variety of problems for which they have sought treatment is referred to as problem-solving therapy. This approach focuses on teaching people how to proceed through logical reasoning to satisfactory solutions to personal problems. D'Zurilla and Goldfried (1971) outlined the following six general steps in personal problem-solving.

1. *General Orientation*   The client is encouraged to recognize problems and to realize that it is possible to deal with them by acting systematically rather than impulsively. For example, when faced with a problem, the client might be taught to make statements such as "I know I can work this out if I just proceed step-by-step."
2. *Problem Definition*   When asked to specify the problem, most clients reply in vague terms—for example, "I've been very upset lately." By specifying the history of the problem and the variables that seem to be controlling it, it is generally possible to define the problem more precisely. For example, a close analysis of a client's concern might indicate that what is upsetting the client is feeling forced to live in a mess created by an untidy roommate.
3. *Generation of Alternatives*   After defining the problem precisely, the client is instructed to brainstorm possible solutions—that is, to "let one's mind run free" and to think of as many solutions as possible, no matter how far-fetched. For example, possible solutions might be to (a) move, (b) learn to accept messiness, (c) speak assertively to the roommate about keeping the place neat, (d) negotiate a behavioral contract with the roommate, (e) throw the roommate's things out the window, and (f) throw the roommate out the window.
4. *Decision Making*   The next step is to examine the alternatives carefully, eliminating those that are obviously unacceptable, such as (e) and (f). The client should then consider the likely short-term and long-term consequences of the remaining alternatives. On the basis of these considerations, the client should select the alternative that seems most likely to provide the optimum solution.
5. *Implementation*   Initially with the help of the therapist, the client devises a plan for carrying out the best solution to the problem. Sometimes this requires learning new skills. If, for example, the client who decided that the best alternative from those listed in Step 3 was (d), then the client might need to learn about behavioral contracting (see pages 243, 267–269).
6. *Verification*   When the plan is put into effect, the client is encouraged to keep track of progress to ensure that it solves the problem. If it doesn't, the problem-solving sequence must be restarted and another solution attempted.

Evaluation of Problem-Solving Therapy

Nezu, Nezu, & D'Zurilla (2013) described how the problem-solving approach might be applied to a variety of clinical problems. Although evidence indicates that adults and children can readily learn problem-solving skills, they do not always apply them appropriately to achieve satisfactory solutions to personal problems.

Questions for learning

13. Briefly list the five steps of self-instructional training that Meichenbaum and others used with children.
14. Briefly describe the three phases of Meichenbaum's stress inoculation training.
15. Does self-instructional training rely largely on contingency-shaped behavior or rule-governed behavior? Justify your choice.
16. In a sentence each, outline the six steps of problem-solving therapy.

Mindfulness and Acceptance Strategies

Recall the mindfulness-based intervention for aggression that was taught to James (the lead case in Chapter 18). When he experienced anger, he would focus on the sensations that he felt in the soles of his feet. From a behavioral point of view, *mindfulness* involves nonjudgmental awareness, observation, and description of one's covert or overt behaviors as they occur and, in some cases, observation of the antecedents and consequences of those behaviors.

Mindfulness is an ancient concept considered to be "at the heart of Buddha's teachings" (Nhat Hanh, 1998, p. 59). It involves paying close attention to the sights, smells, tastes, and tactile sensations of an experience as it occurs. Suppose that you made arrangements to meet your friend Sasha at a particular restaurant at noon. At 12:30, Sasha still hasn't arrived. Feeling angry, you might think to yourself, "This really upsets me. I hate it when Sasha's late! I can't stand it when Sasha's so unreliable! Why do I put up with this? The people in the restaurant must think I'm an idiot for standing here for half an hour." Alternatively, you might practice mindfulness, thinking to yourself, "I'm standing in front of a restaurant. I notice that my heart is beating faster. I feel a queasiness in my stomach. I'm clenching my fists and my forearms feel tense. I'm wondering what people in the restaurant are saying about me. I'm visualizing Sasha apologizing to me." As this example illustrates, mindfulness involves becoming fully aware of one's sensations, thoughts, feelings, and observable behavior on a moment-to-moment basis.

Acceptance, also called *experiential acceptance* to distinguish it from other types of acceptance in psychotherapy (see Block-Lerner, Wulfert, & Moses, 2009), refers to refraining from judging one's sensations, thoughts, feelings, and behaviors as good or bad, pleasant or unpleasant, useful or useless, and so on. Mindfulness and acceptance go hand in hand. While mindfulness focuses on one's behaviors and sensations, acceptance focuses on not judging those behaviors and sensations. One's thoughts are viewed as just responses, just passing events. Feelings, both positive and negative, are accepted as part of life. Acceptance-based procedures are used to teach individuals that they can feel their feelings and think their thoughts, even though they might be aversive, and still take constructive action that is consistent with their values and life goals. An excellent manual for the layperson to learn and practice mindfulness and acceptance-based techniques is the book by Williams, Teasdale, Segal, and Kabat-Zinn (2007) titled *The Mindful Way Through Depression: Freeing Yourself from Chronic Unhappiness.*

In the late 1980s and early 1990s, several therapists began incorporating mindfulness and acceptance-based procedures into behavior therapy (Hayes, Jacobson, Follette, & Dougher, 1994; Linehan, 1993; Teasdale, Segal, & Williams, 1995). As indicated earlier, therapists who incorporate such experiential change strategies in therapy have been described as the third wave or third generation of behavior therapists (Hayes, 2004; Hayes, Follette, & Linehan, 2004; Herbert & Forman, 2013). One such approach to treatment is acceptance and commitment therapy (ACT).

Acceptance and Commitment Therapy (ACT)

ACT (pronounced "act", not "A-C-T"), developed by Hayes and colleagues (Hayes et al., 1999), proceeds through three main phases. First, through the use of metaphors, paradox, stories, and other verbal techniques presented by the therapist, the client learns that past attempts to control troublesome thoughts and emotions have often served only to increase the frequency of such thoughts and emotions. If someone tells you not to think of a pink elephant, what are you likely to think about? A pink elephant. Similarly, if someone tells you or you tell yourself to stop thinking a particular debilitating thought, you are likely to think it even more. Second, through the use of mindfulness training and acceptance exercises, the client learns to experience and nonjudgmentally embrace thoughts and emotions, including those that are troublesome. In one such exercise, for example, a client is encouraged to imagine his or her thoughts as they "float by like leaves on a stream" (Hayes, 2004). Thus, rather than trying to recognize and change troublesome thoughts and feelings as might occur in cognitive restructuring, the goal of mindfulness and acceptance training is to simply "be with" one's worrisome thoughts and unpleasant feelings. A phrase recommended for clients to repeat to themselves is, "It's OK. . . whatever it is, it's already here: Let me feel it" (Williams et al., 2007, p. 84). This is the acceptance portion of ACT. Third, regardless of whether the troublesome thoughts and emotions are eliminated, clients are encouraged to identify values in various life domains, such as work, family, health, and intimate relationships. The client is then encouraged to translate these values into achievable, concrete goals, and to identify and emit specific behaviors to achieve those goals. This is the commitment portion of ACT: Clients are encouraged to identify valued goals in their lives

NOTE 1 and commit to actions to pursue those goals.

ACT differs from the cognitive therapy (CT) of Ellis and Beck in several ways. First, CT assumes that troublesome thoughts constitute the primary cause of disturbing emotions whereas ACT considers both thoughts and emotions simply as responses and assumes that both are caused by various environmental contingencies. Second, a major focus of CT is the use of cognitive restructuring to change **NOTE 2** troublesome thoughts directly while ACT teaches the client to embrace and accept various thoughts and emotions. ACT also teaches clients that, in spite of experiencing troublesome thoughts and aversive feelings, they can still take constructive action to pursue valued goals. A third difference is the focus of the behavioral homework assignments. With CT, a primary purpose of behavioral homework assignments is to help the client overcome distorted thinking. With ACT, behavioral homework assignments are used to build larger patterns of effective action in the pursuit of valued goals.

Evaluation of ACT   Research has provided evidence that ACT is effective for treating a variety of problems including addictions, anxiety, depression, diabetes management, eating disorders, epilepsy **NOTE 3** control, smoking cessation, psychosis, workplace safety, and several other types of problems (Hayes & Lillas, 2012; Ruiz, 2010).

Dialectical Behavior Therapy (DBT)

DBT, originally developed by Marsha Linehan (1987) to treat borderline personality disorder (a disorder characterized by unstable moods, overt behavior, and relationships), is another approach that incorporates mindfulness and acceptance procedures. Dialectics is a philosophy that goes back thousands of years and was revived in the early 1800s by the German philosopher Hegel. While there are many aspects to the philosophy, one of its assumptions is that many aspects of reality are composed of opposing forces or arguments—thesis and antithesis—which, when combined into a synthesis, lead to a new approach (Weiss, 1974). Linehan added the term *dialectical* to her approach to behavior therapy partly because the therapeutic relationship often involves opposing views of the therapist and the client that must eventually come together, and partly because of the logical conflict between acceptance and change. The client initially has very negative views about him or herself and important others that eventually must be mindfully viewed and accepted so that the client can learn to take constructive action to change in spite of such views. In short, several aspects of DBT can be viewed as thesis and antithesis that must be eventually integrated into a synthesis (Robins, Schmidt III, & Linehan, 2004).

DBT typically involves individual weekly sessions between the therapist and client, and weekly group sessions with clients, and therapy typically consists of several phases. The early part of therapy focuses on helping the client express what he or she hopes to get out of therapy. Next, a client is encouraged to nonjudgmentally observe and describe his or her overt and covert behaviors, especially those that are potentially harmful to the client or others, or that might interfere with the course of treatment. Through the use of discussion, role playing, and observation of others in both group and individual sessions, the client learns to identify, label, and accept various previously troubling emotions and thoughts. Next, interpersonal skills are eventually targeted so that clients learn to say no, ask for what they need, and appropriately interact with others in their lives. Finally, after clients have learned to accept aspects of their lives without distortion, judgment, or evaluation, they are much more likely to be able to learn and follow specific behavioral strategies for achieving their therapeutic goals. For a practical guide describing the details of the steps for conducting DBT, see Koerner (2012).

Evaluation of DBT   Studies indicate that DBT is effective for treating people with borderline personality disorder (Kliem, Kroger, & Kossfelder, 2010), women with bulimia nervosa (Telch, Agras, & Linehan, 2001), and elderly people with depression (Lynch, Cheavens, Cukrowicz, Thorp, Bronner, & Beyer, 2007).

Questions for Learning

17. What is *mindfulness* as Buddhists and behavior therapists use the term?
18. What is *acceptance* as cognitive behavior therapists use the term?
19. Briefly describe the three phases of ACT.
20. What are three differences between cognitive therapy and ACT?
21. Briefly explain one of the assumptions of the philosophy of dialectics.
22. What are two of the reasons that Linehan added the term *dialectical* to her approach to behavior therapy?
23. Briefly describe several of the therapeutic phases of DBT.

A Behavioral Interpretation of Aspects of the Therapies in This Chapter

As indicated in Chapter 3, two important categories of behaviors are respondent and operant. As discussed in Chapter 15, much of what we call "thinking" and "feeling" in everyday life can be described in terms of these two fundamental behavioral categories. Also, as indicated in Chapter 15, we assume that the principles and procedures of operant and respondent conditioning apply to private as well as to public behavior. In a number of examples in this book, private behavior was modified to bring about desired changes in public behavior. In no case, however, was it necessary to assume that private behavior is fundamentally different from public behavior. On the contrary, the treatments used were based on the assumption that the same general principles and procedures are applicable to both private and public behavior. From this point of view, we reexamine some aspects of the therapies in this chapter.

Why Might Cognitive Restructuring Be Effective?

As previously discussed in this chapter, cognitive therapists believe that faulty thinking is the cause of emotional and behavioral problems, and thus the primary focus of cognitive therapy is to change faulty thinking. Although research has indicated that the cognitive restructuring is not the effective component of cognitive therapy, Beck and his colleagues (e.g., Hofmann, Asmundson, & Beck, 2013) have argued that this research is invalid. There may be some cases in which cognitive restructuring is effective. As discussed in Chapter 15, it is possible that some self-statements could function as CSs to elicit the respondent components of anxiety, anger, and other emotions. Consider the case of Jim, the student who overslept, cut himself while shaving, and later got stuck in traffic. Instances of Jim's irrational self-talk such as "I'm a walking disaster!" or "Why does the worst always happen to me?" might function as CSs to elicit the respondent components of anxiety or anger. His self-statements might also be analyzed in terms of rule-governed behavior. You will recall from Chapter 17 that a *rule* is a description of a contingency in which in a given situation a certain response will produce certain consequences. The statement of a rule such as "If I study my behavior modification text for 3 hours tonight, I'll do well on my behavior modification test tomorrow" can exert control over behavior as it can influence you to study your behavior modification text for 3 hours. From a behavioral perspective, cognitive restructuring deals largely with rule-governed behavior (Poppen, 1989; Zettle & Hayes, 1982). Jim's irrational self-talk might be thought of as faulty rules. His statement "I always screw up" implies the rule: "If I attempt this task I will encounter failure." Such a rule might cause him to avoid a variety of tasks that he is capable of performing. A cognitive therapist might dispute such irrational self-statements, challenge Jim to replace them with rational self-statements, and give him homework assignments that would support rational thinking. For example, Jim might rehearse such rules as "I do some things quite well. I'll follow the computer assignment instructions carefully so that I can complete the assignment by the deadline." Such rules would counteract his irrational self-talk ("I always screw up") and would likely lead to behavior that will be reinforced. The therapist will have helped Jim to replace inaccurate rules with more accurate ones, and the natural environment is likely to maintain behavior appropriate to the more accurate rules.

Now consider other types of irrational thinking. According to Ellis and Grieger (1977), irrational thinking also includes categories referred to as "awfulizing" (e.g., "It's absolutely awful that I lost my job") and "musterbation" (e.g., "I must get a job or I'm a rotten person"). When a client expresses such thoughts, an REBT therapist might challenge the client ("Why is it awful?" or "Just because you don't have a job doesn't make you a rotten person"). Even though the client might learn to express that being without work is not awful, she still is out of work, which is not good. In such cases, cognitive restructuring is unhelpful (e.g., see Figure 27.1). The client has not been given a set of rules (e.g., "I'll check the want ads," "I'll go to the employment agency") that are likely to lead to effective action that the natural environment will maintain. Even if the client has been given clear rules for effective behavior, he or she might be deficient in the necessary behaviors such as time management, assertiveness, or persistence, that are needed to find a job. Thus, in some cases of cognitive restructuring, the rules might be ineffective because (a) they don't identify specific circumstances for specific behaviors that lead to supportive environmental consequences or (b) the client is deficient in the behaviors specified by the rules.

In summary, cognitive restructuring techniques from a behavioral point of view might be effective when (a) they decrease the frequency of irrational self-statements that elicit the respondent component of troublesome emotions and (b) they teach a client to rehearse rules through verbal discourse and homework assignments that identify specific circumstances for specific behaviors that are likely to be maintained in the natural environment.

Why Might Self-Instruction and Problem-Solving Training Be Effective?

These approaches teach rule-governed behavior that leads to effective consequences. Teaching a student who is nervous about giving a speech in class to (a) recognize the fact that she is nervous, (b) emit some coping self-statements, and (c) self-instruct the steps for taking appropriate action is essentially giving the student a set of rules to follow. If the rules govern the behavior successfully (the student gives the speech and receives positive feedback), then the use of those rules will have been strengthened. Because there is a focus on performing the behavior successfully, there is a greater chance of successful behavior change than if the focus had just been on self-instructions alone. Similarly, in problem-solving, whereas the first three steps (general orientation, problem definition, and generation of alternatives) involve self-talk, the last three steps (decision making, implementation, and verification) require the individual to take action and solve the problem. Once again, self-talk that is appropriately linked to overt behaviors and to supportive environmental consequences is more likely to be effective than self-talk that is not.

Why Might Mindfulness and Acceptance-Based Procedures Be Effective?

One possibility is that nonjudgmentally observing ongoing sensations displaces the behavior of irrational thinking and the negative emotions elicited by it. In Jim's case, if he had observed mindfully how his heart was racing or how tightly he was gripping the steering wheel, when he was stuck in traffic, he might have been less likely to make irrational statements to himself (e.g., "Why does the worst always happen to me?") that had previously elicited negative emotions. As another example, in the lead case in Chapter 18 in which James was taught to mindfully focus on the soles of his feet when he felt anger, doing so likely replaced the thoughts that elicited angry feelings.

A second possibility relates to the differences between contingency-shaped and rule-governed behavior. Mindfulness and acceptance involve exposure to natural contingencies, and the awareness and nonjudgmental acceptance of one's sensations would appear to be largely contingency-shaped behavior (Hayes, 2004). In contrast, cognitive restructuring deals largely with rule-governed behavior. Contingency-shaped behavior has been described as natural, reactive, and intuitive (Baldwin & Baldwin, 2000) whereas rule-governed behavior tends to be inflexible and rigid (Hayes, 1989). Thus, when a client can accept the sensations characteristic of troublesome thoughts and emotions as experiences to be embraced, exposure to natural contingencies is more likely to modify such behavior.

A third possibility is that once the client accepts the sensations characteristic of troublesome thoughts and emotions as simply responses and nothing more, that person might then be more amenable to identifying various life values, articulating concrete goals (i.e., rules) that represent those values, and committing to specific behaviors to achieve those goals. In this way the person has broken a vicious cycle in which negative thoughts elicit negative emotions which evoke further negative thoughts, and so on. Stated simply, it might be that once a client accepts irrational thinking and troublesome emotions as "no big deal," then the person can more easily "get on with life." Thus, it appears that ACT and DBT use strategies to enhance contingency-shaped behavior early in therapy, and then capitalize on both rule-governed and contingency-shaped behavior later in therapy.

Concluding Comments

Although cognitive restructuring and mindfulness and acceptance procedures are often said to be directed toward modifying thoughts, beliefs, and attitudes, their distinguishing characteristic seems to be that they deal with private verbal behavior and imagery as well as with public behavior. They do not appear to involve any behavior principles besides those discussed in the previous chapters of this book. All behavior practitioners should be open to innovative procedures for helping people change their behavior. At the same time, as this chapter has pointed out, looking at such procedures from a consistent behavioral viewpoint has practical as well as theoretical advantages. In addition, it is especially important that, whenever possible, practitioners use procedures that have been validated in the research literature and avoid those that have not been validated. This point receives further emphasis in the following chapter.

Questions for Learning

24. Give an example that illustrates how a person's self-statements (operant thinking) can function as CSs to elicit the respondent components of an emotion. (You might want to review Chapter 15.)
25. Give an example that illustrates how a person's self-statements might exert rule-governed control over that person's behavior. (You might want to review Chapter 17.)
26. Give an example that illustrates how cognitive therapists capitalize on rule-governed behavior to help their clients.
27. From a behavioral point of view, summarize why cognitive restructuring techniques might be effective.
28. What is one explanation of why both self-instruction and problem-solving training might be effective therapeutic techniques?
29. Briefly describe three behavioral explanations that might explain why mindfulness and acceptance-based procedures are therapeutic.
30. Discuss whether reputable behavior modifiers deny the existence and importance of thoughts and feelings.

Application Exercise

Self-Modification Exercise

Consider a situation in which you sometimes experience negative thinking (e.g., thinking about your future, a relationship, work, your performance in a course). In a sentence, describe the general theme around which negative thinking occurs. Then write down 10 different types of thoughts (these could be self-statements, images, or a mixture of the two) that you experience when thinking negatively about that particular topic or theme. Next, for each negative thought, describe an alternative positive thought or coping self-statement that you might practice to counteract the negative thought. Your coping thoughts should be realistic, positive, and specific, and should relate to specific positive outcomes.

Notes for Further Learning

1. ACT is based on an approach referred to as *relational frame theory* (RFT; Hayes, Barnes-Holmes, & Roche, 2001). RFT builds on research on forming equivalence classes discussed in Chapter 9. In general, relational framing is responding in certain ways to a set of arbitrary stimuli that are related to each other by some linguistic phrase or "frame" (e.g., a dime *is worth more than* a nickel). In other words, even though a dime is smaller than a nickel in terms of actual size, we have arbitrarily designated the dime as being worth more.
   Relational frames exhibit three characteristics. First, they exhibit *bidirectionality* also referred to as *mutual entailment*. For example, if you have learned that two nickels equal a dime, then you will have also learned that a dime equals two nickels. Second, relational frames show *combinatorial entailment*. If a child learns that a dime is worth more than a nickel and a quarter is worth more than a dime, the child will also have learned that a quarter is worth more than a nickel. Third, relational frames display *transformation of stimulus functions*. Suppose that the written word *dog*, the spoken word *dog,* and an actual dog have through training become a stimulus equivalence class for a child. Suppose further that a dog approaches the child and barks loudly, scaring the child. The sight of the dog now functions to cause fear. That function will also be transferred to related stimuli so that the child will now feel fear when hearing someone say "dog" or when reading the word *dog*. For Hayes and colleagues, relational framing is the essence of verbal behavior and is the characteristic that sets humans apart from other animals. Nonhuman animals show stimulus generalization to different stimuli provided that the stimuli have some physical characteristic in common, such as learning the concepts red, tree, or people (see Chapter 9). Humans, however, show stimulus generalization across members of an equivalence class even though the members are very different physically. This effect, along with the transformation of stimulus functions among related stimuli, leads to relational framing, which allows us to talk and think about events that are not present, to analyze pros and cons of possible outcomes, and to select courses of action to solve problems. Unfortunately, relational framing can also cause troublesome emotions with respect to stimuli that are not present, such as excessive regret or remorse about events in the remote past and excessive and unproductive worrying about potential events in the distant future. For reviews of RFT, see Volume 19 (2003) of *The Analysis of Verbal Behavior* and Palmer (2004). For a professional level book covering RFT and its applications, see Dymond and Roche (2013)

2. Another method for treating persistent disturbing thoughts is *thought-stopping* (Wolpe, 1958). Consider the case of Carol (Martin, 1982). After being engaged for 3 years, Carol's fiancé, Fred, left her for another woman. Carol suffered from frequent, obsessive thoughts about Fred. She agreed to try thought-stopping. To teach Carol how to use this process, the therapist first instructed her to close her eyes, think about Fred, and raise her finger when she was beginning to feel unhappy. When she did so, the therapist yelled, "Stop!" Carol was startled, immediately opened her eyes, and thoughts about Fred ceased. The therapist and Carol repeated this routine twice more. The therapist then instructed Carol to think about Fred, and when she visualized him clearly, she should yell, "Stop!" herself. Carol followed this routine, and once again, thoughts of Fred immediately ceased. Carol followed this routine on two more trials, which taught her that she could at least temporarily cease thinking about Fred by yelling "Stop!" The therapist then instructed Carol to once more think about Fred, but this time, when clearly visualizing him, she should imagine yelling "Stop!" silently to herself. Carol followed this instruction successfully and repeated it on two more trials. The therapist then explained to Carol that thought-stopping involves two phases: (a) first terminating the distressing thoughts and (b) then thinking competing adaptive thoughts. To implement these phases, Carol agreed that each time she experienced a thought characteristic of those that upset her, she would stop doing what she was doing, clasp her hands, close her eyes, and silently yell "Stop!" to herself. Then she would open her eyes and from her purse take five photographs of herself in a happy mood or situation. She would look at each of the photographs, one at a time, and then turn them over and read statements on the back that prompted her to think positive thoughts. The therapist also instructed her to vary the positive thoughts when viewing the photographs at different times. After following this procedure for several weeks, thoughts about Fred decreased to a very low level, and Carol decided that she no longer needed help. Thought-stopping is often used as part of a treatment package for decreasing troublesome thoughts.

3. At the beginning of this chapter, we indicated that behavior therapy has been referred to as the first wave or generation of behavioral approaches to therapy, cognitive behavior therapy as the second wave or generation, and ACT as a major example of the third wave or generation. How do representatives of each wave or generation perceive the others? In 2007 at the annual meeting of the Association for Behavioral and Cognitive Therapies, two representatives of each wave or generation participated in a panel discussion. Their comments reflected interesting agreements and disagreements, which can be found in the Winter, 2008 issue (No. 8) of the *Behavior Therapist* (see DiGiuseppe, 2008; Hayes, 2008; Leahy, 2008; Moran, 2008; O'Brien, 2008; and Salzinger, 2008). In 2013, the journal *Behavior Therapy* published a series edited by David M. Fresco (2013) in which therapists from the ACT and the traditional cognitive behavior therapy perspectives (Hayes, Levin, Plumb-Vilardaga, Villatte, & Pistorello, 2013; Hofmann, Asmundson, & Beck, 2013) provided target articles. The target articles were followed by the responses of commentators from each perspective (Dobson, 2013; Herbert & Forman, 2013; Kanter, 2013; Rector, 2013), and finally by a synthesis of the series articles (Mennin, Ellard, Fresco, & Gross, 2013). As with the 2007 panel discussion, their comments reflected interesting agreements and disagreements, which can be found in the March 2013 issue (No. 2) of *Behavior Therapy*. The major point of agreement for both cognitive behavior and ACT therapists is that cognitions can affect overt behavior. Points of contention included whether there really are three clearly defined waves or generations of behavior therapy, whether there is convincing evidence that ACT is more effective than other forms of cognitive or cognitive behavior therapy, whether cognitive behavior therapists already do what ACT therapists do although under different labels, and whether ACT is defined with sufficient rigor to be reliably applied and scientifically tested. For a study of the similarities and differences between practitioners of second- and third-wave/generation behavior therapies, see Brown, Gaudiano, and Miller (2011).

Questions for Further Learning

1. With an example, illustrate the bidirectionality aspect of relational framing.
2. With an example, illustrate the combinatorial entailment aspect of relational framing.
3. With an example, illustrate how relational framing involves transformation of stimulus functions among related stimuli.
4. Briefly describe the three steps that a therapist might follow in teaching a client to use thought-stopping to terminate distressing thoughts.

CHAPTER 28

Psychological Disorders Treated by Behavioral and Cognitive Behavioral Therapies

LEARNING OBJECTIVES

After studying this chapter, you will be able to briefly describe common behavioral treatments for:

- specific phobias.
- panic disorder and agoraphobia.
- generalized anxiety disorder.
- obsessive-compulsive disorder.
- posttraumatic stress disorder.
- depression.
- alcohol problems.
- obesity.
- couple distress.
- low sexual desire.
- habit disorders.

From the early 1900s to the present, many types of psychotherapy have been developed. Each proponent of a particular type of psychotherapy, from Freud on, has argued that his or her treatment is effective and that the others are less effective or ineffective. Over time, persistent questions have been raised regarding which psychological treatments, if any, are effective, for which kinds of disorders are they effective, and for which types of clients. To address these questions, the American Psychological Association (APA) has started promoting the policy that decisions regarding the professional activities of psychologists should be based on scientifically valid data. In 2005, APA established a task force to make recommendations and provide guidelines on how best to incorporate scientific research evidence into psychological practice (APA Presidential Task Force on Evidence-Based Practice, 2006). A major recommendation of the task

NOTE 1 force was that clinical psychologists should use **empirically supported treatments (ESTs)**—"specific treatments that have been shown to be efficacious in controlled clinical trials" (p. 273 of the report). Often ESTs are behavioral or cognitive behavioral treatments, primarily because—as discussed in Chapter 1— the behavioral approach emphasizes basing treatments on well-established principles, measuring the outcomes of treatments in objectively defined behaviors, and altering treatments that are not producing satisfactory results.

Following the report of the above-mentioned task force, the clinical division of APA—Division 12, Society of Clinical Psychology—set up the following website to inform a wide audience—including psychologists, potential clients, students, and the general public—about research-supported treatments for various psychological disorders: www.psychologicaltreatments.org/

This website lists a number of psychological disorders, treatments that have been applied to those disorders, and the level of published research support for those treatments. For each disorder and treatment listed, two levels of research support are indicated: (a) strong research support and (b) modest research support. *Strong research support* is defined as a treatment for which "well-designed studies conducted by independent investigators...converge to support a treatment's efficacy." *Modest research support* is defined as a treatment for which "one well-designed study or two or more adequately designed studies... support [the] treatment's efficacy." A treatment not being listed as having research support does not necessarily mean that the treatment is ineffective. It simply means that there is not enough published research evidence to support its efficacy at either the first or second levels at this time. It should also be noted that even if a treatment is listed as having strong or modest research support for treating a given disorder, this does not mean that it will be effective for all individuals suffering from that disorder. It only means that under certain controlled conditions the treatment has been demonstrated to be more effective than no treatment or an appropriate control procedure.

This chapter provides examples of disorders that have been treated with behavior and cognitive behavior therapies. Information about treatments and their research support provided by the above website was used extensively in preparing this chapter. Because the Society of Clinical Psychology Website on Research-Supported Psychological Treatments is updated regularly, it is important to note the date the website was accessed on April 29, 2014, just before this book went to press. Individuals who are interested in the most up-to-date information on this topic are encouraged to consult above website.

As with the previous chapter, the intention of this chapter is not to teach you how to assess, diagnose, or treat the disorders discussed in this chapter. Only trained professionals must perform these activities. Instead, the purpose of this chapter is to provide general information about how qualified behavior therapists treat various disorders and to relate that information to the behavioral principles and procedures discussed in previous chapters. Behavioral and cognitive behavioral treatments of the disorders discussed in this chapter have received detailed coverage elsewhere (e.g., Antony & Barlow, 2010; Barlow, 2008; Beck, 2011; Lambert, 2013; Pear & Simister, in press).

It should be noted that pharmaceutical treatments are available for some of the problems covered in this chapter. While drugs alone can sometimes be an effective treatment, many studies show that they are more effective in combination with behavior therapy or cognitive behavior therapy. Given that drugs often have unwanted side effects, it is usually considered desirable to avoid their use when behavioral or cognitive behavior therapy is a viable alternative. See Flora (2007) for an excellent discussion of how drugs are frequently overused in the treatment of psychological problems that would be more safely and effectively treated by behavioral procedures alone.

The clinical disorders covered in this chapter are representative of the types of disorders behavior and cognitive behavior therapists treat. Because these clinical problems are not independent, clients often have more than one—a condition known as *co-morbidity*. Treatment is generally not as straightforward when co-morbidity is present. For simplicity, this chapter assumes the client suffers from only one of the conditions discussed.

Specific Phobias

Many people have such intense fears that they become virtually incapacitated by them. A person might have such an intense fear of heights that walking up a single flight of stairs or looking out a second-story window causes acute anxiety. Another person might be afraid to go into public places because of being terrified of crowds. Trying to convince these people that their fears are irrational often has no beneficial effect. They usually know that their fears have no rational basis and would like to eliminate them, but they cannot because the fears are automatically elicited by specific stimuli. An intense, irrational, incapacitating fear of a stimulus class is called a *specific phobia*. Specific phobias are classed as animal type (e.g., fear of dogs, birds, spiders), natural environment type (e.g., fear of heights, storms), blood–injury–injection type (e.g., fear of seeing blood, having an operation), situational type (e.g., enclosed spaces, flying), and other type (any specific phobia not included in the preceding list).

Questions for Learning

1. What are empirically supported therapies (ESTs)?
2. Why do empirically supported therapies often turn out to be behavioral or cognitive behavioral therapies?
3. What is a specific phobia?
4. List three classes of specific phobias, and give two examples of each.

Treatment   The Division 12 website on research-supported psychological treatments lists exposure therapies as having strong research support for the treatment of specific phobias. According to the website, "Exposure-based therapies reflect a variety of behavioral approaches that are all based on exposing the phobic individuals to the stimuli that frighten them." The major behavior treatments for specific phobias are discussed below (for additional information on the treatment of specific phobias, see Emmelkamp, 2013, pp. 345–346; Zalta & Foa, 2012, pp. 80–83).

Systematic Desensitization   Joseph Wolpe (1958) developed the earliest behavioral treatment for specific phobias. He hypothesized that the irrational fear characteristic of a phobia is a respondently conditioned response to the feared object or situation (described in Chapter 15). From this hypothesis Wolpe reasoned that he could eliminate the irrational fear response if he could establish a response to the feared stimulus that counteracted or opposed the fear response. In other words, he decided to treat the phobia by exposing the client to the feared stimulus while conditioning another response to it. You may recall from Chapter 3 that this process is called *counterconditioning*. A fear-antagonistic response that Wolpe found suitable for this purpose was relaxation. He further reasoned that when counterconditioning the fear response, the therapist should be careful not to elicit the fear response all at once in its full intensity, as too much fear in the therapy session would interfere with the process. Given this rationale, Wolpe might have called his treatment *systematic counterconditioning*. However, he gave it the name *systematic desensitization*.

Systematic desensitization is a procedure for overcoming a phobia by having a client in a relaxed state successively imagine the items in a fear hierarchy. A **fear hierarchy** is a list of fear-eliciting stimuli arranged in order from the least to the most fear-eliciting. In the first phase of systematic desensitization, the therapist helps the client construct a fear hierarchy—a list of approximately 10–25 stimuli related to the feared stimulus. With help from the therapist, the client orders the stimuli from those that cause the least fear to those that cause the most. An actual example of a fear hierarchy constructed with a client is shown in Table 28.1.

In the next phase, the client learns a deep-muscle relaxation procedure that requires tensing and relaxing a set of muscles. This tension–relaxation strategy is applied to muscles of all major areas of

---

TABLE 28.1   Example of a Fear-of-Flying Hierarchy

1. The plane has landed and stopped at the terminal. I get off the plane and enter the terminal, where I met my friends.
2. A trip has been planned, and I have examined the possible methods of travel and decided "out loud" to travel by plane.
3. I have called the travel agent and told him of my plans. He gives me the times and flight numbers.
4. It is the day before the trip. I pack my suitcase, close it, and lock it.
5. It is 10 days before the trip. I receive the tickets in the mail. I note the return address, open the envelope, and check the tickets for the correct dates, times, and flight numbers.
6. It is the day of the flight. I am leaving home. I lock the house, put the bags in the car, and make sure that I have the tickets and money.
7. I am driving to the airport for my flight. I am aware of every plane I see. As I get close to the airport, I see several planes—some taking off, some landing, and some just sitting on the ground by the terminal.
8. I am entering the terminal. I am carrying my bags and tickets.
9. I proceed to the airline desk, wait in line, and have the agent check my tickets and then weigh and check my bags.
10. I am in the lounge with many other people, some with bags also waiting for flights. I hear the announcements over the intercom and listen for my flight number to be called.
11. I hear my flight number announced, and I proceed to the security checkpoint with my hand luggage.
12. I approach the airline desk beyond the security checkpoint, and the agent asks me to choose a seat from the "map" of the plane.
13. I walk down the ramp leading to the plane and enter the door of the plane.
14. I am now inside the plane. I look at the interior of the plane and walk down the aisle, looking for my seat number. I then move in from the aisle and sit down in my assigned seat.
15. The plane is in flight, and I decide to leave my seat and walk to the washroom at the back of the plane.
16. I notice the seat-belt signs light up, so I fasten my seat belt and I notice the sound of the motors starting.
17. The passengers have their seat belts fastened and the plane slowly moves away from the terminal.
18. I notice the seat-belt signs are again lighted, and the pilot announces that we are preparing to land.
19. I am looking out the window and suddenly the plane enters clouds and I cannot see out the window.
20. The plane has stopped at the end of the runway and is sitting, waiting for instructions to take off.
21. The plane is descending to the runway for a landing. I feel the speed and see the ground getting closer.
22. The plane has taken off from the airport and banks as it changes direction. I am aware of the "tilt."
23. The plane starts down the runway, and the motors get louder as the plane increases speed and suddenly lifts off.

Source: This example is based on a case described by Roscoe, Martin, and Pear (1980).

the body (arms, neck, shoulders, and legs). After several sessions, the client is able to relax deeply in a matter of minutes. During the third phase, the actual therapy begins. At the direction of the therapist, the client while relaxing clearly imagines the least fear-eliciting scene in the hierarchy for a few seconds, then stops imagining it and continues relaxing for about 15–30 seconds. This is repeated. Then the next scene is presented and repeated in the same way. This continues over sessions until the last scene in the hierarchy is presented. If at any point the client experiences anxiety (communicated to the therapist by raising the index finger), the therapist returns the client to a previous step or inserts an intermediate scene. When all the scenes in the hierarchy have been completed, the client can usually encounter the feared stimuli without distress. The positive reinforcement the client then receives for interacting with the previously feared stimuli helps to maintain continued interactions with those stimuli.

Although systematic desensitization is normally carried out by having the client imagine the feared stimuli, it can also be conducted *in vivo*—from the Latin "in life" or, in other words, in the presence of the actual stimuli that elicit fear in the natural environment. *In vivo* exposure is often used when clients have difficulty imagining scenes. It also has the advantage of eliminating the need to program generalization from imagined scenes to actual situations. However, it is usually less time-consuming and less costly for a client to imagine feared scenes in a hierarchical order than to arrange *in vivo* hierarchical exposure to them.

For reasons that are not entirely clear given its proven effectiveness in numerous studies, systematic desensitization has lost popularity among therapists. One reason might be its emphasis on covert or private behavior (i.e., imagery) as opposed to overt behavior, which tends to be favored by behaviorists. In addition, because of its stimulus-response emphasis, systematic desensitization does not appeal to cognitively oriented therapists. (For further discussion of these points, see McGlynn, Smitherman, & Gothard, 2004.)

Flooding   Flooding is a method for extinguishing fear by exposure to a strongly feared stimulus for an extended period of time. Whereas the model for systematic desensitization is counterconditioning, the model for flooding is extinction. That is, the basic assumption behind flooding is that if the client is exposed to the feared stimulus, is not allowed to escape from it, and no aversive event follows, then the fear response to that stimulus will extinguish. Flooding is carried out either *in vivo* or through imagery. *In vivo* is generally preferred because in theory it should maximize generalization, there is evidence that both methods are equally effective (Borden, 1992).

As the name *flooding* suggests, the treatment involves eliciting the fear at or close to its full intensity. However, the procedure may involve graded levels of exposure if the distress experienced by the client is too overwhelming. A fear of heights, for example, might be treated by having the client look out the window on the first floor, then the third floor, then the seventh floor, and finally the top of a 10-story building. Thus, except for the absence of an explicit relaxation procedure, flooding can be very similar to desensitization. (For a special issue on new methods in exposure therapy for anxiety disorders, see *Behavior Modification*, 2013, Vol. 37, No. 3.)

Participant Modeling   Participant modeling is a method for decreasing fear in which a client imitates another individual approaching a feared object. As the procedure's name suggests, both the client and therapist are participating together in the feared situation. Participant modeling is typically carried out in a graded fashion. For example, if a client has a fear of birds, the client watches the therapist observe a budgie in a cage about 10 feet away. The client is then encouraged to imitate this behavior and is praised for doing so. After several trials, the process is repeated at a distance of 5 feet from the bird, then 2 feet, then beside the cage, then with the cage door open, and finally ending with the budgie perched on the client's finger.

Nonexposure Approaches   Systematic desensitization, flooding, and participant modeling are NOTE 2 *exposure-based therapies,* in that they involve exposure—either in imagination or *in vivo*—of the client to the feared stimulus or stimuli. Although nonexposure methods have been used, they are not listed on the Division 12 website for research-supported treatments as being efficacious. However, if an individual with claustrophobia (fear of being in closed spaces, such as elevators) is making self-statements such as "I'm going to be trapped" or "I'm going to suffocate," cognitive therapy is a nonexposure therapy that may reduce the believability of these self-statements and thus eliminate or greatly reduce the phobia (Booth & Rachman, 1992; Shafran, Booth, & Rachman, 1993). ACT, another nonexposure therapy, described in Chapter 27, has also been used in the treatment of specific phobias. Forsyth and Eifert (2007) have prepared a self-help guide for individuals to use ACT to overcome anxiety, phobias, and excessive worrying. Also, Antony and Norton (2009) have described step-by-step strategies for individuals suffering from anxiety problems, including phobias, to use cognitive behavioral procedures to overcome their anxiety problems.

Questions for Learning

5. What is a fear hierarchy?
6. Define systematic desensitization.
7. Using an example, briefly describe the three phases of systematic desensitization of a specific phobia.
8. Describe the fundamental difference between flooding and systematic desensitization.
9. Briefly illustrate an example of how *in vivo* flooding might be used to treat a specific phobia.
10. Briefly illustrate an example of how participant modeling might be used to treat a specific phobia.
11. What is the defining characteristic of exposure-based therapies? Give an example of a nonexposure therapy?

Other Anxiety Disorders

Anxiety disorders are characterized by (a) fear or anxiety that results in physiological changes such as sweaty hands, trembling, dizziness, and heart palpitations; (b) the escape and/or avoidance of situations in which the fear is likely to occur; and (c) interference by the unwanted behaviors with the individual's life. For a discussion of how contemporary learning principles and research can explain the etiology of anxiety disorders, see Mineka and Zinbarg (2006) and Mineka and Oehlberg (2008). Anxiety disorders are classified into several broad categories, including specific phobias, panic disorder and agoraphobia, generalized anxiety disorder, obsessive-compulsive disorder, and posttraumatic stress disorder. Having already considered specific phobias, we now consider the other four.

Panic Disorder and Agoraphobia

Panic disorder is a susceptibility to panic attacks, which are intense fear experiences that seem to come "out of the blue" with no precipitating stimulus or cue. These attacks include four or more of the following symptoms: (a) heart-rate abnormalities, including extremely rapid heart beat, heart palpitations, and pounding heart; (b) sweating; (c) trembling; (d) shortness of breath or feeling of being smothered; (e) feelings of choking; (f) chest pain or discomfort; (g) nausea or extreme abdominal discomfort; (h) dizziness or feeling light-headed or faint; (i) feeling of unreality; (j) numbness or tingling sensation; (k) chills or hot flushes; (l) fear of going crazy or losing control; and (m) fear of dying.

Agoraphobia—which literally means fear of the marketplace—is an intense fear of going out in public or leaving the confines of one's home. People who suffer from panic disorder frequently also have agoraphobia because they are afraid of having a panic attack in public or outside of their home. This can lead to a self-fulfilling prophecy in which the fear of having a panic attack actually generates the attack. To paraphrase Franklin D. Roosevelt's famous words, what a person with panic disorder fears most is fear itself.

Treatment The Division 12 website on research-supported psychological treatments lists cognitive behavioral therapy as having strong research support and applied relaxation as having modest research support for the treatment of panic disorder with or without agoraphobia.

Cognitive behavioral treatment typically includes a behavioral component involving exposure to feared situations, and a cognitive component to help change the client's misconceptions about panic attacks (Craske & Barlow, 2008). For example, a client may believe that a panic attack will precipitate a heart attack, whereas in fact this outcome is extremely unlikely. In addition, the client may be taught relaxation and thought-stopping techniques to lessen the intensity of a panic attack. (Thought-stopping was described in Note 2 of Chapter 27.)

The behavioral component of treatment would include exposure therapy carried out *in vivo* (Bouman & Emmelkamp, 1996; Emmelkamp, 2013, pp. 346–348; Zalta & Foa, 2012, pp. 83–84). This may be accomplished by having the client first make short trips from home, followed by gradually longer and longer trips.

Generalized Anxiety Disorder

A person with *generalized anxiety disorder* is constantly worrying and feeling intensely anxious about potential events that most people would consider trivial. Such a person is so consumed with anxiety that it interferes with normal functioning, often including the inability to sleep at night.

Treatment   The Division 12 website on research-supported psychological treatments lists cognitive and behavioral therapies as having strong research support for the treatment of generalized anxiety disorder.

The most effective therapies for generalized anxiety disorder appear to be treatment packages that combine cognitive and behavioral strategies (Borkovec & Sharpless, 2004; Dugas & Robichaud, 2006; Emmelkamp, 2013, pp. 352–354; Zalta & Foa, 2012, pp. 86–88). One of the behavioral components is usually exposure therapy. The therapist teaches the client relaxation techniques and then has the client use the start of worrying as a stimulus to relax, which competes with or suppresses worrying. It is difficult to worry while relaxed. In addition, cognitive techniques may be used to challenge and change the client's belief in the importance of the things worried about. Acceptance techniques (see Chapter 27) may also help the client realize that worrying will not make bad events less likely to occur—that is, the client is taught to make self-statements to the effect that worry by itself has no effect on things worried about.

Obsessive-Compulsive Disorder

A person suffering from *obsessive-compulsive disorder* may experience unwanted intrusive thoughts (called an *obsession*) or feel impelled to engage in unproductive repetitive behavior (called a *compulsion*), or both. Unlike a person with a generalized anxiety disorder, a person with obsessive-compulsive disorder worries about a specific thing. In addition, obsessions and compulsions tend to go together in that obsessions seem to cause anxiety that can only be reduced by engaging in compulsive behavior. For example an office worker leaving work might worry about someone breaking into the office overnight, feel extremely anxious about it, and check and recheck the office door many more times than the average person would before finally leaving.

Some other common examples of obsessive-compulsive behaviors are obsessing about catching a terrible disease from germs, resulting in constant hand washing; obsessing about hitting a pedestrian, leading to constantly retracing one's route while driving to make sure there are no injured pedestrians lying on or beside the road; and obsessing about hurting one's children, leading to avoiding using knives and other potentially dangerous objects in their presence.

Treatment   The Division 12 website on research-supported psychological treatments lists exposure and response prevention and cognitive therapy as having strong research support and ACT as having modest research support for the treatment of obsessive-compulsive disorder.

During *in vivo* exposure and response prevention (Emmelkamp, 2013, pp. 354–356; Franklin & Foa, 2008; Zalta & Foa, 2012, pp. 88–89), the client is encouraged to engage in behavior leading to the obsession while being prevented from engaging in the compulsive behavior. Suppose that a client experiences obsessive thoughts about germs when touching unwashed objects, which causes considerable anxiety. Suppose further that engaging in a variety of compulsive washing rituals appears to be maintained by anxiety reduction. An exposure-and-response-prevention treatment would involve asking the client to touch particular "contaminated" objects while refraining from performing the washing ritual. The rationale behind this approach is that having the obsession occur without the subsequent anxiety-reducing compulsive behavior allows the anxiety elicited by the obsession to occur in full strength and hence to extinguish. Often a graduated approach is used. For example, a parent who is obsessed with the fear of harming his children with a knife may be encouraged to go through steps that involve first holding a butter knife in the presence of the children until he or she can do so without thinking harmful thoughts, then a table knife, then a small sharp knife, and finally a large knife.

Cognitive therapy might also be used to change the self-statements the client makes that help to maintain the obsession (Taylor, Abramowitz, & McKay, 2010). For example, a person who is deathly afraid of germs might be taught to say privately that proper hand washing for 20 seconds is sufficient to protect against germs. Acceptance procedures (see Chapter 27) may help an individual learn that thoughts are not powerful controllers of behavior. The parent who obsesses about harming his children may be taught to regard these thoughts simply as normal "mental garbage" or "mental background noise," with no bearing on the parent's actual feelings about or behavior toward his or her children.

Posttraumatic Stress Disorder

The classic cases of posttraumatic stress disorder occurred during World War I, when many soldiers exposed to artillery bombardment exhibited what was then called "shell shock" (Jones & Wessely, 2005). The ability of these soldiers to function was extremely impaired, and many were branded as cowards. It is now recognized that not only battlefield conditions, but also any severe trauma—such as being physically or sexually abused, being in a serious traffic accident, or witnessing catastrophic events—can produce posttraumatic stress disorder. There are a number of symptoms of posttraumatic stress disorder, including re-experiencing the intense fear that occurred during the trauma, exhibiting other intense psychological reactions such depression, difficulty sleeping, lack of concentration, and impaired daily functioning. The impaired functioning by someone with this disorder appears to be due to the individual's attempts to avoid thinking about the trauma and hence to avoid stimuli that remind the individual of the event. Since there are many such stimuli, the effort to avoid them consumes a large proportion of the individual's time and energy.

Treatment　The Division 12 website on research-supported psychological treatments lists prolonged exposure therapy and cognitive processing therapy as having strong research support for the treatment of posttraumatic stress disorder.

Prolonged exposure therapy involves long-term vicarious exposure to the event(s) that caused the problem (Emmelkamp, 2013, pp. 357–359; Foa, 2000; Zalta & Foa, 2012, pp. 89–91). This may be done in imagination, talking about the traumatic event(s) with a therapist, writing about the traumatic event(s), or both. In this way, the emotionality elicited by stimuli related to the trauma will extinguish and the debilitating attempts to avoid those stimuli will decrease. Cognitive processing therapy (Resick & Schnicke, 1992) combines exposure with cognitive therapy. The cognitive component is directed toward helping the client learn to challenge faulty thinking about the traumatic event(s) and to generate alternative, more balanced thoughts. Research on these and other variations of behavioral treatments for posttraumatic stress disorder are reviewed by Resick, Monson, and Rizvi (2008).

Questions for Learning

12. List and briefly describe four types of anxiety disorder.
13. Briefly describe an effective treatment for panic disorder with agoraphobia.
14. What is the distinction between obsessions and compulsions, and how might they be related?
15. Briefly describe an effective treatment for obsessive-compulsive disorder.
16. Briefly describe, with reference to an example, how cognitive therapy might be used in the treatment of an obsessive-compulsive disorder.
17. Briefly describe, with reference to an example, how acceptance procedures might be used in the treatment of an obsessive-compulsive disorder.
18. In several sentences, describe an effective treatment for posttraumatic stress disorder.

Depression

Everyone has felt depressed at some point. Usually the feeling occurs when some significant or potential reinforcer has been removed from our lives. For example, a poor grade on a test may cause a student to feel depressed because of the potential loss of the prospect of a good grade in a course. Most people get over their depressions fairly quickly as they find other reinforcers to compensate for the lost reinforcers. Some people, however, suffer from what is referred to as clinical depression. For such individuals, their appetite is usually reduced, they experience decreased energy and increased fatigue, they report an impaired ability to think, concentrate, or make decisions, and they often experience a sense of worthlessness or guilt. Moreover, these feelings can last for weeks.

There are two major theories about depression. One is Beck's cognitive theory (Beck, Rush, Shaw, & Emery, 1979), discussed in the previous chapter, which states that depression results from core beliefs called cognitive schemas that lead to negative interpretations of life events. The other, a behavioral theory called *behavioral activation*, states that "individuals become depressed when there is an imbalance of punishment to positive reinforcement in their lives" (Martell, 2008, p. 40). (For a discussion of a behavioral analysis of the causes of depression, see Kantor, Busch, Weeks, & Landes, 2008.)

Treatment   The Division 12 website on research-supported psychological treatments lists a number of treatments with strong and modest research support for depression. Three treatments with strong research support are: behavior therapy/behavioral activation; cognitive therapy; and problem solving therapy.

Behavioral approaches in the 1970s demonstrated some success treating depression by increasing the contingent reinforcers in chronically depressed individuals' lives (Ferster, 1993; Lewinsohn, 1975). One way they did that was by encouraging depressed individuals to seek out reinforcers such as taking up hobbies, reading books, or going to movies. Moreover, Tkachuk and Martin (1999) reported that encouraging individuals with clinical depression to participate in exercise programs is also helpful in reducing depression. Enlisting significant others, such as spouses, to reinforce the behavior of seeking and sampling new reinforcers is another strategy that behavior therapists have tried. Many of our reinforcers are social; that is, they come from other people, and it takes a certain amount of social skills to access these reinforcers. People with depression are often lacking in these skills. Thus a component of therapy for depression often involves teaching the client social skills.

Although behavioral approaches to the treatment of depression had a promising start in the 1970s, they lost momentum in the 1980s when Beck's cognitive therapy became popular. As described in Chapter 27, a major component of Beck's cognitive therapy for depression is cognitive restructuring to help clients overcome faulty thinking. However, in the late 1990s in the wake of studies (e.g., Gortner, Golan, Dobson, & Jacobson, 1998; Jacobson et al., 1996) indicating that the effective ingredient of Beck's cognitive therapy was the homework assignments, not the cognitive restructuring component, there was a resurgence of the behavioral activation approach to the treatment of depression (Dimidjian et al., 2006; Dimidjian, Martell, Addis, & Herman-Dunn, 2008; Emmelkamp, 2013, pp. 359–361; Jacobson, Martell, & Dimidjian, 2001; Kanter & Puspitasari, 2012; Martell, 2008; Martell, Addis, & Dimidjian, 2004; Martell, Addis, & Jacobson, 2001; Polenick & Flora, 2013). The therapy of behavioral activation, which is based on the theory of behavioral activation described above, consists of homework assignments developed for individual clients from a functional analysis (see Chapter 23) of "the antecedents, behaviors, and consequences that form elements of the client's repertoire contributing to depression" (Martell, 2008, p. 42). In a step-by-step procedure, the treatment is designed to block avoidance behaviors that prevent the individual from coming into contact with reinforcing contingencies and to encourages the client to engage in activities identified as reinforcing in the functional analysis. Research indicates that behavioral activation is at least as effective as cognitive therapy in the treatment of depression and prevention of relapse (Dimidjian et al., 2006; Dobson, Hollon, Dimidjian, Schmaling, & Kohlenberg, 2008). For older adults suffering from depression, associated with aging stemming from the decreasing availability of positive reinforcers, behavioral activation may be particularly indicated (Polenick & Flora, 2013).

As indicated in Chapter 27, ACT has also been shown to be an effective treatment for depression (Forman Herbert, Moitra, Yeomans, & Geller, 2007). For a comparison of behavioral activation and ACT in the treatment of depression, see Kantor, Baruch, and Gaynor (2006).

Alcohol and Other Addictive Substance-Use Disorders

Alcohol abuse can have serious short- and long-term negative effects. Other addictive substances have similar harmful effects. According to a report by the National Center on Addiction and Substance Abuse at Columbia University, almost 40 million Americans (almost 16%) from ages 12 and above are addicted to nicotine, alcohol, and other drugs (*Addiction Medicine: Closing the Gap between Science and Practice*, 2012; also see Winerman, 2013). Over 9% of the U.S. population 12 years and above are addicted to substances other than nicotine. Of these, less than 10% receive any treatment for their addictions. Moreover, very few of these receive evidence-based treatment despite the fact that evidence-based treatments are available (e.g., see *Addiction Medicine: Closing the Gap between Science and Practice*, 2012, pp. 102–107; Winerman, 2013, pp. 31–32).

Treatment   The Division 12 website on research-supported psychological treatments lists *behavioral couple therapy for alcohol-use disorders* as having strong support and moderate drinking treatment for alcohol-use disorders as having modest support. The website lists *contingency management (CM)* as having modest research support for alcohol-use and cocaine-use disorders. The website lists a behavioral treatment called "smoking cessation with weight gain prevention" for nicotine use disorder (smoking).

In behavioral couple therapy for alcohol-use disorder, the therapist teaches the partner without the drinking problem to prompt and reinforce nonalcohol drinking behavior of the person who is abusing alcohol. A variety of behavioral procedures are likely to be used, such as behavioral contracts, in which the alcohol abuser earns various reinforcers for staying sober, and cognitive behavioral procedures A number of behavioral and cognitive-behavioral treatments have been developed for alcohol and other substance use disorders (e.g., see Tucker, Murphy, & Kertesz, 2010; Emmelkamp, 2013, pp. 364–369).

Regarding "moderate drinking for alcohol-use disorders," a variety of behavioral treatment procedures have been successful in helping individuals with alcohol-use disorders to learn to drink in moderation (Emmelkamp, 2013, p. 365; Walters, 2000). A program developed by Sobell and Sobell (1993) teaches problem drinkers to use goal setting to drink in moderation, to control "triggers" (either S^Ds or establishing operations) for drinking, to learn problem-solving skills to avoid high-risk situations, to engage in self-monitoring to detect triggers and maintaining consequences of drinking behaviors, and to practice all of these techniques with various homework assignments.

NOTE 3　CM involves developing ways to measure abstinence of an addictive substance and providing reinforcers powerful enough to compete with the addictive substance. For example, breath analysis or a transdermal alcohol sensor is used as a measure of whether the individual has been abstinent from alcohol over a given period of time (e.g., Barnett, Tidey, Murphy, Swift, & Colby, 2011). Common reinforcers in CM programs are lottery tickets, money, and vouchers that can be exchanged for goods and services (Tuten, Jones, Schaeffer, & Stitzer, 2012).

Behavioral programs have incorporated a number of components to treat alcohol and other addictive-substance-use disorders, including: (a) a *motivational interview* in which the therapist asks the client questions about the problem, the answers to which act as MEOs (see Chapter 19) for change (i.e., reduced substance use becomes reinforcing and therefore strengthens behavior that leads to reduced substance use) (Arkowitz, Westra, Miller, & Rollnick, 2008; Miller, 1996); (b) *functional analysis* (see Chapter 23) to identify the antecedents and consequences that prompt and maintain substance use (McCrady, 2008); (c) *coping-skills training* to teach clients to deal with stressors that are thought to cause excessive substance use; (d) *contingency contracting* (see Chapter 26) to provide reinforcers for work, social, and recreational activities that do not involve substance use; and (e) development of self-control strategies to prevent relapse (see Chapter 26). For discussions of these treatment components see Emmelkamp (2013, pp. 364–369), McCrady (2008), and Tucker, Murphy, & Kertesz (2010).

Eating Disorders

Several distinct eating disorders have been identified: (a) *bulimia nervosa*, (b) *anorexia nervosa*, (c) *binge eating disorder*, and (d) *obesity*. In the first two the client is malnourished and obsessed with being thin. An individual with obesity is sufficiently overweight to have health problems. The chief difference between individuals with bulimia nervosa and those with anorexia nervosa is that the former have frequent episodes of binge eating followed by purges, which consist of self-induced vomiting, taking laxatives or enemas, or engaging in exercise or long periods of fasting in an attempt to counteract the effects of binging; whereas individuals with anorexia nervosa rarely eat or eat very little. (For a discussion of causes of eating disorders, see Farmer & Latner, 2007.)

Treatment　The Division 12 website on research-supported psychological treatments lists cognitive behavioral therapy as having strong research support for the treatment of bulimia nervosa, modest/controversial research support for the treatment of anorexia nervosa, and strong research support for the treatment of binge eating disorder, and behavioral weight loss treatment as having strong research support for the treatment of overweight.

Bulimia nervosa and anorexia nervosa have been extremely resistant to treatment. Some success has been achieved with bulimia nervosa by starting with behavioral procedures followed by cognitive procedures (Fairburn, 2008; Fairburn, Cooper, Shafran, & Wilson, 2008). The behavioral procedures involve reinforcement for going for a specified amount of time, which is gradually increased, between binges, and for eating regular meals at specified times. The cognitive procedures involve attempts to counteract the client's unrealistic beliefs about food, weight, and appearance. Most individuals with bulimia nervosa and anorexia nervosa have poor body images. They see themselves as fat when in fact they are usually thin to the point of being malnourished. Both behavioral and cognitive procedures have been considerably less effective with anorexia nervosa. This may be because individuals with anorexia nervosa tend to experience extreme anxiety at any attempt to get them to behave in a way that would be less than perfect in their belief systems.

For overweight and obese clients, whether they binge or not, behavioral procedures are effective in weight reduction (Craighead & Smith, 2010; Faith, Fontaine, Cheskin, & Allison, 2000; Lundgren, 2006). These procedures focus on long-term lifestyle changes in eating habits and exercise, and in attitudes toward both (Faith et al., 2000). The programs tend to be more effective if the emphasis is on choosing the right foods rather than on calorie reduction. Behavioral components of such programs are likely to include: (a) *self-monitoring*, including daily records of foods eaten and their caloric contents, and body weight; (b) *stimulus control*, such as restricting eating at home to a specific location (e.g., the kitchen table); (c) *changing rate of eating*, by having clients put down utensils between bites or take short breaks between courses; (d) *behavioral contracting*, such as having clients sign a contract in which they agree to lose a certain amount of weight in a specified period of time in return for some desired reinforcer (see Chapter 26); and (e) *relapse prevention strategies* (such as those discussed in Chapter 26).

Couple Distress

Couple distress occurs when at least one of the individuals in an intimate relationship is experiencing dissatisfaction with the relationship. There are probably as many specific reasons for couple distress as there are distressed relationships. Behavior therapists, however, generally start with the premise that the underlying cause is that there are more negative than positive interactions or communications in the relationship. For example, while communicating, one partner may tend to make sarcastic or hostile statements that are reciprocated by hostile statements from the other partner, leading to a breakdown in communication (or worse) between the two individuals.

Treatment   The Division 12 website on research-supported psychological treatments lists behavioral couple therapy as having strong research support for alcohol use disorders and depression. As of this writing, however, couple distress per se is not included on the website.

Behavioral couple therapy typically involves a number of components, including the following (Abbott & Snyder, 2010, 2012; Sexton, Datchi, Evans, LaFollette, & Wright, 2013, pp. 622–624; Snyder & Halford, 2012): (a) *instigation of positive exchanges*—each individual is asked to increase behaviors that are pleasing to the other partner (e.g., displaying affection, showing respect, expressing appreciation; see Figure 28.1); (b) *communication training*—each individual is taught to express thoughts

FIGURE 28.1
What behavioral strategies might be used to help couples increase their rate of positive interactions and decrease their rate of negative interactions with each other?

and feelings concerning what is liked and appreciated about the other, to help the other express his or her feelings and to be an effective listener; (c) *problem-solving training*—couples learn to use their communication skills to systematically identify and solve problems and conflicts in their relationship (see problem-solving training in Chapter 27); and (d) *programming generality*—clients learn to monitor their relationship for specific critical signs of a relapse, and to continue using the problem-solving techniques that they learned in therapy. In an approach called *integrative behavioral couple therapy*, some therapists also incorporate acceptance procedures and exercises (see Chapter 27) to teach partners to accept emotional responses that each partner has to the other (Christensen, Sevier, Simpson, & Gattis, 2004; Christensen, Wheeler, & Jacobson, 2008).

Sexual Dysfunction

There are several types of sexual dysfunction. In males the major types are (a) inability to have an erection and (b) premature ejaculation. In females the major types are (a) vaginismus (involuntary spasms of the vagina musculature that interfere with sexual intercourse), (b) dyspareunia (genital pain related to sexual intercourse), (c) inhibited orgasm, and (d) low sexual desire (Vorvick & Storck, 2010).

Treatment   As of this writing, sexual dysfunction is not included on the Division 12 website on research-supported psychological treatments.

There are a number of medical conditions, such as diabetes, that can cause sexual dysfunction. Therefore, it is important for anyone experiencing sexual dysfunction to have a thorough medical examination before any type of treatment program is undertaken. A reasonable working hypothesis for many cases of sexual dysfunction is that anxiety is an important factor. In males the anxiety may be fear of performing poorly, which therefore becomes a self-fulfilling prophecy. In females the anxiety may be fear of the sex act. In either case, exposure programs appear to be most effective. Based on pioneering work by Masters and Johnson (1970), therapists generally recommend that the couple engage in pleasurable stimulation of each other in a relaxing atmosphere without expectation of, or pressure to, engage in intercourse (Leiblum & Rosen, 2000; Wincze & Carey, 2001). Masturbation by the woman may also be encouraged to help her learn to experience organism if that is one of the issues. Thus, both partners shift the goal from performance to that of experiencing pleasure.

Although a common theoretical assumption is that sexual responses are learned (Plaud, 2007), and although behavioral homework assignments have proven effective in treating many cases of sexual dysfunction, one should be cautious about taking an oversimplistic view of this problem. Sexual dysfunction can result from many causes, including medical diseases, relationship difficulties, lifestyle factors, and age-related changes. Wincze, Bach, and Barlow (2008) have described a range of assessments that should be used by a therapist before attempting to treat a case of sexual dysfunction. Since the development of Viagra and other drugs, sexual dysfunction treatment has become increasingly medicalized. Future research is needed to compare the effects of behavior therapies and medical interventions for a variety of sexual dysfunctions.

Habit Disorders

Many people suffer from frequent and repetitive behaviors that are inconvenient and annoying. These may include nail biting, lip biting, knuckle cracking, hair twirling, hair plucking, excessive throat clearing, muscle tics, and stuttering. In many cases these behaviors are similar to the compulsions described earlier in this chapter, except that they are not linked to obsessive thoughts. Many individuals cope with such behaviors on a daily basis. Sometimes however, such behaviors occur with a sufficient frequency or intensity to cause the individual to seek treatment. When that happens, the behavior is referred to as a *habit disorder* (Hansen, Tishelman, Hawkins, & Doepke, 1990).

Treatment   As of this writing, habit disorders are not included on the Division 12 website on research-supported psychological treatments.

A method called *habit reversal* has been used effectively to treat a number of habit disorders (Azrin & Nunn, 1973; Miltenberger, Fuqua, & Woods, 1998; Tolin & Morrison, 2010, p. 623). This method typically consists of three components. First, the client learns to describe and identify the problem behavior. Second, the client learns and practices a behavior that is incompatible with or competes with the problem behavior. The client practices the competing behavior daily in front of a mirror and also engages in it immediately after an occurrence of the problem behavior. Third, for motivation, the client reviews the inconvenience caused by the disorder, records and graphs the behavior, and has a family member provide reinforcement for engaging in the treatment.

Questions for Learning

19. Briefly describe the behavioral characteristics of clinical depression.
20. What is the behavioral theory of depression referred to as behavioral activation? In a sentence, state what is behavioral activation treatment for depression designed to do?
21. What are the components of Sobell and Sobell's program for problem drinkers.
22. Briefly describe four components of a behavioral treatment for alcohol dependency.
23. Briefly describe four types of eating disorders. For which has behavior therapy been most effective?
24. List and briefly describe four behavioral strategies for treating obesity?
25. List and briefly describe four components of behavioral couples therapy.
26. Describe a general behavioral approach to the treatment of sexual dysfunction.
27. Describe the three components of habit reversal used to treat a habit disorder.

Notes for Further Learning

1. While efforts to establish a list of empirically supported treatments (ESTs) that have proved to be effective in scientifically conducted clinical trials is laudatory, the effort has been met with criticism and has led to recommendations to improve the scientific viability of the process. Discussion of these topics can be found in a special issue of *Behavior Modification* (2003, Vol. 27, No. 3). Also see Hjørland (2011). Two major criticisms of the current emphasis on ESTs is that it detracts from the underlying scientific theory of the treatments and that it tends to decrease the practitioner's autonomy to exercise his or her best expert judgment. There is also the opposite problem; namely, the difficulty of influencing practitioners to learn about the ESTs. For discussions of challenges facing the promotion and dissemination of ESTs, see Kazdin (2008), Rego et al. (2009) and a special issue of *Behavior Modification* (2009, Vol. 33, No. 1) dealing with this topic.

2. A form of exposure therapy that has produced encouraging results is virtual reality therapy (e.g., Emmelkamp, 2013, pp. 345–346; Lamson, 1997; McLay et al., 2012; North, North, & Coble, 1997; Riva, Wiederhold, & Molinari, 1998; Rothbaum et al., 1995; Rothbaum et al., 2006; Wiederhold & Wiederhold, 2004; Winerman, 2005). This involves exposing individuals to realistic computer-generated anxiety-eliciting stimuli, such as images of numerous crawling spiders to treat cases of arachnophobia and traumatic combat experiences to treat posttraumatic stress disorder.

3. Other substance-use disorders that appear also to have been effectively treated with CM include heroin and nicotine use disorders (Emmelkamp, 2013, pp. 368–369; Higgins et al., 2007; also see the *Journal of Applied Behavior Analysis*, 2008, 41[4]—"Special Issue on the Behavior Analysis and Treatment of Drug Addiction"). Accurate measurements of substance use are extremely important in effectively applying CM. Analysis of CO levels in the breath is used as a measure of whether an individual has refrained from smoking, since smoking temporarily increases CO levels in the lungs. Urine samples are used to measure abstinence from opiate drugs. Data indicate that CM increases abstinence dramatically in many individuals with alcohol and substance use disorders. Because CM can be expensive and labor intensive, much research in this area has focused on creative ways to economically measure abstinence and to obtain effective reinforcers. Despite its apparent efficacy, CM is greatly underused by community-based treatment providers. For a discussion of problems relating to the promotion and dissemination of CM for alcohol and substance use disorders, see Roll, Madden, Rawson, and Petry (2009).

Questions for Further Learning

1. What are two criticisms of the current emphasis on ESTs?
2. What is virtual reality therapy? Give an example.
3. In applications of CM approaches to nicotine and opiate addictions, how is substance-use measured?

CHAPTER 29

Giving It All Some Perspective: A Brief History

In Chapter 1, we presented some historical highlights of Behavior Modification. This chapter traces and provides more detail on the remarkable early growth of the field of behavior modification. It should be read with the following qualifications in mind:

1. Although we describe behavior modification as developing primarily through two major separate lines of influence, there are obvious cross-influences, blends, and offshoots.

NOTE 1

2. We identify what we consider to be major highlights of the development of behavior modification during its formative years: the 1950s and 1960s. We also include some highlights of the 1970s. For more complete histories of behavior modification, see Kazdin (1978) and Pear (2007). For a discussion of the difficulties involved in writing a definitive history of behavior modification, see Morris, Altus, and Smith (2013).

NOTE 2

3. We describe mainly historical highlights in North America.

In this chapter, we first consider two major orientations: one that emphasizes classical (Pavlovian or respondent) conditioning and one that emphasizes operant conditioning. Then we discuss mixtures of these with other orientations.

The Pavlovian and Wolpean Orientation

Late in the 19th century, Russian physiologist Ivan P. Pavlov, using dogs as experimental subjects, conducted groundbreaking experiments on digestion. These experiments, which won him the Nobel Prize in Medicine in 1904, involved measuring the secretions of the salivary glands and the other digestive glands including those of the stomach, pancreas, and small intestines. Pavlov observed that the presentation of food to a dog elicited a chain of digestive secretions beginning with salivation. He soon also noticed that the mere sight and smell of food and even the sounds of it being prepared for the experiment elicited digestive gland secretions. Believing in the potential importance of this observation for studying the higher activity of the brain, he decided to use the secretions of the salivary glands as a basis for studying the process by which new reflexes are acquired. He discovered that if a stimulus such as a tone that did not initially elicit salivation was paired with food several times, the presentation of the tone alone would come to elicit salivation. Pavlov called the food–salivation reflex an *unconditional reflex* (i.e., one that is unlearned or not conditional on any pairing process) and the tone–salivation reflex a *conditional reflex* (i.e., one that is learned or conditional on a pairing process). Thus, he embarked on a systematic study of what is now called *Pavlovian, classical,* or *respondent conditioning* (see Chapter 3). Results of this work were published in a classic book titled in its English translation, *Conditioned Reflexes: An Investigation of the Physiological Activity of the Cerebral Cortex* (Pavlov, 1927). In that book, Pavlov's "unconditional reflexes" and "conditional reflexes" were translated into English as *unconditioned reflexes* and *conditioned reflexes,* respectively, which are the terms used today.

Prior to 1913, psychology was defined as the "science of the mind." In 1913, the American psychologist John B. Watson advocated an alternative approach that he called *behaviorism.* Asserting that psychology should be redefined as the science of behavior, he published an influential paper in which he argued that most human activities could be explained as learned habits. After becoming familiar with the work of Pavlov and possibly Vladimir M. Bechterev, another Russian physiologist who studied learned reflexes independently of Pavlov, Watson (1916) adopted the conditioned reflex as the unit of habit. He argued that most complex activities were due to Pavlovian conditioning. Watson followed his 1916 paper with a classic experiment in collaboration with Rosalie Rayner that demonstrated Pavlovian conditioning of a fear response in an 11-month-old infant. In that experiment, Watson and Rayner first demonstrated that the child was not afraid of a white rat. Then, after several pairings of the white rat with a loud noise that caused the infant to cry and show other indications of fear, the child exhibited a conditioned reflex of fear to the rat (Watson & Rayner, 1920). As described in Chapter 1, this experiment was followed up by Mary Cover Jones (1924) who demonstrated the elimination of a child's fear reactions to a rabbit by gradually moving the rabbit closer to the child over trials while the child was engaging in pleasurable activities.

During the next 20 years, a number of somewhat isolated reports of the application of Pavlovian conditioning procedures to various behaviors appeared in the literature (for a list of many of these, see Yates, 1970). Within this Pavlovian tradition, two significant developments occurred in the 1950s. One development happened in South Africa where Joseph Wolpe began some research that drew heavily on Pavlovian conditioning and the work of J. B. Watson, Mary Cover Jones, and British physiologist Sir Charles Sherrington. Following up on the Watson and Rayner study, Sherrington (1947) noted that if one group of muscles is stimulated, an antagonistic muscle group will be inhibited, and vice versa. He called this *reciprocal inhibition* and postulated it to be a general process acting throughout the nervous system. Wolpe extended the principle of reciprocal inhibition to state that if a response that is incompatible with a learned fear or anxiety can be made to occur to a stimulus that had been conditioned to produce that fear, then that stimulus will cease to elicit the fear reaction. Wolpe developed the earliest behavioral treatment for specific phobias, which (as described in Chapter 28) are intense irrational fears, such as an abnormal fear of heights even when there is no danger of falling. In 1958, Wolpe published his first book on reciprocal inhibition. It was to provide a major force in launching the modern era of the Pavlovian tradition of behavior therapy. Wolpe typically used relaxation responses to inhibit a learned fear or anxiety in a procedure called *systematic desensitization* (see Chapter 28).

Also during the 1950s, the British psychologist Hans Eysenck was influential in criticizing traditional Freudian psychoanalytic treatment and in advocating learning theory or conditioning procedures as alternatives. In 1960, Eysenck published a book of readings, *Behaviour Therapy and the Neuroses.* In that book, he presented a number of case histories in which variations of reciprocal inhibition and Pavlovian conditioning procedures were used in clinical therapy. The Pavlovian-conditioning orientation of behavior therapy has occasionally been referred to as the *Wolpe–Eysenck school.*

In the early 1960s, Wolpe moved to the United States where he began a program at Temple University in which he trained therapists in systematic desensitization. In 1963, Eysenck founded the journal *Behaviour Research and Therapy.* On June 30, 1984, the behavior therapy unit at Temple University Medical Center ceased to exist. Wolpe (1985) attributed termination of the unit to misunderstanding of behavior therapy by psychodynamic psychotherapists. Nevertheless, Wolpe continued to contribute actively to the field of behavior therapy until his death in 1997. The highlights of the development of the Pavlovian–Wolpe orientation prior to the 1980s are presented in the bottom panel of Table 29.1.

Questions for Learning

1. Describe how Pavlov demonstrated Pavlovian conditioning with dogs.
2. What are two other names for Pavlovian conditioning?
3. Describe how Watson and Rayner demonstrated Pavlovian conditioning of a fear response in an 11-month-old infant.
4. How did Joseph Wolpe extend the principle of reciprocal inhibition?
5. What did Wolpe call his procedure for using relaxation to inhibit a learned fear?
6. What role did Hans Eysenck play in the development of behavior therapy in the 1950s?

TABLE 29.1	Some Historical Highlights of Behavior Modification and Behavior Therapy Prior to 1980		
	Pre-1950s	**1950s**	**Early and Middle 1960s**
THE OPERANT CONDITIONING ORIENTATION: APPLIED BEHAVIOR ANALYSIS	Some basic research and theory (Skinner, 1938)	Two major texts (Keller & Schoenfeld, 1950; Skinner, 1953) Some human studies and applications: profoundly retarded (Fuller, 1949), schizophrenics (Lindsley, 1956), psychotics (Ayllon & Michael, 1959), verbal conditioning (Greenspoon, 1955), stuttering (Flanagan, Goldiamond, & Azrin, 1958) A basic operant research journal, with some applications (*Journal of the Experimental Analysis of Behavior*, 1958–)	Some major university training centers Several books of readings (e.g., Ulrich, Stachnik, & Mabry, 1966) More applications, many to "resistant" populations: e.g., retardation (Birnbrauer, Bijou, Wolf, & Kidder, 1965; Girardeau & Spradlin, 1964), autism (Ferster & DeMyer, 1962; Lovaas, 1966; Wolf, Risley, & Mees, 1964), hyperactivity (Patterson, 1965), delinquency (Schwitzgebel, 1964), psychotics (Isaacs, Thomas, & Goldiamond, 1960; Haughton & Ayllon, 1965) Child development (Bijou & Baer, 1961)
OFFSHOOTS AND MIXTURES			Premack Principle (Premack, 1965) Coverant control (Homme, 1965) Precision teaching (Lindsley, 1966) Modeling (Bandura & Walters, 1963) A major book of readings (Ullmann & Krasner, 1965) An applied journal (*Behavior Research and Therapy*, 1963–) Covert sensitization (Cautela, 1966)
THE PAVLOVIAN–WOLPEAN ORIENTATION	Some basic research and theory (Pavlov, 1927; Watson & Rayner, 1920) An early application of fear desensitization (Jones, 1924) An early application of assertion training (Salter, 1949)	Two major texts (Dollard & Miller, 1950; Wolpe, 1958) Applications of systematic desensitization, assertion training, and aversion therapy to a variety of phobias and behavioral excesses Comparisons of behavior therapy and psychotherapy (Eysenck, 1959)	Some major university training centers Several books of readings (e.g., Eysenck, 1960; Franks, 1964) More applications of systematic desensitization, assertion training, and aversion therapy to a variety of classic neurotic behaviors and sexual disorders

TABLE 29.1 Continued

	Late 1960s	1970s
THE OPERANT CONDITIONING ORIENTATION: APPLIED BEHAVIOR ANALYSIS	Additional major university training centers	Many "how-to-do-it" books in a variety of areas
	Isolated undergraduate and graduate courses in many universities	Behavior modification procedures described for many "traditional" areas of psychology (e.g., social, developmental, personality, abnormal, and clinical)
	Additional books describing applied research and procedures applicable to a variety of areas: e.g., education (Skinner, 1968), parenting (Patterson & Gullion, 1968), community work (Tharp & Wetzel, 1969), mental hospitals (Schaefer & Martin, 1969)	Many other helping professions adopting behavior modification procedures (see Chapter 2)
	Additional applications to a variety of areas, including self-control, delinquency, university teaching, marriage counseling, sexual behaviors, and academic skills	Wide variety of individual, institutional, and community applications and research
	An applied journal (*Journal of Applied Behavior Analysis*, 1968–)	
OFFSHOOTS AND MIXTURES	Token economies (Ayllon & Azrin, 1968)	Emergence of cognitive behavior modification, social learning theory, and eclectic behavior therapy
	Contingency contracting (Homme, Csanyi, Gonzales, & Rechs, 1969)	Numerous behavior modification–behavior therapy conferences and workshops
	Formulation of social learning theory (Bandura, 1969)	Concern for behavior modification–behavior therapy as a profession, and for controls against misapplications
	Two major books (Bandura, 1969; Franks, 1969)	Mixed paraprofessional and professional organizations (e.g., Association for Behavior Analysis, 1974–)
	Implosive therapy (Stampfl & Levis, 1967)	Professional organizations (Association for the Advancement of Behavior Therapy, 1970–; Behavior Research and Therapy Society, 1970–; European Association of Behavior Therapy, 1971–)
		More journals specializing in behavior modification (see Note 2 in Chapter 2)
THE PAVLOVIAN–WOLPEAN ORIENTATION	Several major university training centers	Many additional books, publications, and training workshops; much additional research
	Additional books (e.g., Wolpe, 1969)	
	More applications to phobias, anger, asthmatic attacks, frigidity, homosexuality, insomnia, speech disorders, exhibitionism, and other behaviors	

The Operant-Conditioning Orientation: Applied Behavior Analysis

Pavlovian conditioning is a type of learning that involves reflexes—automatic responses to prior stimuli. However, much of our behavior is influenced by its consequences rather than by prior stimuli. B. F. Skinner was the first psychologist to make a clear distinction between behavior that is elicited by stimuli and behavior that is controlled by its consequences. The former he termed *respondent behavior* and the latter he termed *operant behavior*. Hence, Skinner's term for Pavlovian conditioning was *respondent conditioning* (which is the term that we frequently use for Pavlovian conditioning in the other chapters of this text and in the remainder of this chapter).

Skinner was strongly influenced by Watson's behaviorism and by Pavlov's experimental approach but believed that a different methodology was needed to study operant behavior. In 1932, he described an apparatus that contained a lever that a laboratory rat could press and a mechanism for dispensing food pellets to reinforce the rat's lever pressing. Others have since called his experimental chamber a *Skinner box*.

NOTE 3   In 1938, B. F. Skinner described his early research in the book *The Behavior of Organisms: An Experimental Analysis* in which he outlined the basic principles of operant conditioning—a type of learning in which behavior is modified by its consequences. This pioneering work influenced other experimental psychologists to begin studying operant conditioning.

In 1950, Fred S. Keller and William N. Schoenfeld wrote an introductory psychology text, *Principles*
NOTE 4 *of Psychology: A Systematic Text in the Science of Behavior.* This text differed from other introductory psychology texts in that it discussed traditional topics in psychology—such as learning, perception, concept formation, motivation, and emotion—in terms of respondent and operant conditioning principles. Keller and Skinner had been graduate students together at Harvard University, and the Keller and Schoenfeld text was inspired largely by the work and writings of Skinner. *Principles of Psychology* had an important impact within the operant tradition.

In 1953, Skinner published his book *Science and Human Behavior.* Like the Keller and Schoenfeld text, this book was also written as an introductory psychology text; however, it extended to topics—such as government and law, religion, economics, education, and culture—not usually covered in introductory psychology texts. In this book, he offered his interpretation of how the basic behavior
NOTE 5 principles (see Part II of this text) influence the behavior of people in all kinds of situations. Although little supporting data existed for Skinner's generalizations to humans at that time, his interpretations influenced others to begin examining the effects of reinforcement variables on human behavior in a number of basic and applied research studies. An important aspect of Skinner's approach is that he rejected the distinction of a mental world that is separate from the physical world. Thus, although he accepted that private speech and covert images exist, he regarded them as being no different in principle from public speech and overt acts of seeing. Moreover, like Watson, he emphasized the importance in a science of behavior of studying the effects of the external environment on overt behavior.

Many of the reports in the 1950s were demonstrations that consequences affect human behavior in predictable ways or single-case demonstrations that an application of a behavioral program could effect a desired behavior change. For example, Fuller (1949) reported a case in which an institutionalized bedridden adult with profound intellectual disability was taught to raise his arm to a vertical position when arm movements were reinforced with a warm sugar-milk solution. Joel Greenspoon (1955) demonstrated that a simple social consequence (saying "mmm-hmm") could influence college students to repeat certain types of words that immediately preceded Greenspoon saying "mmm-hmm," even though the students were unaware of the contingency that was being applied to them. Nathan Azrin and Ogden Lindsley (1956), two of Skinner's graduate students, demonstrated that jelly-bean reinforcement could influence pairs of young children to cooperate in playing a simple game. Each of these experiments demonstrated that consequences influence human behavior in predictable ways. None of these experiments, however, were practically oriented. One of the first published reports of the 1950s that concerned practical, applied problems was that of Teodoro Ayllon and Jack Michael (1959). With Michael as his Ph.D. dissertation advisor, Ayllon conducted a number of behavioral demonstrations at the Saskatchewan Hospital, a psychiatric institution in Weyburn, Saskatchewan, Canada. These demonstrations showed how staff could use behavioral procedures to modify patient behaviors such as delusional talk, refusals to eat, and various disruptive behaviors.

Following Ayllon and Michael's article and several subsequent papers published by Ayllon and his colleagues from their work at Weyburn, similar demonstrations of behavioral control began to appear with some frequency in the early 1960s (see the top panel in Table 29.1). This early work was characterized by two features: (a) Much of it was done with very resistant populations, such as persons with intellectual disabilities, children with autism, and severely regressed psychiatric patients who had not received a great deal of successful input from traditional psychology; and (b) many of the applications took place in institutional or highly controlled settings. A notable exception to this early trend is Sidney Bijou and Donald Baer's (1961) interpretation of child development from a strictly behavioral perspective.

In 1965, Leonard Ullmann and Leonard Krasner published an influential collection of readings, *Case Studies in Behavior Modification.* This was the first book with "behavior modification" in its title. In addition to collecting a number of case histories and research reports by other authors, Ullmann and Krasner compared two models of abnormal behavior. The *behavioral model of abnormal behavior* suggests that abnormal behavior is a function of specifiable environmental causes and that it is possible to rearrange the environment in such a way that the behavior can be changed or improved. In contrast Sigmund Freud's proposed *medical model of abnormal behavior* viewed abnormal behavior as a symptom of an underlying disturbance in a personality mechanism with the implication that one must treat the underlying personality disturbance through Freudian psychoanalysis rather than treating the observed symptoms by rearranging the environment. Freud's model of abnormal behavior was adapted from the model in physical medicine in which germs, viruses, lesions, and other disturbances lead to the production of symptoms in the functioning of normal humans. Ullmann and Krasner's book included studies from both operant and Pavlovian orientations, and it had a significant impact on furthering behavior modification by providing, in a single source, information on much of the preliminary work in this area. In 1965, Krasner and Ullmann followed up their previous book with an edited book of research studies titled *Research in Behavior Modification.*

In the late 1960s, the operant conditioning orientation began to spread throughout the Western Hemisphere. Several university training centers were developed; many universities initiated at least one or two courses in behavior modification at both the graduate and undergraduate levels, and applications spread to normal school settings, university teaching, homes, and other populations and locations (e.g., see Walters & Thomson, 2013).

By the 1970s, the operant orientation had grown considerably. As discussed in Chapter 1, this approach is frequently referred to as *applied behavior analysis.* It is surprising to find contemporary textbooks that suggest that this approach has been used primarily on client populations with "limited cognitive capacity" and where considerable environmental control is a potential characteristic of the treatment procedures. Although this was true in the 1950s and 1960s, applications now occur with virtually all populations and settings (see Chapters 2, 27, and 28).

It has also been claimed that behavior analysts ignore the causes of problem behavior. In the early stages of behavior modification, there was some justification for this charge because behavior analysts emphasized that managing consequences could alleviate problem behavior regardless of its causes. During the 1970s, some behavior analysts (e.g., Carr, 1977; Johnson & Baumeister, 1978; Rincover, 1978; Rincover, Cook, Peoples, & Packard, 1979) began to stress the importance of understanding the causes of—that is, the conditions producing or maintaining—problem behavior. Indeed, the first edition of this text, published in 1978, contained a section titled "It Helps to Know the Causes of Behavior" in a chapter that evolved into Chapter 23 of this edition.

The growing emphasis on understanding the causes of problem behavior led to the pioneering of functional analysis by Brian Iwata and his colleagues (Iwata, Dorsey, Slifer, Bauman, & Richman, 1982). Functional analysis is the discovery of controlling variables (antecedents and consequences) for behavior by directly assessing their effects on behavior. A number of prominent behavior analysts hailed functional analysis as a major new development in the field. In 1994, the *Journal of Applied Behavior Analysis* published a special issue (Vol. 27, No. 2) devoted to functional analysis approaches to behavioral assessment and treatment (discussed in Chapter 23), and this area continues to be a highly active area of research and application (e.g., Betz & Fisher, 2011; Wacker, Berg, Harding, & Cooper-Brown, 2011). It should be noted that the causes that functional analysis uncovers are environmental causes, not hypothetical inner causes of the medical model that are often speculated about by nonbehavioral (e.g., psychoanalytic) approaches.

The highlights of the development of the operant orientation prior to the 1980s are presented in the top panel of Table 29.1.

Questions for Learning

7. What is operant conditioning?
8. In what way was the Keller and Schoenfeld book *Principles of Psychology* unlike other introductory psychology texts of its day?
9. How did Skinner's *Science and Human Behavior* influence the initial development of behavior modification?
10. Many of the early reports in the operant tradition in the 1950s were straightforward experiments that demonstrated that consequences influence human behavior. Briefly, describe two such experiments.
11. Briefly describe one of the first published reports (a very influential one) that concerned practical applications within the operant tradition.
12. The publications of the early 1960s within the operant orientation seem to have been characterized by two features. What were they?

13. Was the influential book *Case Studies in Behavior Modification* strictly within the operant orientation? Why or why not?
14. Distinguish between the behavioral model and the medical model of abnormal behavior.
15. What is another name for the operant orientation?

Mixtures and Offshoots of the Two Major Orientations

Much of the early history of behavior modification and behavior therapy clearly falls within either the operant orientation or the Pavlovian–Wolpean orientation. Most other early developments tended to be offshoots of one or the other of these traditions or fall in a gray area somewhere between (see the middle panel of Table 29.1).

One major "mixture" was *social learning theory,* first outlined by Julian Rotter in 1954 in his book *Social Learning and Clinical Psychology.* The most influential of the social learning theorists, however, has been Albert Bandura (1969, 1977). His approach is "social" in the sense that it places great emphasis on the social contexts in which behavior is acquired and maintained. In addition to basic principles of respondent and operant conditioning, Bandura has strongly emphasized the importance of *observational learning.* By watching other people act and by observing what happens to them, we can then imitate their behavior (see the discussion of modeling in Chapter 18). Bandura emphasizes cognitive processes as an important influence on behavior. *Cognitive processes* refer to things that we say to ourselves or imagine, which are frequently called "believing," "thinking," and "expecting." In fact, Bandura has emphasized cognitive variables to the extent that he renamed his social learning theory to "social cognitive theory," and the term *social learning theory* does not appear in his later books (Bandura, 1986, 1997). An important cognitive process for Bandura is *self-efficacy* (Bandura, 1982, 1997). This refers to the fact that individuals are more likely to perform adequately in a particular situation if they perceive or believe that they can perform adequately in that situation. In Bandura's words, "Given appropriate skills and adequate incentives…efficacy expectations are a major determinant of peoples' choices of activities, how much effort they will expend, and how long they will sustain effort in dealing with stressful situations" (1977, p. 194). (See Chapter 27 for discussion of how cognitions can be explained in terms of operant and respondent conditioning.)

Another mixture that emerged in the 1960s and 70s is referred to as *cognitive behavior modification* or *cognitive behavior therapy* (see Chapter 27). Therapists such as Albert Ellis (1962) and Aaron Beck (1970) believe that faulty cognitive processes, faulty thinking, causes emotional, and behavioral problems. Ellis and Beck independently developed approaches to therapy that focused on helping clients recognize and change faulty thinking. Cognitive behavior modification, now more commonly called *cognitive behavior therapy,* is to be distinguished from social learning theory. Social learning theory, with its emphasis on the regulation of behavior by Pavlovian conditioning, operant conditioning, and cognitive processes, provides a way of explaining behavior. Cognitive behavior therapy has focused mainly on explaining maladaptive behaviors in terms of dysfunctional thinking and includes a method called *cognitive restructuring* as the primary treatment component for modifying dysfunctional thinking.

In addition to these theoretical models of behavior modification—the Pavlovian–Wolpean orientation, the operant orientation, and the mixtures and offshoots of each—some early practicing behavior therapists subscribed to an eclectic approach that includes more traditional components. Arnold Lazarus is representative of this position. Referring to what he called *multimodal behavior therapy,* Lazarus (1971, 1976) argued that practicing clinicians should not restrict themselves to a particular theoretical framework but should use a variety of behavioral and nonbehavioral techniques provided that the techniques have some empirical support.

As indicated by this brief discussion of various conceptualizations of behavior modification, although there is some disagreement among behavior modifiers on theoretical issues, there is also considerable agreement.

Questions for Learning

16. What are the names of two major behavior modification/behavior therapy journals first published in the 1960s (see Table 29.1)?
17. What does the term *cognitive processes* mean?
18. Briefly, how did cognitive therapists Ellis and Beck explain emotional problems, and how did they propose to treat them?
19. What is a major emphasis of social learning theory, and who was its most influential proponent?

The Terms *Behavior Modification, Behavior Therapy, Cognitive Behavior Modification, Cognitive Behavior Therapy,* and *Applied Behavior Analysis*

Some writers use the terms *behavior modification* and *behavior therapy* interchangeably. Other writers use *applied behavior analysis* as synonymous with behavior modification. What is the historical use of these terms? It appears that Lindsley, Skinner, and Solomon (1953) were the first to use the term *behavior therapy*. They did so in a report describing some research in which psychotic patients in a mental hospital were reinforced with candy or cigarettes for pulling a plunger. (For a discussion of the early laboratory contributions of Lindsley and Skinner to the formation of behavior therapy, see Reed & Luiselli, 2009.) However, those within the operant orientation subsequently made little use of the term. Although Lazarus (1958) next used the term *behavior therapy* when he applied it to Wolpe's reciprocal inhibition framework, the term became popular among those within the Pavlovian–Wolpean orientation after Eysenck (1959) used it to describe procedures published by Wolpe.

The first use of the term *behavior modification* appears to be as a section heading in a chapter by R. I. Watson (1962). In the 1960s and 70s, many writers distinguished between behavior modification, with its roots in operant conditioning, and behavior therapy, with its roots in Pavlovian conditioning. Others, however, did not make that distinction. For example, Ullmann and Krasner (1965) frequently used *behavior modification* and *behavior therapy* interchangeably. However, citing Watson (1962, p. 19), Krasner (2001) wrote, "[i]n a broader sense, the topic of behavior modification is related to the whole field of learning" (p. 214). This accords with how we use the term in this book, as explained in Chapter 1 and later in this chapter.

There are some interesting historic connections between behavior modification and humanistic psychology. Watson (1962) credited Carl Rogers, a founder of humanistic psychology, with having "launched the research approach in behavioral modification through psychotherapy" (p. 21); and Ullmann (1980), reflecting on his and Krasner's decision to use *behavior modification* in the title of their case-studies book, credited Rogers for the idea to use that term as opposed to behavior therapy.

Skinner's subtitle for his 1938 book *The Behavior of Organisms* was *An Experimental Analysis*. The words *behavior* and *analysis* were to become prominent in the operant orientation. In 1957, a group of Skinner's followers founded the Society for the Experimental Analysis of Behavior (SEAB). In 1958, SEAB began to publish the *Journal of the Experimental Analysis of Behavior,* which, as stated in the inside cover of each issue, "is primarily for the original publication of experiments relevant to the behavior of individual organisms." In 1968, SEAB began to publish the *Journal of Applied Behavior Analysis,* which, as stated in the inside cover of each issue, "is primarily for the original publication of experimental research involving applications of the experimental analysis of behavior to problems of social importance." In 1974 in Chicago, a group of psychologists interested in behavior analysis founded the Midwestern Association of Behavior Analysis, which, as its membership expanded, became the Association for Behavior Analysis (ABA) in 1978 and finally the Association for Behavior Analysis International (ABAI) in 2007. ABAI publishes several journals: *The Behavior Analyst* (begun in 1978), *The Analysis of Verbal Behavior* (purchased by ABAI in 1994), and *Behavior Analysis in Practice* (begun in 2008). In 1991, recognizing the importance of upholding certain standards in the training of behavior analysts, ABA established a process for accrediting graduate programs in behavior analysis. In 1998, another group of behavior analysts established a nonprofit corporation called the Behavior Analyst Certification Board, whose purpose, as stated on its website, is "to meet professional credentialing needs identified by behavior analysts, governments, and consumers of behavior analysis services."

Some of the distinctions that have tended to characterize the uses of the terms *behavior therapy, behavior modification, cognitive behavior modification,* and *applied behavior analysis* are presented in Table 29.2.

In spite of the historical distinctions, the terms are often used interchangeably. In our view, *behavior modification* has acquired a broader meaning than the other terms. *Behavior therapy* and *cognitive behavior therapy* are clearly less appropriate than *applied behavior analysis* or *behavior modification* when dealing with nondysfunctional behavior. As indicated in Chapter 1, we suggest that the term *behavior modification* subsume *cognitive behavior therapy, behavior therapy,* and *applied behavior analysis. Behavior therapy* or *cognitive behavior therapy* is behavior modification carried out on dysfunctional behavior, generally in a clinical setting. *Applied behavior analysis* emphasizes the application of operant conditioning principles and is *behavior modification* in which there often is an attempt to analyze or clearly demonstrate controlling variables of the behavior of concern. *Behavior modification* includes

TABLE 29.2	A Comparison of the Uses of the Terms *Behavior Therapy, Cognitive Behavior Modification, Behavior Modification,* and *Applied Behavior Analysis*

1960s and 1970s

Behavior Therapy/Cognitive Behavior Modification	Behavior Modification
1. Terms used most often by followers of the Pavlovian–Wolpean orientation and followers of the cognitive orientation	1. Term used most often by followers of the operant orientation
2. Terms tended to be used by behavioral psychologists and psychiatrists who were concerned primarily with treatment in traditional clinical settings; for a historical time line of behavior therapy in psychiatric settings, see Malatesta, AuBuchon, and Bluch, 1994	2. Term tended to be used by behavior specialists in schools, homes, and other settings that were not primarily the domain of the clinical psychologist and psychiatrist
3. Terms tended to be used to refer to behavioral treatments conducted in the therapist's office by means of verbal interaction ("talk therapy") between therapist and client	3. Term tended to be used for behavioral treatments carried out in the natural environment as well as in special training settings
4. Terms were associated with an experimental foundation that was based primarily on human studies in clinical settings	4. Term was associated with an experimental foundation in basic operant research with animals and humans in addition to experimental studies in applied settings

1980s to the Present

- The terms **behavior therapy** and **cognitive behavior modification** have generally been replaced by the term **cognitive behavior therapy**, which continues to be used as described in the left column.
- The term **applied behavior analysis** is used increasingly by followers of the operant orientation as described in the right-hand column.
- The term **behavior modification** tends to have a somewhat broader meaning and includes behavior therapy, cognitive behavior therapy, and applied behavior analysis.

all explicit applications of behavior principles to improve specific behavior—whether or not in clinical settings and whether or not controlling variables have been explicitly demonstrated—which is how we have used the term in this book.

The Future of Behavior Modification

Behavior modification has been applied to a wide variety of individual and social problems. In addition, more and more of these applications have been concerned with the prevention and amelioration of existing problems. There is no doubt that the helping professions including social work, medicine, rehabilitation, nursing, education, dentistry, psychiatry, public health, and clinical and community psychology have adopted behavior modification procedures. Applications are also occur in areas such as business, industry, sports, recreation, and the promotion of healthy lifestyles (see Chapter 2). Someday a thorough knowledge of behavioral techniques might become an accepted necessity in our culture. Children will grow up to see a world in which the positive applications of behavior principles will result in a happy, informed, skillful, productive society without war, poverty, prejudice, or pollution.

Questions for Learning

20. Who first used the term *behavior therapy* and in what context?
21. Describe four differences in the usage of the terms *behavior therapy/cognitive behavior modification* versus *behavior modification* during the 1960s and 1970s (Table 29.2).
22. In a sentence for each, distinguish between the terms *cognitive behavior therapy, applied behavior analysis,* and *behavior modification* as they tend to be used today.

Notes for Further Learning

1. The history of behavior modification is as long as the history of psychology from which it emerged. For a complete discussion of the early history of psychology and the major systems that developed during the 20th and early 21st centuries, see Pear (2007). Some of the more important precursors to the emergence of behavior modification are identified next.

   Plato (427–347 B.C.) attributed behavior to something called the *psyche* (soul), which he believed is separate from the body and continues to exist even after death. His student Aristotle (384–322 B.C.) argued that the soul is the "form" or functioning of the body, apparently including its behavior. Plato's view of the soul had a greater influence than Aristotle's did on early Western European theologians and philosophers.

   The French philosopher René Descartes (1595–1650) was the first to articulate a clear distinction between the body and the soul. He maintained that the body is essentially a machine operating on the basis of reflexes and guidance from a *mente* (soul or mind) comprised of an immaterial, nonspatially extended substance. A long line of philosophers in Britain—from John Locke (1632–1704) to John Stuart Mill (1806–1873)—known as the *British empiricists* contested his philosophy. In their discourses, these individuals replaced the word *soul* with the more scientific-sounding word *mind,* which stems from an Old English word pertaining to memory or thought.

   A group of physiologists known as the *Russian reflexologists* or *psychoreflexologists*—most notably Ivan M. Sechenov (1829–1905) and his followers Ivan P. Pavlov (1849–1936) and Vladimir M. Bechterev (1857–1927)—picked up on Descartes' concept of reflexes and the British empiricists' focus on associations. Bechterev and Pavlov independently performed experiments on establishing new reflexes, which Bechterev called "association reflexes" and Pavlov called "conditional reflexes."

   In the United States, a group of psychologists called *functionalists,* led primarily by William James (1842–1910) at Harvard and John Dewey (1859–1952) at the University of Chicago, basing their approach on Darwin's theory of evolution, advocated studying the mind's role in the adaptation of the individual to the environment. This included both animal and human studies on learning, such as those of E. L. Thorndike (1874–1949).

   John B. Watson (1878–1958) took functionalism a step further. He asserted that psychology, rather than being about the mind, should be purely the science of behavior. Following Watson's exit from academic psychology, the behavioral approach opened to a new generation of leaders.

2. In the 1950s, important historical developments in behavior modification occurred concurrently in three countries: in South Africa, where Wolpe conducted his pioneering work on systematic desensitization; in England, where Eysenck spurred on the behavior modification movement by emphasizing dissatisfaction with traditional methods of psychotherapy; and in the United States, where Skinner and his colleagues were working within the operant conditioning orientation. During the 1960s and 1970s, however, most of the major books and research papers in behavior modification and behavior therapy were based on developments in the United States. For example, three of the first four major behavior therapy journals were published in the United States, and most of their articles were written in the United States (*Journal of Applied Behavior Analysis,* 1968–the present; *Behavior Therapy,* 1970; *Behavior Therapy and Experimental Psychiatry,* 1970–the present. Although the fourth journal (*Behaviour Research and Therapy,* 1963–the present) was edited by Eysenck in England, it too contained a large number of U.S. research reports. Since the 1970s, however, behavior modification has become a truly worldwide movement. Significant developments occurred in Argentina (Blanck, 1983); in Asia (Oei, 1998); in Australia (Brownell, 1981; King, 1996; Schlesinger, 2004); in Brazil (Ardila, 1982; Grassi, 2004); in Canada (Martin, 1981); in Chile (Ardila, 1982); in Colombia (Ardila, 1982; Lopez & Aguilar, 2003); in Costa Rica (Pal-Hegedus, 1991); in Cuba (Dattilio, 1999); in the Dominican Republic (Brownell, 1981); in England (Brownell, 1981); in France (Agathon, 1982; Cottraux, 1990); in Germany (Stark, 1980); in Ghana (Danguah, 1982); in Holland (Brownell, 1981); in Hungary (Tringer, 1991); in Israel (Brownell, 1981; Zvi, 2004); in Italy (Moderato, 2003; Sanivio, 1999; Scrimali & Grimaldi, 1993); in Ireland (Flanagan, 1991); in Japan (Sakano, 1993; Yamagami, Okuma, Morinaga, & Nakao, 1982); in Mexico (Ardila, 1982); in New Zealand (Blampied, 1999, 2004); in Norway (Brownell, 1981); in Poland (Kokoszka, Popiel, & Sitarz, 2000; Suchowierska & Kozlowski, 2004); in Romania (David & Miclea, 2002); in Singapore (Banerjee, 1999); in Spain (Caballo & Buela-Casal, 1993); in South Korea (Kim, 2003); in Sri Lanka (DeSilva & Simarasinghe, 1985); in Sweden (Brownell, 1981; Carter, 2004); in Thailand (Mikulis, 1983); in the United Kingdom (Dymond, Chiesa, & Martin, 2003); in Uruguay (Zamora & Lima, 2000); and in Venezuela (Ardila, 1982). In the September 2009 issue of *Inside Behavior Analysis,* discussion can be found of behavior analysis in Brazil, China, Colombia, India, Ireland, Israel, Italy, Japan, Mexico, New Zealand, the Philippines, Poland, Sweden, Taiwan, and the United Kingdom.

3. Burrhus Frederick Skinner (1904–1990) had a remarkable career and received numerous awards, including the Distinguished Scientific Award from the American Psychological Association (1958), the President's National Medal of Science (1968), and the Humanist of the Year Award from the American Humanist Society (1972). In addition to his basic theoretical and experimental contributions, Skinner published

a utopian novel, *Walden Two* (1948b), worked on a project to teach pigeons to guide missiles during World War II (Skinner, 1960), and developed the concept of programmed instruction and teaching machines (Skinner, 1958). He continued to be active throughout his academic career, publishing his last book in 1989.

4. Fred S. Keller (1899–1996), B. F. Skinner's friend and colleague, made other major contributions. In 1961, he accepted a position at the University of São Paulo, Brazil, where he established the first operant conditioning course and developed the personalized system of instruction, a behavior modification approach to university teaching (see Chapter 2). Keller contributed immeasurably to the development of behavior modification in Brazil. Former students of his and their academic descendents continue to advance behavioral psychology in that country (e.g., see Grassi, 2004).

5. Clark Hull (1884–1952), an early contemporary of Skinner, developed a learning theory that meshed together operant and respondent conditioning into a theory that did not fundamentally distinguish between the two types of conditioning. According to Hull (1943, 1952), reinforcement was involved in respondent as well as in operant conditioning. Hull did not attempt to interpret a wide variety of human behavior to the extent done by Skinner (1953, 1957). Instead, he attempted to develop an elaborate mathematical theory of learning or conditioning. Two other psychologists, John Dollard and Neal Miller (1950), however, translated Freudian psychodynamic concepts into the language of Hull's learning theory. Dollard and Miller's book was influential in the Pavlovian and Wolpean orientation – mainly because they saw no fundamental distinction between respondent and operant (or, in the terminology they used, classical and instrumental) conditioning.

Questions for Further Learning

1. How did Aristotle's view of the soul differ from that of Plato's?
2. Briefly state a contribution each of the following made to the behavioral approach:
   a. Descartes
   b. the British empiricists
   c. the Russian reflexologists
   d. the functionalists
3. Name three countries that were important in the development of behavior modification in the 1950s and the person most associated with this development in each of these countries.
4. Cite three of Skinner's contributions other than his basic research and theoretical writings.
5. In what Latin American country did Keller accept an academic position in 1961, and what contribution did he make to behavior modification while there?
6. To which of the two major orientations did Hull and his followers Dollard and Miller mainly contribute, and briefly what were their contributions?

CHAPTER 30

Ethical Issues

Throughout this book, we have emphasized the ethical or moral concerns that one should always bear in mind when applying behavior modification. It would be a great tragedy if this powerful scientific technology were used in ways that harmed rather than helped humanity. Because this is a real danger, it is fitting that we devote the final chapter of this book to a more detailed discussion of ethical concerns.

The history of civilization is a continuous story of the abuse of power. Throughout the ages, powerful people have used the reinforcers and punishers at their disposal to control the behavior of people who had fewer reinforcers and punishers to deliver or the means to deliver them contingent on selected target behaviors. The effect of this tradition has been to increase the reinforcements occurring to the more powerful at the expense of those occurring to the less powerful. From time to time, as the proportion of total reinforcement allotted to them steadily dwindled, people subjected to this abuse of power have successfully revolted against their oppressors and have modified existing social structures or established new ones to check or eliminate the possibility of future abuses. Constitutions, bills of rights, and related political documents of modern states can be viewed as formal specifications of contingencies designed to control the behavior of those who control the behavior of others. In Western democracies, for example, we have moved from the era of the divine right of monarchs to one of "government by laws." Moreover, with the introduction of periodic popular elections, people who are controlled by those who make the laws can exert a certain measure of reciprocal control. They can vote them out of office. In socialist and communist countries, the revolutionary process concentrated on eliminating economic abuses. In the absence of democracy, other abuses developed, and in reaction to these abuses former communist countries have become more democratic. Nevertheless, power continues to be abused throughout the world.

Because of this cultural history and because of people's personal experiences with others who have abused their power, people have learned to react negatively to overt attempts to manage behavior. It should not be surprising, therefore, that in its early years, the term *behavior modification* evoked many negative reactions ranging from suspicion to outright hostility. These early reactions were exacerbated by the tendency to mistakenly equate behavior modification with such invasive procedures as electroconvulsive shock therapy, brainwashing, and even torture. For example, a survey of the *New York Times* indicated that over a 5-year period in the 1970s, the term *behavior modification* was used incorrectly approximately 50% of the time (Turkat & Feuerstein, 1978). Today, as reports in newspapers, television, and movies illustrate, the general public is more aware that behavior modification—including behavior therapy, cognitive behavior therapy, and applied behavior analysis (discussed in Chapters 1 and 29)—helps individuals manage their behavior.

Systematic applications of learning or conditioning principles and techniques are based on two assumptions: (a) behavior can be controlled and (b) it is desirable to do so to achieve certain objectives. Whether behavior is completely or only partially determined by environmental and genetic factors makes for interesting philosophical discussions. From a practical point of view, however, it makes little difference one way or the other. The important point is that the amount of potential control over behavior is steadily increasing as a result of new discoveries in behavioral science, refinements in behavioral and electronic technology, and advances in Internet communication that makes these discoveries increasingly available to people around the world.

Extreme wariness is a healthy reaction to any new advance in science or technology. Perhaps civilization would be in less danger today if more precautions had been taken early in the development of atomic energy. The solution to the present problems stemming from scientific and technological advances, however, does not lie in attempting to turn the clock back to a seemingly more secure, prescientific era. Science and technology are not the problem. They are merely highly sophisticated means that people have developed for solving problems. The real problem is that people frequently misuse these tools. This is, of course, a behavioral problem. It would seem, therefore, as Skinner (1953, 1971) argued, that the science of behavior is the logical key to the solution of that problem. As with other powerful sciences and technologies, however, behavior modification can be misused. It therefore is important to have ethical guidelines to ensure that it is used for the good of society. In the next section, we discuss ethics from a behavioral perspective. Then we examine some common arguments against deliberately changing behavior. Finally, we turn to the question of how safeguards can be imposed on behavior modification to ensure that it will always be used in the best interests of humanity.

Questions for Learning

1. Describe in behavioral terms how the history of civilization is a story of the continuous abuse of power. From your knowledge of history or current events, give an example of this abuse.
2. From your knowledge of history or current events, give an example of what often happens when the reinforcements occurring to one group in a society fall below a certain critical level relative to the reinforcements occurring to another group in that society.
3. From a behavioral point of view, how might we account for constitutions, bills of rights, and related political documents of modern states?
4. Explain why we tend to react negatively to all overt attempts to control our behavior.
5. Why and how do people who would control our behavior disguise their aims? Give an example of this that is not in the text.
6. State two propositions on which behavior modification is based.
7. Why is extreme wariness a healthy reaction to any new development in science or technology? Discuss an example of this.

A Behavioral View of Ethics

From a behavioral point of view, the term *ethics* refers to certain standards of behavior that a culture developed to promote the survival of that culture (Skinner, 1953, 1971). For example, stealing is considered unethical or wrong in many cultures because of the disruptive effect it has on the culture. Many ethical guidelines likely evolved during prehistoric times. It might be that among a number of cultures that existed before recorded history, respecting the possessions of others happened to be socially reinforced and stealing happened to be punished. Cultures in which respecting others' possessions was not reinforced, however, tended not to survive. There are a number of possible reasons for this. Perhaps the members of cultures that did not reinforce respecting others' possessions put so much effort into fighting each other that they were vulnerable to invasions from other cultures or they did not have enough time or energy to provide an adequate amount of food for themselves. Perhaps these cultures were so unreinforcing to their members that the members defected in large numbers to other groups, so that their former cultures became extinct due to lack of membership. Whatever the case, many cultures that reinforced respecting others' possessions—that is, cultures that considered not stealing ethical or right and stealing unethical or wrong—survived.

Thus, ethics evolved as part of our culture in much the same way that parts of our bodies evolved; that is, ethics contributed to the survival of our culture in much the same way that fingers and an opposable thumb have contributed to the survival of our species. This is not to say that people do not, at times, deliberately decide to formulate ethical rules for their culture. It is part of a cultural evolutionary process that at some point members of a culture begin to engage in such behavior because they have been conditioned to work toward the survival of their culture. One way in which to work toward the survival of one's culture is to formulate and enforce a code of ethics that strengthens that culture through reinforcement as well as punishment.

Ethical guidelines are important sources of behavioral control when immediate reinforcers influence an individual to behave in a way that leads to aversive stimuli for others. For example, whereas a thief is immediately reinforced by possession of the stolen goods, loss of those goods is aversive to the victim. To influence its members to be honest with each other, a culture might therefore develop and enforce the ethical guideline "You shall not steal." Sometimes such guidelines are formulated into rules that specify legal contingencies (e.g., "If you steal, you will be fined or sent to jail"). Sometimes such guidelines are formulated into rules that imply contingencies based on religious beliefs (e.g., "If you obey God's commandments such as to not steal, you will go to heaven"). When members of a culture learn to follow such ethical guidelines, the guidelines exert rule-governed control over behavior (see Chapter 17). This is one way that people learn to emit behavior that is ethical and to refrain from behavior that is unethical.

With this behavioral view of ethics in mind, let's examine whether behavior modifiers should attempt to deliberately change the behavior of others.

Arguments Against Deliberately Controlling Behavior

As we indicated earlier, because of our knowledge of the abuse of power throughout history and because of our personal experience with others who have abused their power, we have learned to react negatively to overt attempts to change our behavior. Perhaps for these reasons it is sometimes argued that all **NOTE 1** attempts to control behavior are unethical. However, a little reflection shows that the goal of any social help profession (e.g., education, psychology, and psychiatry) can be achieved only to the extent that the practitioners of that profession exert control over behavior. For example, the goal of education is to change behavior so that students respond differently to their environment. To teach a person to read is to change the way that person responds to signs, newspapers, books, email, and other items containing written or printed words. The goals of counseling, psychological treatment, and psychiatry likewise involve changing people's behavior so that they can function more effectively than they did prior to receiving professional help.

Perhaps because of people's negative reactions to overt attempts to change behavior, many members of the helping professions do not like to think that they are controlling behavior. They prefer to see themselves as merely helping their clients achieve control over their own behavior. Establishing self-control, however, is also a form of behavioral control. One teaches someone to emit behavior that controls that individual's other behavior in some desired fashion (see Chapter 26). To do this, it is necessary to manage the behavior involved in self-control. The helping practitioner might object that this is nevertheless not control because the external influence over the client's behavior is withdrawn as soon as the practitioner is sure that the client is able to manage his or her own behavior. Actually, as we emphasize repeatedly throughout this book, the practitioner has shifted the control to the natural environment. One may speak of this as "withdrawing control," but the control still continues although its form has changed. If the practitioner has been successful in achieving the behavioral objectives, the desired behavior will be maintained and in that sense, the practitioner's initial influence over the behavior will persist.

Some people argue that deliberately planning to change behavior is "cold" and "mechanical" and believe that it interferes with "warm," "loving," "spontaneous" relationships that should exist between persons. Determining where this objection to planning comes from is difficult because we know of no logical or empirical evidence that supports it. On the contrary, most behavior modification programs that we know about are characterized by friendly, warm interactions between the individuals involved. Good applied behavior analysts and behavior therapists are genuinely interested in people and find the time to interact with their clients on a personal level just as other helping practitioners do. Moreover, in the absence of an empathic relationship, clients will resist complying with behavior therapists' requests for conducting various self-monitoring and homework assignments (Hersen, 1983; Martin & Worthington, 1982; Messer & Winokur, 1984). It also appears that therapist empathy may help in making behavior therapy more effective in general (Joice & Mercer, 2010; Thwaites & Bennett-Levy, 2007). Although some people in all professions appear to be cold and mechanical, such people are no more common among behavior modifiers than they are among any other group in the helping professions.

Conversely, a lack of planning can be disastrous. For illustrations of this, refer to the "Pitfalls" sections in Part II in which we give numerous examples of how behavior principles and processes can work to the disadvantage of those who are ignorant of them or who do not plan for them. A practitioner who is not skillful in constructing programs for developing desirable behavior is apt to unwittingly introduce contingencies that develop undesirable behavior.

Questions for Learning

8. From a behavioral point of view, what does the term *ethics* mean?
9. Describe how ethics has evolved as a part of our culture.
10. In a sentence explain when, from a behavioral point of view, ethical guidelines represent an important source of behavioral control.
11. Using an example, explain how ethical guidelines involve rule-governed control over behavior.
12. Explain why all helping professions are involved in the control of behavior whether or not their practitioners realize it. Give an example.
13. Discuss the relative merits of planning versus not planning for behavior change.

Ethical Guidelines

Having a set of guidelines that describe ethical applications of behavior modification is important. However, simply resolving to treat various individuals and groups in ethical ways is not a sufficient guarantee that this will occur. Contingencies of reinforcement must be arranged to make this happen. One way to arrange such contingencies is through *countercontrol*. This is "the reciprocal of control; it is the influence the controllee has on the controller by virtue of access to suitable reinforcers" (Stolz & Associates, 1978, p. 19). For example, in a democracy, voters exert countercontrol over elected officials because they can vote them out of office. Similarly, a client can stop seeing a therapist as a form of countercontrol if the therapist does not conform to prearranged treatment guidelines. Some individuals in treatment programs, however, such as children, psychiatric patients, geriatric patients, and persons with severe developmental disabilities, might lack meaningful forms of countercontrol. In such cases, other ethical safeguards are necessary. These safeguards require that behavior modifiers be held accountable to a recognized individual or group for applying acceptable procedures and producing satisfactory results.

Various groups and organizations have addressed the ethical issues involved in the application of behavior modification. Three highly reputable organizations that have done so are the Association for the Advancement of Behavior Therapy (AABT), now called the Association for Behavioral and Cognitive Therapies (ABCT); the American Psychological Association (APA); and the Association for Behavior Analysis (ABA), now called the Association for Behavior Analysis International (ABAI).

In 1977, in its journal *Behavior Therapy,* AABT published a set of basic ethical questions that should always be asked with regard to any behavioral program. These questions are reprinted in Table 30.1, and they continue to be an excellent set of questions for consideration. Most of these points are made

---

TABLE 30.1   Ethical Issues for Human Services

The focus of this statement is on critical issues of central importance to human services. The statement is not a list of prescriptions and proscriptions.

On each of the issues described, ideal interventions would have maximum involvement by the person whose behavior is to be changed, and the fullest possible consideration of societal pressures on that person, the therapist, and the therapist's employer. It is recognized that the practicalities of actual settings sometimes require exceptions and that there certainly are occasions when exceptions can be consistent with ethical practice.

In the list of issues, the term "client" is used to describe the person whose behavior is to be changed; "therapist" is used to describe the professional in charge of the intervention; "treatment" and "problem," although used in the singular, refer to any and all treatments and problems being formulated with this checklist. The issues are formulated so as to be relevant across as many settings and populations as possible. Thus, they need to be qualified when someone other than the person whose behavior is to be changed is paying the therapist, or when that person's competence or the voluntary nature of that person's consent is questioned. For example, if the therapist has found that the client does not understand the goals or methods being considered, the therapist should substitute the client's guardian or other responsible person for "client," when reviewing the issues listed.

A Have the goals of treatment been adequately considered?
  1 To ensure that the goals are explicit, are they written?
  2 Has the client's understanding of the goals been assured by having the client restate them orally or in writing?
  3 Have the therapist and client agreed on the goals of therapy?
  4 Will serving the client's interests be contrary to the interests of other persons?
  5 Will serving the client's immediate interests be contrary to the client's long term interest?

TABLE 30.1   Continued

B Has the choice of treatment methods been adequately considered?
  1 Does the published literature show the procedure to be the best one available for that problem?
  2 If no literature exists regarding the treatment method, is the method consistent with generally accepted practice?
  3 Has the client been told of alternative procedures that might be preferred by the client on the basis of significant differences in discomfort, treatment time, cost, or degree of demonstrated effectiveness?
  4 If a treatment procedure is publicly, legally, or professionally controversial, has formal professional consultation been obtained, has the reaction of the affected segment of the public been adequately considered, and have the alternative treatment methods been more closely reexamined and reconsidered?

C Is the client's participation voluntary?
  1 Have possible sources of coercion on the client's participation been considered?
  2 If treatment is legally mandated, has the available range of treatments and therapists been offered?
  3 Can the client withdraw from treatment without a penalty or financial loss that exceeds actual clinical costs?

D When another person or an agency is empowered to arrange for therapy, have the interests of the subordinated client been sufficiently considered?
  1 Has the subordinated client been informed of the treatment objectives and participated in the choice of treatment procedures?
  2 Where the subordinated client's competence to decide is limited, have the client as well as the guardian participated in the treatment discussions to the extent that the client's abilities permit?
  3 If the interests of the subordinated person and the superordinate persons or agency conflict, have attempts been made to reduce the conflict by dealing with both interests?

E Has the adequacy of treatment been evaluated?
  1 Have quantitative measures of the problem and its progress been obtained?
  2 Have the measures of the problem and its progress been made available to the client during treatment?

F Has the confidentiality of the treatment relationship been protected?
  1 Has the client been told who has access to the records?
  2 Are records available only to authorized persons?

G Does the therapist refer the clients to other therapists when necessary?
  1 If treatment is unsuccessful, is the client referred to other therapists?
  2 Has the client been told that if dissatisfied with the treatment, referral will be made?

H Is the therapist qualified to provide treatment?
  1 Has the therapist had training or experience in treating problems like the client's?
  2 If deficits exist in the therapist's qualifications, has the client been informed?
  3 If the therapist is not adequately qualified, is the client referred to other therapists, or has supervision by a qualified therapist been provided? Is the client informed of the supervisory relation?
  4 If the treatment is administered by mediators, have the mediators been adequately supervised by a qualified therapist?

Note: Adopted May 22, 1977, by the board of directors of the Association for Advancement of Behavior Therapy.

This statement on Ethical Issues for Human Services was taken from the Membership Directory of the Association for Advancement of Behavior Therapy and is reprinted by permission of the association.

frequently throughout this book, especially in Chapter 24. If you are conducting a behavior modification program and answer no to any of these questions, it is extremely likely that the ethics of what you are doing would be considered questionable by any recognized group of applied behavior analysts or behavior therapists. It should be noted that these ethical questions are relevant not only to behavior modifers, but also to all providers of human services.

In 1978, a commission appointed by APA published a comprehensive report (Stolz & Associates, 1978) on the ethical issues involved in behavior modification. A primary conclusion of the commission was that persons engaged in any type of psychological intervention should subscribe to and follow the ethics codes and standards of their professions. For members of APA and the Canadian Psychological Association, the current version of the ethics code is APA's *Ethical Principles of Psychologists and Code of Conduct* (2010, which can be retrieved from http://www.apa.org/ethics/code/index.aspx). This document includes a set of general principles that are intended to guide psychologists toward the very highest ethical ideals of the profession and a detailed set of standards to encourage ethical behavior by psychologists and their students.

In 1988, in its journal *The Behavior Analyst,* ABA published a statement of clients' rights (Van Houten et al., 1988) to direct both the ethical and appropriate application of behavioral treatment. In 1998 the Behavior Analyst Certification Board (BACB) was formed to identify and advance the "competent and ethical practice of behavior analysis" (Shook & Favell, 2008, p. 47). In 2001 the BACB produced a set of Guidelines for Responsible Conduct for Behavior Analysts. Minor revisions to these guidelines were made in 2004 and 2010. Bailey and Burch (2011) provide an excellent discussion of the BACB Guidelines for Responsible Conduct for Behavior Analysts including practical advice, illustrated with numerous examples, on how to adhere to the guidelines. An important point that they make is that at the base of all ethics is the golden rule: treat others as you would like to be treated or treat others as you would want people significant to you to be treated under similar circumstances. The following discussion points for the ethical application of behavior modification are based on the reports by Stolz and Associates (1978) and Van Houten and colleagues (1988), and the 2010 revision of the BACB Guidelines for Responsible Conduct for Behavior Analysts.

1. Qualifications of the Behavior Modifier

Applied behavior analysts and behavior therapists must receive appropriate academic training. They must also receive appropriate supervised practical training to ensure competence in behavioral assessment, designing and implementing treatment programs, evaluating their results, and ensuring a thorough understanding of professional ethics (see Shook & Johnston, 2011). Van Houten and colleagues (1988) argued that in cases in which a problem or treatment is complex or might pose risks, clients have a right to direct involvement by an appropriately trained doctoral-level applied behavior analyst or behavior therapist. Regardless of the level of training, the behavior modifier should always ensure that the procedures being used are consistent with the most up-to-date literature in the recognized behavior modification, behavior therapy, and applied behavior analysis journals.

If you want to carry out a behavior modification project and are not a recognized professional, you should obtain the appropriate academic training and supervision from a recognized professional in the field. Such professionals are likely to be members of ABAI or ABCT and certified by BACB; for more information, go to http://www.abainternational.org, and http://www.bacb.com. Practitioners can also be certified in cognitive and behavioral psychology by the American Board of Professional Psychology (http://www.abpp.org/i4a/pages/index.cfm?pageid=3418). The American Board of Professional Psychology developed the examination content and examination instrument used by all 50 states in the United States to license psychologists. In order to offer professional services as an applied behavior analyst or behavior therapist, a practitioner must hold a professional credential from a recognized certifying agency such as BACB (e.g., see Shook & Johnston, 2011, and the above-mentioned websites).

2. Definition of the Problem and Selection of Goals

NOTE 2

Target behaviors selected for modification must be those that are the most important for the client and society. The emphasis should be on establishing functional, age-appropriate skills that will enable the client greater freedom to pursue preferred activities. For individuals with severe handicaps especially, the focus should be on teaching skills that promote independent functioning. Even when improved functioning requires the elimination of problem behaviors, the goals should include developing desirable alternative behaviors. The goals should also be consistent with the basic rights of the client to dignity, privacy, and humane care.

Defining the problem and selecting the goals depend on the values of the individuals involved. One form of countercontrol, therefore, is to require a behavior modifier to clearly specify his or her values relating to the client's target behaviors. Ideally, the values on which the goals are based should be consistent with those of the client and with the long-term good of society. A second form of countercontrol is for the client to be an active participant in selecting goals and identifying target behaviors. In situations in which this is not possible (such as cases of persons with severe developmental disabilities), competent impartial third parties (e.g., ombudspersons, representatives of the community) authorized to act on behalf of a client can ensure accountability by being involved in crucial decisions concerning the selection of goals and the intervention methods.

3. Selection of Treatment

Behavior modifiers should use the most effective, empirically validated intervention methods with the least discomfort and fewest negative side effects. It is generally agreed that the least intrusive and restrictive interventions should be used wherever possible; however, there is no clear agreement on a continuum of intrusiveness or restrictiveness. These terms appear to be used in at least three ways.

First, interventions based on positive reinforcement are generally considered to be less intrusive and restrictive than interventions based on aversive control. As discussed in Chapters 13 and 14, that does not mean that aversive procedures should never be used. It might not be in the client's best interest for behavior modifiers to apply a slow-acting procedure if available research indicates that more aversive procedures would be more effective. As Van Houten and colleagues (1988, p. 114) expressed, "In some cases, a client's right to effective treatment might dictate the immediate use of quicker-acting, but temporarily more restrictive procedures."

Second, *intrusive* and *restrictive* sometimes refer to the extent to which clients are given choices and allowed freedom of movement in a therapeutic environment. In a work-training program for persons with developmental disabilities, for example, the assignment of specific tasks might be considered more intrusive or restrictive than allowing clients to choose among several optional work activities.

Third, *intrusive* and *restrictive* sometimes refer to the extent to which consequences are deliberately managed as opposed to naturally occurring. As indicated in Chapter 4, natural reinforcers are unprogrammed reinforcers that occur in the normal course of everyday living. Chapter 16 and elsewhere in this text stress the desirability of using natural contingencies of reinforcement whenever possible. If it is necessary to use contrived or deliberately programmed reinforcers early in a program, the behavior modifier should transfer control to natural reinforcers as quickly as possible.

While recognizing the desirability of selecting treatments that are the least intrusive and restrictive, the most effective treatment is likely to be based on a functional assessment of the causes of problem behavior as discussed in Chapter 23. When a functional analysis indicates the use of aversive methods, it is important to ensure countercontrol (Bailey & Burch, 2011, pp. 32–33). One way to ensure countercontrol is to stipulate that no program is to be carried out on a client who has not given informed consent to participate in that program. Stated differently, the behavior modifier should explain alternative treatments that could be used, state their pros and cons, and give the client a choice. This collaboration between the behavior modifier and an informed client is an essential element of behavior modification, and one that serves to protect clients' rights. A mechanism to facilitate informed consent is the signing of a treatment contract that clearly outlines the objectives and methods of treatment, the framework for the service to be provided, and the contingencies for the remuneration that might be forthcoming to the therapist (as described in Chapter 24). However, informed consent involves verbal behavior that, like other behavior, is under the control of the environment. Hence, verbal behavior might be manipulated in a particular fashion that might not be in the best interests of the client. The stipulation of informed consent thus provides only a partial check on the ethics of a program. In addition for many individuals, such as those with severe developmental disabilities, informed consent is inapplicable. Therefore, an additional way to help ensure that clients' rights are protected is by having ethical review committees composed of professionals and members of the community evaluate the ethics of proposed programs.

4. Record Keeping and Ongoing Evaluation

An important component of ensuring ethical treatment of clients is the maintenance of accurate data throughout a program. This includes a thorough behavioral assessment before the intervention is developed; ongoing monitoring of target behaviors as well as possible side effects; and appropriate follow-up evaluation after the treatment is concluded. Whereas behavior modifiers should always take good records, they should exercise utmost discretion in whom they permit to see those records. Confidentiality must be respected at all times.

Given the preceding caution, an important form of countercontrol is to provide frequent opportunities for a client to discuss with the applied behavior analyst or behavior therapist the data that tracks progress throughout the program. For this, of course, the client must have access to his or her own records. Another strategy is for the behavior modifier, with the client's permission, to share the client's records with those who are directly concerned with the client's progress. Feedback on the program's effectiveness from those who are concerned directly with the client's welfare is an important accountability mechanism. As indicated in Chapter 1, the most important characteristic of behavior modification is its strong emphasis on defining problems in terms of behavior that can be measured in some way and using changes in the behavioral measure of the problem as the best indicator of the extent to which the problem is being helped. Sharing these data with concerned parties and periodic evaluation of the data by all concerned is the cornerstone for ensuring ethical and effective treatment programs by behavior modifiers. For detailed discussion of ethical issues, see Bailey and Burch (2011), O'Donohue and Ferguson (2011), and Shook and Johnston (2011, pp. 503–504).

Conclusions

Behavior modification has great potential to be used for the good of society. An important responsibility of applied behavior analysts and behavior therapists is to develop ethical safeguards to ensure that behavior modification is always used wisely and humanely and does not become a new tool in the oppression that has thus far characterized the human species. Of all the safeguards discussed, the most fundamental is countercontrol. Perhaps the best way for behavior modifiers to help develop effective countercontrol throughout society is to spread their skills as widely as possible and to help educate the general public with respect to behavior modification. It should be difficult to use behavioral science to the disadvantage of any group whose members are well versed in the principles and tactics of behavior modification.

Questions for Learning

14. Discuss countercontrol. Why is it important?
15. What was a primary conclusion of the comprehensive report by Stolz & Associates on the ethical issues involved in behavior modification?
16. What steps can be taken to help ensure that an applied behavior analyst or behavior therapist is appropriately qualified?
17. State two countercontrol measures regarding the definition of problems and selection of goals.
18. In a sentence, what should be the characteristics of the intervention methods used by behavior modifiers?
19. Discuss three possible meanings of *intrusive* and *restrictive* interventions.
20. Describe a mechanism to facilitate informed consent.
21. What constitutes the cornerstone for ensuring ethical and effective treatment programs by behavior modifers?
22. Briefly explain why it should be difficult to use behavior modification to the detriment of any group whose members are well versed in the principles and tactics of behavior modification.

Notes for Further Learning

1. Skinner (1971) argued that we can trace the negative reaction to behavior control, at least in part, to the influence of 18th-century revolutionaries and social reformers. To counteract the aversive control utilized by tyrants, these activists developed the concept of freedom as a rallying cry. It was, said Skinner, a worthwhile concept in its time, for it spurred people to break away from aversive forms of control. Now, however, we have moved into an era in which positive reinforcement is a more predominant means of control and will perhaps become increasingly so with the growth of behavior modification. The concept of freedom has therefore outlived its social usefulness. Indeed, it is harmful, in that it tends to prevent us from seeing how our behavior is controlled by positive reinforcement. For example, many states and provincial governments in North America have turned to lotteries and casinos as ways to raise funds. Most people who happily buy lottery tickets or gamble in a casino feel that they are "free" to do so and fail to recognize that their behavior is being controlled to the same extent as it would be if they were being "forced" to pay the same amount in taxes. But the mechanism of control is different (i.e., positive reinforcement versus avoidance conditioning). Moreover, the concept of freedom encourages the view that some people deserve more "dignity" than others because of their achievements, whereas in actuality one's achievements or lack thereof are due to one's conditioning history and genetic predispositions. Hence, Skinner titled his book *Beyond Freedom and Dignity* (1971).

2. Prilleltensky (2008) has argued that psychologists who truly wish to help their clients should not focus only on the presenting problem of individual clients. He argues that psychologists should also focus on two other levels: the relational level and the political level. The relational level consists of the members of the community with whom the client interacts. The political level consists of the laws and regulations that affect the client. Clients who are seen by community psychologists are typically members of disadvantaged groups—that is, groups with less power, as discussed in this chapter, than the more dominant groups in the culture. By working only at the individual level, Prilleltensky argues, psychologists tend to maintain the status quo in which the clients remain permanently disadvantaged. In contrast, by working at all three levels psychologists may be able to help shift the balance of power more toward their clients, thereby truly helping them to function more fully in society.

Questions for Further Learning

1. Discuss Skinner's view that we must go "beyond freedom and dignity" if civilization is to solve some of its most difficult problems.
2. Give an example illustrating how governments use positive reinforcement to control behavior without citizens feeling that they are being controlled.
3. Discuss Prilleltensky's approach for how psychologists can best help their clients.

GLOSSARY

(The following are the main technical terms used in behavior modification. Please note that the definitions of many of these terms differ from common English dictionary definitions. For further information about these terms, check the index of this text.)

ABA   See *applied behavior analysis.*

ABAB design   See *reversal-replication design.*

Acceptance   See *experiential acceptance.*

Acceptance and commitment therapy (ACT)   A behavior therapy procedure in which the client: (a) learns to nonjudgmentally accept troublesome thoughts and emotions; and (b) commits to actions to pursue valued goals.

Adventitious chain   A behavioral chain that has some components that are functional in producing the reinforcer and at least one component (called the *superstitious component*) that is not.

Adventitious reinforcement   Strengthening of a behavior when it is followed by a reinforcer that it did not cause to occur.

Alternating-treatments design   An experimental design that involves alternating two or more treatment conditions. Also called a *multielement design.*

Antecedent stimulus   A stimulus that occurs before a behavior and exerts control over the behavior. Also see *discriminative stimulus.*

Applied behavior analysis (ABA)   Behavior modification that emphasizes the application of operant conditioning principles to individuals, and in which there often is an attempt to analyze or clearly demonstrate controlling variables of the behavior of concern using single-subject research designs. Also see *dimensions of applied behavior analysis.*

Aversive stimulus   Either a punisher or a negative reinforcer.

Avoidance conditioning, principle of   See *principle of avoidance conditioning.*

Backup reinforcer   A positive reinforcer that is presented in exchange for another stimulus to cause it to become a conditioned reinforcer.

Backward chaining   A method for establishing a behavioral chain in which the last step of the chain is taught first, then the next-to-last step is linked to the last step, and so on, until the entire chain is learned.

Behavior   Any muscular, glandular, or electrical activity of an organism. More generally, anything an individual says or does.

Behavior analysis   The study of the scientific principles that govern the behavior of individuals.

Behavior model of self-control   A theory that self-control occurs when an individual deliberately arranges the environment to manage his or her subsequent behavior.

Behavior modification   The systematic application of principles and techniques of learning to improve individuals' covert and overt behaviors in order to enhance their daily functioning. It includes applied behavior analysis, behavior therapy, and cognitive behavior modification or therapy.

Behavior therapy/cognitive behavior therapy   Behavior modification carried out on dysfunctional covert or overt behavior, generally in a psychological or psychiatric clinical or office setting. Also see *cognitive behavior modification.*

Behavioral assessment   The collection and analysis of information and data in order to (a) identify and describe target behaviors, (b) identify possible causes of the behavior, (c) guide the selection of an appropriate behavioral treatment, and (d) evaluate treatment outcome.

Behavioral chain   A consistent sequence of stimuli and responses that occur closely to each other in time and is maintained by reinforcement of the last response in the sequence. Also called a *stimulus-response chain.*

Behavioral contract   A written agreement that provides a clear statement of what behaviors of which individuals will produce what consequences and who will deliver those consequences.

Behavioral deficit   Too little behavior of a particular type.

Behavioral excess   Too much behavior of a particular type.

Behavioral rehearsal   Engaging in particular behaviors (playing a role) in a practice setting to increase the likelihood that those behaviors will occur appropriately outside the practice setting.

Behavioral trap   A contingency in which behavior that has been developed by programmed reinforcers is "trapped" (i.e., maintained) by natural reinforcers.

Chain   See *behavioral chain.*

Changing-criterion design   A research design in which the control that a treatment exerts on an individual's behavior is evaluated by introducing sequential changes in the behavioral criterion for reinforcement.

Classical conditioning   See *respondent conditioning.*

Cognition   Covert verbalizations and imagery; frequently called *believing, thinking, expecting,* and *perceiving.*

Cognitive behavior modification   An approach to treatment that focuses mainly on changing overt behavior by modifying covert behavior such as dysfunctional thinking.

Cognitive behavior therapy   See *behavior therapy/cognitive behavior therapy.*

Cognitive processes   Covert verbalizations and/or imagery that are frequently called *believing, thinking, expecting,* or *perceiving.* Also see *thinking.*

Cognitive restructuring   Strategies for recognizing maladaptive thinking and replacing it with adaptive thinking.

Commitment to change   Statements or actions by an individual that indicate that it is important to change his/her behavior, that the individual recognizes the benefits of doing so, and will work toward doing so.

Common-element stimulus class   A set of stimuli that have some physical characteristics in common.

Competing behaviors   See *incompatible behaviors.*

Concurrent schedules of reinforcement   Two or more different schedules of reinforcement operating at the same time.

Conditioned aversive stimulus   See *warning stimulus.*

Conditioned punisher   A stimulus that is a punisher as a result of having been paired with another punisher.

Conditioned reflex   A stimulus–response relationship in which a stimulus elicits a response because of prior respondent conditioning.

Conditioned reinforcer A stimulus that was not originally reinforcing but has become a reinforcer from being paired or associated with another reinforcer.

Conditioned response (CR) Either a respondent response elicited by a conditioned stimulus or an operant response that has been strengthened by reinforcement.

Conditioned stimulus (CS) A stimulus that elicits a response because that stimulus has been paired with another stimulus that elicits that or a similar response.

Conditioning Establishing a response through either respondent or operant conditioning.

Contingency An arrangement for reinforcement or punishment to occur when a specific response occurs on a given schedule in a given situation.

Contingency contract See *treatment contract*.

Contingency-shaped behavior Behavior that develops because of its immediate consequences.

Contingent Said of a stimulus with respect to a behavior if the behavior must occur before the stimulus will occur or be removed.

Continuous recording Recording every instance of a behavior during a designated observation period.

Continuous reinforcement An arrangement in which each instance of a particular response is reinforced.

Counterconditioning Conditioning a new response that is incompatible with a conditioned response at the same time that the latter is being extinguished.

CR See *conditioned response*.

CS See *conditioned stimulus*.

Dependent variable A measure of behavior that is studied as a function of an independent variable. See *independent variable*.

Deprivation The nonoccurrence of a positive reinforcer for a period of time resulting in its increased strength.

Dialectical behavior therapy An approach to behavior therapy based on Hegelian dialectics.

Differential reinforcement Reinforcement contingent on a given response rate, typically designed to lower the response rate.

Differential reinforcement of alternative (DRA) behavior Extinction of a problem behavior combined with reinforcing a behavior that is topographically dissimilar to but not necessarily incompatible with the problem behavior.

Differential reinforcement of incompatible (DRI) responding Withholding reinforcement for a particular response and reinforcing an incompatible response.

Differential reinforcement of low (DRL) rates A reinforcer is presented *only* if a particular response occurs at a low rate; can be programmed as limited-responding DRL or spaced-responding DRL.

Differential reinforcement of other (DRO) responding See *differential reinforcement of zero responding*.

Differential reinforcement of zero (DRO) responding A reinforcer is presented *only* if a specified response does *not* occur during a specified period of time. Also called *differential reinforcement of other responding*.

Dimensions of applied behavior analysis Characteristics of ABA, including: (a) a focus on measurable behavior that is socially significant; (b) a strong emphasis on operant conditioning to develop treatment strategies; (c) an attempt to clearly demonstrate that the applied treatment was responsible for the improvement in the behavior that was measured; and (d) a demonstration of generalizable and long-lasting improvements in behavior.

Direct assessment Judgment based on information about a behavior by directly observing it.

Direct-acting effect of a reinforcer Strengthening of a response that is followed immediately by a reinforcer.

Discriminative stimulus (S^D) A stimulus in the presence of which a response will be reinforced.

Discriminative stimulus (S^Δ) A stimulus in the presence of which a response will not be reinforced.

Discriminative stimulus (S^{Dp}) A stimulus in the presence of which a response will be punished.

DRA See *differential reinforcement of alternative behavior*.

DRI See *differential reinforcement of incompatible responding*.

DRL See *differential reinforcement of low rates*.

DRO See *differential reinforcement of zero responding*.

Echoic A vocal response that has a point-to-point correspondence with an antecedent vocal stimulus and is reinforced by a generalized conditioned reinforcer (see Skinner, 1957).

Effective stimulus control A strong correlation between the occurrence of a particular stimulus and a particular response. Also called *good stimulus control*.

Empirically supported therapies (ESTs) Therapies that have proved to be effective in scientifically conducted clinical trials.

Elicit The production of a response by an unconditioned or respondently conditioned stimulus. See *evoke* and *emit*.

Emit To produce an operant response (said of an individual). See *elicit* and *evoke*.

Error A response to an S^Δ or a failure to respond to an S^D.

Errorless discrimination training The use of a fading procedure to establish a stimulus discrimination so that no errors occur. Also called *errorless learning*.

Errorless learning See *errorless discrimination training*.

Escape conditioning A contingency in which an aversive stimulus is removed immediately following a response. Also called *negative reinforcement*.

Escape conditioning, principle of See *principle of escape conditioning*.

Establishing operation See *motivating establishing operation*.

ESTs See *empirically supported therapies*.

Evoke The production of an operant response by a discriminative stimulus. See *elicit* and *emit*.

Exclusionary timeout Removal of an individual briefly from a reinforcing situation contingent on a response.

Experiential acceptance Refraining from judging one's own thoughts, sensations, feelings, and behaviors as good or bad, pleasant or unpleasant, useful or useless, etc. Also called *acceptance*.

External validity The extent to which a finding of a study or experiment can be generalized to other behaviors, individuals, settings, or treatments.

Extinction burst An increase in responding during extinction.

Extinction (operant) The withholding of a reinforcer following a previously reinforced response that weakens the response.

Extinction (operant), principle of See *principle of extinction (operant)*.

Extinction (respondent)   Presenting a CS while withholding the US with the result that the CS gradually loses its capability of eliciting the CR.

Extinction (respondent), principle of   See *principle of extinction (respondent)*.

Fading   The gradual change over successive trials of an antecedent stimulus that controls a response so that the response eventually occurs to a partially changed or completely new stimulus.

FD schedule   See *fixed-duration schedule*.

Fear hierarchy   A list of fear-eliciting events arranged in order from the least to the most fear-eliciting.

FI/LH   See *fixed-interval-with-limited-hold schedule*.

Final desired behavior   In a shaping program a behavior that does not currently occur but is targeted or desired to do so at the end of the shaping process. Also called the *target behavior*.

Final desired stimulus   In a fading procedure the stimulus that does not currently evoke the response but is targeted or desired to do so at the end of the fading process. Also called the *target stimulus*.

FI schedule   See *fixed-interval schedule*.

Fixed-duration (FD) schedule   A schedule in which reinforcement occurs only if a behavior occurs continuously for a fixed period of time.

Fixed-interval (FI) schedule   A schedule in which reinforcement occurs following the first instance of a specific response after a fixed period of time.

Fixed-interval-with-limited-hold (FI/LH) schedule   A schedule of reinforcement in which a limited hold has been added to a fixed interval schedule.

Fixed-ratio (FR) schedule   A schedule in which reinforcement occurs each time a fixed number of responses of a particular type is emitted.

Flooding   A method for extinguishing fear by exposure to the feared stimulus for an extended period of time.

Forward chaining   A method for establishing a behavioral chain in which the initial step of the chain is taught first, then the initial step is linked to the second step, and so on until the entire chain is learned.

Frequency of behavior   The number of instances of a behavior that occurs in a given period of time. Also called *rate of behavior*.

Functional analysis   The systematic manipulation of environmental events to experimentally test their role as antecedents or as consequences in controlling and maintaining specific problem behaviors.

Functional assessment   A variety of procedures for attempting to identify antecedents and consequences of problem behaviors.

Generalized conditioned reinforcer   A conditioned reinforcer that is paired with more than one kind of unconditioned or backup reinforcer.

Generalized imitation   Occurs when, after learning to imitate a number of behaviors (perhaps with some shaping, fading, physical guidance, and reinforcement), an individual imitates a new response on the first trial without reinforcement.

Good stimulus control   See *effective stimulus control*.

Higher-order conditioning   A procedure in which a stimulus becomes a conditioned stimulus by being paired with another conditioned stimulus instead of with an unconditioned stimulus.

Independent variable   A treatment or intervention introduced to study its influence or effect on a dependent variable.

Indirect-acting effect of a reinforcer   Strengthening of a response that is followed by a delayed reinforcer whose reinforcing effect is mediated by self-directed verbal behavior.

Intermittent reinforcement   An arrangement in which a behavior is reinforced only occasionally rather than every time it occurs.

Internal validity   Said of a study or experiment if it convincingly demonstrated that the independent variable caused the observed change in the dependent variable.

Interobserver agreement (IOA)   See *interobserver reliability*.

Interobserver reliability (IOR)   A measure of the extent to which two observers agree on the occurrences of a behavior after independently observing and recording it during a specified period of time. Also called *interobserver agreement (IOA)*.

Interval recording   A recording method that logs the behavior as either occurring or not occurring during short intervals of equal duration during the specified observation period.

Latency   The time between the occurrence of a stimulus and the beginning of a response elicited or evoked by that stimulus.

Learning   A change in behavior that occurs as a result of respondent and operant condiioning.

LH   See *limited hold*.

Limited hold (LH)   A finite amount of time after a reinforcer becomes available that a response will produce it.

Limited-responding DRL   A contingency that specifies the maximum allowable number of responses during a certain time interval in order for reinforcement to occur.

Mand   A verbal response that is under the control of a motivating operation and is reinforced by the corresponding reinforcer or removal of the corresponding aversive stimulus (see Skinner, 1957).

MAO   See *motivating abolishing operation*.

Mastery criterion   A specific guideline for performing a skill so that if the guideline is met the skill is likely to be mastered.

MEO   See *motivating establishing operation*.

Method of successive approximations   See *shaping*.

Mindfulness   Awareness, observation, and description in a nonjudgmental way of one's covert and overt behaviors as they occur; in some cases, observation of the antecedents and consequences of those behaviors.

MO   See *motivating operation*.

Modeling   Demonstrating a sample of a given behavior to an individual to induce that individual to engage in a similar behavior.

Motivating abolishing operation (MAO)   An event or operation that temporarily decreases the effectiveness of a reinforcer or punisher and decreases the likelihood of behaviors that normally lead to that reinforcer or increases the likelihood of behaviors that lead to that punisher.

Motivating establishing operation (MEO)   An event or operation that temporarily increases the effectiveness of a reinforcer or punisher and increases the likelihood of behaviors that lead to that reinforcer or decreases the likelihood of behaviors that lead to that punisher.

Motivating operation (MO)   An event or condition that (a) temporarily alters the effectiveness of a reinforcer or punisher, and (b) influences behavior that normally leads to that reinforcer or punisher.

Multielement design   See *alternating-treatments design*.

Multiple-baseline-across-behaviors design   A research design that involves establishing baselines for two or more of an individual's behaviors followed by introducing the treatment in a staggered manner across those behaviors.

Multiple-baseline-across-people design   A research design that involves establishing baselines for a behavior of two or more individuals followed by introducing the treatment in a staggered manner across those individuals.

Multiple-baseline-across-situations design   A research design that involves establishing baselines for a behavior of an individual in two or more situations followed by introducing the treatment in a staggered manner across those situations.

Natural environment   Setting in which natural reinforcers occur.

Natural reinforcers   Unprogrammed reinforcers that occur in the normal course of everyday living.

Negative reinforcement, principle of   See *principle of escape conditioning*.

Negative reinforcer   A stimulus whose removal immediately after a response causes the response to be strengthened or to increase in frequency.

Noncontingent   Said of a stimulus if it is presented regardless of the preceding behavior.

Nonexclusionary timeout   Presenting a stimulus associated with less reinforcement contingent on a response.

Operant behaviors   Behavior that operates on the environment to generate consequences and is in turn influenced by those consequences.

Operant conditioning   The process of strengthening a behavior by reinforcing it or weakening it by punishing it.

Operant extinction   See *extinction (operant)*.

Operant responses   See *operant behaviors*.

Pain-inducing punisher   A stimulus immediately following a behavior that activates pain receptors or other sense receptors that typically evoke feelings of discomfort. Also called a *physical punisher*.

Participant modeling   A method for decreasing fear in which a client imitates another individual approaching a feared object.

Pavlovian conditioning   See *respondent conditioning*.

Physical guidance   The application of physical contact to induce an individual to go through the motions of a desired behavior. Also called a *physical prompt*.

Physical prompt   See *physical guidance*.

Physical punisher   See *pain-inducing punisher*.

Positive reinforcement, principle of   See *principle of positive reinforcement*.

Positive reinforcer   A stimulus which, when presented immediately following a behavior, causes the behavior to increase in frequency.

Preference assessment   A test to determine which among several potential reinforcers are preferred by an individual in order to find an effective reinforcer for that individual.

Premack principle   The opportunity to engage in a highly probable behavior can be used to reinforce a behavior that has a lower probability of occurring.

Primary reinforcer/primary punisher   See *unconditioned reinforcer* or *unconditioned punisher*.

Principle of avoidance conditioning   A contingency in which a response prevents or postpones an aversive stimulus from occurring, thereby resulting in an increase in the frequency of that response.

Principle of escape conditioning   The removal of certain stimuli, called aversive stimuli, immediately after the occurrence of a response will increase the likelihood of that response. Also called *principle of negative reinforcement*.

Principle of extinction (operant)   (a) If, in a given situation, someone emits a previously reinforced response and that response is not followed by a reinforcer, (b) then that person is less likely to do the same thing again when next encountering a similar situation.

Principle of extinction (respondent)   If a CS is presented and not followed by the US the CS will gradually loses its capability of eliciting the CR.

Principle of negative reinforcement   See *principle of escape conditioning*.

Principle of positive reinforcement   If, in a given situation, someone does something that is followed immediately by a positive reinforcer, then that person is more likely to do the same thing again when he or she next encounters a similar situation.

Principle of punishment   If, in a given situation, someone does something that is immediately followed by a punisher or the removal of a reinforcer, then that person is less likely to do the same thing again when she or he next encounters a similar situation.

Principle of respondent conditioning   If a neutral stimulus is followed closely in time by an unconditioned stimulus that elicits a specific unconditioned response, then the previously neutral stimulus will also tend to elicit that response in the future.

Programmed reinforcers   Reinforcers that are arranged systematically in behavior modification programs.

Prompt   A supplemental antecedent stimulus provided to increase the likelihood that a desired behavior will occur but that is not a part of the final desired stimulus to control that behavior.

Punisher   A stimulus whose presentation immediately after a behavior causes that behavior to decrease in frequency.

Punishment   Presentation of a punisher or the removal of a reinforcer immediately following a behavior with the effect that the behavior decreases in frequency. Also see *principle of punishment*.

Punishment, principle of   See *principle of punishment*.

Rate of behavior   See *frequency of behavior*.

Rational-emotive behavioral therapy (REBT)   A behavior therapy method that combines challenging the client's debilitating irrational beliefs and more traditional behavior therapy procedures such as behavioral homework assignments.

Reinforcement   Presentation of a positive reinforcer or removal of a negative reinforcer contingent on a response.

Reinforcer   Either a positive or a negative reinforcer. Usually the former unless otherwise specified.

Relapse   The return of a treated behavior to its level prior to treatment.

Relative duration of behavior   The length of time that a behavior occurs within some period.

Reprimand   Negative verbal stimuli presented contingent on behavior.

Respondent behaviors   Behaviors elicited by prior stimuli and that are not affected by their consequences.

Respondent conditioning   Establishing a response to a new stimulus by pairing that stimulus with another stimulus that elicits that response. Also called *Pavlovian conditioning* and *classical conditioning*.

Respondent conditioning, principle of   See *principle of respondent conditioning*.

Respondent extinction   See *extinction (respondent)*.

Response cost   The removal of a specified amount of a reinforcer immediately following a particular behavior. Can also refer to an increase in the effort needed to emit the response.

Response generalization   Increased probability of a response as a result of the reinforcement of another response.

Response topography   The specific movements involved in making a response.

Reversal-replication design   An experimental design consisting of a baseline phase, followed by a treatment phase, followed by a reversal back to baseline, followed by replication of the treatment phase. Also called an *ABAB design*.

Role-playing   See *behavioral rehearsal*.

Rule   A verbal stimulus describing a three-term contingency of reinforcement (antecedent–behavior–consequence).

Rule-governed behavior   Behavior controlled by the presentation of a rule.

S^D See *discriminative stimulus (S^D)*.

S^Δ See *discriminative stimulus (S^Δ)*.

S^{Dp} See *discriminative stimulus (S^{Dp})*.

Satiation   Condition in which an individual has experienced a reinforcer to such an extent that the reinforcer is temporarily ineffective.

Schedule of reinforcement   A rule specifying which occurrences of a given behavior, if any, will be reinforced.

Self-control program   A strategy for using principles of behavior modification to change or control one's own behavior. Also called a *self-management program* and a *self-modification program*.

Self-management program   See *self-control program*.

Self-modification program   See *self-control program*.

Shaping   The development of a new behavior by the reinforcement of successive approximations of that behavior and the extinction of earlier approximations of that behavior until the new behavior occurs. Also called the *method of successive approximations*.

Simple conditioned reinforcer   A conditioned reinforcer paired with a single backup reinforcer.

Spaced-responding DRL   A contingency in which a specified behavior must not occur during a specified interval, and after the interval has passed, an instance of that behavior must then occur for a reinforcer to occur. Also see *differential reinforcement of low rates*.

Spontaneous recovery   The reappearance of an extinguished behavior following a rest or period in which the behavior does not have an opportunity to occur.

Starting behavior   A behavior that reliably occurs, is an approximation of the final desired behavior in a shaping procedure, and is used to begin the process of developing the final desired behavior.

Starting stimulus   In a fading procedure a stimulus that reliably evokes the response and is used to begin the process of bringing the response under the control of the final desired stimulus.

Stimuli   Plural of *stimulus*; the people, animals, objects, and events currently present in an one's immediate surroundings that impinge on one's sense receptors and that can affect behavior.

Stimulus   Singular of *stimuli*.

Stimulus control   The degree of correlation between an antecedent stimulus and a subsequent response.

Stimulus discrimination   A response occurs to an S^D and not to an S^Δ.

Stimulus discrimination training   The procedure of reinforcing a response in the presence of an S^D and extinguishing that response in the presence of an S^Δ.

Stimulus equivalence class   A set of completely dissimilar stimuli that an individual has learned to group or match together.

Stimulus generalization   Refers to the *procedure* of reinforcing a response in the presence of a stimulus or situation and the *effect* of the response becoming more probable in the presence of another stimulus or situation.

Stimulus-response chain   See *behavioral chain*.

Superstitious behavior   Behavior that is strengthened by adventitious reinforcement.

Systematic desensitization   A procedure for overcoming a phobia by having a client while in a relaxed state successively imagine the least to most feared items in a fear hierarchy.

Tact   A verbal response that is under the control of a nonverbal antecedent stimulus and is reinforced by a generalized conditioned reinforcer (see Skinner, 1957).

Target behavior   Behavior to be improved in a behavior modification program. Also see *final desired behavior*.

Target stimulus   See *final desired stimulus*.

Task analysis   The process of breaking a task down into smaller steps or component responses to facilitate training.

Thinking   Covert or private verbalizations and imagery.

Time sampling recording   An observational procedure in which a behavior is scored as occurring or not occurring during very brief observation intervals that are separated from each other by a much longer period of time.

Timeout   A period of time immediately following a particular behavior during which an individual loses the opportunity to earn reinforcers.

Token economy   A behavioral program in which individuals in a group can earn tokens for a variety of desirable behaviors and can cash in their tokens for backup reinforcers.

Token system   A behavior modification program in which an individual can earn tokens for performing desirable behaviors and can cash in the tokens for backup reinforcers.

Tokens   Conditioned reinforcers that can be accumulated and exchanged for backup reinforcers.

Topography   See *response topography*.

Total-task presentation   A chaining method in which an individual attempts all of the steps from the beginning to the end of the chain on each trial until that person learns the chain.

Treatment contract   A written agreement between the client and the behavior modifier that clearly outlines the objectives and methods of treatment, the framework of the service to be provided, and contingencies for remuneration that may be forthcoming to the behavior modifier. Also called a *contingency contract*.

Unconditioned punisher   A stimulus that is a punisher without prior learning. Also called a *primary punisher*.

Unconditioned reflex   A stimulus–response relationship in which a stimulus automatically elicits a response apart from any prior learning.

Unconditioned reinforcer   A stimulus that is reinforcing without prior learning or conditioning. Also called a *primary reinforcer*.

Unconditioned response (UR)   A response elicited by an unconditioned stimulus.

Unconditioned stimulus (US)   A stimulus that elicits a response without prior learning or conditioning.

UR   *See unconditioned response.*

US   *See unconditioned stimulus.*

Variable-duration (VD) schedule   A schedule in which reinforcement occurs only if a behavior occurs continuously for a fixed period of time, and the interval of time from reinforcer to reinforcer changes unpredictably.

Variable-interval (VI) schedule   A schedule in which reinforcement occurs following the first instance of a specific response after an interval of time, and the length of the interval changes unpredictably from one reinforcement to the next.

Variable-interval-with-limited-hold   schedule   (VI/LH)   A variable-interval schedule with an added limited hold.

Variable-ratio (VR) schedule   A schedule in which reinforcement occurs after a certain number of responses of a particular type is emitted, and the number of responses required for reinforcement changes unpredictably from one reinforcer to the next.

VD   *See variable-duration schedule.*

VI/LH schedule   *See variable-interval-with-limited-hold schedule.*

VI schedule   *See variable-interval schedule.*

VR schedule   *See variable-ratio (VR) schedule.*

Warning stimulus   A stimulus that signals a forthcoming aversive stimulus. Also called a *conditioned aversive stimulus*.

REFERENCES

Abbott, B. V., & Snyder, D. K. (2010). Couple distress. In M. M. Antony & D. H. Barlow (Eds.), *Handbook of assessment and treatment planning for psychological disorders* (2nd ed., pp. 439–476). New York: The Guilford Press.

Abbott, B. V., & Snyder, D. K. (2012). Integrative approaches to couple therapy: A clinical case illustration. *Journal of Family Therapy, 34,* 306–320.

Abernathy, W. B. (2013). Behavioral approaches to business and industrial problems: Organization behavior management. In G. J. Madden (Ed.), *APA handbook of behavior analysis: Volume 2, translating behavioral principles into practice* (pp. 501–522). Washington, DC: American Psychological Association.

Addiction Medicine: Closing the Gap between Science and Practice. New York: The National Center on Substance Abuse at Columbia University.

Addison, L., & Lerman, D. C. (2009). Descriptive analysis of teachers' responses to problem behavior following training. *Journal of Applied Behavior Analysis, 42,* 485–490.

Ader, R., & Cohen, N. (1982). Behaviorally conditioned immunosuppression and murine systemic lupis erythematosus, *Science, 215,* 1534–1536.

Ader, R., & Cohen, N. (1993). Psychoneuroimmunology: Conditioning and stress. *Annual Review of Psychology, 44,* 53–85.

Afifi, T. O., Mota, N. P., Dasiewicz, P., MacMillan, H. L., & Sareen, J. (2012). Physical punishment and mental disorders: Results from a nationally representative U.S. sample. *Pediatrics, 130,* 1–9.

Agarwal, S. K. (2012). Cardiovascular benefits of exercise. *International Journal of General Medicine, 5,* 541–545.

Agathon, M. (1982). Behavior therapy in France: 1976–1981. *Journal of Behavior Therapy and Experimental Psychiatry, 13,* 271–277.

Agras, W. S., Taylor, C. B., Feldman, D. E., Losch, M., & Burnett, K. F. (1990). Developing computer-assisted therapy for the treatment of obesity. *Behavior Therapy, 21,* 99–109.

Ahearn, W. H., & Tiger, J. J. (2013). Behavioral approaches to the treatment of autism. In G. J. Madden (Ed.), *APA handbook of behavior analysis: Volume 2, translating behavioral principles into practice* (pp. 301–328). Washington, DC: American Psychological Association.

Airapetyantz, E., & Bykov, D. (1966). Physiological experiments and the psychology of the subconscious. In T. Verhave (Ed.), *The experimental analysis of behavior* (pp. 140–157). New York: Appleton-Century-Crofts.

Alberto, P. A., & Troutman, A. C. (2012). *Applied behavior analysis for teachers* (9th ed.). Upper Saddle River, NJ: Pearson.

Albion, F. M., & Salzburg, C. L. (1982). The effects of self-instruction on the rate of correct addition problems with mentally retarded children. *Education and Treatment of Children, 5,* 121–131.

Allen, G. J. (1973). Case study: Implementation of behavior modification techniques in summer camp settings. *Behavior Therapy, 4,* 570–575.

Allen, K. D., & Stokes, T. F. (1987). Use of escape and reward in the management of young children during dental treatment. *Journal of Applied Behavior Analysis, 20,* 381–390.

American Psychiatric Association. (1952). *Diagnostic and statistical manual of mental disorders: DSM-I.* Washington, DC: Author.

American Psychiatric Association. (2013). *Diagnostic and statistical manual of mental disorders: DSM-5* (5th ed.). Washington, DC: Author.

American Psychological Association. (2010). *Ethical principles of psychologists and code of conduct.* Washington, DC: Author.

Anderson, C. M., & Freeman, K. A. (2000). Positive behaviour support: Expanding the application of applied behaviour analysis. *The Behavior Analyst, 23,* 85–94.

Anderson, W. H. (1978). A comparison of self-distraction with self-verbalization under moralistic versus instrumental rationales in a delay-of-gratification paradigm. *Cognitive Therapy and Research, 2,* 299–303.

Antony, M. M., & Barlow, D. H. (Eds.). (2010). *Handbook of assessment and treatment planning for psychological disorders* (2nd ed.). New York: The Guilford Press.

Antony, M. M., & Norton, P. J. (2009). *The anti-anxiety workbook.* New York: The Guilford Press.

APA Presidential Task Force on Evidence-Based Practice. (2006). Evidence-based practice in psychology. *American Psychologist, 61,* 271–285.

Ardila, R. (1982). International developments in behavior therapy in Latin America. *Journal of Behavior Therapy and Experimental Psychiatry, 13,* 15–20.

Arkowitz, H., Westra, H., Miller, W. R., & Rollnick, S. (2008). *Motivational interviewing in the treatment of psychological problems.* New York: The Guilford Press.

Arnold, M. L., & Van Houten, R. (2011). Increasing following headway with prompts, goal setting, and feedback in a driving simulator. *Journal of Applied Behavior Analysis, 44,* 245–254.

Arrick, C. M., Voss, J., & Rimm, D. C. (1981). The relative efficacy of thought-stopping and covert assertion. *Behaviour Research and Therapy, 19,* 17–24.

Asch, S. E. (1948). The doctrine of suggestion, prestige and imitation in social psychology. *Psychological Review, 55,* 250–276.

Ash, D. W., & Holding, D. H. (1990). Backward versus forward chaining in the acquisition of a keyboard skill. *Human Factors, 32,* 139–146.

Asher, M. J., Gordon, S. B., Selbst, M. C., & Cooperberg, M. (2010). *The behavior problems resource kit: Forms and procedures for identification, measurement, and intervention.* Champagne, IL: Research Press.

Ashford, S. J., & De Stobbeleir, K. E. M. (2013). Feedback, goal setting, and task performance revisited. In E. A. Locke & G. P. Latham (Eds.), *New developments in goal setting and task performance* (pp. 51–64). New York: Routledge.

Athens, E. S., Vollmer, T. R., & St. Peter Pipkin, C. C. (2007). Shaping academic task engagement with percentile schedules. *Journal of Applied Behavior Analysis, 40,* 475–488.

Aubuchon, P. G., Haber, J. D., & Adams, H. E. (1985). Can migraine headaches be modified by operant pain techniques? *Journal of Behavior Therapy and Experimental Psychiatry, 16,* 261–263.

Austin, J. L., & Bevan, D. (2011). Using differential reinforcement of low rates to reduce children's requests for teacher attention. *Journal of Applied Behavior Analysis, 44,* 451–461.

Austin, L. (2000). Behavioral approaches to college teaching. In J. Austin & J. E. Carr (Eds.), *Handbook of applied behavior analysis* (pp. 321–350). Reno, NV: Context Press.

Axe, J. B., & Sainato, D. M. (2010). Matrix training of preliteracy skills with preschoolers with autism. *Journal of Applied Behavior Analysis, 43,* 635–652.

Ayllon, T. (1999). *How to use token economy and point systems* (2nd ed.). Austin, TX: Pro-Ed, Inc.

Ayllon, T., & Azrin, N. H. (1968). *The token economy: A motivational system for therapy and rehabilitation.* New York: Appleton-Century-Crofts.

Ayllon, T., & Michael, J. (1959). The psychiatric nurse as a behavioral engineer. *Journal of the Experimental Analysis of Behavior, 2,* 323–334.

Ayllon, T., & Milan, M. A. (1979). *Correctional rehabilitation and management: A psychological approach.* New York: Wiley.

Azrin, N. H. (1967). Pain and aggression. *Psychology Today, 1*(1), 27–33.

Azrin, N. H., & Lindsley, O. R. (1956). The reinforcement of cooperation between children. *Journal of Abnormal and Social Psychology, 52,* 100–102.

Azrin, N. H., & Nunn, R. G. (1973). Habit reversal: A method of eliminating nervous habits and tics. *Behaviour Research and Therapy, 11,* 619–628.

Azrin, N. H., Rubin, H., O'Brien, F., Ayllon, T., & Roll, D. (1968). Behavioral engineering: Postural control by a portable operant apparatus. *Journal of Applied Behavior Analysis, 1,* 99–108.

Azrin, N. H., Sisson, R. W., Meyers, R., & Godley, N. (1982). Alcoholism treatment by disulfiram and community reinforcement therapy. *Journal of Behavior Therapy and Experimental Psychiatry, 13*(2), 105–112.

Babel, D., Martin, G. L., Fazzio, D., Arnal, L., & Thomson, K. (2008). Assessment of the reliability and validity of the Discrete-Trials Teaching Evaluation Form. *Developmental Disabilities Bulletin, 36,* 67–80.

Bachmeyer, M. H., Piazza, C. C., Frederick, L. D., Reed, G. K., Rivas, K. D., & Kadey, H. J. (2009). Functional analysis and treatment of multiply controlled inappropriate mealtime behavior. *Journal of Applied Behavior Analysis, 42,* 641–658.

Baer, D. M., & Wolf, M. M. (1970). The entry into natural communities of reinforcement. In R. Ulrich, T. Stachnik, & J. Mabry (Eds.), *Control of human behavior* (Vol. 2, pp. 319–324). Glenview, IL: Scott Foresman.

Baer, D. M., Peterson, R. F., & Sherman, J. A. (1967). The development of imitation by reinforcing behavioral similarity to a model. *Journal of the Experimental Analysis of Behavior, 10,* 405–416.

Baer, D. M., Wolf, M. M., & Risley, T. R. (1968). Some current dimensions of Applied Behavior Analysis. *Journal of Applied Behavior Analysis, 1,* 91–97.

Bailey, J. S., & Burch, M. R. (2002). *Research methods in applied behavior analysis.* Thousand Oaks, CA: Sage Publications, Inc.

Bailey, J. S., & Burch, M. R. (2006). *How to think like a behavior analyst: Understanding the science that can change your life.* Mahwah, NJ: Lawrence Erlbaum Associates.

Bailey, J. S., & Burch, M. R. (2011). *Ethics for behavior analysts* (2nd ed.). New York: Routledge.

Bailey, J. S., Hughes, R. G., & Jones, W. E. (1980). *Applications of backward chaining to air-to-surface weapons delivery training.* Williams Airforce Base, AZ: Operations training division, Human Resources Laboratory.

Bailey, J. S., & Pyles, D. A. M. (1989). Behavioral diagnostics. *Monographs of the American Association on Mental Retardation, 12,* 85–106.

Bailey, J. S., Timbers, G. D., Phillips, E. I., & Wolf, M. M. (1971). Modification of articulation errors of pre-delinquents by their peers. *Journal of Applied Behaviour Analysis, 3,* 265–281.

Baldwin, J. D., & Baldwin, J. I. (2000). *Behavior principles in everyday life* (4th ed.). Upper Saddle River, NJ: Prentice Hall.

Bambara, L. M., & Kern, L. (2005). *Individualized supports for students with problem behaviors: Designing positive behavior plans.* New York: The Guilford Press.

Bandura, A. (1965). Influence of models' reinforcement contingencies in the acquisition of imitative responses. *Journal of Personality and Social Psychology, 1,* 589–595.

Bandura, A. (1969). *Principles of behavior modification.* New York: Holt, Rinehart & Winston.

Bandura, A. (1977). *Social learning theory.* Upper Saddle River, NJ: Prentice Hall.

Bandura, A. (1982). Self-efficacy mechanism in human agency. *American Psychologist, 37,* 122–147.

Bandura, A. (1986). *Social foundations of thought and action: A social-cognitive theory.* Upper Saddle River, NJ: Prentice Hall.

Bandura, A. (1997). *Self-efficacy: The exercise of control.* New York: W. H. Freeman and Company.

Bandura, A., & Walters, R. H. (1963). *Social learning and personality development.* New York: Holt, Rinehart & Winston.

Banerjee, S. P. (1999). Behavioral psychotherapy in Singapore. *The Behavior Therapist, 22,* 80, 91.

Barker, J. B., Mellalieu, S. D., McCarthy, P. J., Jones, M. V., & Moran, A. (2013). A review of single-case research in sport psychology, 1997–2012: Research trends and future directions. *Journal of Applied Sport Psychology, 25,* 4–32.

Barkley, R. A. (1996). 18 ways to make token systems more effective for ADHD children and teens. *The ADHD Report, 4,* 1–5.

Barkley, R. A. (2005). *Attention-deficit hyperactive disorder: A handbook for diagnosis and treatment* (3rd ed.). New York: The Guilford Press.

Barkley, R. A., & Murphy, K. R. (2005). *Attention-deficit hyperactive disorder: A clinical workbook* (3rd ed.). New York: Guilford Press.

Barlow, D. H. (Ed.). (2008). *Clinical handbook of psychological disorders: A step-by-step treatment manual* (4th ed.). New York: The Guilford Press.

Barlow, D. H., & Hayes, S. C. (1979). Alternating-treatments design: One strategy for comparing the effects of two treatments in a single subject. *Journal of Applied Behavior Analysis, 12,* 199–210.

Barlow, D. H., Nock, M. K., & Hersen, M. (2009). *Single case experimental designs: Strategies for studying behavior change* (3rd ed.). Upper Saddle River, NJ: Pearson.

Barnett, N. P., Tidey, J., Murphy, J. G., Swift, R., & Colby, S. M. (2011). Contingency management for alcohol reduction: A pilot study using a transdermal alcohol sensor. *Drug and Alcohol Dependence, 118,* 391–399.

Baron-Cohen, S. (1995). *Mindblindness: An essay on autism and theory of mind.* Cambridge, MA: MIT Press.

Barone, D. F. (1982). Instigating additional self-modification projects after a personal adjustment course. *Teaching of Psychology, 9,* 111.

Barrios, B. A., & Hartmann, D. P. (1986). The contributions of traditional assessment: Concepts, issues, and methodologies. In R. O. Nelson & S. C. Hayes (Eds.), *Conceptual foundations of behavioral assessment* (pp. 81–110). New York: The Guilford Press.

Batra, M., & Batra, V. (2005/2006). Comparison between forward chaining and backward chaining techniques in children with mental retardation. *The Indian Journal of Occupational Therapy, 37,* 57–63.

Baum, A., Revenson, T. A., & Singer, J. (2011). *Handbook of health psychology* (2nd ed.). London: Psychology Press.

Baum, J. R. (2013). Goals and entrepreneurship. In E. A. Locke & G. P. Latham (Eds.), *New developments in goal setting and task performance* (pp. 460–473). New York: Routledge.

Baum, W. M. (2011). Behaviorism, private events, and the molar view of behavior. *The Behavior Analyst, 34,* 185–200.

Baum, W. M. (2012). Rethinking reinforcement: Allocation, induction, and contingency. *Journal of the Experimental Analysis of Behavior, 97,* 101–124.

Beavers, G. A., Iwata, B. A., & Lerman, D. C. (2013). Thirty years of research on the functional analysis of problem behavior. *Journal of Applied Behavior Analysis, 46,* 1–21.

Beck, A. T. (1970). Cognitive therapy: Nature and relation to behavior therapy. *Behavior Therapy, 1,* 184–200.

Beck, A. T. (1976). *Cognitive therapy and the emotional disorders.* New York: International Universities Press.

Beck, A. T., Emery, G., & Greenberg, R. L. (1985). *Anxiety disorders and phobias: A cognitive perspective.* New York: Basic Books.

Beck, A. T., Rector, N. A., Stolar, N., & Grant, P. (2008). *Schizophrenia: Cognitive theory, research, and therapy.* New York: The Guilford press.

Beck, A. T., Rush, A. J., Shaw, B. F., & Emery, G. (1979). *Cognitive therapy of depression.* New York: The Guilford Press.

Beck, J. S. (2011). *Cognitive behavior therapy: Basics and beyond* (2nd ed.). New York: The Guilford Press.

Bellack, A. S. (1986). Schizophrenia: Behavior therapy's forgotten child. *Behavior Therapy, 17,* 199–214.

Bellack, A. S., & Hersen, M. (1993). Clinical behavior therapy with adults. In A. S. Bellack & M. Hersen (Eds.), *Handbook of behavior therapy in the psychiatric setting* (pp. 3–18). New York: Plenum Press.

Bellack, A. S., & Muser, K. T. (1990). Schizophrenia. In A. S. Bellack, M. Hersen, & A. E. Kazdin (Eds.), *International handbook of behavior modification and behavior therapy* (2nd ed., pp. 353–376). New York: Plenum Press.

Bellack, A. S., Muser, K. T., Gingerich, S., & Agresta, J. (Eds.). (1997). *Social skills training for schizophrenia.* New York: The Guilford Press.

Bellamy, G. T., Horner, R. H., & Inman, D. P. (1979). *Vocational habilitation of severely retarded adults: A direct service technology.* Baltimore: University Park Press.

Bellini, S., & Akullian, J. (2007). A meta-analysis of video modeling and video self-modeling interventions for children and adolescents with autism spectrum disorders. *Exceptional Children, 73,* 264–287.

Bentall, R. P., Lowe, C. F., & Beasty, A. (1985). The role of verbal behavior in human learning. II: Developmental differences. *Journal of the Experimental Analysis of Behavior, 47,* 165–181.

Bergen, A. E., Holborn, S. W., & Scott-Huyghebart, V. C. (2002). Functional analysis of self-injurious behavior in an adult with Lesch–Nyhan Syndrome. *Behavior Modification, 26,* 187–204.

Bergstrom, R., Najdowski, A. C., & Tarbox, J. (2012). Teaching children with autism to seek help when lost in public. *Journal of Applied Behavior Analysis, 45,* 191–195.

Bernfeld, G. A (2006). The struggle for treatment integrity in a "dis-integrated" service delivery system. *The Behavior Analyst Today, 7,* 188–205. (Reprinted from Bernfeld, G. A., Farrington, D. P., & Leschied, A. W. [Eds.] [2001]. *Offender rehabilitation in practice: Implementing and evaluating effective programs* [pp. 167–188]. Hoboken, NJ: John Wiley & Sons.)

Bernfeld, G. A., Blase, K. A., & Fixsen, D. L. (2006). Towards a unified perspective on human service delivery systems: Application of the Teaching-Family Model. *The Behavior Analyst Today, 7,* 168–187. (Reprinted from McMahon, R. J., & Peters, R. DeV. [Eds.] [1990], *Behavior disorders of adolescence: Research, intervention and policy in clinical and school settings* [pp. 191–205]. New York: Plenum Press.)

Bernstein, D., & Chase, P. N. (2013). Contributions of behavior analysis to higher education. In G. J. Madden (Ed.), *APA handbook of behavior analysis: Volume 2, translating behavioral principles into practice* (pp. 523–544). Washington, DC: American Psychological Association.

Betz, A. M., & Fisher, W. W. (2011). Functional analysis: History and methods. In W. W. Fisher, C. C. Piazza, & H. S. Roane (Eds.), *Handbook of applied behavior analysis.* New York: The Guildford Press.

Bicard, D. F., Ervin, A., Bicard, S. C., & Baylot-Casey, L. (2012). Differential effects of seating arrangements on disruptive behavior of fifth grade students during independent seatwork. *Journal of Applied Behavior Analysis, 45,* 407–411.

Biddle, S. J. H., & Mutrie, N. (2008). *Psychology of physical activity: Determinants, well-being & interventions* (2nd ed.). New York: Routledge.

Bierman, K. L., Miller, C. L., & Stabb, S. D. (1987). Improving the social behavior and peer acceptance of rejected boys: Effects of social skill training with instructions and prohibitions. *Journal of Consulting and Clinical Psychology, 55,* 194–200.

Biglan, A., & Glenn, S. S. (2013). Toward prosocial behavior and environments: Behavioral and cultural contingencies in a public health framework. In G. J. Madden (Ed.), *APA handbook of behavior analysis: Volume 2, translating behavioral principles into practice* (pp. 255–276). Washington, DC: American Psychological Association.

Bijou, S. W., & Baer, D. M. (1961). *Child development: A systematic and empirical theory* (Vol. 1). New York: Appleton-Century-Crofts.

Bijou, S. W., & Baer, D. M. (1965). *Child development II: Universal stage of infancy.* Upper Saddle River, NJ: Prentice Hall.

Binder, L. M., Dixon, M. R., & Ghezzi, P. M. (2000). A procedure to teach self-control to children with attention deficit hyperactivity disorder. *Journal of Applied Behavior Analysis, 33,* 233–237.

Birnbrauer, J. S., Bijou, S. W., Wolf, M. M., & Kidder, J. D. (1965). Programmed instruction in the classroom. In L. P. Ullmann &

L. Krasner (Eds.), *Case studies in behavior modification* (pp. 358–363). New York: Holt, Rinehart & Winston.

Bize, R., Johnson, J. A., & Plotnikoff, R. C. (2007). Physical activity level and health-related quality of life in the general adult population: A systematic review. *Preventive Medicine, 45,* 401–415.

Bjorgvinsson, T., & Rosqvist, J. (2009). *Cognitive behavioral therapy for depression: A practical guide to management and treatment.* New York: Routledge.

Blampied, N. (1999). Cognitive-behavior therapy in Aotearoa, New Zealand. *The Behavior Therapist, 22,* 173–178.

Blampied, N. (2004). The New Zealand association for behavior analysis. *Newsletter of the International Association for Behavior Analysis, 27*(2), 27.

Blampied, N. M. (2013). Single-case research designs and the scientist-practitioner ideal in applied psychology. In G. J. Madden (Ed.), *APA handbook of behavior analysis: Volume 1, methods and principles* (pp. 177–198). Washington, DC: American Psychological Association.

Blampied, N. M., & Bootzin, R. R. (2013). Sleep: A behavioral account. In G. J. Madden (Ed.), *APA handbook of behavior analysis: Volume 2, translating behavioral principles into practice* (pp. 425–454). Washington, DC: American Psychological Association.

Blanck, G. (1983). *Behavior therapy in Argentina.* Buenos Aires: AAPC Ediciones.

Block-Lerner, J., Wulfert, E., & Moses, E. (2009). ACT in context: An exploration of experiential acceptance. *Cognitive and Behavioral Practice, 16,* 443–456.

Blount, R. L., Drabman, R. S., Wilson, N., & Stewart, D. (1982). Reducing severe diurnal bruxism in two profoundly retarded females. *Journal of Applied Behavior Analysis, 15,* 565–571.

Boerke, K. W., & Reitman, D. (2011). Token economies. In W. W. Fisher, C. C. Piazza, & H. S. Roane (Eds.), *Handbook of applied behavior analysis* (pp. 370–384). New York: The Guilford Press.

Boniecki, K. A., & Moore, S. (2003). Breaking the silence: Use of the token economy to reinforce classroom participation. *Teaching of Psychology, 30,* 224–227.

Booth, R., & Rachman, S. (1992). The reduction of claustrophobia: I. *Behaviour Research and Therapy, 30,* 207–221.

Borden, J. W. (1992). Behavioral treatment of simple phobia. In S. M. Turner, K. S. Calhoun, & H. E. Adams (Eds.), *Handbook of clinical behavior therapy* (pp. 77–94). New York: Wiley.

Boris, A., Thomson, K., Murphy, C., Zaragoza Scherman, A., Dodson, L., Martin, G., & Yu, C. T. (in press). An evaluation of a self-instructional manual for conducting discrete-trials teaching with children with autism. *Developmental Disabilities Bulletin.*

Borkovec, T. D., & Sharpless, B. (2004). Generalized anxiety disorder: Bringing cognitive-behavioral therapy into the valued present. In S. C. Hayes, V. M. Follette, & M. M. Linehan (Eds.), *Mindfulness and acceptance: Expanding the cognitive-behavioral tradition.* New York: The Guilford Press.

Borrego, J., Ibanez, E. S., Spendlove, S. J., & Pemberton, J. R. (2007). Treatment acceptability among Mexican American parents. *Behavior Therapy, 38,* 218–227.

Bouchard, S., Vallieres, A., Roy, M., & Maziade, M. (1996). Cognitive restructuring in the treatment of psychotic symptoms in schizophrenia: A critical analysis. *Behavior Therapy, 27,* 257–277.

Bouman, T. K., & Emmelkamp, P. M. G. (1996). Panic disorder and agoraphobia. In V. B. Van Hasselt & M. Hersen (Eds.), *Sourcebook of psychological treatment manuals for adult disorders* (pp. 23–64). New York: Plenum Press.

Bourret, J. C., & Pietras, C. J. (2013). Visual analysis in single-case research. In G. J. Madden (Ed.), *APA handbook of behavior analysis: Volume 1, methods and principles* (pp. 199–218). Washington, DC: American Psychological Association.

Bovjberg, D. H., Redd, W. H., Maier, L. A., Holland, J. C., Lesko, L. M., Niedzwiecki, D., & Hakes T. B.. (1990). Anticipatory immune suppression in women receiving cyclic chemotherapy for ovarian cancer. *Journal of Consulting and Clinical Psychology, 58,* 153–157.

Braam, C., & Malott, R. W. (1990). "I'll do it when the snow melts": The effects of deadlines and delayed outcomes on rule-governed behavior in preschool children. *Analysis of Verbal Behavior, 8,* 67–76.

Brantner, J. P., & Doherty, M. A. (1983). A review of time-out: A conceptual and methodological analysis. In S. Axelrod & J. Apsche (Eds.), *The effects of punishment on human behavior* (pp. 87–132). New York: Academic Press.

Braukmann, C. J., & Blase, K. B. (Eds.). (1979). *Teaching-parent training manuals* (2 Vols.). Lawrence, KS: University of Kansas Printing Service.

Braukmann, C., & Wolf, M. (1987). Behaviorally based group homes for juvenile offenders. In E. K. Morris & C. J. Braukmann (Eds.), *Behavioral approaches to crime and delinquency: A handbook of application, research, and concepts* (pp. 135–160). New York: Plenum Press.

Brigham, T. A. (1982). Self-management: A radical behavioral perspective. In P. Karoly & F. H. Canfer (Eds.), *Self-management and behavior change: From theory to practice* (pp. 32–59). New York: Pergamon Press.

Brigham, T. A. (1989a). *Managing everyday problems.* New York: The Guilford Press.

Brigham, T. A. (1989b). *Self-management for adolescents: A skills training program.* New York: The Guilford Press.

Briscoe, R. V., Hoffman, D. B., & Bailey, J. S. (1975). Behavioral community psychology: Training a community board to problem-solve. *Journal of Applied Behavior Analysis, 8,* 157–168.

Brossart, D. F., Parker, R. I., Olson, E. A., & Mahadevan, L. (2006). The relationship between visual analysis and five statistical analyses in a simple AB single-case research design. *Behavior Modification, 30,* 531–563.

Brown, R. (1973). *A first language: The early years.* Cambridge, MA: Harvard University Press.

Brown, L. A., Gaudiano, B. A., & Miller, I. W. (2011). Investigating the similarities and differences between practitioners of second- and third-wave cognitive-behavioral therapies. *Behavior Modification, 35,* 187–200.

Brown, W. H., Pfeiffer, K., McIver, K. L., Dowda, M., Almeida, J., & Pate, R. R. (2006). Assessing preschool children's physical activity: An Observational System for Recording Physical Activity in Children—Preschool version (OSRPAC-P). *Research Quarterly for Exercise and Sport, 77,* 167–176.

Brownell, K. D. (1981). Report on international behavior therapy organizations. *The Behavior Therapist, 4,* 9–13.

Bush, J. P., & Ciocco, J. E. (1992). Behavioral coding and sequential analysis: The portable computer systems for observational use. *Behavioral Assessment, 14,* 191–197.

Butler, A., Chapman, J. M., Forman, E. M., & Beck, A. T. (2006). The empirical status of cognitive behavioral therapy: A review of meta-analyses. *Clinical Psychology Review, 26*, 17–31.

Buzas, H. P., & Ayllon, T. (1981). Differential reinforcement in coaching skills. *Behavior Modification, 5*, 372–385.

Caballo, V. E., & Buela-Casal, G. (1993). Behavior therapy in Spain. *Behavior Therapist, 16*, 53–54.

Caldwell, L. (1971). Behavior modification with children. Paper presented at the 1st Manitoba Behavior Change Conference, Portage la Prairie, Manitoba, Canada.

Cameron, J., Banko, K. M., & Pierce, W. D. (2001). Pervasive negative effects of rewards on intrinsic motivation: The myth continues. *The Behavior Analyst, 24*, 1–44.

Capriotti, M. R., Brandt, B. C., Ricketts, E. J., Espil, F. M., & Woods, D. W. (2012). Comparing the effects of differential reinforcement of other behavior and response-cost contingencies on tics in youth and Tourette Syndrome. *Journal of Applied Behavior Analysis, 45*, 251–263.

Carney, C. E., & Edinger, J. D. (2010). *Insomnia and anxiety.* New York: Springer.

Carp, C. L., Peterson, S. P., Arkel, A. J., Petursdottir, A. I., & Ingvarsson, E. T. (2012). A further evaluation of picture prompts during auditory-visual conditional discrimination training. *Journal of Applied Behavior Analysis, 45*, 737–751.

Carr, E. G. (1977). The origins of self-injurious behavior: A review of some hypotheses. *Psychological Bulletin, 84*, 800–816.

Carr, E. G., & Durand, V. M. (1985). Reducing behavior problems through functional communication training. *Journal of Applied Behavior Analysis, 18*(2), 111–126.

Carr, E. G., Newsom, C. D., & Binkoff, J. A. (1980). Escape as a factor in the aggressive behavior of two retarded children. *Journal of Applied Behavior Analysis, 13*, 101–117.

Carr, J. E., & Miguel, C. F. (2013). The analysis of verbal behavior and its therapeutic applications. In G. J. Madden (Ed.), *APA handbook of behavior analysis: Volume 2, translating behavioral principles into practice* (pp. 329–352). Washington, DC: American Psychological Association.

Carr, J. E., & Sidener, T. M. (2002). In response: On the relation between applied behavior analysis and positive behavior support. *The Behavior Analyst, 25*(1), 425–253.

Carter, N. (2004). Swedish Association for Behavior Analysis. *Newsletter of the International Association for Behavior Analysis, 27*(2), 29.

Carter, S. L. (2010). *The social validity manual: A guide to subjective evaluation of behavior interventions in applied behavior analysis.* Boston: Elsevier.

Catania, A. C. (1975). The myth of self-reinforcement. *Behaviorism, 3*, 192–199.

Catania, A. C. (2011). Basic operant contingencies: Main effects and side effects. In W. W. Fisher, C. C. Piazza, & H. S. Roane (Eds.), *Handbook of applied behavior analysis* (pp. 34–54). New York: The Guilford Press.

Cattell, R. B., Eber, H. W., & Tatsuoka, M. M. (1970). *Handbook for the 16-Personality Factor Questionnaire.* Champaign, IL: Institute for Personality and Ability Testing.

Cautela, J. R. (1966). Treatment of compulsive behavior by covert desensitization. *Psychological Record, 16*, 33–41.

Cautela, J. R., & Kearney, A. (1993). *The covert conditioning handbook.* Pacific Grove, CA: Brooks/Cole.

Cautela, J. R., Kastenbaum, R., & Wincze, J. P. (1972). The use of the Fear Survey Schedule and the Reinforcement Survey Schedule to survey possible reinforcing and aversive stimuli among juvenile offenders. *Journal of Genetic Psychology, 121*, 255–261.

Charlop, M. H., Burgio, L. D., Iwata, B. A., & Ivancic, M. T. (1988). Stimulus variation as a means of enhancing punishment effects. *Journal of Applied Behavior Analysis, 21*, 89–95.

Chen, C. P. (1995). Counseling applications of RET in a Chinese cultural context. *Journal of Rational-Emotive and Cognitive Behavior Therapy, 13*, 117–129.

Choi, J. H., & Chung, K. (2012). Effectiveness of a college-level self-management course on successful behavior change. *Behavior Modification, 36*, 18–36.

Chomsky, N. (1959). A review of B. F. Skinner's *Verbal Behavior. Language, 35*, 26–58.

Christensen, A., Sevier, M., Simpson, L. E., & Gattis, K. S. (2004). Acceptance, mindfulness, and change in couple therapy. In S. C. Hayes, V. M. Follette, & M. M. Linehan (Eds.), *Mindfulness and acceptance: Expanding the cognitive behavioural tradition.* New York: The Guilford Press.

Christensen, A., Wheeler, J. G., & Jacobson, N. S. (2008). Couple distress. In D. H. Barlow (Ed.), *Clinical handbook of psychological disorders: A step-by-step treatment manual* (4th ed., pp. 662–690). New York: The Guilford Press.

Christner, R. W., Stewart, J., & Freeman, A. (Eds.). (2007). *Handbook of cognitive-behavior group therapy with children and adolescents: Specific settings and presenting problems.* New York: Routledge Mental Health.

Chung, S. H. (1965). Effects of delayed reinforcement in a concurrent situation. *Journal of the Experimental Analysis of Behavior, 8*, 439–444.

Cipani, E. (2004). *Punishment on trial.* Reno, NV: Context Press.

Cipani, E., & Schock, K. M. (2007). *Functional behavioral assessment, diagnosis, and treatment.* New York: Springer Publishing Company. Retrieved from www.ecipani.com/PoT.pdf.

Cipani, E., & Schock, K. M. (2011). *Functional behavioral assessment, diagnosis, and treatment: A complete system for education and mental health settings* (2nd ed.). New York: Springer Publishing Company.

Clark, D. A., & Beck A. T. (2010). *Cognitive therapy of anxiety disorders: Science and practice.* New York: The Guilford Press.

Clarke, I., & Wilson, H. (2008). *Cognitive Behavior Therapy for acute in-patient mental health units.* London: Routledge.

Clayton, M. C., & Helms, B. T. (2009). Increasing seatbelt use on a college campus: An evaluation of two prompting procedures. *Journal of Applied Behavior Analysis, 42*, 161–164.

Cohen, R., DeJames, P., Nocera, B., & Ramberger, M. (1980). Application of a simple self-instruction procedure on adult exercise and studying: Two case reports. *Psychological Reports, 46*, 443–451.

Cone, J. D. (Ed.). (1999). Special section: Clinical assessment applications of self-monitoring. *Psychological Assessment, 11*, 411–497.

Conyers, C., Martin, T. L., Martin, G. L., & Yu, D. C. T. (2002). The 1983 AAMR manual, the 1992 AAMR manual, or the Developmental Disabilities Act: Which is used by researchers? *Education and Training in Mental Retardation and Developmental Disabilities, 37*, 310–316.

Conyers, C., Miltenberger, R., Maki, A., Barenz, R., Jurgens, M., Sailor, A., & Kopp, B. (2004). A comparison of response cost and differential reinforcement of other behavior to reduce disruptive behavior in a preschool classroom. *Journal of Applied Behavior Analysis, 37*, 411–415.

Corrigan, P. W. (1995). Use of a token economy with seriously mentally ill patients: Criticisms and misconceptions. *Psychiatric Services, 46*, 1258–1263.

Cottraux, J. (1990). "Cogito ergo somme": Cognitive behavior therapy in France. *Behavior Therapist, 13*, 189–190.

Cowdery, G. E., Iwata, B. A., & Pace, G. M. (1990). Effects and side-effects of DRO as treatment for self-injurious behavior. *Journal of Applied Behavior Analysis, 23*, 497–506.

Cox, B. S., Cox, A. B., & Cox, D. J. (2000). Motivating signage prompts: Safety belt use among drivers exiting senior communities. *Journal of Applied Behavior Analysis, 33*, 635–638.

Cracklen, C., & Martin, G. (1983). To motivate age-group competitive swimmers at practice, "fun" should be earned. *Swimming Techniques, 20*(3), 29–32.

Craighead, L. W., & Smith, L. (2010). Obesity and eating disorders. In M. M. Antony & D. H. Barlow (Eds.), *Handbook of assessment and treatment planning for psychological disorders* (2nd ed., pp. 390–438). New York: The Guilford Press.

Craske, M. G., & Barlow, D. H. (2008). Panic disorder and agoraphobia. In D. H. Barlow (Ed.), *Clinical handbook of psychological disorders: A step-by-step treatment manual* (4th ed., pp. 1–64). New York: The Guilford Press.

Craske, M. G., Hermans, D., & Vansteenwegen, D. (Eds.). (2006). *Fear and learning: From basic processes to clinical implications*. Washington, DC: American Psychological Association.

Critchfield, T. S., & Fienup, D. M. (2010). Using stimulus equivalence technology to teach statistical inference in a group setting. *Journal of Applied Behavior Analysis, 43*, 763–768.

Cunningham, T. R., & Austin, J. (2007). Using goal setting, task clarification, and feedback to increase the use of the hands-free technique by hospital operating room staff. *Journal of Applied Behavior Analysis, 40*, 673–677.

Cuvo, A. J., & Davis, P. K. (2000). Behavioral acquisition by persons with developmental disabilities. In J. Austin & J. E. Carr (Eds.), *Handbook of applied behavior analysis* (pp. 39–60). Reno, NV: Context Press.

Cuvo, A. J., Davis, P. K., O'Reilly, M. F., Mooney, B. M., & Crowley, R. (1992). Promoting stimulus control with textual prompts and performance feedback for persons with mild disabilities. *Journal of Applied Behavior Analysis, 25*, 477–489.

Dallery, J., Meredith, S., & Glenn, I. M. (2008). A deposit contract method to deliver abstinence reinforcement for cigarette smoking. *Journal of Applied Behavior Analysis, 41*, 609–615.

Damasio, A. R. (2000). A second chance for emotions. In R. D. Lane & L. Nadel (Eds.), *Cognitive neuroscience of emotion* (pp. 12–23). New York: Oxford University Press.

Danguah, J. (1982). The practice of behavior therapy in West Africa: The case of Ghana. *Journal of Behavior Therapy and Experimental Psychiatry, 13*, 5–13.

Daniels, A. C., & Daniels, J. E. (2005). *Performance management: Changing behavior that drives organizational effectiveness*. Atlanta, GA: Performance Management Publications.

Dardig, J. C., & Heward, W. L. (1976). *Sign here: A contracting book for children and their parents*. Kalamazoo, MI: Behaviordelia.

Daruna, J. H. (2004). Introduction to psychoneuroimmunology. St. Louis, MO: Elsevier, Academic Press.

Dattilio, F. M. (1999). Cognitive behavior therapy in Cuba. *The Behavior Therapist, 22*, 78, 91.

David, D., & Miclea, M. (2002). Behavior therapy in Romania: A brief history of theory, research, and practice. *The Behavior Therapist, 25*, 181–183.

Davies, G., Chand, C., Yu, C. T., Martin, T., & Martin, G. L. (2013). Evaluation of multiple-stimulus preference assessment with adults with developmental disabilities. *Education and Training in Autism and Developmental Disabilities, 48*, 269–275.

Day, H. R., & Ballard, D. (2005). *The Classroom Mini-Economy*. New York: National Council for Economic Education.

Deci, E. L., Koestner, R., & Ryan, R. M. (1999). A meta-analytic review of experiments examining the effects of extrinsic rewards on intrinsic motivation. *Psychological Bulletin, 125*, 627–668.

Deitz, S. M., & Repp, A. C. (1973). Decreasing classroom misbehavior through the use of DRL schedules of reinforcement. *Journal of Applied Behavior Analysis, 6*, 457–463.

Dekker, E., & Groen, J. (1956). Reproducible psychogenic attacks of asthma: A laboratory study. *Journal of Psychosomatic Research, 1*, 58–67.

DeLeon, I. G., & Iwata, B. A. (1996). Evaluation of a multiple-stimulus presentation format for assessing reinforcer preferences. *Journal of Applied Behavior Analysis, 29*, 519–533.

DeLeon, I. G., Bullock, C. E., & Catania, A. C. (2013). Arranging reinforcement contingencies in applied settings: Fundamentals and implications of recent basic and applied research. In G. J. Madden (Ed.), *APA handbook of behavior analysis: Volume 2, translating behavioral principles into practice* (pp. 47–76). Washington, DC: American Psychological Association.

DeLuca, R. V., & Holborn, S. W. (1992). Effects of a variable ratio reinforcement schedule with changing-criteria on exercise in obese and non-obese boys. *Journal of Applied Behavior Analysis, 25*, 671–679.

Demchak, M. (1990). Response prompting and fading methods: A review. *American Journal on Mental Retardation, 94*, 603–615.

Demchak, M. A., & Bossert, K. W. (1996). *Innovations: Assessing problem behaviors*. Washington, DC: American Association on Mental Retardation.

Den Boer, P. C., Wiersma, D., & Van Den Bosch, R. J. (2004). Why is self-help neglected in the treatment of emotional disorders? A meta-analysis. *Psychological Medicine, 34*, 959–971.

DeRicco, D. A., & Niemann, J. E. (1980). In vivo effects of peer modelling on drinking rate. *Journal of Applied Behavior Analysis, 13*, 149–152.

DeRisi, W. J., & Butz, G. (1975). *Writing behavioral contracts: A case simulation practice manual*. Champaign, IL: Research Press.

DeRiso, A., & Ludwig, T. D. (2012). An investigation of response generalization across cleaning and restocking behaviors in the context of performance feedback. *Journal of Organizational Behavior Management, 32*, 140–151.

Desilva, P., & Simarasinghe, D. (1985). Behavior therapy in Sri Lanka. *Journal of Behavior Therapy and Experimental Psychiatry, 16*, 95–100.

Desrochers, M. N., Hile, M. G., & Williams-Mosely, T. L. (1997). Survey of functional assessment procedures used with individuals who display mental retardation and severe problem behaviors. *American Journal on Mental Retardation, 101*, 535–546.

DeWiele, L., Martin, G. L., Martin, T. L., Yu, C. T., & Thomson, K. (2012). *The Kerr-Meyerson assessment of basic learning abilities revised: A self-instructional manual* (2nd ed.). St.

Amant Research Centre, Winnipeg, MB, Canada. Retrieved from http://stamantresearch.ca/abla/.

Dickerson, F. B., Tenhula, W. N., & Green-Paden, L. D. (2005). The token economy for schizophrenia: Review of the literature and recommendations for future research. *Schizophrenia Research, 75*, 405–416.

Didden, R. (2007). Functional analysis methodology in developmental disabilities. In P. Sturmey (Ed.), *Functional analysis in clinical treatment* (pp. 65–86). London, UK: Elsevier.

Digiuseppe, R. (2008). Surfing the waves of behavior therapy. *The Behavior Therapist, 31*, 154–155.

Dimidjian, S., Barrerra, M., Martell, C., Munoz, R. F., & Lewinsohn, P. M. (2011). The origins and current status of behavioral activation treatments for depression. *Annual Review of Clinical Psychology, 7*, 1–38.

Dimidjian, S., Hollon, S. D., Dobson, K. S., Schmaling, K. B., Kohlenberg, R. J., Addis, M. E., & Jacobson, N. S. (2006). Randomized trial of behavioral activation, cognitive therapy, and antidepressant medication in the acute treatment of adults with major depression. *Journal of Consulting and Clinical Psychology, 74*, 658–670.

Dimidjian, S., Martell, C. R., Addis, M. E., & Herman-Dunn, R. (2008). In D. H. Barlow (Ed.), *Clinical handbook of psychological disorders: A step-by-step treatment manual* (4th ed., pp. 328–364). New York: The Guilford Press.

Dishon, T. J., Stormshak, E., & Kavanagh, G. (2012). *Everyday parenting: A professional's guide to building family management skills.* Champagne, IL: Research Press.

DiTomasso, R. A., Golden, B. A., & Morris, H. J. (Eds.). (2011). *Handbook of cognitive-behavioral approaches in primary care.* New York: Springer Publishing Company.

Dixon, D. R., Vogel, T., & Tarbox, J. (2012). A brief history of functional analysis and applied behavior analysis. In J. L. Matson (Ed.), *Functional assessment for challenging behaviors* (pp. 3–24). New York: Springer Publishing Company.

Dobson, K. S. (2012). *Cognitive therapy.* Washington, DC: American Psychological Association.

Dobson, K. S. (2013). The science of CBT: Toward a metacognitive model of change? *Behavior Therapy, 44*, 224–227.

Dobson, K. S., Hollon, S. D., Dimidjian, S., Schmaling, K. B., Kohlenberg, Gallop, R. J., & Jacobson, N. S. (2008). Randomized trial of behavioral activation, cognitive therapy, and antidepressant medication in the prevention of relapse and recurrence in major depression. *Journal of Consulting and Clinical Psychology, 76*, 468–477.

Doleys, D. M., Meredith, R. L., & Ciminero, A. R. (Eds.). (1982). *Behavioral psychology and medicine and rehabilitation: Assessment and treatment strategies.* New York: Plenum Press.

Dollard, J., & Miller, N. E. (1950). *Personality and psychotherapy.* New York: McGraw-Hill.

Donaldson, J. M., & Vollmer, T. R. (2011). An evaluation and comparison of time-out procedures with and without release contingencies. *Journal of Applied Behavior Analysis, 44*, 693–706.

Donaldson, J. M., Vollmer, T. R., Krous, T., Downs, S., & Berard, K. P. (2011). An evaluation of the good behavior game in kindergarten classrooms. *Journal of Applied Behavior Analysis, 44*, 605–609.

Donny, E. C., Caggiula, A. R., Weaver, M. T., Levin, M. E., & Sved, A. F. (2011). The reinforcement-enhancing effects of nicotine: Implications for the relationship between smoking, eating and weight. *Physiology & Behavior, 104*, 143–148.

Dorsey, M. F., Iwata, B. A., Ong, P., & McSween, T. E. (1980). Treatment of self-injurious behavior using a water mist: Initial response suppression and generalization. *Journal of Applied Behavior Analysis, 13*, 343–353.

Dougher, M. J. (1997). Cognitive concepts, behavior analysis, and behavior therapy. *Journal of Behavior Therapy and Experimental Psychiatry, 28*, 65–70.

Drash, P. W., & Tudor, M. (1993). A functional analysis of verbal delay in preschool children: Implications for prevention and total recovery. *The Analysis of Verbal Behavior, 11*, 19–29.

Dryden, W., DiGiuseppe, R., & Neenan, M. (2010). *A primer on rational-emotive behavior therapy* (3rd ed.). Champage, IL: Research Press.

Dube, W. V., Ahearn, W. H, Lionello-DeNolf, K., & McIlvane, W. J. (2009). Behavioral momentum: Translational research in intellectual and developmental disabilities. *The Behavior Analyst Today, 10*, 238–253.

Dugas, M. J., & Robichaud, M. (2006). *Cognitive-behavioral treatment for generalized anxiety disorder: From science to practice.* New York: Routledge.

Durand, V. M., & Crimmins, D. B. (1988). Identifying the variables maintaining self-injurious behavior. *Journal of Autism and Developmental Disorders, 18*, 99–117.

Durrant, J., & Ensom, R. (2012). Physical punishment of children: Lessons from 20 years of research. *Canadian Medical Association Journal, 184*(2), 1373–1377.

Dymond, S., & Barnes, D. (1997). Behavior analytic approaches to self-awareness. *The Psychological Record, 47*, 181–200.

Dymond, S., Chiesa, M., & Martin, N. (2003). An update on providing graduate level training in applied behavior analysis in the UK. *Newsletter of the International Association for Behavior Analysis, 26*(3), 10.

Dymond, S., & Rehfeldt, R. A. (2000). Understanding complex behavior: The transformation of stimulus functions. *The Behavior Analyst, 23*, 239–254.

Dymond, S., & Roche, B. (Eds.). (2013). *Advances in relational frame theory.* Reno, NV: Context Press.

D'Zurilla, T. J., & Goldfried, M. R. (1971). Problem-solving and behavior modification. *Journal of Abnormal Psychology, 78*, 107–126.

Edinger, J., & Carney, C. (2008). *Overcoming insomnia: A cognitive-behavioral therapy approach therapist guide.* New York: Oxford University Press.

Ellingson, S. A., Miltenberger, R. G., & Long, E. S. (1999). A survey of the use of functional assessment procedures in agencies serving individuals with developmental disabilities. *Behavioral Interventions, 14*, 187–198.

Ellis, A. (1962). *Reason and emotion in psychotherapy.* New York: Lyle Stewart.

Ellis, A. (1993). Changing rational-emotive therapy (RET) to rational-emotive behavior therapy (REBT). *The Behavior Therapist, 16*, 257–258.

Ellis, A., & Bernard, M. E. (Eds.). (1985). *Clinical applications of rational-emotive therapy.* New York: Plenum Press.

Ellis, A., & Dryden, W. (1997). *The practice of rational-emotive behavior therapy* (2nd ed.). New York: Springer Publishing Company.

Ellis, A., & Grieger, R. (1977). *Handbook of rational-emotive therapy.* New York: Springer Publishing Company.

Elwood, R. W., & Appel, M. (2009). Pain experience in hermit crabs? *Animal Behaviour, 77*(5), 1243–1246.

Emmelkamp, P. M. G. (2013). Behavior therapy with adults. In M. J. Lambert (Ed.), *Bergin and Garfield's handbook of psychotherapy and behavior change* (6th ed., pp. 343–392). Hoboken, NJ: John Wiley & Sons.

Emmelkamp, P. M. G., Bouman, T. K., & Scholing, A. (1992). *Anxiety disorders: A practitioner's guide*. Chichester, UK: Wiley.

Esch, J. W., Esch, B. E., & Love, J. R. (2009). Increasing vocal variability in children with autism using a lag schedule of reinforcement. *Analysis of Verbal Behavior, 25*, 73–78.

Eysenck, H. J. (1959). Learning theory and behavior therapy. *Journal of Mental Science, 105*, 61–75.

Eysenck, H. J. (Ed.). (1960). *Behaviour therapy and the neuroses*. London: Pergamon.

Fabiano, G. A., Pelham, W. E., Jr., Manos, M. J., Gnagy, E. M., Chronis, A. M., Onyango, A. N. & Swain, S. (2004). An evaluation of three time-out procedures for children with attention-deficit/ hyperactive disorder. *Behavior Therapy, 35*, 449–469.

Fairburn, C. G. (2008). *Cognitive behavior therapy and eating disorders*. New York: The Guilford Press.

Fairburn, C. G., Cooper, Z., Shafran, R., & Wilson, G. T. (2008). Eating disorders: A transdiagnostic protocol. In D. H. Barlow (Ed.), *Clinical handbook of psychological disorders: A step-by-step treatment manual* (4th ed., pp. 578–614). New York: The Guilford Press.

Faith, M. S., Fontaine, K. R., Cheskin, L. J., & Allison, D. B. (2000). Behavioral approaches to the problems of obesity. *Behavior Modification, 24*, 459–493.

Fantino, E. (2008). Choice, conditioned reinforcement, and the Prius effect. *The Behavior Analyst, 31*, 95–111.

Farmer, R. F., & Latner, J. D. (2007). Eating disorders. In P. Sturmey (Ed.), *Functional analysis in clinical treatment* (pp. 379–402). London, UK: Elsevier.

Farrell, A. D. (1991). Computers and behavioral assessment: Current applications, future possibilities, and obstacles to routine use. *Behavioral Assessment, 13*, 159–179.

Favell, J. E., Azrin, N. H., Baumeister, A. A., Carr, E. G., Dorsey, M. F., Forehand, R., & Romanczyk, R. G. (1982). The treatment of self-injurious behavior. *Behavior Therapy, 13*, 529–554.

Fazzio, D., Arnal, L., & Martin, G. L. (2010). *Discrete-Trials Teaching Evaluation Form (DTTEF): Scoring manual*. St. Amant Research Centre, Winnipeg, MB, Canada. Retrieved from http://stamantresearch.ca/abla/.

Fazzio, D., & Martin, G. L. (2012). *Discrete-trials teaching with children with autism: A self-instructional manual*. Winnipeg, Canada: Hugo Science Press.

Fazzio, D., Martin, G. L., Arnal, L., & Yu, D. (2009). Instructing university students to conduct discrete-trials teaching with children with autism. *Journal of Autism Spectrum Disorders, 3*, 57–66.

Feldman, M. A. (1990). Balancing freedom from harm and right to treatment in persons with developmental disabilities. In A. Repp & N. Singh (Eds.), *Current perspectives in use of nonaversive and aversive interventions with developmentally disabled persons*. Sycamore, IL: Sycamore Press.

Fellner, D. J., & Sulzer-Azaroff, B. (1984). A behavioral analysis of goal setting. *Journal of Organizational Behavior Management, 6*, 33–51.

Ferreri, S. (2013). Token economy. In F. R. Volkmar (Ed.), *Encyclopedia of autism spectrum disorders* (pp. 3131–3138). New York: Springer Publishing Company.

Ferster, C. B. (1993). A functional analysis of depression. *American Psychologist, 28*, 857–870.

Ferster, C. B., & Demyer, M. K. (1962). A method for the experimental analysis of the behavior of autistic children. *The American Journal of Orthopsychiatry, 32*, 89–98.

Ferster, C. B., & Skinner, B. F. (1957). *Schedules of reinforcement*. New York: Appleton-Century-Crofts.

Filcheck, H. A., McNeil, C. B., Greco, L. A., & Bernard, L. S. (2004). Using a whole-class token economy and coaching of teacher skills in a preschool classroom to manage disruptive behavior. *Psychology in the Schools, 41*, 351–361.

Filter, K. J. (2007). Positive behavior support: Considerations for the future of a model. *The Behavior Analyst, 30*, 87–89.

Fisch, G. S. (1998). Visual inspection of data revisited: Do the eyes still have it? *The Behavior Analyst, 21*, 111–123.

Fischer, J., & Corcoran, K. (2007a). *Measures for clinical practice: A sourcebook* (Vol. 1, 4th ed.). Couples, families and children. New York: Free Press.

Fischer, J., & Corcoran, K. (2007b). *Measures for clinical practice: A sourcebook* (Vol. 2, 4th ed.). Adults. New York: Free Press.

Fisher, E. B. (1979). Overjustification effects in token economies. *Journal of Applied Behavior Analysis, 12*, 407–415.

Fisher, W. W., Kelley, M. E., & Lomas, J. E. (2003). Visual aids and structured criteria for improving visual inspection and interpretation of single-case designs. *Journal of Applied Behavior Analysis, 36*, 387–406.

Fisher, W. W., Piazza, C. C., & Roane, H. S. (Eds.). (2011). *Handbook of applied behavior analysis* (Chapters 9–13). New York: The Guilford Press.

Fixsen, D. L., & Blase, K. A. (1993). Creating new realities: Program development and dissemination. *Journal of Applied Behavior Analysis, 26*, 597–615.

Fixsen, D. L., Blase, K., Timbers, G. D., & Wolf, M. M. (2007). In search of program implementation: 792 replications of the Teaching-Family Model. *The Behavior Analyst Today, 8*, 96–110. (Reprinted from Bernfeld, G. A., Farrington, D. P., & Leschied, A. W. [Eds.] [1999]. *Offender rehabilitation in practice: Implementing and evaluating effective programs* [pp. 149–166]. London. Wiley.)

Flanagan, B., Goldiamond, I., & Azrin, N. (1958). Operant stuttering: The control of stuttering behavior through response-contingent consequences. *Journal of the Experimental Analysis of Behavior, 1*, 173–177.

Flanagan, C. (1991). Behavior therapy and cognitive therapy in Ireland. *The Behavior Therapist, 14*, 231–232.

Flora, S. R. (1990). Undermining intrinsic interest from the standpoint of a behaviorist. *The Psychological Record, 40*, 323–346.

Flora, S. R. (2000). Praise's magic: Reinforcement ratio five-one gets the job done. *Behavior Analyst Today [Online], 1*(4), 64–69. Retrieved from www.behavior.org.

Flora, S. R. (2007). *Taking America off drugs: Why behavior therapy is more effective for treating ADHD, OCD, depression, and other psychological problems*. New York: State University of New York Press.

Flora, S. R., & Flora, D. B. (1999). Effects of extrinsic reinforcement for reading during childhood on reported reading habits of college students. *The Psychological Record, 49*, 3–14.

Foa, E. B. (2000). Psychosocial treatment of posttraumatic stress disorder. *Journal of Clinical Psychiatry, 61*(Suppl. 5), 43–48.

Fonagy, P., Target, M, Cottrell, D., Phillips, J., & Kurtz, Z. (2002). *What works for whom? A critical review of treatments for children and adolescents*. New York: The Guilford Press.

Forman, E. M., Herbert, J. D., Moitra, E., Yeomans, P. D., & Geller, P. A. (2007). A randomized controlled effectiveness trial of Acceptance and Commitment Therapy and Cognitive Therapy for anxiety and depression. *Behavior Modification, 31,* 772–799.

Forsyth, J. P., & Eifert, G. H. (2007). *The mindfulness and acceptance workbook for anxiety: A guide to breaking free from anxiety, phobias, and worry using Acceptance and Commitment Therapy.* Oakland, CA: New Harbinger.

Foxx, R. M., & Shapiro, S. T. (1978). The timeout ribbon: A non-exclusionary timeout procedure. *Journal of Applied Behavior Analysis, 11,* 125–136.

Franklin, M. E., & Foa, E. B. (2008). Obsessive compulsive disorder. In D. H. Barlow (Ed.), *Clinical handbook of psychological disorders: A step-by-step treatment manual* (4th ed., pp. 164–215). New York: The Guilford Press.

Franks, C. M. (1964). *Conditioning techniques in clinical practice and research.* New York: Springer Publishing Company.

Franks, C. M. (Ed.). (1969). *Behavior therapy: Appraisal and status.* New York: McGraw-Hill.

Frederiksen, L. W., & Lovett, F. B. (1980). Inside organizational behavior management: Perspectives on an emerging field. *Journal of Organizational Behavior Management, 2,* 193–203.

Fresco, D. M. (2013). Theories and directions in behavior therapy: ACT and contemporary CBT. Tending the garden and harvesting the fruits of behavior therapy. *Behavior Therapy, 44*(2), 177–179.

Friman, P. C., & Piazza, C. C. (2011). Behavioral pediatrics: Integrating applied behavior analysis with behavioral medicine. In W. W. Fisher, C. C. Piazza, & H. S. Roane (Eds.), *Handbook of applied behavior analysis* (pp. 433–450). New York: The Guilford Press.

Friman, P. C., & Poling, A. (1995). Making life easier with effort: Basic findings and applied research on response effort. *Journal of Applied Behavior Analysis, 28,* 583–590.

Friman, P. C., Osgood, D. W., Smith, G., Shanahan, D., Thompson, R. W., Larzelere, R., & Daly, D. L. (1996). A longitudinal evaluation of prevalent negative beliefs about residential placement for troubled adolescents. *Journal of Abnormal Child Psychology, 24,* 299–324.

Fritz, J. N., Iwata, B. A., Hammond, J. L., & Bloom, S. E. (2013). Experimental analysis of precursors to severe problem behavior. *Journal of Applied Behavior Analysis, 46,* 101–129.

Fuller, P. R. (1949). Operant conditioning of a vegetative human organism. *American Journal of Psychology, 62,* 587–590.

Ganz, J. B., Earles-Vollrath, T. L., & Cook, K. E. (2011). Video modeling: A visually based intervention for children with autism spectrum disorder. *Teaching Exceptional Children, 43*(6), 8–19.

Gelfand, D. M., Hartmann, D. P., Lamb, A. K., Smith, C. L., Mahan, M. A., & Paul, S. C. (1974). Effects of adult models and described alternatives on children's choice of behavior management techniques. *Child Development, 45,* 585–593.

Geller, E. S., Winett, R. A., & Everett, P. B. (1982). *Preserving the environment: New strategies for behavior change.* New York: Plenum Press.

Gena, A., Krantz, P. J., McClannahan, L. E., & Poulson, C. L. (1996). Training and generalization of effective behavior displayed by youth with autism. *Journal of Applied Behavior Analysis, 29,* 291–304.

Gershoff, E. T. (2002). Corporal punishment by parents and associated child behaviors and experiences: A meta-analytic and theoretical review. *Psychological Bulletin, 128,* 539–579.

Gimpel, G. A., & Holland, N. L. (2003). *Emotional and behavioral problems of young children.* New York: The Guilford Press.

Girardeau, F. L., & Spradlin, J. E. (1964). Token rewards on a cottage program. *Mental Retardation, 2,* 345–351.

Global Initiative to End All Corporal Punishment of Children. (2010). *Ending legalized violence against children: Global report 2010.* Retrieved from http://www.endcorporalpunishment.org/pages/pdfs/reports/globalreport2010.pdf.

Glynn, E. L., & Thomas, J. D. (1974). Effect of cueing on self-control of classroom behavior. *Journal of Applied Behavior Analysis, 7,* 299–306.

Glynn, S. N. (1990). Token economy approaches for psychiatric patients: Progress and pitfalls over 25 years. *Behavior Modification, 14,* 383–407.

Goetz, E. M., & Baer, D. M. (1973). Social control of form diversity and the emergence of new forms in children's block building. *Journal of Applied Behavior Analysis, 6,* 105–113.

Goldenring, J. (2011). *Infant reflexes.* MedlinePlus medical encyclopedia. Retrieved January 14, 2013, from http://www.nlm.nih.gov/medlineplus/ency/article/003292.htm

Goldiamond, I. (1965). Self-control procedures in personal behavior problems. *Psychological Reports, 17,* 851–868.

Goldiamond, I. (1976a). Self-reinforcement. *Journal of Applied Behavior Analysis, 9,* 509–514.

Goldiamond, I. (1976b). Fables, armadyllics, and self-reinforcement. *Journal of Applied Behavior Analysis, 9,* 521–525.

Gormally, J., Black, S., Daston, S., & Rardin, D. (1982). The assessment of binge eating severity among obese persons. *Addictive Behaviors, 7,* 47–55.

Gortner, E. T., Golan, J. K., Dobson, K. S., & Jacobson, N. S. (1998). Cognitive behavior treatment for depression. *Relapse Prevention, 66,* 377–384.

Gossette, R. L., & O'Brien, R. M. (1989, May). Efficacy of rational-emotive therapy with children: Fact or artifact? Paper presented at the meeting of the Association for Behavior Analysis, Nashville, TN.

Gossette, R. L., & O'Brien, R. M. (1992). The efficacy of rational-emotive therapy in adults: Clinical fact or psychometric artifact? *Journal of Behavior Therapy and Experimental Psychiatry, 23,* 9–24.

Gould, D. (2010). Goal setting for peak performance. In J. M. Williams (Ed.), *Applied sport psychology: Personal growth to peak performance* (6th ed., pp. 211–220). New York: McGraw-Hill.

Gould, R. A., & Clum, G. A. (1993). A meta-analysis of self-help treatment approaches. *Clinical Psychological Review, 13,* 167–189.

Graaf, I. D., Speetjens, P., Smit, F., Wolff, M. D., & Tavecchio, L. (2008). Effectiveness of the Triple P Positive Parenting Program on behavioral program in children: A meta-analysis. *Behavior Modification, 32,* 714–735.

Graff, R. B., & Karsten, A. M. (2012). Evaluation of a self-instruction package for conducting stimulus preference assessments. *Journal of Applied Behavior Analysis, 45,* 69–82.

Grant, A., Townend, M., Mulhern, R., & Short, N. (2010). *Cognitive behavioral therapy in mental health care* (2nd ed.). Thousand Oaks, CA: Sage Publications, Inc.

Grassi, T. C. C. (Ed.). (2004). *Contemporary challenges in the behavioral approach: A Brazilian overview.* Santo André, Brazil: Esetec Editores Associados.

Greenspoon, J. (1951). The effect of verbal and nonverbal stimuli on the frequency of members of two verbal response classes.

Unpublished doctoral dissertation, Indiana University, Bloomington.

Greenspoon, J. (1955). The reinforcing effect of two spoken words on the frequency of two responses. *American Journal of Psychology, 68*, 409–416.

Greenspoon, J. (1976). *The sources of behavior: Abnormal and normal.* Monterey, CA: Brooks/Cole.

Gregory, R. J., Canning, S. S., Lee, T. W., Wise, J. C. (2004). Cognitive bibliotherapy: A meta-analysis. *Professional Psychology: Research and Practice, 35*, 275–280.

Gresham, F. M., & MacMillan, D. L. (1997). Autistic recovery? An analysis and critique of the empirical evidence on the early intervention project. *Behavioral Disorders, 22*, 185–201.

Grey, I., Healy, O., Leader, G., & Hayes, D. (2009). Using a Time Timer™ to increase appropriate waiting behavior in a child with developmental disabilities. *Research in Developmental Disabilities, 30*, 359–366.

Griffen, A. K., Wolery, M., & Schuster, J. W. (1992). Triadic instruction of chained food preparation responses: Acquisition and observational learning. *Journal of Applied Behavior Analysis, 25*, 193–204.

Groff, R. A., Piazza, C. C., Zeleny, J. R., & Dempsey, J. R. (2011). Spoon-to-cup fading as treatment for cup drinking in a child with intestinal failure. *Journal of Applied Behavior Analysis, 44*, 949–954.

Guess, D., & Carr, E. (1991). Emergence and maintenance of stereotopy and self-injury. *American Journal on Mental Retardation, 96*, 299–319.

Guess, D., Helmstetter, E., Turnbull, H. R., III, & Knowlton, S. (1986). *Use of aversive procedures with persons who are disabled: An historical review and critical analysis.* Seattle, WA: Association for Persons with Severe Handicaps.

Guess, D., Sailor, W., Rutherford, G., & Baer, D. M. (1968). An experimental analysis of linguistic development: The productive use of the plural morpheme. *Journal of Applied Behavior Analysis, 1*, 297–306.

Guevremont, D. C., Osnes, P. G., & Stokes, T. F. (1986). Preparation for effective self-regulation: The development of generalized verbal control. *Journal of Applied Behavior Analysis, 19*, 99–104.

Guinther, P. M., & Dougher, M. J. (2013). From behavioral research to clinical therapy. In G. J. Madden (Ed.), *APA handbook of behavior analysis: Volume 2, translating behavioral principles into practice* (pp. 3–32). Washington, DC: American Psychological Association.

Hackenberg, T. D. (2009). Token reinforcement: A review and analysis. *Journal of the Experimental Analysis of Behavior, 91*, 257–286.

Haddad, A. D. M., Pritchett, D., Lissek, S., & Lau, J. Y. F. (2012). Trait anxiety and fear responses to safety cues: Stimulus generalization or sensitization? *Journal of Psychopathology and Behavioral Assessment, 34*, 323–331.

Hagopian, L. P., Piazza, C. C., Fisher, W. W., Thibault Sullivan, M., Acquisto, J., & Leblanc, L. A. (1998). Effectiveness of functional communication training with and without extinction and punishment: A summary of 21 inpatient cases. *Journal of Applied Behavior Analysis, 12*(2), 273–282.

Hains, A. H., & Baer, D. M. (1989). Interaction effects in multi-element designs: Inevitable, desirable, and ignorable. *Journal of Applied Behavior Analysis, 22*, 57–69.

Hanley, G. P., Heal, N. A., Tiger, J. H., & Ingvarsson, E. T. (2007). Evaluation of a classwide teaching program for developing preschool life skills. *Journal of Applied Behavior Analysis, 40*, 277–300.

Hanley, G. P., Piazza, C. C., Fisher, W. W., & Maglieri, K. A. (2005). On the effectiveness of and preference for punishment and extinction components of function-based interventions. *Journal of Applied Behavior Analysis, 38*(1), 51–65.

Hansen, D. J., Tishelman, A. C., Hawkins, R. P., & Doepke, K. (1990). Habits with potential as disorders: Prevalence, severity, and other characteristics among college students. *Behavior Modification, 14*, 66–88.

Haring, T. G., & Kennedy, C. H. (1990). Contextual control of problem behavior in students with severe disabilities. *Journal of Applied Behavior Analysis, 23*, 235–243.

Harris, C. S., & McReynolds, W. T. (1977). Semantic cues and response contingencies in self-instructional control. *Journal of Behavior Therapy and Experimental Psychiatry, 8*, 15–17.

Harris, F. R., Wolf, M. M., & Baer, D. M. (1964). Effects of adult social reinforcement on child behavior. *Young Children, 20*, 8–17.

Hatch, M. L., Friedman, S., & Paradis, C. M. (1996). Behavioral treatment of obsessive-compulsive disorder in African Americans. *Cognitive and Behavioral Practice, 3*, 303–315.

Haughton, E., & Ayllon, T. (1965). Production and elimination of symptomatic behavior. In L. P. Ullmann & L. Krasner (Eds.), *Case studies in behavior modification* (pp. 94–98). New York: Holt, Rinehart & Winston.

Hawkins, R. C., & Clement, P. (1980). Development and construct validation of a self-report measure of binge eating tendencies. *Addictive Behaviors, 5*, 219–226.

Hawkins, R. P. (1979). The functions of assessment: Implications for selection and development of devices for assessing repertoires in clinical, educational, and other settings. *Journal of Applied Behavior Analysis, 12*, 501–516.

Hawkins, R. P., & Dotson, V. A. (1975). Reliability scores that delude: An Alice in Wonderland trip through the misleading characteristics of interobserver agreement scores in interval recording. In E. Ramp & G. Semp (Eds.), *Behavior analysis: Areas of research and application* (pp. 359–376). Upper Saddle River, NJ: Prentice Hall.

Hawkins, R. P., & Forsyth, J. P. (1997). Bridging barriers between paradigms: Making cognitive concepts relevant for behavior analysis. *Journal of Behavior Therapy and Experimental Psychiatry, 28*, 3–6.

Hayes, S. C. (1989). *Rule-governed behavior: Cognition, contingencies, and instructional control.* New York: Plenum Press.

Hayes, S. C. (2004). Acceptance and commitment therapy, relational frame theory, and the third wave of behavior therapy. *Behavior Therapy, 35*, 639–666.

Hayes, S. C. (2008). Avoiding the mistakes of the past. *The Behavior Therapist, 31*, 150–153.

Hayes, S. C., Barnes-Holmes, D., & Roche, B. (Eds.). (2001). *Relational frame theory: A post-Skinnerian account of human language and cognition.* New York: Plenum Press.

Hayes, S. C., Follette, V. M., & Linehan, M. M. (Eds.) (2004). *Mindfulness and acceptance: Expanding the cognitive-behavioral tradition.* New York: Guilford Press.

Hayes, S. C., Jacobson, N. S., Follette, V. M., & Dougher, M. J. (Eds.). (1994). *Acceptance and change: Content and context in psychotherapy.* Reno, NV: Context Press.

Hayes, S. C., Levin, M. E., Plumb-Vilardaga, J., Villatte, J. L., & Pistorello, J. (2013). Acceptance and commitment therapy and contextual behavioral science: Examining the progress of a distinctive model of behavioral and cognitive therapy. *Behavior Therapy, 44*, 180–198.

Hayes, S. C., & Lillas, J. (2012). *Acceptance and commitment therapy*. Washington, DC: American Psychological Association.

Hayes, S. C., Rosenfarb, I., Wulfert, E., Munt, E. D., Korn, D., & Zettle, R. D. (1985). Self-reinforcement effects: An artifact of social standard setting? *Journal of Applied Behavior Analysis, 18*, 201–214.

Hayes, S. C., Strosahl, K. D., & Wilson, K. G. (1999). *Acceptance and commitment therapy: An experiential approach to behavior change*. New York: The Guilford Press.

Hayes, S. C., Strosahl, K. D., & Wilson, K. G. (2011). *Acceptance and commitment therapy: The process and practice of mindful change* (2nd ed.). New York: The Guilford Press.

Haynes, S. N. (1998). The changing nature of behavioral assessment. In A. S. Bellack & M. Hersen (Eds.), *Behavioral assessment: A practical handbook* (4th ed., pp. 1–21). Boston: Allyn & Bacon.

Hefferline, R. F., Keenan, B., & Harford, R. A. (1959). Escape and avoidance conditioning in human subjects without their observation of the response. *Science, 130*, 1338–1339.

Henrich, J., & Gil-White, F. J. (2001). The evolution of prestige: Freely conferred deference as a mechanism for enhancing the benefits of cultural transmission. *Evolution and Human Behavior, 22*, 165–196.

Herbert, J. D., & Forman, E. M. (2013). Caution: The differences between CT and ACT may be larger (and smaller) than they appear. *Behavior Therapy, 44*, 218–223.

Herrnstein, R. J., & DeVilliers, P. A. (1980). Fish as a natural category for people and pigeons. In G. H. Bower (Ed.), *The psychology of learning and motivation* (Vol. 14, pp. 60–97). New York: Academic Press.

Herrnstein, R. J., Loveland, D. H., & Cable, C. (1976). Natural concepts in pigeons. *Journal of Experimental Psychology: Animal Behavior Processes, 2*, 285–302.

Hersen, M. (1976). Historical perspectives in behavioral assessment. In M. Hersen & A. S. Bellack (Eds.), *Behavioral assessment: A practical handbook* (pp. 3–17). New York: Pergamon Press.

Hersen, M. (Ed.). (1983). *Outpatient behavior therapy: A clinical guide*. New York: Grune & Stratton.

Heyes, C. (2010). Where do mirror neurons come from? *Neuroscience and Biobehavioral Reviews, 34*, 575–583.

Higgins, S. T., Silverman, K., Heil, S. H. (2007). *Contingency management in substance abuse treatment*. New York: Guilford.

Hildebrand, R. G., Martin, G. L., Furer, P., & Hazen, A. (1990). A recruitment of praise package to increase productivity levels of developmentally handicapped workers. *Behavior Modification, 14*, 97–113.

Hile, M. G. (1991). Hand-held behavioral observations: The Observer. *Behavioral Assessment, 13*, 187–196.

Himle, M. B., Chang, S., Woods, D. W., Pearlman, A., Buzzella, B., Bunaciu, L., & Piacentini, J. C. (2006). Establishing the feasibility of direct observation in the assessment of tics in children with chronic tic disorders. *Journal of Applied Behavior Analysis, 39*, 429–440.

Himle, M. B., Woods, D. W., & Bunaciu, L. (2008). Evaluating the role of contingency analysis of vocal stereotypy and therapist fading. *Journal of Applied Behavior Analysis, 41*, 291–297.

Hineline, P. N., & Rosales-Ruiz, J. (2013). Behavior in relation to aversive events: Punishment and negative reinforcement.

In G. J. Madden (Ed.), *APA handbook of behavior analysis: Volume 1, methods and principles* (pp. 483–512). Washington, DC: American Psychological Association.

Hirai, M., & Clum, G. A. (2006). A meta-analytic study of self-help interventions for anxiety problems. *Behavior Therapy, 37*, 99–111.

Hjørland, B. (2011). Evidence based practice: An analysis based on the philosophy of science. *Journal of the American Society for Information Science and Technology, 62*, 1301–1310.

Hoeksma, J. B., Oosterlaan, J., & Schipper, E. M. (2004). Emotion regulation and the dynamics of feelings: A conceptual and methodological framework. *Child Development, 75*(2), 354–360.

Hoekstra, R., Kiers, H. A. L., & Johnson, A. (2012). Are assumptions of well-known statistical techniques checked, and why (not)? *Frontiers in Psychology, 3*, article 137.

Hofmann, S. G., Asmundson, G. J. G., & Beck, A. T. (2013). The science of cognitive therapy. *Behavior Therapy, 44*, 199–212.

Hofmann, S. G., & Otto, M. W. (2008). *Cognitive behavioral therapy for social anxiety disorder: Evidence-based and disorder-specific treatment techniques (practical clinical guidelines)*. New York: Routledge.

Homme, L. E. (1965). Perspectives in psychology: XXIV. Control of coverants, the operants of the mind. *Psychological Record, 15*, 501–511.

Homme, L. E., Csanyi, A. P., Gonzales, M. A., & Rechs, J. R. (1969). *How to use contingency contracting in the classroom*. Champaign, IL: Research Press.

Honig, W. K., & Stewart, K. (1988). Pigeons can discriminate locations presented in pictures. *Journal of the Experimental Analysis of Behavior, 50*, 541–551.

Horan, J. J., & Johnson, R. G. (1971). Coverant conditioning through a self-management application of the Premack principle: Its effect on weight reduction. *Journal of Behavior Therapy and Experimental Psychiatry, 2*, 243–249.

Horner, R. (2005). General case programming. In M. Hersen, J. Rosqvist, A. Gross, R. Drabman, G. Sugai, & R. Horner (Eds.), *Encyclopedia of behavior modification and cognitive behavior therapy: Volume 1: Adult clinical applications, Volume 2: Child clinical applications, Volume 3: Educational applications* (Vol. 3, pp. 1343–1348). Thousand Oaks, CA: Sage Publications, Inc.

Horner, R. D., & Keilitz, I. (1975). Training mentally retarded adolescents to brush their teeth. *Journal of Applied Behavior Analysis, 8*, 301–309.

Horner, R. H., Dunlap, G., Koegel, R. L., Carr, E. G., Sailor, W., Anderson, J., & O'Neil, R. E. (1990). Toward a technology of "nonaversive" behavioral support. *Journal of the Association for Persons with Severe Handicaps, 15*, 125–132.

Horner, R. H., Sprague, T., & Wilcox, B. (1982). General case programming for community activities. In B. Wilcox & G. T. Bellamy (Eds.), *Design of high school programs for severely handicapped students* (pp. 61–98). Baltimore: Paul Brookes.

Horner, R. H., Sugai, G., Todd, A. W., & Lewis-Palmer, T. (2005). School-wide positive behavior support: An alternative approach to discipline in schools. In L. Bambara & L. Kern (Eds.), *Individualized supports for students with problem behavior: Designing positive behavior plans* (pp. 359–390). New York: The Guilford Press.

Hrycaiko, D., & Martin, G. L. (1996). Applied research studies with single-subject designs: Why so few? *Journal of Applied Sport Psychology, 8*, 183–199.

Hrydowy, E. R., & Martin, G. L. (1994). A practical staff management package for use in a training program for persons with developmental disabilities. *Behavior Modification, 18,* 66–88.

Huang, W., & Cuvo, A. J. (1997). Social skills training for adults with mental retardation in job-related settings. *Behavior Modification, 21,* 3–44.

Hull, C. L. (1943). *Principles of behavior.* New York: Appleton-Century-Crofts.

Hull, C. L. (1952). *A behavior system.* New Haven, CT: Yale University Press.

Hume, K. M., Martin, G. L., Gonzales, P., Cracklen, C., & Genthon, S. (1985). A self-monitoring feedback package for improving freestyle figure skating performance. *Journal of Sport Psychology, 7,* 333–345.

Hur, J., & Osborne, S. (1993). A comparison of forward and backward chaining methods used in teaching corsage making skills to mentally retarded adults. *The British Journal of Developmental Disabilities, 39* (Part 2, No. 77), 108–117.

Hustyi, K. M., Normand, M. P., & Larson, T. A. (2011). Behavioral assessment of physical activity in obese preschool children. *Journal of Applied Behavior Analysis, 44,* 635–639.

Ice, G. H. (2004). Technological advances in observational data collection: The advantages and limitations of computer-assisted data collection. *Field Methods, 16,* 352–375.

Irey, P. A. (1972). *Covert sensitization of cigarette smokers with high and low extraversion scores.* Unpublished master's thesis, Southern Illinois University, Carbondale.

Isaacs, W., Thomas, J., & Goldiamond, I. (1960). Application of operant conditioning to reinstate verbal behavior in psychotics. *Journal of Speech and Hearing Disorders, 25,* 8–12.

Israel, A. C., Stolmaker, L., & Adrian, C. A. G. (1985). The effects of training parents in general child management skills on a behavioral weight loss program for children. *Behavior Therapy, 16,* 169–180.

Iwamasa, G. Y. (1999). Behavior therapy and Asian Americans: Is there a commitment? *The Behavior Therapist, 10,* 196–197, 205–206.

Iwamasa, G. Y., & Smith, S. K. (1996). Ethic diversity in behavioral psychology: A review of the literature. *Behavior Modification, 20,* 45–59.

Iwata, B. A., DeLeon, I. G., & Roscoe, E. M. (2013). Reliability and validity of the functional analysis screening tool. *Journal of Applied Behavior Analysis, 46,* 271–284.

Iwata, B. A., Dorsey, M. F., Slifer, K. J., Bauman, K. E., & Richman, G. S. (1982). Toward a functional analysis of self-injury. *Analysis and Intervention in Developmental Disabilities, 2,* 3–20.

Iwata, B. A., Dorsey, M. F., Slifer, K. J., Bauman, K. E., & Richman, G. S. (1994). Toward a functional analysis of self-injury. *Journal of Applied Behavior Analysis, 27,* 197–209. (Reprinted from *Iwata, Dorsey, Slifer, Bauman, & Richman* [Eds.]. [1982]. *Analysis and Intervention in Developmental Disabilities, 2,* 3–20.)

Iwata, B. A., Kahng, S. W., Wallace, M. D., & Lindberg, J. S. (2000). The functional analysis model of behavioral assessment. In J. Austin & J. E. Carr (Eds.), *Handbook of applied behavior analysis* (pp. 61–90). Reno, NV: Context Press.

Iwata, B. A., Pace, G. M., Cowdery, G. E., & Miltenberger, R. G. (1994). What makes extinction work? An analysis of procedural form and function. *Journal of Applied Behavior Analysis, 27,* 131–144.

Iwata, B. A., Pace, G. M., Dorsey, M. F., Zarcone, J. R., Vollmer, T. R., Smith, R. G., & Willis, K. D. (1994). The functions of self-injurious behavior: An experimental-epidemiological analysis. *Journal of Applied Behavior Analysis, 27,* 215–240.

Iwata, B. A., Pace, G. M., Kalsher, M. J., Cowdery, G. E., & Cataldo, M. F. (1990). Experimental analysis and extinction of self-injurious escape behavior. *Journal of Applied Behavior Analysis, 23,* 11–27.

Izard, C. E. (1991). *The psychology of emotions.* New York: Plenum Press.

Jackson, D. A., & Wallace, R. F. (1974). The modification and generalization of voice loudness in a 15-year-old retarded girl. *Journal of Applied Behavior Analysis, 7,* 461–471.

Jacobson, N. S., Dobson, K. S., Truax, P. A., Addis, M. E., Koerner, K., Gollan, J. K., & Prince, S. E. (1996). A component analysis of cognitive behavioral treatment for depression. *Journal of Consulting and Clinical Psychology, 64,* 295–304.

Jacobson, N. S., Martell, C. R., & Dimidjian, S. (2001). Behavioral activation for depression: Returning to contextual roots. *Clinical Psychology: Science & Practice, 8,* 255–270.

Jeanson, B., Thiessen, C., Thomson, K., Vermeulen, R., Martin, G. L., & Yu, C. T. (2010). Field testing of the Discrete-Trials Teaching Evaluation Form. *Research in Autism Spectrum Disorders, 4,* 718–723.

Johnson, C. R., Hunt, F. M., & Siebert, M. J. (1994). Discrimination training in the treatment of pica and food scavenging. *Behavior Modification, 18,* 214–229.

Johnson, K. R., & Ruskin, R. S. (1977). *Behavioral instruction: An evaluative review.* Washington, DC: American Psychological Association.

Johnson, S. P., Welch, T. M., Miller, L. K., & Altus, D. E. (1991). Participatory management: Maintaining staff performance in a university housing cooperative. *Journal of Applied Behavior Analysis, 24,* 119–127.

Johnson, T. E., & Dixon, M. R. (2009). Altering response chains in pathological gamblers using a response-cost procedure. *Journal of Applied Behavior Analysis, 42,* 735–740.

Johnson, W. G. (1971). Some applications of Homme's coverant control therapy: Two case reports. *Behavior Therapy, 2,* 240–248.

Johnson, W. L., & Baumeister, A. (1978). Self-injurious behavior: A review and analysis of methodological details of published studies. *Behavior Modification, 2,* 465–484.

Johnston, J. M. (2006). "Replacing" problem behavior: An analysis of tactical alternatives. *The Behavior Analyst, 29,* 1–11.

Johnston, J. M., & Pennypacker, H. S. (Eds.). (2009). *Strategies and tactics of behavioral research* (3rd ed.). New York: Routledge.

Johnston, J. M., Foxx, R. M., Jacobson, J. W., Green, G., & Mulick, J. A. (2006). Positive behavior support and Applied Behavior Analysis. *The Behavior Analyst, 29,* 51–74.

Joice, A., & Mercer, S. W. (2010). An evaluation of the impact of a large group psycho-education programme (Stress Control) on patient outcome: Does empathy make a difference? *The Cognitive Behaviour Therapist, 3,* 1–17.

Jones, E., & Wessely, S. (2005). *Shell shock to PTSD: Military psychiatry from 1900 to the Gulf War.* Hove, East Sussex: Psychology Press.

Jones, M. C. (1924). The elimination of children's fears. *Journal of Experimental Psychology, 7,* 383–390.

Jones, R. R., Weinrott, M. R., & Howard, J. R. (1981). *The national evaluation of the teaching family model.* Final Report R01 MH Grants 25631 and MH 31018 awarded by the Center for Studies of Crime and Delinquency, National Institute of Mental Health. Eugene, OR: Evaluation Research Group, Inc.

Juliano, L. M., Donny, M., Houtsmuller, E. J., & Stitzer, M. L. (2006). Experimental evidence for a causal relationship between smoking lapse and relapse. *Journal of Abnormal Psychology, 11*, 166–173.

Kadey, H. J., & Roane, H. S. (2012). Effects of access to a stimulating object on infant behavior during tummy time. *Journal of Applied Behavior Analysis, 45*, 395–399.

Kahng, S., Ingvarsson, E. T., Quigg, A. M., Seckinger, K. E., & Teichman, H. M. (2011). Defining and measuring behavior. In W. W. Fisher, C. C. Piazza, & H. S. Roane (Eds.), *Handbook of applied behavior analysis* (pp. 113–131). New York: The Guilford Press.

Kahng, S. W., & Iwata, B. A. (2000). Computer systems for collecting real-time observational data. In T. Thompson, D. Felce, & F. Symons (Eds.), *Behavioral observation: Technology and applications in developmental disabilities* (pp. 35–46). Baltimore. MD: Brookes.

Kanter, J. W. (2013). The vision of a progressive clinical science to guide clinical practice. *Behavior Therapy, 44*, 228–233.

Kanter, J. W., Baruch, D. E., & Gaynor, S. T. (2006). Acceptance and Commitment Therapy and behavioral activation for the treatment of depression: Description and comparison. *The Behavior Analyst, 29*, 161–185.

Kanter, J. W., Busch, A. M., Weeks, C. E., & Landes, S. J. (2008). The nature of clinical depression: Symptoms, syndromes, and behavioral analysis. *The Behavior Analyst, 31*, 1–21.

Kanter, J. W., & Puspitasari, A. J. (2012). Behavioral activation. In W. T. O'Donohue & J. E. Fisher (Eds.), *Cognitive behavior therapy: Core principles for practice* (pp. 215–250). Hoboken, NJ: John Wiley & Sons.

Karol, R. L., & Richards, C. S. (1978, November). Making treatment effects last: An investigation of maintenance strategies for smoking reduction. Paper presented at the meeting of the Association for the Advancement of Behavior Therapy, Chicago.

Kau, M. L., & Fischer, J. (1974). Self-modification of exercise behavior. *Journal of Behavior Therapy and Experimental Psychiatry, 5*, 213–214.

Kazbour, R. R., & Bailey, J. S. (2010). An analysis of a contingency program on designated drivers at a college bar. *Journal of Applied Behavior Analysis, 43*, 273–277.

Kazdin, A. E. (1973). The effect of vicarious reinforcement on attentive behavior in the classroom. *Journal of Applied Behavior Analysis, 6*, 72–78.

Kazdin, A. E. (1977). *The token economy: A review and evaluation.* New York: Plenum Press.

Kazdin, A. E. (1978). *History of behavior modification.* Baltimore: University Park Press.

Kazdin, A. E. (1985). The token economy. In R. M. Turner & L. M. Ascher (Eds.), *Evaluating behavior therapy outcome* (pp. 225–253). New York: Springer Publishing Company.

Kazdin, A. E. (2008). Evidence-based treatment and practice: New opportunities to bridge clinical research and practice, enhance the knowledge base, and improve patient care. *American Psychologist, 63*, 146–159.

Kazdin, A. E. (2011). *Single-case research designs: Methods for clinical and applied settings* (2nd ed.). New York: Oxford University Press.

Kazdin, A. E., & Erickson, L. M. (1975). Developing responsiveness to instructions in severely and profoundly retarded

residents. *Journal of Behavior Therapy and Experimental Psychiatry, 6*, 17–21.

Kazdin, A. E., & Polster, R. (1973). Intermittent token reinforcement and response maintenance in extinction. *Behavior Therapy, 4*, 386–391.

Keller, F. S. (1968). Good-bye, teacher... *Journal of Applied Behavior Analysis, 1*, 79–89.

Keller, F. S., & Schoenfeld, W. N. (1950). *Principles of psychology.* New York: Appleton-Century-Crofts.

Keller, F. S., & Sherman, J. G. (1982). *The PSI handbook: Essays on personalized instruction.* Lawrence, KS: T.R.I. Publications.

Kennedy, C. H. (2002a). The maintenance of behavior change as an indicator of social validity. *Behavior Modification, 26*, 594–604.

Kennedy, C. H. (2002b). Toward a socially valid understanding of problem behavior. *Education and Treatment of Children, 25*, 142–153.

Kennedy, C. H. (2005). *Single-case designs for educational research.* Boston: Allyn and Bacon.

Kerr, S., & LePelley, D. (2013). Stretch goals: Risks, possibilities, and best practices. In E. A. Locke & G. P. Latham (Eds.)., *New Ddevelopments in Ggoal Ssetting and Ttask Pperformance* (pp. 21–31). New York: Routledge.

Keyers, C., & Gazzola, V. (2009). Unifying social cognition. In Jaime A. Pineda (Ed.), *Mirror neuron systems: The role of mirroring processes in social cognition* (pp. 3–37). New York: Springer Publishing Company.

Kim, J. (2003). History of Korean ABA. *Newsletter of the International Association for Behavior Analysis, 26*(3), 20–21.

King, N. (1996). The Australian Association for Cognitive and Behavior Therapy. *The Behavior Therapist, 19*, 73–74.

Kingsley, D. E. (2006). The Teaching-Family Model and post-treatment recidivism: A critical review of the conventional wisdom. *International Journal of Behavioral and Consultation Therapy, 2*, 481–497.

Kirby, F. D., & Shields, F. (1972). Modification of arithmetic response rate and attending behavior in a seventh grade student. *Journal of Applied Behavior Analysis, 5*, 79–84.

Kircher, A. S., Pear, J. J., & Martin, G. (1971). Shock as punishment in a picture-naming task with retarded children. *Journal of Applied Behavior Analysis, 4*, 227–233.

Kirigin, K. A., Braukmann, C. J., Atwater, J. D., & Wolf, M. M. (1982). An evaluation of Teaching-Family (Achievement Place) group homes for juvenile offenders. *Journal of Applied Behavior Analysis, 15*, 1.

Klein, H. J. Cooper, J. T., & Monahan, C. A. (2013). Goal commitment. In E. A. Locke & G. P. Latham (Eds.), *New developments in goal setting and task performance* (pp. 65–89). New York: Routledge.

Kleinke, C. L. (1986). Gaze and eye-contact: A research review. *Psychological Bulletin, 100*, 78–100.

Kleinman, K. E., & Saigh, P. A. (2011). The effects of the good behavior game on the conduct of regular education New York City high school students. *Behavior Modification, 35*, 95–105.

Kliem, S., Kroger, C., & Kossfelder, J. (2010). Dialectical behavior therapy for borderline personality disorder: A meta-analysis using mixed-effects modeling. *Journal of Consulting and Clinical Psychology, 78*, 936–951.

Knight, M. F., & McKenzie, H. S. (1974). Elimination of bedtime thumb-sucking in home settings through contingent reading. *Journal of Applied Behavior Analysis, 7*, 33–38.

Knoster, T. P. (2000). Practical application of functional behavioral assessment in schools. *Journal of the Association for Persons with Severe Handicaps, 25,* 201–211.

Kodak, T., & Grow, L. L. (2011). Behavioral treatment of autism. In W. W. Fisher, C. C. Piazza, & H. S. Roane (Eds.), *Handbook of applied behavior analysis* (pp. 401–416). New York: The Guilford Press.

Koegel, L. K., Kuriakose, S., Singh, A. K., & Koegel, R. L. (2012). Improving generalization of peer socialization games in inclusive school settings using initiations training. *Behavior Modification, 36,* 361–378.

Koegel, R. L., & Williams, J. A. (1980). Direct versus indirect response-reinforcer relationships in teaching autistic children. *Journal of Abnormal Child Psychology, 8,* 537–547.

Koerner, K. (2012). *Doing dialectical behavior therapy, a practical guide.* New York: The Guilford Press.

Kohler, F. W., & Greenwood, C. R. (1986). Toward technology of generalization: The identification of natural contingencies of reinforcement. *The Behavior Analyst, 9,* 19–26.

Kohn, A. (1993). *Punished by rewards: The trouble with gold stars, incentive plans, A's, praise, and other bribes.* New York: Houghton Mifflin.

Kokoszka, A., Popiel, A., & Sitarz, M. (2000). Cognitive-behavioral therapy in Poland. *The Behavior Therapist, 23,* 209–216.

Komaki, J., & Barnett, F. T. (1977). A behavioral approach to coaching football: Improving the play execution of the offensive backfield on a youth football team. *Journal of Applied Behavior Analysis, 7,* 199–206.

Koop, S., Martin, G., Yu, D., & Suthons, E. (1980). Comparison of two reinforcement strategies in vocational-skill training of mentally retarded persons. *American Journal of Mental Deficiency, 84,* 616–626.

Koritzky, G., & Yechiam, E. (2011). On the value of non-removable reminders for behavior modification: An application to nail-biting. *Behavior Modification, 35,* 511–530.

Krasner, L. (2001). Cognitive behavior therapy: The oxymoron of the century. In W. T. O'Donohue, D. A. Henderson, S. C. Hayes, J. E. Fisher, & L. J. Hayes (Eds.), *A history of the behavioral therapies: Founders' personal histories* (pp. 207–218). Reno, NV: Context Press.

Krasner, L., & Ullmann, L. T. (Eds.) (1965). *Research in Behavior Modification.* New York: Holt, Rinehart, & Winston.

Kraus, A. J., Hanley, G. P., Cesana, L. L. Eisenberg, D., & Jarvie, A. C. (2012). An evaluation of strengthening precursors to increase preschooler compliance. *Journal of Applied Behavior Analysis, 45,* 131–136.

Kuhn, D. E., Chirighin, A. E., & Zelenka, K. (2010). Discriminated functional communication: A procedural extension of functional communication training. *Journal of Applied Behavior Analysis, 43,* 249–264.

Kurtz, P. F., & Lind, M. A. (2013). Behavioral approaches to treatment of intellectual and developmental disabilities. In G. J. Madden (Ed.), *APA handbook of behavior analysis: Volume 2, translating behavioral principles into practice* (pp. 279–302). Washington, DC: American Psychological Association.

Lam, D. C. K. (2008). *Cognitive behavior therapy: A practical guide to helping people take control.* New York: Routledge.

Lambert, M. J. (2013). *Bergin & Garfield's Handbook of psychotherapy and behaviour change* (6th ed.). Hoboken, NJ: John Wiley & Sons.

Lamson, R. (1997). *Virtual therapy.* Montreal, Canada: Polytechnic International Press.

Lancioni, G. E., Bellini, D., Oliva, D., Singh, N. H., O'Reilly, M. F., Lang, R., & Didden, R. (2011). Camera-based microswitch technology to monitor mouth, eyebrow, and eyelid responses of children with profound multiple disabilities. *Journal of Behavioral Education, 20,* 4–14.

Lang, R., O'Reilly, M., Sigafoos, J., Lancioni, G. E., Machalicek, W., Rispoli, M., & White, P. (2009). Enhancing the effectiveness of a play intervention for abolishing the reinforcing value of stereotypy: A pilot study. *Journal of Applied Behavior Analysis, 42,* 889–894.

Laraway, S., Snycerski, S., Michael, J., & Poling, A. (2003). Motivating operations and terms to describe them: Some further reinfinements. *Journal of Applied Behavior Analysis, 36,* 407–414.

Larkin, K. T., & Zayfert, C. (1996). Anger management training with essential hypertensive patients. In V. B. Van Hasselt & M. Hersen (Eds.), *Sourcebook of psychological treatment manuals for adult disorders* (pp. 689–716). New York: Plenum Press.

LaRue, R. H., Stewart, V., Piazza, C. C., Volkert, V. M., Patel, M. R., & Zeleny, J. (2011). Escape as reinforcement and escape extinction in the treatment of fading problems. *Journal of Applied Behavior Analysis, 44,* 719–735.

Larzelere, R. E., Daly, D. L., Davis, J. L., Chmelka, M. B., & Handwerk, M. L. (2004). Outcome evaluation of Girls and Boys Town's Family Home Program. *Education and Treatment of Children, 27,* 130–149.

Larzelere, R. E., Dinges, K., Schmidt, M. D., Spellman, D. F., Criste, T. R., & Connell, P. (2001). Outcomes of residential treatment: A study of the adolescent clients of Girls and Boys Town. *Child & Youth Care Forum, 30,* 175–184.

Latham, G. P., & Arshoff, A. S. (2013). The relevance of goal setting theory for human resource management. In E. A. Locke & G. P. Latham (Eds.), *New developments in goal setting and task performance* (pp. 331–342). New York: Routledge.

Latimer, P. R., & Sweet, A. A. (1984). Cognitive vs. behavioral procedures in cognitive behavior therapy: A critical review of the evidence. *Journal of Behavior Therapy and Experimental Psychiatry, 15,* 9–22.

Latner, J. D., & Wilson, G. T. (2002). Self-monitoring and the assessment of binge eating. *Behavior Therapy, 33,* 465–477.

Lattal, K. A. (2012). Schedules of reinforcement. In N. M. Seel (Ed.), *Encyclopedia of the sciences of learning* (pp. 2929–2933). New York: Springer Publishing Company.

Lattal, K. A., & Metzger, B. (1994). Response acquisition by Siamese fighting fish with delayed visual reinforcement. *Journal of the Experimental Analysis of Behavior, 61,* 35–44.

Lattal, K. A., St. Peter, C., & Escobar, R. (2013). Operant extinction: Elimination and generation of behavior. In G. J. Madden (Ed.), *APA handbook of behavior analysis: Volume 2, translating behavioral principles into practice* (pp. 77–108). Washington, DC: American Psychological Association.

Lattal, K. M. (2013). Pavlovian conditioning. In G. J. Madden (Ed.), *APA handbook of behavior analysis: Volume 1, methods and principles* (pp. 283–308). Washington, DC: American Psychological Association.

Lazarus, A. A. (1958). New methods in psychotherapy: A case study. *South African Medical Journal, 32,* 660–664.

Lazarus, A. A. (1971). *Behavior therapy and beyond.* New York: McGraw-Hill.

Lazarus, A. A. (1976). *Multi-model behavior therapy.* New York: Springer Publishing Company.

Lazarus, A. A., & Lazarus, C. N. (2005). *Multimodal life history inventory.* Champagne, ILL: Research Press.

Lazarus, R. S. (2007). Stress and emotion: A new synthesis. In A. Monat, R. S. Lazarus, & G. Reevy (Eds.), *The Praeger handbook on stress and coping.* (pp. 33–53). Westport, CT: Praeger.

Leahy, R. L. (2008). A closer look at ACT. *The Behavior Therapist, 31,* 148–150.

Leahy, R. L., Holland, S. J. F., & McGinn, L. K. (2011). *Treatment plans and interventions for depression and anxiety disorders* (2nd ed.). New York: The Guilford Press.

Leal, J., & Galanter, M. (1995). The use of contingency-contracting to improve outcome in methadone maintenance. *Substance Abuse, 16,* 155–167.

LeBlanc, L. A., Raetz, P. B., & Feliciano, L. (2011). Behavioral gerontology. In W. W. Fisher, C. C. Piazza, & H. S. Roane (Eds.), *Handbook of applied behavior analysis* (pp. 472–488). New York: The Guilford Press.

LeBow, M. D. (1989). *Adult obesity therapy.* New York: Pergamon Press.

LeBow, M. D. (1991). *Overweight children: Helping your child to achieve lifetime weight control.* New York: Insight Books/Plenum Press.

LeBow, M. D. (2013). *The teenager's guide to understanding and healthfully managing weight: Questions, answers, tips, and cautions.* St. Louis: Sciences and Humanities Press.

Ledford, J. R., & Wolery, M. (2011). Teaching imitation to children with disabilities: A review of the literature. *Topics in Early Childhood Special Education, 30,* 245–255.

Lee, N. S. H., Yu, C. T., Martin, T. L., & Martin, G. L. (2010). On the relation between reinforcer efficacy and preference. *Journal of Applied Behavior Analysis, 43,* 95–100.

Lee, R., Sturmey, P., & Fields, L. (2007). Schedule-induced and operant mechanisms that influence response variability: A review and implications for future investigations. *The Psychological Record, 57,* 429–455.

Lehrer, P. M., Woolfolk, R. L., & Sime, W. E. (Eds.). (2007). *Principles and practice of stress management* (3rd ed.). New York: The Guilford Press.

Leiblum, S. R., & Rosen, R. C. (Eds.). (2000). *Principles and practice of sex therapy* (3rd ed.). New York: The Guilford Press.

Lennox, D. B., Miltenberger, R. G., & Donnelly, D. (1987). Response interruption and DRL for the reduction of rapid eating. *Journal of Applied Behavior Analysis, 20,* 279–284.

Lerman, D. C., & Iwata, B. A. (1995). Prevalence of the extinction burst and its attenuation during treatment. *Journal of Applied Behavior Analysis, 28,* 93–94.

Lerman, D. C., & Iwata, B. A. (1996). Developing a technology for the use of operant extinction in clinical settings: An examination of basic and applied research. *Journal of Applied Behavior Analysis, 29,* 345–382.

Lerman, D. C., Iwata, B. A., Shore, B. A., & DeLeon, I. G. (1997). Effects of intermittent punishment on self-injurious behavior: An evaluation of schedule thinning. *Journal of Applied Behavior Analysis, 30,* 187–201.

Lerman, D. C., Iwata, B. A., Shore, B. A., & Kahng, S. (1996). Responding maintained by intermittent reinforcement: Implications for the use of extinction with problem behavior in clinical settings. *Journal of Applied Behavior Analysis, 29,* 153–171.

Lerman, D. C., Iwata, B. A., & Wallace, M. D. (1999). Side effects of extinction: Prevalence of bursting and aggression during the treatment of self-injurious behavior. *Journal of Applied Behavior Analysis, 32,* 1–8.

Lerman, D. C., & Toole, L. M. (2011). Developing function-based punishment procedures for problem behavior. In W. W. Fisher, C. C. Piazza, & H. S. Roane (Eds.), *Handbook of applied behavior analysis* (pp. 370–384). New York: The Guilford Press.

Lerman, D. C., & Vorndran, C. M. (2002). On the status of knowledge for using punishment: Implications for treating behavior disorders. *Journal of Applied Behavior Analysis, 35,* 431–464.

Leslie-Toogood, A., & Martin, G. L. (2003). Do coaches know the mental skills of their athletes? Assessments from volleyball and track. *Journal of Sport Behavior, 26,* 56–68.

Lewinsohn, P. M. (1975). The behavioral study and treatment of depression. In M. Hersen, R. M. Eisler, & P. M. Miller (Eds.), *Progress in behavior modification* (Vol. 1, pp. 19–65). New York: Academic Press.

Liberman, R. P. (2000). The token economy. *American Journal of Psychiatry, 157,* 1398.

Lima, E. L., & Abreu-Rodrigues, J. (2010). Verbal mediating responses: Effects on generalization of say-do correspondence and noncorrespondence. *Journal of Applied Behavior Analysis, 43,* 411–424.

Lindsley, O. R. (1956). Operant conditioning methods applied to research in chronic schizophrenia. *Psychiatric Research Reports, 5,* 118–139.

Lindsley, O. R. (1966). An experiment with parents handling behavior at home. *Johnstone Bulletin, 9,* 27–36.

Lindsley, O. R., Skinner, B. F., & Solomon, H. C. (1953). *Studies in behavior therapy: Status report. I.* Waltham, MA: Metropolitan State Hospital.

Linehan, M. M. (1987). Dialectical behavior therapy: A cognitive-behavioral approach to parasuicide. *Journal of Personality Disorders, 1,* 328–333.

Linehan, M. M. (1993). *Cognitive behavioral treatment of borderline personality disorder.* New York: The Guilford Press.

Lines, J. B., Schwartzman, L., Tkachuk, G. A., Leslie-Toogood, S. A., & Martin, G. L. (1999). Behavioral assessment in sport psychology consulting: Applications to swimming and basketball. *Journal of Sport Behavior, 4,* 558–569.

Linscheid, T. R., Iwata, B. A., Ricketts, R. W., Williams, D. E., & Griffin, J. C. (1990). Clinical evaluation of the Self-Injurious Behavior Inhibiting System (SIBIS). *Journal of Applied Behavior Analysis, 23,* 53–78.

Linscheid, T. R., Pejeau, C., Cohen, S., & Footo-Lenz, M. (1994). Positive side-effects in the treatment of SIB using the Self-Injurious Behavior Inhibiting System (SIBIS): Implications for operant and biochemical explanations of SIB. *Research in Developmental Disabilities, 15,* 81–90.

Lippman, M. R., & Motta, R. W. (1993). Effects of positive and negative reinforcement on daily living skills in chronic psychiatric patients in community residences. *Journal of Clinical Psychology, 49,* 654–662.

Lipsey, M. (1999a). Juvenile delinquency treatment: A meta-analytic inquiry into the viability of effects. In T. D. Cook, H. Cooper, D. Cordray, H. Hartman, L. V. Hedges, R. J. Light, T. A. Louis, & F. Mosteller (Eds.), *Meta-analysis for evaluation: A casebook* (pp. 83–128). New York: Russell Sage Foundation.

Lipsey, M. W. (1999b). Can intervention rehabilitate serious delinquents? *Annals of the American Academy of Political and Social Science(s), 564,* 142–199.

Lipsey, M. W., & Wilson, D. B. (1998). Effective intervention for serious juvenile offenders: A synthesis of research. In R. Loeber & D. P. Farrington (Eds.), *Serious and violent juvenile offenders: Risk factors and successful interventions* (pp. 315–345). Thousand Oaks, CA: Sage Publications, Inc.

Lloyd, K. E. (2002). A review of correspondence training: Suggestions for a revival. *The Behavior Analyst, 25,* 57–73.

Locke, E. A., & Latham, G. P. (2002). Building a practically useful theory of goal setting and task motivation: A 35-year odyssey. *American Psychologist, 57,* 705–717.

Locke, E. A., & Latham, G. P. (2013). Goal setting theory: The current state. In E. A. Locke & G. P. Latham (Eds.), *New developments in goal setting and task performance* (pp. 623–630). New York: Routledge.

Longmore, R., & Worrell, M. (2007). Do we need to challenge thoughts in cognitive behavioural therapy? *Clinical Psychology Review, 27,* 173–187.

Lopez, W. L., & Aguilar, M. C. (2003). Reflections on the history of ABA Columbia: Five years of experience and development. *Newsletter of the International Association for Behavior Analysis, 26*(3), 14–15.

Loprinzi, P. D., & Cardinal, B. J. (2011). Measuring children's physical activity and sedentary behaviors. *Journal of Exercise Science & Fitness, 9,* 15–23.

Lovaas, O. I. (1966). A program for the establishment of speech in psychotic children. In J. K. Wing (Ed.), *Early childhood autism* (pp. 115–144). Elmsford, NY: Pergamon Press.

Lovaas, O. I. (1977). *The autistic child: Language development through behavior modification.* New York: Irvington.

Lovaas, O. I. (1987). Behavioral treatment and normal educational and intellectual functioning in young autistic children. *Journal of Consulting and Clinical Consulting, 55,* 3–9.

Lovaas, O. I., Newsom, C., & Hickman, C. (1987). Self-stimulatory behavior and perceptual development. *Journal of Applied Behavior Analysis, 20,* 45–68.

Lowe, C. F., Beasty, A., & Bentall, R. P. (1983). The role of verbal behavior in human learning: Infant performance on fixed interval schedules. *Journal of the Experimental Analysis of Behavior, 39,* 157–164.

Lubetkin, B. S., Rivers, P. C., & Rosenberg, C. N. (1971). Difficulties of disulfiram therapy with alcoholics. *Quarterly Journal of Studies on Alcohol, 32,* 118–171.

Lubow, R. E. (1974). High-order concept formation in pigeons. *Journal of the Experimental Analysis of Behavior, 21,* 475–483.

Luce, S. C., Delquadri, J., & Hall, R. V. (1980). Contingent exercise: A mild but powerful procedure for suppressing inappropriate verbal and aggressive behavior. *Journal of Applied Behavior Analysis, 13,* 583–594.

Luiselli, J. K., & Reed, D. D. (Eds.). (2011). *Behavioral sport psychology: Evidence-based approaches to performance enhancement.* New York: Springer Publishing Company.

Lundgren, J. D. (2006). Behavior therapy and its contributions to obesity treatment. *The Behavior Therapist, 29,* 28–29.

Lutz, J. (1994). *Introduction to learning and memory.* Pacific Grove, CA: Brooks/Cole.

Lynch, T. R., Cheavens, J. S., Cukrowicz, K. C., Thorp, S. R., Bronner, L., & Beyer, J. (2007). Treatment of older adults with comorbid personality disorders and depression: A dialectical behavior therapy approach. *International Journal of Geriatric Psychiatry, 2,* 131–143.

Ma, H. (2006). An alternative method for quantitative synthesis of single-subject researches: Percentage of data points exceeding the median. *Behavior Modification, 30,* 598–617.

MacDonald, R., Sacrimone, S., Mansfield, R., Wiltz, K., & Ahearn, W. H. (2009). Using video modeling to teach reciprocal pretend play to children with autism. *Journal of Applied Behavior Analysis, 42,* 43–55.

Mace, F. C., & Belfiore, P. (1990). Behavioral momentum in the treatment of escape-motivated stereotypy. *Journal of Applied Behavior Analysis, 23,* 507–514.

Mace, F. C., Belfiore, P. J., & Hutchinson, J. M. (2001). Operant theory and research on self-regulation. In B. J. Zimmerman & D. H. Schunk (Eds.), *Self-regulated learning and academic achievement: Theoretical perspectives* (2nd ed., pp. 39–65). Mahwah, NJ: Lawrence Erlbaum Associates.

Mace, F. C., Hock, M. L., Lalli, J. S., West, B. J., Belfiore, P., Pinter, E., & Brown, D. K. (1988). Behavioral momentum in the treatment of noncompliance. *Journal of Applied Behavior Analysis, 21,* 123–141.

Mace, F. C., Lalli, J., Lalli, E. P., & Shey, M. C. (1993). Function analysis and treatment of aberrant behavior. In R. Van Houten & S. Axelrod (Eds.), *Behavior analysis and treatment* (pp. 75–99). New York: Plenum Press.

Madsen, C. H., Becker, W. C., Thomas, D. R., Koser, L., & Plager, E. (1970). An analysis of the reinforcing function of "sit down" commands. In R. K. Parker (Ed.), *Readings in educational psychology* (pp. 71–82). Boston: Allyn & Bacon.

Madsen, C. H., Jr., & Madsen, C. R. (1974). *Teaching discipline: Behavior principles towards a positive approach.* Boston: Allyn & Bacon.

Mager, R. F. (1972). *Goal analysis.* Belmont, CA: Fearon.

Mahoney, K., VanWagenen, K., & Meyerson, L. (1971). Toilet training of normal and retarded children. *Journal of Applied Behavior Analysis, 4,* 173–181.

Mahoney, M. J. (1974). *Cognition and behavior modification.* Cambridge, MA: Ballinger.

Maier, S. F., Watkins, L. R., & Fleshner, M. (1994). Psychoneuroimmunology: The interface between behavior, brain, and immunity. *American Psychologist, 49,* 1004–1017.

Maletsky, B. M. (1974). Behavior recording as treatment: A brief note. *Behavior Therapy, 5,* 107–111.

Malott, R. W. (1989). The achievement of evasive goals: Control by rules describing contingencies that are not direct-acting. In S. C. Hayes (Ed.), *Rule-governed behavior: Cognition, contingencies, and instructional control* (pp. 269–324). New York: Plenum Press.

Malott, R. W. (1992). A theory of rule-governed behavior and organizational behavior management. *Journal of Organizational Behavior Management, 12,* 45–65.

Malott, R. W. (2008). *Principles of behavior* (6th ed.). Upper Saddle River, NJ: Pearson Prentice-Hall.

Malott, R. W., & Whaley, D. L. (1983). *Psychology.* Holmes Beach, FL: Learning Publications.

Malouff, J. M., & Rooke, S. E. (2007). Empirically supported self-help books. *The Behavior Therapist, 30,* 29–131.

Marion, C., Martin, G. L., Yu, C. T., Buhler, C., & Kerr, D. (2012). Teaching children with autism spectrum disorder to mand "Where?" *Journal of Behavioral Education, 21,* 273–294.

Marion, C., Martin, G. L., Yu, C. T., Buhler, C., Kerr, D., & Claeys, A. (2012). Teaching children with autism spectrum disorder to mand for information using "Which?" *Journal of Applied Behavior Analysis, 45,* 865–870.

Marion, C., Vause, T., Harapiak, S., Martin, G. L., Yu, D., Sakko, G., & Walters, K. L. (2003). The hierarchical relationship between several visual and auditory discriminations and three verbal operants among individuals with developmental disabilities. *The Analysis of Verbal Behavior, 19*, 91–105.

Marlatt, G. A., & Parks, G. A. (1982). Self-management of addictive disorders. In P. Karoly & F. H. Kanfer (Eds.), *Self-management and behavior change: From theory to practice* (pp. 443–488). New York: Pergamon Press.

Marr, M. J. (2003). The stitching and the unstitching: What can behavior analysis have to say about creativity? *The Behavior Analyst, 26*, 15–27.

Martell, C. R. (2008). Behavioral activation treatment for depression. In W. O'Donohue & J. E. Fisher (Eds.), *Cognitive behavior therapy: Applying empirically supported techniques in your practice* (2nd ed., pp. 40–45). Hoboken, NJ: John Wiley & Sons.

Martell, C. R., Addis, M. E., & Jacobson, N. S. (2001). *Depression in context: Strategies for guided action.* New York: Norton.

Martell, C., Addis, M., & Dimidjian, S. (2004). Finding the action in behavioral activation: The search for empirically supported interventions and mechanisms of change. In S. C. Hayes, V. M. Follette, & M. M. Linehan (Eds.), *Mindfulness and acceptance: Expanding the cognitive behavioral tradition* (pp. 152–167). New York: The Guilford Press.

Martens, B. K., Daily III, E. J., Begeny, J. C., & VanDerHeyden, A. (2011). Behavioral approaches to education. In W. W. Fisher, C. C. Piazza, & H. S. Roane (Eds.), *Handbook of applied behavior analysis* (pp. 385–401). New York: The Guilford Press.

Martin, G. A., & Worthington, E. L. (1982). Behavioral homework. In M. Hersen, R. M. Isler, & P. M. Miller (Eds.), *Progress in behavior modification* (Vol. 13, pp. 197–226). New York: Academic Press.

Martin, G. L. (1981). Behavior modification in Canada in the 1970's. *Canadian Psychology, 22*, 7–22.

Martin, G. L. (1982). Thought stopping and stimulus control to decrease persistent disturbing thoughts. *Journal of Behavior Therapy and Experimental Psychiatry, 13*(3), 215–220.

Martin, G. L. (1999). *A private consultation with a professional golfer,* unpublished report.

Martin, G. L. (2015). *Sport psychology: Practical guidelines from behavior analysis* (5th ed.). Winnipeg, Canada: Sport Science Press.

Martin, G. L., England, G. D., & England, K. G. (1971). The use of backward chaining to teach bed-making to severely retarded girls: A demonstration. *Psychological Aspects of Disability, 18*, 35–40.

Martin, G. L., England, G., Kaprowy, E., Kilgour, K., & Pilek, V. (1968). Operant conditioning of kindergarten-class behavior in autistic children. *Behaviour Research and Therapy, 6*, 281–294.

Martin, G. L., & Ingram, D. (2001). *Play golf in the zone: The psychology of golf made easy.* San Francisco: Van der Plas.

Martin, G. L., Koop, S., Turner, C., & Hanel, F. (1981). Backward chaining versus total task presentation to teach assembly tasks to severely retarded persons. *Behavior Research of Severe Developmental Disabilities, 2*, 117–136.

Martin, G. L., & Osborne, J. G. (1993). *Psychological adjustment and everyday living* (2nd ed.). Upper Saddle River, NJ: Prentice Hall.

Martin, G. L., & Osborne, J. G. (Eds.). (1980). *Helping in the community: Behavioral applications.* New York: Plenum Press.

Martin, G. L., & Thomson, K. (2010). A self-instructional manual for figure skaters. Winnipeg, Canada: Sport Science Press.

Martin, G. L., & Thomson, K. (2011). Overview of behavioral sport psychology. In J. K. Luiselli & D. D. Reed (Eds.), *Behavioral sport psychology: Evidence-based approaches to performance enhancement* (pp. 3–25). New York: Springer Publishing Company.

Martin, G. L., Thomson, K., & Regehr, K. (2004). Studies using single-subject designs in sport psychology: 30 years of research. *The Behavior Analyst, 27*, 123–140.

Martin, G. L., & Tkachuk, G. (2000). Behavioral sport psychology. In J. Austin & J. E. Carr (Eds.), *Handbook of applied behavior analysis* (pp. 399–422). Reno, NV: Context Press.

Martin, G. L., & Toogood, A. (1997). Cognitive and behavioral components of a seasonal psychological skills training program for competitive figure skaters. *Cognitive and Behavioral Practice, 4*, 383–404.

Martin, T. L., Pear, J. J., & Martin, G. L. (2002a). Analysis of proctor grading accuracy in a computer-aided personalized system of instruction course. *Journal of Applied Behavior Analysis, 35*, 309–312.

Martin, T. L., Pear, J. J., & Martin, G. L. (2002b). Feedback and its effectiveness in a computer-aided personalized system of instruction course. *Journal of Applied Behavior Analysis, 35*, 427–430.

Martin, G. L., Thomson, K., & Regehr, K. (2004). Studies using single-subject design is sports psychology: 30 years of research. *The Behavior Analyst, 27*, 123–140.

Martin, G. L., Thorsteinsson, J. R., Yu, C. T., Martin, T. L., & Vause, T. (2008). The Assessment of Basic Learning Abilities Test for predicting learning of persons with intellectual disabilities: A review. *Behavior Modification, 32*, 228–247.

Martin, G. L., Toogood, S. A., & Tkachuk, G. A. (Eds.). (1997). *Behavioral assessment forms for sport psychology consulting.* Winnipeg, Canada: Sport Science Press.

Marzullo-Kerth, D., Reeve, S. A., Reeve, K. F., & Townsend, D. B. (2011). Using multiple-exemplar training to teach a generalized repertoire of sharing to children with autism. *Journal of Applied Behavior Analysis, 44*, 279–294.

Masia, C. L., & Chase, P. N. (1997). Vicarious learning revisited: A contemporary behavior analytic interpretation. *Journal of Behavior Therapy and Experimental Psychiatry, 28*, 41–51.

Mason, W. A., & Capitanio, J. P. (2012). Basic emotions: A reconstruction. *Emotion Review, 4*, 238–244.

Masters, J. C., Burrish, T. G., Hollon, S. D., & Rimm, D. C. (1987). *Behavior therapy: Techniques and empirical findings* (3rd ed.). Orlando, FL: Harcourt Brace Jovanovich.

Masters, W. H., & Johnson, V. E. (1970). *Human sexual inadequacy.* Boston: Little, Brown.

Mathews, J. R., Friman, P. C., Barone, V. J., Ross, L. V., & Christophersen, E. R. (1987). Decreasing dangerous infant behavior through parent instruction. *Journal of Applied Behavior Analysis, 20*, 165–169.

Matson, J. L., Bielecki, J., Mayville, E. A., Smolls, Y., Bamburg, J. W., & Baglio, C. S. (1999). The development of a reinforcer choice assessment scale for persons with severe and profound mental retardation. *Research in Developmental Disabilities, 20*, 379–384.

Matson, J. L., & Boisjoli, J. A. (2009). The token economy for children with intellectual disability and/or autism: A review. *Research in Developmental Disabilities, 30*, 240–248.

Matson, J. L., & Smith, K. R. M. (2008). Current status of intensive behavioral interventions of young children with autism and PDD-NOS. *Research in Autism Spectrum Disorders, 2,* 60–74.

Matson, J. L., & Sturmey, P. (Eds.). (2011). *International handbook of autism and pervasive developmental disabilities.* New York: Springer Publishing Company.

Matson, J. L., & Vollmer, T. R. (1995). *User's guide: Questions About Behavioral Function (QABF).* Baton Rouge, LA: Scientific Publishers.

Mattaini, M. A., & McGuire, M. S. (2006). Behavioral strategies for constructing non-violent cultures with youth: A review. *Behavior Modification, 30,* 184–224.

May, A. C., Rudy, B. M., Davis III, T. E., & Matson, J. L. (2013). Evidence-based behavioral treatment of dog phobia with young children: Two case examples. *Behavior Modification, 37,* 143–160.

Mazaleski, J. L., Iwata, B. A., Vollmer, T. R., Zarcone, J. R., & Smith, R. G. (1993). Analysis of the reinforcement and extinction components in DRO contingencies with self injury. *Journal of Applied Behavior Analysis, 26,* 143–156.

Mazur, J. E. (1991). Choice with probabilistic reinforcement: Effects of delay and conditioned reinforcers. *Journal of the Experimental Analysis of Behavior, 55*(1), 63–77.

McCrady, B. S. (2008). Alcohol use disorders. In D. H. Barlow (Ed.), *Clinical handbook of psychological disorders: A step-by-step treatment manual* (4th ed., pp. 492–546). New York: The Guilford Press.

McDonald, A. J., Wang, N., & Camargo, C. A. (2004). US emergency department visits for alcohol-related diseases and injuries between 1992 and 2000. *JAMA Internal Medicine, 164,* 531–537.

McEachin, J. J., Smith, T., & Lovaas, O. I. (1993). Long-term outcome for children with autism who received early intensive behavioral treatment. *American Journal on Mental Retardation, 97,* 359–372.

McFall, R. M. (1970). The effects of self-monitoring on normal smoking behavior. *Journal of Consulting and Clinical Psychology, 35,* 135–142.

McGinnis, J. C., Friman, P. C., & Carlyon, W. D. (1999). The effect of token rewards on "intrinsic" motivation for doing math. *Journal of Applied Behavior Analysis, 32,* 375–379.

McGlynn, F. D., Smitherman, T. A., & Gothard, K. D. (2004). Comment on the status of systematic desensitization. *Behavior Modification, 28,* 194–205.

McGowan, S. K., & Behar, E. (2013). A preliminary investigation of stimulus control training for worry: Effects on anxiety and insomnia. *Behavior Modification, 37,* 90–112.

McIlvane, W. J. (2013). Simple and complex discrimination learning. In G. J. Madden (Ed.), *APA handbook of behavior analysis: Volume 2, translating behavioral principles into practice* (pp. 129–164). Washington, DC: American Psychological Association.

McIver, K. L., Brown, W. H., Pfeiffer, K. A., Dowda, M., & Pate, R. R. (2009). Assessing children's physical activity in their homes: The Observational System for Recording Physical Activity in Children's Home. *Journal of Applied Behavior Analysis, 42,* 1–16.

McKinney, R., & Fiedler, S. (2004). Schizophrenia: Some recent advances and implications for behavioral intervention. *The Behavioral Therapist, 27,* 122–125.

McLay, R. N., Graap, K., Spira, J., Perlman, K., Johnston, S., & Rotbaum, B. O., & Rizzo, A. (2012). Development and testing of virtual reality exposure therapy for post-traumatic stress disorder in active duty service members who served in Iraq and Afghanistan. *Military Medicine, 177,* 635–642.

Meany-Daboul, M. G., Roscoe, E. M., Bourret, J. C., & Ahearn, W. H. (2007). A comparison of momentary time sampling and partial-interval recording for evaluating functional relations. *Journal of Applied Behavior Analysis, 40,* 501–514.

Meichenbaum, D. H. (1977). *Cognitive behavior modification: An integrative approach.* New York: Plenum Press.

Meichenbaum, D. H. (1985). *Stress inoculation training.* New York: Pergamon Press.

Meichenbaum, D. H. (1986). Cognitive behavior modification. In F. H. Kanfer & A. P. Goldstein (Eds.), *Helping people change: A textbook of methods* (3rd ed., pp. 346–380). New York: Pergamon Press.

Meichenbaum, D. H., & Goodman, J. (1971). Training impulsive children to talk to themselves: A means of developing self-control. *Journal of Abnormal Psychology, 77,* 115–126.

Meichenbaum, D., & Deffenbacher, J. L. (1988). Stress inoculation training. *Counselling Psychologist, 16,* 69–90.

Mennin, D. S., Ellard, K. K., Fresco, D. M., & Gross, J. J. (2013). United we stand: Emphasizing commonalities across cognitive-behavioral therapies. *Behavior Therapy, 44,* 234–248.

Messer, S. B., & Winokur, M. (1984). Ways of knowing and visions of reality in psychoanalytic therapy and behavior therapy. In H. Arkowitz & S. B. Messer (Eds.), *Psychoanalytic therapy and behavior therapy: Is integration possible?* (pp. 63–100). New York: Plenum Press.

Michael, J. (1982). Distinguishing between discriminative and motivational functions of stimuli. *Journal of the Experimental Analysis of Behavior, 37,* 149–155.

Michael, J. (1986). Repertoire-altering effects of remote contingencies. *Analysis of Verbal Behavior, 4,* 10–18.

Michael, J. (1987). Symposium on the experimental analysis of human behavior: Comments by the discussant. *Psychological Record, 37,* 37–42.

Michael, J. (1991). A behavioral perspective on college teaching. *Behavior Analyst, 14,* 229–239.

Michael, J. (1993). Establishing operations. *Behavior Analyst, 16,* 191–206.

Michael, J. (2000). Implications and refinements of the establishing operation concept. *Journal of Applied Behavior Analysis, 33,* 401–410.

Michael, J. (2007). Motivating operations. In J. O. Cooper, T. E. Heron, & W. L. Heward (Eds.), *Applied behavior analysis* (2nd ed., pp. 374–391). Upper Saddle River, NJ: Prentice Hall/Merrill.

Michael, J. C., Belendiuk, K. A., Kuchara, A. M., & Rofey, D. L. (2013). Cognitive behavioral therapy for weight management. *The Behavior Therapist, 36,* 28–38.

Midgley, M., Lea, S. E. G., & Kirby, R. M. (1989). Algorithmic shaping and misbehavior in the acquisition of token deposit by rats. *Journal of the Experimental Analysis of Behavior, 52,* 27–40.

Mikulis, W. L. (1983). Thailand and behavior modification. *Journal of Behavior Therapy and Experimental Psychiatry, 14,* 93–97.

Miller, D. L., & Kelley, M. L. (1994). The use of goal setting and contingency contracting for improving children's homework. *Journal of Applied Behavior Analysis, 27,* 73–84.

Miller, N., & Neuringer, A. (2000). Reinforcing variability in adolescents with autism. *Journal of Applied Behavior Analysis, 33*(2), 151–165.

Miller, W. R. (1996). Motivational interviewing: Research, practice and puzzles. *Addictive Behaviors, 21*, 835–842.

Miltenberger, R. G. (2012). *Behavior modification: Principles and procedures* (5th ed.). Delmont, CA: Thompson Wadworth.

Miltenberger, R. G., Fuqua, R. W., & Woods, D. W. (1998). Applying behavior analysis to clinical problems: Review and analysis of habit reversal. *Journal of Applied Behavior Analysis, 31*, 447–469.

Mineka, S., & Oehlberg, K. (2008). The relevance of recent developments in classical conditioning to understanding the etiology and maintenance of anxiety disorders. *Acta Psychologica, 127*, 567–580

Mineka, S., & Zinbarg, R. (2006). A contemporary learning theory perspective on the etiology of anxiety disorders: It's not what you thought it was. *American Psychologist, 61*, 10–26.

Ming, S., & Martin, G. L. (1996). Single-subject evaluation of a self-talk package for improving figure skating performance. *The Sport Psychologist, 10*, 227–238.

Moderato, P. (2003). Behaviorism and behavior analysis in Italy. *Newsletter of the International Association for Behavior Analysis, 26*(3), 17–19.

Moorhead, G., & Griffin, R. W. (2010). *Organizational behavior: Managing people and organizations* (10th ed.). Mason, OH: South-Western Publishing Co.

Moran, D. J. (2008). Charting a collaborative course. *The Behavior Therapist, 31*, 155–157.

Moran, D. J., & Mallott, R. W. (Eds.). (2004). Evidence-based educational methods (pp. 223–243). San Francisco, CA: Elsevier Academic Press.

Morgan, D. L., & Morgan, R. K. (2009). *Single-case research methods for the behavioral and health sciences*. Los Angeles, CA: Sage Publications, Inc.

Morisano, D. (2013). Goal setting in the academic arena. In E. A. Locke & G. P. Latham (Eds.), *New developments in goal setting and task performance* (pp. 495–506). New York: Routledge.

Morris, E. K., Altus, D. E., & Smith, N. G. (2013). A study in the founding of applied behavior analysis through its publications. *The Behavior Analyst, 36*, 73–107.

Morris, R. J., & Kratochwill, T. R. (1983). *Treating children's fears and phobias: A behavioral approach*. New York: Pergamon Press.

Mulaire-Cloutier, C., Vause, T., Martin, G. L., & Yu, D. (2000). Choice, task preference, task performance, and happiness indicators with persons with severe developmental disabilities. *International Journal of Practical Approaches to Disability, 24*, 7–12.

Myerson, J., & Hale, S. (1984). Practical implications of the matching law. *Journal of Applied Behavior Analysis, 17*, 367–380.

Nabeyama, B., & Sturmey, P. (2010). Using behavioral skills training to promote staff and correct staff guarding and ambulance distance of students with multiple physical disabilities. *Journal of Applied Behavior Analysis, 43*, 341–345.

National Institute of Mental Health. Retrieved January 1, 2009, from www.nimh.nih.gov/health/publications/schizophrenia/what-is-schizophrenia.shtml.

Neef, N. A., Mace, F. C., & Shade, D. (1993). Impulsivity in students with serious emotional disturbances: The interactive effects of reinforcer rate, delay, and quality. *Journal of Applied Behavior Analysis, 26*, 37–52.

Neef, N. A., Mace, F. C., Shea, M. C., & Shade, D. (1992). Effects of reinforcer rate and reinforcer quality on time allocation: Extensions of the matching theory to educational settings. *Journal of Applied Behavior Analysis, 25*, 691–699.

Neef, N., & Northup, J. (2007). Attention-deficit-hyperactivity disorder. In P. Sturmey (Ed.), *Functional analysis in clinical treatment* (pp. 87–110). London, UK: Elsevier.

Neef, N. A., Perrin, C. J., & Madden, G. J. (2013). Understanding and treating attention-deficit/hyperactive disorder. In G. J. Madden (Ed.), *APA handbook of behavior analysis: Volume 2, translating behavioral principles into practice* (pp. 387–404). Washington, DC: American Psychological Association.

Neef, N. A., Shade, D., & Miller, M. S. (1994). Assessing influential dimensions of reinforcers on choice in students with serious emotional disturbance. *Journal of Applied Behavior Analysis, 27*, 575–583.

Nelson, R. O. (1983). Behavioral assessment: Past, present, and future. *Behavioral Assessment, 5*, 195–206.

Nevin, J. A. (1988). Behavioral momentum and the partial reinforcement effect. *Psychological Bulletin, 103*, 44–56.

Nevin, J. A., & Grace, R. C. (2000). Behavioral momentum and the law of effect. *Behavioral and Brain Sciences, 23*, 73–130.

Nevin, J. A., & Shahan, T. A. (2011). Behavioral momentum theory: Equations and applications. *Journal of Applied Behavior Analysis, 44*, 877–895.

Nevin, J. A., & Wacker, D. P. (2013). Response strength and persistence. In G. J. Madden (Ed.), *APA handbook of behavior analysis: Volume 2, translating behavioral principles into practice* (pp. 109–128). Washington, DC: American Psychological Association.

Newquist, M. H., Dozier, C. L., & Neidert, P. L. (2012). A comparison of the effects of brief rules, a timer, and preferred toys on self-control. *Journal of Applied Behavior Analysis, 45*, 497–509.

Nezu, A. M., Nezu, C. M., & D'Zurilla, T. (2013). *Problem-solving therapy: A treatment manual*. New York: Springer Publishing Company.

Nhat Hanh, T. (1998). *The heart of the Buddha's teaching: Transforming suffering into peace, joy, and liberation*. Berkeley, CA: Parallax Press.

Nisbet, E. K. L., & Gick, N. L. (2008). Can health psychology help the planet? Applying theory and models of health behavior to environmental actions. *Canadian Psychology, 49*, 296–403.

Norcross, J. C. (2006). Integrating self-help into psychotherapy: Sixteen practical suggestions. *Professional Psychology: Research & Practice, 37*, 383–393.

Nordquist, D. M. (1971). The modification of a child's enuresis: Some response-response relationships. *Journal of Applied Behavior Analysis, 4*, 241–247.

North, M. M., North, S. M., & Coble, J. R. (1997). Virtual reality therapy for fear-of-flying. *American Journal of Psychiatry, 154*, 130.

Northup, J., Wacker, D., Sasso, G., Steege, M., Cigrand, K., Cook, J., & DeRaad, A. (1991). A brief functional analysis of aggressive and alternative behavior in an out-clinic setting. *Journal of Applied Behavior Analysis, 24*, 509–522.

Nyp, S. S., Barone, V. J., Kruger, T., Garrison, C. B., Robertsen, C., & Christophersen, E. R. (2011). Evaluation of developmental surveillance by physicians at the two-month preventive care visit. *Journal of Applied Behavior Analysis, 44*, 181–185.

O'Brien, R. M. (2008). What would have happened to CBT if the second wave had preceded the first? *The Behavior Therapist, 31*, 153–154.

O'Connor, R. T., Lerman, D. C., Fritz, J. N., & Hodde, H. B. (2010). The effects of number and location of bins on plastic recycling at a university. *Journal of Applied Behavior Analysis, 43,* 711–715.

O'Donnell, J. (2001). The discriminative stimulus for punishment or S^Dp. *The Behavior Analyst, 24,* 261–262.

O'Donnell, J., Crosbie, J., Williams, D. C., & Saunders, K. J. (2000). Stimulus control and generalization of point-loss punishment with humans. *Journal of the Experimental Analysis of Behavior, 73,* 261–274.

O'Donohue, W., & Ferguson, K. E. (2011). Behavior analysis and ethics. In W. W. Fisher, C. C. Piazza, & H. S. Roane (Eds.), *Handbook of applied behavior analysis* (pp. 489–497). New York: The Guilford Press.

Oei, T. P. S. (Ed.). (1998). *Behavior therapy and cognitive behavior therapy in Asia.* Glebe, Australia: Edumedia.

Ogden, J. (2010). *The psychology of eating: From healthy to disordered behavior* (2nd ed.). Hoboken, NJ: John Wiley & Sons.

Ohman, A., Dimberg, U., & Ost, L. G. (1984). Animal and social phobias. In S. Reiss & R. Bootzin (Eds.), *Theoretical issues in behavior therapy* (pp. 210–222). New York: Academic Press.

Okouchi, H. (2009). Response acquisition by humans with delayed reinforcement. *Journal of the Experimental Analysis of Behavior, 91,* 377–390.

Olenick, D. L., & Pear, J. J. (1980). Differential reinforcement of correct responses to probes and prompts in picture-naming training with severely retarded children. *Journal of Applied Behavior Analysis, 13,* 77–89.

O'Neill, G. W., & Gardner, R. (1983). *Behavioral principles in medical rehabilitation: A practical guide.* Springfield, IL: Charles C Thomas.

Osborne, J. G., & Powers, R. B. (1980). Controlling the litter problem. In G. L. Martin & J. G. Osborne (Eds.), *Helping in the community: Behavioral applications* (pp. 103–168). New York: Plenum Press.

Otto, T. L., Torgrud, L. J., & Holborn, S. W. (1999). An operant blocking interpretation of instructed insensitivity to schedule contingencies. *The Psychological Record, 49,* 663–684.

Page, T. J., Iwata, B. A., & Neef, N. A. (1976). Teaching pedestrian skills to retarded persons: Generalization from the classroom to the natural environment. *Journal of Applied Behavior Analysis, 9,* 433–444.

Paggeot, B., Kvale, S., Mace, F. C., & Sharkey, R. W. (1988). Some merits and limitations of hand-held computers for data collection. *Journal of Applied Behavior Analysis, 21,* 429.

Pal-Hegedus, C. (1991). Behavior analysis in Costa Rica. *Behavior Therapist, 14,* 103–104.

Palmer, D. C. (2004). Data in search of a principle: A review of Relational Frame Theory: A post-Skinnerian account of human language and cognition. *Journal of the Experimental Analysis of Behavior, 81,* 189–204.

Paradis, C. M., Friedman, S., Hatch, M. L., & Ackerman, R. (1996). Cognitive behavioral treatment of anxiety disorders in orthodox Jews. *Cognitive and Behavioral Practice, 3,* 271–288.

Parker, R. I. (2006). Increased reliability for single-case research results: Is the bootstrap the answer? *Behavior Therapy, 37,* 326–338.

Parker, R. I., & Hagan-Burke, S. (2007). Useful effect-size interpretations for single-case research, *Behavior Therapy, 38,* 95–105.

Pascarella, E. T., & Terenzini, P. T. (1991). *How college affects students: Findings and insights from 20 years of research.* San Francisco: Jossey-Bass.

Patterson, G. R. (1965). An application of conditioning techniques to the control of a hyperactive child. In L. P. Ullmann & L. Krasner (Eds.), *Case studies in behavior modification* (pp. 370–375). New York: Holt, Reinhart & Winston.

Patterson, G. R., & Gullion, M. E. (1968). *Living with children: New methods for parents and teachers.* Champaign, IL: Research Press.

Pavlov, I. P. (1927). *Conditioned reflexes: An investigation of the physiological activity of the cerebral cortex* (G. V. Anrep, Trans.). London: Oxford University Press.

Pear, J. J. (2001). *The science of learning.* Philadelphia: Psychology Press.

Pear, J. J. (2004). A spatiotemporal analysis of behavior. In J. E. Burgos & E. Ribes (Eds.), *Theory, basic and applied research and technological applications in behavior science: Conceptual and methodological issues* (pp. 131–149). Guadalajara: University of Guadalajara Press.

Pear, J. J. (2007). *A historical and contemporary look at psychological systems.* Mahwah, NJ: Lawrence Erlbaum Associates.

Pear, J. J. (2012). Behavioral approaches to instruction. In N. M. Seel (Ed.), *Encyclopedia of the sciences of learning* (Vol. 1, pp. 429–432). New York: Springer Publishing Company.

Pear, J. J., & Crone-Todd, D. E. (2002). A social constructivist approach to computer-mediated instruction. *Computers & Education, 38,* 221–231.

Pear, J. J., & Eldridge, G. D. (1984). The operant–respondent distinction: Future directions. *Journal of the Experimental Analysis of Behavior, 42,* 453–467.

Pear, J. J., & Legris, J. A. (1987). Shaping of an arbitrary operant response by automated tracking. *Journal of the Experimental Analysis of Behavior, 47,* 241–247.

Pear, J. J., & Martin, G. L. (2012). Behavior modification, behavior therapy, applied behavior analysis, and learning. In N. M. Seel (Ed.), *Encyclopedia of the sciences of learning* (Vol. 1, pp. 421–424). New York: Springer Publishing Company.

Pear, J. J., & Martin, T. L. (2004). Making the most of PSI with computer technology. In D. J. Moran & R. W. Malott (Eds.), *Evidence-based educational methods* (pp. 223–243). San Diego: Elsevier Academic Press.

Pear, J. J., Schnerch, G. J., Silva, K. M., Svenningsen, L., & Lambert, J. (2011). Web-based Computer-aided Personalized System of Instruction. In W. Buskist & J. E. Groccia (Eds.), *New directions for teaching and learning: Evidenced-based teaching* (Vol. 128, pp. 85–94). San Franscisco, CA: Jossey-Bass.

Pear, J. J., & Simister, H. D. (in press). Behavior modification. In H. E. A. Tinsley, S. H. Lease, & N. S. G. Wiersma (Eds.), *Contemporary theory and practice of counseling and psychotherapy.* Thousand Oaks, CA: Sage Publications, Inc.

Pelaez, M., Virues-Ortega, J., Gewirtz, J. L. (2011). Reinforcement of vocalizations through contingent vocal imitation. *Journal of Applied Behavior Analysis, 44,* 33–40.

Perin, C. T. (1943). The effect of delayed reinforcement upon the differentiation of bar responses in white rats. *Journal of Experimental Psychology, 32,* 95–109.

Perlis, M. (2012). Why treat insomnia and what is CBT-I? *Cognitive Therapy Today, 17*(2), 4–7.

Perlis, M., Jungquist, C., Smith, M., & Posner, D. (2008). *Cognitive behavioral treatment of insomnia: A session-by-session guide.* New York: Springer Publishing Company.

Perri, M. G., Limacher, M. C., Durning, P. E., Janicke, D. M., Lutes, L. D., Bobroff, L. B., & Martin, A. D. (2008). Extended-care programs for weight management in rural communities: The treatment of obesity in underserved rural settings (TOURS) randomized trial. *Archives of Internal Medicine, 168,* 2347–2354.

Perri, M. G., & Richards, C. S. (1977). An investigation of naturally occurring episodes of self- controlled behaviors. *Journal of Consulting Psychology, 24,* 178–183.

Perry, A., Pritchard, E. A., & Penn, H. E. (2006). Indicators of quality teaching in intensive behavioral intervention: A survey of parents and professionals. *Behavioral Interventions, 21,* 85–96.

Phillips, E. L. (1968). Achievement Place: Token reinforcement procedures in a home-style rehabilitation setting for "pre-delinquent" boys. *Journal of Applied Behavior Analysis, 1,* 213–223.

Phillips, E. L., Phillips, E. A., Fixsen, D. L., & Wolf, M. M. (1973). Behavior shaping works for delinquents. *Psychology Today, 7*(1), 75–79.

Phillips, E. L., Phillips, E. A., Fixsen, D. L., & Wolf, M. M. (1974). *The teaching family handbook* (2nd ed.). Lawrence, KS: University of Kansas Printing Service.

Phillips, E. L., Phillips, E. A., Wolf, M. M., & Fixsen, D. L. (1973). Achievement Place: Development of the elected manager system. *Journal of Applied Behavior Analysis, 6,* 541–546.

Piazza, C. C., Fisher, W. W., Brown, K. A., Shore, B. A., Patel, M. R., Katz, R. M., Sevin, B. M., Goulotta, G. S., & Blakely-Smith, A. (2003). Functional analysis of inappropriate mealtime behaviors. *Journal of Applied Behavior Analysis, 36,* 187–204.

Piazza, C. C., Patel, M. R., Goulatta, G. S., Sevin, B. M., & Layer, S. A. (2003). On the relative contributions of positive reinforcement and extinction in the treatment of food refusal. *Journal of Applied Behavior Analysis, 36,* 309–324.

Piazza, C. C., Roane, H. S., & Karsten, A. (2011). Identifying and enhancing the effectiveness of positive reinforcement. In W. W. Fisher, C. C. Piazza, & H. S. Roane (Eds.), *Handbook of applied behavior analysis* (pp. 151–164). New York: The Guilford Press.

Pierce, K., & Schreibman, L. (1997). Multiple peer use of pivotal response training to increase social behaviors of classmates with autism: Results from trained and untrained peers. *Journal of Applied Behavior Analysis, 30,* 157–160.

Pinker, S. (1994). *The language instinct: How the mind creates language.* New York: William Morrow.

Pi-Sunyer, X. (2009). The medical risks of obesity. *Postgraduate Medicine, 121*(6), 21–33.

Plaud, J. J. (2007). Sexual disorders. In P. Sturmey (Ed.), *Functional analysis in clinical treatment* (pp. 357–378). London, UK: Elsevier.

Plavnick, J. B., & Ferreri, S. J. (2011). Establishing verbal repertoires in children with autism using function-based video modeling. *Journal of Applied Behavior Analysis, 44,* 747–766.

Plimpton, G. (1965). Ernest Hemingway. In G. Plimpton (Ed.), *Writers at work: The Paris Review interviews* (2nd series, pp. 215–239). New York: Viking.

Plutchik, R. (2001). The nature of emotions. *American Scientist, 89,* 344–350.

Polenchar, B. F., Romano, A. G., Steinmetz, J. E., & Patterson, M. M. (1984). Effects of US parameters on classical conditioning of cat hindlimb flexion. *Animal Learning and Behavior, 12,* 69–72.

Polenick, C. A., & Flora, S. R. (2013). Behavioral activation for depression in older adults: Theoretical and practical considerations. *The Behavior Analyst, 36,* 35–55.

Polick, A. S., Carr, J. E., & Hanney, N. M. (2012). A comparison of general and descriptive praise in teaching intraverbal behavior to children with autism. *Journal of Applied Behavior Analysis, 45,* 593–599.

Poling, A. (2001). Comments regarding Olsen, Laraway, and Austin (2001). *Journal of Organizational Behavior Management, 21,* 47–56.

Poling, A. (2010). Progressive ratio schedules and applied behavior analysis. *Journal of Applied Behavior Analysis, 43,* 347–349.

Poling, A., Methot, L. L., & LeSage, M. G. (1995). *Fundamentals of behavior analytic research.* New York: Plenum Press.

Poppen, R. L. (1989). Some clinical implications of rule-governed behavior. In S. C. Hayes (Ed.), *Rule-governed behavior: Cognition, contingencies, and instructional control* (pp. 325–357). New York: Plenum Press.

Pouthas, V., Droit, S., Jacquet, A. Y., & Wearden, J. H. (1990). Temporal differentiation of response duration in children of different ages: Developmental changes in relations between verbal and nonverbal behavior. *Journal of the Experimental Analysis of Behavior, 53,* 21–31.

Powers, R. B., & Osborne, J. G. (1976). *Fundamentals of behavior.* St. Paul, MN: West.

Premack, D. (1959). Toward empirical behavioral laws. I: Positive reinforcement. *Psychological Review, 66,* 219–233.

Premack, D. (1965). Reinforcement theory. In D. Levin (Ed.), *Nebraska symposium on motivation* (pp. 123–180). Lincoln: University of Nebraska.

Prendeville, J. A., Prelock, P. A., & Unwin, G. (2006). Peer play interventions to support the social competence of children with autism spectrum disorders. *Seminars in Speech and Language, 27,* 32–46.

Prilleltensky, I. (2008). The role of power in wellness, depression, and liberation: The promise of psycho-political validity. *Journal of Community Psychology, 36,* 116–136.

Pritchard, R. D., Young, B. L., Koenig, N., Schmerling, D., & Dixon, N. W. (2013). Long-term effects of goal setting on performance with the productivity measurement and enhancement system (ProMES). In E. A. Locke & G. P. Latham (Eds.), *New developments in goal setting and task performance* (pp. 233–245). New York: Routledge.

Public Law, 98–527 (October 19, 1984). *Developmental disabilities act of 1984.* Washington, DC: U.S. Government.

Purcell, D. W., Campos, P. E., & Perilla, J. L. (1996). Therapy with lesbians and gay men: A cognitive behavioral perspective. *Cognitive and Behavioral Practice, 3,* 391–415.

Pyles, D. A. M., & Bailey, J. S. (1990). Diagnosing severe behavior problems. In A. C. Repp & N. N. Singh (Eds.), *Perspectives on the use of nonaversive interventions for persons with developmental disabilities* (pp. 381–401). Sycamore, IL: Sycamore Press.

Quarti, C., & Renaud, J. (1964). A new treatment of constipation by conditioning: A preliminary report. In C. M. Franks (Ed.), *Conditioning techniques in clinical practice and research* (pp. 219–227). New York: Springer Publishing Company.

Querim, A. C., Iwata, B. A., Roscoe, E. M., Schlichenmeyer, K. J., Virués Ortega, J., & Hurl, K. E. (2013). Functional analysis screening for problem maintained by automatic reinforcement. *Journal of Applied Behavior Analysis, 46,* 47–60.

Rachlin, H. (2011). Baum's Private Thoughts. *The Behavior Analyst, 34*, 209–212.

Rae, S., Martin, G. L., & Smyk, B. (1990). A self-management package versus a group exercise contingency for increasing on-task behavior of developmentally handicapped workers. *Canadian Journal of Behavioral Science, 22*, 45–58.

Raiff, B. R., & Dallery, J. (2010). Internet-based contingency management to improve adherence with blood glucose testing recommendations for teens with Type 1 diabetes. *Journal of Applied Behavior Analysis, 43*, 487–491.

Ramsay, M. C., Reynolds, C. R., & Kamphaus, R. W. (2002). *Essentials of behavioral assessment.* New York: Wiley & Sons.

Rasey, H. W., & Iversen, I. H. (1993). An experimental acquisition of maladaptive behavior by shaping. *Journal of Behavior Therapy and Experimental Psychiatry, 24*, 37–43.

Ray, E., & Heyes, C. (2011). Imitation in infancy: The wealth of the stimulus. *Developmental Science, 14*, 92–105.

Rayner, C., Denholm, C., & Sigafoos, J. (2009). Video-based intervention for individuals with autism: Key questions that remain unanswered. *Research in Autism Spectrum Disorders, 3*, 291–303.

Reagon, K. A., & Higbee, T. S. (2009). Parent-implemented script-fading to promote play-based verbal initiations in children with autism. *Journal of Applied Behavior Analysis, 42*, 649–664.

Rector, N. A. (2013). Acceptance and commitment therapy: Empirical considerations. *Behavior Therapy, 44*, 213–217.

Reed, D. D., & Luiselli, J. K. (2009). Antecedents to a paradigm: Ogden Lindsley and B. F. Skinner's founding of "behavior therapy." *The Behavior Therapist, 32*, 82–85.

Rego, S. A., Barlow, D. H., McCrady, B. S., Persons, J. B., Hildebrandt, T. B., & McHugh, R. K. (2009). Implementing empirically supported treatments in real-world clinical settings: Your questions answered! *The Behavior Therapist, 32*, 52–58.

Reid, D. H., O'Kane, N. P., & Macurik, K. M. (2011). Staff training and management. In W. W. Fisher, C. C. Piazza, & H. S. Roane (Eds.), *Handbook of applied behavior analysis* (pp. 281–296). New York: The Guilford Press.

Repp, A. C., Deitz, S. M., & Deitz, D. E. (1976). Reducing inappropriate behaviors in classrooms and individual sessions through DRO schedules of reinforcement. *Mental Retardation, 14*, 11–15.

Repp, A. C., Karsh, K. G., Felce, D., & Ludewig, D. (1989). Further comments on using hand-held computers for data collection. *Journal of Applied Behavior Analysis, 22*, 336–337.

Resick, P. A., & Schnicke, M. K. (1992). Cognitive processing therapy for sexual assault victims. *Journal of Consulting and Clinical Psychology, 60*, 748–756.

Resick, P. A., Monson, C. M., & Rizvi, S. L. (2008). Post-traumatic stress disorder. In D. H. Barlow (Ed.), *Clinical handbook of psychological disorders: A step-by-step treatment manual* (4th ed., pp. 65–122). New York: The Guilford Press.

Reynolds, L. K., & Kelley, M. L. (1997). The efficacy of a response-cost based treatment package for managing aggressive behavior in preschoolers. *Behavior Modification, 21*, 216–230.

Rice, A., Austin, J., & Gravina, N. (2009). Increasing customer service behaviors using manager-delivered task clarification and social praise. *Journal of Applied Behavior Analysis, 42*, 665–669.

Richard, D. C. S., & Bobicz, K. (2003). Computers and behavioral assessment: Six years later. *The Behavior Therapist, 26*, 219–223.

Richards, S. B., Taylor, R. L., & Ramasamy, R. (2014). *Single subject research: Applications in educational and clinical settings* (2nd ed.). Belmont, CA: Wadsworth.

Richman, G. S., Reiss, M. L., Bauman, K. E., & Bailey, J. S. (1984). Training menstrual care to mentally retarded women: Acquisition, generalization, and maintenance. *Journal of Applied Behavior Analysis, 17*, 441–451.

Rincover, A. (1978). Sensory extinction: A procedure for eliminating self-stimulatory behavior in psychotic children. *Journal of Abnormal Child Psychology, 6*, 299–310.

Rincover, A., Cook, R., Peoples, A., & Packard, D. (1979). Sensory extinction and sensory reinforcement principles for programming multiple adaptive behavior change. *Journal of Applied Behavior Analysis, 12*, 221–233.

Rincover, A., & Devaney, J. (1982). The application of sensory extinction procedures to self-injury. *Analysis and Intervention in Developmental Disabilities, 2*, 67–81.

Riva, G., Wiederhold, B. K., & Molinari, E. (1998). *Virtual environments in clinical psychology and neuroscience. Methods and techniques in advanced patient-therapist interaction.* Amsterdam, The Netherlands: IOS Press.

Roane, H. S. (2008). On the applied use of progressive-ratio schedules of reinforcement. *Journal of Applied Behavior Analysis, 41*, 155–161.

Roberts, R. N. (1979). Private speech in academic problem-solving: A naturalistic perspective. In G. Zevin (Ed.), *The development of self-regulation through private speech* (pp. 295–323). New York: Wiley.

Roberts, R. N., & Tharp, R. G. (1980). A naturalistic study of children's self-directed speech in academic problem-solving. *Cognitive Research and Therapy, 4*, 341–353.

Robins, C. J., Schmidt III, H., & Linehan, M. M. (2004). Dialectical behavior therapy: Synthesizing radical acceptance with skillful means. In S. C. Hayes, V. M. Follette, & M. M. Linehan (Eds.), *Mindfulness and acceptance: Expanding the cognitive behavioral tradition.* New York: The Guilford Press.

Rodrigue, J. R., Banko, C. G., Sears, S. F., & Evans, G. (1996). Old territory revisited: Behavior therapists in rural America and innovative models of service delivery. *The Behavior Therapist, 19*, 97–100.

Roll, J. M., Madden, G. M., Rawson, R., & Petry, N. M. (2009). Facilitating the adoption of contingency management for the treatment of substance use disorders. *Behavior Analysis in Practice, 2*, 4–13.

Roscoe, B., Martin, G. L., & Pear, J. J. (1980). Systematic self-desensitization of fear of flying: A case study. In G. L. Martin & J. G. Osborne (Eds.), *Helping in the community: Behavioral applications* (pp. 345–352). New York: Plenum Press.

Rosen, G. M. (1987). Self-help treatment books and the commercialization of psychotherapy. *American Psychologist, 42*, 46–51.

Ross, S. W., & Horner, R. H. (2009). Bully prevention in positive behavior support. *Journal of Applied Behavior Analysis, 42*, 747–759.

Rothbaum, B. O., Anderson, P., Zimand, E., Hodges, L., Lang, D., & Wilson, J. (2006). Virtual reality exposure therapy and standard (in vivo) exposure therapy in the treatment of fear of flying. *Behavior Therapy, 37*, 80–90.

Rothbaum, B. O., Hodges, L. F., Kooper, R., Opdyke, D., Williford, J. S., & North, M. (1995). Effectiveness of computer-generated (virtual reality) graded exposure in the treatment of acrophobia. *American Journal of Psychiatry, 152*, 626–628.

Rotter, J. B. (1954). *Social learning and clinical psychology*. Upper Saddle River, NJ: Prentice Hall.

Rovetto, F. (1979). Treatment of chronic constipation by classical conditioning techniques. *Journal of Behavior Therapy and Experimental Psychiatry, 10*, 143–146.

Roy-Wsiaki, G., Marion, C., Martin, G. L., & Yu, C. T. (2010). Teaching a child with autism to request information by asking "What?" *Developmental Disabilities Bulletin, 38*, 55–74.

Ruiz, F. J. (2010). A review of acceptance and commitment therapy empirical evidence: Correlation, experimental psychopathology, component and outcome studies. *International Journal of Psychology and Psychological Therapy, 10*, 125–162.

Saari, L. M. (2013). Goal setting and organizational transformation. In E. A. Locke & G. P. Latham (Eds.), *New developments in goal setting and task performance* (pp. 262–269). New York: Routledge.

Sajwaj, T., Libet, J., & Agras, S. (1974). Lemon-juice therapy: The control of life-threatening rumination in a six-month-old infant. *Journal of Applied Behavior Analysis, 7*, 557–563.

Sakano, Y. (1993). Behavior therapy in Japan: Beyond the cultural impediments. *Behavior Change, 10*, 19–21.

Sakko, G., Martin, T. L., Vause, T., Martin, G. L., & Yu, C. T. (2004). A visual-visual non-identity matching assessment: A worthwhile addition to the assessment of basic learning abilities test. *American Journal on Mental Retardation, 109*, 44–52.

Salend, S. J., Ellis, L. L., & Reynolds, C. J. (1989). Using self-instructions to teach vocational skills to individuals who are severely retarded. *Education and Training in Mental Retardation, 24*, 248–254.

Salmivalli, C. (2002). Is there an age decline in victimization by peers at school? *Educational Research, 44*, 269–277.

Salmon, D. J., Pear, J. J., & Kuhn, B. A. (1986). Generalization of object naming after training with picture cards and with objects. *Journal of Applied Behavior Analysis, 19*, 53–58.

Salter, A. (1949). *Conditioned reflex therapy*. New York: Creative Age Press.

Salzinger, K. (2008). Waves or ripples? *The Behavior Therapist, 31*, 147–148.

Sanderson, C. (2012). *Health psychology* (2nd ed.). New York: John Wiley & Sons, Inc.

Sanivio, E. (1999). Behavioral and cognitive therapy in Italy. *The Behavior Therapist, 22*, 69–75.

Sarwer, D. B., & Sayers, S. L. (1998). Behavioral interviewing. In A. S. Bellack & M. Hersen (Eds.), *Behavioral assessment: A practical handbook* (4th ed., pp. 63–78). Boston: Allyn & Bacon.

Schaefer, H. H., & Martin, P. L. (1969). *Behavioral therapy*. New York: McGraw-Hill.

Scherer, K. R. (2000). Emotions as episodes of subsystem synchronization driven by nonlinear appraisal processes. In M. D. Lewis & I. Granic (Eds.), *Emotion, development, and self-organization: Dynamic systems approaches to emotional development* (pp. 70–99). Cambridge, England: Cambridge University Press.

Schleien, S. J., Wehman, P., & Kiernan, J. (1981). Teaching leisure skills to severely handicapped adults: An age-appropriate darts game. *Journal of Applied Behavior Analysis, 14*, 513–519.

Schlesinger, C. (2004). Australian association for cognitive and Behavior Therapy. *Newsletter of the International Association for Behavior Analysis, 27*(2), 20–21.

Schlinger, H. D., Derenne, A., & Baron, A. (2008). What 50 years of research tell us about pausing under ratio schedules of reinforcement. *The Behavior Analyst, 31*, 39–60.

Schlinger, H. D., Jr. (2011). Introduction: Private events in a natural science of behavior *The Behavior Analyst, 34*, 181–184.

Schlinger, H. D., Jr., & Normand, M. (2013). On the origin and functions of the term functional analysis. *Journal of Applied Behavior Analysis, 46*, 285–288.

Schloss, P. J., & Schloss, M. A. (1997). *Applied behavior analysis in the classroom* (2nd ed.). Boston: Allyn & Bacon.

Schloss, P. J., Smith, M., Santora, C., & Bryant, R. (1989). A respondent conditioning approach to reducing anger responses of a dually-diagnosed man with mild mental retardation. *Behavior Therapy, 20*, 459–464.

Schmidt, F. L. (2013). The economic value of goal setting to employers. In E. A. Locke & G. P. Latham (Eds.), *New developments in goal setting and task performance* (pp. 16–20). New York: Routledge.

Schoenfeld, W. N., & Farmer, J. (1970). Reinforcement schedules and the "behavior stream." In W. N. Schoenfeld (Ed.), *The theory of reinforcement schedules* (pp. 215–145). New York: Appleton-Century-Crofts.

Schreibman, L. (1975). Effects of within-stimulus and extra-stimulus prompting on discrimination learning in autistic children. *Journal of Applied Behavior Analysis, 8*, 91–112.

Schunk, D. H. (1987). Peer models and children's behavioral change. *Review of Educational Research, 57*, 149–174.

Schwartz, M. S., & Andrasic, F. (2003). *Biofeedback: A practitioner's guide* (3rd ed.). New York: The Guilford Press.

Schwitzgebel, R. L. (1964). *Streetcorner research: An experimental approach to juvenile delinquency*. Cambridge, MA: Harvard University Press.

Scogin, F., Bynum, J., Stephens, G., & Calhoon, S. (1990). Efficacy of self-administered treatment programs: Meta-analytic review. *Professional Psychology: Research and Practice, 21*, 42–47.

Scott, M. A., Barclay, B. R., & Houts, A. C. (1992). Childhood enuresis: Etiology, assessment, and current behavioral treatment. In M. Hersen, R. N. Eisler, & P. M. Miller (Eds.), *Progress in behavior modification* (Vol. 28, pp. 84–119). Sycamore, IL: Sycamore Press.

Scott, R. W., Peters, R. D., Gillespie, W. J., Blanchard, E. B., Edmundson, E. D., & Young, L. D. (1973). The use of shaping and reinforcement in the operant acceleration and deceleration of heart rate. *Behaviour Research and Therapy, 11*, 179–185.

Scrimali, T., & Grimaldi, L. (1993). Behavioral and cognitive psychotherapy in Italy. *The Behavior Therapist, 16*, 265–266.

Seabaugh, G. O., & Schumaker, J. B. (1994). The effects of self-regulation training on the academic productivity of secondary students with learning problems. *Journal of Behavioral Education, 4*, 109–133.

Searight, H. R. (1998). *Behavioral medicine: A primary care approach*. Philadelphia: Brunner-Mazel.

Seigts, G. H., Meertens, R. M., & Kok, G. (1997). The effects of task importance and publicness on the relation between goal difficulty and performance. *Canadian Journal of Behavioural Science, 29*, 54–62.

Seijts, G. H., Latham, G. P., & Woodwark, M. (2013). Learning goals: A qualitative and quantitative review. In E. A. Locke

& G. P. Latham (Eds.), *New developments in goal setting and task performance* (pp. 195–212). New York: Routledge.

Seiverling, L., Williams, K., Sturmey, P., & Hart, S. (2012). Effects of behavioral skills training on parental treatment of children's food selectivity. *Journal of Applied Behavior Analysis, 45*, 197–203.

Seligman, M. E. P. (1971). Phobias and preparedness. *Behavior Therapy, 2*, 307–321.

Seligman, M. E. P. (1994). *What you can change and what you can't.* New York: Knopf.

Semb, G., & Semb, S. A. (1975). A comparison of fixed-page and fixed-time reading assignments in elementary school children. In E. Ramp & G. Semb (Eds.), *Behavior analysis: Areas of research and application* (pp. 233–243). Upper Saddle River, NJ: Prentice Hall.

Sexton, E. L., Datchi, C., Evans, L., LaFollette, J., & Wright, L. (2013). The effectiveness of couple and family-based clinical interventions. In M. J. Lambert (Ed.), *Bergin and Garfield's handbook of psychotherapy and behavior change* (6th ed., pp. 587–639). Hoboken, NJ: John Wiley & Sons.

Shafran, R., Booth, R., & Rachman, S. (1993). The reduction of claustrophobia: II. Cognitive analyses. *Behaviour Research and Therapy, 31*, 75–85.

Shahan, T. A., Bickel, W. K., Madden, G. J., & Badger, G. J. (1999). Comparing the reinforcing efficacy of nicotine containing and denicotinized cigarettes: A behavioral economic analysis. *Psychopharmacology, 147*, 210–216

Shayne, R. K., Fogel, V. A., Miltenberger, R. G., & Koehler, S. (2012). The effects of exergaming on physical activity in a third-grade physical education class. *Journal of Applied Behavior Analysis, 45*, 211–215.

Sherrington, C. S. (1947). *The integrative action of the central nervous system.* Cambridge, UK: Cambridge University Press.

Shilts, M. K., Townsend, M. S., & Dishman, R. K. (2013). Using goal setting to promote health behavior changes: Diet and physical activity. In E. A. Locke & G. P. Latham (Eds.), *New developments in goal setting and task performance* (pp. 415–438). New York: Routledge.

Shimoff, E., Matthews, B. A., & Catania, A. C. (1986). Human operant performance: Sensitivity and pseudosensitivity to contingencies. *Journal of the Experimental Analysis of Behavior, 46*, 149–157.

Shook, G. L., & Favell, J. E. (2008). The Behavior Analyst Certification Board and the profession of behavior analysis. *Behavior Analysis in Practice, 1*, 44–48.

Shook, G. L., & Johnston, J. M. (2011). Training and professional certification in applied behavior analysis. In W. W. Fisher, C. C. Piazza, & H. S. Roane (Eds.), *Handbook of applied behavior analysis* (pp. 498–510). New York: The Guilford Press.

Sidman, M. (1953). Avoidance conditioning with brief shock and no exteroceptive warning signal. *Science, 118*, 157–158.

Sidman, M. (1960). *Tactics of scientific research.* New York: Basic Books.

Sidman, M. (1994). *Equivalence relations and behavior: A research story.* Boston: Authors Cooperative.

Siedentop, D. (1978). The management of practice behavior. In W. F. Straub (Ed.), *Sport psychology: An analysis of athletic behavior* (pp. 42–61). Ithaca, NY: Mouvement.

Siedentop, D., & Tannehill, D. (2000). *Developing teaching skills in physical education* (4th ed.). Mountain View, CA: Mayfield.

Sigurdsson, V., Saevarsson, H., & Foxall, G. (2009). Brand placement and consumer choice: An in-store experiment. *Journal of Applied Behavior Analysis, 42*, 741–745.

Silber, J. M., & Martens, B. K. (2010). Programming for the generalization of oral reading fluency: Repeated readings of entire text versus multiple exemplars. *Journal of Behavioral Education, 19*, 30–46.

Simek, T. C., & O'Brien, R. M. (1981). *Total golf: A behavioral approach to lowering your score and getting more out of your game.* Huntington, NY: B-Mod Associates.

Simó-Pinatella, D., Font-Roura, J., Planella-Morató, J., McGill, P., Alomar-Kurz, E., & Giné, C. (2013). Types of motivating operations in interventions with problem behavior: A systematic review. *Behavior Modification, 37*, 3–38.

Singer, G. H., Singer, J. S., & Horner, R. H. (1987). Using pre-task requests to increase the probability of compliance for students with severe disabilities. *Journal of the Association for Persons with Severe Handicaps, 12*, 287–291.

Singh, N. N., Wahler, R. G., Adkins, A. D., & Myers, R. E. (2003). Soles of the feet: A mindfulness-based self-control intervention for aggression by an individual with mild mental retardation and mental illness. *Research in Developmental Disabilities, 24*(1), 58–169.

Sirard, J. R., & Pate, R. R. (2001). Physical activity assessment in children and adolescents. *Sports Medicine, 31*, 439–454.

Skinner, B. F. (1938). *The behavior of organisms.* New York: Appleton-Century-Crofts.

Skinner, B. F. (1948a). "Superstition" in the pigeon. *Journal of Experimental Psychology, 38*, 168–172.

Skinner, B. F. (1948b). *Walden Two.* New York: Macmillan.

Skinner, B. F. (1953). *Science and human behavior.* New York: Macmillan.

Skinner, B. F. (1957). *Verbal behavior.* New York: Appleton-Century-Crofts.

Skinner, B. F. (1958). Teaching machines. *Science, 128*, 969–977.

Skinner, B. F. (1960). Pigeons in a pelican. *American Psychologist, 15*, 28–37.

Skinner, B. F. (1968). *The technology of teaching.* New York: Appleton-Century-Crofts.

Skinner, B. F. (1969). *Contingencies of reinforcement: A theoretical analysis.* New York: Appleton-Century-Crofts.

Skinner, B. F. (1971). *Beyond freedom and dignity.* New York: Knopf.

Skinner, B. F. (1974). *About behaviorism.* New York: Knopf.

Skinner, B. F. (1977). Why I am not a cognitive psychologist. *Behaviorism, 5*, 1–10.

Skinner, B. F. (1989). *Recent issues in the analysis of behavior.* Columbus, OH: Charles E. Merrill.

Skinner, B. F., & Vaughan, N. E. (1983). *Enjoy old age: A program of self-management.* New York: W. W. Norton.

Slocom, S. K., & Tiger, J. H. (2011). An assessment of the efficiency of and child preference for forward and backward chaining. *Journal of Applied Behavior Analysis, 44*, 793–805.

Smith, G. J. (1999). Teaching a long sequence of behavior using whole task training, forward chaining, and backward chaining. *Perceptual and Motor Skills, 89*, 951–965.

Smith, M. T., Perlis, M., Park, A., Smith, M. S., Pennington, J., Giles, G. E., & Buysse, D. J. (2002). Comparative meta-analysis of pharmacotherapy and behavior therapy for persistent insomnia. *American Journal of Psychiatry, 159*(1), 5–11.

Smith, R. E. (1988). The logic and design of case study research. *The Sport Psychologist, 2*, 1–12.

Smith, R. G. (2011). Developing antecedent interventions for problem behavior. In W. W. Fisher, C. C. Piazza, & H. S. Roane (Eds.), *Handbook of applied behavior analysis* (pp. 297–316). New York: The Guilford Press.

Smith, R., Michael, J., & Sundberg, M. L. (1996). Automatic reinforcement and automatic punishment in infant vocal behavior. *The Analysis of Verbal Behavior, 13,* 39–48.

Snyder, D. K., & Halford, W. K. (2012). Evidence-based couple therapy: Current status and future directions. *Journal of Family Therapy, 34,* 229–249.

Snyder, J., Schrepferman, L., & St. Peter, C. (1997). Origins of antisocial behavior: Negative reinforcement and affect disregulation of behavior as socialization mechanisms in family interaction. *Behavior Modification, 21,* 187–215.

Sobell, M. B., & Sobell, L. C. (1993). *Problem drinkers: Guided self-change treatment.* New York: The Guilford Press.

Sommer, R. (1977, January). Toward a psychology of natural behavior. *APA Monitor, 8,* 13–14.

Spiegel, T. A., Wadden, T. A., & Foster, G. D. (1991). Objective measurement of eating rate during behavioral treatment of obesity. *Behavior Therapy, 22,* 61–67.

Spiegler, M. D., & Guevremont, D. C. (2010). *Contemporary behavior therapy* (5th ed.). Belmont, CA: Wadsworth/ Thompson Learning.

Spinelli, P. R., & Packard, T. (1975, February). Behavioral self-control delivery systems. Paper presented at the National Conference on Behavioral Self-Control, Salt Lake City, UT.

Spira, A. P., & Edelstein, B. A. (2006). Behavioral interventions for agitation in older adults with dementia: An evaluative review. *International Psychogeriatrics, 18,* 195–225.

Spooner, F. (1984). Comparisons of backward chaining and total task presentation in training severely handicapped persons. *Education and Training of the Mentally Retarded, 19,* 15–22.

Spooner, F., & Spooner, D. (1984). A review of chaining techniques: Implications for future research and practice. *Education and Training of the Mentally Retarded, 19,* 114–124.

Spradlin, J. E., & Simon, J. L. (2011). Stimulus control and generalization. In W. W. Fisher, C. C. Piazza, & H. S. Roane (Eds.), *Handbook of applied behavior analysis* (pp. 76–91). New York: The Guilford Press.

Sprague, J. R., & Horner, R. H. (1984). The effects of single-instance, multiple-instance, and general case training on generalized vending machine use by moderately and severely handicapped students. *Journal of Applied Behavior Analysis, 17,* 273–278.

Staats, A. W. (1996). *Behavior and personality.* New York: Springer Publishing Company.

Staats, A. W., Staats, C. K., & Crawford, H. L. (1962). First-order conditioning of meaning and the parallel conditioning of a GSR. *Journal of General Psychology, 67,* 159–167.

Stainback, W. C., Payne, J. S., Stainback, S. B., & Payne, R. A. (1973). *Establishing a token economy in the classroom.* Columbus, OH: Charles E. Merrill.

Stampfl, T. G., & Levis, D. J. (1967). Essentials of implosive therapy: A learning-theory-based psychodynamic behavioral therapy. *Journal of Abnormal Psychology, 72,* 496–503.

Stark, M. (1980). The German association of behavior therapy. *Behavior Therapist, 3,* 11–12.

Steege, M. W., & Watson, T. S. (2009). *Conducting school-based functional behavioral assessments: A practitioner's guide.* (2nd ed.). New York: The Guilford Press.

Stephens, C. E., Pear, J. J., Wray, L. D., & Jackson, G. C. (1975). Some effects of reinforcement schedules in teaching picture names to retarded children. *Journal of Applied Behavior Analysis, 8,* 435–447.

Stevens, C., Sidener, T. M., Reeve, S. A., & Sidener, D. W. (2011). Effects of behavior-specific and general praise on acquisition of tacts in children with pervasive developmental disorders. *Research in Autism Spectrum Disorders, 5,* 666–669.

Stevenson, J. G., & Clayton, F. L. (1970). A response duration schedule: Effects of training, extinction, and deprivation. *Journal of the Experimental Analysis of Behavior, 13,* 359–367.

Stickney, M., & Miltenberger, R. (1999). Evaluation of procedures for the functional assessment of binge-eating. *International Journal of Eating Disorders, 26,* 196–204.

Stickney, M., Miltenberger, R., & Wolff, G. (1999). A descriptive analysis of factors contributing to binge eating. *Journal of Behavior Therapy and Experimental Psychiatry, 30,* 177–189.

Stokes, J. V., Luiselli, J. K., & Reed, D. D. (2010). A behavioral intervention for teaching tackling skills to high school football athletes. *Journal of Applied Behavior Analysis, 43,* 509–512.

Stokes, T. F., & Baer, D. M. (1977). An implicit technology of generalization. *Journal of Applied Behavior Analysis, 10,* 349–367.

Stokes, T. F., & Osnes, P. G. (1989). An operant pursuit of generalization. *Behavior Therapy, 20,* 337–355.

Stolz, S. B., & Associates. (1978). *Ethical issues in behavior modification.* San Francisco: Jossey-Bass.

Strack, B. W., Linden, M. K., & Wilson, V. S. (Eds.). (2011). *Biofeedback and neurofeedback applications in sport psychology.* Wheatridge, CO: Association for Applied Psychophysiology and Biofeedback.

Stromer, R., Mackay, H. A., & Remington, B. (1996). Naming: The formation of stimulus classes, and applied behavior analysis. *Journal of Applied Behavior Analysis, 29,* 409–431.

Stromer, R., McComas, J. J., & Rehfeldt, R. A. (2000). Designing interventions that include delayed reinforcement: Implications of recent laboratory research. *Journal of Applied Behavior Analysis, 33,* 359–371.

Stuart, R. B. (1967). Behavioral control of overeating. *Behaviour Research & Therapy, 5,* 357–365.

Stuart, R. B. (1971). Assessment and change of the communication patterns of juvenile delinquents and their parents. In R. D. Rubin, H. Fernsterheim, A. A. Lazarus, & C. M. Franks (Eds.), *Advances in behavior therapy* (pp. 183–196). New York: Academic Press.

Sturmey, P. (1994). Assessing the functions of aberrant behaviors: A review of psychometric instruments. *Journal of Autism and Developmental Disabilities, 24,* 293–303.

Sturmey, P. (Ed.). (2007). *Functional analysis in clinical treatment.* London, UK: Elsevier.

Suchowierska, M., & Kozlowski, J. (2004). Behavior analysis in Poland: A few words on Polish ABA. *Newsletter of the International Association for Behavior Analysis, 27*(2), 28–29.

Sullivan, M. A., & O'Leary, S. G. (1990). Maintenance following reward and cost token programs. *Behavior Therapy, 21,* 139–149.

Sulzer-Azaroff, B., & Reese, E. P. (1982). *Applying behavior analysis: A program for developing professional competence.* New York: Holt, Rinehart & Winston.

Sundberg, M. L. (2004). A behavioral analysis of motivation and its relation to mand training. In W. L. Williams (Ed.), *Advances in developmental disabilities: Etiology, assessment, intervention, and integration* (pp. 199–220). Reno, NV: Context Press.

Sundberg, M. L., & Michael, J. (2001). The benefits of Skinner's analysis of verbal behavior for children with autism. *Behavior Modification, 25,* 698–724.

Sundberg, M. L., & Partington, J. W. (1998). *Teaching language to children with autism and other developmental disabilities.* Pleasant Hill, CA: Behavior Analysts.

Sundberg, M. L., Michael, J., Partington, J. W., & Sundberg, C. A. (1996). The role of automatic reinforcement in early language acquisition. *The Analysis of Verbal Behavior, 13,* 21–37.

Sweet, A. A., & Loizeaux, A. L. (1991). Behavioral and cognitive treatment methods: A critical comparative review. *Journal of Behavior Therapy and Experimental Psychiatry, 22,* 159–185.

Tanaka-Matsumi, J., & Higginbotham, H. N. (1994). Clinical application of behavior therapy across ethnic and cultural boundaries. *The Behavior Therapist, 17,* 123–126.

Tanaka-Matsumi, J., Higginbotham, H. N., & Chang, R. (2002). Cognitive behavioral approaches to counselling across cultures: A functional analytic approach for clinical applications. In P. B. Pedersen, J. G. Draguns, W. J. Lonner, & J. E. Trimble (Eds.), *Counselling across cultures* (5th ed., pp. 337–354). Thousand Oaks, CA: Sage Publications, Inc.

Tarbox, J., Madrid, W., Aguilar, B., Jacobo, W., & Schiff, A. (2009). Use of chaining to increase complexity of echoics in children with autism. *Journal of Applied Behavior Analysis, 42,* 901–906.

Tarbox, J., Wallace, M. D., Tarbox, R. S. F., Landaburu, H. J., & Williams, W. L. (2004). Functional analysis and treatment of low rate problem behavior in individuals with developmental disabilities. *Behavioral Interventions, 19,* 187–204.

Tarbox, J., Zuckerman, C. K., Bishop, M. R., Olive, M. L., O'Hora, D. P. (2011). Rule-governed behavior: Teaching a preliminary repertoire of rule-following to children with autism. *The Analysis of Verbal Behavior, 27,* 125–139.

Taub, E., Crago, J. E., Burgio, L. D., Groomes, T. E., Cook, E. W., III, Deluca, S. C., & Miller, N. E. (1994). An operant approach to rehabilitation medicine: Overcoming learned nonuse by shaping. *Journal of the Experimental Analysis of Behavior, 61,* 281–293.

Taylor, B. A., & DeQuinzio, J. A. (2012). Observational learning and children with autism. *Behavior Modification, 36,* 341–360.

Taylor, C. B., Fried, L., & Kenardy, J. (1990). The use of real-time computer diary for data acquisition and processing. *Behavior Research and Therapy, 28,* 93–97.

Taylor, S. E. (2011). *Health psychology* (8th ed.). New York: McGraw-Hill.

Taylor, S., Abramowitz, J. S., & McKay, D. (2010). Obsessive-compulsive disorder. In M. M. Antony & D. H. Barlow (Eds.), *Handbook of assessment and treatment planning for psychological disorders* (2nd ed., pp. 267–300). New York: The Guilford Press.

Teasdale, J. D., Segal, Z. V., & Williams, J. M. G. (1995). How does cognitive therapy prevent depressive relapse and why should attentional control (mindfulness) training help? *Behavior Research and Therapy, 33,* 25–39.

Telch, C. F., Agras, W. S., & Linehan, M. M. (2001). Dialectical behavior therapy for binge-eating disorder. *Journal of Consulting Clinical Psychology, 69,* 1061–1065.

Tews, L. (2007). Early intervention for children with autism: Methodologies critique. *Developmental Disabilities Bulletin, 35,* 148–168.

Tharp, R. G., & Wetzel, R. J. (1969). *Behavior modification in the natural environment.* New York: Academic Press.

Thierman, G. J., & Martin, G. L. (1989). Self-management with picture prompts to improve quality of household cleaning by severely mentally handicapped persons. *International Journal of Rehabilitation Research, 12,* 27–39.

Thiessen, C., Fazzio, D., Arnal, L., Martin, G. L., Yu, C. T., & Kielback, L. (2009). Evaluation of a self-instructional manual for conducting discrete-trials teaching with children with autism. *Behavior Modification, 33,* 360–373.

Thomas, D. L., & Miller, L. K. (1980). Helping college students live together. Democratic decision-making versus experimental manipulation. In G. L. Martin & J. G. Osborne (Eds.), *Helping in the community: Behavioral applications* (pp. 291–305). New York: Plenum Press.

Thompson, R. H., & Iwata, B. A. (2000). Response acquisition under direct and indirect contingencies of reinforcement. *Journal of Applied Behavior Analysis, 33,* 1–11.

Thompson, R. H., Iwata, B. A., Conners, J., & Roscoe, E. M. (1999). Effects of reinforcement for alternative behavior during punishment of self-injury. *Journal of Applied Behavior Analysis, 32,* 317–328.

Thompson, R. W., Smith, G. L., Osgood, D. W., Dowd, T. P., Friman, P. C., & Daly, D. L. (1996). Residential care: A study of short- and long-term educational effects. *Children and Youth Services Review, 18,* 221–242.

Thompson, T., Felce, D., & Symons, F. (Eds.). (2000). *Behavioral observation: Technology and applications in developmental disabilities.* Baltimore, MD: Brookes.

Thomson, K. M., Martin, G. L., Fazzio, D., Salem, S., Young, K., & Yu, C. T. (2012). Evaluation of a self-instructional package for teaching tutors to conduct discrete-trials teaching with children with autism. *Research in Autism Spectrum Disorders, 6,* 1073–1082.

Thomson, K., Martin, G. L., Arnal, L., Fazzio, D., & Yu, C. T. (2009). Instructing individuals to deliver discrete-trials teaching to children with autism spectrum disorders: A review. *Research in Autism Spectrum Disorders, 3,* 590–606.

Thorndike, E. L. (1911). Animal intelligence: An experimental study of the associative processes in animals. *Psychological Review Monograph Supplement, 2,* Whole No. 8.

Thwaites, R., & Bennett-Levy, J. (2007). Conceptualizing empathy in cognitive therapy: Making the implicit explicit. *Behavioural and Cognitive Psychotherapy, 35,* 591–612.

Tiffany, S. T., Martin, C., & Baker, R. (1986). Treatments for cigarette smoking: An evaluation of the contributions of aversion and counselling procedures. *Behavior Research and Therapy, 24,* 437–452.

Timberlake, W., & Farmer-Dougan, V. A. (1991). Reinforcement in applied settings: Figuring out ahead of time what will work. *Psychological Bulletin, 110,* 379–391.

Tincani, M. J., Gastrogiavanni, A., & Axelrod, S. (1999). A comparison of the effectiveness of brief versus traditional functional analyses. *Research in Developmental Disabilities, 20,* 327–338.

Tingstrom, D. H., Sterling-Turner, H. E., & Wilczynski, S. M. (2006). The good behavior game: 1969–2002. *Behavior Modification, 30,* 225–253.

Tkachuk, G. A., & Martin, G. L. (1999). Exercise therapy for psychiatric disorders: Research and clinical implications. *Professional Psychology: Research and Practice, 30,* 275–282.

Todd, F. J. (1972). Coverant control of self-evaluative responses in the treatment of depression: A new use for an old principle. *Behavior Therapy, 3,* 91–94.

Tolin, D. F., & Morrison, S. (2010). Impulse control disorders. In M. M. Antony & D. H. Barlow (Eds.), *Handbook of assessment and treatment planning for psychological disorders* (2nd ed., pp. 606–632). New York: The Guilford Press.

Torgrud, L. J., & Holborn, S. W. (1990). The effects of verbal performance descriptions on nonverbal operant responding. *Journal of the Experimental Analysis of Behavior, 54,* 273–291.

Toussaint, K. A., & Tiger, J. H. (2012). Reducing covert self-injurious behavior maintained by automatic reinforcement through a variable momentary DRO procedure. *Journal of Applied Behavior Analysis, 45,* 179–184.

Travers, C. J. (2013). Using goal setting theory to promote personal development. In E. A. Locke & G. P. Latham (Eds.), *New developments in goal setting and task performance* (pp. 603–619). New York: Routledge.

Travis, R., & Sturmey, P. (2010). Functional analysis and treatment of the delusional statements of a man with multiple disabilities: A four year follow-up. *Journal of Applied Behavior Analysis, 43,* 745–749.

Tringer, L. (1991). Behavior therapy in Hungary. *The Behavior Therapist, 14,* 13–14.

Tucker, J. A., Murphy, J. G., & Kertesz, S. G. (2010). Substance use disorders. In M. M. Antony & D. H. Barlow (Eds.), *Handbook of assessment and treatment planning for psychological disorders* (2nd ed., pp. 529–570). New York: The Guilford Press.

Tucker, M., Sigafoos, J., & Bushell, H. (1998). Use of non-contingent reinforcement in the treatment of challenging behavior. A review and clinical guide. *Behavior Modification, 22,* 529–547.

Turk, D. C., & Okifuji, A. (1997). Evaluating the role of physical, operant, cognitive, and affective factors in the pain behaviors of chronic pain patients. *Behavior Modification, 21,* 259–280.

Turkat, I. D., & Feuerstein, M. (1978). Behavior modification and the public misconception. *American Psychologist, 33,* 194.

Turner, J., & Mathews, M. (2013). Behavioral gerontology. In G. J. Madden (Ed.), *APA handbook of behavior analysis: Volume 2, translating behavioral principles into practice* (pp. 545–562). Washington, DC: American Psychological Association.

Tuten, L. M., Jones, H. E., Schaeffer, C. M., & Stitzer, M. L. (2012). *Reinforcement-based treatment for substance-use disorders: A comprehensive behavioral approach.* Washington, DC: American Psychological Association.

Tyron, W. W. (1998). Behavioral observation. In A. S. Bellack & M. Hersen (Eds.), *Behavioral assessment: A practical handbook* (4th ed., pp. 79–103). Boston: Allyn & Bacon.

Tyron, W. W., & Cicero, S. D. (1989). Classical conditioning of meaning—I. A replication and higher order extension. *Journal of Behavior Therapy and Experimental Psychiatry, 20,* 137–142.

Ullmann, L. P. (1980). This week's citation classic, *Case Studies in Behavior Modification. Current Contents/Social and Behavioral Sciences* (No. 11), 255. Retrieved from http://garfield.library.upenn.edu/classics.html.

Ullmann L. P., & Krasner, L. (Eds.). (1965). *Case studies in behavior modification.* New York: Holt, Rinehart & Winston.

Ulrich, R., Stachnik, T., & Mabry. J. (Eds.). (1966). *Control of human behavior* (Vol. 1). Glenview, IL: Scott Foresman.

Underwood, L. A., Talbott, L. B., Mosholder, E., & von Dresner, K. S. (2008). Methodological concerns of residential treatment and recidivism for juvenile offenders with disruptive behavioral disorders. *The Journal of Behavior Analysis of Offender and Victim Treatment and Prevention, 1,* 222–236.

Urcuioli, P. J. (2013). Stimulus control and stimulus class formation. In G. J. Madden (Ed.), *APA handbook of behavior analysis: Volume 1, methods and principles* (pp. 361–386). Washington, DC: American Psychological Association.

U.S. Centers for Disease Control and Prevention (2014). Prevalence of autism spectrum disorder among children aged 8 years – autism and developmental disabilities monitoring network, 11 sites, United States, 2010. *Morbidity and Mortality Weekly Report.* Accessed at http://www.cdc.gov/mmwr/preview/mmwrhtml/ss6302a1.htm?s_cid=ss6302a1_w on April 13, 2014.

Van Acker, R., Boreson, L., Gable, R. A., & Potterton, T. (2005). Are we on the right course? Lessons learned about current FBA/BIP practices in schools. *Journal of Behavioral Education, 14,* 35–56.

Van Houten, R. (1983). Punishment: From the animal laboratory to the applied setting. In S. Axelrod & J. Apsche (Eds.), *The effects of punishment on human behavior* (pp. 13–44). New York: Academic Press.

Van Houten, R., & Doleys, D. M. (1983). Are social reprimands effective? In S. Axelrod & J. Apsche (Eds.), *The effects of punishment on human behavior* (pp. 45–70). New York: Academic Press.

Van Houten, R., Axelrod, S., Bailey, J. S., Favell, J. E., Foxx, R. M., Iwata, B. A., & Lovaas, O. I. (1988). The right to effective behavioral treatment. *Journal of Applied Behavior Analysis, 21,* 381–384.

Van Houten, R., Malenfant, J. E., Austin, J., & Lebbon, A. (2005). The effects of a seatbelt-gearshift delay prompt on the seatbelt use of motorists who do not regularly wear seatbelts. *Journal of Applied Behavior Analysis, 38,* 195–203.

Van Houten, R., Malenfant, J. E. L., Reagan, I., Sifrit, K., Compton, R., & Tenenbaum, J. (2010). Increasing seatbelt use in service vehicle drivers with a gearshift delay. *Journal of Applied Behavior Analysis, 43,* 369–380.

Vaughan, M. (1989). Rule-governed behavior in behavior analysis: A theoretical and experimental history. In S. C. Hayes (Ed.), *Rule-governed behavior: Cognition, contingencies, and instructional control* (pp. 97–118). New York: Plenum Press.

Vaughan, M. E., & Michael, J. L. (1982). Automatic reinforcement: An important but ignored concept. *Behaviorism, 10,* 217–227.

Vaughan, W., Jr., & Herrnstein, R. J. (1987). Choosing among natural stimuli. *Journal of the Experimental Analysis of Behavior, 47,* 5–16.

Vause, T., Regehr, K., Feldman, M., Griffiths, D., & Owen, F. (2009). Right to behavioral treatment for individuals with intellectual disabilities: Issues of punishment (219–239). In F. Owen & D. Griffiths (Eds.), *Challenges to the human rights of people with intellectual disabilities.* London & Philadelphia: Jessica Kingsley Publishers.

Vause, T., Yu, C. T., & Martin, G. L. (2007). The assessment of basic learning abilities test for persons with intellectual disability: A valuable clinical tool. *Journal of Applied Research in Intellectual Disabilities, 20,* 483–489.

Velentzas, K., Heinen, T., & Schack, T. (2011). Routine integration strategies and their effects on volleyball serve performance and players' movement mental representation. *Journal of Applied Sport Psychology, 23,* 209–222.

Verbeke, A. K., Martin, G. L., Thorsteinsson, J. R., Murphy, C., & Yu, C. T. (2009). Does mastery of ABLA Level 6 make it easier for individuals with developmental disabilities to learn to name objects? *Journal of Behavioral Education, 18,* 229–244.

Verbeke, A. K., Martin, G. L., Yu, C. T., & Martin, T. L. (2007). Does ABLA test performance predict picture name recognition with persons with severe developmental disabilities? *The Analysis of Verbal Behavior, 23,* 35–39.

Virues-Ortega, J., & Martin, G. L. (2010). Guidelines for sport psychologists to evaluate their interventions in clinical cases using single-subject designs. *Journal of Behavioral Health and Medicine, 3,* 158–171.

Vollmer, T. R., & Iwata, B. A. (1992). Differential reinforcement as treatment for behavior disorders: Procedural and functional variations. *Research in Developmental Disabilities, 13,* 393–417.

Vollmer, T. R., Borrero, J. C., Lalli, J. S., & Daniel, D. (1999). Evaluating self-control and impulsivity in children with severe behavior disorders. *Journal of Applied Behavior Analysis, 32,* 451–466.

Vollmer, T. R., Iwata, B. A., Zarcone, J. R., Smith, R. G., & Mazaleski, J. L. (1993). The role of attention in the treatment of attention-maintained self-injurious behavior: Non-contingent reinforcement and differential reinforcement of other behavior. *Journal of Applied Behavior Analysis, 26,* 9–21.

Vollmer, T. R., Roane, H. S., Ringdahl, J. E., & Marcus, B. A. (1999). Evaluating treatment challenges with differential reinforcement of alternative behavior. *Journal of Applied Behavior Analysis, 32,* 9–23.

Vorvick, L. J., & Storck, S. (2010). Sexual problems overview. MedlinePlus [Internet]. Bethesda (MD): National Library of Medicine (US); [updated 2010 September 11; cited 2013 June 9]. Retrieved from http://www.nlm.nih.gov/medlineplus/.

Vygotsky, L. S. (1978). *Mind and society.* Cambridge, MA: Harvard University Press.

Wacker, D. P., Berg, W. K., Harding, J. W., & Cooper-Brown, L. J. (2011). Functional and structural approaches to behavioral assessment of problem behavior. In W. W. Fisher, C. C. Piazza, & H. S. Roane (Eds.), *Handbook of applied behavior analysis.* New York: The Guilford Press.

Wahler, R. G. (2007). Chaos, coincidence, and contingency in the behavior disorders of childhood and adolescence. In P. Sturmey (Ed.), *Functional analysis in clinical treatment* (pp. 111–128). London, UK: Elsevier.

Wahler, R. G., Winkel, G. H., Peterson, R. F., & Morrison, D. C. (1965). Mothers as behavior therapists for their own children. *Behaviour Research and Therapy, 3,* 113–124.

Walker, B. D., & Rehfeldt, R. A. (2012). An evaluation of the stimulus equivalence paradigm to teach single-subject designs to distance education students via Blackboard. *Journal of Applied Behavior Analysis, 45,* 329–344.

Walker, B. D., Rehfeldt, R. A., & Ninness, C. E. (2010). Using the stimulus equivalence paradigm to teach course material in an undergraduate rehabilitation course. *Journal of Applied Behavior Analysis, 43,* 615–633.

Walker, H. M., & Buckley, N. K. (1972). Programming generalization and maintenance of treatment effects across time and across setting. *Journal of Applied Behavior Analysis, 5,* 209–224.

Wallace, I. (1971). *The writing of one novel.* Richmond Hill, ON, Canada: Simon & Schuster.

Wallace, I., & Pear, J. J. (1977). Self-control techniques of famous novelists. *Journal of Applied Behavior Analysis, 10,* 515–525.

Walls, R. T., Zane, T., & Ellis, W. D. (1981). Forward and backward chaining, and whole task methods: Training assembly tasks in vocational rehabilitation. *Behavior Modification, 5,* 61–74.

Walsh, J. (2012). The psychological person. In E. D. Hutchison (Ed.), *Essentials of human behavior: Integrating person, environment, and the life course* (pp. 109–152). Thousand Oaks, CA: Sage Publications, Inc.

Walters, G. D. (2000). Behavioral self-control training for problem drinkers: A meta-analysis of randomized control studies. *Behavior Therapy, 31,* 135–149.

Walters, K., & Thomson, K. (2013). The history of behavior analysis in Manitoba: A sparsely-populated Canadian province with an international behavior-analytic influence. *The Behavior Analyst, 36,* 57–72.

Walton, K. M., & Ingersoll, B. R. (2012). Evaluation of a sibling-mediated imitation intervention for young children with autism. *Journal of Positive Behavior Interventions, 14,* 241–253.

Wang, S., Cui, Y., & Parrila, R. (2011). Examining the effectiveness of peer-mediated and videomodeling social skills interventions for children with autism spectrum disorders: A meta-analysis in single-case research using HLM. *Research in Autism Spectrum Disorders, 5,* 562–569.

Wanlin, C., Hrycaiko, D., Martin, G. L., & Mahon, M. (1997). The effects of a goal-setting package on performance of speed skaters. *Journal of Sport Psychology, 9,* 212–228.

Ward, P. (2005). The philosophy, science, and application of behavior analysis in physical education. In D. Kirk, D. MacDonald, & M. O'Sullivan (Eds.), *The handbook of physical education.* Thousand Oaks, CA: Sage Publications, Inc.

Ward, P. (2011). Goal setting and performance feedback. In J. K. Luiselli & D. D. Reed (Eds.), *Behavioral sport psychology: Evidence-based approaches to performance enhancement.* New York: Springer Publishing Company.

Ward, W. D., & Stare, S. W. (1990). The role of subject verbalization in generalized correspondence. *Journal of Applied Behavior Analysis, 23,* 129–136.

Warren, S. F. (2000). Mental retardation: Curse, characteristic, or coin of the realm? *American Association on Mental Retardation News and Notes, 13,* 10–11.

Warzak, W. J., Floress, M. T., Kellen, M., Kazmerski, J. S., & Chopko, S. (2012). Trends in time-out research: Are we focusing our efforts where our efforts are needed? *The Behavior Therapist, 35,* 30–33.

Watkins, P. L., & Clum, G. A. (Eds.). (2008). *Handbook of self-help therapies.* Mahwah, NJ: Erlbaum.

Watson, D. L., & Tharp, R. G. (1997). *Self-directed behavior: Self-modification for personal adjustment* (7th ed.). Monterey, CA: Brooks/Cole.

Watson, D. L., & Tharp, R. G. (2007). *Self-directed behavior: Self-modification for personal adjustment* (9th ed.). Monterey, CA: Brooks/Cole.

Watson, J. B. (1913). Psychology as the behaviorist views it. *Psychological Review, 20,* 158–177.

Watson, J. B. (1916). The place of the conditioned reflex in psychology. *Psychological Review, 23,* 89–116.

Watson, J. B. (1930). *Behaviorism* (Rev. ed.). Chicago: University of Chicago Press.

Watson, J. B., & Rayner, R. (1920). Conditioned emotional reactions. *Journal of Experimental Psychology, 3,* 1–14.

Watson, R. I. (1962). The experimental tradition and clinical psychology. In A. J. Bachrach (Ed.), *Experimental foundations of clinical psychology* (pp. 3–25). New York: Basic Books.

Wearden, J. H. (1988). Some neglect problems in the analysis of human operant behavior. In G. Davey & C. Cullen (Eds.), *Human operant conditioning and behavior modification* (pp. 197–224), Chichester, UK: Wiley.

Weiss, F. G. (1974). *Hegel: The essential writings.* New York: Harper and Row.

Weiss, K. M. (1978). A comparison of forward and backward procedures for the acquisition of response chains in humans. *Journal of the Experimental Analysis of Behavior, 29,* 255–259.

Welch, M. W., & Gist, J. W. (1974). *The open token economy system: A handbook for a behavioral approach to rehabilitation.* Springfield, IL: Charles C Thomas.

Welch, S. J., & Pear, J. J. (1980). Generalization of naming responses to objects in the natural environment as a function of training stimulus modality with retarded children. *Journal of Applied Behavior Analysis, 13,* 629–643.

Wexler, D. (1981). *Manual for the Wexler Adult Intelligence Scale—Revised.* New York: Psychological Corporation.

White, K. G. (2013). Remembering and forgetting. In G. J. Madden (Ed.), *APA handbook of behavior analysis: Volume 1, methods and principles* (pp. 411–438). Washington, DC: American Psychological Association.

Whiting, S. W., & Dixon, M. R. (2012). Creating an iPhone application for collecting continuous ABC data. *Journal of Applied Behavior Analysis, 45,* 643–656.

Whitman, T. L., Spence, B. H., & Maxwell, S. (1987). A comparison of external and self-instructional teaching formats with mentally retarded adults in a vocational training setting. *Research in Developmental Disabilities, 8,* 371–388.

Wiederhold, B. K., & Wiederhold, M. D. (2004). *Virtual reality therapy for anxiety disorders: Advances in evaluation and treatment.* Washington, DC: American Psychological Association.

Wilder, D. A., & Wong, S. E. (2007). Schizophrenia and other psychotic disorders. In P. Sturmey (Ed.), *Functional analysis in clinical treatment* (pp. 283–306). London, UK: Elsevier.

Wilder, L. K., & King-Peery, K. (2012). *Family hope: Positive behavior support for families of children with challenging behavior.* Champagne, IL: Research Press.

Williams, B., Myerson, J., & Hale, S. (2008). Individual differences, intelligence, and behavioral analysis. *Journal of the Experimental Analysis of Behavior, 90,* 219–231.

Williams, C. D. (1959). The elimination of tantrum behavior by extinction procedures. *Journal of Abnormal and Social Psychology, 59,* 269.

Williams, J. E., & Cuvo, A. J. (1986). Training apartment upkeep skills to rehabilitation clients: A comparison of task analysis strategies. *Journal of Applied Behavior Analysis, 19,* 39–51.

Williams, K. J. (2013). Goal setting in sports. In E. A. Locke & G. P. Latham (Eds.), *New developments in goal setting and task performance* (pp. 375–396). New York: Routledge.

Williams, M., Teasdale, J., Segal, Z., & Kabat-Zinn, J. (2007). *The mindful way through depression: Freeing yourself from chronic unhappiness.* New York: The Guilford Press.

Williams, W. L. (Ed.). (2004). *Advances in developmental disabilities: Etiology, assessment, intervention, and integration.* Reno, NV: Context Press.

Williams, W. L., Jackson, M., & Friman, P. C. (2007). Encopresis and enuresis. In P. Sturmey (Ed.), *Functional analysis in clinical treatment* (pp. 171–192). London, UK: Elsevier.

Wilson, G. T. (1991). Chemical aversion conditioning in the treatment of alcoholism: Further comments. *Behavior Research and Therapy, 29,* 415–419.

Wilson, J. Q., & Herrnstein, R. J. (1985). *Crime and human nature.* New York: Simon & Schuster.

Wilson, K. G., Hayes, S. C., & Gifford, E. V. (1997). Cognition in behavior therapy: Agreements and differences. *Journal of Behavior Therapy and Experimental Psychiatry, 28,* 53–63.

Wincze, J. P., Bach, A. K., & Barlow, D. H. (2008). Sexual dysfunction. In D. H. Barlow (Ed.), Clinical handbook of psychological disorders: A step-by-step treatment manual (4th ed., pp. 615–662). New York: The Guilford Press.

Wincze, J. P., & Carey, M. P. (2001). *Sexual dysfunction: A guide for assessment and treatment* (2nd ed.). New York: The Guilford Press.

Winerman, L. (2004). Back to her roots. *Monitor on Psychology, 35*(8), 46–49.

Winerman, L. (2005). Fighting phobias: A virtual cure. *Monitor on Psychology, 36*(7), 87–89.

Winerman, L. (2013). Breaking free from addiction. *Monitor on Psychology: A Publication of the American Psychological Association, 44*(6), 30–34. [Open article at http://www.apamonitor-digital.org/apamonitor/201306/#pg48]

Wirth, K. (2014). *How to get your child to go to sleep and stay asleep: A practical guide for parents to sleep train young children.* Victoria, BC: FriesenPress.

Witt, J. C., & Wacker, D. P. (1981). Teaching children to respond to auditory directives: An evaluation of two procedures. *Behavior Research of Severe Developmental Disabilities, 2,* 175–189.

Wolf, M. M. (1978). Social validity: The case for subjective measurement or how applied behavior analysis is finding its heart. *Journal of Applied Behavior Analysis, 11,* 203–214.

Wolf, M. M., Braukmann, C. J., & Ramp, K. A. (1987). Serious delinquent behavior as part of a significantly handicapping condition: Cures and supportive environments. *Journal of Applied Behavior Analysis, 20,* 347–359.

Wolf, M. M., Hanley, E. L., King, L. A., Lachowicz, J., & Giles, D. K. (1970). The timer-game: A variable interval contingency for the management of out-of-seat behavior. *Exceptional Children, 37,* 113–117.

Wolf, M. M., Kirigin, K. A., Fixsen, D. L., Blase, K. A., & Braukmann, C. J. (1995). The teaching-family model: A case study in data-based program development and refinement (and dragon wrestling). *Journal of Organizational Behavior Management, 15,* 11–68.

Wolf, M. M., Risley, T., & Mees, H. (1964). Application of operant conditioning procedures to the behavior problems of an autistic child. *Behavior Research and Therapy, 1,* 305–312.

Wolfe, V. F., & Cuvo, A. J. (1978). Effects of within-stimulus and extra-stimulus prompting on letter discrimination by mentally retarded persons. *American Journal of Mental Deficiency, 83,* 297–303.

Wolko, K. L., Hrycaiko, D. W., & Martin, G. L. (1993). A comparison of two self-management packages to standard coaching for improving practice performance of gymnasts. *Behavior Modification, 17,* 209–223.

Wolpe, J. (1958). *Psychotherapy by reciprocal inhibition.* Stanford, CA: Stanford University Press.

Wolpe, J. (1969). *The practice of behavior therapy.* Elmsford, NY: Pergamon Press.

Wolpe, J. (1985). Requiem for an institution. *Behavior Therapist, 8,* 113.

Wood, S. J., Murdock, J. Y., & Cronin, M. E. (2002). Self-monitoring and at-risk middle-school students: Academic performance improves, maintains, and generalizes. *Behavior Modification, 25,* 605–626.

Woody, D. J. (2012). Infancy and toddlerhood. In E. D. Hutchison (Ed.), *Essentials of human behavior: Integrating person, environment, and the life course* (pp. 415–459). Thousand Oaks, CA: Sage Publications, Inc.

Yamagami, T., Okuma, H., Morinaga, Y., & Nakao, H. (1982). Practice of behavior therapy in Japan. *Journal of Behavior Therapy and Experimental Psychology, 13,* 21–26.

Yates, A. J. (1970). *Behavior therapy.* New York: Wiley.

Yoder, P. J., & Symons, F. J. (2010). *Observational measurement of behavior.* New York: Springer Publishing Company.

Young, J. E., Rygh, J. L., Weinberger, A. D., & Beck, A. T. (2008). Cognitive therapy for depression. In D. H. Barlow (Ed.), *Clinical handbook of psychological disorders: A step-by-step treatment manual* (4th ed., pp. 250–305). New York: The Guilford Press.

Young, K. L., Boris, A. L., Thomson, K. M., Martin, G. L., & Yu, C. T. (2012). Evaluation of a self-instructional package on discrete-trials teaching to parents of children with autism. *Research in Autism Spectrum Disorders, 6,* 1321–1330.

Yu, C. T., Martin, T. L., Vause, T., & Martin, G. L. (2013). Kerr-Meyerson Assessment of Basic Learning Abilities Revised: Recent findings and a conceptual analysis of ordering. In C. Goyos, T. Higbee, & C. Miguel (Eds.), *Advances in research and treatment of autism.* In preparation.

Yu, D., Martin, G. L., Suthons, E., Koop, S., & Pallotta-Cornick, A. (1980). Comparisons of forward chaining and total task presentation formats to teach vocational skills to the retarded. *International Journal of Rehabilitation Research, 3,* 77–79.

Zalta, A. K., & Foa, E. B. (2012), Exposure therapy: Promoting emotional processing of pathological anxiety. In W. T. O'Donohue & J. E. Fisher (Eds.), *Cognitive behavior therapy: Core principles for practice* (pp. 75–104). Hoboken, NJ: John Wiley & Sons.

Zamora, R., & Lima, J. (2000). Cognitive behavioral therapy in Uruguay. *The Behavior Therapist, 23,* 98–101.

Zettle, R. D., & Hayes, S. C. (1982). Rule-governed behavior: A potential theoretical framework for cognitive behavioral therapy. In P. C. Kendall (Ed.), *Advances in cognitive behavioral research and therapy* (Vol. 1, pp. 73–118). New York: Academic Press.

Ziegler, S. G. (1987). Effects of stimulus cueing on the acquisition of groundstrokes by beginning tennis players. *Journal of Applied Behavior Analysis, 20,* 405–411.

Zvi, M. B. (2004). IABA: The new Israeli ABA Chapter. *Newsletter of the International Association for Behavior Analysis, 27*(2), 24–25.

Zweig, R. D., & Leahy, R. L. (2012). *Treatment plans and interventions for bulimia and binge-eating disorder.* New York: The Guilford Press.

AUTHOR INDEX

SUBJECT INDEX